"Whilst there has been extensive research on the peace agreements themselves, the processes that led to specific outcomes are often ignored or regarded as 'too difficult'. As this book shows the processes themselves are not only worthy of study, but critical in the determination of the peaceful outcomes of each case. A valuable framework facilitates comparison across a very broad selection of cases that should provide the standard text on this subject for some years."

Paul Jackson, University of Birmingham, UK

"Two of Britain's leading scholars of conflict resolution and peace building have assembled a first-class group of contributors in a seminal volume on comparative peace processes in no fewer than 18 different settings. The essays contain a wealth of new material and conceptual insights into the multiple challenges of peace building. It is a book that will appeal to scholars and practitioners of conflict resolution and peacebuilding, not least because it offers a major theoretical advancement to our understanding of the social, economic and political dynamics of peace process. The volume will appeal to students and practitioners alike not least because it challenges our basic assumptions about the workings of any peace process."

Fen Osler Hampson, Carleton University, Canada

"The issue of peace process design is a central one for mediators and international organisations supporting peace processes. However, until now it has not been the subject of sustained academic inquiry. This book provides an extensive and systematic comparative case study approach to understanding process design. The book sets out an overall framework for understanding process design and is vital reading for students and practitioners alike."

Christine Bell, University of Edinburgh, UK

COMPARING PEACE PROCESSES

This book offers a comparative survey of 18 contemporary peace processes conducted by leading international scholars.

There is no standard model of peace processes and all will vary according to the context, type of conflict, timing, national and global economic climate, and factors like natural disasters. Therefore, making comparisons between peace processes is difficult, but it is beneficial – indeed, imperative – and is the principal motivation behind this volume. What works in one context may not work in another, but it can be modified and adapted to fit another context.

The book is structured to maximise comparison between processes, and the case studies chosen are topical and span the major regions of the world. The concluding chapter systematically compares the case studies around 11 variables that cover the conflict context, peace process procedures, the responsiveness of the peace process to demands, and levels of participation and inclusion. Each peace process is then given a numeric score according to each of these variables, and the book thereby reaches judgements on whether each case can be termed a 'success' or a 'failure'.

This book will be essential reading for students of peace studies, conflict resolution, war and conflict studies, security studies, and IR.

Alpaslan Özerdem is Associate Pro-Vice Chancellor Research at Coventry University, UK. He is co-editor of *Local Ownership in International Peacebuilding* (Routledge, 2015), co-author of *Peacebuilding: An Introduction* (Routledge, 2016), and co-editor of *Conflict Transformation and the Palestinians* (Routledge, 2017).

Roger Mac Ginty is Professor of Defence, Diplomacy and Development at the Durham Global Security Institute, Durham University, UK. He edits the journal *Peacebuilding* and co-directs the Everyday Peace Indicators project.

Routledge Studies in Peace and Conflict Resolution

Series Editors: Tom Woodhouse and Oliver Ramsbotham

University of Bradford

The field of peace and conflict research has grown enormously as an academic pursuit in recent years, gaining credibility and relevance amongst policy makers and in the international humanitarian and NGO sector. The Routledge Studies in Peace and Conflict Resolution series aims to provide an outlet for some of the most significant new work emerging from this academic community, and to establish itself as a leading platform for innovative work at the point where peace and conflict research impacts on International Relations theory and processes.

UN Intervention Practices in Iraq
A Discursive Approach to International Relations
Kerstin Eppert

Comparing Peace Processes
Edited by Alpaslan Özerdem and Roger Mac Ginty

State Domination and the Psycho-Politics of Conflict
Power, Conflict and Humiliation
Daniel Rothbart

Gender, Nationalism and Conflict Transformation
New Themes and Old Problems in Northern Ireland
Fidelma Ashe

For more information about this series, please visit: www.routledge.com/Routledge-Studies-in-Peace-and-Conflict-Resolution/book-series/RSPCR

COMPARING PEACE PROCESSES

Edited by Alpaslan Özerdem and Roger Mac Ginty

Routledge
Taylor & Francis Group
LONDON AND NEW YORK

First published 2019
by Routledge
2 Park Square, Milton Park, Abingdon, Oxon OX14 4RN

and by Routledge
52 Vanderbilt Avenue, New York, NY 10017

Routledge is an imprint of the Taylor & Francis Group, an informa business

British Library Cataloguing-in-Publication Data
A catalogue record for this book is available from the British Library

Library of Congress Cataloging-in-Publication Data
Names: Özerdem, Alpaslan, editor. | Mac Ginty, Roger, 1970– editor.
Title: Comparing peace processes / Edited by Alpaslan Özerdem and Roger Mac Ginty.
Description: First edition. | London ; New York, NY : Routledge/Taylor & Francis Group, 2019. | Series: Routledge studies in peace and conflict resolution | Includes bibliographical references and index.
Identifiers: LCCN 2018054393 (print) | LCCN 2018055465 (ebook) | ISBN 9781315436609 (Web PDF) | ISBN 9781315436593 (ePub) | ISBN 9781315436586 (Mobi) | ISBN 9781138218963 (hardback) | ISBN 9781138218970 (pbk.) | ISBN 9781315436616 (e-book)
Subjects: LCSH: Pacific settlement of international disputes. | Peace-building.

ISBN: 978-1-138-21896-3 (hbk)
ISBN: 978-1-138-21897-0 (pbk)
ISBN: 978-1-315-43661-6 (ebk)

Typeset in Bembo
by Apex CoVantage, LLC

CONTENTS

ACKNOWLEDGEMENTS

We would like to acknowledge Dr Elly Harrowell's great assistance in the overall editing work of this volume as well as the diligent formatting assistance we received from Muğla Sıtkı Koçman University MA/PhD students Yunus Emre Çakmak, Damla Yıldız, and Deniz Ekşi.

TABLES AND FIGURES

Tables

Figures

ABBREVIATIONS

21CPC	21st Century Panglong Conference
AA	Arakan Army
AFL	Armed Forces of Liberia
AHJAG	Ad Hoc Joint Action Group
AKP	Justice and Development Party
AMM	Aceh Monitoring Mission
ANC	African National Congress
APLA	Azanian People's Liberation Army
ARENA	Republican National Alliance
ARMM	Autonomous Region in Muslim Mindanao
ARSA	Arakan Rohingya Salvation Army
ASEAN	Association of Southeast Asian Nations
ASNLF	Aceh–Sumatra National Liberation Front
AUC	United Self Defence Group of Colombia
BBL	Bangsamoro Basic Law
BDF	Bong Defense Force
BDP	Peace and Democracy Party
BGF	Border Guard Forces Plan
BIMPT-EAGA	Brunei Darussalam Indonesia Malaysia Philippines–East Asia Growth Area
BPP	Basque Peace Process
BTC	Bangsamoro Transition Commission
CAB	Comprehensive Agreement on the Bangsamoro
CBMs	Confidence-Building Measures
CELAC	Community of Latin American and Caribbean States
CERAC	Centre for Resources for Analysis of Conflicts
CFA	Ceasefire Agreement

CGDK	Coalition Government of Democratic Kampuchea
CHP	Republican People's Party
CIEDP	Commission of Investigation on Enforced Disappeared Persons
CMI	Crisis Management Initiative
CODESA	Convention for a Democratic South Africa
COHA	Cessation of Hostilities Framework Agreement
COP	Consolidation for Peace
CPA	Comprehensive Peace Agreement
CPB	Communist Party of Burma
CPN-Maoist	Communist Party of Nepal–Maoist
CPP	Communist Party of Philippines
CRC	Central Revolutionary Council
CSO	Civil Society Organization
DAG	Dialogue Advisory Group
DDR	Disarmament Demobilization and Reintegration
DF	Democratic Front
DOM	Military Operation Area
DoP	Declaration of Principles
DPR	People's Representative Council
DRC	Danish Refugee Council
DTP	Democratic Society Party
DUP	Democratic Unionist Party
EAOs	Ethnic Armed Organizations
EC	European Community
ECOMOG	Economic Community Cease-Fire Monitoring Group
ECOWAS	Economic Community of West African States
EEC	The European Economic Community
EITI	Extractive Industries Transparency Initiative
ELN	Army of National Liberation
EPL	Eritrean People's Liberation
EPLF	Eritrean People's Liberation Front
ERP	Revolutionary Army of the People
ETA	Basque Homeland and Freedom
EU	European Union
FAB	Framework of Agreement on the Bangsamoro
FAES	Armed Forces of EI Salvador
FAN	Broad National Front
FARC	Revolutionary Armed Forces of Colombia
FMLN	Farabundo Marti National Liberation Front
FPA	Final Peace Agreement
FPL	Armed Forces of Liberation
FPNCC	Federal Political and Negotiation Consultative Committee
FUNCINPEC	National United Front for an Independent, Neutral, Peaceful and Cooperative Cambodia

FUSADES	Salvadoran Foundation for Social and Economic Development
GAL	Anti-Terrorist Liberation Groups
GAM	Free Aceh Movement
GAO	Organized Armed Groups
GPH	Government of the Philippines
GRP	Republic of Philippines
HD	Humanitarian Dialogue
HDP	People's Democratic Party
HDZ	Croatian Democratic Union
HSZ	High Security Zones
ICG	International Contact Group
ICJ	International Court of Justice
ICTY	International Criminal Tribunal for the Former Yugoslavia
IFOR	Implementation Force
IFP	Inkatha Freedom Party
IGAD	Inter-Governmental Authority for Development
IMF	International Monetary Fund
IMT	International Monitoring Team
INGO	International Non-Governmental Organizations
INPFL	Independent National Patriotic Front of Liberia
INTERFET	Australian-led International Force East Timor
IPKF	Indian Peacekeeping Force
IPPP	Israel–Palestinian Peace Process
IRA	Irish Republican Army
IRP	Interim Relief Programme
IS	Islamic State
ISGA	Interim Self-Governing Administration
ISIS	Islamic State of Iraq and the Levant
ISO	International Organization for Standardization
IVC	International Verification Commission
JHU	Jathika Hela Urumaya
JICA	Japan International Cooperation Agency
JRG	Revolutionary Governing Junta
JVP	Janatha Vimukthi Peramuna
KCK	Kurdistan Communities Union
KIO	Kachin Independence Organization
KNU	South-East Myanmar
KPNLF	Khmer People's National Liberation Front
KSPP	Kachin State Progressive Party
KUFNS	Kampuchean United Front for National Salvation
LDCs	Least Developed Countries
LDF	Lofa Defense Force
LGBTI	Lesbian, Gay, Bisexual, Transgender and/or Intersex
LNH	Liberia New Horizons

LOGA	Law on Governing Aceh
LPC	Liberian Peace Council
LTTE	Liberation Tigers of Tamil Eelam
LURD	Liberians United for Reconciliation and Democracy
MEC	Myanmar Economic Corporation
MHP	Nationalist Movement Party
MILF	Moro Islamic Liberation Front
MIM	Muslim Independence Movement
MINUSAL	United Nations Mission in El Salvador
MİT	National Intelligence Agency
MK	Spear of the Nation in Zulu
MNDAA	Myanmar National Democratic Army Alliance
MNLF	Moro National Liberation Front
MOA-AD	Memorandum of Agreement on Ancestral Domain
MODEL	Movement for Democracy in Liberia
MoU	Memorandum of Understanding
MP	Member of Parliament
MPC	Myanmar Peace Centre
MPC	Mindanao People's Caucus
MPIGO	Mouvement Populaire Ivoirien du Grand-Ouest
MPNF	Multi-Party Negotiating Forum
MPR	Indonesian Parliament
NAD	Nanggroe Aceh Darussalam
NATO	North Atlantic Treaty Organization
NC	Nepal Congress Party
NCA	Nationwide Ceasefire Agreement
NCCT	Nationwide Ceasefire Coordination Team
NCP	National Congress Party
NDAA	National Democratic Army Alliance
NDDC	National Disarmament and Demobilisation Commission
NGO	Non-Governmental Organization
NIS	National Intelligence Service
NLD	National League for Democracy
NPA	New People's Army
NPFL	National Patriotic Front of Liberia
NPFL-CRC	NPFL-Central Revolutionary Council
NPRC	National Reconciliation and Peace Center
NSO	National Statistics Office
NTGL	National Transitional Government of Liberia
NVS	Afghan Intelligence Service
OAU	Organisation of African Unity
OBOR	One Belt One Road
ODIN	Delinquent Organizations Linked to Drug Trafficking
OHCHR	High Commissioner for Human Rights

OHR	Office for High Representative
OIAP	Observatory for Monitoring the Peace Accord
OIC	Organization of Islamic Conference
ONUSAL	Observer Mission of the United Nations El Salvador
ONUV	United Nations Office for Verification
OPAPP	Office of the Presidential Adviser on the Peace Process
OPT	Palestinian Territories and Occupied Palestinian Territories
ORDEN	Democratic Nationalist Organization
OSCE	Organization for Security and Cooperation in Europe
PA	Institution of the Palestinian Authority
PAC	Pan Africanist Congress
PDC	Christian Democratic Party
PEP	Paris Economic Protocol
PIC	Peace Implementation Council
PKK	Kurdistan Workers' Party
PLO	Palestine Liberation Organisation
PNC	Party National Conciliation
PP	Popular Party
PPA	Paris Peace Accords
PRC	The People's Redemption Council
PRK	Republic of Kampuchea
PSOE	Spanish Socialist Workers' Party
P-TOMS	Post-Tsunami Operational Management Structure
PYD	Democratic Union Party
RA	Republic Act
RAW	Research and Analysis Wing
RCSS	Restoration Council of Shan State
REP-USM	Research and Education for Peace
RNA	Royal Nepali Army
RRU	Rapid Response Units
RUF	Revolutionary United Front
SACP	South African Communist Party
SADF	South African Defence Force
SAF	Special Action Forces
SANDF	South African National Defence Force
SCO	Schangai Cooperation Organisation
SCOPP	Secretariat for Coordination of the Peace Process
SDA	Bosniak Party of Democratic Action
SDLP	Social Democratic and Labour Party
SDP	Social Democratic Party
SEACSN	Southeast Asian Conflict Studies Network
SGBV	Sexual and Gender Based Violence
SLFP	Sri Lankan Freedom Party
SLMC	Sri Lankan Muslim Congress

SLMM	Sri Lanka Monitoring Mission
SNC	Supreme National Council
SNM	Somali National Movement
SNSD	Serb Alliance for Independent Social Democrats
SPA	Sub-committee on Political Affairs
SPA	Seven Party Alliance
SPLA	Sudan People's Liberation Army
SPLM/A	Sudan People's Liberation Movement and Army
SSPP	Shan State Progressive Party
SSR	Security Sector Reform
TNI	Indonesian Armed Forces
TNLA	Ta'ang National Liberation Army
TRC	Truth and Reconciliation Commission
TRCAct	Enforced Disappearances Enquiry, Truth and Reconciliation Commission Act
TRO	Tamil Rehabilitation Organisation
TSE	Supreme Electoral Tribunal
UC	Unity Centre
UDF	United Democratic Front
UK	United Kingdom
ULIMO	United Liberation Movement of Liberia for Democracy
ULIMO-K	United Liberation Movement of Liberia for Democracy–Kromah Faction
UMEHL	Union of Myanmar Economic Holdings Limited
UML	United Marxist Leninist
UN	United Nations
UNAMET	United Nations Mission in East Timor
UNDHA-HACO	United Nations Department of Humanitarian Affairs Humanitarian Assistance Coordination Office in Liberia
UNDP	United Nations Development Programme
UNFC	United Nationalities Federal Council
UNMIL	UN Peacekeeping Mission in Liberia
UNMIN	UN Mission in Nepal
UNMIS	United Nations Mission in Sudan
UNOMIL	United Nations Observer Mission in Liberia
UNP	United National Party
UNPROFOR	United Nations Protection Force
UNRWA	UN Relief and Works Agency for Palestinian Refugees in the Near East
UNSC	United Nations Security Council
UNTAC	United Nations Transnational Authority in Cambodia
UNTAET	United Nations Transitional Administration in East Timor
UP	Patriotic Union Party
UPFN	United People's Front Nepal

US	United States
USA	United States of America
USAID	United States Agency for International Development
USDP	Union Solidarity and Development Party
USSR	Union of Soviet Socialist Republics
UUP	Ulster Unionist Party
UWSA	United Wa State Army
WB	World Bank
YPG	People's Protection Unit

AUTHOR BIOGRAPHIES

The editors

Alpaslan Özerdem is Associate Pro-Vice Chancellor Research at Coventry University and holds the post of Professor of Peacebuilding. With nearly 20 years of field research experience in Afghanistan, Bosnia-Herzegovina, El Salvador, Kosovo, Lebanon, Liberia, Nigeria, Philippines, Sierra Leone, Solomon Islands, Sri Lanka, and Turkey, he is author of one monograph, co-author of five books, and co-editor of seven books, including the Routledge titles *Human Security in Turkey* (2013), *Local Ownership in International Peacebuilding* (2015), *Peacebuilding: An Introduction* (2016), *Conflict Transformation and the Palestinians: The Dynamics of Peace and Justice under Occupation* (2016) and *Routledge Handbook of Turkish Politics* (2019).

Roger Mac Ginty is Professor at the School of Government and International Affairs, Durham University. He works on the interface between top-down and bottom-up peace. He directs the Everyday Peace Indicators project (with Pamina Firchow) and edits the journal *Peacebuilding* (with Oliver Richmond). He also edits the Palgrave book series Rethinking Political Violence.

Chapter contributors

Ayesah Abubakar is Senior Lecturer at the Universiti Malaysia Sabah. Her main fields of research include development management, human rights, and peace and conflict studies. Ayesah was a recipient of the Japan International Cooperation Agency (JICA) Presidential Recognition Award in 2014 for her work on Peacebuilding in Southeast Asia. She is the author of *Peacebuilding and Sustainable Human Development: Pursuit of Bangsamoro Right to Self-Determination* (2019).

Kamarulzaman Askandar is Professor of Peace and Conflict Studies and former Coordinator for Research and Education for Peace (REP-USM) in the School of Social Sciences at the Universiti Sains Malaysia. He is the Regional Coordinator for the Southeast Asian Conflict Studies Network (SEACSN) and an awardee of the JICA Presidential Recognition Award (2014) for his contributions to peacebuilding in the region. In 2018, he was appointed as the Malaysian Representative to the ASEAN Institute for Peace and Reconciliation (ASEAN-IPR).

Bahar Başer is Senior Research Fellow at the Centre for Trust, Peace and Social Relations. She is also an associate research fellow at the Security Institute for Governance and Leadership in Africa (SIGLA), Stellenbosch University, South Africa. She completed a PhD in Social and Political Sciences at the European University Institute in Florence, Italy.

Daniele Conversi is Research Professor at Ikerbasque (the Basque Foundation for Science) at the University of the Basque Country (UPV/EHU). His current areas of research include social and political theory, comparative democratisation, and theories of nationalism.

Gorka Espiau is currently Visiting Professor of Practice at the Center for Interdisciplinary Research in Montreal (McGill University) and Senior Fellow at the Agirre Center for Social and Political Studies (University of the Basque Country). He was previously Director of Places and International Affairs at the Young Foundation and has also worked as an advisor to the Basque Government on peace and reconciliation issues.

Adrian Guelke is Emeritus Professor in the School of History, Anthropology, Philosophy, and Politics at Queen's University Belfast. He is the author of *Politics in Deeply Divided Societies*, published by Polity, and of *Rethinking the Rise and Fall of Apartheid*.

Dejan Guzina is Associate Professor in Political Science at Wilfrid Laurier University in Waterloo (Ontario, Canada). His major research interest intersects comparative democratisation, ethnic conflict management, and external state and nation building in post-conflict states. Dr Guzina's current research project is on the European Union's accession policies and state-building in the Western Balkans.

Varsha Gyawali is a PhD researcher with the Centre for Trust, Peace and Social Relations at Coventry University. She is currently carrying out research into transitional justice processes and conceptions of victimhood in Nepal.

Elly Harrowell is a research associate at the Centre for Trust, Peace and Social Relations at Coventry University. Her work focuses on reconstruction processes following conflict and disaster and the role of memory in post-conflict societies.

She has published on post-conflict processes in a range of contexts, including Nepal, Sri Lanka, and Kyrgyzstan.

SungYong Lee is Senior Lecturer in Peace and Conflict Studies at the University of Otago, New Zealand and serves as a regional council member of the Royal Society of New Zealand. Dr Lee's current research mainly focuses on conflict resolution and post-conflict peacebuilding in civil war.

David G. Lewis is Associate Professor of International Relations in the Department of Politics at the University of Exeter. His research focuses on international relations and peace and conflict studies, with a particular interest in the politics of authoritarian states.

Anatol Lieven is Professor at Georgetown University School of Foreign Service, Qatar, Visiting Professor in the War Studies Department of King's College London, and Senior Fellow of the New America Foundation in Washington, DC.

Louise Wiuff Moe has a PhD from the University of Queensland and has worked for the Danish Institute for International Studies. She is based at the Helmut Schmidt University.

Jenny Pearce is Research Professor in the Latin American and Caribbean Centre at the London School of Economics. She is a specialist on issues of violence, conflict, social change, and social agency in Latin America and has published widely on these themes. She is particularly interested in participatory research methods in contexts of violence and insecurity. She is currently working on a book on politics and violence.

Sukanya Podder is Senior Lecturer in Defence Studies at Kings College London. Her primary areas of research are post-conflict reconstruction, civil wars, and youth in peacebuilding, on which she has co-authored two books: *Child Soldiers: From Recruitment to Reintegration* and *Youth in Conflict and Peacebuilding: Mobilization, Reintegration and Reconciliation.*

Stefano Ruzza is Assistant Professor of Conflict, Security and Statebuilding at the University of Turin and a co-founder of T.wai (Torino World Affairs Institute). He also lectures regularly for the Italian Army. His research interests mainly focus around Myanmar's transition, non-state armed actors in international relations, and private military and security companies.

Nathan Shea is Senior Program Officer on The Asia Foundation's regional Conflict and Fragility program. His research focuses predominantly on sub-national and border conflicts in South and Southeast Asia. Previously, he was a founding partner on the Australian International Conflict Resolution Project at the University of Melbourne. He is currently based in Myanmar.

William Stanley is Professor of Political Science and directs the Latin American and Iberian Institute at the University of New Mexico. His scholarship addresses the interactions of international and domestic political actors in armed conflict and peace processes in Central America, with particular attention to military, police, and justice institutions.

Mandy Turner is Director of the Kenyon Institute (Council for British Research in the Levant) in East Jerusalem. Her research and publications focus thematically on the politics of international intervention, particularly the political economy of peacebuilding and development in war-torn societies, with a current country focus on the occupied Palestinian territory.

Alex de Waal is Executive Director of the World Peace Foundation at Tufts University. His two most recent books are *The Real Politics of the Horn of Africa: Money, War and the Business of Power* (Polity, 2015) and *Mass Starvation: The History and Future of Famine* (2017).

INTRODUCTION

Why compare peace processes?

Roger Mac Ginty and Alpaslan Özerdem

Introduction

A peace process is an attempt to reach a negotiated outcome in a violent conflict. It is not an attempt to reach a peace of rainbows and unicorns. Instead, it is a calculated attempt by the parties to a conflict to recalibrate the conflict in order to lower the conflict costs. Often it is a way to end the most overt forms of violence and channel the conflict into political contestation. Most peace processes can be regarded as conflict management as opposed to conflict transformation (Ramsbotham et al. 2016: 10–110). That is, they accept that the conflict is irresolvable, so they seek to re-organise it. They do not seek to eliminate the conflict through conflict transformation – a lengthy and costly endeavour that requires confronting one's own identity and stance (Lederach 2003). In a conflict management approach, parties often maintain their original nationalist, secessionist, or identity beliefs but express them in different and less virulent ways.

All peace processes are experimental, and parties to a process might pursue it with differing degrees of conviction. It is rational for parties to a conflict to be suspicious of the motives of the other side (Richmond 1998), and so they may seek assurances as to the seriousness of the other side's involvement in a process. Such Confidence-Building Measures (CBMs) may be minor or symbolic but could develop into more significant measures. Often the start of peace processes is secretive and occurs at a deniable level. After years or decades of demonising the other side, it may take significant media and expectation management to convince politicised and mobilised populations that it is worth finding a negotiated outcome to the conflict. Moreover, parties might use ceasefires and peace processes as a chance to rearm and then pursue a battlefield advantage. When Sri Lanka's peace process stalled, the Sri Lankan government used it as an opportunity to rearm and subsequently defeated the Tamil Tigers in 2009. But conflict termination through military victory often involves very significant human costs: an estimated 40,000 civilians died in the final months of the war (Mundy 2017).

There is no standard model of a peace process. All will vary according to context and type of conflict, timing, the strength of parties, the national and global economic climate, and factors like natural disasters. Fundamentally, conflicts differ in terms of scale, causes, and their strategic importance. The highly contextualised nature of peace processes means that we must be very wary of making generalisations between peace processes. What works in one peace process may not work in another. Sections of the media are fond of asking, 'Where is the Palestinian Nelson Mandela?' (Linton 2014). Mandela was a product of a particular time and place that is not replicable. In a similar way, the interlocuters, mediators, electoral cycle, political economy, and issue agenda of one context are likely to be very different from those of another.

Although comparison between peace processes is difficult, it is useful – indeed, imperative – and is the principal motivation behind this book. What works in one context may not work in another, but it can be modified and right-sized to fit another context. Peace processes are assemblages of multiple elements addressing different security, political, territorial, economic, social, cultural, and symbolic issues. Each peace process must find its own path but may be influenced by other processes and engage in selective lending and borrowing. Perhaps the main lesson that one peace process can offer another is a realisation that a peace process and a negotiated settlement are possible. Often in the midst of a violent conflict, when recriminations and a sense of revenge are in the ascendant, the possibility of a peace process or any form of negotiation may seem remote. Yet, long-running and apparently intractable conflicts have managed to produce peace processes and reach situations in which the costs of the conflict have been lowered. A mere three years before the 1994 ceasefires that were foundational for the Northern Ireland peace process, no one could have considered a peace process to be feasible. Yet a peace process did take root (not without difficulty) and resulted in a major peace accord and significant quality of life improvements for many. The key lesson is that a peace process can be possible even if the immediate circumstances look unpromising.

The nature of a book on peace processes may mean that we focus too much on the process and not enough on the peace. In other words, we might pay attention to the 'how' without giving adequate bandwidth to the 'why' and the 'what happened next?' Certainly, procedural issues are crucial. It is of scholarly, practical, and policy importance that we have a clear understanding of what works and what does not work when adversaries attempt to reach a negotiated settlement in a conflict. But it is also worth investigating the kind of peace that they will deliver. A peace that leaves people insecure and economically precarious may not be worth the term 'peace'. Take the example of El Salvador, where a series of peace accords ended a decade-long civil war in 1992. Yet El Salvador's homicide rate is among the worst on the planet (Jaramillo 2018). The peace process failed to address a series of issues – such as an imbalanced economy and corruption in the police – that have fuelled a sky-high crime rate. Or consider the example of Bosnia-Herzegovina, where most violence ended as a result of the 1995 Dayton Accords. Despite massive international intervention in support of the Accords, many people in Bosnia remain politically disaffected and economically marginalised (IMF 2016). The key point is that the quality of peace must also be taken into account when we consider peace processes and peace accords. To take a straightforward approach that regards peace as a situation prevailing once a peace accord has been reached overlooks the importance of peace accord implementation and the legacy of a conflict.

How to compare peace processes

Given the variety in peace processes, the task of comparison is tricky – but not impossible. There are three key ways to compare across peace processes, and this book will use all three. The first is to identify peace processes as conflict case studies – for example Aceh or Nepal – and view the cases side-by-side. The second is to identify issue areas within peace processes, such as how to deal with the exclusion of a minority from the polity or how to address the problem of a surfeit of small arms left after violent conflict. Comparison can then be made between how different peace processes address similar issues. A third avenue of comparison is to examine procedural issues – such as negotiations, confidence-building measures, or the symbolism of signing ceremonies. For example, peace processes have used mediators in a variety of roles to attempt to get beyond the problems of face-to-face talks between adversaries.

This book organises its chapters according to conflict cases but then seeks, in the case study chapters and in the concluding chapter, to identify particular points of issue and procedural comparison. The organisation of the book around case studies is justified as peace processes are usually identified according to a particular conflict or location for that conflict. For example, the term 'Colombian peace process' has a readily identifiable meaning, even though many observers would agree that most conflict and peace processes have an international and transnational dimension. Moreover, understanding peace processes is enhanced when they are placed in a regional context. Understanding the Cambodian and Afghan cases, for example, is difficult unless one takes into account the regional dynamics and power-brokers.

In this book, our case study-led approach delves into issues areas in peace processes as well as procedural issues. To maximise comparison, we take a structured approach: the chapters – on the instruction of the editors – touch upon a set of key peace process elements (such as the pre-peace process context, or the negotiations). Since there is significant variety between peace processes, not all chapters will cover exactly similar ground, but there are enough points of comparison to ensure rigour. Crucially, the concluding chapter is organised around 11 variables that will have a bearing on the success or failure of the peace process. These 11 variables can be grouped into four broad categories: context, procedural factors, responsiveness of the peace process and peace accord, and participation and inclusion of the process and accord. As befits socio-political contexts that are often in flux, we should not see these variables and categories as fixed. They overlap with one another to co-produce an assemblage. In the conclusion chapter, and based on the analysis in each chapter, we give a numeric score to each of the variables in order to judge the extent to which a peace process can be judged a 'success' or 'failure'. As discussed elsewhere in this Introduction, the notion of success and failure in relation to peace processes is very subjective.

The variables listed below are not exhaustive, but based on the case study chapters in the book they are often significant.

Context

Level of symmetry between the parties
Level of engagement and supportiveness by the international community

Procedural

Existence and effectiveness of confidence-building measures
Level and supportiveness of third-party engagement

Responsiveness

Ability of the process and accord to deal with security issues
Ability of the process and accord to deal to produce effective governance
Ability of the process and accord to deal with justice and legacy issues
Ability of the process and accord to deal with the political economy of peace and conflict

Participation and inclusion

Level of public participation in the process and accord
Level of gender inclusion in the process and accord
Level of youth inclusion in the process and accord

The rest of this section unpacks the variables, while the concluding chapter reveals how the different peace processes covered in this book score in relation to the variables.

Context

Level of symmetry between the parties

This variable is about power and the extent to which the parties to a peace process exercise their relative power against other parties. In a situation of extreme asymmetry, the most powerful parties to a peace process or peace accord may be able to impose the rules of the process and the provisions in the accord to suit themselves.

In the 'Oslo process' between Israel and Palestinians, Israel was clearly the most powerful actor and was able to dictate many of the terms of the subsequent Oslo Accords. The Israeli power advantage then manifested itself in the lopsided implementation of those Accords. Yet, to some extent, the Israeli power advantage was something of a double-edged sword. The Israeli willingness to use their power advantage to turn the peace process into a win/lose rather than win/win process guaranteed the elongation of the conflict and the disaffection of many Palestinians. Of course, Palestinian powerlessness is only part of the story; the incompetence of their negotiating team (gathered around a stale and out-of-touch Palestinian Liberation Organisation clique) also played a large part in the fraying and eventual collapse of the Oslo Process (Said 2001).

If parties have relative symmetry in terms of power, then they may be able to negotiate with some level of parity. In an ideal case, such a context may allow for the give and take that might lead to a sustainable agreement: a sense that all sides have had to make compromises but also have been able to make some gains. It is worth noting that judgements on the power of actors also need to take into account their external sponsors. Israeli power, while very considerable and with a strong independent streak, ultimately has a backstop in the form of the United States. Indeed, a large number of the cases covered in this volume show how external sponsorship of conflict parties has been crucial in determining the pacific or aggressive intent of those parties. It is fair to say that the Serbian government was bombed to the negotiating table in 1995. External parties, and the United States in particular, enabled Croat and Bosniak forces to mount offensives against Serb forces in the run-up to the negotiations. This, together with Operation Deliberate Force – a 1995 NATO bombing campaign against Serbian military targets – had the effect of compelling the Serbian leadership to the negotiating table (Paczukla 2009). This 'thump and talk' sequencing has been quite common in peace processes whereby parties to the conflict seek to achieve battlefield advantage before engaging in negotiations.

Level of engagement and supportiveness by the international community

A supportive neighbourhood is widely regarded as being a crucial determinant of a successful peace process (Francis 2009). Most conflicts have a transnational and regional context in which neighbouring countries can act as patrons for regimes and armed groups, and can play a stabilising or destabilising role in the conflict. As the chapter on Afghanistan illustrates, a 'bad neighbourhood' can hamper the prospects of a viable peace process. India, Pakistan, Iran, and Russia all play a significant role in sponsoring their favoured actors. On top of this, out of area actors, such as the United States and European Union, are also involved. The result is a mix of moves and counter-moves that mean that internal actors do not have autonomy. Indeed, the current situation has shades of the 'Great Game' of the nineteenth century (Becker 2012). At a minimum, the medley of actors complicates matters. More grievously, there is deliberate and provocative meddling at the expense of

Afghanistan itself. It is fair to say that India's increasing involvement in the conflict is a function of their wish to keep an eye on their rivals Pakistan (Mitton 2017; Akbarzadeh 2003).

In other cases, however, 'good neighbours' can be supportive of a peace process and accord. One reason for the relative success of the Northern Ireland peace process was that the neighbours – the United Kingdom, Republic of Ireland, and European Union – were not only supportive of a negotiated settlement but were all actively engaged in the process. The external actors were not always aligned, yet they largely acted in concert to provide a supportive political and economic environment for the peace process, peace accord, and its subsequent implementation. While some conflicts can be described as 'proxy conflicts' (such as Lebanon, Syria, or Yemen, whereby external actors sponsor regimes or militant groups), we can also conceive of 'proxy peace', whereby external actors encourage peace negotiations and the reaching of an agreement. As described in Chapter 5, the changing stance of China in relation to the Khmer Rouge, for example, was a turning point in reaching an agreement.

Procedural

Existence and effectiveness of confidence-building measures

It is entirely rational for parties to a nascent peace process to distrust one another. Years or decades of demonisation, violent outrages and mobilisation mean that the default response towards an out-group is likely to be distrust. As a result, peace processes often begin in tentative ways so that parties to the process can assess the seriousness of the other side. Crucial here are confidence-building measures or indicators of trustworthiness (Leiven 2008). Initially, these might take the form of largely symbolic gestures that might, over time, develop into something more substantive. In the case of Northern Ireland, for example, the main pro-united Ireland militant group, the Irish Republican Army (IRA), staged a number of unofficial ceasefires to show its bona fides in relation to developing a viable peace process (Maloney 2002). In return, the British government inserted phrases suggested by the IRA (and their political cousins, Sinn Féin) into a speech made by the British Minister for Northern Ireland. In other peace processes, confidence-building measures have included the release of prisoners and demilitarisation measures. Perhaps the ultimate confidence-building measures are elite level gestures aimed at encouraging support constituencies to place their faith in the peace process or peace accord. Although occurring after the transition of power, South African President Nelson Mandela wore a Springboks jersey at the 1995 Rugby World Cup (The Economist 1995: 81). While a seemingly inconsequential act, it was actually full of symbolism. The Springboks – the South African rugby team – were strongly and almost exclusively associated with the white population. Mandela's act was a statement to both white and non-white South Africans. To whites it said: I respect your culture and want you to feel part of the new South Africa. To non-whites it said: we have to embrace out-group members if we are to make this new South Africa work.

Level and supportiveness of third-party engagement

This is more specific than the contextual variable above of a supportive neighbourhood. It refers to third parties who act as go-betweens and mediators for the peace process (Curle 1990). Their role is usually procedural and facilitative, and is highly contingent on the particularities of the peace process. It is often the case that third parties might play a significant role at particular moments in a peace process and a less significant role at other points. Third parties can be insiders and outsiders (and a mix of the two) (Mitchell 2003: 81–82). They can be states, international organisations, or be drawn from civil society, and can play a variety of roles. In some peace processes, Nepal being a good example, third-party involvement was relatively limited as the government and Maoists largely preferred to restrict the role of outsiders (Westendorf 2018). In other peace processes, for example Mindanao, they have played a more significant role (Özerdem 2012).

Third parties will have varying degrees of interest in the conflict. In the case of Norway's mediation role in the Sri Lankan peace process, it is difficult to suggest that the Norwegians had anything other than altruistic reasons for being involved. Certainly, they would have received some reflective glory and soft power enhancement if the peace process succeeded, but there was no strategic interest for Norway (Stokke 2012). In other cases, however, third parties do have a direct interest and make little pretence to neutrality. If the context and their power allows, third parties will engage in a range of activities stretching from cajoling and encouragement, to technical support for the peace process (such as provision of a venue for talks), to inducements such as the promise of economic support for reconstruction or the reconfiguration of the post-conflict state or security sector (Mitchell 2003: 82–84). Can third parties cross the line from inducement and encouragements, towards coercion? That depends on how one interprets the role of third parties, but certainly 'mediation with muscle' can be in the toolkit of some mediators (Svensson 2007).

Responsiveness

Ability of the process and accord to deal with security issues

Violent conflict distorts societies in multiple ways, not least in relation to security. In addition to engaging in actual violence and human rights abuses, a state may enlarge its security apparatus, enact emergency legislation, and engage in securitised messaging. Populations and areas under the control of armed groups may be similarly mobilised, militarised, and securitised. A peace process and peace accord may provide the opportunity for demilitarisation and normalisation whereby the military–civilian balance in government, governance, legal codes, and the general orientation of society can be recalibrated. This, of course, is easier said than done. Demilitarisation and disarmament rest on trust between parties to a peace process or peace accord that they will not be needing their weaponry in the future. Elements in state militaries and in militant groups may have vested interests in the continuation of the conflict, and so there may be resistance to demilitarisation. In contexts like Afghanistan, the military, militias, and police are mass employers, and a normalisation of security would mean a threat to the income in millions of households (Sedra 2013).

It is worth noting that the challenge facing peace processes and peace accords is not just the stemming of the violence of the conflict. In a large number of peace process cases, criminal violence has become a significant post-conflict factor. South Africa, Nicaragua, El Salvador, and many other contexts now face criminal violence that is on a larger scale than the conflict that preceded it (Steenkamp 2011). To some extent, this violence has roots in the political economies of the civil war or authoritarianism that preceded the peace deal. Societies emerging from violent conflict may have a surfeit of small arms as well as a large number of young men who know how to use them and have limited opportunities from the licit economy. Stemming post-conflict criminal violence requires an economy able to offer opportunities – something that often relies on the global economy and is therefore outside of the control of national politics. It also requires a state competent and powerful enough to impose a monopoly of violence on its own citizens. This is not always possible, and so a peace process and peace accord may usher in an era of less rather than more security for many citizens.

Ability of the process and accord to deal to produce effective governance

This issue is crucial to peace processes and peace accords. Often issues of governance lie at the heart of conflicts. Communities might feel excluded or unrepresented. Systems of governance might be corrupt, discriminatory, or repressive. Many peace processes and peace accords revolve around seeking to change the state in fundamental ways, and this is where governance comes in. Parties to a peace process may wish to change how the state is governed, how it responds to citizens, and how it represents them. Other parties may wish to resist such changes. In many cases, peace accord provisions revolve around the state and its responsibilities (Richmond 2014). The state and its sub-units, such as municipalities, are the central clearing house for conflict management. How it distributes public goods (like healthcare and education) and how it deals with perceptions of discrimination are crucial to how political actors can stoke or calm fears of a conflict.

International support for peace accords implementation also tends to revolve around the state. In many cases, this involves state-building activities that are concerned with governance. The logic among international interveners runs as follows:

if the state is well-run and responsive to citizen needs, then there is less likelihood of a resumption of violent conflict, the peace accord will bed down, and international interveners can pursue an exit strategy in the knowledge that the post-peace accord dispensation is stable and sustainable (Rwanda Research Group 2009; Stockemer 2009). A common criticism of international support for peace accord implementation is that it becomes too focused on reforming and right-sizing the state to the detriment of other aspects of peacebuilding. The state-centric approach might be too capital city-focused, leaving those living outside of the metropolis feeling overlooked. An over-focus on state-building and what became known as 'good governance' might also mean that interveners concentrate on rigid technocratic goals rather than the more social and empathetic aspects of peace that a society moving away from conflict might require (Mac Ginty 2018).

Ability of the process and accord to deal with justice and legacy issues

At heart, violent conflict involves multiple emotions of hurt, fear, trauma, and grievance. Dealing with these issues is complex given the depth and variety of feelings and the different timelines that people that people may have. To some extent, justice and peace can be seen to be contradictory (Schuett 1997). In order to achieve a peace accord, parties may have to accept that their adversaries' past behaviour will go unpunished. For example, there may be an amnesty or the release of prisoners. To victims of violence and their families, this may be too high a price to pay for peace – they may rather have justice. Others, however, may be prepared for the 'hard swallow and weak smile' that a peace process or peace accord may require. This might require negotiating with people and groups that they find repugnant, or accepting that individuals they regard as 'terrorists' or 'perpetrators' receive rights and representation. Clearly, all such issues have an emotional edge.

Most peace processes and accords address justice issues. This might involve reform of a judicial system that may be regarded as being biased in favour of the regime or a particular community. Many peace accords have involved transitional justice provisions that seek to navigate a way through the messy endings of the violent phase of a conflict (Maddison and Shepherd 2014). The transitional justice toolkit can include truth and justice commissions, amnesty and reparations, and the deployment of indigenous and traditional reconciliation and truth-telling practices. Alongside such measures, reforms are often made to the formal judicial system.

Two further points are worth listing in relation to justice and legacy issues. The first is that while efforts may be made at the formal and national scale to reform the judicial system, most often justice and legacy issues have to be dealt with at the informal and societal level. While a state can introduce a new constitution, reform the courts system, and make sure that the new police force are cognisant of human rights law, it cannot legislate for forgiveness and tolerance. If it takes place at all, this occurs at the everyday level. It occurs in the queue at the bakery or on the bus when people from different backgrounds might come into contact with one another. This 'everyday peace', or more likely everyday tolerance and co-existence, involves emotional intelligence and a form of everyday diplomacy that might draw on the spirit of a peace accord (Berents 2015).

The second point to make is that there is no set end date on legacy. Conflicts that occurred centuries ago can still be used as mobilisation tools by politicians who may wish to capitalise on a community's sense of grievance. Those involved in a peace process and peace accord may wish to recalibrate the conflict-affected society so that it looks forward rather than back. The symbolism and messaging around peace processes often encourages communities to leave behind the past and embrace a new future. This, of course, is easier said than done.

Ability of the process and accord to deal with the political economy of peace and conflict

Economics lies at the heart of many conflicts, and it can be crucial to a peace process and peace accord (Distler et al. 2018). Conflicts often develop because of perceived or real grievances felt by one community. They may feel, for example, that another community gets preferential treatment when it comes to the distribution of public goods by the state. Violent conflict often distorts an economy. In the licit sector, this might involve the direction of state resources towards the security sector and away from social goods. It may also involve the state becoming further indebted in order to pay for the war. The security sector may become a significant employer. In the illicit sector, there may be the smuggling of goods and people, illegal mining, or the imposition of 'revolutionary taxes'. These conflict economies are often complex, will develop as the conflict develops, and will contain vested interests who may be threatened by a peace process. The 'resource curse' suffered in some conflict-affected contexts, whereby the conflict is sparked by the unfair distribution of primary products like oil, will not go away unless redistributive efforts are made.

Crucial in all of this is the economic security of everyday people. While some might be impoverished and displaced by conflict, others might flourish economically. A peace process and peace accord thus faces navigating a delicate path. In some cases, a peace process and accord might be accompanied by internationally sponsored economic reconstruction packages. This might involve the physical reconstruction of damaged infrastructure, debt relief, or foreign direct investment. In all cases, however, the exigencies of the global economy will prevail and will do much to influence how a post-peace accord context fares. Although parties to a peace accord may wish to push the 'reset' button, the global economy will take its course. Bosnia-Herzegovina and Kosovo, for example, have benefited from peace assistance packages from international donors, yet these do not offset the structures and dynamics of the wider economic context. Both states suffer from significant out-migration simply because their economies cannot provide enough jobs. Without sought-after primary products, and not situated on major trading routes or benefiting as tourist destinations, their economies are poorly placed. This has contributed to a sense of disillusionment among many in the post-peace accord years.

Participation and inclusion

Level of public participation in the process and accord

Peace processes, especially in their early phases, often require secrecy. The first tentative steps towards a peace process might require subterranean talks involving intermediaries. To make such talks public, especially if conflict is still ongoing, may be incendiary. Moreover, should such a peace process take off, the negotiations need to be restricted to a reasonably narrow range of personnel simply to keep the process manageable. In a number of cases, peace accords have been negotiated 'off-site' so that the negotiators have the space to thrash out a deal away from the 24/7 glare of the local news media. Yet there does come a time when a peace process and peace accord will require public buy-in to be legitimate. This may be difficult, as the issues involved in a peace process, indeed the very existence of a peace process, may be very divisive.

While peace processes ultimately involve inter-group bargaining, the intra-group level is crucial. Few parties in a conflict are monolithic. Instead, they often involve coalitions and factions. Parties to a peace process often need to spend immense energy on consulting within their own group in order to assess the support in the in-group for the peace process. The risk of moving too far beyond what the support base is willing to support is that there could be a split. In extreme cases, this might manifest itself in violent spoiler activity. More zealous actors within a group may brand the peace process as traitorous and a betrayal of fundamental goals.

A key form of participation in a peace process is through a referendum that will endorse or reject the deal. This is a high-risk strategy, as Colombia's President Santos found to his cost when the public rejected the 2016 peace accord. The nature of a referendum, and its binary yes/no question, means that it is a one-off form of consultation. Other forms of inclusion and consultation can include the involvement of civil society in negotiations. This might broaden the parties to a process beyond a government, militant groups, and established political parties, and it may broaden the issues under discussion. The Colombian negotiations, for example, included extensive representations from victims of violence – a device that had a large impact on the seriousness with which victims' issues were treated in the final peace accord.

The ultimate test of inclusion and participation in a peace accord is the nature of the polity that might stem from a peace accord. In many cases, there is a tendency for political actors to seek to maximise their own position and minimise the space for others. Peace accords can seek to preserve space for various groups and move beyond majoritarianism or the exclusion of some groups. The most obvious inclusion device is a formal power-sharing arrangement that may be part of a peace accord. Under power-sharing (found in Lebanon and Northern Ireland among other contexts), the parties to the conflict will agree to share power. This might mean setting aside the central constitutional dispute in order to ensure that public services function. Other tests of inclusion and participation include the extent to which civil society and minorities can access the polity. This is difficult even in societies that have not been affected by conflict.

Level of gender inclusion in the process and accord

Just as conflict is gendered, so is peace. Violent conflict affects men and women in different ways, with Sexual and Gender-Based Violence (SGBV) often playing a prominent role in how war is perpetrated (Oriolo 2017). The gendered nature of conflict is often subtle and insidious. It can be manifest in the political economies, cultural and political expression, and social expectations in a conflict-affected society. Prescribed and expected gender roles during conflict often continue into and beyond the peace process. Women are often expected to play a secondary role in peace talks, and there is strong evidence that women often play a marginal role in negotiations. In many cases, those who shout loudest and have guns (usually men) receive most of the attention in peace processes. This can lead to a skewed peace accord that makes provision for issues like Disarmament, Demobilisation and Reintegration, and Security Sector Reform that are overwhelmingly directed at males. Other issues that do not directly minister to the needs and demands of combatants may receive less attention.

At the heart of the issue of gender inclusion is the ability of those involved in peace negotiations to recognise the needs of the conflict-affected society. This means looking beyond hard political, security, and constitutional issues to embrace a more sociological understanding of conflict and peace. This is not to say that hard political, security, and constitutional issues are somehow male and apparently soft issues like the needs of victims and the need to reform the education system are somehow female. It is, instead, to underscore the need for those involved in a conflict-affected context to have a holistic understanding of that context. This includes a recognition that there may be a preponderance of female-headed households, or that it is women who are the main breadwinners.

There have been a number of initiatives to increase female participation in peace processes. The rationale behind these initiatives is that a more gendered peace accord will have a greater chance of acceptance and that the peace that ensues will be more sustainable. It is too early to tell if these initiatives will bear fruit.

Level of youth inclusion in the process and accord

In many societies, a substantial conflict burden falls upon youth. They may be subject to mobilisation, radicalisation, abduction, and conscription. Yet, the patriarchal and hierarchical nature of many societies means that, despite the high conflict burden they bear, youth may be excluded from key decisions relating to the conflict and peace process (Berents and McEvoy-Levy 2015). In some conflict-affected societies there may be a 'youth bulge' or a high birth-rate and large numbers of youths. This may be problematic if the economy is unlikely to offer adequate education, employment, and prospects. In some cases, youths may have been radicalised and traumatised during their time as combatants. They may find reintegration into civilian life difficult, and communities may remain wary of them. As well as being victims, many of these youths may also be perpetrators. The dislocations and displacements of war may mean that the family structures that may offer rootedness (but also possibly stultifying control) are absent.

While a peace process and peace accord may offer the opportunity for a society to recalibrate its gender relations, and the relations of the youth to the rest of society, this rarely occurs on a wholesale basis. Power-holders such as political parties or representatives of militant groups may be wary of a substantial ceding of power. As a result, in most cases, dealing with youth is often seen as an afterthought in peace processes. A number of post-peace accord societies are host to large numbers of disaffected youth who feel little investment in the peace accord and the post-accord dispensation. For many, for example in Bosnia-Herzegovina and Kosovo, out-migration becomes a principal life goal – something that has implications for the sustainability of the economy (Efendic 2016).

The study of peace processes

Three factors are worth taking on board in relation to the study of peace processes. The first relates to the increasing breadth of peace processes, the second to the time range of our studies, and the third to the critical or problem-solving dispositions of many scholars.

The systematic study of peace processes is a relatively young endeavour. Indeed, before the end of the Cold War, the systematic study of violent conflict, particularly civil war, was very much a specialist academic interest (Horowitz 1985; Azar 1990). A rise in conflicts after the end of the Cold War – and particularly their visibility, high body counts, and, in some cases, their proximity to Europe – meant that there was a rush to explain the causes and possible ways out of conflict (Darby and Mac Ginty 2000, 2003; Crocker et al. 1999, 2005, 2007). This was the genesis of the study of peace processes, with many of these studies being systematic and comparative. Over the years, the study of armed conflict and peace processes has become more sophisticated and has broadened considerably. The inter-linkages between peace, conflict, development, and wider political economies has become more apparent (Mac Ginty and Williams 2016: 20–24; Keen 2008; Kaldor 2012). Peace processes themselves have broadened. In the early post-Cold War days, many peace processes were primarily concerned with constitutional, territorial, and security matters. Peace processes and accords have become more expansive, in recognition of the economic, societal, and cultural dimensions of conflict.

It is now possible to find a range of studies on dimensions of peace processes that were once considered marginal. Indeed, some aspects of peace processes – such as transitional justice and disarmament, demobilisation, and reintegration (DDR) – have spawned enormous literatures (Williams et al. 2012; Berdal 1996; Özerdem 2002). The long-neglected issue of gender and peace processes has finally received attention, although some issues (such as media coverage and peace processes, and the impact of macro-economics on negotiations) have yet to attract significant scholarly attention.

Alongside the burgeoning academic study of peace processes, there has also been a growing body of practitioner insights from those involved in negotiation and implementation and from those working in the international organisation and international non-governmental spheres. Some of the memoirs from peace process participants risk being self-congratulatory, although given the relatively small number of people involved in negotiations, they offer invaluable insights. From the NGO and INGO practitioner world, the Accord series published by Conciliation Resources has provided wonderful primary documentation and analyses of a long list of peace processes and issues (www.c-r.org/accord). Also worth mentioning are two datasets that allow both qualitative and quantitative investigation. The Peace Accords Matrix (PAM) is a dataset derived from 34 comprehensive peace accords reached in the 1989–2012 period (https://peaceaccords.nd.edu/). Its emphasis on comprehensive agreements (that is, agreements involving the major conflict parties and main issues) means that it covers landmark agreements that have inspired other peace accords. It can be searched according to issue areas to allow comparison between peace accords and has been contracted to monitor the implementation of the 2016 Colombian peace accord. The second dataset is PA-X and contains around 1,500 agreements (many of them partial and temporary) that were reached between 1990 and 2016. The concentration of data in PA-X has allowed longitudinal and comparative data to become more apparent (such as the fact that peace accords are becoming wordier – reflecting their coverage of a broader range of issues) (www.politicalsettlements.org/portfolio/pa-x-database/).

A second point to make in relation to the study of peace processes relates to the temporal range: when does a peace process begin and end? The question does not have an easy answer. The beginnings of a peace process may be hard to discern, as it may take the form of informal overtures conducted 'under cover'. These overtures may be to a more substantive peace process that becomes public and, in time, to negotiations and a peace accord. It is unclear which of those markers might be identified as the starting point of the peace process. Similarly, the end point of a peace process is likely to be indistinct. If the process collapses and the parties revert back to violent conflict (as in the case of Sri Lanka), then the peace process can be said to be over. In other cases, there might be drift – a 'no war, no peace' situation in which no party formally walks away from the peace process, yet at the same time, there is no willingness to reinvigorate the process. Even in successful cases in which a peace accord is reached, it is difficult to identify a terminal point, as the implementation of the accord may take many years. Indeed, the act of studying a particular context and identifying it as 'post-conflict' risks reinforcing the conflict-related character of a context. Scholars still refer to Bosnia-Herzegovina as a 'post-conflict' area over two decades after the Dayton Accords.

A final issue to note in relation to the study of peace processes is to alert readers to the divide between critical and problem-solving scholarship (Pugh 2013; Ryan 2013). This divide (which has fuzzy edges) pertains across the social sciences, but is particularly noticeable in relation to the study of peace. The problem-solving approach, as the name suggests, is interested in real-world problems and how to address them. For those of a critical persuasion, however, the problem-solving approach may focus too heavily on conflict manifestations rather than on the underlying causes of conflict. Critical approaches are primarily concerned with the structural conflict drivers and rationalise that dealing with conflict manifestations merely kicks the can down the road. Consider the case of the Israeli–Palestinian conflict. There are regular eruptions in that conflict, particularly in relation Gaza, with Israeli air assaults on Gaza that frequently cause large numbers of civilian casualties. A problem-solving approach would see a ceasefire as a worthy endeavour as it may dampen down the direct violence and save lives. For critical scholars, however, such an approach is a half-measure. It does not address the wider Israel–Palestinian conflict, power imbalance, and the identity politics that undergird the conflict. In this view, problem-solving might deal with the immediate problem but leave unaddressed the wider conflict and indirect violence (discrimination, exclusion, avoidable poverty) with occasional flare-ups of direct violence.

These academic debates are important because they influence how we might interpret 'success', 'failure', and the end goal in a peace process. For some actors and observers, stopping the immediate violence in a conflict might be the principal objective. Other issues such as rights, fairer political representation, and access to public goods may be regarded as of secondary importance or not important at all. In Myanmar and India, for example, the governments have made numerous ceasefire agreements with armed groups. In both cases, the follow-through with a meaningful peace process has been painfully slow, suggesting that the governments are really only interested in stopping the violence rather than addressing the grievances of the conflict actors. For other actors, the end goal of a peace process should be much more ambitious than a ceasefire or peace accord. In this view, the goal should be positive peace or conflict transformation whereby the underlying conflict causes are addressed and social and economic relations are recalibrated in order to ensure smooth inter-group relations. Such a whole of society approach, however, would entail a dramatic revolution of society and would likely face opposition from vested interests. The 2016 peace agreement between the Colombian government and the FARC guerrilla group was a remarkable achievement with far-reaching political and security implications. Yet many powerful interests remain entrenched in Colombia, not least powerful landowners who were suspicious of the peace process, and so without land reform and taking some land away from current landowners, there are limits to how far the Colombian peace process can address underlying conflict causes.

Bibliography

Akbarzadeh, Shahram. 2003. "India and Pakistan's Geostrategic Rivalry in Central Asia." *Contemporary South Asia* 12 (2): 219–228.

Azar, Edward E. 1990. *The Management of Protracted Social Conflicts*. London: Dartmouth Publishing Company.

Becker, Seymour. 2012. "The 'Great Game': The History of an Evocative Phrase." *Asian Affairs* 43 (1): 61–80.

Berdal, Mats. 1996. *Disarmament and Demobilisation After Civil Wars: Arms, Soldiers and the Termination of Armed Conflicts*. London: International Institute for Strategic Studies.

Berents, Helen. 2015. "An Embodied Everyday Peace in the Midst of Violence." *Peacebuilding* 3 (2): 1–14.

Berents, Helen, and Siobhan McEvoy-Levy. 2015. "Theorising Youth and Everyday Peace(Building)." *Peacebuilding* 3 (2): 115–125.

Crocker, Chester A., Fen Osler, and Pamela Aall. (Eds.). 1999. *Herding Cats: Multiparty Mediation in a Complex World*. Washington, DC: United States Institute of Peace Press.

Crocker, Chester A., Fen Osler, and Pamela Aall. (Eds.). 2005. *Grasping the Nettle: Analyzing Cases of Intractable Conflict*. Washington, DC: United States Institute of Peace Press.

Crocker, Chester A., Fen Osler, and Pamela Aall. (Eds.). 2007. *Leashing the Dogs of War: Conflict Management in a Divided World*. Washington, DC: United States Institute of Peace Press.

Curle, Adam. 1990. "Third Party Peace Making." *Interdisciplinary Peace Research* 2 (2): 62–73.

Darby, John, and Roger Mac Ginty. (Eds.). 2000. *The Management of Peace Processes*. Houndmills: Palgrave Macmillan.

Darby, John, and Roger Mac Ginty. (Eds.). 2003. *Contemporary Peacemaking: Conflict, Violence and Peace Processes*. Houndmills: Palgrave Macmillan.

Distler, Werner, Elena B. Stavrevska, and Birte Vogel. 2018. "Economies of Peace: Economy Formation Processes and Outcomes in Conflict-Affected Societies." *Civil Wars* 20 (2): 139–150.

Economist. 1995. "Mandela's 'boks'." *The Economist*, 1 July, 336 (7921): 81.

Efendic, Adnan. 2016. "Emigration Intentions in a Post-Conflict Environment: Evidence from Bosnia and Herzegovina." *Post-Communist Economies* 28 (3): 335–352.

Francis, David J. 2009. "Peacekeeping in a Bad Neighbourhood." *African Journal of Conflict Resolution* 9 (3): 87–116.

Horowitz, Donald L. 1985. *Ethnic Groups in Conflict*. Berkeley, CA: University of California Press.

IMF. 2016. "Bosnia-Herzegovina: Turning the Economy Around." *IMF News*, 9 (9).

Jaramillo, Krishna. 2018. "El Salvador Homicides Increase in the First Month of 2018." *Latin American Post* 26 January.

Kaldor, Mary. 2012. *New and Old Wars: Organized Violence in a Global Era*, 3rd edn. Cambridge: Polity Press.

Keen, David. 2008. *Complex Emergencies*. Cambridge: Polity Press.

Lederach, John Paul. 2003. *The Little Book of Conflict Transformation*. Intercourse, PA: Good Books.

Leiven, Anatol. 2008. "Confidence-Building Measures: Lessons for the Middle East." *International Relations* 22 (3): 369–374.

Linton, Martin. 2014. "Release Marwan Barghouti: He Can Be Palestine's Nelson Mandela." *Guardian*, 28 March.

Maddison, Sarah, and Laura J. Shepherd. 2014. "Peacebuilding and the Postcolonial Politics of Transitional Justice." *Peacebuilding* 2 (3): 253–269.

Mac Ginty, Roger. 2018. "The Limits of Technocracy and Local Encounters: The European Union and Peacebuilding." *Contemporary Security Policy* 39 (1): 166–179.

Mac Ginty, Roger, and Andrew Williams. 2016. *Conflict and Development*, 2nd edn. London: Routledge.

Maloney, Ed. 2002. *A Secret History of the IRA*. London: Penguin.

Mitchell, Christopher. 2003. "Mediation and the Ending of Conflicts." In John Darby, and Roger Mac Ginty (Eds.), *Contemporary Peacemaking: Conflict, Violence and Peace Processes*, 77–86. Basingstoke: Macmillan.

Mitton, John Logan. 2017. "Rivalry Intervention in Civil Conflicts: Afghanistan (India-Pakistan), Angola (USSR-USA), and Lebanon (Israel-Syria)." *Canadian Foreign Policy Journal* 23 (3): 277–291.

Mundy, Simon. 2017. "Sri Lanka Counts High Cost of War and Peace." *Financial Times*, 7 November.

Paczukla, Julla. 2009. "The Long, Difficult Road to Dayton." *International Journal* 60 (1): 235–272.

Pugh, Michael. 2013. "The Problem-Solving and Critical Paradigms." In Roger Mac Ginty (Ed.), *Routledge Handbook of Peacebuilding*, 11–24. Abingdon: Routledge.

Oriolo, Temitope B. 2017. "'Unwilling Cocoons': Boko Haram's War Against Women." *Studies in Conflict & Terrorism* 40 (2): 99–121.

Özerdem, Alpaslan. 2002. "Disarmament, Demobilisation and Reintegration of Former Combatants in Afghanistan: Lessons Learned from a Cross-Cultural Perspective." *Third World Quarterly* 23 (5): 961–975.

Özerdem, Alpaslan. 2012. "The Contribution of the Organisation of the Islamic Conference to the Peace Process in Mindanao." *Civil Wars* 14 (3): 393–413.

Ramsbotham, Oliver, Tom Woodhouse, and Hugh Miall. 2016. *Contemporary Conflict Resolution*, 4th edn. Cambridge: Polity Press.

Richmond, Oliver, P. 1998. "Devious Objectives and the Disputants' View of International Mediation: A Theoretical Framework." *Journal of Peace Research* 35 (6): 707–722.

Richmond, Oliver P. 2014. *Failed Statebuilding: Intervention, the State, and the Dynamics of Peace Formation*. New Haven: Yale University Press.

Rwanda Research Group. 2009. "Peace-Building Through Good Governance and Capable Statehood." *Peace Review* 21 (3): 286–295.

Ryan, Stephen. 2013. "The Evolution of Peacebuilding." In Roger Mac Ginty (Ed.), *Routledge Handbook of Peacebuilding*, 25–35. Abingdon: Routledge.

Said, Edward. 2001. *The End of the Peace Process: Oslo and After*. London: Vintage.

Schuett, Oliver. 1997. "The International War Crimes Tribunal for Former Yugoslavia and the Dayton Peace Agreement: Peace Versus Justice?" *International Peacekeeping* 4 (2): 91–114.

Sedra, Mark. 2013. "The Hollowing-Out of the Liberal Peace Project in Afghanistan: The Case of Security Sector Reform." *Central Asian Survey* 32 (3): 1–17.

Steenkamp, Christina. 2011. "In the Shadows of War and Peace: Making Sense of Violence After Peace Accords." *Conflict, Security & Development* 11 (3): 357–383.

Stockemer, Daniel. 2009. "Does Democracy Lead to Good Governance? The Question Applied to Africa and Latin America." *Global Change, Peace & Security* 21 (2): 241–255.

Stokke, Kristian. 2012. "Peace-Building as Small State Foreign Policy: Norway's Peace Engagement in a Changing International Context." *International Studies* 49 (3–4): 207–231.

Svensson, Isak. 2007. "Mediation with Muscles or Minds? Exploring Power Mediators and Pure Mediators in Civil Wars." *International Negotiation* 12 (2): 229–248.

Westendorf, Jasmine-Kim. 2018. "Challenges of Local Ownership: Understanding the Outcomes of the International Community's 'Light Footprint' Approach to the Nepal Peace Process." *Journal of Intervention and Statebuilding* 12 (2): 228–252.

Williams, Melissa, Rosemary Nagy, and Jon Elster. 2012. *Transitional Justice*. New York: University of New York Press.

1

ACEH

Nathan Shea

Introduction

The signing of the Memorandum of Understanding (MoU) peace agreement between the government of Indonesia and the Free Aceh Movement (*Gerakan Aceh Merdeka* in Bahasa Indonesia; GAM) on 15 August 2005 brought an end to a civil war that had seized the Aceh province for nearly three decades. The agreement was finalised just seven months after a return to talks between the two parties, following the Indian Ocean tsunami which devastated the region on 26 December 2004, radically altering the dynamics of the peace process.

Since 1976, GAM had fought for independence for the province which it saw as wrongly subsumed into the Indonesian state. Commanding popular sympathies through the 1990s in the face of a repressive military campaign by the Indonesian armed forces (*Tentara Nasional Indonesia*; TNI), the civil war was caught in the maelstrom of democratic political reform (*reformasi*) that swept across Indonesia following the Asian Financial Crisis. Spurred by the successful (yet violent) referendum and independence that birthed Timor Leste in 1999, widespread demonstrations for Acehnese sovereignty threatened the potential balkanisation of the Indonesian archipelago. The 1998 ouster of President Suharto, who had ruled the country for 31 years, and the dismantling of his New Order period appeared to be the catalyst for the reclaiming of ethnic identities that had been previously constricted. An increase in violence was also witnessed in the provinces of Papua, Maluku and North Maluku, Central Sulawesi, and in West and Central Kalimantan (Braithwaite et al. 2010; Shea 2016).

The Aceh Peace Process, mediated by two International NGOs – The Centre for Humanitarian Dialogue from 1999 to 2003 and Crisis Management Initiative in 2005 – helped usher in a generation where international non-governmental organizations (INGOs) now play a significant role in peacemaking efforts. For nearly six years, Indonesian officials negotiated in Geneva and then Helsinki with GAM leaders in exile, far removed from the remote areas where armed groups clashed with Indonesian security forces over territory and influence. Ceasefires were regularly and often flagrantly ignored, until a sustainable political solution was negotiated over the first half of 2005. While the Helsinki Agreement offered limited enhancements over the autonomy already enjoyed by the province, it provided the inducements necessary for the demilitarisation of GAM and its evolution into a political party under the framework of 'self-government'. Since signing the agreement the province has experienced more than a decade of relative peace, despite ongoing concerns on human rights violations and historical injustices.

This chapter examines the peacemaking process in Aceh, delving into how and why International NGOs became the preferred mediators in the conflict, and the difficult path they took to bring an end to violence in the region. First it outlines the origins of the conflict in Aceh, detailing the evolution of GAM as an independence movement born out of centuries of ethnic identity formation and fuelled by a modern history of harsh military suppression and exploitative regional policies. An examination of the peace process shows how local, national, and international efforts eventually led to the significant and rapid developments in late 2004 and 2005. Lastly, reflections are offered to help expand on some of the key takeaways from the peace process as a contained peacemaking exercise and its broader implications for the long-term socio-political environment in Aceh and Indonesia.

Conflict analysis

The province of Aceh sits at the northernmost tip of the Indonesian state on the island of Sumatra, separated from Malaysia by the Malacca Strait to its east and the Indian islands of Andaman and Nicobar across the Andaman Sea to its north. It is home to a largely homogeneous ethnic population; over 70 per cent of the population are ethnically Acehnese, while over 98 per cent of the population are Muslim (Ananta et al. 2015). Islam arrived in the region by 1250 AD, and for centuries Aceh acted as a gateway port between Southeast Asia and the Middle East, earning the region the nickname the Verandah of Mecca (*Serambi Mekkah*). Though the Dutch first established the Dutch East Indies Company in modern Indonesia in 1602, the Acehnese Sultanate withstood colonisation for centuries, only incorporated into the Dutch colony in the late nineteenth century.

Acehnese resistance to Dutch and then Japanese imperialism continued until the end of the Second World War, when there was real optimism that Aceh might gain sovereign status. However, Aceh's incorporation into the newly independent Indonesian state in 1949 triggered persistent nationalist conflict that would span across the following six decades.

The precursor to GAM was the independence group Darul Islam, established in 1949 and led by Aceh's first governor, Teungku Daud Beureu'eh. Darul Islam engaged in regular conflict with the Indonesia government throughout the 1950s, leading to the imposition of martial law by President Sukarno in 1957. Sustained military pressure eventually forced rebels into a negotiated settlement for the establishment of Aceh as autonomous province with special rights to Islamic laws in 1962.

These special autonomy provisions would, however, be slowly wound back over the years, leading to the resurfacing of nationalist aggression in the 1970s. Responding to increased popular dissatisfaction with Jakarta, a group of around 70 ideologically driven and well-educated professionals established in December 1976 the Aceh–Sumatra National Liberation Front (ASNLF), the precursor to the Free Aceh Movement (GAM).

GAM was led by Hasan di Tiro, a grandson of Teungku Cik di Tiro, a revered Indonesian 'national hero' who led the Acehnese fight against the Dutch colonial forces in the late nineteenth century. Hasan had studied in New York for a period and even worked at the Indonesian Mission to the United Nations; however, he was stripped of the position and his Indonesian citizenship after declaring his support for the Darul Islam movement in 1953. He would return to Indonesia eventually in 1974, reconnecting with contacts gained during his time with Darul Islam to begin the GAM movement.

At first glance, GAM was almost entirely an independence movement – grounded in the international fervour experienced in the 1970s and 1980s decolonisation movement and the UN's mandated right to self-determination. Its 1976 independence manifesto reads:

> The people of Acheh, Sumatra, exercising our right of self-determination, and protecting our historic right of eminent domain to our fatherland, do hereby declare ourselves free and independent from all political control of the foreign regime of Jakarta and the alien people of the island of Java.

In this sense, GAM sought to construct (or preserve) a sense of Acehnese nationalism encoded in the legacy of the sultanate as distinct from the Indonesian state created after the Second World War (Ansori 2012; Na Thalang 2009). It rejected the idea of Indonesian nationhood, instead seeing the country as a Javanese colonialist construct aimed at subjugating differing peoples in the archipelago. The suppression of Acehnese national identity became a key contestation over the course of the conflict. The Indonesian government prohibited the public display of symbols connected with GAM and Acehnese independence; the flag of the Free Aceh Movement was particularly targeted for repression and removal, often with punitive force (Schulze 2004).

The aspirations for independent nationhood were also driven by perceived resource exploitation and dispossession from Jakarta (Aspinall 2007). Di Tiro is said to have returned to Aceh in 1974 to bid for an oil pipeline project with the new Mobil Oil gas plant in the northwest of the province. With his bid unsuccessful, di Tiro alleged interference by Jakarta, and competition for access to natural resources remained a continuing concern of GAM as it pursued independence (Schulze 2004). As evidence of this, the Declaration of Independence of Acheh[1] reads:

> During these last thirty years the people of Acheh, Sumatra, have witnessed how our fatherland has been exploited and driven into ruinous conditions by the Javanese neo-colonialists: they have stolen our properties; they have robbed us from our livelihood . . . while Acheh, Sumatra, has been producing a revenue of over 15 billion US dollars yearly for the Javanese neo-colonialists, which they used totally for the benefit of Java and the Javanese.

In essence, it makes clear the direct connection not only with the territorial memory of Aceh but also a perceived grievance at the collection of natural resources and the maldistribution of profits gained from the lands' exploitation. It makes direct correlations between the poor living conditions of Acehnese people and the lack of development of the region, despite perceived wealth. The nation-building project undertaken throughout Indonesia and driven by Jakarta was seen by GAM as the mere continuation of the exploitative practices implemented by the Dutch East Indies Company.

Following on from declaration of independence in 1976, the first iteration of GAM would be sustained until 1979, by which time most of the original members had fled into exile, been arrested, or been killed. Di Tiro himself had fled to Malaysia, and from 1980 moved to Sweden with a small group of the GAM leadership, where he would lead the movement in exile for the next 25 years.

By the late 1980s, GAM would again begin to radically disrupt the security environment in Aceh. Starting in 1986, GAM rebels underwent training in Libya, and in turn returning fighters would train others in the combat skills they had acquired overseas. In response, the Indonesia military launched in 1990 the 'Military Operation Area' or *Daerah Operasi Militer* (DOM), a heavy-handed counterinsurgency campaign targeting communities seen as sympathetic or providing sanctuary to the GAM. The military campaign, which lasted until 1998, was brutal in its implementation, described as a 'systematic campaign of terror' with the purpose of 'strik[ing] fear into the population' and pressuring them to withdraw support for GAM (Kelly 1995: 74, quoted in Schulze 2004: 4). By the end of the campaign, some 1,258 to 2,000 people had been killed, and nearly 3,500 tortured (Schulze 2004). There were 625 cases of rape and torture of women, while the number of persons disappeared varied between 500 and as many as 39,000. Twelve mass graves were investigated and over 7,000 human rights violations documented (International Crisis Group 2001; Schulze 2004).

Yet, while DOM was largely successful in repressing GAM as a rebel organisation, the movement was able to continue because: (1) the organisation's leadership remained safe in exile in Sweden; (2) large numbers of GAM combatants were able to seek refuge in Malaysia, and (3) the heavy-handed military tactics deployed by the Indonesian military in the 1990s were significant in giving rise to a new generation of GAM fighters, those with close, personal experiences of the military crackdown (Schulze 2004). Under the significant civil repression employed by the government, the legitimacy of GAM as an alternative voice for a free and independent Aceh was strengthened.

It took the collapse of the Suharto government in May 1998 in the wake of the Asian Financial Crisis and Indonesia's democratic reform process for space to be carved for the possibility of peace talks with GAM. The shift in power precipitated in Aceh an increase in the expression of anti-Jakarta and anti-military sentiments. Throughout 1998 and 1999, large-scale rallies and province-wide strikes were held in support of holding a referendum on independence similar to the one granted to Timor Leste. At the same time, a relaxing of punitive military operations allowed GAM fighters to return and regroup, particularly in the rural areas and small towns away from major cities. As a result, the number of violent incidents and associated deaths rose sharply during the *reformasi* period and through the six years that covered the peace process (see Figure 1.1).

Widespread public celebrations of the 23rd anniversary of the founding of GAM on 4 December 1999 were of such a scale that the Indonesian government and military were unable to intervene. At the same time, efforts by the Indonesian parliament (*Majelis Permusyawaratan Rakyat*, MPR) to re-establish special autonomy within the province and to grant greater law-making power to the regional government did little to appease activists.

Despite the lifting of direct military operations in mid-1998, 447 civilians and almost 90 members of the security force were killed in the 19 months between the resignation of Suharto in 1998 and early 2000 (Aspinall and Crouch 2003). It was the election of President Abdurrahman Wahid in October 1999, seen as a reformist and part of the Democracy Forum opposition that opposed President Suharto,

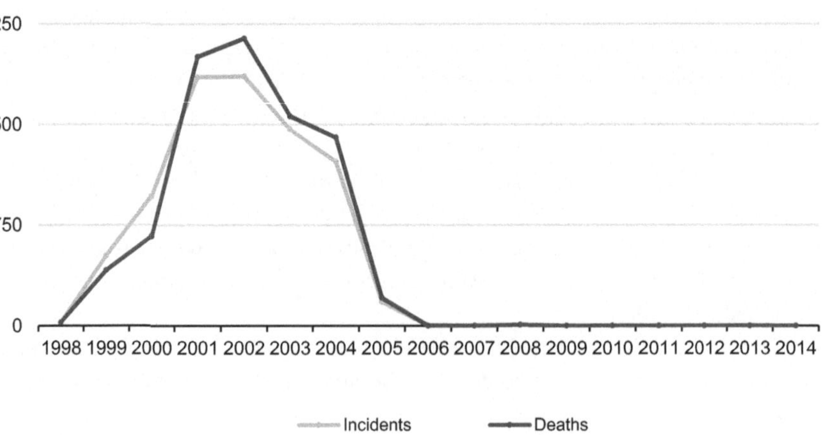

FIGURE 1.1 Separatist incidents and deaths, Aceh, 1998–2014

Source: (Kemenko PMK 2015; Barron et al. 2016)

that would pave the way for negotiations between the Indonesian government and GAM.

The conflict resolution process

Moves towards peace talks took place in late 1999. The Henry Dunant Centre, now more commonly known as the Centre for Humanitarian Dialogue (HD) – a new international non-government organization established in August 1999 in Geneva – approached President Wahid with the offer of dialogue. This came after several months of investigation and contact-building.

HD staff at the time had little experience in Indonesia; however, the organisation recognised space for peacebuilding interventions in the wake of democratic change and the referendum in Timor Leste. Connections within Indonesian government and civil society eventually led to a meeting between President Wahid and HD's director Martin Griffiths in November 1999, where the organisation was able to raise its interests in facilitating dialogue between the government and GAM (Huber 2004).

The involvement of an NGO such as HD appealed to Indonesia for a number of reasons. International intervention in the 30 August 1999 Timor Leste independence referendum shamed the Indonesian government, with the United Nations Mission in East Timor (UNAMET) negotiated by Secretary-General Kofi Annan overseeing the vote that led to the former Portuguese colony's secession. The TNI in particular were embarrassed, having come under significant international criticism in the violent aftermath of the referendum that forced the establishment of the Australian-led International Force East Timor (INTERFET) peacekeeping mission. In the face of strong anti-UN sentiment in Jakarta, HD were seen as a viable alternative, sufficiently international so as to appeal to the GAM leadership, while lacking official diplomatic status so as not to be able to bring coercive pressure (and embarrassment) to the government.

For GAM, there was an immediate interest in the negotiations, as they were seen to afford important international recognition of the struggle, particularly in Europe, where the senior leadership had been in exile for two decades. At the same time the internationalisation of the armed struggle helped the exiled leadership gain greater legitimacy for their position among GAM militias and Acehnese in Indonesia. The start of talks necessitated that the GAM leadership consolidate its command over its forces in Aceh, strengthening communication lines and coordination between local units.

HD facilitated the first meeting between the Indonesian Ambassador to the UN in Geneva, Hassan Wirajuda, and Hasan di Tiro in Geneva on 27 January 2000. Both acknowledged that they were unable to achieve a military victory in the conflict, and that the most productive method for resolving the stalemate was through negotiations (Aspinall and Crouch 2003). HD's offer to mediate dialogue between the parties would then be officially accepted on 30 January by President Wahid on a state visit to Geneva.

The Humanitarian Pause

Further talks would take place between the Indonesian government and GAM in Geneva on 24 March and 14–17 April 2000. Initial discussions were aimed at forming a ceasefire for ending direct military confrontations between the parties and creating an environment perceived to be more amenable for discussion of a long-term political solution.

The talks culminated in the agreement of the 'Joint Understanding on Humanitarian Pause for Aceh' (referred to more commonly as the Humanitarian Pause), signed on 12 May 2000, and which came into effect on 2 June. The agreement comprised two components: humanitarian access, aimed at ensuring relief in rehabilitating areas of Aceh which had been affected by the decades of conflict and limited development; and security modalities for the purpose of monitoring the cessation in hostilities between the parties and preventing outbreaks in violence. The agreement established Joint Committees for implementing each component, as well as attached monitoring mechanisms. For the ceasefire, this consisted of five persons agreed to by the Indonesian government and GAM, to eventually be based in the Kuala Tripa hotel in Banda Aceh. Sitting above these would be a Joint Forum based in Geneva.

The Humanitarian Pause was met with enthusiasm internationally, and USAID and Norway provided the financial support for the maintenance of the ceasefire support mechanisms. However, the reception to the agreement in Jakarta was much less warm, bordering on hostile. The speaker of the People's Representative Council (DPR) criticised the level of recognition the agreement gave to GAM by concluding and signing the agreement abroad. There were concerns that the agreement set a precedent of recognising GAM as a legitimate international actor that placed the group's military wing on the same standing as the TNI (Aspinall and Crouch 2003).

Despite these reservations, the signing precipitated a temporary but noticeable decrease in the level of hostilities compared to the first four months of the year. Still, violent contact between TNI and GAM forces continued, and as the three-month deadline for the renewal of the Humanitarian Pause approached in August, the number of incidents rose sharply. The parties had delayed the resumption of talks to renew the Humanitarian Pause, both placing conditions for the extension of the ceasefire. On the day it was due to expire, President Wahid announced an extension until 15 January 2001. Regardless, the security situation continued to deteriorate through the remainder of 2000, though the formal dialogue process would continue. A new round of talks held on 6–10 January 2001 concluded with an agreement that HD would push ahead with facilitating talks on substantive issues, summarised across four broad points: human rights and humanitarian law, socio-economic development, security arrangements, and democratic process (Aspinall and Crouch 2003). At the same time, the Humanitarian Pause was extended for a month, though the language of the ceasefire changed to that of a 'moratorium', and then indefinitely to a process labelled 'peace through dialogue', despite all semblance of a functioning ceasefire now eroded.

The January 2001 meeting also saw an expansion of the peace process mediation team. HD introduced William Ury from the Harvard University Negotiation Project into the negotiations, to be followed by others through 2001: retired US General Anthony Zinni, former Foreign Minister of Yugoslavia Budimir Loncar, former Foreign Minister of Thailand Surin Pitsuan, British parliamentarian Lord Avebury, and Swedish diplomat Bengt Soderberg. Together, this group of esteemed politicians and peace practitioners, who would come to be known as 'the Wise Men', would attend all future negotiations held by HD. While the Wise Men would participate within their own private capacities, their inclusion within the dialogues signalled the further internationalisation of the peace process, with the hope of putting greater pressure on the parties to engage with the talks in an honest and substantive manner. Indeed, despite both parties notionally committing to negotiations, neither appeared willing to make concessions so that the talks might proceed constructively. GAM remained steadfast in its insistence for a referendum on Aceh's independence, and the Indonesian government appeared increasingly unwilling (and unable) to prevent TNI military operations.

The Cessation of Hostilities Agreement

Two key developments would shift the direction of the peace process in the latter half of 2001. On 23 July, Abdurrahman Wahid was impeached and removed from office, to be replaced by his Vice President Megawati Sukarnoputri. President Sukarnoputri took office with a stronger articulation of Indonesian nationalism and the insistence on the maintenance of national unity. At the same time, the MPR unilaterally passed the Nanggroe Aceh Darussalam law (NAD), new legislation that extended special autonomy provisions to the Aceh province. The law was seen as a move to ameliorate Acehnese resentment against central authority by providing for a significant return of revenue from oil and gas, while also providing for direct elections for provincial governors and district heads (Aspinall and Crouch 2003). At best, it was hoped the law would appease and accommodate GAM's requests, though many perceived the law as an effort to undermine GAM's legitimacy and shift public perceptions.

After a seven-month delay, fresh talks would take place on 2–3 February 2002, with the Indonesian delegation represented by retired diplomat Sastrohandoyo Wiryono, after Hassan Wirajuda had become President Sukarnoputri's new foreign minister. While no major outcomes were gained from the meeting, the government, buoyed by significant military advances over the past months, put greater pressure on GAM to accept negotiations under the premise of renouncing independence and accepting the enhanced autonomy framework established by the NAD law. Further rounds of negotiations on 25–26 April and 8–9 May saw GAM making several concessions, including agreeing to negotiations using the NAD law as the starting point – though both parties disagreed on what exactly was agreed, with GAM insisting that the statement did not prevent the pursuit of a referendum as a necessary recourse for Acehnese concerns. Frustrated by what it saw from GAM as an unwillingness to cooperate under significant military and diplomatic pressure, the Indonesian government announced an ultimatum that GAM undertake serious dialogue within the framework of special autonomy and the cessation of hostilities by the end of Ramadan (6 December 2002) or face aggressive military action. HD appeared increasingly unable to exert influence over the peace process, with the direction of the talks being led more by developments in the security situation on the ground and unilateral demands from Jakarta than by dialogue in Geneva.

Regardless, HD continued to shuttle between the two parties through the later months of 2002, resulting in a final text agreed and signed on 9 December, three days after the deadline set by the Indonesian government. The Cessation of Hostilities Framework Agreement (COHA) set out the details for a ceasefire and phased demobilisation process for GAM, with their arms to be deposited at mandated sites within 'peace zones', to be secured by HD acting as the key guarantor. The Indonesian government relented to requests for international third-party monitoring of the ceasefire, with Thai military officer Major General Tanongsuk Tuvinun appointed to co-chair the revised Joint Security Committee. Fifty monitors from HD would also join members from the TNI and GAM to develop local ceasefire monitoring teams, while a small contingent of international peacekeepers from Thailand and the Philippines were also added to the monitoring mechanism (Braithwaite et al. 2010). No progress was made on political issues, only that the parties agreed to 'all-inclusive dialogue' to be facilitated by HD.

The COHA, as a more accomplished ceasefire agreement than the Humanitarian Pause, was seen as a significant achievement for long-term peace and was met with widespread enthusiasm in Aceh and Jakarta. Both TNI and GAM forces undertook to uphold the ceasefire upon its signing, and while sporadic clashes continued in the first few weeks after signing, by and large the security situation stabilised over December. Progress was made on implementing some of the conditions of the agreement, with peace zones identified throughout the province in late January and March. Yet, while these ceasefire mechanisms were taking nascent steps, through March and April the Indonesian government again began to pursue a more bellicose rhetoric, deploying larger numbers of police and military personnel to Aceh in contravention to the COHA. Similarly, GAM was criticised for being seen to extend both its reach and depth of influence through Aceh, collecting taxes in regional areas and recruiting greater numbers of fighters into its armed wing.

Once again HD appeared to be losing control of the peace process; the impasse over Indonesia's demands for political negotiations within the maintenance of Indonesian territorial integrity and for GAM to drop its calls for an independence referendum led to continued breakdowns and misunderstandings over what had and had not been agreed at the negotiating table. David Gorman of HD was eventually pressured by the Indonesian government to hold a press conference in Banda Aceh clarifying that the COHA did not in any way make a determination on the matter of independence or a referendum (Aspinall and Crouch 2003).

By April 2003, widespread clashes between government forces and GAM fighters were again taking place. Susilo Bambang Yudhuyono, the government's representative to the main body in charge of the ceasefire implementation, put forward two non-negotiable demands: that GAM accept negotiations solely under the enhanced autonomy framework, and that it warehouse its weapons. Government demands for talks in late April fell through, and in an attempt to save the peace process, HD compelled the parties to meet in Tokyo on 17 May. The talks, seen as a last-ditch effort to resurrect the COHA, were strongly encouraged by the international community – particularly the United States, Japan, the European Union, and the World Bank – helping to secure pressure on Indonesia's participation and GAM's agreement to attend.

While the talks in Tokyo would take place, the hardened position of the government was near unacceptable for GAM. HD attempted again to shuttle between the two parties, with GAM proposing text that committed the movement to 'dropping the armed struggle . . . [and] refrain[ing] from advocating independence', a significant concession considering the circumstances. Still the government rejected this position, and with neither side willing to shift, the talks were scuttled. Martial law was declared in Aceh just hours later, taking effect at midnight on 18 May. The collapse in the talks would bring about the end of HD's official involvement in the peace process, and usher in a new period of intense conflict.

Crisis Management Initiative and the 2004 Indian Ocean tsunami

Despite the widespread fighting that took place in the months that followed the collapse of the COHA, backchannel efforts towards restarting the peace process persisted. Jusuf Kalla, Coordinating Minister for People's Welfare under President Sukarnoputri, travelled to Sweden in the hope of meeting with GAM's leadership in Stockholm. Kalla had by this time gained experience in resolving intra-state and communal violence elsewhere in Indonesia, having been involved in peace negotiations on behalf of the government in Sulawesi, Ambon, and Maluku. When the GAM leadership refused to meet in Stockholm, Kalla instead met with former Finnish president Martti Ahtisaari, who had been lauded for his peace efforts in Kosovo in 1999. Since stepping down as president in 2000, Ahtisaari had founded a new Finnish NGO Crisis Management Initiative with the aim of forging lasting peace through informal dialogue and mediation. Ahtisaari had been in talks in 1999 about the possibility of mediating in Aceh, though ultimately these conversations came to little, particularly as the HD process appeared more promising and further developed. With the sustained violence in the wake of the failed COHA, GAM suffered significant military and territorial losses, to the point where continued armed resistance was becoming increasingly difficult. As such, there was an opportunity for Ahtisaari and CMI to become involved.

The election of President Yudoyono and his vice president Kalla in September 2004 shifted the political calculations in Jakarta. Further backchannel work in Sweden and Finland undertaken between Ahtisaari, Kalla, and Finnish businessman Juha Christensen, who had close connections with the GAM leadership, meant that by early December 2004 there were informal commitments from both parties for a resumption of negotiations to be led by CMI. With arrangements for talks made, formal invitations were sent out on 24 December.

Yet just two days later, the Indian Ocean earthquake and tsunami would hit, bringing incredible destruction to Aceh as well as many other countries caught in its path. The death toll in Aceh alone was estimated at as many as 180,000, killing more people in one day than had died from three decades of conflict (Merikallio 2006).

The impact of the tsunami on the conflict was immediate. Days after the tsunami, GAM announced a unilateral ceasefire, calling on the international community to assist in a formal ceasefire agreement. The government, for its worth, saw an opportunity to frame the new peace talks within the broader humanitarian response and international assistance which had flowed into the country post-tsunami. In this sense, the tsunami provided an opportunity for the government to save face, while bringing the level of internationalisation and humanitarian assistance long sought by GAM (Aspinall 2005). On the ground, it provided a circuit breaker to ongoing conflict, with the province wrought with destruction and overrun by international humanitarian agencies providing emergency relief.

The Helsinki Agreement

The first round of talks under CMI began on 27 January, held at Königstedt Manor on the northern outskirts of Helsinki. Justice and Human Rights Minister Hamid Awaluddin and Deputy Minister for People's Welfare Farid Husain attended on behalf of the government, while GAM were represented by 'Prime Minister' Malik Mahmud and 'Foreign Minister' Zaini Abdullah, as Hasan di Tiro was now too frail to play a major role in the negotiations.

Martti Ahtisaari had invested significant effort preparing for the negotiations, keen to learn from the lessons and experiences of HD's mediation and to avoid the missteps and pitfalls experienced under the Humanitarian Pause and COHA. Though Ahtisaari initially met with the Indonesian and GAM representatives separately, he quickly convened a joint session, breaking with previous conventions where the facilitator shuttled between the two parties. The change was made to allow the parties to speak directly with one another and in Bahasa Indonesia if preferred, in order to build mutual esteem and trust. The location for the talks, in lush surrounds by the Vantaa river, also allowed for the negotiating parties to go for private walks and talk informally outside of the primary negotiations.

A further significant change implemented by CMI was the adoption of a principle where 'nothing is agreed until everything is agreed'. Where the HD process had sought to secure incremental gains, starting primarily with the ceasefire and security mechanisms before tackling the political questions, Ahtisaari instead wanted only one final solution, similar in style to that adopted by Bill Clinton in the Camp David talks in 2000 (Aspinall 2005). While the method carried significant risk, not least because it meant complex political bargains were being discussed early in the negotiations, it meant that compromises could be made without fear that these would weaken bargaining leverage in other areas.

This meant that in spite of the humanitarian emergency that followed the tsunami and the objections of GAM, a formal ceasefire was kept off the table until a full political agreement was reached. Though President Yudoyono announced the TNI would adopt a defensive posture following the tsunami, the lack of a formal ceasefire meant the government's military ascendancy that had been established through 2003 and 2004 remained in place.

The continued military pressure made it clear that Indonesia was unwilling to accept anything less than the certainty that Aceh would remain a part of Indonesian territory, remaining committed to negotiations around the NAD law and special autonomy. While GAM had shown itself progressively more willing to bend to demands to relinquish its aims of Aceh independence, the terminology of special autonomy remained unpalatable due to its connections with the unilateral decisions made by Jakarta that had driven military rule within the province for decades. A compromise was found during the second round of discussions on 21–23 February 2005, when GAM proposed that talks be based around 'self-government', accepting that the demand for independence was no longer part of the negotiations. The concept has been characterised as a breakthrough, allowing the conversation to move beyond past rhetorical roadblocks. As part of self-government, GAM pushed forward with its demands for changes in Indonesian law to allow for local political parties; at the time, restrictive association laws meant broad national constituencies were needed in order to form political parties necessary for election and political engagement, a legacy of the concerns surrounding the potential for Indonesian territorial disintegration. This demand would prove to be a major sticking point, and as progress was made over the third and fourth rounds of negotiations, a solution to local democratic participation remained elusive. Ostensibly, any agreement that failed to allow local political parties was seen as paramount to GAM abandoning its military campaign without avenues for it to continue political involvement through legitimate legal means – effectively, surrender.

The fifth and final round of negotiations took place from 12 to 17 July 2005, with the parties still yet to agree on security modalities and local political parties. GAM remained anxious about the number of Indonesian military and security personnel to remain in Aceh; however, the establishment of the Aceh Monitoring Mission (AMM) – a collaborative peacekeeping mission with the European Union (EU) and the Association of Southeast Asian Nations (ASEAN) – was put forward as being able to effectively monitor the on-the-ground security situation. The AMM, secured by Ahtisaari and CMI through discussions with the EU in Brussels, was a substantially more resourced and prominent monitoring mechanism than had been established under the COHA. It represented a significant concession on behalf of the Indonesian government, considering its experiences with INTERFET and the United Nations Transitional Administration in East Timor (UNTAET).

At the 11th hour of the negotiations, the government would also back down and allow local political parties to assemble and contest elections, agreeing to pass the necessary legislation through the MPR. With that, agreement on all major elements of the complete peace resolution had been reached, achieved in just six months of negotiations across five rounds of talks.

The Memorandum of Understanding between the government of the Republic of Indonesia and the Free Aceh Movement (commonly referred to as the Helsinki Agreement or MoU) was signed on 15 August 2005 in Helsinki. It marked the resolution of the civil war between the Indonesian government and GAM and charted a course for an agreed path towards 'self-governance' for the Aceh region through provisions on political participation, economy, and the guidelines for a new governing law. Provisions Arrangements were also made for the AMM and the amnesty and disbanding of GAM forces. Only minor reference was made to rights protections and historical injustices; Section 2 of the MoU states that a Human Rights Court and a Commission for Truth and Reconciliation would be established, but no further elaboration on modalities or timeframes were provided.

At only seven pages in total, the Helsinki Agreement is modest considering the decades through which the conflict had persisted and the years in which a negotiated resolution appeared elusive. It has been pointed out that aside from the provisions allowing for local political parties, in the end the agreement proposed only minor amendments to the current NAD autonomy law governing the territory (Aspinall 2008; International Crisis Group 2007). The Law on Governing Aceh (LOGA) adopted by the MPR in May 2006 in fulfilment of the MoU only partially met some the conditions agreed in Helsinki, excluding some constitutionally questionable parameters surrounding security and government authority. The key provisions on local political parties were maintained, however, and the implementation of the AMM starting in September 2005 successfully oversaw the demilitarisation of GAM forces and the destruction of weapons. GAM officials returned from exile and established *Partai Aceh* (Aceh Party), successfully participating in gubernatorial elections in 2006 and provincial elections in 2009 (International Crisis Group 2011, 2006; Morfit 2007).

Lessons to be learned from the case study

While many of the conditions surrounding the successful resolution to the peace process between the government of Indonesia and the Free Aceh Movement are unique, the Aceh conflict shares many relatable experiences among post-colonial states. Aceh for decades had been a relatively dormant yet violent subnational conflict, until given new life by rapid national political change in the wake of the fall of the Suharto government. Colonial legacies in Indonesia were wrought anew by international norms of self-determination, and identities, ethnicities, and nationalities were challenged and reimagined through the process of state formation and disintegration. Competing power structures drove contestation between state and non-state institutions at the nation's periphery. And through it all, a highly sensitive central government remained averse to international involvement in what it maintained were domestic security concerns.

This last condition is often the most difficult to counteract, when states are reticent to enter into mediation for fear of legitimising non-state groups and insurgencies. There is a conventional understanding that (international) NGOs are well positioned to act as mediators because they are able to work at a lower profile and stay invested in a conflict for a longer period of time than other, more traditional mediation actors (Ban Ki-Moon 2009; Beardsley 2009; Bercovitch and Jackson 2009; Lanz et al. 2009). In many ways, it was these characteristics that first drew President Wahid to HD, and what made their involvement palatable to the Indonesian government and TNI.

In comparison, CMI appeared to act as an NGO only in name. Ahtisaari was clear with the parties that he was not invested in spending significant time facilitating the peace process; the limiting of negotiations to just five rounds was a deliberate tactic, especially once significant progress on previous sticking points was made. Similarly, Ahtisaari would not hesitant to exercise a fierce temper with the negotiating parties, and is known to have shouted and thrown his pen when losing his patience (Kingsbury 2006; Merikallio 2006). Such traits are not commonly expected from an NGO third party, particularly when not possessing the coercive 'sticks and carrots' particularly necessary to maintain the commitment of a belligerent state. Undoubtedly Ahtisaari, as a former head of state, commanded significantly more respect than Martin Griffiths and HD, a deficiency that appeared to be a concern considering the injection of the 'Wise Men' in 2001 (many of whom were distinguished statesmen in their own right). Nevertheless, to attribute the success of the CMI process solely to the cult of personality of Ahtisaari would be disingenuous.

Overall, international actors were inconsistent in their capacity to pressure the parties to compromise. The US, Japan, Norway, and others were seen to play a significant diplomatic role in supporting the HD and CMI peace negotiations; the organisation of a summit in Tokyo sponsored by Japan, the United States, the European Union, and the World Bank attended by 38 countries on the eve of the signing of the COHA was seen as useful for marshalling international support for the peace process. However, similar international activities five months later, as the COHA was collapsing, proved impotent. Ahtisaari's strong connections with Brussels were said to be telling in securing the EU's agreement to co-lead the AMM, but international peacekeepers had already been deployed in 2003, though to a much smaller extent. Indeed, international guarantees appeared useful at certain times in securing concessions and commitments to the peace process, but the record is uneven.

At the other end of the spectrum, Acehnese civil society played a very minor role in the peace process. Both the HD and CMI processes kept the scope for local involvement in the formal peace process to a minimum; Ahtisaari explicitly rejected overtures by some within the organisation to strengthen the involvement of local CSOs, instead preferring to work with expedience than to broaden the constituency at the peace table. While some CSOs were involved in the on-the-ground security and humanitarian mechanisms as part of the Humanitarian Pause, there was also concern that civil society was co-opted in the political contest between the government and GAM (Aguswandi and Large 2008). This is not to exclude the more pronounced role played by CSOs in peacebuilding in the post-negotiation phase, including in the drafting of the LOGA.

Regardless, it is simplistic to conclude that the successes of the Aceh peace process are owed to a narrow, pressured, elite bargain between the Indonesian government and a group of a few Acehnese leaders in exile. Following the tsunami, the conflict appeared ripe for resolution, and CMI were successful in capitalising on this moment to achieve a solution that went far enough to accomplish GAM's demilitarisation and its transformation into a political party. At the same time, the Helsinki Agreement cannot solely be attributed to the tsunami; Sri Lanka was similarly devastated, yet distinct forces at play meant the conflicts took starkly different paths in the aftermath. Natural disasters can help to create opportune moments for conflict resolution, but they are not the *fait accompli* often assumed when discussing peace process trajectories (Akcinaroglu et al. 2011; Beardsley and McQuinn 2009). In the case of Aceh, the election of key individuals in Yudoyono and Kalla, in addition to the sustained military pressure that had been built over the period since the collapse of the COHA, played a significant role in creating the conditions for both parties to be able to make the necessary compromises. Ahtsaari and CMI were essential in ensuring such favourable conditions were capitalised upon.

At the same time, it is worth considering the sacrifices made by expediting the process in 2005. While the MoU was successful in bringing a clear end to separatist violence (see Figure 1.1), the agreement only briefly touched on issues of human rights and post-conflict justice, with short provisions included in the hope that these issues could be tackled in the period following. In reality, these institutions have been limited or non-existent, meaning that issues of post-conflict justice remain (Aspinall 2008; Cornish 2014). In certain areas, a lack of guarantees and guidelines has left an environment that has permitted serious human rights abuses, particularly against vulnerable minorities in Acehnese society, including LGBTI communities. Indeed, while separatist 'vertical' conflict incidents more or less stopped in 2005, in the ten years since other 'horizontal' conflict incidents have grown (see Figure 1.2). Rather than the centre–periphery conflict that characterised the years of civil war, conflict today focuses around the contestation between different political elites, particularly among the former leaders of GAM in the wake of *Partai Aceh*'s split (Barron et al. 2013). Further, too, domestic violence and popular justice conflicts – violence perpetrated to respond to or punish actual or perceived wrong – have risen sharply since the conclusion of the official peace process (Kemenko PMK 2015). Over a decade since the conclusion of the Helsinki Agreement, these issues

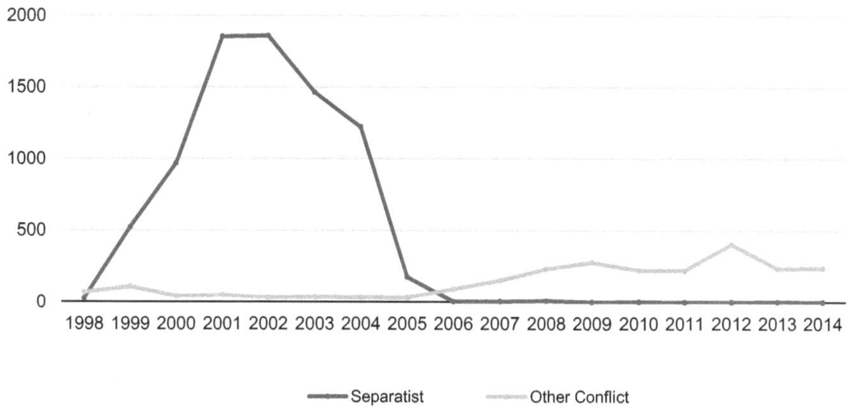

FIGURE 1.2 Separatist conflict versus other conflict incidents, Aceh, 1998–2014

Source: (Kemenko PMK 2015)

continue the dominate in a region where punitive religious ideologies remain the overarching a significant concern.

As such, the effects of the peace are less clear when it comes to development and people's wellbeing in Aceh. The international response to the Indian ocean tsunami meant that unprecedented levels of ODA flowed into the region, with over USD 8 billion in post-tsunami assistance for the period 2005–2008. Direct government and international donor assistance for the peace process for the same period was USD 360 million (Barron et al. 2013). However, by 2012 annual aid had reduced by 40 per cent on 2005–2008, with much of the programming now funded directly by government, both from Jakarta and locally, linked with the special autonomy funds negotiated in the peace agreement.

These aid commitments have failed to have a demonstrable effect on the overall poverty and development profile of the province, with Human Development Indicators roughly in line with or slightly behind national growth trajectories (Badan Pusat Statistik 2018; United Nations Development Programme 2010; World Bank 2008). While combatants have benefited from reintegration and training programmes, leading to increased levels of employment, the impact of the retreat of international aid has seen development programming increasingly come under the control of former GAM apparatchiks. As such, the amount of programming for building the capacity of local government institutions has diminished, with claims of patronage and corruption widespread (Barron et al. 2013). Ultimately, outside of the direct gains related to resolving the direct civil war between the Indonesian government and GAM, developments towards a more 'positive' peace have been relatively marginal and disparate.

Overall, the Aceh Peace Process is one built of peculiar dynamics: a near one-dimensional independence struggle addressed through a peace process that, due to a confluence of factors, at times defies comparison. Its legacy, however, in a now more unified Indonesia, points to the capacity for harmonising national ambition within a diverse multi-ethnic state.

Note

1 Acheh is the traditional spelling adopted by GAM for the region.

References, further reading, and links to key primary documents

References

Aguswandi, J. Large. 2008. *Reconfiguring Politics: The Indonesia – Aceh Peace Process, Accord: An International Review of Peace Initiatives*. London: Conciliation Resources.

Akcinaroglu, Seden, M. Jonathan Dicicco, and Elizabeth Radzisewski. 2011. "Avalanches and Olive Branches: A Multimethod Analysis of Disasters and Peacemaking in Interstate Rivalries." *Political Research Quarterly* 64 (2): 260–275.

Ansori, Mohammad Hasan. 2012. "Linking Identity to Collective Action: Islam, History and Ethnicity in the Aceh Conflict." *Studia Islamika* 19 (1).

Ananta, Aris, Evi Nurvidya Arifin, M. Sairi Hasbullah, Nur Budi Hundayani, and Wahyu Pramono. 2015. *Demography of Indonesia's Ethnicity*. Singapore: Institute of Southeast Asian Studies.

Aspinall, Edward. 2005. "The Helsinki Agreement: A More Promising Basis for Peace in Aceh?" *East–West Center Washington* 20.

Aspinall, Edward. 2007. "The Construction of Grievance: Natural Resources and Identity in a Separatist Conflict." *Journal of Conflict Resolution* 51: 950–972.

Aspinall, Edward. 2008. "Peace Without Justice? The Helsinki Peace Process in Aceh." April. www.hdcentre.org/wp-content/uploads/2016/08/56JusticeAcehfinalrevJU NE08-May-2008.pdf.

Aspinall, Edward, and A. Harold Crouch. 2003. "The Aceh Peace Process: Why It Failed." *East–West Center* 1.

Badan Pusat Statistik (Statistics Indonesia). 2018. "(Metode Baru) Indeks Pembangunan Manusia [(New Method) Human Development Index]." Jakarta.

Barron, P., A. Engvall, and A. Morel. 2016. *Understanding Violence in Southeast Asia: The Contribution of Violent Incident Monitoring Systems*. San Francisco: The Asia Foundation.

Barron, Patrick, Anders Engvall, and Adrian Morel. 2013. "The Case of Aceh, Indonesia, the Contested Corners of Asia: Subnational Conflict and International Development Assistance." *The Asia Foundation*, 7 October. https://asiafoundation.org/publication/the-contested-corners-of-asia-subnational-conflict-and-international-development-assistance/.

Beardsley, Kyle. 2009. "Intervention Without Leverage: Explaining the Prevalence of Weak Mediators." *International Interactions* 35: 272–297.

Beardsley, Kyle, and Brian McQuinn. 2009. "Rebel Groups as Predatory Organizations: The Political Effects of the 2004 Tsunami in Indonesia and Sri Lanka." *Journal of Conflict Resolution* 53 (4): 624–645.

Bercovitch, Jacob, and Richard Jackson. 2009. *Conflict Resolution in the Twenty-First Century: Principles, Methods, and Approaches*. Ann Arbor: University of Michigan Press.

Braithwaite, John, Valeria Braithwaite, Michael Cookson, and Leah Dunn. 2010. "Anomie and Violence: Non-Truth and Reconciliation in Indonesian Peacebuilding." *Jstor*. www.jstor.org/stable/j.ctt24hf62.

Cornish, Michael. 2014. "Contemporary Politics in Aceh." *Peace and Conflict Monitor*, 21 January. www.monitor.upeace.org/archive.cfm?id_article=1027.

The Economist. 2011. "Privatising Peace." *Economist*, 30 June. www.economist.com/international/2011/06/30/privatising-peace.

Huber, Konrad. 2004. "The HDC in Aceh: Promises and Pitfalls of NGO Mediation and Implementation." *Policy Studies* 9.

International Crisis Group. 2001. "Aceh: Can Autonomy Stem the Conflict?" *ICG*, 27 June. www.crisisgroup.org/asia/south-east-asia/indonesia/aceh-can-autonomy-stem-conflict.

International Crisis Group. 2006. "Aceh's Local Elections: The Role of the Free Aceh Movement (GAM)." *ICG*, 29 November. www.crisisgroup.org/asia/south-east-asia/indonesia/aceh-s-local-elections-role-free-aceh-movement-gam.

International Crisis Group. 2007. "Aceh: Post-Conflict Complications, Asia Report." *ICG*, 4 October. www.crisisgroup.org/asia/south-east-asia/indonesia/aceh-post-conflict-complications.

International Crisis Group. 2011. "Indonesia: GAM vs GAM in the Aceh Elections, Asia Briefing." *ICG*, 15 June. www.crisisgroup.org/asia/south-east-asia/indonesia/indonesia-gam-vs-gam-aceh-elections.

Kemenko, P.M.K. 2015. "National Violence Monitoring System." Kemenko PMK; World Bank; Habibie Center, Jakarta.

Ki-Moon, Ban. 2009. "Enhancing Mediation and Its Support Activities." *Peace Maker*, April. https://peacemaker.un.org/node/85.

Kingsbury, Damien. 2006. *Peace in Aceh: A Personal Account of the Helsinki Peace Process*. Jakarta: Equinox Pub.

Lanz, David, Damiano Sguaitamatti, and Matthias Siegfried. 2009. *Towards Realizing the Strengths and Mitigating the Challenges of NGO Mediators*. ETH, Zurich: Center for Security Studies.

Merikallio, Katri. 2006. *Making Peace: Ahtisaari and Aceh*. Helsinki: W. Söderström.

Morfit, Michael. 2007. "The Road to Helsinki: The Aceh Agreement and Indonesia's Democratic Development." *International Negotiation* 12 (1): 111–143.

Na Thalang, Chanintira. 2009. "The Fluidity of Nationalistic and Ethnic Aspirations in Aceh." *Nations and Nationalism* 15: 319–339.

Schulze, E. Kristen. 2004. "The Free Aceh Movement (GAM): Anatomy of a Separatist Organization." *Policy Studies* 2.

Shea, Nathan. 2016. "Nongovernment Organisations as Mediators: Making Peace in Aceh, Indonesia." *Global Change Peace & Security* 28 (2): 177–196.

United Nations Development Programme. 2010. "Provincial Human Development Report Aceh 2010: Human Development and People Empowerment." Jakarta: UNDP. http://hdr.undp.org/en/content/provincial-human-development-report-aceh.

World Bank. 2008. *Aceh Poverty Assessment 2008: The Impact of the Conflict, the Tsunami and Reconstruction on Poverty in Aceh*. Jakarta: World Bank.

Further reading

Aspinall, Edward. 2009. *Islam and Nation: Separatist Rebellion in Aceh, Indonesia*. Stanford, CA: Stanford University Press.

Braithwaite, John, Valeria Braithwaite, Michael Cooksoni, and Leah Dunn. 2010. *Anomie and Violence: Non-Truth and Reconciliation in Indonesian Peacebuilding*. Acton, ACT: ANU E Press.

Kingsbury, Damien. 2006. *Peace in Aceh: A Personal Account of the Helsinki Peace Process*. Jakarta: Equinox Pub.

Merikallio, Katri. 2006. *Making Peace: Ahtisaari and Aceh*. Helsinki: W. Söderström.

Reid, Anthony. (Ed.). 2006. "Verandah of Violence: The Background to the Aceh Problem." *Pacific Affairs* 80 (3): 548–550.

Reports and journal articles

Aguswandi, Large, and Judith Large. 2008. *Reconfiguring Politics: The Indonesia – Aceh Peace Process*. London: Conciliation Resources.

Aspinall, Edward. 2005. *The Helsinki Agreement: A More Promising Basis for Peace in Aceh?* Washington, DC: East-West Center.

Aspinall, Edward. 2008. *Peace Without Justice? The Helsinki Peace Process in Aceh*. Geneva: HD Centre.

Aspinall, Edward, and Harold Crouch. 2003. *The Aceh Peace Process: Why It Failed*. Washington, DC: East-West Center.

Huber, Konrad. 2004. *The HDC in Aceh: Promises and Pitfalls of NGO Mediation and Implementation*. Washington, DC: East-West Center.

International Crisis Group. 2003. *Aceh: A Fragile Peace*. Jakarta, Brussels: ICG.

International Crisis Group. 2007. *Aceh: Post-Conflict Complications*. Jakarta, Brussels: ICG.

Schulze, E. Kirsten. 2004. *The Free Aceh Movement (GAM): Anatomy of a Separatist Organization*. Washington, DC: East-West Center.

Shea, Nathan. 2016. "Nongovernment Organisations as Mediators: Making Peace in Aceh, Indonesia." *Global Change, Peace & Security* 28 (2): 177–196.

Key primary documents

"Cessation of Hostilities Agreement Between the Government of the Republic of Indonesia and the Free Aceh Movement." Signed in Geneva, Switzerland, 9 December 2002. https://peacemaker.un.org/sites/peacemaker.un.org/files/ID_021209_Cessation%20of%20Hostilities%20Framework%20Gov%20of%20Indonesia%20and%20Free%20Aceh%20Movement.pdf.

"Declaration of Independence of Acheh – Sumatra." Aceh, Sumatra, 4 December 1976. http://acehnet.tripod.com/declare.htm.

"Joint Understanding on Humanitarian Pause in Aceh." Signed Between the Government of the Republic of Indonesia and the Leadership of the Free Aceh Movement signed in Bavois, Switzerland, 12 May 2000. www.hdcentre.org/wp-content/uploads/2016/10/Joint-Understanding-for-a-Humanitarian-Pause-12-May-2000.pdf.

"Joint Statement by the Government of the Republic of Indonesia and the Free Aceh Movement." Signed in Switzerland, 10 May 2002. www.hdcentre.org/wp-content/uploads/2016/10/Joint-Statement-by-The-Government-of-the-Republic-of-Indonesia-and-The-Free-Aceh-Movement-10-May-2002.pdf.

"Memorandum of Understanding Between the Government of the Republic of Indonesia and the Free Aceh Movement." Signed in Helsinki, Finland, 15 August 2005. www.acehpeaceprocess.net/pdf/mou_final.pdf.

2

AFGHANISTAN

Anatol Lieven

Introduction

Hopes of peace in Afghanistan rest on the belief – based on many years of inconclusive warfare – that neither the Afghan state nor the Taliban can win a definitive victory, and that if the war is not to go on forever, sooner or later both will have to recognise this and seek a compromise.[1] Afghanistan also has a long history of apparently implacable foes reaching pragmatic compromises.[2]

Scepticism about the prospects for peace stems firstly from the fact that any settlement would have to involve some degree of power-sharing in Afghanistan, and the hatred and distrust between Kabul and the Taliban makes this very hard to imagine (though such arrangements have been achieved in unpromising internal circumstances in Lebanon, Bosnia, and Northern Ireland).

Equally importantly, the Afghan conflict involves a multiplicity of players, internal and external. Both the Kabul state and the Taliban are coalitions, including elements bitterly hostile to any settlement. On both sides there are fears that any serious moves towards peace would dissolve these coalitions, with diehard Taliban elements breaking away to join the Islamic State and hard-line Tajik elements in the Afghan Army seizing power to block a settlement.

A range of outside players also play key roles, and their mutual hostility has encouraged them to play the role of spoilers. Afghanistan is being sucked into the growing geopolitical rivalry between the USA and China, just as previously it was sucked into the rivalry between the USA and the USSR during the Cold War and the British and Russian empires in the nineteenth century. So far, therefore, while Kabul, the USA, and the Taliban have all made gestures in the direction of peace, none have gone beyond what could best be defined as a call to the other side to surrender on terms. In early 2019 the Trump administration began direct talks with the Taliban. Agreement in principle seems to have been reached on US military withdrawal in return for Taliban renunciation of terrorism. However, no progress has apparently yet been made on the most difficult issue, the contours of a political settlement with the Afghan government. At the time of writing, the general expectation is that this process will probably take a long time to reach agreement - unless the USA decides simply to withdraw.

Nonetheless, all the major internal and external players have at least expressed their support in principle for a political solution to the conflict. In February 2018 President Ashraf Ghani issued a call for peace talks with the Taliban 'without preconditions', including promises of amnesty and government posts for the Taliban.[3] The Taliban replied with their usual demand for the withdrawal of foreign (i.e. mainly US) forces as a precondition of talks: 'If Ashraf Ghani dreams of peace in the presence of the invaders, he must understand that such efforts have not resulted in anything in the past 17 years'. However, they also welcomed the tone of President Ghani's speech.

The Taliban position has generally been that they will only talk to the American 'invaders' and not their 'puppets' in Kabul, though it is not clear if this position is in fact absolute. Pakistan, which is generally considered to give at least limited shelter to the Taliban, has urged them to begin talks.

The vast majority of experts on Afghanistan agree that neither side can win, if by 'winning' is meant achieving their maximal objectives. As of the end of 2017, an estimated 30,000 government troops and police had been killed, together with 42,000 Taliban (though this could be a considerable exaggeration and include many civilians), 31,000 civilians, and 3,500 US and NATO troops.[4] Yet despite these sacrifices by the Afghan state forces, there are no conceivable circumstances for the foreseeable future in which they will be able to extend real control over the rural areas now controlled by the Taliban, nor force the Taliban to lay down their arms and surrender on terms.

Equally, it is highly unlikely that even in the event of a collapse of the present Afghan state, the Taliban would be able to establish their rule over the whole of Afghanistan and prevent the continuation of the present civil war along new lines (as was the case after the Taliban took Kabul in 1996). Nor do the great majority of the key actors on both sides wish to see a permanently partitioned Afghanistan. This marks an important difference between Afghanistan and ethno-religious conflicts like those in Lebanon and Bosnia in the past and Syria and Yemen today, where key actors have either aimed at separation or would be willing to settle for it as a last resort.

In Afghanistan, the different ethnicities have no history of separate statehood. Prior to the creation of the Durrani Pashtun Afghan monarchy in the mid-eighteenth century, they were subject to a range of outside empires: Iranian, Mughal, and Central Asian. Moreover, even by Lebanese or Bosnian standards, the different ethnicities are mixed up together, with not a single clearly defined border between them. This would make ethnic separation particularly hellish even by the miserable historical standards of such processes.

The Taliban for their part are determined that in all circumstances they will maintain control of their own core territories (including de facto control over the security forces), and an acceptance of this will have to form part of any conceivable peace settlement. They are also, however, heirs to the tradition of Pashtun-Afghan nationalist state-building and are categorically opposed to breaking up the existing

Afghan state. The idea of partition has sometimes been raised by Western analysts as a solution to the Afghan conflict. Every Taliban member or sympathiser with whom I have spoken has categorically rejected it.[5]

Finally, the emergence in Afghanistan of the Islamic State means the appearance of a force that should in principle help bring all the other parties together, since IS is in the remarkable position of being detested by *all* the other internal and external actors in Afghanistan: the government, the Taliban, the USA, Pakistan, India, Iran, Russia, and China.

As for the ordinary people of Afghanistan, their deep war weariness and desire for peace has been shown by the Peace March initiative of 2018, calling on the government and Taliban to negotiate peace and denouncing both for continuing the war. This movement began in Helmand in March 2018 and spread to several other provinces, including some in non-Pashtun areas of the north. In Helmand, the peace marchers have relied both on respected local religious figures and elders and on the Pashtun tradition of *nenawati*, whereby groups of women can go to the houses of enemy clans to intercede for compromise or mercy. This peace initiative seems to have embarrassed both the Taliban and the government. The Taliban leadership in Helmand told the peace marchers that they

> should go to Shurab and Kandahar airbases of [the] American forces and ask them for peace instead of coming to Musa Qala. . . . It's now the duty of the whole nation including you [the protestors] to raise your voice against invaders.
>
> *(Sabawoon 2018)*

Conflict analysis

The underlying reality of the power balance in Afghanistan, however, is unfortunately at variance with these positive indications. Figures on the government side in particular have very strong economic incentives to prefer a continuation of the conflict to a peace settlement, since they very largely depend for their income on western aid, which would have to be shared with the Taliban in the event of a settlement.

Any peace settlement will have to include a very significant share of power for the Taliban, at both national and regional level, and the intense bitterness and distrust between the actors involved makes it extremely difficult to imagine them working together without conflict. Most analysis assumes that as in other such peace settlements, the Taliban would have to be given a guaranteed and permanent share of power in Kabul. Most such settlements, however, require an outside power – backed by military force – to hold them in place and resolve disputes, as with the British government in Northern Ireland and NATO and the European Union in Bosnia.

In Afghanistan, however, the withdrawal of US forces is a condition of peace, and it is difficult to see who could replace them, at least until China and the Shanghai Cooperation Organisation (SCO) come to play a vastly greater role than hitherto.

Moreover (as is all too likely, given the attitudes of the US Congress both to the Taliban and to foreign aid in general), if a peace settlement with the Taliban led to a drastic reduction in US aid, then there would be nothing to hold the Afghan state together and no patronage to motivate the different sides together, and the settlement would collapse – unless China were prepared to step in an replace the USA as the major donor.

As long as the US military presence and US financial support remain, the wishes of Washington will be of decisive importance for any peace process. It seems highly probable (and is the assessment of the Pentagon) that only US airpower and special forces have saved the Kabul state from military collapse. The poverty of Afghanistan and the inability of the Afghan state to extract taxes from the population means that the USA also pays the entirety of Afghanistan's security budget and a majority of its civilian budget, so that no Afghan government can conceivably ignore US wishes.

The US security establishment is deeply unwilling to contemplate the loss of prestige that a genuine deal with the Taliban would imply, and may also be unwilling to give up its bases in Afghanistan as part of a deal. The enormous reduction in US troops since 2014 and their confinement to limited actions by the US air force, drones, and special forces means that US casualties have diminished to a level where they are hardly noticed by the US public and create no public pressure to seek peace and withdraw.

Pakistan for its part is categorically unwilling to try to force the Afghan Taliban to surrender. China and Russia do not have nearly enough of a stake in the conflict to seek a decisive peacemaking role and are also highly sceptical of their own or anyone else's ability to bring about a settlement.

Finally – and perhaps most importantly – any real moves towards a peace settlement would increase internal tensions among both the Kabul state elites and the Taliban to the point where the disintegration of both would become a real possibility. As a US Institute of Peace report of 2011 stated, 'the core players in the conflict are complex and potentially incoherent actors who may have difficulty cohering round stable negotiating positions and delivering on agreements' (Schirch 2011). The succeeding years have only confirmed this judgement. Faced with this danger, the leaderships on both sides may both see a continuation of the conflict as the lesser evil. Nor do the physical risks involved affect them. No coward is likely to have volunteered for the Taliban; and anyone on the government side with weak nerves took the money and ran a long time ago.

The impossibility of military victory

As of early 2018, the military situation in Afghanistan appears to have reached a stalemate that cannot be resolved by military means – or rather not by military means alone. The reason for this is rooted in a specifically military dynamic, the difference between guerrilla warfare and siege warfare. The Taliban's skilful use of guerrilla tactics, backed by the active or passive support of a large part of the rural Pashtun population and elements of other ethnic groups, has driven government forces and officials from most of the countryside in southern and eastern Afghanistan, and parts of the north as well. Government forces backed by the USA sometimes retake some of these territories, but they are facing too many challenges in too many areas to hold them for long.

In the words of Barnett Rubin, a former US diplomat and Afghan expert who has negotiated with the Taliban:

> More troops, more training, more bombing, and more money might budge the front lines, but the main problems are not at the front but in the rear – in the political divisions in the Afghan government, in the sanctuary the Afghan Taliban have enjoyed in Pakistan, and in the hostility of many regional countries to the U.S. presence. More troops, in the absence of an effective diplomatic strategy, could make Afghanistan less rather than more stable.
>
> *(Rubin 2017)*

The Taliban, whose annual budget is generally estimated at around one-tenth of the security budget of the Afghan state ($300 to $500 million per year) is more than capable of maintaining its existing level of spending on the war from a combination of taxing the heroin trade (something on which parts of the Afghan state security forces and their leaders also depend), contributions from private sympathisers in the Gulf, and (allegedly) limited financial support from the Pakistani intelligence services.

The Taliban have, however, proved incapable of capturing even medium-sized towns (on the one occasion that they did so, the fall of Kunduz in September 2016, they were forced to pull out again after a few days). Central to guerrilla warfare is the dispersal of forces in the face of the superior firepower of the other side. Forces that come together for attacks have to scatter again soon afterwards. Regular attacks on heavily defended towns, by contrast, require the concentration of attacking forces for a considerable period of time, during which they can be decimated by the defenders' firepower and airpower.

As long as the United States continues to pay the Afghan state armed forces, therefore, and provide it with sufficient support from the air, and those armed forces hold together, it will probably not be possible for the Taliban to seize and hold major towns. The purely military situation therefore replicates in key respects that between the Soviet military withdrawal from Afghanistan in early 1989 and the collapse of the Soviet-backed Afghan state in early 1992.

Then, too, the Afghan Mujahedin swept by far the greater part of the countryside but were unable to capture any major towns. When they tried, at Jalalabad in the spring of 1989, they were beaten back with very heavy casualties. This was despite the fact that the Mujahedin had received vastly more outside assistance than the Taliban (including US anti-aircraft missiles), and that the USSR had withdrawn all its forces from Afghanistan (though they continued to provide covert air support from Soviet Central Asia). The Kabul regime only collapsed in 1992 when the USSR itself collapsed and Soviet supplies of arms, money and fuel dried up, leading in turn to the defection of key forces from the regime to the opposition.

The hope of Taliban leaders (though not necessarily all of them) is that in this respect too history will repeat itself, with the USA abandoning its clients in Afghanistan as it previously abandoned them in Vietnam. As already noted, however, US casualties in Afghanistan today are a tiny fraction of those of the USA in Vietnam or the USSR in Afghanistan. There is no serious domestic pressure to withdraw, and even before the Trump administration took office, the Pentagon had persuaded President Barack Obama to retain US air forces and special forces in Afghanistan, arguing that otherwise the Afghan state forces would collapse.

The USA has landed itself with one problem that the Soviet-backed regime did not face: regular 'democratic' elections in Afghanistan. Given the profound ethnic, political, and personal differences among the groups supporting the regime, this is a recipe for recurrent crisis; a collapse of the Kabul state due to its own internal divisions seems a much more likely cause of state demise than Taliban military victory. Following the Afghan presidential elections of 2014, only long, intense mediation and pressure by US Secretary of State John Kerry and his staff brought the losing candidate, Abdullah Abdullah, to accept the results and join a power-sharing agreement. If, as seems all too likely, such crises recur, such engagement by future US administrations cannot be guaranteed. A collapse of Afghan democracy would also give Americans tired of the endless Afghan imbroglio a good excuse to withdraw US forces. This gives the Taliban hope that they may still win, despite their failure to make greater progress on the battlefield.

However, even if the Americans do withdraw and the Kabul regime and political order do collapse, they will not do so as one single and conclusive disintegration, like the South Vietnamese state in 1975. Even if Kabul falls, this is very unlikely to allow the Taliban to fulfil their ambition of recreating an Islamic emirate across the whole of Afghanistan, or even the 85 per cent or so that they controlled by September 2001. For while the Taliban are by no means an exclusively Pashtun force, they are certainly closely associated with that ethnicity. Other ethnic groups in Afghanistan are determined to resist their hegemony. This is especially true of the Shia Hazaras, a Farsi-speaking people of Mongolian origin who live in the central mountains and have extremely bitter memories of their past oppression by Pashtun rulers of Afghanistan; and the Farsi-speaking Tajiks.

Both of these ethnicities gained an unprecedented share of power as a result of the overthrow of the Taliban in 2001, which they have no intention of surrendering. Even if the Taliban took Kabul, they would continue to resist in their own areas, as they did in the years between the Taliban's capture of Kabul in 1996 and their overthrow in 2001. The Hazara can expect help from their Shia co-religionists and patrons in Iran.

It is true that in recent years the Iranians have sought contact with the Taliban and offered them limited help, but this appears to be only a precautionary strategy. In case the USA or Israel attack Iran in an effort to destroy its nuclear programme, the Iranians feel that they need to have a capacity to hit back at the USA via the Taliban, and they are pre-positioning help to that end. Iranian officials have, however, assured me in private that in the long run, their strategy will remain the old one: to support fellow Shia and to make sure that Herat, an ancient centre of Iranian culture, does not fall into the hands of the Taliban or any other potential enemies of Iran. The Tajiks, for their part, will be able to rely on help from India, which has a strong desire to keep Afghanistan from falling under the full control of the Taliban (viewed in Delhi simply as Pakistani clients) and which has established close relations with the Tajik elites and particularly with the Tajik commanders of the Afghan intelligence service (the NVS).

War would therefore probably continue and complete Taliban victory be as far away as ever. In my own conversations with Taliban members and people close to the Taliban, it has seemed to me that the key division between categorical opponents of any peace settlement and those who would favour one in principle is precisely that between those who believe that complete victory is possible and those who do not believe this.

To describe the latter as 'moderates' is not necessarily accurate. They may be just as conservative (in the Western view, 'extreme') in ideological terms as the others. Rather, they should be described as 'pragmatists'. They have made an intellectual judgement and drawn pragmatic conclusions from it. These pragmatists were in the past chiefly associated with the name of Mullah Akhtar Mansour, the Taliban leader who covertly succeeded the Taliban's founding Emir, Mullah Omar, during his illness leading to his (long concealed) death in 2013.

The killing of Mansour by a US drone strike on 21 May 2016 greatly weakened the pragmatist strain within the Taliban and cast severe doubt on the seriousness of the US military's desire for a peace settlement. Mullah Mansour was replaced by a collective Taliban leadership, composed of Maulvi Habitullah Akhunzada as Emir, and as deputies Mullah Omar's son Mullah Mohammed Yaqoob and Sirajuddin Haqqani, successor to his father Jalaluddin as leader of the famous 'Haqqani network'. The Haqqanis are generally viewed as the most powerful and most implacable fighting group aligned with the Taliban and have had especially close links to Al-Qaeda. Nothing in their almost half-century of warfare suggests a readiness to accept anything short of victory.

The conflict resolution process

Victory admittedly need not be unqualified. The history of the Taliban's negotiations during their rise and period of government between 1994 and 2001 was a good deal more nuanced and complicated than the standard Western picture of ignorant fundamentalist savages.[6] Moreover, while official talks have never taken place between the Kabul government and the Taliban, the nature of Afghan society and the Afghan tradition means that there are innumerable personal contacts between lower level figures on both sides. These could in the long run provide a basis for peace or at least – as on many occasions in the past – for individual or collective arrangements to surrender on terms or go over to the other side.[7]

The Taliban have never publicly formulated their own ideas for peace in concrete terms, partly because of their repeated insistence that US troops must leave the country and an 'independent Islamic system' be established before they will even agree to join talks on peace.[8] It has occasionally been suggested by sources close to the Taliban that they might agree to a long-term presence of US forces out of fear of some of Afghanistan's neighbours, but this seems highly unlikely.[9] This demand has been stated too often as the most important element of the Taliban's 'struggle for the liberation of Afghanistan' to be abandoned without catastrophic loss of face and the defection of major Taliban elements to join IS. What seems more plausible is that they might abandon this as a *precondition* if it were stated that (as proposed for example by the Pugwash Group) a peace settlement would lead to the withdrawal of US troops according to a strict and fairly short timetable.[10]

Beyond the demand for the withdrawal of foreign troops, the Taliban have called for the restoration of an 'Islamic system of government' in Afghanistan, and a change in the Afghan constitution to reflect this. What they mean by this is unclear, and the movement still continues to describe itself as the Islamic Emirate of Afghanistan', implying a claim to represent the sole legitimate state. Some analyses have described the Taliban as weak and internally divided, with major elements ready to make peace.[11] However, very little of this has appeared in public, and in any case the struggle between the Kabul state and the Taliban has always been more a battle of weaknesses than a battle of strengths: that is to say, not a fight for victory but a competition to see who disintegrates first.

Under Hamid Karzai (President 2004–2014), the Afghan government insisted that as a precondition of any peace agreement the Taliban must accept the Afghan constitution as it stands, as well as laying down their arms. In return, they would receive an amnesty and be allowed to establish themselves as a legal political party. These offers were simply non-starters, being equivalent in the eyes of the Taliban to surrender. The Afghan official High Peace Council was therefore widely seen as a failure even before the Taliban assassinated its leader, former President Burhanuddin Rabbani, in 2011.

In February 2018, President Ashraf Ghani considerably expanded the state's peace terms, with the abandonment of preconditions, the proposal of a ceasefire during negotiations, the dropping of sanctions against Taliban leaders, and a 'review' of the Afghan constitution followed by new elections. However, the terms still included Taliban recognition of the government as the legitimate government of Afghanistan in return for the government's recognition of the Taliban only as a political movement (Deutsche Welle). These proposals were supported by Russia, China, and Iran, as well as the USA – somewhat half-heartedly – despite President Trump's earlier statement that the USA would not negotiate with the Taliban. The Taliban's response was reserved, repeating the familiar line that Afghanistan is under occupation and that the withdrawal of foreign forces is a condition of talks. Observers were encouraged, however, by the fact that this rejection appeared less harsh and categorical than on previous occasions.

Most Western discussion of the Afghan peace process has focused on the issues of the constitution and women's rights. Given a desire for compromise on both sides, however, these can be fudged. After all, President Karzai himself said in 2004 that 'the Constitution is not the Koran' – in other words, it can be amended (Rubin 2004). The constitution already guarantees the Islamic character of the Afghan state, and the Taliban have said that they will accept the education of women as long as men and women are educated separately.

National elections would be necessary to ratify any peace process – but the results of those elections would be largely dictated by those parties holding armed power in given areas. It would therefore be no good whatsoever expecting either an elected parliament or a specially convened grand national assembly (*loya jirga*) to take the lead in peacemaking. The history of *loya jirgas* in Afghanistan is that they ratify deals already made. Any deal would have to be made in advance by the main power-holders.

Decisive in the end is likely to prove the issue of security. Fundamental to US fears of a peace deal with the Taliban involving the withdrawal of US troops is the memory of the US peace deal with North Vietnam in 1973, which led to the North's conquest of the South two years later. At the same time, there is no chance whatsoever in my view of the Taliban disarming as part of any peace settlement. Nobody ever disarms in Afghanistan unless they are forced at gunpoint to do so – take for example the miserable failure of the West's 'DDR' (disarmament, demobilisation, and reintegration) programme to disarm Afghan warlords and militias in the years after 2001.[12]

The Taliban would be literally suicidal to give up their arms, given the hatred and desire for revenge they have inspired in other sections of the population. A means would therefore have to be found to recognise the continued existence of the Taliban as autonomous units formally incorporated into the Afghan security forces. This in turn would form part of what is bound to be an inflexible demand of any Taliban leadership: for control – de facto if not de jure – of their core areas in Greater Kandahar in the south, Greater Pakhtia in the east, and Kunduz in the north. This control would guarantee the safety of the Taliban, and also that they would control elections to a future Afghan parliament from these regions, ensuring a major political stake in Afghanistan's future.

The co-existence within the same country of different armed forces with different sources of legitimacy is an offence against Max Weber's definition of the modern state, but it is not unknown in other peace processes (Lebanon being a leading example) and is certainly in tune with Afghan history. Only for a very brief period from the 1940s to the 1970s did the state enjoy a monopoly even of large-scale armed force (Giustozzi 2015). Parts of the Afghan security services are already to a considerable degree divided between different warlords.[13]

Some of these warlords, including Razzaq, form a key obstacle to peace. Warlords from non-Pashtun nationalities in the north and west, like General Atta Mohammed and General Rashid Dostum, would probably be able to co-exist with the Taliban if these gained a share of power in Kabul. This is not true of pro-government Pashtun warlords in the Taliban-dominated areas of the south and east. Taliban members have emphasised in conversation with me that during the wars of the 1990s, they spared enemies who made peace in good time and, following Afghan tradition, allowed them to go home with their weapons. However, they also said that there had been and would be certain leading figures whose 'crimes against the Afghan people' meant that they could not be pardoned.

The role of outside actors

An unsympathetic summary of America's role in relation to the Afghan peace process is that successive US administrations have been incapable of imposing their version of a peace settlement on Afghanistan and unwilling to let anyone else try. The unwillingness stems from America's understanding of its status and role as a superpower, from the complexity and contradictions of its motives in Afghanistan, and from the way in which these conflicting motives interact with other US agendas and rivalries in the region.

One feature distinguishing the Afghan conflict and peace process is the sheer number of outside players involved, their ability to bring influence to bear, and in several cases the extent of their mutual hostility. What they all have in common is their profound indifference to the interests of Afghanistan itself. Several have also more than once already demonstrated their willingness to 'fight to the last Afghan' as part of proxy wars in that country.

In the case of Lebanon, the outside players were France, the USA, Israel, and Syria, and in the end in the mid-1980s the first three effectively withdrew and allowed the Syrians to partly broker and partly enforce a peace settlement. In Bosnia, the USA and the European Union managed after long hesitation to work together, to exclude Russia from any effective role (helped by Russia's extreme weakness at the time), to isolate and defeat the proxy forces of Serbia, and to impose a settlement backed by US military force and Croat and Bosnian Muslim military success. In Northern Ireland, the outside players were Britain, the Irish Republic, and the USA. By the 1990s, their interests were congruent, and they worked together to push the Northern Irish combatants into a settlement.

In Afghanistan, by contrast, the USA, Pakistan, Iran, India, Russia, and China all have not only important stakes in the country and its conflict (in the case of Iran, dating back literally thousands of years) but also a very considerable capacity to bring influence to bear. Curiously enough, none of them have an interest in the Taliban as such, and all have a very strong interest in combating international Islamist terrorism. To date, however, their fear, distrust, and ambition vis-à-vis each other has proved even stronger. The result has been a tangled combination that has worked to help obstruct peace rather than further it.

For almost two hundred years, the weakness of the Afghan state has made Afghanistan the object of interference by stronger neighbours. Central to this dynamic has been the fact that since the Portuguese and their European successors from the 1490s on diverted the trade from South Asia to Europe from the overland route via Afghanistan to the sea route via the Cape of Good Hope, Afghanistan has lacked the wealth to support a strong state authority, since Afghan agriculture in the arid and mountainous terrain of Afghanistan (with the important but recent exception of the opium poppy) certainly cannot do so.[14]

The brief flowering of the Durrani Afghan monarchy in the second half of the eighteenth century was based not on Afghanistan's own resources but on the successful plunder of the collapsing Safavid empire in Iran and Mughal empire in India. When Iran recovered under the Qajars and north-western India fell first to the Sikhs and then to the British, this plunder ceased, Afghan revenue dried up, and the authority of the Durrani dynasty shrank drastically. A combination of the weakness and internal feuds of the Durranis and British fear of Russian imperial expansion then led to repeated British interventions in the country. After the second Afghan war of 1878–1879, the British adopted a different approach, that of building up an Afghan state as a buffer against Russia under the rule of an Afghan strongman, Emir Abdurrahman. His success in laying the basis for a limited modern Afghan state was due to his own ruthless ability but also to British guns and money.

After the British withdrawal from South Asia in 1947, for three decades Afghanistan was able to benefit from the superpower competition between the USA and the USSR, drawing significant amounts of aid from both. This relatively happy situation came crashing down in 1978, when Communist officers carried out a coup, leading to an Islamist and tribal rebellion and the military intervention of the USSR to rescue its Afghan clients (just as 15 years earlier the USA had sent troops to rescue its South Vietnamese clients). The USA, Pakistan, and Saudi Arabia then threw their support behind the Afghan Mujahedin anti-Soviet guerrillas. The resulting conflict between a Kabul-based state backed by one set of outside states and rural Islamist guerrillas backed by other states has continued up to the present, albeit with shifting sets of battle-lines and casts of actors.

A constant throughout this period, however, has been the role and the underlying interests of Pakistan. Seen from Islamabad (and still more importantly from Rawalpindi, where the Pakistani Army and intelligence service have their headquarters), the actual or potential threat from Afghanistan has always been twofold. First, the Pakistani establishment is made uneasy by the fact that Afghanistan since 1947 has maintained a territorial claim to the Pashtun territories taken from Afghanistan by the British Empire and now forming part of Pakistan, and in the 1950s and early 1960s supported Pashtun nationalist tribal rebels in Pakistan.

The fact that despite the US domination of Afghanistan since 2001 Washington has not been willing or able to persuade Kabul to drop this claim has been another source of suspicion and resentment of the USA in Pakistan – though interestingly enough, Pakistani sponsorship of the Taliban has also not resulted in the latter abandoning this claim, either, since the Taliban are in their way strong Afghan Pashtun nationalists.

This Afghan territorial claim obviously gives Pakistan a very strong motive either to try to bring about a pro-Pakistani government in Kabul or to keep Afghanistan weak and divided. And over the past four decades, Afghanistan has indeed been so riven by internal conflict that any serious attempt to abolish the 'Durand Line' (the frontier between Afghanistan and Pakistan imposed by the British) has been in abeyance. Pakistani fears of Afghan ambition however, have never been rooted solely or even mainly in fear of Afghanistan itself. Rather, the Pakistani establishment has feared that Afghanistan may become the instrument of a much more powerful enemy against Pakistan. During the Cold War, this meant the USSR. More recently, it has meant India.

Pakistani fear of Afghanistan becoming a base for India to encircle, destabilise, and possibly break up Pakistan has been a prime (though not the only) motive for Pakistani shelter for the Taliban since they were ousted from power in Kabul in 2001. Over time, this has led to an important shift in Pakistani attitudes to the crucial issue of the continuation of US bases in Afghanistan. For the first decade or so of the US presence, Pakistan, while favouring a peace settlement involving a share of power for the Taliban, did not wish for a complete withdrawal of US forces precisely out of fear that they would be replaced by the Indians.

More recently, however, this issue has become disastrously enmeshed with the wider geo-politics of Asia and the growing rivalry between the USA and China. As the USA in response to this rivalry has forged a closer and closer relationship with India to counterbalance China, so Pakistan has drawn even closer to its ally, China (and even, in recent years, to its old enemy Russia). As Barnett Rubin has written,

> General John Nicholson, the top American commander in the country, said that the additional troops are needed 'to maintain a regional counterterrorism platform' in Afghanistan. This might sound unthreatening to Americans, but it sounds different in the region. Washington used counterterrorism as a rationale for regime change in Iraq and other interventions. American bases in Afghanistan enable the U.S. to enhance electronic surveillance of neighboring countries.
>
> *(Rubin, 2017)*

The result is that US bases in Afghanistan are increasingly seen by the Pakistani security establishment not only as the source of a potential US threat to Pakistan (a fear obviously reinforced by the long-running US campaign of drone strikes against Taliban targets in Pakistan's tribal areas) but also as part of a hostile US–Indian alliance aimed at Pakistan and China. As a result, it would appear that the Pakistani establishment has become more sympathetic to the Taliban demand that US bases be withdrawn as part of a peace settlement.

> Pakistan in the past promoted peace talks between the Kabul government and the Taliban at Murree in 2015, but these broke down when Kabul revealed (after promising Islamabad that it would not do so) that Mullah Omar had been dead for two years. This drastically undermined the authority of the de facto Taliban leader, Mullah Akhtar Mansour, and led to Taliban withdrawal from the talks. It was seen by Pakistan as deliberate sabotage by the Kabul government. The subsequent killing of Mansour (widely seen as the leader of the pragmatic strain of the Taliban) by the USA was seen by the Pakistani

> establishment as confirmation that the USA is not interested in any settlement short of Taliban surrender.

The growth of hostility between the USA and China has also meant that in recent years nothing more has been heard of previous US calls for China to play a stronger role in Afghanistan and in the search for peace there. China was always extremely wary of responding to such requests, both because – as Chinese officials stated candidly in private – China has no 'magic formula' to end the conflict, and because of a feeling that the USA created this mess and should be responsible for clearing it up. The threat of permanent US bases threatening Pakistan and China, however, is likely to mean that in any future peace process involving China, Beijing is likely to give at least tacit support to Taliban demands that US forces be withdrawn as part of a settlement.

Afghanistan has also been affected by the growing hostility between the USA and Russia. In the years immediately following the US overthrow of the Taliban in 2001, Russia not only allowed US supplies to Afghanistan to pass through Russian territory and facilitated the establishment of US bases in Central Asia but also offered Russian participation in the international effort in Afghanistan (for which it was firmly snubbed by the Bush administration). With the steady deterioration of US–Russian relations as a result of President Bush's decision to continue NATO expansion, the wars in Georgia and Ukraine, and the various crises that followed the election of Donald Trump as US president, Russian support for the USA, such as it was, has been withdrawn, and Russia has moved closer to China.

As a result, Russia has sought rapprochement with Pakistan – including the beginning of arms sales – and has opened talks with the Taliban (though Moscow firmly denies US accusations that it is supplying them with arms and money).[15] This new diplomatic strategy of Moscow is also driven by three other convictions: that the Taliban can be a useful ally against IS, which Moscow regards as a mortal enemy that has recruited several thousand volunteers from Russia and the countries of the former USSR into its ranks; that the US campaign in Afghanistan will never succeed in defeating the Taliban, and that sooner or later there will be a peace settlement in which they will gain a major share of power; and that if the conflict can be ended, the Taliban might be persuaded to renew their offer of 1999–2001 and suppress the Afghan heroin trade, much of which goes to Russia. In the words of the Russian special envoy for Afghanistan, Zemir Kabulov, in December 2015,

> Taliban interests objectively coincide with ours. . . . Both the Afghan and the Pakistani Taliban have said they don't recognize ISIS and they don't recognize the ISIS leader [Abu Bakr] al-Baghdadi as the caliph; that is very important.
> *(Kaura 2018; Lewis 2017)*

The Russian interest in talking to the Taliban about the heroin threat (which is also an important Iranian interest) stems from the recognition that since 2001

US-backed governments in Kabul have failed utterly to control heroin production, from which many supporters of the Kabul state (including key US allies) benefit, and that the Taliban have been the only Afghan force in the past four decades which has in fact managed to suppress the trade, albeit for their own reasons. Finally, the talks with the Taliban have apparently convinced Moscow that the Taliban is sincere in its promise not to support international terrorism, and that their ambitions are confined to Afghanistan.[16]

The Moscow peace process has gained the participation of Pakistan, Iran, China, the Central Asian states, India, and the Afghan government. The USA initially refused to take part but agreed to do so once the meetings moved to Kabul. The Taliban also refused to take part on the basis of their standard position that foreign troops must be withdrawn before talks can begin. It seems likely that only greatly intensified pressure from Pakistan could get them to change their position on this.

In its attitude to Afghan peace, Pakistan has since 2001 become influenced by another consideration, that of peace in Pakistan itself. In 2004, US pressure to crackdown on militants who had taken refuge in Pakistan's tribal areas led to a botched military campaign which sparked an Islamist and tribal rebellion (which in 2007 named itself the Tehreek-e-Taliban Pakistan). In the years that followed, this rebellion and its suppression cost the lives of tens of thousands of Pakistanis, including more than 8,000 soldiers and police. Pakistan, however, has always been careful to restrict this campaign to Pakistani rebels and certain categories of international terrorist, and not to target the Afghan Taliban's bases within Pakistan.

This is not only because of a belief that the Taliban retain value as a proxy against India but also out of fear that to attack them would begin a new war within Pakistan itself as Pakistani Pashtuns rally to the cause of their Afghan brothers. It should be noted that while in the end, the Pakistani state and army were able to rally sufficient public support to defeat the Pakistani Taliban, the Afghan Taliban continue to enjoy much more widespread sympathy as a supposed war of resistance or 'defensive jihad' against foreign, non-Muslim 'occupation' of their country.[17]

Given the fact that Pakistan has stood up to repeated and intense US pressure on this issue, there seems no chance that Pakistani policy will change and that the Pakistanis will bring enough pressure to bear on the Taliban to persuade them to surrender on terms. Equally, there has been no sign of Pakistan increasing military help to the Taliban to the point that they could win in Afghanistan – something that would risk a truly ferocious US response. Pakistan will only back an Afghan peace offer that they think the Taliban have some chance of accepting at least as a basis for negotiation – and so far, no such offer has emerged from Kabul.[18]

As for the Indian establishment, it has been consistently opposed to any peace settlement with the Taliban that would give them a share of power in Kabul, and has sought to support the Afghan state in various ways. Delhi certainly does see Afghanistan as a useful weapon against Pakistan and would probably be glad in principle to replace the USA as Afghanistan's principal outside sponsor. In practice, India's willingness to play a more active role has been limited by a consciousness of India's own limited resources. The $4 billion or so needed to finance the Afghan security forces each year is a tiny proportion of America's military budget of some $690 billion dollars in 2018, but a much bigger proportion of India's budget of $62.8 billion – which is already under severe pressure from the perceived need to compete with China's much larger budget.

The more intelligent members of the Indian establishment are also influenced by an awareness that, as a retired Indian general once told me, 'You do not have to be a historical genius to know that for an outside power to get involved in Afghanistan does not usually turn out well'.[19] India's ability to play an active role in Afghanistan is therefore limited, but the close links between the Indian intelligence service (the Research and Analysis Wing, or RAW) and Afghan intelligence, together with the growing influence of the Indian lobby in Washington, means that it does have a certain capacity to help frustrate moves towards peace.[20]

Finally, Iran's policy towards Afghanistan is balanced between two different and partially conflicting imperatives: on the one hand to support the Hazara, its traditional Shia allies, against Pashtun Sunni domination and to combat anti-Shia Sunni extremism – now represented more by IS than by the Taliban; and on the other hand, to establish relations with the Taliban that will allow Iran to use them to attack US forces in Afghanistan if Iran is attacked by the USA or Israel, and also to put pressure on the USA to withdraw its bases from Afghanistan so that they can no longer threaten Iran. This means that Iran is in effect compelled to support the Taliban position that US forces must leave Afghanistan as part of any peace settlement, and it has led Iran to participate in the peace initiatives launched by Pakistan and Russia. In the end, therefore, Iran, like Russia and China, is happy enough to see the present situation continue, and the USA to continue to wriggle on the Afghan hook on which it has impaled itself.

Lessons to be learned from the case study

Externally, the Afghan peace process is bedevilled by a multiplicity of outside actors, none of whom have the power to bring about a peace settlement, but all of whom can help to block one. This is above all true of the two most important players, the USA and Pakistan. For the USA, the imperatives of the fight against international Islamist terrorism would suggest a deal with the Taliban to fight IS, and cooperation with Pakistan, Russia, and China to the same end. The need to make savings (however small) in US money and US lives, and to extract the USA from embroilment in future Afghan disasters, would also suggest a deal with the Taliban and withdrawal.

This is, however, blocked both by considerations of US prestige, by pressure from India (seen as an increasingly important US ally), and by the perceived need for Afghanistan as a base in the geopolitical struggle against Russia and China. For Pakistan, an end to the war is in principle desirable, since the Afghan war since 2001 has had extremely severe effects on Pakistan. However, for the Pakistani establishment this cannot mean either a Pakistani war with the Taliban to force them to the negotiating table, or a situation in which Afghanistan may become an Indian client state. It must mean a settlement in which the Taliban have enough power to block such a development.

Concerning the internal actors, even Taliban pragmatists have an obvious motive to get the US forces to withdraw, as this would put them in a vastly stronger bargaining position vis-à-vis Kabul. Moreover, the Taliban have stated so publicly and so repeatedly that US withdrawal is a condition of peace that it would be extremely difficult for them to abandon this without disastrous loss of face. The most that might change is that they would set US withdrawal as an essential *result* of talks rather than a *precondition* of talks. Assuming that the Taliban hold together (admittedly a big and possibly false assumption), this would still leave the Kabul state in a catastrophically weakened military situation and quite possibly open the way for a much greater Taliban seizure of power later.

There is no chance whatsoever of the Taliban disarming as a result of peace talks, let alone as a precondition of them. Given the number of commanders of the Afghan security forces who hate and fear them and also often have family reasons to take revenge on them, they would be literally suicidal to do so. So, any peace deal will have to involve the Taliban forces continuing to exist but now forming part – officially at least – of the Afghan security forces. This would form part of de facto Taliban control over their core areas in Greater Kandahar, Greater Pakhtia, and Kunduz, which in turn would mean that the chief enemies of the Taliban would have to leave these areas or die, even if their followers could remain as long as they submitted to Taliban authority.

An Afghan peace settlement would therefore in important respects resemble an armed truce more than a full peace settlement in the modern sense. However, the peace settlements in Bosnia, Lebanon, and elsewhere were also in their ways armed truces which left the armed forces of the domestic combatants largely intact. Such an arrangement would also be in keeping with Afghan history, by far the greater part of which has involved very weak central authority and a multiplicity of armed groups and overlapping legitimacies.

For even such a tenuous peace to be achieved, however, the USA would not only have to be prepared to withdraw its forces, but to work with China, Russia, Iran, Pakistan, and India both to convince the Taliban that they could not win an absolute victory and to uphold the resulting settlement both politically and financially. The only development that seems likely to bring the USA to this point would be an implosion of the Kabul regime due to its own internal divisions – which of course would open up a new set of obstacles to peace. If, therefore, the existing configuration of Afghanistan and its region continues unchanged, there are few grounds of hope for peace.

Notes

1 See Jones 2018; Singh 2018.
2 For general studies of the Afghan peace process, see Lieven (2016); Lakhdar and Thomas (2011); Jarvenpaa (2013); Nixon (2011).
3 See Reuters (2018).

4 Figures from Ben (2017).
5 For the changing character of the Taliban since their overthrow in 2001, see Giustozzi (2009a); Gopal (2009).
6 See Linschoten and Kuehn (2018); Dorronsoro (2005); Mike (2017); Malkassian (2013).
7 See Gannon (2017).
8 See for example the statement to this effect by the then Taliban chief negotiator, Sher Mohammed Abbas Stanekzai, at the Pugwash track 2 meeting in Kabul in January 2016, in Gul (2016).
9 See Semple et al. (2012).
10 See the Pugwash (2017).
11 See for example Farrell and Semple (2017).
12 See Giustozzi (2012); Dirksen (2017).
13 For the roots of warlord power in Afghanistan, see Giustozzi (2009b).
14 See Hopkins (2008), Barfield (2010).
15 See Gurganus (2018).
16 For the Taliban promise not to allow Afghanistan not to be used as a base for attacks on other countries, see the Taliban presentation to the Pugwash talks in Doha on Afghan peace, May 2015, in van Linschoten and Kuehn (2018: 501).
17 See for example the works and speeches of Imran Khan, who on this point at least does reflect the views of many of his fellow Pakistanis (Khan 2012: 235–276).
18 For Pakistani policy in Afghanistan, see Lieven (2016); Aziz (2009: 207–216), Nawaz (2009: 538–546), Rashid (2009: 84–108, 219–239). For the background to Pakistani strategy in the wars of the 1980s and 1990s, see Khan (2011); Coll (2005).
19 For Indian strategy in Afghanistan, see Larry Hanauer and Chalk (2012); Yadav and Barwa (2011).
20 For the India-Pakistan relationship in the context of Afghanistan, see Lieven (2012: 186–197); Cohen (2013: 29–30, 170–171, 189–191); Ganguly and Horenstein (2009); MacDonald (2016: 83–102).

References, further reading, and links to key primary documents

"19 Points Afghan Peace Proposal." *Pugwash*, 8 January 2017. https://pugwash.org/2017/01/08/consultations-on-afghanistan/.Aziz, Sartaz. 2009. *Between Dreams and Realities: Some Milestones in Pakistan's History*. Karachi: Oxford University Press.

"Afghan President Ashraf Ghani Offers Taliban Peace Talks and Political Recognition." *Deutsche Welle*. www.dw.com/en/afghan-president-ashraf-ghani-offers-taliban-peace-talks-and-politic al-recognition/a-42764769.

"Afghan President Ghani Makes Offer to Taliban for Peace Talks." *Reuters*, 28 February 2018. www.reuters.com/article/afghanistan-taliban/afghan-president-ghani-makes-offer-to-taliban-for-peace-talks-idUSL8N1QI0LE.

Barfield, Thomas. 2010. *Afghanistan: A Political and Cultural History*. Princeton: Princeton University Press.

Brahimi, Lakhdar, and R.P. Thomas 2011. "Afghanistan: Negotiating Peace." *The Century Foundation*, 31 March. https://tcf.org/content/book/afghanistan/.

Cohen, P.S. 2013. *Shooting for a Century: The India-Pakistan Conundrum*. Washington, DC: Brookings Institution Press.

Coll, Steve. 2005. *Ghost Wars: The Secret History of the CIA, Afghanistan and Bin Laden*. London: Penguin.

Dirksen, L.D. 2017. "Commanders in Control, Disarmament, Demobilisation and Reintegration under the Karzai Administration." PhD diss., King's College London.

Dorronsoro, Gilles. 2005. *Revolution Unending: Afghanistan 1979 to the Present*. London: Hurst & Company.

Farrell, Theo, and Michael Semple. 2017. "Ready for Peace? The Afghan Taliban After a Decade of War." *Rusi*, January. https://rusi.org/sites/default/files/rusi-briefing-afghanistan-310117.pdf.

Ganguly, Sumit, and Nicholas Horenstein. 2009. "India–Pakistan Rivalry in Afghanistan." *Journal of International Affairs* 63 (1): 127–140.

Gannon, Kathy. 2017. "Afghan Officials Said to Talk Every Day with the Taliban: Here Are Their Demands." *Associated Press*, 30 August. www.chicagotribune.com/news/nation world/ct-afghan-officials-taliban-20170830-story.html.

Giustozzi, Antonio. 2009a. *Decoding the New Taliban: Insights from the Afghan Field*. Columbia: Columbia University Press.

Giustozzi, Antonio. 2009b. *Empires of Mud: Wars and Warlords in Afghanistan*. London: Hurst & Company.

Giustozzi, Antonio. 2012. *Post-Conflict Disarmament, Demobilisation and Reintegration: Bringing the State Back*. London: Routledge.

Giustozzi, Antonio. 2015. *The Army of Afghanistan: The Political History of a Fragile Institution*. London: Hurst & Company.

Gopal, Anand. 2009. *The Battle for Afghanistan: Militancy and Conflict in Kandahar*. Washington, DC: New America Foundation.

Gul, Ayaz. 2016. "Taliban Skeptical of Four-Way Afghan Peace Process." *Voa News*, 24 January. www.voanews.com/a/taliban-skeptical-of-four-way-afghan-peace-process/3160382.html.

Gurganus, Julia. 2018. "Russia's Afghanistan Strategy: How Moscow Is Preparing to Go It Alone." *Foreign Affairs*, 2 January. www.foreignaffairs.com/articles/afghanistan/2018-01-02/russias-afghanistan-strategy.

Hanauer, Larry, and Barry Chalk. 2012. *India's and Pakistan's Strategies in Afghanistan: Implications for the United States and the Region*. Washington, DC: Rand Corporation.

Hopkins, B.D. 2008. *The Making of Modern Afghanistan*. Cambridge: Cambridge University Press.

Jarvenpaa, Minna. 2013. "Making Peace in Afghanistan." *US Institute of Peace*, 15 March. www.usip.org/sites/default/files/SR267Jarvenpaa.pdf.

Jones, S.G. 2018. "Why the Taliban Isn't Winning in Afghanistan." *Foreign Affairs*, 3 January. www.foreignaffairs.com/articles/afghanistan/2018-01-03/why-taliban-isnt-winning-afghanistan.

Kaura, Vinay. 2018. "Russia and Afghanistan Align Their Afghanistan Policies." *Middle East Institute*, 8 March. www.mei.edu/content/article/russia-and-pakistan-are-aligning-their-afghan-policies.

Khan, Imran. 2012. *Pakistan: A Personal History*. London: Bantam.

Khan, M.R. 2011. *Afghanistan and Pakistan: Conflict, Extremism and Resistance to Modernity*. Washington, DC: Johns Hopkins University Press.

Lewis, David. 2017. "Why Russia Is Back in Afghanistan." *Business Insider*, 15 November. www.businessinsider.com/why-russia-is-back-in-afghanistan-2017-11.

Lieven, Anatol. 2012. *Pakistan: A Hard Country*. London: Penguin.

Lieven, Anatol. 2016. "What Change for Afghanistan?" *The New York Review of Books*, 21 April. www.nybooks.com/articles/2016/04/21/what-chance-for-afghanistan/.

Macdonald, Myra. 2016. *Defeat Is an Orphan: How Pakistan Lost the Great South Asian War*. London: Hurst & Company.

Malkassian, Carter. 2013. *War Comes to Garmser: Thirty Years of Conflict in the Afghan Frontier*. London: Hurst & Company.

Martin, Mike. 2017. *An Intimate War: An Oral History of the Helmand Conflict 1978–2012*. London: Hurst & Company.

Nixon, Hamish. 2011. "Achieving Durable Peace: Afghan Perspectives on a Peace Process." *Peace Research Institute Oslo (PRIO)*. www.usip.org/sites/default/files/ccm/Nixon,%20 H%20(2011)%20Achieving%20Durable%20Peace%20(PRIO%20Paper).pdf.

Rashid, Ahmed. 2009. *Descent Into Chaos. The World's Most Unstable Region and the Threat to Global Security*. London: Penguin.

Rubin, Barnett. 2004. "Crafting a Constitution for Afghanistan." *Journal of Democracy* 15 (3): 5–19.

Rubin, Barnett. 2017. "Why More Troops Won't Help Afghanistan." *The New Yorker*, 5 June. www.newyorker.com/news/news-desk/why-more-troops-wont-help-afghanistan.

Sabawoon, A.M. 2018. "Going Nationwide: The Helmand Peace March Initiative." *Afghanistan Analysts Network*, 23 April. www.afghanistan-analysts.org/going-nationwide-the-helmand-peace-march-initiative/.

Semple, Michael, Theo Farrell, Anatol Lieven, and Rudra Chaudhuri. 2012. "Taliban Perspectives on Reconciliation." *Rusi*, 7 September. https://rusi.org/publication/briefing-papers/taliban-perspectives-reconciliation.

Schirch, Lisa. 2011. "Designing a Comprehensive Peace Process for Afghanistan." *United States Institute of Peace*, 19 September. www.usip.org/publications/2011/09/designing-comprehensive-peace-process-afghanistan.

Shuja, Nawaz. 2009. *Crossed Swords: Pakistan, Its Army, and the Wars Within*. Karachi: Oxford University Press.

Singh, V.J. 2018. "Why Peace Talks Are Washington's Best Bet in Afghanistan." *Foreign Affairs*, 21 March. www.foreignaffairs.com/articles/afghanistan/2018-03-21/why-peace-talks-are-washingtons-best-bet-afghanistan.

van Linschoten, A.S., and Felix Kuehn. (Ed.). 2018. *The Taliban Reader: War, Islam and Politics*. London: Hurst & Company.

Westcott, Ben. 2017. "Afghanistan: 16 Years, Thousands Dead and No Clear End in Sight." *CNN World*, 1 November. https://edition.cnn.com/2017/08/21/asia/afghanistan-war-explainer/index.html.

Yadav, Vikash, and Conrad Barwa. 2011. "Relational Control: India's Grand Strategy in Afghanistan and Pakistan." *India Review* 10 (2): 93–125.

3

BASQUE COUNTRY

Daniele Conversi and Gorka Espiau

Introduction

The majority of peace processes around the world need to include all actors and parts involved in the conflict. The Basque peace process (BPP) is, however, remarkable as it provides a glimpse of a peace process in which one of the key actors, the central state, in particular the incumbent government, has been largely absent – at least in a formal capacity. The BPP can be said to have developed *unilaterally* as only the non-state armed group, ETA (*Euzkadi Ta Askatasuna*, Homeland and Freedom), sat at the internationally led negotiating table pressured by a civil society that was firmly demanding an end to violence.

ETA's decision to end its armed campaign should be comprehended in its relative *longue durée* and contextualised within the framework of deepening federalisation, successful socio-economic transformation, democratisation, and the concession of widening levels of autonomy within the Spanish state. These changes configured the emergence of a set of institutions, which granted a certain amount of power to the Basque nationalists, resulting in the development of new forms of multilevel local sovereignty and a successful cultural assertion and socio-economic transformation. This framework, we argue, was essential in the development of the broader BPP.

We also argue that the BPP lasted from the transition to democracy (1975) and the approval of the statute of autonomy (1979) to the 2011 definitive ceasefire, the subsequent disarmament in April 2017 and ETA's final dissoution in April–May 2018. During this time, we suggest, there were two significant processes: the disbanding of the main of the two branches of ETA in 1981 and the final abandonment of violence by ETA in 2011, culminating in its dissolution in 2018 and its disapperance as a political 'trademark'. The latter cannot be understood without the former, and both are related to the process of democratisation and transference of powers in most fields, including the revival of the Basque language and several other aspects of the local culture (Woodworth 2007). Finally, in line with recent research (Murua 2016, 2017; Tellidis 2010, 2011; Whitfield 2014), we argue that the intensive participation of civil society facilitated this process and its unilateral thrust.

Conflict analysis

Until the late nineteenth century, a system of *fueros* (local statutes codified as agreements between the Spanish Crown and Basque regional powers) allowed each province to keep a separate administration. However, Basque defeat in the last Carlist Wars (1872–1876) led to the abolition of the *fueros* – followed by a rapid, massive industrialisation. The reaction to this double process of state centralisation and rapid economic development resulted in the birth of Basque nationalism. Like other nationalists in Europe at that time, the founder of the first Basque nationalist party, Sabino Arana y Goiri (1865–1903), defined the Basque nation, renamed Euskadi, mostly on the basis of race. This was at a time when heavy industries attracted thousands of immigrants turning the Basque Country, particularly the province of Bizkaia/Vizcaya, into Spain's richest and most developed region along with Catalonia (Conversi 1997). But nationalism remained peaceful until new socio-political changes created the conditions for the emergence of terrorist political violence.

After the Spanish Civil War (1936–1939), Francisco Franco's dictatorship (1939–1975) unleashed a wave of political repression persecuting Basque cultural and political activities. But in 1959 an underground group of university students founded ETA: inadvertently, it was Franco's success in weakening the Basque Nationalist Party that led a group of frustrated youths to form the organisation (Jeram and Conversi 2014). Despite an initial rejection of violence, ETA's First Assembly (1962) adopted a Declaration of Principles structuring ETA into cells of full-time activists totally dedicated to secrecy. ETA's first full political programme was conveyed in *Vasconia* (1963) by Federico Krutwig (1921–1998), who incidentally was never a member of ETA. It incorporated Marxism, 'third-worldism', secularism, and a rejection of the Church as an agent of de-nationalisation (Krutwig Sagredo 1973: 75). Following in the footsteps of the Algerian and Cuban revolutions, *Vasconia* proposed guerrilla war as the only means to liberate Euskadi, incorporating Franz Fanon's (1925–1961) emphasis on anti-colonial violence as a liberating and purifying principle, essential to the psychological wellbeing of the 'oppressed'.

ETA subsequently adopted a clandestine guerrilla manual with echoes of Mao-Tse-Tung and Ho-Chi-Minh, dividing Euskadi into six operative zones (*herrialdes*) with the aim of conducting a revolutionary war (Conversi 1993).[1] Armed struggle became a primary concern, with violence now considered to be the only available solution to the 'awakening' of the nation.

The first armed attack was an assault on a bank courier in 1965, followed by a series of bank robberies. In one of these, in June 1968, an ETA activist was killed at a roadblock following the murder of a member of the security forces, the *Guardia Civil*.[2] As anticipated by ETA's theorists, popular indignation about the killing broke out in illegal mass demonstrations in support of the fallen 'martyr', and 'ETA's ranks swelled with new arrivals' (Clark 1984: 49). This engendered a spiral of state violence and counter-violence, which, in turn, contributed to further radicalising Basque politics for several decades (Ibarra Güell 1987).

The next step was a fully premeditated political murder. In 1968, ETA chose a highly symbolic target, the police commissioner Melitón Manzanas, widely identified as a torturer of political prisoners. The government response was swift and ruthless. After declaring a 'state of emergency', several suspected ETA sympathisers were rounded up, detained, and intimidated. In 1969, the structure of ETA was severely disrupted by a further wave of arrests, and most of its leaders were forced into exile. In the meantime, people filled the streets in mass demonstrations.

With nearly all the leaders either arrested or in exile, ETA's Executive Committee became controlled by inexperienced youth. In December 1970, 16 ETA members were judged in the Burgos Trial (*Proceso de Burgos*), a showcase trial that became a defining moment in Spanish history by exposing the regime's ferocity and causing widespread international condemnation.

ETA rapidly regrouped, swiftly reborn from its ashes. In 1972, the kidnapping of the Basque industrialist Lorenzo Zabala indicated a new type of non-military 'legitimate target' (Darby 1994), chosen with the goal of attracting working-class support.

ETA had thus regained considerable strength after the difficult days of the Burgos trial, initiating an unprecedented wave of guerrilla attacks and unleashing renewed police repression upon the whole of the Basque Country.[3] ETA reached a period of unequalled expansion: in December 1973, the killing of Admiral Carrero Blanco eliminated Franco's expected successor.

As soon as Francisco Franco died (20 November 1975), the process of democratisation began and proceeded swiftly, but ETA's death toll continued to rise. Spain as a whole changed in the 1970s, and the milestone was the drafting and approval of a new Constitution in 1978 (Conversi 1998, 2002).

The legacy of state repression survived the demise of the regime and contributed to creating a 'culture of violence' within the radical left (*Izquierda Abertzale*) 'reproduced within a broad social network of organisations, groups, initiatives or media through rituals, rites of passage, symbols and belief systems which convey transcendent meaning' (Mees 2003: 184). This culture was pervasive and remained the main obstacle to a move towards a peacemaking agenda.

The BPP must be understood as a long process beginning with the end of the dictatorship and becoming articulated in two main phases: first, the dissolution of ETA-pm and, second, the unilateral declaration of cessation of armed struggle in 2011 and the internationally verified disarmament in 2017. ETA-pm was then the mainstream faction within ETA and differed from ETA-m (which thereafter seized the acronym ETA for itself) by acting simultaneously as a paramilitary group and politically as an organiser of strikes and clandestine labour mobilisations (Fernández Soldevilla 2010).

As with the demise of many authoritarian regimes, Spain's *democratisation* was tightly bound up with the accommodation of nationalist aspirations. The Constitution's gestation phase lasted 16 months, its draft passing through over a thousand amendments for its 169 articles – the majority of which revolved around issues of national identity. The Constitution combined a pluralist vision of Spain's constituent 'nationalities' (*nacionalidades*) with a persisting stress on shared 'Spanishness' within an indivisible Spanish 'nation' (*nación*). The three 'historical nationalities' – Catalonia, Euskadi (Basque Country), and Galicia – are not explicitly mentioned in the Constitution. The homogeneity ideal was thus replaced by the recognition of regional differences, with the monarchy supposedly acting as a supra-national unitary symbol (Conversi 1998, 2002).

However, the organisations gravitating around ETA invited a 'no' vote in the referendum on the Constitution, and 46.7 per cent of the Basque and Navarre's electorate abstained (Linz et al. 1981: 88–91), showing the extent to which the Spanish state had gained little local legitimacy – a state of affairs that provided fertile ground for the continuation of violence.[4] All the same, regional statutes of autonomy were approved soon after the 1978 Constitution, and in due course, the Basque Autonomous Community government acquired considerable powers through its own Statute (*Statute of Gernika* 1979). In the early 1980s, it was endowed with its own parliament, school system, television channels, social welfare, a police force (the *Ertzaintza*), and, most importantly, a special tax regime and economic agreement, the *Concierto económico* (Alonso Olea 1995, 2010).

Even in this context of extended democratisation and decentralisation, ETA's attacks and police repression continued to catalyse public opinion, attracting new recruits to the organisation. As the spiral theory of violence and counter-violence seemed to be translated into reality, hundreds of disaffected youth joined ETA. Henceforth, the death toll continued to rise, reaching its peak during the transition to democracy and just before the Basque statute of autonomy could be implemented in the decades following its approval (1979).

According to the Spanish and French security forces, ETA has always been a relatively small organisation, while its numbers steadily and slowly declined since the 1990s.[5] It remained internally self-structured into cells and operationally controlled by a central command (the military leadership). The political decisions were taken by another group (the political leadership). These were loosely connected with the pro-independence, but fully legalised, political parties, unions, and associations gravitating around the broader *Movimiento de Liberación Nacional Vasco* (MLNV, Basque National Liberation Movement) (Bullaín López 2011). The military leadership and the political leadership shared collaborative decision-making in order to avoid the possible emergence of any form of individual charismatic leadership.

Why violence?

Several scholars have investigated the origins of Basque political violence. The overwhelming majority tend to agree that the particular conditions of political and cultural oppression under the dictatorship were the main catalyst (Alimi et al. 2015: 261; Conversi 1997; De La Calle 2015: 72–78; Della Porta 2013, 2014; Irvin 1999; Jáuregui Bereciartu 1981; Letamendia 1991, 2000; Llera et al. 1993; Watson 2007; Woodworth 2007; Zirakzadeh 1991; Zulaika 1988). The combination of weak state legitimacy, police repression, economic expansion, and resentment against cultural oppression provided an explosive mix. The loss of traditional culture, especially the Basque language, was accompanied by cultural and ideological fragmentation (Conversi 1997; Lecours 2007; Woodworth 2007).

In most respects, Spain's long-term effort to impose a homogeneous, uniform culture along the lines of the Jacobin model had failed (Conversi 2008, 2012). Above all, its overarching goal of creating more streamlined, loyal, and obedient citizens only superficially succeeded through the imposition of a common language and patterns of behaviour, but not shared attitudes, loyalties, and identifications. While homogenising policies did destroy part of the region's cultural specificity, they could hardly break up the defiant sense of underlying identity, which was caused in part by those very efforts. In fact, the more the state tried to proscribe and persecute Basque culture and national symbols, the more anti-Spanish sentiment grew and, eventually, radicalised.[6]

The 'socialization of suffering' and civic opposition

Once ETA began to turn to political violence in the mid-1960s, the state's response was uncompromisingly violent, extending police repression to most spheres of Basque society, either directly or indirectly. This led to increasing human rights abuses, including the use of torture during police interrogations – a practice that had previously been used in nearly all of Spain's internal and international conflicts (Watson 2007: 83–84).[7] As a guerrilla organisation, ETA's main aim was to mobilise the maximum number of Basque citizens, even at the cost of human rights deterioration. Thus, ETA's leaders were fully cognisant that more armed attacks would be translated into further pain and sorrow, often through random state violence and human rights abuses. Inspired by the Algerian revolution, as well as the Cuban and Vietnamese mass mobilisations, ETA sought to reproduce the same conditions in a highly developed industrial society (Conversi 1993). Such an unrealistic task seemed initially to succeed because the state's ferocious response led more people, particularly youth, to join ETA's rank and file, creating an aura of political legitimacy around the organisation, which would last decades after the end of the dictatorship.

But slowly the pendulum began to swing the other way. In its early years, under the Francoist dictatorship, ETA considered all members of the security forces as 'legitimate targets' – to paraphrase a military term which has been used to explain the IRA's restrictive choice of targets (Darby 1994) and extended to describe the tendency to abjure 'attacks on civilians except as parts of its campaign against economic targets' (Horowitz 2003: 498). However, the definition of 'legitimate target' changed over the years, and in the 1980s non-military targets began to be included. Professionals such as the nuclear engineers José María Ryan and Angel Pascual

Múgica (1981 and 1982, respectively) and senior politicians such as Enrique Casas (1984) were part of a long list of more than 800 victims.[8]

A most significant change took place in January 1995, when Gregorio Ordoñez, the president of the local Popular Party (PP) – which in 1996 would become Spain's ruling party – was killed in San Sebastian. One year later, Francisco Tomás y Valiente, President of the Spanish Constitutional Court, and Fernando Múgica Herzog, President of the local Socialist Party, were also assassinated. The list of murdered politicians includes Ernest Lluch (1937–2000), former Minister of Health and Consumption in the first Spanish Socialist Workers' Party (PSOE) government, Professor of Economics at the University of Barcelona, and among those who were seeking dialogue. The extension of 'legitimate targets' fomented revulsion against any form of violence to the point that even among radical nationalists the belief became widespread 'that it is possible to make greater advances without, rather than with, armed activity' (Zabalo and Saratxo 2015: 362).

The new strategy adopted by ETA in 1995 was described as the '*socialization of suffering*'.[9] For ETA's younger leaders, if violence were experienced by only a small segment of the population, the Spanish Government would never engage in true negotiations. Scaling up this logic, everybody had to directly suffer in the conflict. From that moment on, local politicians, judges, business leaders, journalists, and even academics began to be targeted. A third of the 85 murders committed by ETA since the end of the truce in 1999 were councillors and members of the PP and the PSOE. Under this strategy, the number of attacks decreased, but the non-military profile of the targets caused a much bigger impact in social and political terms.

The 'socialization of suffering' strategy inflamed Basque streets. Thousands of local politicians, judges, journalists, and academics lived their daily lives escorted by bodyguards. Although the numbers of directly affected victims may have diminished, the number of potential targets – and with it the disruptive threat on society as a whole – increased.

The Basque region has a large number of family-owned small- and medium-sized industrial firms. ETA has used the kidnapping of prominent business leaders to extract revenues as a high-impact tactic, requesting them to make regular payments to support ETA's activities.[10] If a company refused to pay, its cadres, owners, and relatives risked becoming targets of physical attacks or kidnapping.[11] Historically, only business leaders who had refused to pay the 'revolutionary tax' were kidnapped. The goal was to demonstrate the dramatic consequences of not collaborating with the rest of the local business community. But under the new strategy, kidnapping was also used for non-financial purposes. The kidnapping of Jose Antonio Ortega Lara in 1996, an ordinary prison warden, led to 532 days of political and social confrontation.[12]

Shortly after, ETA kidnapped Miguel Angel Blanco, a local PP chancellor in the city of Ermua, and killed him 48 hours later. This watershed assassination provoked a mass movement of social revulsion throughout Basque society, in which moderate nationalists joined forces with other local and Spanish parties, through recurrent and huge street demonstrations.

The conflict resolution process

ETA announced the definitive end to its violent campaign on 20 October 2011, responding to an International Peace Conference that took place in the Aiete Palace (Donostia–San Sebastian). This decision was the result of a complex combination of circumstances, including massive popular demonstrations against violence, new political strategies, and successful international security operations. Within ETA's rank and file, the decision had to be reached unanimously, in unison, otherwise it could have once more resulted in the creation of a splinter group (Zulaika and Murua 2017). The likelihood of spoilers emerging in such difficult phases is a long-studied phenomenon (Newman and Richmond 2006; Nilsson and Söderberg Kovacs 2011), and it was considered a possibility in the Basque case itself (Reiter 2016a, 2016b). This required a long work of conviction within the support basis and its leaders. Thanks to these non-lineal efforts, Basque society has been offered the most significant opportunity for transforming the conflict dynamics since the end of dictatorship.

As described in the previous sections, the 'socialization of suffering' strategy designed by younger ETA leaders did not generate the expected outcome. As never before, huge numbers of citizens mobilised against ETA, uniting Basque nationalists and non-nationalists alike. The disaffection of ETA's own constituency towards the use of political violence reached unprecedentedly high levels.

In 2004, almost ten years after the killing of Gregorio Ordoñez, senior members of the pro-independence movement led by Arnaldo Otegi and Rafael Diez Usabiaga offered 'a commitment to settle differences during the process in a peaceful and democratic way' by proposing a *dual track negotiation strategy*.[13] This duality referred to the simultaneous search for an agreement between Basque political forces and a separate negotiation process between ETA and the Spanish and French states – largely on 'technical' issues such as the decommissioning of weapons and the release of prisoners who had renounced violence – a measure still supported by 72 per cent of Basque residents a few years later (Sociometro vasco 2012). Eighteen months later, ETA announced a total ceasefire to support this new strategy that lasted from March 2006 until June 2007.

The influence of the peace movement

It is difficult to delineate a precise chronology for the events leading up to the beginning of a mass peace movement in Basque society. Labour unions and political organisations initiated the first public initiatives against violence. Many union meetings and political events provided opportunities to speak out against the use of violence. Public protests had already erupted in 1981 against the assassination of the nuclear engineer José María Ryan, while students from the University of Duesto promoted public rallies following the assassination in 1984 of the Socialist militant Enrique Casas. Simultaneously, social movements also mobilised against the violent activity of the secret paramilitary 'anti-terrorist' organisation, *Grupos Antiterroristas de Liberación* (GAL), which assassinated an estimated 27 people and wounded several others (Clark 1990: 59; Murua 2016: 28–29).

Since the 1980s, a multitude of entities have acted as peace promoters, chiefly *Gesto por la paz de Euskal Herria* and the social movement for dialogue with ecologist roots *Elkarri* (f. 1992, later transformed into *Lokarri*, f. 2006). Although their discourses and repertories of action sharply differed, they contributed to the same aims and goals – the definitive cessation of violence. Through protests, events, and meetings, they created the context within which the organisation of the 2011 Aiete Peace Conference could eventually take place.

The decline in ETA's popularity had begun as far back as the 1980s, that is, soon after the dismantling of ETA-pm and concomitantly with the implementation of the autonomy statute. As Table 3.1 shows, the contrast between two surveys, taken respectively in 1981 and 2005 testifies to the steady decline in support for ETA.[14]

More recently, the vast majority of Basque society has shown overwhelming opposition to ETA's activities, with less than 5 per cent declaring total or 'critical' support.[15] This hostility is clearly articulated throughout all Basque provinces, both by those who consider themselves as Basque nationalists and by those who support Spanish-wide parties. Almost unanimously, Basque society has come to disapprove of ETA as a highly harmful organisation.

This public opposition, reinforced by the new 'totally unarmed strategy' adopted by the pro-independence political movement, together with anti-terrorist operations, including various arrests of members of ETA's leadership, created the conditions for the unilateral ceasefire declaration in 2006.

Since then, on numerous occasions, ETA has tried to establish conversations with the Spanish government with the support of international mediators, but the Spanish government refused to discuss a possible peace process even after ETA had decided to terminate the armed campaign.[16] The most substantial attempts involved international mediators such as Jonathan Powell,[17] the Center for Humanitarian Dialogue in Geneva, the *Comunita' di Sant'Egidio* in Rome, the South African

TABLE 3.1 Changes in public support for ETA from 1981 to 2005

Attitudes towards ETA in Basque society	*1981 (%)*	*2005 (%)*
Complete support	8	–
Ambivalent support	4	2
Support for goals only	3	11
Support in the past, not in the present	12	22
Indifference	1	2
Fear	1	4
Complete opposition	23	56
Don't know	48	3

(*Source*: *Euskobarometro*. https://www.ehu.eus/es/web/euskobarometro/aurkezpenak)

Human Rights lawyer Brian Currin, and Father Alec Reid from Ireland.[18] These efforts could not facilitate an agreement with the central government, but they had a deep impact on the evolution of the pro-independence movement. The peace process in Northern Ireland, in particular, offered the experience, narrative, and political support that the Basque pro-independence movement needed to transition towards a totally unarmed strategy – although some authors speak about a 'misrepresentation of the Irish model' (Alonso 2004). Reciprocally, Irish Republicans, such as the Sinn Féin councillor Eoin Ó Broin, have viewed Basque society as a model for organisational efficiency and the effectiveness of street social mobilisations (Ó Broin 2003). Retrospectively, we can consider the contributions from Ireland as aspects of an 'internal and partial mediation' process (Espiau 2010).[19]

In the absence of a formal negotiation process, this evolution, brought about by civil society, mass demonstrations, and campaigns, created the conditions for ETA to disarm unilaterally. Although there have been secret talks and negotiations throughout most of Spain's democratic history (Clark 1990), the Spanish state never formally recognised the validity of the international negotiating efforts, and most Spanish media close to successive incumbent governments continued to stress that ETA had been militarily and morally defeated and had no choice but to lay down its arms. A considerable body of Basque public opinion interpreted this unilateralism as one of the many aspects of state inaction. Indeed, recent studies clearly explain that the Spanish state in practice sabotaged the BPP by incarcerating the leaders who were more prone to dialogue (Murua 2016: 50–66, 70–89; Whitfield 2014: 215–220; Zulaika and Murua 2017).

In 2017, the geo-localisation of ETA's arsenal (weapons, ammunitions, and explosives depots) was transmitted to a group of ordinary citizens, *Bakearen Artisauak* (the *Peace Artisans*). This group, also called *Luhuso* (from the name of a town across the French border host to the first attempt to destroy ETA's weaponry) was established and led by the ecologist Jean-Noel ('Txetx') Etcheverry to support the demilitarisation process. In other words, ETA announced through civilian intermediaries its solemn promise of unilateral and unconditional disarmament. This publicly took place in Bayonne (France) on 8 April 2017 before the eyes of a broad public from a variety of sectors of civil society (Tremlett 2017). The French authorities initially reacted by arresting some of the peace activists, accusing them of assisting ETA to disarm – although they were all later released. The disarmament took place under the international supervision of the Dialogue Advisory Group (DAG), founded and led by Ram Manikkalingam (Sri Lanka). DAG set up an International Verification Commission (IVC) to monitor ETA's ceasefire and work towards its disarmament by the announced date of 8 April 2017 – although the first sealing of weapons by ETA dates back to February 2014.[20]

Current situation and future perspectives

After the permanent ceasefire and cessation of armed activity in 2011, ETA announced that it had 'completely dissolved all its structures and ended its political initiatives' (letter dated 16 April 2018, but made public on 2 May 2018).[21] The remaining challenges include the reintegration of remaining prisoners and formulas to allow the participation of victims and their relatives in the new post-conflict scenario, despite the scarcity of deliberative discussions during and after the BPP (Jeram and Conversi 2014). A continuous effort of cross-partisan acknowledgement of mutual suffering would no doubt enrich the discussions and honour the victims' memories. Granting non-partisan support for specific initiatives, such as a project for collecting testimonies, would also contribute significantly to the healing process and help all political narratives to be democratically expressed.

After ETA's dissolution, there is no reason to hinder all narratives being recorded and disseminated to reach beyond their original audiences. Such a vast storytelling exercise will undoubtedly provide much-needed psychological support to those who have suffered losses and simultaneously overcome instrumental efforts of persistent victimisation. Basque society still needs to discuss how to represent a new social reality and how to accommodate all existing narratives. Only by allowing the free expression of contrasting narratives can a shared narrative eventually be allowed to emerge.

The former negotiating parts are likely to endorse the defence of human rights principles similar to those that have successfully guided previous peace negotiations in other parts of the world: an unequivocal commitment to exclusively peaceful means in defending political ideas, honouring the memory of the victims and guaranteeing the participation of their relatives in the process, the participation of all political traditions in all-party talks, and new initiatives regarding the situation of remaining prisoners.

Lessons to be learned from the case study

Several hundred books, articles, and reports have been published on terrorism in Spain. However, until recently the atmosphere created by indiscriminate terrorist attacks, intimidations, and violence was so tense that it seemed impossible to write a balanced account of recent events.[22] We argue that the following lessons can be drawn from the BPP. Saturated by years of violence, Basque civil society played a pivotal role in the peace process. Despite the limits in the process of democratic transition, the relatively high level of autonomy achieved rendered the use of violence politically illegitimated and anachronistic. By the late twentieth century, ETA's loss of internal support was increasingly becoming a key factor in the end of its violent campaign. ETA-pm first dissolved in the early 1980s, just when regional autonomy was being implemented (Fernández Soldevilla 2010). In this context, those who decided to continue the use of violence had to face a society that was increasingly hostile to their methods – if not necessarily to their goals. At the same time, sustained police action and cross-border cooperation between the Spanish and French services dealt a series of military blows to ETA – to the point that some authors consider cross-border police coordination as the single most important catalyst in bringing about ETA's defeat (Alonso 2010).

The BPP was, however, *unilateral*, as the state remained largely absent at the negotiating able. This contrasts with mainstream assumptions, exemplified by Tony

Blair's confused and superficial declaration exalting the role of 'the Spanish administration' in handling ETA – by which he mostly referred to Zapatero's efforts, but also lauded the PP's 'seriousness and responsibility' (Blair 2011). This absence of the state in the peace process originates from its hard stance and official refusal to negotiate with terrorists. While violent methods seem to have become universally discredited in the wake of 9/11, successive conservative government since Aznar's second term in office (2000–2004) have consistently exploited this to their advantage (Conversi 2006; Whitfield 2014: 96–105), while Basque civil society began to mobilise autonomously against terrorism. Even as recently as March 2017, Franz Valli, former president of Emmaus France, declared: 'We have to get out of this absurd situation where we have, on one side, ETA which wants to be a disarmed organization as quickly as possible and, on the other, [two] states that refuse to realize this'.[23]

The positive evolution of the BPP should be interpreted as long term, articulated in several phases, some of which date back to the transition years (1975–1979). In this chapter, we have first considered the institutional progresses developing around the statute of autonomy, whose roots lie in the Spanish Constitution's initial attempt to implement an Iberian interpretation of a quasi-federal state (Moreno 2001). Second, we focused on ETA's slow drift towards isolation and social de-legitimacy, largely as a consequence of the widespread violence and the negotiated transfer of powers from Madrid to the new Basque institutions year by year. Third, we suggest that the state's security offensive must be read in tandem with ETA's social, as well as military, weakening caused by the disaffection of its own constituency: ETA's internal decline and inner debilitation was accompanied by police infiltration at all levels of the organisation, from the grassroots to the vertex. Fourth, we have shown that the participation of international actors emerging from outside the conflict area, sharing their experiences of other conflicts, has been vital in the decisive negotiation phases. Finally, the peace process should be seen in the broader context of cultural recovery, which has provided new spaces for social interaction well beyond radical politics. Cultural revival has thus worked as a powerful connection, incentive, and bond in the overcoming of political–ideological divides (Conversi 2010, 2017; De La Calle 2015: 72–78; Medeiros 2015).

Historically, this conflict has been deeply influenced by the nation–state's incapacity to accommodate multiple nationalities aspiring to some form of self-government. Through the years, the key political actors – the Spanish government, ETA, and the Basque government – have substantially modified their run-of-the-mill positions regarding territorial organisation and national sovereignty. Current leaders have contemplated more flexible formulas and strategies, like the one exposed by Juan José Ibarretxe Markuartu, former *lehendakari* (President of the Basque autonomous community, 1999–2009) on 'shared sovereignty' and 'sustainable human development', which could potentially become the subject of a compromise based on a broader consensus than that enjoyed by the current Statute of Autonomy (Ibarretxe 2011, 2015).[24]

In fact, the democratic transition process has been successful enough that it has been possible to envisage a specific 'Basque social model' (Ibarretxe 2011). Many economic, labour, and social rights have been maintained in the Basque Country, while they have been drastically curtailed in the rest of Spain, as the central government embraced neoliberal globalisation while responding to the post-2008 economic recession. Such a 'Basque social model' may be considered a variation of the 'European social model' (Moreno 2014), but the region's unique achievements have been made possible largely thanks to a taxation regime and other specific powers which the Basque administration enjoys. This means that the Basque Country finds itself in a political space relatively free of manoeuvring in comparison with other Autonomous Communities such as Catalonia, where 'neoliberal recentralization' radicalised public opinion through cuts in public services and the erosion of citizens' social rights.

This new approach to conflict resolution is relevant to the international debate on new creative solutions to similar conflicts. A successful outcome of the process can deepen and intensify the trend begun elsewhere in the pursuit of alternative solutions that are able to transcend the hidebound limits of 'nation–statism'. Emerging from the positive experience of building the European Union, new formulas for complex interdependence no longer seem unrealistic (Espiau 2006). The broader positive context offered by the European Union should not be underestimated (Zabalo and Saratxo 2015), despite the multiple threats emanating from xenophobic anti-Europeanism – one of the many consequences of unregulated globalisation (Conversi 2014). In fact, European engagement has been identified as one of the key factors in both conflict resolution and the maintenance of plurinational federations within the European Union (Loizides 2016: 183–184).

In general, the involvement of international actors was a central, and perhaps peculiar, aspect of the BPP. Rather than discussing what motivated these actors to get involved (on this and other aspects of the international mediation, see Whitfield 2014), we have shown that actors on the ground and Basque public opinion in general perceived their contribution as decisive to the entire BPP – despite the fact that the Spanish state has persistently refused to acknowledge their involvement.

The milestone events of the peace process since the Spanish transition were possibly identifiable as follows. First, the self-dissolution of ETA-pm, the main branch of the organisation in 1981, presented a viable precedent; subsequently, ETA's adoption of a campaign of almost indiscriminate targeting of public figures (1995) resulted in the emergence of massive public opposition to terrorism, culminating in the 2011 Aiete conference the 2017 surrender of weapons caches and ETA's complete dissolution of all its structures and political initiatives in April 2018.

The Basque self-government experience and, in particular, its long but ultimately successful peace process, provides a context and an example which seems well fitted to an argument for the conjunction of multiple positive forces. In the end, the BPP can provide a set of illustrations about the power of civic initiatives beyond (and despite) the state and the spectre of simplistic military solutions – as exemplified by the ruthless termination of the Tamil conflict in Sri Lanka (see David G. Lewis' chapter in this book). Finally, we have also shown how an entire 'culture of violence' can become increasingly de-legitimised and unrecognised by the very society in whose name the violence is carried out.

Notes

1 José Luís Zalbide's (Kumbeltz) 46-page booklet, *La Insurrección en Euskadi,* published anonymously as *Cuadernos ETA*, no. 20 (Zalbide 1963).
2 The *Civil Guard* is a gendarmerie-style military force founded in 1844 and charged with police duties among civilian populations.
3 A new generation of leaders emerged, among them 'Txomin' and 'Argala'. Four ETA members were killed on separate occasions.
4 Basque Government Electoral Records: www.euskadi.net/elecciones
5 'The U.S. State Department's 2010 global terrorism report estimates ETA still has some 300 active militants; at its peak, membership was in the thousands' (see Cala 2010).
6 While, prior to 1939, the Spanish state did not have the means to articulate a far-reaching process of nation building, Franco's regime adopted the most radical politics of assimilation against non-Castilian cultures in modern Spanish history (Lecours 2007).
7 This is well documented until the late 2000s, with a few isolated incidents emerging even more recently.
8 Ryan and Múgica were engineers building a nuclear power plant within the greater Bilbao area (Lemoniz); ETA identified them as military targets.
9 In Spanish, '*socialización del sufrimiento*' (Zallo 2001: 33–38). The term was used in English in a briefing by the Committee to Protect Journalists (CPJ 2001).
10 The kidnapping of Julio Iglesias Zamora and José Maria Aldaya, local business leaders, were the longest-lasting and most significant ones.
11 There is no evidence that ETA has been significantly funded by the Basque Diaspora (Oiarzabal 2012) or any other illegal activity, such as drug trafficking.
12 In return for his freedom, ETA demanded the end of the Spanish penitentiary policy of isolating Basque prisoners and taking them away from their home areas. The Spanish security forces identified and arrested the cell that was in charge of this kidnapping and Jose Antonio Ortega Lara was liberated.
13 Anoeta Proposal, *Batasuna*, 14 November 2004.
14 *Euskobarometro*, 'Evolución de la actitud ante ETA', 1981: https://www.ehu.eus/es/web/euskobarometro/aurkezpenak.
15 *Euskobarometro*, University of the Basque Country Periodical Political Opinion Survey: www.ehu.es/euskobarometro/.
16 The International Contact Group Press Release. Wednesday 14 December 2011. (www.basquepeaceprocess.info/2011/12/14/the-international-contact-group-press-release/).
17 Jonathan Powell served as the first Downing Street Chief of Staff under British Prime Minister Tony Blair from 1997 to 2007.
18 Father Alec Reid (1931–2013) was an Irish Catholic Redemptorist priest from the charitable and philanthropic Congregation of the Most Holy Redeemer (C.Ss.R.), who had played a key role in the Northern Ireland peace process (Crutchley 2014).
19 An exhaustive treatment of ETA's international ramifications can be found in Teresa Whitfield's book (Whitfield 2014).
20 Ram Manikkalingam served as an advisor to the former President of Sri Lanka, Chandrika Kumaratunga, to help broker peace in the Tamil areas.
21 'ETA anuncia su disolución. La banda comunica el "final de su trayectoria" y que "ha desmantelado totalmente sus estructuras"', *El País*, 3 May 2018; 'ETA releases statement announcing its complete dissolution Historic declaration puts an end to the organization 59 years after it first launched its violent campaign for Basque independence', *El País*, 3 May 2018

22 Probably, the most complete balanced and well-researched history of the long peace process has been published in English by a non-academic researcher: Theresa Whitfield's remains the most important book published so far on the BPP from the transition to the 2011 Aiete conference (Whitfield 2014). The next most important book in English is, not by chance, written by a professional journalist (Murua 2016). Both provide essential information for anyone wanting to explore the end of terrorism in the Basque Country. Journalists have been special targets during the most extreme phases of terrorism.

23 Pantxika Delobel, 'Désarmement d'ETA: ils appellent à participer à la journée du 8 avril à Bayonne', *Sud Ouest*, publié le 23/03/2017.

24 On this, see Keating and Bray (2006).

References

Alimi, Y. Eitan, Lorenzo Bosi, and Chares Demetriou. 2015. *The Dynamics of Radicalization: A Relational and Comparative Perspective*. Oxford: Oxford University Press.

Alonso Olea, J. Eduardo. 1995. *El concierto económico 1878–1937: orígenes y formación de un derecho histórico [The Economic Concert 1878–1937: Origins and Formation of a Historical Right]*. Oñati: Instituto Vasco de Administración Pública.

Alonso Olea, J. Eduardo. 2010. *El concierto económico: desde la abolición foral hasta su recuperación (1839–1981) [The Economic Concert: From Abolition to Recovery (1839–1981)]*. Bilbao: Bilbao Bizkaiko Foru Aldundia= Diputación Foral de Bizkaia.

Alonso, Rogelio. 2004. "Pathways Out of Terrorism in Northern Ireland and the Basque Country: The Misrepresentation of the Irish Model." *Terrorism and Political Violence* 16 (4): 695–713.

Alonso, Rogelio. 2010. "Confronting Terrorism in Northern Ireland and the Basque Country: Challenges for Democracy and Legitimacy." In Martha Crenshaw (Ed.), *The Consequences of Counterterrorism*, 213–254. New York: Russell Sage Foundation.

Blair, Tony. 2011. "A Basque Peace." *The New York Times*, 21 October. www.nytimes.com/2011/10/22/opinion/22iht-edblair22,1.html.

Broin, Ó. Eoin. 2003. *Matxinada. Basque Nationalism & Radical Basque Youth Movements*. Belfast: Left Republican Books.

Bullaín, López Ini. 2011. *Revolucionarismo Patriótico. El Movimiento De Liberación Nacional Vasco (MLNV) [Patriotic Revolutionary. The Basque National Liberation Movement (MLNV)]. Origen, Ideología, Estrategia y Organización*. Madrid: Tecnos.

Cala, Andrés. 2010. "Is the End Near for Basque Separatist Group ETA?" *Time Magazine*, 25 September. http://content.time.com/time/world/article/0,8599,202 1333,00.html

Clark, P. Robert. 1984. *The Basque insurgents: ETA, 1952–1980*. Madison, WI: University of Wisconsin Press.

Clark, P. Robert. 1990. *Negotiating with ETA: Obstacles to Peace in the Basque Country, 1975–1988*. Reno: University of Nevada Press.

Conversi, D. 1993. "Domino Effect or Internal Developments? The Influences of International Events and Political Ideologies on Catalan and Basque Nationalism." *West European Politics* 16 (3): 245–270.

Conversi, Daniele. 1997. *The Basques, the Catalans and Spain: Alternative Routes to Nationalist Mobilization*. London: Hurst & Company, Reno, University of Nevada Press.

Conversi, Daniele. 1998. "The Spanish Federalist Tradition and the 1978 Constitution." *Telos* 112: 125.

Conversi, Daniele. 2002. "The Smooth Transition: Spain's 1978 Constitution and the Nationalities Question." *National Identities* 4 (3): 223–244.

Conversi, Daniele. 2006. "Why Do Peace Processes Collapse? The Basque Conflict and the Three 'spoilers' Perspective'." In Edward Newman, and Oliver Richmand (Eds.), *Challenges to Peacebuilding: Managing Spoilers During Conflict Resolution*, 173–200. Tokyo, New York: United Nations University Press.

Conversi, Daniele. 2008. "'We are all equals!' Militarism, Homogenization and 'egalitarianism' in Nationalist State-Building (1789–1945)." *Ethnic and Racial Studies* 31 (7): 1286–1314.

Conversi, Daniele. 2010. "Building Bridges on the Road to Peace. Centralism, Resistance and the Basque Revival." *Political Geography* 29 (8): 463–465.

Conversi, Daniele. 2012. "Nación, estado y cultura. Para una historia política y social de la homogeneización cultural (1789–1945) [Nation, State and Culture. For a Political and Social History of Cultural Homogenization (1789–1945)]." *Historia Contemporánea* 45 (3): 429–473.

Conversi, Daniele. 2014. "Between the Hammer of Globalization and the Anvil of Nationalism: Is Europe's Complex Diversity Under Threat?" *Ethnicities* 14 (1): 25–49.

Conversi, Daniele. 2017. "Sovereignty, Boundaries and Violence: Constructing the Basque National Self (1959–2011)." In Ibarra Güell Pedro, and Kolås As (Eds.), *Sovereignty Revisited: The Basque Case*, 18–44. London: Routledge.

CPJ. 2001. *Spain Briefing: The Socialization of Suffering*. New York: Committee to Protect Journalists.

Crutchley, Peter. 2014. "IRA Ceasefire 20 Years on: The Priest Who Brokered the Peace." *BBC News*, 31 August. www.bbc.com/news/uk-28812366.

Darby, John. 1994. "Legitimate Targets: A Control on Violence?" In Adrian Guelke (Ed.), *New Perspectives on the Northern Ireland Conflict*, 46–64. Aldershot: Avebury.

De La Calle, Luis. 2015. *Nationalist Violence in Postwar Europe*. Cambridge: Cambridge University Press.

Della Porta, Daniella. 2013. *Clandestine Political Violence*. Cambridge: Cambridge University Press.

Della Porta, Daniella. 2014. "On Violence and Repression: A Relational Approach." *Government and Opposition* 49 (2): 159–187.

Espiau, Gorka. 2006. *The Basque Conflict. New Ideas and Prospects for Peace*. Washington, DC: USIP (U.S. Institute of Peace).

Espiau, Gorka. 2010. *The Peace Processes in the Basque Country and Northern Ireland (1994–2006): A Comparative Approach*. Barcelona: Institut Català Internacional per la Pau.

Fernández, Gaizka, Soldevilla. 2010. "Agur a las armas. EIA, Euskadiko Ezkerra y la disolución de ETA político-militar (1976–1985) [Greetings to Guns. EIA, the Basque Country Left and the Dissolution of Political-Military ETA (1976–1985)]." *Sancho el sabio: Revista de cultura e investigación vasca* 3355–3396.

Horowitz, L. Donald. 2003. *The Deadly Ethnic Riot*. Berkeley, CA: University of California Press.

Ibarra, P. Güell. 1987. *La evolución estratégica de ETA: de la "Guerra revolucionaria" (1963) a la negociación (1987) [The Strategic Evolution of ETA: from the "Revolutionary War" (1963) to the Negotiation (1987)]*. Donostia: Kriselu.

Ibarretxe, Juan Jose. 2011. *The Basque Case: A Comprehensive Model of Sustainable Human Development*. Arlington, VA: SCAR (The School for Conflict Analysis and Resolution), George Mason University.

Ibarretxe, Juan Jose. 2015. *The Basque Experience: Constructing Sustainable Human Development*. Reno, Nevada: Center for Basque Studies.

Irvin, L. Cynthia. 1999. *Militant Nationalism: Between Movement and Party in Ireland and the Basque Country*. Minneapolis: University of Minnesota Press.

Jáuregui, G. Bereciartu. 1981. *Ideología y estrategia política de ETA: análisis de su evolución entre 1959 y 1968 [Ideology and Political Strategy of ETA: Analysis of Its Evolution Between 1959 and 1968]*. Madrid: Siglo Veintiuno Editores.

Jeram, Sanjay, and Daniele Conversi. 2014. "Deliberation and Democracy at the End of Armed Conflict: Post-Conflict Opportunities in the Basque Country." In Juan Ugarizza, and Didier Clauwaerts (Eds.), *Democratic Deliberation in Deeply Divided Societies: From Conflict to Common Ground*, 53–72. Houndmills, Basingstoke: Palgrave Macmillan.

Keating, Michael, and Zoe Bray. 2006. "Renegotiating Sovereignty: Basque Nationalism and the Rise and Fall of the Ibarretxe Plan." *Ethnopolitics* 5 (4): 347–364.

Krutwig, F. Sagredo. 1973. *Vasconia*. Buenos Aires: Norbait (Originally published as Sarrailh de Ihartza, Fernando.Vasconia. Buenos Aires: Norbait, 1962.

Lecours, André. 2007. *Basque Nationalism and the Spanish State*. Reno: University of Nevada Press.

Letamendia, Francisco. 1991. *Euskadi: pueblo y nación [Euskadi: People and Nation]*. San Sebastian: Editorial Sendoa (7 volumes).

Letamendia, Francisco. 2000. *Game of Mirrors: Centre-Periphery National Conflicts*. Aldershot: Ashgate.

Linz, Juan, Jose, M. Gomez-Reino, D. Vila, et al. 1981. *Atlas electoral del Paìs Vasco y Navarra [Electoral Atlas of the Basque Country and Navarre]*. Madrid: Centro de Investigaciones Sociológicas.

Llera, J. Francisco, José M. Mata, and Cynthia L. Irvin. 1993. "ETA: From Secret Army to Social Movement – The Post-Franco Schism of the Basque Nationalist Movement." *Terrorism and Political Violence* 5 (3): 106–134.

Loizides, Neophytos. 2016. *Designing Peace: Cyprus and Institutional Innovations in Divided Societies*. Philadelphia, PA: University of Pennsylvania Press.

Medeiros, Mike. 2015. "The Language of Conflict: The Relationship Between Linguistic Vitality and Conflict Intensity." *Ethnicities* 17 (5): 627–645.

Mees, Ludger. 2003. *Nationalism, Violence and Democracy: The Basque Clash of Identities*. New York: Palgrave Macmillan.

Moreno, Luis. 2001. *The Federalization of Spain*. London: F. Cass.

Moreno, Luis. 2014. *Europa sin Estados. Unión política en el (des) orden global [Europe without States. Political union in the global (dis) order]*. Madrid: Catarata.

Murua, Imanol. 2016. *Ending ETA's Armed Campaign. How and Why the Basque Armed Group Abandoned Violence*. London: Taylor & Francis.

Murua, Imanol. 2017. "No More Bullets for ETA: The Loss of Internal Support as a Key Factor in the End of the Basque Group's Campaign." *Critical Studies on Terrorism* 10 (1): 93–114.

Newman, Edward, and Oliver Richmond. (Eds.). 2006. *Challenges to Peacebuilding: Managing Spoilers During Conflict Resolution*. Tokyo, New York: United Nations University Press.

Nilsson, Desirée, and Mimmi Söderberg Kovacs. 2011. "Revisiting an Elusive Concept: A Review of the Debate on Spoilers in Peace Processes." *International Studies Review* 13 (4): 606–626.

Oiarzabal, J. Pedro. 2012. "Diaspora Basques and Online Social Networks: An Analysis of Users of Basque Institutional Diaspora Groups on Facebook." *Journal of Ethnic and Migration Studies* 38 (9): 1469–1485.

Reiter, G. Andrew. 2016a. "Introduction: When Peace Begets Violence." In Andrew G. Reiter (Ed.), *Fighting Over Peace: Spoilers, Peace Agreements, and the Strategic Use of Violence*, 1–20. Cham: Springer International /Palgrave Macmillan.

Reiter, G. Andrew. 2016b. "Who Spoils and Why." In Andrew G. Reiter (Ed.), *Fighting Over Peace: Spoilers, Peace Agreements, and the Strategic Use of Violence*, 21–50. Cham: Springer International/Palgrave Macmillan.

Sociometro, Vasco. 2012. *Sociometro vasco 48. Fin del terrorismo (marzo 2012) / 48. euskal soziometroa. Tterrorismoaren amaiera (2012ko martxoa) [Basque Sociologist 48. End of Terrorism (March 2012) / 48. Basque Sociologist. End of Terrorism (March 2012)].* Vitoria-Gasteiz: Eusko Jaurlaritza (Gobierno Vasco).

Tellidis, Ioannis. 2010. "Terrorist Conflict vs. Civil Peace in the Basque Country." In Oliver Richmond (Ed.), *Palgrave Advances in Peacebuilding*, 415–438. London: Palgrave Macmillan.

Tellidis, Ioannis. 2011. "Orthodox, Criticals and the Missing Context: Basque Civil Society's Reaction(s) to Terrorism." *Critical Studies on Terrorism* 4 (2): 181–197.

Tremlett, Giles. 2017. "Exclusive: Eta Documents Reveal Details of Weapons Dumps as Group Disarms." *The Guardian*, 8 April. www.theguardian.com/world/2017/apr/08/eta-basque-separatist-group-formally-disarms-arms-cache.

Watson, Cameron. 2007. *Basque Nationalism and Political Violence: The Ideological and Intellectual Origins of ETA*. Reno, Nevada: University of Nevada Press, Center for Basque Studies.

Whitfield, Teresa. 2014. *Endgame for ETA. Elusive Peace in the Basque Country*. New York: Oxford University Press.

Woodworth, Paddy. 2007. *The Basque Country: A Cultural History*. Oxford: Signal Books, Oxford University Press.

Zabalo, Julen, and Mikel Saratxo. 2015. "ETA Ceasefire: Armed Struggle vs. Political Practice in Basque Nationalism." *Ethnicities* 15 (3): 362–384.

Zalbide, J.L. 1963. *La Insurrección en Euskadi*. Bayonne: Goiztiri.

Zallo, RamÓn. 2001. *El país de los vascos. Desde los sucesos de Ermua al segundo gobierno de Ibarretxe [The Country of the Basques. From the Events of Ermua to the Second Ibarretxe Government]*. Madrid: Alberdania, Editorial Fundamentos.

Zirakzadeh, Ernesto Cyrus. 1991. *A Rebellious People: Basques, Protests and Politics*. Reno: University of Nevada Press.

Zulaika, Joseba. 1988. *Basque Violence: Metaphor and Sacrament*. Reno: University of Nevada Press.

Zulaika, Joseba, and Imanol Murua. 2017. "How Terrorism Ends – And Does Not End: The Basque Case." *Critical Studies on Terrorism* 1–19.

4

BOSNIA-HERZEGOVINA

Dejan Guzina

Introduction

For more than 20 years, Bosnia-Herzegovina has been a prominent case in the peacebuilding literature, a benchmark by which other conflict-ridden societies have been evaluated or to which they have been compared. Its significance in the realm of peacebuilding and state making stems from several interrelated factors. First, the Bosnian War began at the threshold of a post-Cold War era when new international rules were in the process of being formed. The Bosnian war shattered the European peace architecture that had emerged after the Second World War, resulting in frantic efforts by the international community to create an alternative conceptual framework that later became known under the moniker of liberal peacebuilding (Mac Ginty 2011; Campbell et al. 2011; Newman et al. 2009).

Second, the daily coverage by major international news agencies and the TV images of the siege of Sarajevo and ethnic cleansing brought home to North American and European households the realities of the Bosnian War. Even though an effective international peacemaking campaign took years to put together, pressure by Western publics to 'do something' was present from the first days of the war in the spring of 1992. Moreover, the sheer brutality of the war, which left close to 100,000 people dead in three and half years (Tokaca 2018; Guzina and Marijan 2013), raised questions about the actual costs of peace and the limits of peacebuilding operations in the supposedly liberal world order.

For all these reasons, the entire first generation of post-Cold War scholars, humanitarian workers, and policy analysts have been heavily influenced by the Bosnian peacebuilding experience. Indeed, it is hard to find an edited collection of chapters or a monograph on peacebuilding that does not refer to the international involvement in Bosnia-Herzegovina. In general, there are two schools of thought on the case of Bosnia-Herzegovina. Foreign policy makers and pragmatically oriented scholars are quick to praise the stability brought about by the newly created, internationally orchestrated power-sharing structures in Bosnia-Herzegovina (Tonge 2014; Durch 2006). From this perspective, one of the central achievements of the Dayton Peace Agreement (also known as Dayton Peace Accords), which brought an end to the war in Bosnia-Herzegovina, is the lack of violent conflicts in more than 20 years. A more critically oriented scholarship instead argues that Bosnian peacebuilding offers a cautionary tale where the prescribed goals of liberal peacebuilding have produced a political system based on rigid power-sharing, lack of local ownership, disempowered citizenship, and a deeply fractured civil society (Merdzanovic 2017; Richmond 2014; Donais 2012).

Bosnia-Herzegovina is an ideal case study for understanding the complexities of post-Cold War conflict resolution. The chapter provides an overview and an evaluation of the lessons that can be drawn from the Bosnian peace process. More specifically, it addresses the following questions: how can the Dayton peace process be evaluated from the perspective of the past 20-some years? Can Bosnia-Herzegovina be genuinely upheld as the 'gold standard' of peacebuilding? And, does Bosnia-Herzegovina lend itself to easy comparisons?

Conflict analysis

The descent of Bosnia-Herzegovina into fratricidal war should be situated within a broader context of the geopolitical transformation sparked by the implosion of the global communist system. Without the changes in the geopolitical map of Europe, it is doubtful that Yugoslavia would have collapsed and Bosnia-Herzegovina would have ended up in war. One of the central tenets of the European Cold War structure has been the critical role played by the former Yugoslavia as a bridge between the liberal West and the communist East. With the implosion of the Soviet Union and the bloodless revolutions in Eastern Europe, the need of the international community for such a bridge disappeared, leaving Yugoslav actors in the position to pursue their respective policies without regard for the broader implications of their actions.

Serbian President Slobodan Milosevic, Croatian President Franjo Tudjman, and Chairman of the Presidency of Bosnia-Herzegovina Alija Izetbegovic each relied on nationalist ideology to legitimise their respective political agendas. In particular, Milosevic's orchestration of the so-called anti-bureaucratic revolution in Serbia, in a series of mass rallies across the republic, allowed him to bypass both the Serbian and Yugoslav constitutions and to undermine the territorial autonomy of the multi-ethnic Serbian provinces of Vojvodina and Kosovo (Ramet 2006; Popov 1996). Milosevic sought to unify Serbs living within Croatia and Bosnia-Herzegovina; both regions had a substantial percentage of local Serbs (according to the last Yugoslav Census in 1991, Serbs constituted 12.2 per cent of the population in Croatia, and 31.4 per cent in Bosnia-Herzegovina). Likeminded Tudjman also sought to carve up Bosnia-Herzegovina and incorporate those areas with a substantial Croat majority (in particular, Western Herzegovina) into Croatia. Izetbegovic, on the other hand, was never able to attract Bosnian Serb or Croat allegiances; his legitimacy was deeply rooted in the Bosnian Muslim constituency.

Unfortunately, a peaceful dissolution of a multinational federation in the context of the former Yugoslavia was only possible in regions that were ethnically almost entirely homogenous. Slovenia, with a tiny percentage of non-ethnic Slovenians, was the only republic that fulfilled this condition. Thus, after brief skirmishes with the Yugoslav Army (the so-called Ten Days War for Independence from 27 June to 7 July 1991), the Yugoslav military withdrew, and Slovenia effectively became an independent state. In all other cases, the dissolution of the multinational one-party federal state would not only fail to open the door to peaceful self-determination and democratic transition but would also bring bloody wars to Croatia, Bosnia-Herzegovina, and Kosovo.

The European Economic Community's (EEC; as of 1993, European Community – EC) initial strategy centred around the recommendations of the Arbitration Commission of the International Conference on Yugoslavia (the so-called Badinter Commission) set up on 27 August 1991 to provide the Conference with legal advice. The EEC's Badinter Commission set forth criteria based on principles of liberal democracy, including widespread support for independence through democratically organised referenda and protection of national minority rights. Once these criteria were fulfilled, the regions could legitimately secede and establish themselves as independent states. But, the Commission also applied the post-colonial principle of *uti posseditis*, which effectively legitimised and imposed Yugoslav provincial borders as the borders of those newly emerging states (Caplan 2005; Radan 2002). This principle was not acceptable to Serbia and local Serbian leadership in Croatia and Bosnia-Herzegovina. Their interpretation of the principle of self-determination was as belonging to the people rather than to territories. Accordingly, they sought to redraw regional borders in their fight for self-determination by any means necessary.

The case of Bosnia-Herzegovina, in particular, exemplifies the tensions and limits of the Commission's recommendations. The republic was divided among three national communities, none of which had full majority status. Bosniaks (as of 1993, the historical term used to refer to Bosnian Muslims) were the most numerous, comprising 43.7 per cent of the population according to the 1991 Census. Bosnian Serbs accounted for 31.4 per cent and Croats 17.3 per cent of the population (Burg and Shoup 1999: 27). To secure representation and peace within the region, the Bosnian Constitution declared all three groups as collectively the founding nations in Bosnia-Herzegovina, and thus no one group could be treated as a minority. The Constitution also ensured that the combined majority vote of two ethnic groups would not undermine nor impose decisions on the third national community in the country.

Be that as it may, following the Badinter Commission's ruling, Bosnia-Herzegovina held a referendum on the question of independence that took place on 29 February and 1 March 1992. By then, Bosnians of all ethnic stripes were caught in a circle of escalating violence and deep mistrust. Even before Bosnia's recognition as an independent state, Bosnian Serb forces, with the support of the Serbian Army (then still operated under the official name of the Yugoslav Army), engaged in aggressive military actions against Bosniaks and Croats (Hoare 2007; Ramet 2006). When the referendum was finally organised, Bosnian Muslims and Croats voted overwhelmingly in favour of independence, while Bosnian Serbs boycotted it. Despite the constitutionally problematic character of the vote, the Bosnian Muslim politician Alija Izetbegovic, as the Chairman of the Presidency of Bosnia-Herzegovina, declared independence on 6 April 1992. Ironically, this date came to represent the birth of a new state, but also the formal beginning of the war. The following day, both the United States and the EEC nominally committed themselves to the unity of Bosnia-Herzegovina by recognising it as a new European state. While doing so, they underestimated the ethnic divisions pervading the region.

In response, Bosnian Serbs intensified military campaigns and laid a three-year-long siege of Sarajevo, which became a symbol of the entire Bosnian war. Bosnian Serb military and political objectives in the ensuing conflict were made public from the very beginning; if a Serb-dominated Yugoslavia were not possible, the second-best solution was to establish a territory of their own. Already on 7 April 1992, Bosnian leaders in the Bosnian Serb stronghold of Pale declared the creation of Republika Srpska (RS) within Bosnia-Herzegovina. On 12 May, during the session of the assembly of the RS in Banja Luka, the Bosnian Serb leader, Radovan Karadzic, announced that the 'belt along the Drina [the river separating Serbia and Bosnia-Herzegovina] must basically belong to Serbian Bosnia-Herzegovina' (Karcic 2015). At the same assembly, the delegates adopted Karadzic's 'Six Strategic Objectives of the Serbian People in Bosnia and Herzegovina' (the document was later published in the Republika Srpska's Official Gazette on 26 November 1993). The most strategic objective was a proposal to delineate a new state that would connect the corridors of all 'Serb territories' into one coherent area. In other words, as early as April 1992, Bosnian Serb leaders officially inaugurated the politics of ethnic cleansing as both a war tool and political objective. After all, according to the 1991 Bosnian Census, there was not one single municipality at the territory that later became known as Republika Srpska where Bosnian Serbs, Croats, and Bosniaks did not live together.

In the early stages of the war, the Bosniak position was much more precarious. Faced with the heavily armed Bosnian Serb forces, they focused their efforts on securing international support (from the UN, USA, EEC, OSCE, and Islamic states) for the preservation of a unified Bosnia-Herzegovina. Diplomatically, this proved to be a successful strategy given the international outrage against the Bosnian Serb practice of ethnic cleansing. Yet, despite international support, an arms embargo was imposed on all warring sides in Bosnia-Herzegovina, which effectively precluded Bosniaks from arming themselves with heavy weaponry. Similarly, external military assistance to Bosniak forces was not deployed until the last stages of the war. Thus, throughout most of the war, the United Nations mission on the ground (UNPROFOR) was best understood as peacekeeping and humanitarian intervention rather than peacebuilding. In the words of the Bosnia-Herzegovina

UNPROFOR commander, Michael Rose, 'the UN was not ready to cross "the Mogadishu line" between peacekeeping and warfighting' (Durch 2006).

Bosnian Croats, the smallest of three communities, had the most difficulties in creating a coherent strategy. They were territorially dispersed; western Herzegovina was an overwhelmingly Croat region, yet the rest of Bosnian Croats were spread out through many Bosnian municipalities. Herzegovinian Croats had the same objectives as Bosnian Serbs – the creation of an exclusively Croat entity, the so-called Herzeg Bosnia. However, despite Croats' eight-month war against Bosniaks in 1993, they failed to create a so-called third entity in Bosnia-Herzegovina, which effectively marginalised their war efforts until 1995.

In light of the military preponderance of the Bosnian Serb forces (already by mid-1992, they were able to control 70 per cent of the Bosnian territory), the incompatible political objectives of all three sides in the conflict, and the reluctance of the external agencies to cross 'the Mogadishu line', all peace initiatives succumbed to what James Gow describes as 'the triumph of the lack of will' (Gow 1997). The target of Gow's critique was international mediators, in particular, the US dispirited interest to become more actively engaged in the peace process until later in 1994. This lack of interest was particularly manifest with the jointly sponsored UN-EEC initiative, also known as the Vance–Owen Plan, in late 1992 and early 1993. Even though at one point all three sides were in principle supportive of the programme, it was shattered by disagreements between the Clinton Administration and the UN-EEC representatives over the Plan's sustainability on the ground (Burg and Shoup 1999; Owen 1995).

In hindsight, the Plan offered a vision of Bosnia-Herzegovina to which the later-signed Dayton Accords never aspired: an administrative division of the country into nine ethnic cantons, each controlling policing, education, and transport, albeit within the framework of a weak unified central government. More importantly, the Plan maintained the principle of ethnic proportionality and pushed back against the Bosnian Serbs' objective to have contiguous borders with Serbia. It also suggested the rolling back of Serb territorial gains by 30 per cent (Tonge 2014: 139; Owen 1995). Still, as Gow (1997: 313) maintains, 'the Clinton Administration effectively destroyed the Vance–Owen plan through allegations that it rewarded aggression and condoned ethnic cleansing'.[1] But perhaps the most important implication of the Plan was that it, for the first time, revealed a split in Serbian leadership. As much as a Serbian president, Slobodan Milosevic, supported the Plan (no matter how problematic that support might be), Bosnian Serb leaders were adamantly against it, a division that would become ever more significant in the later stages of the war and during the Dayton peace talks. The apple of discord was that Bosnian Serbs did not want to give up on the independently run Bosnian Serb territory and contiguous borders with Serbia.

Different pieces of the peace puzzle were finally put together in the summer and fall of 1995. What accelerated the process was the UN's failure to prevent the Bosnian Serb massacre of Bosniaks in the UN-designated safe area, the town of Srebrenica, in July 1995, when more than 7,000 Bosnian men were killed (Nettelfield and Wagner 2013; Honig and Both 1997). The United States was forced to act more decisively by launching the NATO air campaign, Operation Deliberate Force, against Bosnian Serb positions. Already, a year before, the Contact Group (comprising of USA, Britain, France, Germany, and Russia) had been created, which led to the Washington Framework Agreement of 1 March 1994. The Agreement established a joint Bosnian Muslim and Croat Federation; it also laid the groundwork for a new Bosnia-Herzegovina that would include the Bosnian Muslim and Croat Federation along with the Bosnian Serb Republic.

Ultimately, with the Croatian Army regaining control over Croatia in 1995, followed by ethnic cleansing of Serbs from Croatia, the Bosnian Serbs' military luck started to change in Bosnia-Herzegovina as well. The moment was at last ripe for a peace. No one has explained this better than the top American negotiator, Holbrooke (1998):

> the success of the Croatian (and later, in similar circumstances, the Bosnian–Croat Federation) offensive was a classic illustration of the fact that the shape of the diplomatic landscape will usually reflect the balance of forces on the ground. In concrete terms, this meant that as diplomats we could not expect the Serbs to be conciliatory at the negotiating table as long as they had experienced nothing but success on the battlefield.
>
> *(pp. 72–73)*

By mid-October 1995, the Serb-held territory was scaled down from 70 per cent to roughly 50 per cent of the Bosnian land.

The Western bombing campaign was simultaneously followed by the very successful American-initiated shuttle-diplomacy. First, on September 14, Milosevic and the Bosnian Serb leaders agreed to sign the document that effectively put an end to the Bosnian Serbs' siege of Sarajevo. Second, by October 5, Holbrooke successfully negotiated a ceasefire that was for the first time since the beginning of the war respected by Bosnian Serb and Bosniak forces (Pomfret 1995). Finally, after almost four years of fighting, all sides were genuinely ready to pursue peace talks, even though each of the warring parties entered the negotiations with radically opposing expectations.

The conflict resolution process

The Bosnian peace talks lasted a total of 21 days, from 1 to 21 November 1995. At first, the place chosen for the negotiations seemed rather peculiar – the Wright–Peterson Air Force Base in Dayton, Ohio. This site was selected deliberately to keep the warring sides away from the press, thereby reducing the possibility of any one party outbidding the other in the public war of words. At the end of the 'lock everyone up until they reach agreement' (Holbrooke 1998: 232) style of negotiations, the General Framework for Peace with its 11 annexes (the so-called Dayton Peace Accords), was agreed to and officially signed a month later in Paris on 14 December. The peace process was achievable because all parties, both international and regional powers, accepted the peace process as in their mutual interest. As Hampson (1996: 217) points out, peace settlements require 'a combination of international and regional strategies', and they are always 'inextricably tied to the interests of neighbouring regional powers and their overall commitment to the peace process'.

A series of prior events (some previously discussed) laid the conditions that would allow for all parties to come to the negotiation table. These included the creation of the Bosnian Muslim-Croat Federation a year earlier, the military defeat and the cleansing of local Serbs from Croatia, NATO bombing of Bosnian Serb positions, and, most importantly, the American decision to replace the Europeans and the UN as principal architects, engineers, and guarantors of the entire peace process. Furthermore, what made those talks possible was the emerging congruence of interests between principal regional actors (Serbia and Croatia) and the United States' strategy to address violent conflict in Bosnia-Herzegovina. Serbia and Croatia sought respectively to lift international sanctions against Serbia and regain control over eastern Slavonia, an area in Croatia that was not yet firmly integrated with the rest of the country. Both sides also gave up their resolve to carve up Bosnia-Herzegovina and, instead, began to support institutional arrangements that will allow them to retain their interests in Bosnia-Herzegovina (Bildt 1999; Holbrooke 1998). Moreover, both presidents were forced into agreeing to a political compromise, a negotiated outcome that local Serb or Croat delegations were less likely to accept.

The peace process resembled an intricate chess game with continuous moving parts that ultimately converged with the peace talks and the Dayton Agreement. From the very beginning of the war, the position of external actors has been twofold – to reach permanent peace and preserve Bosnia-Herzegovina as a multi-ethnic state. These two interrelated goals were best integrated in the joint EC–UN initiative (the previously discussed Vance–Owen Plan), which revolved around preserving the multi-ethnic character of the Bosnian state by reversing the effects of the ethnic cleansing campaign that uprooted half of the pre-war Bosnian population. The Plan proposed dividing the country into cantons, each of which would retain demographic diversity even though nominally identified as Bosnian Serb, Croat, or Bosniak (Owen 2013, 1995). The Americans rejected such a plan because the proposed programme of action was not feasible, but also for the 'ethical reasons' of not wanting to territorially reward the Bosnian Serbs that the Clinton Administration perceived as aggressors in the war.

And yet, a year later, the American approach to the Bosnian war shifted in two fundamental aspects. First, the United States actively supported the creation of the Bosnian Muslim-Croat Federation (1994). At the same time, they also implicitly recognised the need for territorial separation between the Federation and Republika Srpska, albeit within a federal structure that would keep the Bosnian state formally multi-ethnic. Second, the US compromised on its initial position regarding the delineation of borders within the country. More than a year before the Dayton talks, the proposed border formula called for 51 per cent for Bosniak-Croat territory and 49 per cent for Republika Srpska; in other words, already at that time, all external actors accepted this proposal as the most realistic as for how to end the war. However, with the US firmly behind such a plan, this meant that American negotiators acknowledged Republika Srpska's contiguous borders with Serbia. By 1995, during the Dayton talks, the goal of achieving a peace accord overshadowed any American previous ethical concerns. It would be shown later that this effectively led to the acceptance of the ethnic cleansing as an acceptable tool in the Bosnian war.

How should one understand such a 'pragmatic' shift in the American approach to the Bosnian conflict? Part of the answer is already provided in Hampson's recognition that peace settlements require that major external peace strategies should be aligned with the interests of neighbouring regional powers and their overall commitment to the peace process. American readiness to accept Serbia and Croatia as legitimate actors in any deal on peace in Bosnia-Herzegovina goes a long way to explaining the outcome of the Dayton peace talks. Belloni adds another dimension to the international efforts to achieve the peace. In his insightful analysis of statebuilding and international intervention in Bosnia-Herzegovina, Belloni (2008) has identified three major lessons for international peacekeepers. First, the multiple objectives of all actors involved in conflict complicate reaching a genuinely agreed-upon solution to such a conflict. Second, contrary to the rhetoric of moral arguments, 'the focus of international actors has been to preserve stability as much as possible while neglecting the more important need for a long-term change' (p. 5). Third, the focus on stability goes 'hand-in-hand' with the 'preoccupation with visible and concrete short-term results' (p. 5).

Once American negotiators identified peace between Serbia and Croatia as strategically essential for the stability of the entire region, the Bosnian delegation had no choice but to accept the agreement, even though they recognised that the particulars of the deal would undermine an integrated multi-ethnic state and, instead, result in deep ethnic divisions. Indeed, the country that emerged out of Dayton (usually referred to as a Dayton Bosnia) is a nation that walks a fine line between partition and reintegration. Formally, Bosnia-Herzegovina preserved its internationally recognised borders. But it is also internally divided in a threefold way: administratively, ethnically, and territorially. Each of these aspects is fully elaborated upon in Annex 4 of the Dayton Peace Accords, which became recognised as a new Bosnia-Herzegovinian Constitution.

The Dayton Agreement hinged on the ability of the international community to enforce and oversee the peace process. It contained an additional eleven annexes covering such a wide variety of issues, ranging from military aspects and regional stabilisation (annex 1), inter-ethnic boundary lines (annex 2), elections (annex 3), human rights and refugees and displaced persons (annexes 6 and 7), to civilian implementation and an international police task force (annexes 10 and 11). Each of these annexes was supported by key external implementers with a NATO-led implementation force and the newly created Office of the High Representative.

Also, especially in the first years of Dayton Bosnia, the OSCE – Organization for Security and Cooperation in Europe – and the UN High Commissioner for Refugees played an essential role in organising the first elections and in securing the framework for a safe return of refugees and protection of human rights. Finally, even though not part of the Dayton structure, both the International Court of Justice (ICJ) and the International Criminal Tribunal for the Former Yugoslavia (ICTY, already created in 1993) have become central agencies through which the issues of transitional justice and the responsibility for war crimes have been addressed.

The peace process was successful in ending the war. Within ten years, the international military presence downsized from 60,000 to fewer than 6,000 troops (Cousens and Harland 2006: 83–87; Durch 2006). The leaders responsible for war crimes were arrested and sent to The Hague for prosecution at the ICTY, including the former president of Serbia, Slobodan Milosevic, and Bosnian Serb political and military leaders Radovan Karadzic and Ratko Mladic. Moreover, a series of post-war elections in the past 20 years were organised peacefully. Finally, the country rebuilt its destroyed infrastructure, and it has been engaged in formal negotiations to join the European Union (EU). In other words, the objectives that have been identified within each of the signed annexes have been fully implemented. And yet, Bosnia-Herzegovina did not emerge as a fully integrated, democratic, federal state. Quite the contrary, the achieved results of international intervention are ambiguous at best.

To understand this apparent paradox, one needs to separate the international intervention in terms of the short-term, easily identifiable goals of the peace process from post-conflict peacebuilding, which requires a more ambitious project of 'state making from scratch', a simultaneous process of rebuilding state institutions, democratic transition, and inter-ethnic integration. Most of the achievements reflect what Belloni has described as short-term goals of the international community's approach to peacebuilding (Belloni 2009, 2008). The rest of this section outlines three outstanding long-term issues that external and local actors still struggle with, specifically, the question of local ownership; the permanent shift in the demographic structure of Bosnian society; and the competing narratives over the responsibility for the war in Bosnia-Herzegovina. Finally, these raise the critical question of citizens' satisfaction with the post-Dayton period in Bosnia-Herzegovina. A focus on these challenges underscores the limits of the peace process and questions the extent to which post-war peacebuilding has achieved the presumed long-term stability of the region.

Without relying on massive international military and civil presence, Bosnia-Herzegovina would not have achieved peace, understood in terms of stability and security. The multinational troops were employed with the primary task to secure the *status quo* on the ground. However, such 'realist concerns with stability merged uneasily' with the broader objectives of Dayton to guarantee human rights protection, rebuild civic structures, and reverse wartime ethnic cleansing (Belloni 2008: 173). Thus, in the early years of international engagement in Bosnia-Herzegovina, such a stability-oriented strategy necessitated the primacy of robust military structures (IFOR) at the expense of a strong civilian mandate from the Office of the High Representative. Later, the roles reversed, and the OHR became overinvolved in a top-down Bosnian state and social engineering, undermining the development of a genuine Bosnian civil society and local political structures (Donais 2017, 2005; Chandler 2000). This new strategy of intrusive institution-building was inaugurated at the Peace Implementation Council (PIC, the organisation in charge of implementing the Dayton Accords) meeting in December 1997. It allowed the PIC to legitimise the UN High Representative's request to use his administrative powers and impose a solution despite strong disagreement between local Bosnian parties. The so-called Bonn powers permitted the practice of external imposition of the rule of law in the country, thereby allowing for the dismissal of elected politicians and the external imposition of constitutional principles, laws, and regulations (Merdzanovic 2017; Caplan 2005).

Even though the Bonn powers were initially upheld as central to the future success of Bosnia, many scholars have argued that they blocked domestic political debate on the flaws of the Dayton Agreement. Moreover, the external bureaucratic interventions in Bosnian affairs worked against the very democratic principle of self-government that the Office of the High Representative sought to achieve. The focus of such critique was in particular that the international community imposed a 'culture of dependency' among the local population, resulting in a 'paternalistic, authoritarian manner' by which international agencies undermined local grassroot incentives for more democratic involvement in politics (Chandler 2017, 2000). In essence, the interventionist template imposed on Bosnia-Herzegovina has hollowed out the public space for any local agencies attempting to challenge the imposed consociational system (Donais 2017, 2012, 2005).

Another (un)intended peacebuilding outcome is the failure of external actors to address the growing territorial fragmentation among ethnic groups that began with ethnic cleansing during the war. Population trends suggest increased ethnic fragmentation following the war. For instance, in 1991, what is now Republika Srpska had a mixed population composed of 55 per cent Serb, 28 per cent Bosniak, 9 per cent Croat, 5 per cent Yugoslav, and 3 per cent the so-called other. Census data for 2013 reveal that Serbs increased their representation from 55 to 81 per cent in this region and Bosniaks dropped from 28 to 14 per cent, and Croats to 2.5 per cent. Likewise, in the Bosniak–Croat Federation of Bosnia-Herzegovina, in 1991, the area was composed of 52 per cent Bosniaks, 22 per cent Croats, 18 per cent Serbs, 6 per cent Yugoslavs, and 3 per cent others. In 2013, in the Bosniak–Croat parts of Bosnia-Herzegovina, 70 per cent identified as Bosniaks, 22 per cent as Croats, and 2.5 per cent as Serbs. (Bosnia-Herzegovina Statistics Agency, Rezultati Popisa 2013: p. 54)

The official 2013 Census results (the first since the 1992–1995 war) only confirm that the legacies of ethnic cleansing remain a permanent fixture of the Bosnian state. These demographic shifts in ethnic composition were just in part a result of the ethnic cleansing war strategy. They were also a product of the peace agreement itself. Indeed, the Bosnian territorial divisions, as enshrined in Dayton, rewarded the nationalist parties for their territorial feuds and ethnic cleansing policies. Despite initial efforts to encourage refugees and internally displaced persons to return and settle roots in their homeland, people sold their lands in favour of moving to areas where they felt more secure among their respective ethnic majority. Hence, rather than fostering ethnic integration in each of the cantons and within RS, the peace arrangements intensified divisions between ethnic groups, thereby undermining long-term regional stability.

A final and most damaging limitation on peacebuilding in Bosnia-Herzegovina has been the complete failure of the international actors to challenge the competing local narratives over the causes and consequences of the war in Bosnia-Herzegovina. This issue, more than any other, betrays the tensions between Dayton's short-term peace objectives and long-term goals of reintegrating Bosnian society. At the heart of this tension is the very structure of the Dayton Accords – its territorial and institutional solutions to peace in Bosnia-Herzegovina. In particular, it revolves around the Dayton Accords support for the internal territorial integrity of Republika Srpska. But the emerging post-war Bosniak narrative is that of being the victims of Bosnian Serb genocide against them. On their side, Bosnian Serbs' representation of the war is as the fight for national self-determination and protection from possible retaliation by other communities in Bosnia.

From the very beginning of Dayton Bosnia, Bosniaks hoped that the international community would prosecute Bosnian Serbs for engaging in genocide in the war. Accordingly, Bosniaks were much more interested in the genocide case against Serbia in front of the International Court of Justice (ICJ) than in the individual cases before the ICTY (Subotic 2009). The ICJ's decision against Serbia would have recognised the Bosnian war as a war of aggression and resulted in the abolition of Republika Srpska. In other words, Bosniaks hoped that the ICJ ruling would achieve what could not have been accomplished during the Dayton negotiations. However, in February 2007, the ICJ issued a ruling that cleared Serbia of direct responsibility for the genocide and any complicity in the genocide that happened between 1992 and 1995. The verdict reiterated the ICTY decision that the only confirmed case of genocide in Bosnia is the one committed by Bosnian Serb forces in Srebrenica (Guzina and Marijan 2013).

The Courts outcome intensified deep-seated tensions between these ethnic groups. It also reinforced local public perceptions that the ICTY has done little to support or inspire reconciliation between the communities. Instead, the joint ICJ and ICTY ruling appears to have intensified those divisions. Or, as Meernik (2005: 287) has put it, 'more often than not, ethnic groups responded with increased hostility towards one another after an arrest or judgement'. In the end, there is still a widespread sense of a continuing conflict shared by Bosnians irrespective of which community they belong to. Within the environment of the 'incomplete peace' in Bosnia-Herzegovina, 'everyday peace politics' has almost naturally resulted in conflict over the symbols and competing narratives over the causes of war (Marijan 2017). In 2019, as much as was the case in 1995, Bosniaks perceive RS as a 'genocidal creation', while for Bosnian Serbs it is a 'legitimate outcome' of the Bosnian Serbs' struggle for the right to self-determination.

In the end, the identified three Dayton Bosnia's challenges oblige every student of Bosnian affairs to address, however briefly, two interlocked questions: whether any local agency has the leverage and power to make necessary changes to Bosnia-Herzegovina's political system? And, exactly how viable is Bosnia-Herzegovina in the long term? With hindsight of more than 20 years, the answer to both questions appears to be ambiguous at best. Despite constant emphasis on the need for change reiterated during every single Bosnian election, the changes in the system merely reinforce the status quo, allowing 'Bosnian oligarchs to stay as they are' (Calori 2014).

The Bosnian election of 2014 is an excellent example of the pretext of such 'changes'. Only months prior to the 2014 elections, thousands of citizens in Bosniak majority areas took part in massive street protests to express frustration against political and economic corruption and the astronomic unemployment crippling the country (GDP growth rate averaged only 0.31 per cent from 2009 to 2017; the average unemployment rate from 2007 until 2017 was at a staggering 42.65 per cent; and about 150,000 young people have left their homes since the end of the war, with 10,000 leaving every year) (Trading Economics 2018; BalkanInsight 2013). Thus, the so-called Bosnian Spring street protest reflected deep-seated dissatisfaction with Bosnian political elites at all levels of government. However, they also revealed the territorial divisions within Bosnia-Herzegovina, for citizens of Republika Srpska were much less prone to join the street protests (Marijan and Guzina 2014). Only a few months after the street protests, radical demands for social and economic changes all but disappeared, and nationalist parties resumed their dominance in the political domain. The Bosniak, Croat, and Serb nationalist parties (respectively, SDA – Bosniak Party of Democratic Action; HDZ – Croatian Democratic Union; SNSD – Serb Alliance for Independent Social Democrats) did manage to incorporate some of the protestors' requests for change in their political platforms, thereby securing their triumph once again in the 2014 general elections. However, these changes were minimal and did little to disrupt existing political structures that reinforce ethnic divisions.

The Dayton plan, in part, is responsible for constraining the rise of multi-ethnic parties that could disrupt nationalist political divisions. The Bosnian party system is defined by intra-ethnic electoral competition among parties representing a single ethnic group, typically Bosniak, Bosnian Serb, and Bosnian Croat, with rare cases of inter-ethnic cooperation. And even when they occur, as is the case between the leaders of the two major Bosnian Serb and Croat parties (SNSD and HDZ), such cooperation is motivated primarily by reasons of political expediency and effort to outbid or block the third Bosniak side in its determination to change the Dayton structure (Korzeniewska-Wiszniewska and Zdeb 2015: 102–106). Overall, the political system is designed to push voters to choose nationalist candidates as a less risky option than voting for the moderate candidate that might shift the precarious balance imposed by Dayton.

That said, one momentary window of opportunity occurred during the 2010 elections, which saw the rise of the Bosnian Social Democrats, and when the Social Democratic Party (SDP) rose to power in the 2010 elections as the only genuinely cross-ethnic party in Bosnia-Herzegovina (Korzeniewska-Wiszniewska and Zdeb 2015). However, the structure of the Dayton Agreement entrenched the dominance of nationalist identity politics, making it difficult for intra-ethnic parties like the SDP to disrupt existing political structures. Nor was the SDP able to tackle the significant socio-economic problems gripping the country (Bieber 2014). The SDP subsequently suffered a crushing defeat in 2014. It is important to note that the SDP's defeat should have been anticipated months earlier because the street protest first erupted in Tuzla, an SDP stronghold. Citizens in the area were dissatisfied with nationalist politics but saw no possibility or hope in the SDP's ability to challenge existing political structures. The internal fragmentation of the SDP following the 2014 election led to the creation of a new social democratic party, the Democratic Front (DF). Whether this will lead to a further split within the moderate vote in Bosnia-Herzegovina, or whether DF might prove to be more successful than SDP, remains to be seen.

Despite the continuing presence of nationalism and the nationalist victory in 2014, it would be wrong to assume that the majority of Bosnian citizens are supportive of their respective nationalist parties. Apart from venting their dissatisfaction on the streets in February 2014, citizens' protest was evident in the low voter turnout, with 46 per cent of the electorate abstaining from voting. This highlights the level of political apathy among citizens, but it also reflects divisions between those who already lost their jobs and support protests or boycott elections, versus those who enjoy the benefits of the overinflated public sector and fear potential reforms that might cost them their jobs (Calori 2014). For the latter, there is still something to lose, for, on balance, a poorly paid job is still better than no job at all.

Finally, while the Dayton Agreement plays a significant role in maintaining a political structure that reinforces nationalist ethnic divisions, this alone cannot explain the current context in Bosnia-Herzegovina. The economic stagnation and the failure of any meaningful socio-economic reforms cut through most of the Western Balkans and the broader area of former communist countries (Milanovic 2018). Bosnian politicians are not the only ones in the region that proved very capable of maintaining their position of control over their respective societies. Similar practice is spread across the region, in particular, in Serbia, Montenegro, and Macedonia. Nor was such development of 'elastic authoritarianism' possible without the active insistence of the EU on twofold goals of political stability and the IMF- and World Bank-inspired economic reforms (Mujanovic 2018). For many regional scholars, what has emerged should best be described in terms of stabilitocracies. As Bieber has poignantly defined it, these are 'governments that claim to secure stability, pretend to espouse EU integration and rely on informal, clientelist structures, control of the media, and the regular production of crises to undermine democracy and the rule of law' (Bieber 2018a).

The future of Bosnia-Herzegovina is tenuous at best. One possibility is the continuation of the EU-inspired policies of support for external stability of the Western Balkans in general, and the territorial integrity of Bosnia-Herzegovina in particular. But this comes at the cost of stabilising a political system that legitimises itself by relying on the rhetoric of democracy, while internally being supportive of ethnic tensions and identity politics. At least, this is what many authors fear while evaluating the EU initiatives in support of the Western Balkans. Many would like to see renewed EU engagement in the Balkans that 'could break the downward spiral of authoritarianism and escalating crises and restore faith in the EU model' (Bieber 2018b). However, the continuing EU focus on external stability of the Western Balkans could further legitimise a rise in autocracy in the region. Under such conditions, fragmentation without democratisation will continue to define the events in Bosnia-Herzegovina and elsewhere in the region.

Mujanovic, in his book *Hunger and Fury*, offers an alternative scenario. Endemic poverty and widespread corruption will eventually spark a new wave of street protests across the countries emerging out of the former Yugoslavia, and not only in Bosnia-Herzegovina. If successful, in Mujanovic's words, 'the popular fury will leave in its wake fresh soil from which genuinely reformed societies may emerge' (2018: 174). To the extent that this outcome is possible, Bosnia-Herzegovina and other Western Balkans states might be finally starting to come together and to integrate their societies within the region and under the broader architecture of the EU. The first test for those two scenarios were the latest Bosnian general elections in the fall of 2018. However, as one might have expected, the alternative scenario failed to materialise. Rather, by voting for nationalist parties and thus keeping the Dayton status quo unchallenged, Bosnian citizens have once more caught themselves in a *Groundhog Day* scenario that makes them relive the same election results over and over again.

Lessons to be learned from the case study

What lessons can we glean from international involvement in Bosnia-Herzegovina? Once peace accords are signed, the day after brings the same uncertainties as the day before signing them. Short of a clear victory of one side over the other in an intra-state conflict, the former combatants end up in the driver's seat as to how to interpret those agreements. In other words, a delicate and unstable compromise is usually the outcome of the peace accords. Too often, particularly in the case of Bosnia-Herzegovina, international peace agreements obscure the deep-seated tensions that continue to permeate societies, tensions that fuel instability in these regions and that are always at the brink of erupting. Thus, we should not search for generalisable, ready-made solutions that can be transferable to conflicts that were caused by radically different circumstances. Instead, we should recognise that what peace operations have in common are not necessarily shared lessons but shared challenges.

The best way to approach those challenges is by separating peacebuilding as a peace process from peacebuilding as post-conflict state making. The peace process is built by achieving an international consensus on possible steps towards peace. In the context of Bosnia-Herzegovina, it took a full three and half years before international actors agreed to act in unison. Moreover, without an orchestrated NATO air campaign against Serb positions in Bosnia-Herzegovina in the summer of 1995, it is doubtful that Serbian President Slobodan Milosevic would have reigned in local Serb leaders on the ground and accepted the Dayton peace framework (Holbrooke 1998). International mediators were also careful not to take sides and declare a winner, despite the atrocities perpetrated by some players. Finally, the peace process was built on the clear understanding that no party would be rewarded with more than its 'fair' share.

Post-conflict state making, however, requires a more enduring long-term process that seeks to ensure not only stability and peace but also a democratic consolidation of post-conflict states; a process that major external agencies and international humanitarian organisations are often ill-equipped or lack sustained interest to pursue. Post-conflict state making incorporates various negotiated strategies, such as security transition, political transformation, societal integration, and economic recovery, to name a few (Castillo 2017). Security transition and internationally mediated political change have brought 20-plus years of peace in the region, albeit the political institutions envisioned in the Dayton Agreement were engineered to end the war (Paris and Sisk 2009; Paris 2004) and required the consent of those who were fighting on the ground. Thus, they most benefited those who were directly responsible for the war in the first place.

In sum, the international solution to the destruction of Yugoslavia's federation and the war in Bosnia-Herzegovina was the creation of yet another ethnic federation, that of Bosnia-Herzegovina. The rigidly imposed power-sharing federal structure of a Bosnian state, with its elaborate system of regional veto powers at the expense of the federal institutions, is perilously close in its design to the one of the former Yugoslavia. In both instances, these institutions are overshadowed by 'thick' ethnic tensions that underscore the entire political system. Nowadays, as was the case 20-plus years ago, the question of Bosnian partition remains open. From the Bosniak perspective, the Dayton Accords are just a set of documents to be changed in the direction of building stronger central institutions. For Bosnian Serbs and Croats, with no small help from their neighbouring kin-states (Serbia and Croatia), Dayton is 'the ceiling that should not be further developed' (Belloni 2008: 42).

Note

1 See Owen (1995).

References, further reading, and links to key primary documents

References

BalkanInsight. 2013. "Youth Emigration Causing Balkan 'Brain Drain'." 1 August 2013. www.balkaninsight.com/en/article/young-people-leave-serbia-bosnia-the-most.

Belloni, Roberto. 2008. *State Building and International Intervention in Bosnia*, 1st edn. New York: Routledge.

Belloni, Roberto. 2009. "Bosnia: Dayton Is Dead! Long Live Dayton!" *Nationalism and Ethnic Politics* 15 (3–4): 355–375.

Bieber, Florian. 2014. "Is Change Coming (Finally)? Thoughts on the Bosnian Protests." *Balkan Insight*, 10 February. Accessed 15 February 2018. www.balkaninsight.com/en/blog/is-change-coming-finally-thoughts-on-the-bosnian-protests.

Bieber, Florian. 2018a. "The Rise (and Fall) of Balkan Stabilitocracies." *Belgrade: CIRSD*. www.cirsd.org/en/horizons/horizons-winter-2018-issue-no-10/the-rise-and-fall-of-balkan-stabilitocracies.

Bieber, Florian. 2018b. "A Way Forward for the Balkans?" *Foreign Affairs*, 6 February. Accessed 31 March 2018. www.foreignaffairs.com/articles/southeastern-europe/2018-02-06/way-forward-balkans.

Bildt, Carl. 1999. *Peace Journey: The Struggle for Peace in Bosnia*. London: Orion Pub Co.

Burg, Steven L., and Paul Shoup. 1999. *The War in Bosnia-Herzegovina: Ethnic Conflict and International Intervention*. Armonk, NY: M.E. Sharpe.

Calori, Anna. 2014. "Is There Life After the (Bosnian) Elections? Poverty as a Weapon of Mass Destruction." *Open Democracy*, 13 November. Accessed 29 March 2018. www.opendemoc racy. net/can-europe-make-it/anna-calori/is-there-life-after-bosnian-elections-poverty-as-weapon-of-mass-destr.

Campbell, Susanna, David Chandler, and Meera Sabaratnam. (Eds.). 2011. *A Liberal Peace? The Problems and Practices of Peacebuilding*. London, New York: Zed Books.

Caplan, Richard. 2005. *Europe and the Recognition of New States in Yugoslavia*. Cambridge, New York: Cambridge University Press.

Castillo, Graciana del. 2017. *Obstacles to Peacebuilding*. London, New York: Routledge.

Chandler, David. 2000. *Bosnia: Faking Democracy After Dayton*, 2nd edn. London, Sterling, VA: Pluto Press.

Chandler, David. 2017. *Peacebuilding: The Twenty Years' Crisis, 1997–2017*. Rethinking Peace and Conflict Studies. Cham, Switzerland: Palgrave Macmillan.

Cousens, Elizabeth, and David Harland. 2006. "Post-Dayton Bosnia and Herzegovina." In William J. Durch (Ed.), *Twenty-First-Century Peace Operations*, 49–140. Washington, DC: United States Institute of Peace and the Henry L. Stimson Center.

Donais, Timothy. 2005. *The Political Economy of Peacebuilding in Post-Dayton Bosnia*. Contemporary Security Studies. London, New York: Routledge.

Donais, Timothy. 2012. *Peacebuilding and Local Ownership: Post-Conflict Consensus-Building*. Studies in Conflict, Development and Peacebuilding 5. London, New York: Routledge.

Donais, Timothy A. 2017. "Dayton +20: Peacebuilding and the Perils of Exclusivity." *Peacebuilding* 5 (1): 7–21.

Durch, William J. (Ed.). 2006. *Twenty-First-Century Peace Operations*. Washington, DC: United States Institute of Peace and the Henry L. Stimson Center.

Gow, James. 1997. *Triumph of the Lack of Will: International Diplomacy and the Yugoslav War*. New York: Columbia University Press.

Guzina, Dejan, and Branka Marijan. 2013. "Local Uses of International Criminal Justice in Bosnia-Herzegovina: Transcending Divisions or Building Parallel Worlds?" *Studies in Social Justice* 7 (2): 245–263.

Hampson, Fen Osler. 1996. *Nurturing Peace: Why Peace Settlements Succeed or Fail.* Washington, DC: United States Institute of Peace Press.

Hoare, Marko Attila. 2007. *The History of Bosnia: From the Middle Ages to the Present Day.* London, Berkeley, CA: Saqi.

Holbrooke, Richard C. 1998. *To End a War.* New York: Random House.

Honig, Jan Willem, and Norbert Both. 1997. *Srebrenica: Record of a War Crime.* New York: Penguin Books.

Karcic, Hikmet. 2015. "Blueprint for Genocide: The Destruction of Muslims in Eastern Bosnia." *Open Democracy*, 11 May. Accessed 21 March 2018. www.opendemocracy.net/can-europe-make-it/hikmet-karcic/blueprint-for-genocide-destruction-of-muslims-in-eastern-bosnia.

Korzeniewska-Wiszniewska, Mirella, and Aleksandra Zdeb. 2015. *Bosnia and Herzegovina and Its Political Kaleidoscope: General Elections 2014: Report.* Krakow: Ksiegarnia Akademicka. Accessed 17 January 2018. www.academia.edu/17658157/BOSNIA_AND_HERZEGOVINA_AND_ITS_POLITICAL_KALEIDOSCOPE._General_elections_2014_report.

Mac Ginty, Roger. 2011. *International Peacebuilding and Local Resistance: Hybrid Forms of Peace.* Rethinking Peace and Conflict Studies. Houndmills, Basingstoke, Hampshire, New York: Palgrave Macmillan.

Marijan, Branka. 2017. "The Politics of Everyday Peace in Bosnia and Herzegovina and Northern Ireland." *Peacebuilding* 5 (1): 67–81.

Marijan, Branka, and Dejan Guzina. 2014. "An Early 'Spring in Bosnia'?" *Centre for International Governance Innovation*, 20 February. Accessed 29 March 2018. www.cigionline.org/publications/early-spring-bosnia.

Meernik, James. 2005. "Justice and Peace? How the International Criminal Tribunal Affects Societal Peace in Bosnia." *Journal of Peace Research* 42 (3): 271–289.

Merdzanovic, Adis. 2017. "'Imposed Consociationalism': External Intervention and Power Sharing in Bosnia and Herzegovina." *Peacebuilding* 5 (1): 22–35.

Milanovic, Branko. n.d. 2018. "For Whom the Wall Fell? A Balance-Sheet of Transition to Capitalism." *Global Inequality*, 3 November. Accessed 14 March 2018. http://glineq.blogspot.com/2014/11/for-whom-wall-fell-balance-sheet-of.html.

Mujanovic, Jasmin. 2018. *Hunger and Fury: The Crisis of Democracy in the Balkans.* Oxford: Oxford University Press.

Nettelfield, Lara J., and Sara Wagner. 2013. *Srebrenica in the Aftermath of Genocide.* Cambridge: Cambridge University Press.

Newman, Edward, Roland Paris, and Oliver P. Richmond. (Eds.). 2009. *New Perspectives on Liberal Peacebuilding.* Tokyo, New York: United Nations University Press.

Owen, David. 1995. *Balkan Odyssey*, 1st U.S. edn. New York: Harcourt Brace.

Owen, David. (Ed.). 2013. *Bosnia-Herzegovina: The Vance/Owen Peace Plan.* Liverpool: Liverpool University Press.

Paris, Roland. 2004. *At War's End: Building Peace After Civil Conflict.* Cambridge: Cambridge University Press.

Paris, Roland, and Timothy D. Sisk. (Eds.). 2009. *The Dilemmas of Statebuilding: Confronting the Contradictions of Postwar Peace Operations*, 1st edn. London: Routledge.

Pomfret, John. 1995. "Bosnian Balance Shifted Since Last Truce." *Washington Post*, 6 October. Accessed 29 March 2018. www.washingtonpost.com/archive/politics/1995/10/06/bosnian-balance-shifted-since-last-truce/5ba7bf1e-9495-4fbb-b98b-6f65dabf809e/.

Popov, Nebojsa. 1996. *Srpska Strana Rata: Trauma i Katarza u Istorijskom Pamćenju* [Serbian Wartland: Trauma and Catarrh in Historic Memory]. Beograd: Republika.

Radan, Peter. 2002. *The Break-Up of Yugoslavia and International Law*. Routledge Studies in International Law 2. London, New York: Routledge.

Ramet, Sabrina P. 2006. *The Three Yugoslavias: State-Building and Legitimation, 1918–2005*. Washington, DC, Bloomington, IN: Woodrow Wilson Center Press, Indiana University Press.

Richmond, Oliver P. 2014. *Failed Statebuilding: Intervention and the Dynamics of Peace Formation*. New Haven: Yale University Press.

Subotic, Jelena. 2009. *Hijacked Justice: Dealing with the Past in the Balkans*. Ithaca, London: Cornell University Press.

Tokaca, Mirsad. 2018. "Preko Osamdeset Odsto Civilnih Žrtava Su Bošnjaci [Over Eighty Percent of Civil Victims Are Bosniaks]." Accessed 15 February 2018. www.monit or.co.me/index.php?option=com_content&view=article&id=6749:mirsad-tokaa-direktor-istraivako-dokumentacionog-centra-u-sarajevu-preko-osamdeset-odsto-civilnih-rtava-su-bonjaci-&catid=4650:broj-1328&Itemid=5994.

Tonge, Jonathan. 2014. *Comparative Peace Processes*. Cambridge: Polity Press.

Trading Economics. 2018. "Bosnia and Herzegovina Unemployment Rate | 2007–2018 | Data | Chart." *Trading Economics*, Accessed 29 March 2018. https://tradingeconomics.com/bosnia-and-herzegovina/unemployment-rate.

Further reading

Many sources have been already identified in the chapter. The suggested list represents just a glimpse into the vast literature on the varied aspects of the war and peacebuilding in Bosnia-Herzegovina.

Borger, Julian. 2016. *The Butcher's Trail: How the Search for Balkan War Criminals Became the World's Most Successful Manhunt*. LLC: Other Press.

Delpla, Isabelle, Xavier Bougarel, and Jean-Louis Fournel. (Eds.) 2012. *Investigating Srebrenica: Institutions, Facts, Responsibilities*, 1st edn. New York: Berghahn Books.

Hromadzic, Aida. 2015. *Citizens of an Empty Nation*. Philadelphia: University of Pennsylvania Press.

Keil, Soeren, and Valery Perry. 2017. *State-Building and Democratization in Bosnia and Herzegovina*. New York: Routledge.

Merdzanovic, Adis. 2015. *Democracy by Decree: Prospects and Limits of Imposed Consociational Democracy in Bosnia and Herzegovina*. Stuttgart: Ibidem-Verlag.

Nettelfield, Laura J. 2010. *Courting Democracy in Bosnia and Herzegovina: The Hague Tribunal's Impact in a Postwar State*. New York: Cambridge University Press.

Sebastián-Aparicio, Sofía. 2014. *Post-War Statebuilding and Constitutional Reform: Beyond Dayton in Bosnia*. Rethinking Peace and Conflict Studies. Houndmills, Basingstoke, Hampshire: Palgrave Macmillan.

Toal, Gerard, and Carl Dahlman. 2011. *Bosnia Remade: Ethnic Cleansing and Its Reversal*. New York: Oxford University Press.

Online resources

Census – Census - ethnicity, nationality, religion, mother tongue (2013). Bosnian Statistics Agency, Rezultati Popisa. At http://www.popis.gov.ba/popis2013/doc/RezultatiPopisa_SR.pdf. In 2013, Bosnia-Herzegovina organized the first official census since 1991, when it recorded 4.4 million citizens. Data in 2013 recorded 3.8 million people living in the country.

EUFOR – European Union Force in Bosnia-Herzegovina. www.euforbih.org/eufor/index.php/about-eufor/background.

ICTY – International Crime Tribunal for Former Yugoslavia. http://icr.icty.org. It is located in The Hague in the Netherlands, and it had authority to prosecute individuals for serious violations of international humanitarian law committed in the former Yugoslavia since 1991. The United Nations Security Council passed Resolution 827 establishing the court on 25 May 1993. It officially dissolved in December 2017, but the court documents are still available.

Office of the High Representative. At www.ohr.int/?lang=en. The Office of the High Representative (OHR) is an ad hoc international institution responsible for overseeing implementation of civilian aspects of the Peace Agreement ending the war in Bosnia and Herzegovina.

OSCE Mission to Bosnia-Herzegovina. www.osce.org/mission-to-bosnia-and-herzegovina. The Mission's principal aim is to promote stability and reconciliation while assisting Bosnia and Herzegovina on its path to regional political, economic, and social integration. Its activities focus on reforming systems of governance, justice, and education, as well as upholding human rights and the rule of law for all citizens.

Peace Accords Matrix (PAM), Kroc Institute for International Peace Studies, University of Notre Dame. https://peaceaccords.nd.edu. The PAM project hosts the largest existing collection of implementation data on intra-state peace agreements. In addition to the wealth of information and links to primary documents on Bosnia-Herzegovina, the PAM database is a source of qualitative and quantitative data on the implementation of 34 Comprehensive Peace Agreements (CPAs) negotiated after 1989.

RECOM. At http://recom.link. RECOM is a regional commission for the establishment of facts about war crimes and other serious violations of human rights committed in the former Yugoslavia from 1 January 1991 until 31 December 2001.

UNMIBH – United Nations Mission in Bosnia-Herzegovina. http://peacekeeping.un.org/mission/past/unmibh/index.html. Provides general information about the UN mission in Bosnia-Herzegovina during its mandate (December 1995–December 2002).

5

CAMBODIA

SungYong Lee

Introduction

The peace process in Cambodia has been discussed in academic discourse as a representative example of the new form of intervention and peacebuilding. It was one of the first international peace-supporting activities in the post-Cold War period and demonstrated typical features of the externally driven mega-size peacebuilding that aimed to transform the sources of conflicts (Mayall 1994; Doyle et al. 1997). The considerable achievements during the 1990s in implementing demilitarisation, a 'fair and free' election, and the reconstruction of state institutions in Cambodia raised people's optimism for the international community's contributions to such processes. The objectives of the Western interveners for reconstructing peace through democratisation seemed to be gradually materialising (Richmond and Franks 2009).

However, as of the late 2010s, the hope for developing democratic governance in the country has proved to be stunted, and the situation seems to be deteriorating. Prime Minister Hun Sen has remained in power for longer than 30 years, making him the longest reigning government head in Asia. His political dominance has become more intense since the death of his long-time rival, Chea Sim, in 2015; moreover, international actors' hope of developing a democratic governance system has been severely compromised by Cambodian resistance to this (Morgenbesser 2017). Meanwhile, the limited space for inclusive political participation is shrinking further, and the government's violations of human rights have continued if not increased (Lilja 2008; HRW 2017).

The striking contrast between the optimism of the mid-1990s and the realities of political and social development in the late 2000s reflects the discrepancies between the visions of Cambodia's future held by the international peacebuilders and those of the Cambodian factional leaders at the signing of the Paris Peace

Agreement in 1991. Since then, peacebuilding and development in the country have been undertaken based on the interaction and compromises between these two distinct visions. In most cases, moreover, the outcomes of such interactions were formed in favour of the Hun Sen party's desires.

So, what was the gap in the views of the two parties, and how was this gap presented and addressed in the peace processes? How did it determine the political space in post-war Cambodia? This chapter aims to examine these questions by considering the interaction between external mediators and the key Cambodian parties during the process of peace negotiations in Cambodia, 1989–1993. Of various factors, it will highlight the negative consequences of external mediators' failure to develop close and constant channels of communication. Due to a lack of such channels, the mediators and their Cambodian counterparts could not deliver clear messages to each other and so made many decisions based on their own assumptions. Moreover, when things failed to develop as they had hoped, the interveners tended to apply coercive pressure without the opportunity to comprehend the motivations of Cambodian resistance to their directions.

Conflict analysis

The civil war in Cambodia was a military conflict between four national leaderships that had governed the country. After gaining its independence from France in 1953, Prince Norodom Sihanouk ruled the Kingdom of Cambodia as a prince (*de facto* king), prime minister, and head of state until 1970. Then, with support from the US, General Lon Nol deposed Sihanouk and established the Khmer Republic. The Republic was overthrown by a socialist military group called the Khmer Rouge in 1975.[1] During its four years of rule, the Khmer Rouge launched radical socialist projects such as a collective agricultural system, depopulation of cities, and prohibition of markets, which caused the deaths of between 1.5 and 2 million people. A group of Khmer Rouge officers who were opposed to the direction the party had taken escaped to Vietnam and formed an anti-Khmer Rouge movement called the Kampuchean United Front for National Salvation (KUFNS) (Chandler 1998).

When the KUFNS, headed by Heng Samrin, Chea Sim, and Hun Sen, with backing from Vietnam, overthrew the Khmer Rouge regime and established the People's Republic of Kampuchea (PRK) in 1979, the Cambodian civil war began.[2] Although Hun Sen was the youngest of the PRK's top leaders, his political leadership and skills enabled him to become the prime minister in 1985. Initially, the government operated under strong Vietnamese influence. Most bureaucratic issues were managed by people trained in Vietnam, and Vietnamese soldiers controlled the major cities (Slocomb 2004; Gottesman 2004).

Against the PRK government, three major military movements led by former national leaders emerged, basing themselves near the Thai border (see Table 5.1). First, soon after it lost Phnom Penh on January 7, 1979, the Khmer Rouge began

TABLE 5.1 Actors in the Cambodian Civil War*

	PRK	*The Khmer Rouge*	*FUNCINPEC*	*KPNLF*
Governmental identity	People's Republic of Kampuchea	Democratic Kampuchea	United Front for an Independent, Neutral, Peaceful, and Cooperative Cambodia	Khmer People's National Liberation Front
		Coalition Government of Democratic Kampuchea (CGDK)		
Core negotiator	Hun Sen	Khieu Samphan	Prince Sihanouk	Son Sann
Leaders	Hun Sen Heng Samrin Chea Sim	Pol Pot Ieng Sary	Prince Sihanouk Prince Ranariddh	Son Sann
Regional supporters	Vietnam	Thailand	ASEAN	
Aligned outside powers	USSR	China	Australia, France, USA, China	
Number of soldiers	30,000 (150,000)**	30,000 ~40,000**	7,000	15,000

* This table is partly quoted from Brown and Zasloff (1998: xiii, 32) and updated by the author.

** The numbers of solders are the estimated number in 1985. The PRK's troops include the Vietnamese forces fighting in Cambodia. There are no agreed figures for the number of troops commanded by the resistance groups. Although many previous studies accept the figures given above, other studies contend that the number differed markedly from the above totals. For instance, Turner insists on the following figures: the Khmer Rouge 25,000, FUNCINPEC 1,200–1,500, the KPNLF 7,000 (2004: 56).

to undertake guerrilla operations. Its military strength and support from China remained a grave threat to the PRK (Slocomb 2004). Second, the National United Front for an Independent, Neutral, Peaceful, and Cooperative Cambodia (FUNCINPEC) was formed by Prince Sihanouk. Although it lacked substantial military and financial resources, the king's perceived legitimacy and his intimate relationship with China made the party an important actor in the resistance movement. Finally, the former prime minister, Son Sann, established the Khmer People's National Liberation Front (KPNLF), which apparently claimed to develop a liberal democratic politics in the country. Chiefly supported by and composed of refugees from near the Thai border, the KPLNF conducted guerrilla operations and received moderate support from the US and ASEAN.

Three anti-Vietnamese military movements established a coalition group, the Coalition Government of Democratic Kampuchea (CGDK) in 1981 and proclaimed that they would 'avoid any clashes among themselves' (Joint Statement of the Three Khmer Leaders 4 September, 1981, cited in Sihanouk 2005, appendix).

The CGDK was a loose gathering of three factions that allowed each group to operate with a certain degree of freedom and to maintain autonomy. Both FUNCINPEC and the KPNLF had a deep-seated distrust of the Khmer Rouge, and there was also keen rivalry between the KPNLF and FUNCINPEC. However, their common goal to resist Vietnamese imperialism enabled them to work together. The CGDK controlled a number of refugee camps near the border with Thailand but had never been a government that could claim to govern a significant portion of Cambodian territory.

In the mid-1980s, it became more evident that ending the war through one party's military victory was impossible. Although the PRK–Vietnam alliance dominated the combat in the initial phase of the civil conflict, it failed to control territories effectively. Although the heavily armed PRK–Vietnam joint forces were able to attack and destroy the Khmer Rouge's military bases during its dry-season campaigns, the resistance groups were successful in organising counteroffensives during the rainy season. Gradually, both sides began to worry that the war might become a protracted affair.

The PRK–Vietnam alliance's dry-season campaign in 1984–1985 heightened the concerns of both sides. In fact, the alliance had achieved its greatest conventional victory since 1979. It destroyed most major KPNLF and the Khmer Rouge bases and forced the majority of the Khmer Rouge troops to retreat to the border (Bilveer 1985). As a result, all the resistance groups realised that their forces were unlikely to prevail and that an outright military victory was improbable. Particularly, the Khmer Rouge and the KPNLF, which had pursued a policy of 'total victory' over the PRK–Vietnam, were shaken by the destruction of most of their bases. As Hun Sen recalls, however, the campaign also strained the PRK and caused it to re-evaluate its potential to militarily bring about an end to the war and to consider peace talks as a supplementary (if not an alternative) way of resolving the conflict (Haas 1991).

Hun Sen became the new prime minister of the PRK in 1987, and there were some signs of a peace process beginning (Osborne 1994; Brown and Zasloff 1998). Nevertheless, although a few formal and informal meetings between the PRK and the CGDK (mainly Prince Sihanouk and his envoys) were conducted, the parties failed to reach any substantial agreement. Primarily, the withdrawal of the Vietnamese military troops from Cambodia was an issue that was critical to the resolution of the conflict. The CGDK and many external interveners, including China, Thailand, and Singapore, demanded Vietnamese withdrawal as a prerequisite for negotiation or as a non-negotiable condition. Moreover, one main issue at stake was on whether the Khmer Rouge should be allowed to participate in the new political institutions. (Haas 1991; Gottesman 2004; Um 1990).

The collapse of the Cold War system opened a new phase of peace talks. With encouragement from the Soviet Union and Vietnam, the PRK showed signs of changes in its posture. China in particular applied strong pressure on the Khmer Rouge. The US also encouraged the Khmer Rouge by announcing the withdrawal of its support for the CGDK's continued possession of its UN seat and did not seek the return of the Khmer Rouge.

The greatest momentum for a peace process was provided by the withdrawal of the Vietnamese army in September 1989, which removed a huge obstacle to the peace process. Losing its largest military resource and seeing that Vietnam had more important national interests than supporting its Cambodian ally, the PRK began more earnestly to work towards the success of the negotiation. For the resistance groups, the withdrawal meant that they achieved their primary goal (the removal of Vietnamese imperialism). After realising that the Vietnamese 'puppet' regime was still strong despite Vietnam's withdrawal, the CGDK finally acknowledged Hun Sen as a negotiation partner.

However, Vietnam and the PRK's concession did not immediately or directly result in a stable and productive negotiation. In contrast, believing that the PRK had been weakened, the CGDK conducted vigorous military operations during the rainy season in 1989–1990. However, although these operations achieved relative success, the PRK recovered most of its lost territories in the next dry-season campaign (Turner 2004). All Cambodian provincial capitals and all but two district towns remained under PRK rule (Kiernan 1992). It was obvious that the PRK's military strength was stronger than the resistance groups had estimated. Finally, FUNCINPEC and the KPNLF more actively engaged in negotiation.

The conflict resolution process

More serious peace talks began at the end of 1989 under the advocacy of the international actors, and the development of the peace processes was largely determined by the interactions between the Cambodian factional leaders and their international counterparts in mediation. Hence, this section will overview the development in the peace processes by focusing on the interplay between the national factions, who were reluctant to make concessions, and the third parties, who attempted to convince them to compromise.

When the negotiation started, the two most important issues at stake were demilitarisation and the establishment of the interim authority. National factions remained stubborn with their views on how much the military forces should be purged, and by whom and with what mechanisms the process should be supervised and monitored. Regarding the interim authority, although the establishment of an authority that represented the Cambodian sovereignty was widely supported, the controversial issue was whether it would be a quadripartite government that would grant the four factions equal numbers of seats or a bipartite body, with the PRK and the CGDK each having 50 per cent of the seats.

The PRK had two fundamental goals: the removal of the Khmer Rouge and maintaining its superiority in the post-conflict Cambodian political arena. The former goal was set when the KUFNS was established in 1978 and had been a core principle of its movement. The second goal emerged when it became clear that the PRK could not eliminate its opponents militarily. Hence, if it could not stand as the sole legitimate authority, the PRK needed to continue to be a leading political organisation (Turner 2004: 163).

A common goal of the three internal factions of the CGDK was the withdrawal of Vietnamese imperialism from Cambodia (Sihanouk 2005; Brown and Zasloff 1998). However, there were contradictory views between the internal factions regarding the political roles of the Khmer Rouge in post-war Cambodia: while the Khmer Rouge's first goal was to return to power, KPNLF insisted on the elimination of the Khmer Rouge from the political arena (Ashley 1998; Heder 1999; Corfield 1991; Ieng Mouly 2009, author's interview).

Phase I (late 1989–late 1990)

During the first phase of the peace negotiation, third-party mediators succeeded in pressurising the Cambodian factions (excluding the Khmer Rouge) to consent to their core demands on demilitarisation and the transitional authority. While Indonesia, France, Japan, and China contributed to the Cambodian peace negotiations by providing good offices and applying diplomatic pressure on the national factions, Australia and the United States produced comprehensive peace proposals (Lizée 1999).

Of the external mediators, the US played a particularly important role. First, the country prepared detailed UN-centred peace proposals based on ideas suggested by Australia (Solomon 2000: 34). The US peace proposals were formed by the UN Security Council's peace initiatives, which comprised a 'Framework Document' (August 1990) and an 'Implementation Plan' (November 1990) and offered a bedrock for the subsequent negotiation. Regarding demilitarisation and interim authority, the documents made four recommendations: the UN would control the processes of a national election; a Supreme National Council (SNC) would be established in order to represent Cambodian sovereignty; the composition of the SNC would be decided by the national factions; and although the bureaucratic structure of the PRK would remain, all military forces would be dissolved (Lizée 1999: 68; Haas 1991: 287). The document also declared that UNTAC would be the central governing body during the transitional period and that the SNC would play only a nominal role. Moreover, the US made various economic and diplomatic efforts to bring the parties to the negotiation table. For instance, the US applied economic pressure by withdrawing its support for the Khmer Rouge and restricting its aid to non-military support of the two non-communist resistance factions. In addition, American economic cooperation with Vietnam became more direct and active (Haas 1991; Solomon 2000; Brown and Zasloff 1998; Richardson 2009).

In entering negotiation with its counterpart, the PRK was not greatly attracted by the proposals set by mediators since it considered the Framework Document's proposals, especially those on the transitional authority, harmful to its goals. Although the preservation of its organisation was good news for the PRK, the UN's control over electoral processes would remove the privileges that the PRK's governmental status had afforded. Moreover, it believed that the Khmer Rouge's guerrilla forces would be easier to avoid if the UN verification of their demobilisation and the dissolution of all military forces were likely to benefit the Khmer Rouge.

Despite the PRK's reservations, the strengthened incentives and pressure from the US, together with the transformation in its advocate state's diplomatic position, convinced the PRK to adopt more a flexible attitude in the peace negotiations (Solomon 2000). Accepting the SNC as an unavoidable reality, the PRK changed its main strategy from claiming legitimacy as the sole government to maximising its interest in the council. For example, two weeks after the announcement of the UN's Framework Document, the Cambodian national factions agreed to form a 12-member Supreme National Council (Solomon 2000) and endorsed the Framework Document (Accords 1998; Doyle 1995).

In contrast, the CGDK's commitment to the peace process in this period was significantly deterred by the Khmer Rouge's refusal to participate. Despite economic and diplomatic pressure calling for peace dialogue, the Khmer Rouge continued to conduct a nationwide military campaign, sabotaging the ongoing negotiation.

Lying behind the Khmer Rouge's stubborn attitude were three self-delusions. First, the Khmer Rouge was convinced of its domestic popularity, blindly believing that it had the unconditional support of Cambodian peasants (Heder 1999: 96). Second, the Khmer Rouge considered Vietnam's announcement of the withdrawal of its military forces in 1989 to be a straightforward lie. They believed that most Vietnamese troops still remained in Cambodia, without wearing uniforms (Brown and Zasloff 1998; Chhin Kim Thong 2009, author's interview). Third, the Khmer Rouge did not notice the changes in China's diplomatic priorities in support of the negotiation. The direct communications between these two sides decreased, and the Khmer Rouge's Beijing representatives failed to convey comprehensive reports to their leaders (a former Khmer Rouge leader who requested anonymity 2009, author's interview).

Hence, the negotiations in Phase I was conducted mostly without meaningful participation of the Khmer Rouge throughout 1990. A main issue at stake was the transitional authority. The CGDK initially demanded that each faction should hold 25 per cent of the SNC membership, whereas the PRK insisted on a membership formula comprising a 50:50 distribution. A diplomatic breakthrough came in April 1990, when Prince Sihanouk of the CGDK accepted a 6:6 distribution of seats (Haas 1991). Two weeks later, in exchange for these developments, the PRK accepted that the Khmer Rouge should be included as part of the authority. These proposals were reconfirmed when Sihanouk and Hun Sen met in Japan in June 1990 (Lizée 1999; Haas 1991). While the PRK gained a concession from the CGDK on the composition of the SNC's membership, the CGDK convinced the PRK to include the Khmer Rouge in the forthcoming authority (Solomon 1999: 312).

Nevertheless, the national factions' collaboration on ending the conflict, based as it was on diplomatic and economic incentives and pressure from the US and other impartial interveners, would not last long.

Phase II (late 1990 and October 1991)

In the next phase of the peace process, China began to assume a greater role, while the Western mediators exhibited much less enthusiasm in promoting the progress of the conflict resolution. These changes brought the Khmer Rouge to the negotiations and opened a new opportunity for the PRK to push forward its own agenda in the peace process.

The Khmer Rouge, which had a strong but misguided belief in China's unwavering support, was surprised by China's cessation of military support in late 1990.[3] Diplomatically, however, China began to make open calls for the Khmer Rouge's participation in the negotiation. Moreover, the latter believed that the UN P-5's Framework Document was consistent with its core interests for three reasons. First, it thought that the composition of SNC would prevent the PRK's dominance in post-war Cambodia. Second, UNTAC's control of the transitional period seemed beneficial to the Khmer Rouge in directing its political campaigns. Third, the complete demilitarisation of all factions would enable it to use more manpower to rebuild its political units. Based on these assumptions, Pol Pot considered the proposals to be the Khmer Rouge's 'best bet for regaining power' and achieving victory (Heder 1999: 105).

The Khmer Rouge gradually escaped from its half-hearted commitment with China, accepting the proposals from other negotiators as long as these were not fundamentally inconsistent with its long-term survival. At a negotiation in Pattaya in August 1991, for instance, the Khmer Rouge compromised its previous position and explicitly agreed with the ceasefire, the discontinuation of military aid from external actors, and demilitarisation; it also pledged cooperation between the SNC and UNTAC (Brown 1992; Brown and Zasloff 1998).

In the same period, the PRK aimed to utilise the Khmer Rouge's increasing commitment to the peace negotiations and the decreased involvement of Western mediators, as well as the increased Chinese support for more independent roles for the national factions, as an opportunity to resist the UNTAC arrangement that it had previously agreed to under strong international pressure.

In pursuing his goals, Hun Sen firstly improved his relationship with China and attempted to gain its support for the PRK's position in the negotiation. Moreover, he tried to convince non-Khmer Rouge leaders of resistance groups to agree to his proposals, which aimed to minimise the negotiating power of the Khmer Rouge. These strategies frequently worked in making deals in favour of the PRK. For instance, at the meeting in Jakarta in early June 1991, the Khmer Rouge refused to accept the proposal on Sihanouk's role as SNC chairman and the composition of the SNC (7:7), to which the other factions had agreed. On this occasion, Hun Sen ignored the opposition while accepting continued participation of the Khmer Rouge in the negotiations. Moreover, the party took advantage of improving its relationship with Vietnam and China to apply pressure to the Khmer Rouge (Lizée 1999).

Eventually, the long process of peace negotiation was concluded by the second Paris Conference on Cambodia in October 1991. A number of important decisions related to the transitional authority were made, which benefited the PRK's pursuit of its interests and ran contrary to the proposals suggested by the UN. First, it was agreed that resolution of all disagreements within the SNC should occur through its internal conflict resolution mechanism rather than by simply complying with the decisions of UNTAC. Second, the SNC should assume greater legitimacy than a nominal representative of Cambodian sovereignty and should play an increased role in the peace process. In addition, each faction's military capacity should be reduced by 70 per cent rather than undergoing complete dissolution (Final Communiqué of the Supreme National Council of Cambodia, 29 August 1991, U.N. document A/46/494 and S/23066, 24 September 1991; PCC Co-Chairs report, A/46/418 and S/23011, 4 September 1991). While the first two decisions provided the PRK with grounds to intervene and refuse to accept UNTAC's implementation policies, the last decision enabled the PRK to possess a military capability, which it considered essential in order to defend itself against possible attacks by the Khmer Rouge. In short, the PRK was able to maintain its superior status in terms of administrative and military organisation during the transitional period.

However, the decisions would make realisation of the UN P-5's ideas very difficult, if not impossible. First, establishing a neutral political environment for the election by eliminating the existing political powers would be difficult because the UN had consented to the retention of the PRK's administration in its Framework Document of August 1990, and the PRK could exploit its position as the *de facto* government by drawing on the relatively autonomous power of the SNC. Second, although the PRK's preservation of 30 per cent of its military forces was crucially important to the pursuit of its interests, this decision made UNTAC's verification of the demilitarisation process very difficult. Thus, the Cambodian national factions were able to keep military forces in reserve in order to resist UNTAC's implementation with force if necessary.

Nevertheless, the US and other international interveners did not play an active role. Rather, they left the decisions on the detailed issues of the proposal to the factions themselves rather than making sustained efforts to develop a blueprint for the transitional authority (Brown and Zasloff 1998). For instance, although the US had chances to raise its concerns about the Pattaya agreements at the P-5 session on the last day of the Pattaya meeting, at a final SNC meeting convened by the P-5 in late September, and at the meeting between President Bush and Sihanouk in September, it failed to do so (Solomon 2000).

To summarise, the reduced enthusiasm of the US and other external third parties allowed the PRK to renegotiate and modify the pre-agreed provisions in the second phase of the negotiation. As the interveners simply adopted these changed ideas without considering their outcomes at the Paris Conference on Cambodia, the final peace agreements became a poorly coordinated mixture of Western ideas of peace and the Cambodian national factions' determination to resist the ideas.

Phase III (October 1991–June 1993)

After the signing of Paris Peace Agreements, the efforts of the Cambodian national factions to challenge the UN's proposal became more evident. During this period, external actors did not pay much attention to the Cambodian peace processes, assuming that the negotiation process had ended and the remaining issues were solely about 'implementation' of the agreed processes. However, the Cambodian national factions continued to try to renegotiate or redefine the details of the agreement in order to achieve their fundamental goals (Heder 1999).

As for the PRK's efforts, Hun Sen first tried to justify and expand the PRK's power in the SNC through an alliance with FUNCINPEC (especially, Prince Sihanouk). Consulting closely in a power-sharing arrangement, Sihanouk and Hun Sen collaborated to exclude the Khmer Rouge from playing a part in the implementation of the PPAs. While Sihanouk turned his back against the Khmer Rouge and called for an international tribunal on the rule of the Khmer Rouge and its atrocities, Hun Sen allowed (if not organised) a violent attack by Cambodian mobs on the Khmer Rouge representatives to take place in the same month (Gottesman 2004: 345).

Second, after gaining a firm powerbase in the SNC, Hun Sen made efforts to reduce UNTAC's authority and to secure real administrative power for the transitional government. The PRK's efforts to hamper the effectiveness of UNTAC activities included ignoring orders from UNTAC, conducting attacks on UNTAC contingents and refusing to provide necessary facilities to the authority (Brown and Zasloff 1998; Mu Sochua 2009, author's interview).

Third, the PRK tried to renegotiate the popular vote principle agreed upon at the Paris Peace Agreements. As the political violence between the PRK and the Khmer Rouge became serious enough for international interveners to anticipate a return to civil war, international actors, including China and France, expressed the need to seek an alternative approach to forming a new government. Based on these prominent international actors' concerns, in January 1993, the SNC decided to 'reconsider the peace agreement' and to establish a government of national reconciliation (Lizée 1999). Although the SNC's proposition failed to materialise because of strong opposition from the US, which insisted that any future government should reflect the people's democratic will, the PRK did not abandon its desire to secure its prominence (Brown and Zasloff 1998).

In the same period, the Khmer Rouge realised that its expectations of the interim political authority, the UN's roles, its popular support, and the external aid from China were not going to be met. First, it was clear that, in his collaboration with Hun Sen, Sihanouk would not advocate the Khmer Rouge's interests in the SNC. Second, the arrival of the external controlling body – UNTAC – was delayed for more than six months, allowing the PRK to manipulate power politics at central and local levels. Moreover, once it arrived, the Khmer Rouge felt that UNTAC simply demanded the Khmer Rouge's full collaboration with the PPAs without serious consideration of the Khmer Rouge's security concerns in the post-demilitarisation period (Peou 1997; Heder 1999). Third, the Khmer Rouge realised its assumption of high popularity was mere self-delusion and that attempts to rally popular support by invoking the image of Pol Pot or Khieu Samphan were counterproductive (Heder 1999). Finally, the Khmer Rouge had to abandon its hope of reclaiming Chinese support by agreeing to China's demand to remain in the peace process. After that, the bilateral communication with China stopped, and the termination of the aid was reconfirmed in early 1992. Deeply disappointed and betrayed by these developments, in June 1992 the Khmer Rouge decided to withdraw from the peace process and continue its 'revolutionary movement' (Heder 1999; Lee 2013).

Hence, the first general election was conducted without the Khmer Rouge in May 1993. Despite all its machinations, the PRK failed to secure victory; the Cambodian People's Party (the political wing of the PRK) gained 38 per cent of the votes and FUNCINPEC 45 per cent (Solomon 2000). When the election outcome was released, Cambodian politics went into another round of negotiations because Hun Sen refused to accept the result and threatened to resume military operations. Eventually, Hun Sen and Prince Ranariddh (a son of Sihanouk and the leader of FUNCINPEC) assumed co-premiership and the 50:50 power-sharing between them was agreed. Therefore, although the election was supposed to reflect the democratic will of Cambodians, the government was actually formed in accordance with the factional leaders' objective of establishing a government of national reconciliation.

During this period, external interveners, with the exception of the UN, did not play significant roles in the implementation of the Cambodian peace process. The international interveners regarded the Paris Peace Agreements as having concluded the negotiations and wanted to declare peace and withdraw from involvement in the Cambodian issue as soon as possible (Lizée 1999; Lee 2013). Rather than devising and employing additional strategies to persuade or coerce the Cambodian national factions to implement the peace agreements, the interveners paid most attention to technical issues related to the dispatch of UNTAC, which included mobilisation of resources, recruitment of staff and military forces, and logistics. Hence, when the national factions 'violated' the agreement and changed the conditions related to the election, international actors did nothing more than simply call for 'keeping the internationally consented agreement' or accepting the changed situation as a reality.

Lessons to be learned from the case study

The Paris Peace Agreement was a hybrid of the UN P-5's proposal and the national factions' modifications, comprising a simple mixture of the ideas that had been moulded by the actors' differing perceptions rather than a coordinated merge between them. In addition, UNTAC's mandate, which was one of the first and largest of its kind in UN history, achieved only partial success. Although the UN seemed to achieve most of the immediate mandates, more fundamental objectives lying behind these mandates were compromised or challenged by the Cambodian actors' resistance. In particular, the PRK – the *de facto* government – managed to redirect the peace negotiation to maintain its supremacy in the post-war political sphere.

In terms of supervising the national election and overseeing the transitional period, UNTAC succeeded in enabling 90 per cent of registered voters to exercise their franchise and in encouraging the Cambodian politicians to establish a new assembly and government. However, the UN's more ambitious vision of establishing and maintaining a neutral political environment for the free and fair election of a new government based on a popular democratic mandate could not be realised. In other words, through its incessant efforts to overcome the obstacles posed by the UN's peace proposal, the PRK finally achieved its goal, gaining a prominent position in the new government.

Although the agreements generally heeded the P-5's call for UNTAC's central role in administrative issues, the SNC became a nationalist authority that would not permit the foreign power to become the dominant force in Cambodia. In fact, the power of the SNC expanded beyond the level that the UN had envisioned in its original proposal, which had limited the role of the SNC to mere 'consultation' (Lizée 1999: 92).

In addition, the UN P-5's decision to entrust administration to the PRK structure during the transitional period was made with the expectation of utilising the structure for UNTAC's work. However, once the SNC was allowed to play a relatively independent role, and since the PRK had influence over the majority of seats in the SNC, the UN's expectation turned out to be naïve (Brown 1992; Brown and Zasloff 1998). From then, while the institutional/procedural democracy in the country seemed to be constantly developing, Hun Sen's political dominance became more obvious as time went by (Morgenbesser 2017). In 1997, Hun Sen overturned the co-premiership through a violent coup and became the sole prime minister. Since then, he has managed to undermine the international donor groups' demands for 'democratic governance' by using various strategies such as flat rejection, smoke and mirror techniques, partial acceptance, and superficial implementation.

In this sense, the third-party mediators achieved a partial success in convincing the Cambodian party to abide by the external vision for complete demilitarisation, politically neutral interim authority, and a free and fair election for new leadership. Moreover, the tension between the international donors' demand for democratisation and Hun Sen government's power consolidation over the past decades (starting with the initiation of the peace process in 1989) continued in the following political process for peacebuilding and development.

One outstanding factor behind this outcome was the limited communications between the third-party mediators and the Cambodian military factions. When the peace process was initiated, no external mediators or advocates had maintained close and multiple channels for communication with the Cambodian factions. Even China, which had played a key role in the civil war as the biggest supporter of the Khmer Rouge, did not maintain regular communication meetings.

Hence, many mediating actors, including the US and China, relied on coercive mediations without having proper chances to develop mutual understanding with their Cambodian counterparts. Under such circumstances, the coercive methods that seemed to work from a short-term perspective eventually failed to direct the Cambodian factions to pursue the mediators' goals. The behavioural pattern of the PRK in the peace negotiation presents a good example. When the incentives and pressures from external interveners were strong, the PRK seemed to accept the suggested proposal. However, when it saw a possibility to pursue its objectives in the third phase of the negotiation, the faction tried to change the UN proposal by excluding external actors from the national factions' negotiation processes, by convincing other national leaders, and by using the power of regional states, including China and Vietnam. As a result, the peace agreement became a confused mix of incompatible ideas based on Western or Cambodian perceptions of violence, peace, and negotiation.

Moreover, during the implementation period, the PRK's attempts to secure its own interests became more direct and obvious during the implementation phase. Although the interveners considered the negotiations concluded by the peace agreements, the Cambodian national factions wanted to continue their negotiation. Eventually, although UNTAC succeeded in conducting a nationwide election, the shape of the Cambodian central power was decided mainly by the national factions' negotiation. In short, a coercive intervention may enforce a military faction to remain in the negotiation, but it cannot make that faction agree with the proposals.

In the decision-making process, a lack of communication prevented the conveyance of accurate messages between national factions and third parties. Hence, key negotiating parties were subject to 'bounded awareness' based on their ethnocentric cultural values and perceptual limitations (Chugh and Bazerman 2006). In the above case study, China's ineffective mediation on behalf of the Khmer Rouge from August 1990 was discussed as an example of this. Although China had formal and informal communication routes with the Khmer Rouge leadership, its continued economic and military aid, regardless of its revised diplomatic stance, led the Cambodian faction to believe that China would not withdraw its advocacy. Moreover, China failed to clearly express to the Khmer Rouge the fundamental nature of its policy changes in 1991. Hence, when there was finally a dramatic reduction in Chinese material assistance (if not a complete withdrawal of aid) in 1992, the Khmer Rouge regarded this change as an unexpected betrayal and felt that it had lost its external ally. This misunderstanding was an important factor in convincing the Khmer Rouge to return to military action.

All in all, this chapter revisits the previous research on third-party mediation, which tended to pay primary attention to how to improve the effectiveness of third-party intervention. Hence, it was unavoidable that these earlier studies should underplay the role of national factions, under the assumption that the latter behave as reactive actors. However, in Cambodia at least, it was revealed that the procedures and the outcomes of peace negotiations are the result of the mutual influence between the two sides, and it was ultimately the national factions that finally decided the outcomes of the peace negotiations. No external interveners succeeded in compelling the national factions to accept proposals that the domestic actors considered critically harmful to their long-term goals. Hence, further studies need to be conducted to understand the dynamics of the interplay between mediators and national factions, as well as the correlation between the dynamics, procedures, and outcomes of the peace process.

Notes

1 Although the group's official name is the Party of Democratic Kampuchea, this chapter uses the Khmer Rouge (meaning Red Khmer in French) as it is a widely utilised term to denote this faction in both Cambodia and the West.
2 The government changed its official name to the State of Cambodia in 1989. To pursue consistency with terminology, this chapter will use the PRK.
3 It remains a matter of dispute whether China stopped its military aid completely in 1990. However, it appears to be the case that the amount of military aid post-1990, if any, was significantly less than previously (Chhin Kim Thong and a former Khmer Rouge commander who requested anonymity 2009, author's interview).

References, further reading, and links to key primary documents

Ashley, David. 1998. "Between War and Peace: Cambodia 1991–1998." *Accord* 5: 20–30.

Bilveer, S. 1985. "Vietnam's War Against the Khmer Rouge." *Asian Defence Journal* 5: 28–36.

Brown, Frederick Z. 1992. "Cambodia 1991: An Uncertain Peace." *Asian Survey* 32 (1): 88–96.

Brown, Macalister, and Joseph Zasloff. 1998. *Cambodia Confounds the Peacemakers, 1979–1998*. Ithaca, NY: Cornell University Press.

Chandler, David. 1998. "Cambodia's Historical Legacy." *Conciliation Resources*. www.c-r.org/our-work/accord/cambodia/historical-legacy.php.

Chugh, Dolly, and Max H. Bazerman. 2006. "Bounded Awareness: Focusing Failures in Negotiation." In Leigh L. Thompson (Ed.), *Negotiation Theory and Research*, 7–26. Frontiers of Social Psychology. New York: Psychology Press.

Collier, Paul, and Nicholas Sambanis. (Eds.). 2005. *Understanding Civil War: Evidence and Analysis*. Washington, DC: The World Bank.

Conciliation Resources. 1998. *Safeguarding Peace: Cambodia's Constitutional Challenge*. Accord 5. London: Conciliation Resources.

Corfield, Justin. 1991. "A History of the Cambodian Non-Communist Resistance 1975–1983." Working Paper, 72. Clayton: Centre of Southeast Asian Studies, Monash University.

Doyle, W. Michael. 1995. *UN Peacekeeping in Cambodia: UNTAC's Civil Mandate*. Boulder and London: Lynne Rienner Publishers.

Doyle, Michael W., Ian Johnstone, and Robert C. Orr. (Ed.). 1997. *Keeping the Peace: Multidimensional UN Operations in Cambodia and El Salvador*. Cambridge: Cambridge University Press.

Gottesman, Evan. 2004. *Cambodia after the Khmer Rouge: Inside the Politics of Nation Building*. New Haven: Yale University Press.

Haas, Michael. 1991. *Genocide by Proxy: Cambodian Pawn on a Superpower Chessboard*. New York: Praeger Publisher.

Heder, Stephen. 1999. "Pol Pot at Bay: People's War and the Breakdown of the 1991 Paris Agreements." PhD diss., School of Oriental and African Studies, University of London.

Human Rights Watch (HRW). 2017. "World Report 2017 – Cambodia: Events of 2016." www.hrw.org/world-report/2017/country-chapters/cambodia.

Jones, Lee. 2007. "ASEAN Intervention in Cambodia: From Cold War to Conditionality." *The Pacific Review* 20 (4): 523–550.

Kaufinann, Chaim. 1996. "Possible and Impossible Solutions to Ethnic Conflicts." *International Security* 20 (4): 136–175.

Kiernan, Ben. 1992. "Behind the Peace Agreement in Cambodia." *Viet Nam Generation Journal & Newsletter* 3 (4).

Lee, SungYong. 2013. "Lost in Translation: The Problem of Perceptual Limitations in Civil War Peace Negotiation." *International Interactions: Empirical and Theoretical Research in International Relations* 39 (2): 144–166.

Lilja, Mona. 2008. *Power, Resistance and Women Politicians in Cambodia.* Copenhagen: NIAS Press.

Lizée, P. Pierre. 1999. *Peace, Power and Resistance in Cambodia.* Houndmills: Palgrave Macmillan.

Mayall, James. (Ed.). 1996. *New Interventionism 1991–1994.* Cambridge: Cambridge University Press.

Morgenbesser, Lee. 2017. "The Failure of Democratisation by Elections in Cambodia." *Contemporary Politics* 23 (2): 135–155.

Osborne, Milton. 1994. *Sihanouk: Prince of Light Prince of Darkness.* St Leonards, Australia: Allen & Unwin.

Peou, Sorpong. 1997. *Conflict Neutralization in the Cambodia War: From Battlefield to Ballot-Box.* Oxford: Oxford University Press.

Regan, M. Patrick. 2000. *Civil War and Foreign Powers.* Ann Arbor: The University of Michigan Press.

Richardson, Sophie. 2009. *China, Cambodia, and the Five Principles of Peaceful Coexistence.* New York: Colombia University Press.

Richmond, Oliver, and Jason Franks. 2009. *Liberal Peace Transitions.* Edinburgh: Edinburgh University Press.

Ross, S. Robert. 1991. "China and the Cambodian Peace Process: The Value of Coercive Diplomacy." *Asian Survey* 31 (12): 1170–1171.

Sihanouk, Norodom. 2005. *Shadow Over Angkor.* Phnom Penh: Monument Books.

Slocomb, Margaret. 2004. *The People's Republic of Kampuchea: The Revolution After Pol Pot.* Seattle: University of Washington Press.

Solomon, H. Richard. 2000. *Exiting Indochina: U.S. Leadership of the Cambodia Settlement & Normalization with Vietnam.* Washington, DC: United States Institute of Peace.

Turner, C. Jack. 2004. "The Great Powers and Local Factors in Internal Conflict: The Dynamics of Conflict Termination in Cambodia, 1979–1991." PhD diss., Oxford University.

Um, Khatharya. 1990. "Cambodia in 1989: Still Talking But No Settlement." *Asian Survey* 30 (1): 96–104.

Walter, F. Barbara. 2002. *Committing to Peace: The Successful Settlement of Civil Wars.* Princeton, NJ and Oxford: Princeton University Press.

6

COLOMBIA

Jenny Pearce

Introduction

Colombia is known for the protracted length of its armed conflict, often described as the longest in the Western Hemisphere. Its origins are usually traced to 1964, the year that the ELN (Army of National Liberation, *Ejército de Liberación Nacional*, founded in 1962) set up its first guerrilla camp and when a military offensive, known as *Operation Marquetalia*, was launched against peasant self-defence groups and so-called independent republics. These peasants headed to the lowland jungles and adopted the name FARC (Revolutionary Armed Forces of Colombia, *Fuerzas Armadas Revolucionarias de Colombia*). In 1982, at their seventh conference, they added EP, or *Ejército del Pueblo*, People's Army, to their name. Other guerrilla groups emerged over the next decade and demobilised in the early 1990s, including a group within the ELN. The ELN and the FARC remained the surviving insurgencies, with the FARC by far the strongest. It was the FARC who participated in peace negotiations which began in Havana in December 2012, while negotiations with the ELN were announced in October 2016 and began in February 2017.[1] The successful conclusion of the Peace Accord with the FARC, announced in August 2016, was the culmination of an arduous process of negotiation, whose outcome was never certain. Since the signing of the Accord, the fragility of the transition from making to building peace stands out. Weak state implementation capacity, societal polarisation, and uncertain political will overshadow what is nevertheless an historic process for Colombia, full of learning for the world beyond it.

The 2016 Peace Accord is an extraordinary achievement, and even more so when set in the context of Colombia's long internal warfare and the legacy of the violence that it produces/reproduces. The polarised armed conflict between state and insurgents described above has taken place alongside multipolar violent antagonisms, involving many armed state and non-state actors. Non-state paramilitary groups, who have collaborated with the state military at times, emerged in the course of the 1980s and formed an organised group, the AUC (The United Self Defence Group of Colombia, *Autodefensas Unidas de Colombia*) in 1997. The AUC formally demobilised between 2003 and 2005. A good number of the 30,000 demobilised were also involved in drug trafficking, and many were drug traffickers rather than 'self-defence' combatants. In the wake of this demobilisation, new criminal bands, labelled initially BACRIM (Criminal Bands) and involved in illegal enterprises from drugs to illegal gold mining, proliferated (McDermott 2014). In 2016, these were renamed GAO (Organised Armed Groups) to reflect their growing national significance and structured character. For instance, the *Urabeños* or *Clan de Golfo*[2] began to take over the territorial spaces and trafficking corridors vacated by the FARC demobilisation. After suffering some defeats, they also sought a deal with the State in late 2017 (Ariel and Valencia 2017). The ELN and the dissidents of a former guerrilla group, the EPL, which laid down arms in the early 1990s, also contested territory vacated by the demobilised FARC in Catatumbo, leading to high levels of violence in that area in 2018. Meanwhile, some FARC dissidents frustrated by the slow implementation of the Peace Accords were drawn into criminal activities. At the same time, 80 murders of demobilised FARC combatants took place between November 2016 and August 2018 (El Tiempo, 2018).

Social, criminal, and political violences blur in Colombia, changing form and constantly generating new alliances and territorial disputes. Perea (2016) drew attention to the absence of the city and urban violence in the discussion of peace in Havana. Yet, alongside the ongoing disputes over territory and corridors in rural areas, there was a notable increase in urban violence by 2016 and talk of a new urban phenomenon, the ODIN (*Organizaciones Delincuenciales Integradas al Narcotrafico*, Delinquent Organisations Linked to Drug Trafficking). These chronic and mutating violences are set against a socio-economic backdrop of some of the highest indices of inequality in the world and a political system in which a 'modern'-looking state in the capital Bogota lacks institutional presence or authority in many parts of the country. This has preserved and been preserved by, a transactional form of politics between Bogota elites and regional political elites, into which drug trafficking and paramilitary groups have injected money and violence. Colombia's traditional and emergent elites have failed to invest in an equitable and accessible rule of law. They buy their private security. Without effective and trustworthy public security, some citizens end up relying on criminal actors for 'protection'. Inequality in experiences of insecurity is a serious problem facing peace in Colombia. Afro Colombian and indigenous communities, for instance, have borne a disproportionate impact of war and post-war violences (Amnesty International 2017).

Peace in Colombia remains a deeply contested ideal and purpose, reflecting multiple competing interests and experiences of victimhood and lack of trust amongst and between citizens and between citizens and the State. The Peace Accord signed on 26 September 2016 itself became a source of renewed polarisation in Colombia and was rejected, albeit narrowly and on a low turnout, in the referendum of 2 October 2016. A modified Accord was renegotiated, agreed on 24 November, and ratified in Congress on 30 November 2016 with opposition abstention. The question of legitimising the Peace Accord and enabling legislation to fast track through Congress overshadowed the next months, while the 2018 election created another moment of polarisation in the country. That election was won by the candidate from the right, Ivan Duque, supported by former President Uribe, in which he made clear his intention of addressing perceived 'unfairnesses' in the Peace Accord and the transitional justice mechanisms for the FARC. The election demonstrated that popular support for peace had not been won. A dark shadow hung over the future of the Peace Accord in 2018. On the other hand, the 2018 election was historic for its low level of violence and the 8 million votes cast for Gustavo Petro, the left candidate and former M19 guerrilla, who came second to Duque in the final run-off.

The Colombian peace process is thus a complex story of creative and historic efforts to make peace and construct a turning point in the national narrative. It demonstrates how much a Peace Accord is a necessary but insufficient step toward building peace. It also confirms the proposition that violence, not war or conflict, must be seen as the opposite of peace in order to understand how a Peace Accord can only open the possibility for building the conditions to live without violence (Pearce 2016). The first part of the chapter will explore the roots of Colombia's protracted armed conflict before analysing the peace negotiations and journey towards the Accord. Finally, it will highlight some of the challenges that still overshadow the prospect of building these conditions for peace.

Conflict analysis

The tangled roots and ruptures of Colombia's armed conflict

Colombians often speak of *Colombia Profunda* or 'Deep Colombia' to distinguish areas distant from the urban centres and from socially and infrastructurally connected territorial spaces. Colombia's armed conflict first emerged in such spaces. However, the armed conflict has everything do with the struggles over what kind of *totality* Colombia could be, or what might connect all its people in this geographically as well as socially and politically fragmented country.

The idea of the Colombian nation–state has never been resolved. The two traditional parties, Liberal and Conservatives, emerged in the nineteenth century before the concept of a Colombian 'nation' was articulated. The parties reflected distinct elite economic interests and attitudes towards church and state. They polarised the country before it could be brought together, each mobilising a cross-class sectarian following, which led to violent confrontations as well as electoral contests. Following the assassination in 1948 of Gaitan, a reforming Liberal party leader, a savage civil war known as *La Violencia* (the Violence) broke out, resulting in the deaths of around a quarter of a million people. In the wake of the *Violencia*, an elite pact was forged in 1958, culminating in an exclusionary political formation, in which the two traditional parties agreed to alternate political office for 16 years.

This cemented an elitist and clientelistic political order that never tackled the deep underlying structural problems of the country. Colombia's institutions were not weak as such, but they served only selective interests, both socially and territorially.

An electoral system functioned to preserve this order, giving an appearance of democracy, even though many Colombians ceased to participate electorally during the National Front years and beyond (Pearce 1990: 192). Colombia remained a country where power and wealth were heavily concentrated. However, the elites themselves were deeply divided, regionally and sectorally, as well as socially and politically. A dominant and at times unifying position was readiness to prevent democratic social, political, and economic change with all available means, including dark, tacit alliances with illegal groups. Tensions between reform and counter-reform tendencies in the 1980s had allowed a violent drugs economy to grow, bringing a third criminal force in on the side of the counter-reform. At the same time, the most militaristic wings of the insurgents began to see some involvement in the drugs economy and predation on the oil economy as a means for escalating the war rather than serious engagement with the reforming peace processes initiated first by President Belisario Betancur (1982–1986) and continued in a different form under President Barco (1986–1990).

In 1989, the reforming, anti-cartel presidential candidate of the Liberal Party, Luis Carlos Galan, favourite to win the 1990 elections, was assassinated. When the FARC formed the UP (Patriotic Union party) in 1985 to fight elections, their candidates and members were systematically targeted by the right, and around 3,000 were assassinated. The rise in political violence in the regions reflected elite contestations over reform or counter-reform, and the army's firm foot in the latter camp. Even initiatives aimed at political decentralisation, such as the direct election of mayors in 1988, perversely generated more opportunities for corruption and violence involving regional elites and armed actors. In turn, strengthening the arguments of the more militaristic wings of the insurgents.

Another important reforming moment was the 1990–1991 peace process completed under President Cesar Gaviria (1990–94), in which 3,726 guerrillas gave up their weapons definitively (Nasi 2009:39). The international context at the end of the Cold War favoured a turn to peace. Critical to the process of demobilisation was the Constituent Assembly, which gave space and participation not only to former guerrillas but also to indigenous Colombians as well as recognition to the Afro Colombian population. The traditional elites underestimated the importance of the Constituent Assembly elections and did not mobilise their electoral machines, giving the Assembly a very progressive representation (Rampf and Chavarro 2014). Neither the FARC nor the ELN, who in 1987 had formed the CGSB (Simon Bolivar Guerrilla Coordination), participated, although subsequent reports showed that FARC had been strongly considering participating until their headquarters was bombed (Semana 2013).

Struggles for social and political change grew outside the electoral system, on the one hand through armed struggle and on the other through the rise of social protest movements. State violence was used systematically to contain both. The two traditional political parties gradually lost coherence, fragmenting and weakening during the 1990s. However, while party identities and affiliations declined, interesting new social expressions emerged, including large marches for peace (Garcia Duran 2006), a women's peace movement (founded in 1996 – *Ruta Pacifica*, Pacific Route), and the 1998 Permanent Assembly of Civil Society for Peace. The Citizens' Mandate for Peace led to ten million people voting in 1997 in a non-binding ballot for peace during municipal elections. However, some of these movements subsided once the peace discussions launched by President Pastrana that year were underway, with massive disillusionment when it was clear that the FARC (as well as the paramilitary right, often in collusion with the state army) were expanding their military activities while negotiations were continuing. The Santos government would later resist FARC calls for a ceasefire during the 2012 negotiations, or matching the FARC's unilateral ceasefires. It feared that violations would sap public support, as had bedevilled the Pastrana negotiations, when the FARC had been given a special ceasefire area in Caguan.

Public support for peace never recovered from the failed Pastrana peace talks, and this haunted Santos' efforts. Under President Uribe (2002–2010), a militaristic approach to the guerrilla insurgency prevailed, with the armed forces greatly strengthened and the guerrillas weakened. The United States, fearful not only of Colombia's drugs production in territories controlled by the FARC but also of the fact that the Colombian state was negotiating from a position of military and political weakness, pumped US $6 billion between 2000 and 2010 into Plan Colombia (Isacson 2013). This strengthened the Colombian state's military capacity and effectiveness and controversially targeted coca production, notably in areas of FARC support. Thus, state territorial presence in so-called ungoverned spaces and military power were prioritised over efforts to rethink state–society relationships and alternative economies for peasant coca producers.

The FARC remained rooted in the problematic of rural inequality even as popular support for them waned. The armed conflict, the forced displacement of peasants, and the seizure of their land by paramilitaries and drug traffickers had all led to what some call a violent counter agrarian reform in Colombia (Sánchez 2009). The World Bank's 2004 report on Land Policy in Colombia (World Bank 2004) documented extreme inequality, with land ownership concentrated in the hands of the few and overwhelmingly used for livestock grazing rather than the agriculture needed to support rural populations. It concluded that 'high levels of land inequality may be an important factor that contributes to a vicious cycle of low growth, violence and even greater inequality' (ibid.: 2). The commodity boom that followed the recession of the 1990s bolstered the Colombian economy. However, some sectors, such as African palm and oil production, were in the heartland of zones of armed conflict, including among the most impoverished Afro Colombian communities. The disproportional effects of violent displacement on that population led many to argue that certain business sectors were benefiting from land seized during the armed conflict. Richani talked about a 'war system' in Colombia (2002, 2013), within which a range of elite and other actors position and reposition themselves according to the economic opportunities and limitations offered by armed violence. This included ranching, agriculture, mining, and industrial elites as well as insurgent, military, and paramilitary armed actors. Ranching elites and other regional elites, in particular, collaborated with paramilitary groups, a process exposed in 2006 by the investigation into the 'parapolitics' scandal, which resulted in the conviction of 55 members of Congress who had won seats through funding from drug-financed paramilitaries (Corporación Nuevo Arco Iris, 2007).

President Uribe, whose own father had been killed by the FARC, waged a passionately personal war against them. He preferred to forge a direct relationship with the electorate and declared a 'democratic security' policy while ignoring escalating state human rights violations. His strong personality resonated with many Colombians, particularly in his native Antioquia, who were prepared to ignore the human and social cost of security gains. Some argue, therefore, that Uribe's crusade sacrificed the country's institutional integrity and commitment to democratic processes (Palacios 2012: 201). A series of scandals and the sense of erosion of Colombian institutions led the more modernising urban industrial elites into withdrawing support they had initially given Uribe for his hard-line policies towards the FARC. Despite a 70 per cent popularity rating during 2009, Uribe did not win the backing of the Constitutional Court in 2010 for a referendum on a third term. In the meantime, Uribe had shifted the weight of the war from the paramilitary to the military and funded a tripling of the army's defence budget, while extending army and police presence. FARC kidnapping declined along with the murder rate. However, between 2004 and 2008, evidence began to accumulate of what became the 'False Positives' scandal: extra-judicial killings of civilians committed by the Colombian army but reported as combatants killed in action, thus boosting the statistics of army successes against the guerrillas and allowing soldiers to claim salary benefits.

Historically, the peace process of 2012–2016 could be analysed as an attempt to find ways of resolving the question of state and nation building in Colombia without violent armed conflict, escalating militarisation, and democratic decay. Although Santos had been Uribe's Minister of Defence, he infuriated Uribe by changing course dramatically on becoming president. While Santos strictly limited the peace agenda to the ending of the armed conflict, he nevertheless opened up the possibility for a much wider debate on defining the 'nation', including the participation of the left/communist voice of the FARC as political actors. The military capacity of the FARC had clearly been weakened under President Uribe. By 2012, the FARC was reduced to some 9,000 combatants; thousands had taken advantage of government demobilisation programmes and deserted over the decade. Its territorial reach was down from 377 out of 1,100 municipalities in 2002 to 142 in 2010 (International Crisis Group 2012). The FARC's founder commander, Manuel Marulanda, died of a heart attack in 2009, while Mono Jojoy, the FARC's military leader, was killed in 2010; Alfonso Cano, who took over from Marulanda, was killed in 2011. He was quickly replaced by Rodrigo Londono Echeverri (Timochenko). The new FARC leader would face the newly elected President, Juan Manuel Santos (2010–2018). Why did they agree to negotiate?

The conflict resolution process

From perceived stalemate to persuading the public: peace in a polarised landscape

Ripeness v. readiness

The new president and former Minister of Defence had electoral legitimacy, majorities in Congress, and authority and command over the armed forces, a sound political basis for entering peace negotiations. Direct contacts between the government and the FARC began on January 2011 (Santos Calderon 2014: 23). Crucially, the peace process survived the killing of Alfonso Cano by the army in November of that year, leading President Santos' brother Enrique, involved with the pre-negotiation, to later wonder whether the FARC's decision to continue with the process after Cano's death was due to weakness or rather a deeper commitment to peace than had been assumed (ibid.: 24).

The government prepared the ground for peace with the Victims and Land Restitution Law 1448, which passed through Congress in June 2011 and pledged the government to pay reparations to over four million victims of the armed conflict and return millions of hectares back to peasants forced off the land. This signalled the government's recognition of land as at the heart of the armed conflict. The second preparatory step was the promotion of the Legal Framework for Peace, which passed as a temporary reform in June 2012 and would need to be activated by the Constitutional Court. This was to provide the basis for addressing one of the thorniest problems of the peace process, which is how to deal with crimes against humanity and who should be brought to justice. From 24 February 2012, for six months and in absolute secrecy, the government and the FARC sat down in ten formal sessions until announcing on 26 August that a General Agreement for talks on the ending of the armed conflict in Colombia had been agreed (Santos Calderon 2014: 18).

One of the debates in the field of peace settlements is over the Ripeness Theory, first elaborated by William Zartman in the 1980s (Zartman 1989, updated, 2000, 2013), and the Readiness Theory of Dean Pruitt (2005). Zartman argues that ripeness is a necessary - though not sufficient - condition for the initiation of negotiations, thus redirecting the focus from substantive issues in the conflict to issues of timing. The 'ripe' moment is when parties perceive a 'mutually hurting stalemate' in which neither side can win but continuing the conflict will be harmful to each in different ways. At the same time, a mutually perceived way out presents itself through negotiation. Readiness Theory builds on ripeness theory but unpacks the motives and perceptions of ripeness on each side separately, to grasp the extent to which an individual disputant is interested in negotiation (Pruitt 2005: 6). It suggests that two psychological variables are at play: the motivation to end conflict and optimism about the success of negotiation or simply 'optimism' (ibid.: 7).

The decision to negotiate of the FARC and the government is explained for many by the military weakening of the FARC, on the one hand, and the increasing economic and social costs of the war to the State, on the other. The former was indeed a reality, as discussed. However, while the FARC negotiated from a position of much greater weakness than in 1997, it was by no means from a position of defeat, neither subjective nor objective. They still had sufficient troops, as well as a large back-up militia, to inflict damage. The months leading up to the initiation of peace talks were marked by increased attacks on oil, coal, and gas infrastructure (Rettberg 2015: 7). By 2012, these sectors accounted for 50 per cent of total foreign direct investment in Colombia (ibid.). The FARC had plenty of funds to continue waging war. Much less could they contemplate seizing control of large tracts of the country as they had done in their decade of expansion of the 1990s. From the government's perspective, the costs of the war had escalated hugely, with military spending doubling in real terms between 2000 and 2010, reaching more than 3 per cent of GDP (International Crisis Group 2012: 15). The costs of war and the global image of the country did not convince all sectors of the elite that peace was essential, however.

Ripeness Theory works to explain some of the most visible calculations of the parties. However, Readiness Theory asks us to reflect on less visible variables and to consider the complexities of the wider context. For instance, those who had come to see the FARC as merely a criminalised armed actor with no politics could not appreciate that the FARC may have made a political calculation, that this was a unique moment to end the war and engage in electoral politics. Enrique Santos concluded from his intense pre-negotiation conversations with the FARC, that they no longer considered armed struggle the main nor most realistic means to achieve their political goals (Santos Calderon 2014: 71). At the very least, the negotiations would give them a platform from which to communicate these goals. Indeed, the FARC took the initiative after the talks were first announced in Oslo in October 2012, to reach out publicly in an unprecedented way, with interviews and press conferences, often appearing unaware of their deep unpopularity but intent on exposing how the extractive development model impacted on poverty and inequality, for example. The government found itself taken by surprise (ibid.: 28). It had a very restricted agenda for the peace process. Its main goal was to end the armed conflict and not to enter into details of its causes or the economic model or the status of the armed forces. It also wanted a quick process, one that would not drag on and make itself vulnerable to all kinds of risks. The FARC chief negotiator, Ivan Marquez, on the other hand, made clear in his Oslo remarks that he opposed what he called a 'paz expres' (express peace).

It did not turn out to be an express peace; many tense moments threatened and delayed it. The kidnapping by the FARC of Brig. General Alzate Mora in Choco in November 2014, for instance, led to the suspension of the talks. However, one notable outcome of this event was the quick response of the FARC to secure his release and also to produce a video of the process. The FARC had begun to learn the meaning of communication, with an eye to winning public opinion – not just informing it of their positions. The Readiness Theory, with its emphasis on optimism, thus tends to be confirmed. The FARC embraced the process while not relinquishing its foundational identity and beliefs. As time wore on and trust grew, the leadership showed greater capacity to act with political maturity. However, incidents in 2015, such as the killing of 11 army soldiers in April by a FARC unit, generated more public scepticism towards the talks.

The optimism lens could, nevertheless, be used to analyse the parallel if not convergent aspirations of the Santos government and the FARC in the historical moment in which the talks began. It could be argued that former President Uribe needed the FARC as the 'enemy' that would give identity to his own political project, just as Uribe was the 'enemy' that the FARC could use to justify its militarism and abuses. This changed with President Santos. Santos needed peace in order to make possible his project of state and economic modernisation. His appeal was to that sector of the elites, whose economic interests lay in presenting an open economy and modernising image to the world. Santos has expressed his admiration for Anthony Giddens' 'Third Way'[3] and of the Blair government, whose chief negotiator on Northern Ireland was one of his key advisors. Santos situated the peace process, as distinct from Uribe's approach, in the context of a State willing to criticise its own record and to correct historic injustices (Santos Calderon 2014: 47). Santos gave the FARC the opportunity to recognise they had a common 'enemy' in the right in Colombia, and in particular in agrarian and ranching elites. The argument was strengthened by the way Santos anticipated the talks by reaching out early in his presidency to Chavista Venezuela and Correa's Ecuador to build a new relationship with the left governments of Latin America. The support of Chavez, as well as Cuba, was extremely important to the FARC's trust in the process. The existence of mostly left governments in the region at the time also fostered optimism in the possibility of politics and that the era of armed struggle was truly over. Venezuela and Chile were accompanying countries for the whole process, while Cuba and Norway were appointed 'guarantor countries'.

Thus, Readiness Theory adds dimensions which give deeper insights into the origins of the peace process. What stands out in the Colombian case, also, is that the negotiations seemed to have generated new dynamics and capacities to solve issues as they evolved, despite many difficult moments, including a presidential election in 2014 which was considered by some a kind of plebiscite on the peace talks. Only three of the five agreed topics had reached an agreement by then. Santos' victory in the second round of 51 per cent against the Uribista candidate Oscar Ivan Zuluaga's 45 per cent gave another boost to the process. The grudging support of the left for Santos showed how an implicit progressive alliance had somehow emerged. However, support for Uribismo gave his party, the *Centro Democratico*, 19 seats in Congress, giving them a solid oppositional bloc. The strength of the opposition to the peace process led by the former President, and his ongoing political appeal, would hover over the entire process.

The rocky road towards a peace accord

The Santos government might not have managed to push through a quick agreement, but it did manage to limit the agenda to five substantive issues – rural development, political participation, illicit crops, victims, and conflict termination, and a sixth issue of procedures for implementation of the final agreement. A rule was accepted by the parties that 'nothing is agreed until everything is agreed'.

Each party could appoint up to ten delegates, of which five were plenipotentiaries, with a back-up team of up to 20 more. The FARC delegation was made up of combatants led by the second in command, Ivan Marquez. Over time, the FARC rotated commanders who participated in the talks, ensuring that there was wider and deeper ownership of the process. The government's chief negotiator, Humberto de la Calle, and the peace commissioner, Sergio Jaramillo, proved exceptional negotiators, undoubtedly an important factor in navigating the problems ahead. The government astutely included representatives of the security forces round the table: retired army general Jorge Enrique Mora, and retired police general, Oscar Naranjo. The potential problems with the army were highlighted in February 2014, when it was revealed that a military intelligence unit had illegally monitored the private communications of government negotiators in Havana. Santos was swift to condemn and to act, and two generals, including the head of military intelligence, were dismissed and an investigation begun. The winning of support from the armed forces is one of the achievements of the process, despite a core of retired army generals who remained strongly in the Uribe camp. Business was also represented, and some business groups and foundations began to organise support for the process, arguing that business and the economy would thrive once alleviated from the costs of war. The receptivity to this message was uneven, however, and the attitude of elites from the different sectors remained cautious to ambivalent, on the one hand, and intransigently opposed among landowning elites in particular, on the other.

The absence of women among the delegates, apart from a Dutch-born female FARC combatant, was one of the noticeable weaknesses in the process at the beginning. One of the significant features of the peace process, however, was the gradual emergence of interactions with different civil society organisations and sectors and their impact on the perceptions of the negotiators, including around gender, sexual violence, and sexuality in war. The government's aim for a quick negotiation did not give much space to the participation of civil society organisations, although some gestures in that direction were made with the opening of a web page for citizens to feed in their suggestions. However, the United Nations Development Programme (UNDP) and the National University were commissioned to convene public forums in different parts of the country. The Peace Commissions of the House and Senate also brought people together in roundtables in a number of regions. Other non-governmental organisations and social movements began to organise events and debates. In October 2014 a National Peace Council was created by law. Some public discussion around each of the topics at the table gradually took place.

Colombia's prior history of social activist organising, mostly under threat and under fire, was of great significance to the capacity to insert voices and experiences outside those of the parties at the negotiating table. Women's and victims' organisations contributed significantly to transforming mindsets among the negotiators. Ruta Pacifica, for instance, produced its own truth and memory report from the perspective of womens' experiences in the armed conflict (Ruta Pacifica, 2014). A key moment for the women's organisations was when 450 from all cultural backgrounds and 30 regions of the country came together in October 2013 for the National Summit of Women and Peace (Bouvier 2016). This landmark moment generated an impetus towards tackling the gender impacts of the war and sexual violence in particular. It opened up discussion on violence against LGBTI (lesbian, gay, bisexual, transsexual, and/or intersex) persons also, thus challenging the hegemonic masculinities and traditional assumptions about gender and sexuality that dominate Colombian social life. Evidence of the effectiveness of these developments lay in the strong backlash from evangelical churches and conservative Catholics at the time of the referendum in October 2016, when they condemned what the negotiators called a 'gender focus' of the peace agreement as 'gender ideology'. However, these reactions only highlighted the potential of the peace process to open up debates about the kind of society Colombia is and could be.

The government appointed two women in November 2013 as plenipotentiary negotiators, and the FARC gradually extended the participation of women in their team until it reached 40 per cent by February 2015, including commanders, thus reflecting the actual composition of the armed movement (ibid.: 20). In addition, women gained 25 per cent representation on the Technical Subcommission on Ending the Conflict, set up in 2014 to discuss implementation challenges of a bilateral ceasefire, laying down of weapons, security guarantees, etc. The gender subcommission set up in September 2014 contributed a gendered perspective on peacebuilding itself and was another significant development. Three delegations went to Havana between December 2014 and March 2015, with 18 representatives of women's and LGBTI organisations who gave perspectives on the war from their experiences that appear to have had a deep effect on negotiators.

Parallel to these efforts were the mobilisations of victims' groups on all sides. Under President Uribe, in 2005, a National Centre for Historical Memory had been set up, led by one of Colombia's most distinguished historians, Gonzalo Sanchez. The Centre has produced an impressive range of detailed research and publications on all aspects of the armed conflict. In 2013, they presented their report, *Basta Ya!* (Enough Already!) on 50 years of armed violence. They calculated that 220,000 people died between 1958 (1958 to 1964 was the transition between bipartisan and insurgent violence) and 2012, of whom 18.5 per cent were combatants and 81.5 per cent were civilians (CNMH 2013: 32). The report also highlighted non-lethal violences. Its figures have since been updated further. The Office of the High Commissioner of Peace came to offer a detailed and accessible account through its dedicated web page, on the peace process and each Accord, overcoming a sense at the beginning that there was insufficient communication to wider society from

Havana. Placing the victims at the centre of the peace process became one of its key foundations. This involved hard questions for everyone at the negotiating table. The FARC had to deal with the truth that in the name of the revolution they sought, they had grievously abused the human rights of the people, while the State had to confront its own responsibilities in massive violations.

Statistics revealed a society deeply traumatised by violences of every kind: at least 6.7 million victims of displacement, at least 13,000 victims of sexual violence, at least 74,000 victims of attacks on populations, at least 11,000 victims of anti-personnel mines, at least 45,000 forced disappearances, at least 10,000 victims of torture, at least 30,000 victims of kidnappings, and at least 9,000 victims of forced land evictions (Oficina del Alto Comisionado de la Paz 2016). The government had begun the very difficult process of reparations for victims while the negotiations were underway, through the Unit for Reparations for Victims, created under the 2011 Law on Victims and Land Restitution. Progress was slow, however, and killings of those claiming their land still took place. Perhaps the most remarkable process was the emergent voices of the victims themselves. Victims of state violence were well organised; those of the FARC only began to organise in the course of the peace process. Over 3,000 victims participated in four regional forums, while between August and December 2014 five groups of 12 victims chosen by the UN to represent the diversity of victimhood travelled to Havana. Of these, 60 per cent were women, 8 per cent indigenous, 13 per cent Afro Colombian, and 8 per cent were from municipal, departmental, and national roundtables for victims (ibid.).

The shift in the FARC position around its victims is one of the most compelling indications of how peace talks can transform the mentalities of participants. In November 2015, FARC commander Pastor Alape travelled to Bojayá, where he took responsibility for the killings of 79 members of the community, who had sought shelter in the church and died from a FARC gas cylinder bomb. Ivan Marquez recognised the great pain caused by kidnappings (Semana 2016). On 10 September 2016, before leaving Havana, the FARC met with the families of the 11 deputies of the Valle who they kidnapped in 2002 and executed in 2007. They took complete responsibility for their actions and asked for forgiveness. They subsequently met with the victims of the massacre of 35 people in La Chinita, Uraba. When the peace deal was signed formally in Cartagena on 27 September 2016, Timochenko publicly asked for forgiveness for all the pain the FARC had caused victims of the conflict. President Santos acknowledged that the State had not done enough to avoid the tragedy of the UP members who were assassinated in the 1980s (Semana 2016). Both sides agreed to translate these statements into actions. For instance, the FARC agreed to return possessions of kidnapped victims, and the government agreed to protect and not stigmatise the new formation of the UP. These reciprocal steps showed a willingness to accept group and institutional responsibility on the part of the FARC and the State, rather than blame individual 'rotten apples' (ibid.).

For many, however, the FARC had been too slow in recognising these abuses and showing sincere remorse. Early in the peace process, FARC commander Jesus

Santrich had famously said 'perhaps, perhaps, perhaps' the FARC might recognise their victims (ibid.). Many victims themselves did accept the sincerity of the FARC's shift. Others, often those who had been impacted less directly by the armed conflict, did not. There were many who had been influenced less by the evidence of violence on all sides than by President Uribe's construction of the FARC as a `terrorist` group responsible for all the wrongs. He continued to circulate such messages through social media throughout the peace process.

The protracted character of the talks allowed for the changing of mindsets, as those round the table grappled with the multiple challenges of each item on the agenda. At the same time, it allowed for so-called spoilers to make maximum political capital out of every setback. These encouraged the perception of a distance between those at the negotiating table and the Colombian public. This distance was partly necessary to the process of conducting talks in a space cocooned from media and other interferences. However, the distance was widened by a sense that communication was sporadic and lacked a strong and appealing personality able to persuade and convince. Many depended on information from radio and television channels controlled by right-wing business interests. President Santos was a cerebral rather than passionate president and did not connect well with the electorate.

It is remarkable in the circumstances that progress was made. In December 2014, the FARC declared their fifth unilateral ceasefire since 2012 and their first indefinite one. Throughout 2015, international support for the peace process grew. The US appointed Bernard Aronson as a special envoy in February that year. The de-escalation of the armed conflict began. The government agreed to cease the bombing of FARC camps for a month in March. Despite critical moments of breakdown and re-escalation, which led to plummeting support for the peace process, negotiators pulled back from the brink. On 4 June 2015, a Commission for the Clarification of Truth, Coexistence, and Non-Repetition was created.

A major boost to the process came in the last months of 2015, when progress was made on the transitional justice question, the most difficult task facing the peace process. The FARC would never agree to a peace accord which meant their leaders would go to prison and were adamant on the issue of recognition of state crimes. On the other hand, the International Criminal Court was observing closely the Colombian peace process and its adherence to international criminal law; too many of the cases in which they had intervened had been in Africa, and they were looking for a case outside that region. Thirdly, state armed forces did not want punishment for their crimes to imply equivalence between them and the insurgents. In the end, with the help of international lawyers chosen by both parties, an agreement was made on transitional justice on 23 September 2015, which combined restorative justice with alternative sentences for both guerrillas and state armed actors who had committed crimes. It proposed a Special Jurisdiction for Peace, which would allow individuals accused of crimes to avoid prison if they cooperated with the justice system, and instead would have sentences focused on assisting victims and repairing damage. The final agreement on victims was agreed on

15 December 2015, creating the Comprehensive System of Truth, Justice, Reparation, and Non-Repetition.

The last of the issues facing Havana were those of the bilateral and definitive ceasefire and the monitoring and verification mechanisms. The latter included an international verification component made up of unarmed observers from the Community of Latin American and Caribbean States (CELAC). In an unusual vote in January 2016, the 15 Security Council member states unanimously agreed to endorse the UN's role. The FARC agreed to demobilise in 23 transitory rural settlement normalisation zones (ZVTN) and encampments and eight encampments/transitory normalisation points, in 30 municipalities in 15 departments of the country (a figure later adjusted to 25 municipalities).

The Colombian approach to justice and reconciliation is considered a creative innovation for war-torn countries by international observers. However, it was expected that Colombian society would embrace the advanced spirit of forgiveness and redemption that would satisfy the ICC and the most progressive international opinion on the balance between peace, truth, and justice. This did not take into account the deep scepticism of many Colombians towards the FARC's commitment to peace. The negotiators had imagined that the main problem now facing Colombia would be the building of peace. Already thought had been given to this. Sergio Jaramillo had put forward his idea of '*paz territorial*' or territorial peace (Jaramillio 2013) quite early on in the process. While not much flesh was put on the idea, it signalled an awareness of the tasks that would face Colombia after the ending of the armed conflict. The possibility that Colombians might reject the Peace Accord was not imagined.

The legitimisation of peace

The Peace Accord was finally announced on 24 August 2016. The form of legitimisation had been a source of contention in Havana. The FARC had eventually given up its demand for a Constituent Assembly and accepted the referendum (referred to as a plebiscite in the Spanish literature), which took place on 2 October 2016. The referendum rejected the Accord, with 50.2 per cent voting against it and 49.78 per cent in favour on a very low (37.4 per cent) turnout (Registraduria Nacional de Estado Civil 2016). The 'no' victory was very small, and over 60 per cent had failed to vote. The vote among the nearly 40 per cent revealed the polarisation of the Colombian landscape, with half the 32 departmental capitals voting 'no' and half 'yes'; Bogota voted 56.07 per cent yes, while the second city, Medellin, voted 62.9 per cent 'no' (El Tiempo 2016).

There is much controversy about whether a referendum was the way to secure legitimacy for the Peace Accord and, in particular, the short time to prepare for it. It allowed the Uribista right to run a campaign which its campaign manager, Juan Carlos Velez, subsequently admitted in an interview used lies and encouraged the electorate to vote '*berraca*' (El Espectador 2016), roughly meaning, out of their anger. Many Colombians were furious that the FARC leadership would not go to prison and that they would gain the right to participate in politics, including assigned seats for the first two years.

The government acted swiftly. Within 41 days, it had conducted extensive consultations with representatives of the 'no' vote, who proposed 500 changes to the Accord. This package was taken back to Havana, where the FARC ceded some ground. Penalties for those guilty of committing war crimes were tightened but still did not include prison. The Special Peace Jurisdiction had its scope reduced, with no foreign judges participating. The Accord would not become part of Colombia's constitution, which had been a guarantee for the FARC that any future government would comply with its commitments. The FARC had to reveal its assets, which would be used to pay for reparations of the conflict. The language on gender equity was tightened up to appease the social conservatives, though without changing its basic meaning. The revised Accord, alongside the original 297-page Accord, was uploaded onto the High Commissioner's web site (Oficina del Alto Comisionado de Paz 2016). This revised final Accord was signed and ratified in Congress, but the thorny question of its legitimisation and the fast track needed to get legislation passed to enable implementation remained.

From making to building peace

The referendum result seems to confirm a phrase of the great Colombian writer Garcia Marquez: 'I believe that we are acting, thinking, conceiving and trying to go on making not a real country, but one of paper' (Semana 1989, quoted in Pearce 1990: 11). The prolonged and hard-won negotiation was an extraordinary and creative achievement. It produced an exceptional document (as did the 1991 Constitution). However, it failed to connect sufficiently with the 'real' Colombia, with all its complexities and particularities of history, geography, and experiences of violence. Nevertheless, it created an historic opportunity for rethinking the country. Notably, many of the communities most directly impacted by the war voted in favour of the peace, a tribute to the work on reconciliation which emerged from Havana. The capacity to build a nation at peace with itself remained fragile, however. Violent criminality and the assassination of social activists and human rights defenders continued. The bilateral ceasefire had to be maintained, while FARC combatants remained in a state of uncertainty about the demobilisation process and their own security. When they began to demobilise in early 2017, their camps were not ready. Already, former President Uribe was suggesting that the new accord was bypassing the popular will, as he looked towards the 2018 electoral contest, a contest which his candidate won.

Making peace proved to be an uphill task among its main parties. However, support was bolstered by the international community, epitomised by the Nobel Peace prize awarded to President Santos shortly after the referendum. The rise of the urban middle class was key, with students mobilising on the streets after the referendum defeat for an '*Acuerdo Ya*' (Peace Accord Now). Making peace with the 'other' Colombia, the old order of Colombia, its landowning elites in particular, proved much more difficult. Some suggested that President Santos should have paid attention to preparing a peace with these other elites, a great 'national pact' (Duncan 2016). However, such a pact would have limited the effort to bring historic changes to the country around, for instance, the agrarian question, in turn enabling the state to focus on the criminality that still threatened peace. Even so, implementing the land restitution programme and alternative crop substitution for coca growers and other rural developmental initiatives remained too slow for the survival needs of many peasants. As coca production increased, so did US pressure for a return to fumigation, supported by President Duque.

The Colombian peace process reminds us of the enormous task of transforming socio-political orders without violence. It was recognised that by the end of the first year of the Peace Accord, some 3,000 lives had been saved, according to the Centre for Resources for Analysis of Conflicts (CERAC quoted in Semana 2018), and homicides were at their lowest in 40 years and kidnappings 94 per cent less than in 2000 (ibid.). However, the Observatory for Monitoring the Peace Accord (*Observatorio de Seguimiento al Acuerdo de Paz* OIAP) reported in January 2018 that only 18.3 per cent of the implementation norms of the Accord had so far been fulfilled (El Espectador 2018). The Reports of the Secretary General on the United States Verification Mission in Colombia in December 2017 outlined ongoing concerns about the uneven progress of the peace-related legislative agenda, the way the Constitutional Court had limited the scope of the Special Jurisdiction for Peace with respect to Third Parties (e.g. landowning elites), who are only required to voluntarily present themselves to it. It also expressed serious concern about security guarantees for ex-combatants and for communities in the areas most affected by the conflict (UN Verification Mission in Colombia 2017). Between the November 2016 signing of the Peace Accords and August 2018, 184 social leaders had been assassinated in Colombia, 21 following Ivan Duque's arrival to the presidency (Fundacion para la Paz y Reconciliation 2018). The July 2018 UN Verification Report highlighted that 'the fundamental goal of providing income-generating opportunities for 14,000 former combatants is far from being realised' (2018: 5). The Kroc Institute, charged with an important task of academic evaluation of the Peace Accord Implementation, concluded in its second report in August 2018 that although 39 per cent of the commitments in the Peace Accord had not been initiated, and 31 per cent minimally implemented, this was not so different from comparable comprehensive peace accords (Kroc Institute 2018: 7). However, it drew attention to the same areas emphasised by the UN: security and community protection, the slowness of long-term processes of political, social, and economic reincorporation, and important regulatory and institutional adjustments to guarantee citizen participation and the right to social protest (ibid.: 9). As evidence mounted that the FARC leadership was itself increasingly split between those who remained committed to building the peace and others who had lost faith in its sincerity, it was evident that uncertainty still overshadowed the long-term peace potentialities of the Colombian Peace Accord.

Lessons to be learned from the case study

The Colombian peace process was very open and flexible to learning from the world, with delegations invited to share experiences of armed conflict from many countries. The intelligent selection of key Latin American countries representing somewhat distinct political positions (e.g. Cuba and Venezuela on the one hand, Chile on the other) gave reassurance to the parties around the table, particularly the FARC. The peace process was also open, eventually, to the voices of those Colombians who have formed strong and active associations for human and civil rights. It adapted to the temporalities that made an express peace impossible, despite exposing the process to many risks from acts of war during the peace talks. The mutual learning in the Havana negotiating table on how to manage the risks grew through the process, despite many vulnerable moments. Such openness requires leadership and confidence, and President Santos deserves his Nobel Prize for giving that. However, Santos' form of astute intellectual leadership was not sufficient to cross social divides and communicate with those Colombians more influenced by the emotive leadership of former president Uribe.

The Colombian peace process is rightly recognised for many innovations in conducting peace accords (e.g. Herbolzheimer 2016), such as limiting the agenda to six points, distinguishing between conflict termination and transformation, placing the victims at the centre, including a gender focus, and the balance it sought between peace and justice. However, a peace negotiation cannot address in itself all the multiple dynamics that protracted armed conflict generate in a society. Entrenched interests around power and wealth resist change, while in the globalised economy since the 1990s in particular, illegal actors have created new sets of interests and ever greater capacity to buy and use the instruments of violence. This hovers over the Colombian peace building process.

Two years after the Accord was signed, there was progress but it was far behind expectations. The killing of social leaders, the slow implementation of the comprehensive rural reform agreement in the Accords, the ongoing importance of coca production and insufficient support for crop substitution, and the dynamism of the illegal economy all threatened the sustainability of the peace process. The global context had shifted, with a President in the United States with little interest in peace, and a new President in Colombia, who had been elected with the support of those opposed to it. Ex-combatants had been left frustrated by the slowness of projects to help them build new civic lives and livelihoods; increasing reports of desertions from the demobilisation zones emphasised the problem. The release of a tape by the US Drugs Enforcement Agency purporting to show one of the FARC leaders and negotiators, Jesus Santrich, continuing to deal drugs after the Accord was signed, led to Santrich's imprisonment in April 2018 and fed into the fears and prejudices of the FARC left and the political right. The FARC's efforts to become a political party (it had renamed itself the Common Alternative Revolutionary Force, controversially retaining the Spanish acronym of FARC), were weakened by the poor electoral showing in 2018 and tensions within the leadership. Nevertheless, it was making serious efforts to build its political organisation. President Ivan Duque did not dismantle the peace implementation process on coming to office, although nor did he progress it. The Special Jurisdiction for Peace (JEP in the Spanish acronym), in particular, faced threats to its role, struggling to ensure it took responsibility for the Santrich case and not the Public Prosecutor, known for opposition to the Peace Accord. Yet, the Truth Commission could begin its three year mandate on 28 November 2018, a clear indication that the Colombian peace process was still actively moving forward in the midst of the multiple obstacles. It was consciously aiming to connect to Colombia Profunda, rural and urban, and this remains perhaps the greatest challenge of all.

It was mostly the poorest residents of Colombia's cities who voted 'no' to the Peace Accord in this overwhelmingly urban country. Peace processes need national narratives of inclusion, and practices which make these meaningful and credible to those whose anger can so easily be diverted by the particular agendas of politicians. Those outside and beyond the peace negotiating table cannot be abandoned during a peace process, in particular those who are not organised and socially and educationally connected to wider visions and possibilities.

Notes

1 These talks entered their sixth cycle in July 2018 but were suspended by President Duque, who won the Colombian election in the June run-off. Duque demanded the release of 19 ELN captives, while the ELN announced its willingness to release six. The focus of this chapter will be on the peace talks, agreement, and implementation with the FARC 2012–2018.

2 This criminal organisation also gave itself the name of *Autodefensas Gaitanistas de Colombia*, a bid, it seems, to suggest it was a 'self-defence' group rather than a criminal drug trafficking one and could do deals with the state.

3 Juan Manuel Santos studied at the LSE when Giddens was Director, and when invited to speak there following the announcement of his Nobel Peace Prize, Santos acknowledged this influence. Author's notes, LSE 2 November 2016.

References, further reading, and links to key primary documents

Amnesty International. 2017. *The Years of Solitude Continue. Colombia: The Peace Agreement and Guarantees of Non-Repetition in Choco*. London: Amnesty International.

Ávila, Ariel, and León Valencia. 2017. "El Clan del Golfo y la Suspension de Acciones Militares." *El Espectador*, 15 December. Accessed 1 January 2019. https://colombia2020.elespectador.com/pais/el-clan-del-golfo-y-la-suspension-de-acciones-militares

Bouvier, Virginia. 2016. *Gender and the Role of Women in the Colombian Peace Process*. New York: USIP.

Chernick, Marc. 1999. "Negotiating Peace Amid Multiple Forms of Violence." In Cynthia Arnson (Ed.), *Comparative Peace Processes in Latin America*, 159–200. Washington, DC: Woodrow Wilson Center Press.

Corporación Nuevo Arco Iris (2007) *Parapolítica. La Ruta de la Expansion Paramilitary y los Acuerdos Políticos*. Bogota: Corporación Nuevo Arco Iris.

CNMH. 2013. *Basta Ya*. Colombia Memorias de Guerra y Dignidad. Bogota: CNMH.

Duncan, Gustavo. 2016. "No había de otra [There Was No Other]." *El Tiempo*, 30 November. www.eltiempo.com/opinion/columnistas/gustavo-duncan/no-habia-de-otra-gustavo-duncan-columna-el-tiempo-54126.

El Espectador. 2016. "Tormenta en Uribismo [Storm in Uribismo]." *El Espectador*, 6 October. Accessed 12 January 2018. www.elespectador.com/noticias/politica/torment a-el-uribismo-articulo-658967.

El Espectador. 2018. "Implementación va en 18.3%, Según el Observatorio de Seguimiento al Acuerdo de Paz [Implementation goes at 18.3%, According to the Monitoring Observatory of the Peace Agreement]." *El Espectador*, 4 January. Accessed 13 January 2018. www.elespectador.com/noticias/politica/implementacion-va-en-183-segun-el-obser vatorio-de-seguimiento-al-acuerdo-de-paz-articulo-731595.

El Tiempo. 2016. "Las Capitales Quedaron Divididas tras Votación [The Capitals Were Divided After Voting]." *El Tiempo*, 2 October. Accessed 13 January 2018. www.eltiempo.com/archivo/documento/CMS-16716976.

El Tiempo. 2018 "Los Asesinatos contra desmovilizados de FARC tras firma de la paz." El Tiempo, 6 September, Accesses 1 January 2019. https://www.eltiempo.com/justicia/investigacion/asesinatos-de-exguerrilleros-de-farc-tras-la-firma-de-la-paz-264996

Fundación para la Paz y Reconciliation. 2018. "Estos son los 21 lideres asesinados desde el inicio del gobierno Duque [These Are the 21 Leaders Killed Since the Beginning of the Duque Government]." Accessed 12 September 2018. http://pares.com.co/2018/09/05/estos-son-los-21-lideres-asesinados-desde-el-inicio-del-gobierno-duque/.

Garcia Duran, Mauricio. 2006. *Movimiento por la Paz en Colombia 1978–2003* [Movement for Peace in Colombia 1978–2003*]*. Bogota: CINEP.

Herbolzheimer, Kristian. 2016. *Innovations in the Colombian Peace Process*. Oslo: NOREF.

International Crisis Group. 2012. *Colombia: Peace at Last*. Bogota and Brussels: ICG.

Isacson, Adam, 2013, *Colombia Peace Process Update*, 5 June. Washington: WOLA.

Jaramillo, Sergio. 2013. "Transition in Colombia." *Externado University*, 9 May. Accessed 4 December 2016. www.wola.org/files/1305_jaram_eng.pdf.

Kroc Institute. 2018. "State of Implementation of the Colombia Peace Agreement." 31 May. Accessed 12 September 2018. http://kroc.nd.edu/assets/284862/executive_sum mary_2_with _logos.pdf.

McDermott, Jeremy. 2014. "The BACRIM and Their Position in Colombia's Underworld." *Insight Crime*, 2 May. Accessed 1 January 2019. https://www.insightcrime.org/investigations/bacrim-and-their-position-in-colombia-underworld/

Nasi, Carlos (2009) "Colombia's Peace Processes, 1982-2002, Conditions, Strategies and Outcomes." In Bouvier, Virginia (Ed.), *Building Peace in a Time of War*, 39–64. Washington: USIP.

Oficina del Alto Comisionado de la Paz. 2016. *Acuerdo Sobre las Victimas del Conflicto* [Agreement on the Victims of the Conflict]. Bogota: Oficina del Alto Comisionado de la Paz. Accessed 5 December 2016. www.altocomisionadoparalapaz.gov.co/Prensa/Com unicados/Documents/2016/proceso-paz-colombia-cartilla-acuerdo-victimas.pdf

Palacios, Marcos, 2012. A Historical Perspective on Counterinsurgency and the "War on Drugs" in Colombia, 175-206. In Arnson, C. (ed) *In the Wake of War: Democratization and Internal Armed Conflict in Latin America*. Washington: Woodrow Wilson Center.

Pearce, Jenny 1990. *Colombia: Inside the Labyrinth*. London: Latin America Bureau.

Pearce, Jenny. 2016. "The 'Violence Turn' in Peace Studies and Practice." In Barbara Unger, Véronique Dudouet, Matteo Dressler, and Beatrix Austin (Eds.), *"Undeclared Wars" Exploring a Peacebuilding Approach to Armed Social Violence*, 31–40. Berlin: Berghof Foundation.

Perea, C. Mario. 2016. Vislumbrar la Paz [Glimpse the Peace]. Bogota: Penguin Random House Editorial.

Pizarro, Eduardo. 2016. "Una Lectura Multiple y Pluralista de la Historia [A Multiple and Pluralist Reading of History]." In Eduardo Pizarro, and Victor Moncayo (Eds.), *Contribución al entendimiento del conflicto armado en Colombia*, 2nd edn. Bogota: Ediciones Desde Abajo.

Pruitt, G. Dean. 2005. "Whither Ripeness Theory?" *Institute for Conflict Analysis and Resolution*. https://activity.scar.gmu.edu/sites/default/files/wp_25_pruitt_0.pdf.

Rampf, David, and Diana Chavarro. 2014. *The 1991 Colombian National Constituent Assembly*. Berlin: Berghof Foundation.

Registraduría Nacional de Estado Civil. 2016. "Plebiscito." *Registra Duria*. Accessed 4 December 2016. http://plebiscito.registraduria.gov.co.

Rettburg, Angelika, 2015. *Gold, oil and the lure of violence: the private sector and post-conflict risks in Colombia*. September. Oslo:NOREF

Ruta Pacifica, 2014. La Verdad de las Mujeres Víctimas de Conflicto Armado en Colombia. Informe de Comisión de Verdad y Memoria. (The Truth of the Women Victims of the Armed Conflict in Colombia. Report of the Truth and Memory Commission) Bogota:Ruta Pacifica.

Sánchez, María. 2009. *Guerreros y Campesinos: El Despojo de la Tierra en Colombia*. Bogota: Grupo Editorial Norma.

Santos Calderon, Enrique, 2014, *Así Empezó Todo. El Primer Cara a Cara Secreto Entre el Gobierno y las FARC en la Habana*. Bogota:Intermedio Editores.

Segura, Renata, and Delphine Mechoulan. 2017. *Made in Havana: How Colombia and the FARC Decided to End the War*. New York: International Peace Institute.

Semana. 2013. "Habla Pablo Catatumbo." *Nacion*, 25 May. Accessed 4 December 2016. www.com/nacion/articulo/halba-pablo-catatumbo/344345-3.

Semana. 2016. "La increible fuerza del perdón en el proceso de paz [The Incredible Strength of Forgiveness in the Peace Process]." 17 September. Accessed 4 December 2016. www.semana.com/nacion/articulo/el-perdon-entre-las-farc-el-estado-y-lasvictimas/494040.

Semana. 2018. "¿El Vaso Medio Lleno? [The Half Full Glass]." 6 January. Accessed 13 January 2018. www.semana.com/nacion/articulo/datos-positivos-al-comenzar-2018-que-vale-la-pena-registrar/552621.

UNHCR. 2016. "Comunicado de Prensa: Preocupación por Aumento de la Violencia en Contra de Lideres, Lideresas, Defensores y Población que habita zonas Rurales [Press Release: Concern about Increasing Violence against Leaders, Leaders, Defenders and the Population that lives in rural areas.]" 2 December. Accessed 4 December 2016. www.hchr.org.co/publico/comunicados/2016/8fCEYkS6RNZg.pdf.

UN Verification Mission in Colombia. 2017, 2018. "Report of the Secretary-General on the United Nations Verification Mission in Colombia." https://colombia.unmissions.org/en.

WOLA. 2010. *Plan Colombia: Don't Call It a Model*. Washington, DC: WOLA.

World Bank. 2004. *Colombia: Land Policy in Transition*. Washington, DC: World Bank.

Zartman, William. 1989. *Ripe for Resolution*. Oxford: Oxford University Press.

Zartman, William. 2000. "Ripeness: The Hurting Stalemate and Beyond. In Conflict Resolution After the Cold War. In Daniel Druckman, and Paul C. Stern (Eds.), *International Conflict Resolution After the Cold War 2*, 225–250. Washington, DC: National Academy Press.

Zartman, William. 2013. "Ripeness." *Beyond Intractability*, June. Accessed 4 December 2016. www.beyondintractability.org/essay/ripeness.

7

EL SALVADOR

William Stanley

Introduction

The Central American country of El Salvador suffered a 12-year civil war that claimed at least 75,000 civilian lives. The war ended in 1992 following negotiations mediated by the United Nations. El Salvador's conflict was a classic Cold War proxy war, with the United States backing the Salvadoran government against rebels supported by the Socialist Bloc. In 1990, faced with a strategic stalemate and declining expectations for external support as the Cold War wound down, both the Salvadoran rebels and the government turned to the United Nations to mediate a settlement. Senior UN Secretariat officials brokered a definitive settlement, and the Security Council mandated a verification mission, initially to monitor human rights conditions and subsequently to oversee implementation of the full accords. The Salvadoran accords produced a stable and complete ceasefire, demobilisation of the rebel forces, and halving of the government's military, as well as extensive political reforms that substantially addressed the repression and political exclusion that had contributed to the outbreak of war. The military was excluded from interference in internal political affairs, and a completely new civilian police force was created to provide domestic security. After the war, there was minimal political violence, and the resulting democratic system stands out for its openness and competitiveness. Yet socio-economic inequalities went largely unaddressed, and the country faced a post-war crime wave that peaked four years after the ceasefire, producing violent death rates that exceeded the average rate during the war (Call 2002: 402). Criminal violence, much of it gang-related, persisted at levels that continued to drive out-migration 20 years after the signing of the final accords.

El Salvador's peace process stands out for the absence of armed peacekeepers. The military separation of forces, cantonment, and disarmament were verified by fewer than three hundred unarmed military observers, while unarmed police observers and UN civilian human rights officials monitored internal security forces. The stability of the peace process depended on the two adversaries' relatively high confidence in each other's intentions, reassured by UN verification. Both the rebel leaders and the civilian government substantially shifted their goals and strategies through the negotiations, and both were relatively satisfied with the settlement. While both sides resisted implementing elements of the accords, outright spoiling was confined to specific groups within each side whose grievances were fairly easily resolved.

The timing of the Salvadoran process was propitious. As the Soviet Union crumbled during 1991, the United States shifted to actively supporting a negotiated settlement. During peace implementation in 1992 and 1993, the United States financed side-payments that elicited cooperation from potential spoilers within both rebel and government forces.

The UN innovated successfully in El Salvador by deploying a human rights-monitoring mission before the ceasefire, by incorporating institution-building capacity into the verification mission, and by deploying two successor missions of diminishing scope after the primary peace mission closed. The main lessons from El Salvador are that international peacekeeping adds important value even when conditions are favourable for settlement; that domestic parties to a peace agreement may jointly undermine their own accord; that an international verification mission can only partially prevent such backsliding; that post-war institution-building efforts are likely to achieve relatively little until new leadership emerges; and that deeply reforming the police post-war is a long-term investment that can risk a sharp increase in violent crime in the shorter term.

Conflict analysis

El Salvador's civil war broke out in 1980, driven by a combination of worsening inequality, political exclusion, a revolution in a neighbouring country, and indiscriminate repression by the government's internal security forces. Excessive and ill-targeted state violence was the proximate cause, as unarmed civilians faced slaughter and concluded that their chances improved by taking arms against the state (Mason and Krane 1989). Since the nineteenth century, El Salvador had developed an economy based on labour repressive agriculture, and the government maintained multiple internal security forces whose role was to coerce the rural poor to work for plantations, prevent labour organising of any kind, and suppress the political left (Williams 1986, 1994; Mahoney 2002). The military assumed direct power in 1932, massacring thousands of unarmed civilians in response to a minor rural rebellion. After 1948, the army created an official political party and sought to legitimise its rule through elections and economic development. Over subsequent decades, the army proved unable to manage the contradictions between military rule and 'open' elections. By the 1970s, increasingly blatant electoral frauds and ham-fisted repression led to mass demonstrations and the formation of nascent guerrilla cells.

After revolutionaries overthrew the regime of Anastasio Somoza in neighbouring Nicaragua, a group of reform-minded junior officers in El Salvador organised a coup to remove their own military president, Carlos Romero. The coup on 15 October 1979 replaced Romero with a joint civil–military 'Revolutionary Governing Junta' (JRG), backed by the progressive wing of the Catholic Church (Whitfield 1995: 118–142; Guerra y Guerra 2009). The junior officers' goal was to forestall outright civil war by making socio-economic concessions to the poor, halting excessive repression, and overseeing a transition to a more genuine electoral democracy. The junior officers and their allies shut down a notorious military intelligence organisation and purged officers associated with abuses. They arranged an uneasy truce with one of the rebel groups and explored a more lasting pact (Stanley 1996: 157–161, 17–88). However, senior military hardliners outmanoeuvred their junior colleagues and regained full control over 11 months. Unable to control the hard-line elements of military, the more left-leaning members of the JRG and cabinet resigned in December 1979 and were replaced in a series of short-lived civil–military juntas by members of the Christian Democratic Party (PDC). Military reformists tried three more times during 1980 to reassert control and were defeated each time. Each setback for reformists brought heightened violence against civilians, including the murder of Archbishop Oscar Romero, who had spoken out publicly against the repression.

With all compromise foreclosed, civil war ensued and developed through four phases. Initially (1979 through early 1981), five separate rebel groups sought to organise themselves, while encouraging mass demonstrations against the government. This period saw the most intense civilian casualties, as the military targeted the popular movements. Activists went into hiding, and many fled to rural encampments to receive military training from the rebels. The five groups created a unified command in September 1980, calling themselves the Farabundo Martí National Liberation Front (FMLN). The two dominant groups within the FMLN, the Armed Forces of Liberation (FPL) and the Revolutionary Army of the People (ERP), held two very different philosophies. The FPL favoured a war of attrition dependent on thorough organisation and indoctrination of a peasant and worker social base. The ERP was more eclectic politically, focused on military effectiveness, and insurrectionist. These differences generated internal frictions, but the FMLN overall was able to function with sufficient coordination to be effective. Unity brought international credibility, and the FMLN received significant shipments of arms through the revolutionary regime in Nicaragua.

The second phase began around 1982, when the FMLN was sufficiently organised to be able to move battalion-sized units around the country in vehicles, engaging in major battles against the government Armed Forces of El Salvador (FAES) and often winning (Peceny and Stanley 2010). During this phase, the FMLN focused on forming a large force that peaked at around 10,000 fighters, depending on forced recruitment that they later abandoned. At this stage, the FMLN was armed largely with US-made M-16 rifles, some captured from the FAES, but many previously belonging to the Army of the Republic of Vietnam, captured by Vietnamese

Communist forces, and shipped to El Salvador. The FMLN might have won the civil war outright had this dynamic continued, but the US greatly increased its military aid programme and salvaged the government's position. The army grew from around 14,000 to close to 60,000 by the end of the war, but just as importantly, the US provided El Salvador with dozens of helicopters and fixed wing ground attack aeroplanes, including jets and AC-47 gunships, plus logistical support.[1]

The government build-up led to the third phase of the war, which began in 1984, when the FMLN found it could no longer operate in large units because they were vulnerable to attack from the air. At this stage, the FMLN lacked sophisticated anti-aircraft weapons. Under regular aerial observation and unable to defend adequately against aerial attacks, the rebels divided their forces into small units and focused on a war of economic attrition, punctuated by occasional, carefully prepared larger attacks on military bases. Despite tactical improvements, the FAES could not adequately protect cotton fields, coffee mills, coffee harvests, bridges, or electric posts in the country. By the late 1980s, the FAES often had the upper hand tactically, but it could not defeat the rebels outright. FMLN forces, by this point reduced to about 7,000 combatants, exploited legally disputed territories along the border with Honduras where Salvadoran forces were reluctant to enter.

This military stalemate lasted until November of 1989, when the FMLN conducted a spectacular offensive in which it seized substantial portions of the capital city. The FMLN pre-positioned thousands of small arms in poor neighbourhoods in the eastern side of the capital city. Rebel combatants then rode into town on public buses, dressed as civilians, and blended into the urban population. After gathering at social events the night the offensive was to begin, they collected their weapons and began attacking military and government targets around the city (Smyth 1989). Ultimately, the FAES withstood the attack, most critically fending off the FMLN's attempt to overrun the main air force base at Ilopango, the loss of which could easily have resulted in collapse of government forces. There followed a relentless air force campaign of aerial bombardment against FMLN positions in the city, causing high casualties among the rebels. The popular insurrection that some FMLN leaders had hoped for did not materialise, as most civilians fled the occupied neighbourhoods.

After five days of bombardment and hundreds of casualties, the FMLN abandoned its fixed positions in poor neighbourhoods and began moving about the capital city. One of these manoeuvres resulted in the rebels occupying positions in the upmarket Escalón neighbourhood. Suddenly, the air force was neutralised, unwilling to bomb or rocket the homes of the wealthy. Moreover, the FMLN occupied a hotel housing the Secretary General of the Organization of American States, who had flown to El Salvador in the midst of the offensive hoping to promote talks, as well as a group of United States Special Forces troops. This standoff required direct dialogue between the FMLN and the US to coordinate the separation of forces (Samayoa 2003: 223–235). The occupation of wealthy people's houses also gave rise to direct discussions between FMLN leaders and their ostensible class enemies, setting the stage for formal dialogue later.[2] Overall, the offensive showed that the FMLN was still a potent force and that the army had failed utterly to protect the capital city. Yet the FMLN fell far short of its maximum aim of defeating the army, and its prospects for outright victory faded.

On November 16, five days into the offensive, the FAES high command sent a detachment of soldiers to murder six Jesuit scholars at the Catholic University of Central America. The murdered priests had been prominent critics of both the government and the FMLN and had publicly advocated for a negotiated solution. They were also internationally renowned as academics, with many friends abroad (Doggett 1993). From the perspective of many members of Congress in Washington, these killings proved that the FAES was utterly unreformed: after hundreds of millions of dollars in aid and a decade of human rights training, the Salvadoran army was still murdering priests. The next day, both houses of the US Congress passed resolutions threatening to cut military aid unless the perpetrators were prosecuted. Congressional investigation followed, and the FAES' prospects for indefinite US military assistance were suddenly uncertain.

The fourth and final stage of the war coincided with peace talks that began after the offensive. By this point, fighting focused on bolstering negotiating positions. In a significant escalation, the FMLN acquired shoulder-fired, heat-seeking anti-aircraft missiles (apparently through Nicaragua) and brought down several FAES aircraft of types that had previously been largely immune to ground fire. This new threat made it more difficult for the air force to provide effective close air support for troops on the ground. Forced to fight with less air support, the government army lost the initiative and suffered a number of embarrassing defeats.

The conflict resolution process

Alongside the military stalemate, the political basis for conflict resolution in El Salvador developed slowly over a decade. The key enabling condition was the emergence of a civilian political party with sufficient legitimacy, authority, and autonomy from the military to negotiate seriously with the rebels. That party was the Republican National Alliance (ARENA), and a more unlikely peacemaker has seldom been known. ARENA was founded in 1981 by a group of far-right civilians and former military officers who had separated from the military's official Party of National Conciliation (PCN), initially calling themselves the Broad National Front (FAN). After the junta announced that elections would be held in 1982, these activists formed the ARENA party to compete. ARENA founders included former army major Roberto D'Aubuisson, who had been dismissed from the service by the first JRG for his human rights abuses. Death squad members and shady elements suspected of kidnapping activities figured prominently in the first years of ARENA.[3] The party's social base centred on the paramilitary Democratic Nationalist Organization (ORDEN) that had been established with US help in the 1960s to prevent communist organising in the countryside. ARENA's initial agenda was a radical anti-communist crusade, along with opposition to land reform and economic regulation.

The 1982 Constituent Assembly election was part of an effort by the Reagan administration to mollify the US Congress by demonstrating that the US was promoting democracy, not just helping the army to kill leftists. It was widely touted as a foundational event, and even local television stations in the US sent reporters to cover the long lines of voters who were braving guerrilla attacks to cast their ballots. Little was made of the fact that voting was compulsory and that non-voters were subject to imprisonment or worse. The results produced a plurality for the Christian Democrats (24 per cent), but ARENA and the PCN jointly won 33 per cent, and it appeared likely that D'Aubuisson of all people would be selected interim president. Given his reputation for torture and political murder, this was unacceptable to the US. High-level US officials intervened to block D'Aubuisson (who had to settle for being president of the Constituent Assembly), and the parties chose Alvaro Magaña, personal banker to many military officers, as interim president.[4]

Following this procedurally undemocratic beginning, more regular electoral practices took hold. Christian Democrat José Napoleón Duarte was elected president in 1984, solidly defeating D'Aubuisson with financial and campaign help from the US. The PDC won a majority of legislative seats in 1985. ARENA learned from these defeats, especially from the determined, partially covert opposition from the United States. It began to reinvent itself to become more widely acceptable. With the help of a US Agency for International Development-funded think tank known as the Salvadoran Foundation for Social and Economic Development (FUSADES), ARENA created a softer, social market ideology and programme (Rosa 1993: 75–95). Meanwhile, the PDC suffered predictable erosion of support as a wartime government. The economy stagnated, and there were rumours of considerable corruption on the part of PDC officials. President Duarte held two days of talks with the FMLN in the town of La Palma in 1984, but these led nowhere. The war of economic attrition continued, and private sector interests objected to the PDC's interventions in the economy. The FMLN's kidnapping of the president's daughter and her subsequent exchange for a large number of political prisoners (including a top FMLN commander) contributed to an impression that Duarte and the PDC were ineffective.

Exploiting the PDC's vulnerabilities, ARENA won a majority of legislative seats in the 1988 race, and then in 1989 ran a comparatively moderate, soft-spoken businessman named Alfredo Cristiani as its presidential candidate. Cristiani won decisively (54 per cent) in the first round. Thus, a party that was born as an offshoot of a death squad converted itself into a mainstream party with broad appeal and strong campaigning skills. Most importantly, the private sector elite, which for many decades of the twentieth century had depended on the military to govern on their behalf, had learned how to win political power in their own name (Miles and Ostertag 1989; Paige 1998; Wolf 1992: 25–77).

Cristiani surprised many by announcing in his inaugural address that he would negotiate with the FMLN, and indeed his government began talks with the rebels in San José, Costa Rica in September and October of 1989. During the talks, the military signalled its discontent by holding a press conference in which the entire high command of the military lined up behind the Defence Minister as he announced that there would be no concessions to the 'criminal terrorists'. Shortly thereafter, a bomb detonated in the headquarters of a major labour union sympathetic to the FMLN, killing nine and seriously injuring 40. The FMLN, unsurprised by the military's response, proceeded with its November 1989 offensive.

In the aftermath of the November 1989 offensive, both the Cristiani government and the FMLN independently approached the United Nations and requested assistance in negotiating an end to the conflict. The UN Secretary General, Javier Pérez de Cuellar, assigned a senior official, Alvaro De Soto (Peru), as his personal representative to the peace process, and De Soto assembled an excellent support staff. In April 1990, the parties signed an initial pact in Geneva, committing to negotiate continuously and secretly, under UN auspices, until reaching a definitive resolution of the war. In Caracas in May of 1990, the parties agreed to a comprehensive negotiating agenda that included the armed forces, human rights, the judicial system, the electoral system, constitutional reforms, economic and social issues, provisions for verification, and provisions for the reintegration of FMLN members into national life.

The first substantive topic taken up, at meetings in San José, Costa Rica in July of 1990, was human rights. This seemed surprising at the time given the severity of human rights violations by both sides and the government's appalling record in particular. However, the Salvadoran state was already a party to many international human rights conventions, and to a large extent the language negotiated by the two sides merely reiterated standards to which the government was already obligated. The problem was how the state actually behaved, and to address that problem, the parties agreed that the UN would deploy a human rights verification mission with broad powers to inspect government facilities without prior notice. This was a significant concession by the government, since such intrusive inspections ran counter to the state's rhetoric about sovereignty.

After San José, however, the talks stagnated. The parties began discussing the question of the military, on which the FMLN took two positions, neither acceptable to the government. The rebels called either for the complete abolition of the army, or a merger of military forces under a power-sharing arrangement. The FMLN launched a renewed offensive in November 1990, within one week destroying four FAES aircraft with anti-aircraft missiles and ground fire and outmatching the FAES in a number of actions. In February 1991, the FMLN shot down a helicopter crewed by US military personnel and summarily executed two survivors of the crash. After this incident, the US released military assistance that had been on hold as a result of the Jesuit murders and sent diplomatic signals criticising the UN-led negotiations.

Progress finally resumed in April 1991, when the two sides reached an agreement in Mexico on constitutional reforms. The Mexico accord also included elements that would prove important later, including the idea (underdeveloped at this point) that internal security would be handled by a National Civilian Police force rather than by the military, that the military would be subordinated to civilian authority, and that there would be a Truth Commission to establish a definitive record of what happened during the war. Most importantly, the lame-duck Legislative Assembly promptly approved the reforms by more than the required supermajority. This vote was essential since the constitution required that two consecutive legislatures approve constitutional reforms, and failure to approve at this juncture would have delayed implementation of reforms until 1994. The fact that the government could not only make commitments at the negotiating table but also deliver on them made FMLN leaders more confident in the process.

In July 1991, the UN Security Council took the unprecedented step of deploying a human rights verification mission before the achievement of a ceasefire. The Observer Mission of the United Nations in El Salvador (ONUSAL) established regional offices around the country and began inspecting military and police bases. The presence of the UN's white jeeps and observers 'made it difficult for the two sides to intensify the fighting . . . it was hard to fight in the presence of ONUSAL'.[5]

Perhaps the most critical breakthrough of the negotiations came in September 1991 in New York, when the parties reached an agreement that broke the impasse regarding what to do about the military. Essentially, the FMLN agreed to leave the military intact (though reduced in size and subject to lustration), with the understanding that the PNC would be the *only* armed internal security force with national jurisdiction. This went a step farther than the constitutional reform agreement of April 1991, and it would break the military's source of political power. Moreover, the agreement elaborated a vision of the PNC as a completely different kind of police force, with a new, university-educated officer corps, comparatively high educational requirements even for patrolmen, a doctrine emphasising its apolitical nature and minimal use of violence, and representation of the FMLN constituting up to 20 per cent of the initial force. In an initially secret side agreement, the FMLN agreed to forego demands for power-sharing within, or abolition of, the military, for the duration of the negotiations (it was free to pursue this cause later through legislative channels). A key factor in this breakthrough was assistance from the UN mediation team, who helped convince the FMLN to imagine a democratically governed, genuinely national police force rather than the rebels merely being the 'local sheriff' in their own areas of influence.[6]

After the breakthrough on police and military, talks accelerated rapidly, culminating in a marathon session in New York at the end of 1991, at which President Cristiani participated, with active and favourable engagement by US diplomats and defence officials. There was a perception of urgency, because the term of Secretary General Pérez de Cuellar was ending, and both parties recognised his personal commitment to the Salvadoran peace process. The New York meetings produced little more than a statement that a deal was imminent, to be signed at Chapultepec palace in Mexico City on 16 January, but most of the sticky details had in fact been worked out.

The final accord signed at Chapultepec is impressive, although uneven, in its detail. It provided thorough guidance for the timetable and coordination of the ceasefire and force separation; for the reduction, lustration, and governance of the armed forces; and for the organisation, composition, and governance of the PNC. In contrast, it was comparatively vague on judicial reform, electoral reform, and socio-economic matters (Popkin 2000). Remarkably for a Marxist insurgency that had fought for over a decade in favour of socialism, the FMLN agreed to defer many decisions about socio-economic reform to a tri-partite commission, made up of representatives of the government, business, and labour, which would meet after the ceasefire. Since the incumbent government was closely linked to business, the Socio-Economic Forum was in effect stacked in favour of business, and this was certainly obvious to the FMLN negotiators. Thus, the FMLN strategically negotiated the deal that it *could* negotiate and accepted the risk of deferring economic reforms until later when, FMLN leaders hoped, they could win state power through elections. It used its military leverage to break the power of the armed forces, which ARENA was willing to do, while avoiding demands such as massive land redistribution that ARENA would have opposed.

Peace implementation

Several features of the Salvadoran peace agreements facilitated successful implementation. The disarmament and demobilisation of the FMLN forces was to take place in stages, during which the government had a series of obligations, including downsizing the military overall and demobilising specific units completely; transferring lands to former combatants as well as close civilian supporters of the FMLN; and setting in motion a series of reforms including selection and training of the new civilian police. Although the parties' obligations were theoretically independent of one another, the interlocking timetables in practice allowed either side to sanction the other for noncompliance. Moreover, the timing of the ceasefire allowed for two years of peace implementation before the next national elections, sufficient time for the FMLN to convert from an insurgency into a political party. This cooling off period also allowed the UN to help address serious shortcomings of the voter registration rolls before the vote.

Implementation of the agreements began with a 'cessation of armed conflict' that took effect 1 February 1992. In fact, the FMLN had declared a unilateral ceasefire in November of 1991, and an informal bilateral truce was in effect by mid-January of 1992, so hostilities had wound down before the formal ceasefire. Nonetheless, the separation of forces was delayed by a variety of problems, including inadequate housing and sanitation at the concentration sites, disputes over boundaries of concentration areas, the presence of army troops at some 16 sites not enumerated in the force separation plan, and military over-flights of FMLN concentration areas that triggered fears of aerial attack. Some 292 unarmed ONUSAL military observers monitored the force separation, resided in the FMLN camps, patrolled around them, and oversaw weapons collections (United Nations 1995: 236). By March there were concerns that the peace process was stalling, so the UN sent Under-Secretary General Marrack Goulding (UK) to El Salvador to reassure both parties, clarify the UN's interpretation of what each side had agreed to, and to impress upon both sides, but especially the government, that noncompliance would bring significant reputational costs. Among the main concerns were that instead of demobilising two hated security forces, the National Guard and the Treasury Police, Cristiani had allowed them to be transferred as special units into the army; the government was late in establishing the new civilian police academy; and the government delayed arrangements for land transfers to ex-combatants. The Secretary General followed on 26 May 1992 with a sternly worded assessment of the lack of progress. This catalysed action, and the FMLN demobilised its first contingent in June. ONUSAL and other observers noted with surprise the poor quality of weapons handed in by the first groups of demobilising FMLN fighters (United Nations 1995: 265). This would prove to be significant later.

The land issue had perhaps the greatest potential to result in violence. Many details were insufficiently specified, such as how to adjust the amount of land transferred to take account of varying quality, how to set prices, and who exactly was eligible. The FMLN was less than transparent about who among its supporters qualified, how many they were, and where they were located. It encouraged affiliates to occupy lands, to create a *fait accompli*, while landowners insisted that the government evict the squatters, resulting in numerous angry face-offs between occupiers and police, which ONUSAL officials attempted to mediate. Ultimately, pressured by a second visit by Marrack Goulding, the government and FMLN accepted a 'take-it-or-leave-it' settlement drafted by UN team of agronomists (Wood 2000: 92–97).

A further challenge was an impasse over the FMLN's certification as a political party. The FMLN wanted the Supreme Electoral Tribunal (TSE) to acknowledge its status as a party before it completed demobilisation; the TSE threatened to refuse certification because the FMLN was still armed. ONUSAL finessed these issues by ensuring that the missiles were sequestered and then certifying that the FMLN was disarmed, which allowed the TSE to certify their registration as a political party. With this resolved, the demobilisation phase ended on 15 December with a celebration at the San Salvador fairgrounds, attended by international dignitaries, including US Vice President Dan Quayle (who to the surprise of many observers received a standing ovation from the FMLN delegation in recognition of the United States' generosity).

Negotiations continued after the formal demobilisation. In addition to its remaining anti-aircraft missiles, the FMLN held another bargaining chip related to the future of officers in the military high command. The Ad Hoc Commission had recommended in September 1992 that 103 officers be purged promptly from the armed forces because of their human rights records. High military officials rejected the recommendations and intimated threats of coup d'état. Many of the named officers either retired, were transferred to administrative duties, or were placed on paid leave; however, 15 top-ranking officers remained in positions of authority.[7] The government, nervous about catalysing military insubordination, wanted to delay the purge of the top commanders; it also wanted to transfer two special investigative units from the old National Police wholesale into the new PNC, with minimal re-training. Neither of these proposed actions were in compliance with the accords, and neither were good for long-term democratisation. Yet the FMLN struck a bilateral deal with the government, without consulting the UN, allowing for the transfer of the police units and delayed departure of the officers, in exchange for government consent for a more generous 'social reinsertion' package for 600 mid-level FMLN officers (funded largely by USAID) and guarantee that specific land holdings would transfer to FMLN beneficiaries.[8]

This presented ONUSAL with a challenging situation, as the UN was being more demanding with respect to compliance with the peace accords than the FMLN. To its credit, the UN continued to insist on the departure of the 15 top officers and objected early and often to the police unit transfers (United Nations 1995: 491). In the event, the transferred police units proved to be a disaster. None were acculturated to the new police or its philosophy, and the units engaged in such egregious misconduct, including torture of witnesses and insubordination, that both were eventually disbanded. The top-ranked officers named by the Commission eventually retired in June 1993, amid rumours of clandestine side-payments to them from the United States. The departure of the final 15 was helped along by the release of the Truth Commission report in May 1993, which made clear that the listed officers indeed had atrocious human rights records.

The Truth Commission, as expected, reported that government forces were responsible for the vast majority of civilians killed during the civil war. It found the FMLN responsible for specific killings, including the assassination of mayors and other public officials. Unfortunately, the Commission reported only those crimes that had been openly acknowledged by one of the five FMLN factions. Other well-known crimes, including hundreds of killings by an FPL commander in San Vicente, went unexamined. The Truth Commission also made a series of recommendations, including the removal of Supreme Judicial Court justices who had committed numerous due process violations and fomented impunity for perpetrators of human rights crimes (Betancur et al. 1993). Military and government officials rejected the Truth Commission's report as biased and resisted its recommendations for reform.

On 25 May 1993, an explosion occurred in a vehicle parked at a car repair shop in Managua, Nicaragua. It exposed a massive underground cache of arms, ammunition, explosives, and documents linking the FMLN to the weapons and to international criminal conspiracies. The government protested vehemently, and the UN demanded that the FMLN come clean about its retention of weapons. The FMLN then revealed numerous caches, many of them in El Salvador, equivalent to one-third of the FMLN's original weapons inventory. The UN supervised the destruction of these weapons. It appeared the commanders' initial motive for retaining weapons was as a guarantee against deception by the government. Once caught out, they faced a choice between risking full disarmament or defecting from the accords and renewing hostility. They quickly decided to trust the process. In the end, the timing of the revelations was fortuitous for the rebels, as it allowed them to dispose of weapons that had become a political liability, well before the scheduled electoral campaign during which any fresh revelations would have been even more damaging politically.

An ongoing challenge for ONUSAL was to report accurately on human rights conditions after the ceasefire. While overt repressive acts declined dramatically, there was a surge in ambiguous violent crimes such as carjacking and armed robbery resulting in the deaths of FMLN members. The UN responded by sponsoring the formation of a 'Joint Group for the Investigation of Politically Motivated Illegal Armed Groups'. The Joint Group hired international investigators to ferret out grey-area groups, many of them former soldiers and intelligence personnel who had turned their talents to criminal activity (United Nations 1994). The Joint Group determined that these gangsters also occasionally carried out politically motivated crimes. The Joint Group's investigations appeared to deter violence during the crucial lead-up to the 1994 elections, and its findings confirmed ONUSAL's characterisation of the changing nature and sources of political violence.

In the Salvadoran electoral system, presidential elections occur every five years, while legislative assembly and mayoral polls are every three. The elections of 1994 were particularly foundational because, by coincidence, all levels of government were in play at the same time as the FMLN was to be incorporated into the electoral system. In 1993, ONUSAL's mandate was expanded to provide verification of the conditions for the election. The mission's priority concern was that voter rolls excluded an estimated 700,000 eligible voters who had been displaced during the conflict, or who resided in conflict zones where many government records, including voter rolls, had been destroyed. Moreover, the TSE, whose composition included only the parties already represented in the legislature, had few incentives to help register new voters who were more likely than not to vote for the FMLN. ONUSAL found various ways, including driving local TSE officials to work and providing copying machines, generators, and other logistical support to accelerate the TSE's work. Roughly half of the undocumented eligible voters were added to the rolls, and despite numerous voting day irregularities related to voting roll and identification errors, ONUSAL concluded that the election had been 'acceptable', especially in view of the comparatively wide margins by which most races were decided (Spence et al. 1994: 47–54; United Nations 1995: 531).

To monitor the election itself, ONUSAL mobilised its entire staff, including police observers, to observe campaign events, watch for voter intimidation, and monitor the polls on Election Day. ONUSAL's prompt reporting of exit survey results helped bolster confidence in the results. Presidential elections in El Salvador's multi-party system utilise a run-off if no candidate wins a majority. Among seven candidates in the first round, ARENA presidential candidate Armando Calderón Sol and FMLN candidate Rubén Zamora Rivas came in first and second, respectively, with Calderón netting 49 per cent of the vote. Calderón beat Zamora handily in the second round with 68 per cent of the vote. Nonetheless, the FMLN had emerged in a single election as the country's second-leading party, eclipsing the Christian Democrats and the PCN. The FMLN won 21 of 84 seats in the Legislative Assembly, versus 39 for ARENA. In subsequent elections, FMLN gained legislative seats, winning near parity with ARENA by 2000 and maintaining it thereafter. ARENA would win the next two presidential elections in 1999 and 2004, but in 2009 FMLN candidate Mauricio Funes won the presidency, succeeded in 2014 by one of the FMLN's wartime commanders, Salvador Sánchez Cerén, and in 2019 by a third party candidate, Nayib Bukele.

Perhaps the greatest challenges for ONUSAL arose in its efforts to build and help reform government institutions. It was part of ONUSAL's mandate to help, for example, to build the PNC and the Human Rights Ombudsman's office. Unfortunately, a number of the individuals selected by government to head key agencies were resistant to the values of transparency, due process, and human and civil rights protection promoted by ONUSAL. At one point, ONUSAL withdrew its police observers from working with the PNC because of conflicts with PNC leadership. Thus, ONUSAL's unprecedented efforts to engage in longer-term peacebuilding were only modestly successful.

ONUSAL's mandate, after a one-year extension, was to end in April 1995. However, the UN and the Salvadoran parties recognised that post-war accomplishments were still fragile and that an abrupt UN departure could result in reversals. Therefore, the Security Council mandated a new mission of reduced scale known as the United Nations Mission in El Salvador (MINUSAL) to maintain political accountability and international attention to implementation on police, judicial, and other institutional reforms. In May 1996, the UN followed with an even smaller United Nations Office for Verification (ONUV). By January 1997, remaining peacebuilding tasks shifted to the United Nations Development Programme.

Perhaps the most remarkable aspect of the Salvadoran peace process, at least in comparison to negotiated settlements elsewhere in the world, is that very early in the ceasefire it was clear to most observers that the war was definitively over. Even though the FMLN delayed its demobilisation and then handed over second-rate weapons while keeping some of its best weaponry in secret caches, and despite the bitterness of the war and the history of brutality by both sides, there seemed little risk of the kind of mass violence and spoiling seen in so many other peacekeeping cases. The delays and cheating that did take place were 'limited' spoiling – noncompliance aimed at extracting concessions to address specific grievances (Stedman 1997: 6–11).

El Salvador's peace process delivered on its main promise of demilitarising governance, confining the military largely to external security missions, incorporating the left legally and fully into the nation's electoral politics, and improving many state institutions. From a political point of view, the development of the PNC was extremely important and largely successful as it removed the military's historical base of political power and manipulation – what I have characterised in other writings as a state protection racket. It bears repeating that these reforms were all sharply contested during the implementation phase, and that the UN's insistence on faithful implementation of the agreement was critical to preventing backsliding (Call 2002; Costa 1999: 28–60, 95–130; Stanley 1996: 218–220, 252–255). Notwithstanding various biases on the part of the main newspapers and broadcast stations, the post-war political climate remains comparatively open, with vibrant debate that covers a wide spectrum of political views (Ladutke 2004). Much political discourse remains highly polarised and self-serving, with factually irreconcilable narratives of the causes and conduct of the war and very negative depictions of former enemies (Ching 2016). Yet the FMLN held the presidency from 2009 to 2019, and the military obeyed the authority of its former enemies, an outcome that would have been inconceivable during the war.

Amid these political successes, three areas of failure stand out. The accords were deficient in addressing economic equity and poverty; the transition to the PNC created a public security vacuum that led to a horrific violent crime wave; and the basic problems of poverty, unemployment, and concentration of wealth remained unresolved. For a decade or more after the war ended, public insecurity and lack of economic opportunities dominated public opinion, and the combination has driven continued out-migration to Mexico and the United States (Call 2007; Wade 2016: 148–197).

Lessons to be learned from the case study

El Salvador stands out as among the most successful post-Cold War peace processes, with its absence of large-scale violence after the official ceasefire, full demobilisation of the rebels, extensive state reforms, and robust democratic political competition. The peace process left some long-term problems unresolved, such as socio-economic inequality, and may even have worsened some others, such as crime and insecurity. Yet the democratic transformation of El Salvador from repressive military regime to open democracy is an undeniable achievement. This success was achieved with a relatively light international touch: no armed peacekeepers were needed, and although ONUSAL and its successor missions remained in the country for six years, the missions were small and logistically uncomplicated compared to heavily militarised contemporary missions in Cambodia, Croatia, Bosnia-Herzegovina, Angola, and Mozambique. Three main lessons stand out from this case, demonstrating both the conditions for success and the limitations facing the peacemaking strategies used.

The primary enabling condition for the Salvadoran peace process was the changing international context, especially the shift in the role of external sponsors. The collapse of the Berlin Wall in 1989, the regionally important electoral defeat of the Sandinista Front in Nicaragua (1990), and the unravelling of the Soviet Union in 1991 changed the resources and even ideological rationales of the Salvadoran belligerents. Following the Jesuit murders, the US began to withhold some military assistance from the government, and though it never cut off military aid completely, long-term prospects for continued support declined. The electoral defeat of the Sandinista front in Nicaragua cut two ways. While the Sandinistas still controlled the military, the civilian government – and budgetary authority – was now in the hands of the pro-US opposition. Ironically, previous political constraints on the Sandinista military appeared to vanish, and delivery of anti-aircraft weapons to the FMLN began. Nonetheless, the Sandinista military's ability to facilitate future logistical flows declined.

More important than the change in direct support, however, was the shift in goals and expectations of both sides. With the erosion and then collapse of the Socialist Bloc, the FMLN shifted from being a client of a global power network to being an isolated insurgency in the neighbourhood of the United States. Accordingly, the FMLN accommodated itself to the necessity of competing electorally under internationally supported liberal rules. ARENA, in turn, had fewer grounds to view the FMLN as an instrument of a foreign power, which made it more acceptable to negotiate with the rebels.[9] With the FMLN transformed into a mostly domestic political problem, ARENA assumed the political authority and willingness to subordinate the army as needed to win the disarmament of the FMLN. Thus, the changing international context fundamentally changed the goals, strategies, and even identities of the domestic parties. A clear lesson is that international peacemakers should not under-estimate the extent to which changes in international alignments may significantly transform the parties to civil wars in ways that open up settlement possibilities that would have been previously unthinkable.[10]

It is also difficult to imagine the Salvadoran war ending as quickly as it did, with as stable and transformative an outcome, had the United Nations secretariat not played multiple roles as fair broker, verifier, and upholder of the letter and spirit of the agreement. UN mediation enabled the parties to clearly state their priority concerns and provided international normative pressure to keep negotiating even as the process encountered impasses. In practice, it went beyond mediation to propose specific language and solutions to key problems, most notably in generating the vision of a democratically controlled national police force. That proposal, which meant that the PNC could effectively replace and displace the military's historical role in internal security, broke the impasse over the future of the military and allowed the negotiations to advance (Costa 1999: 84–95). Once the ceasefire began, ONUSAL did all the things that Page Fortna (2008) has identified as the mechanisms by which peacekeeping works: reducing fear and uncertainty through observation and information; preventing political violence and abuses through human rights monitoring; and preventing accidents and involuntary defection by timely, on-the-spot mediation and communication. Without these services, it seems probable that any one of dozens of incidents could have resulted in noncompliance or armed clashes. In addition to the risks associated with separation of forces and cantonment of the FMLN, there were innumerable potential flash points, including labour protests and land occupations, that could have led to violence had ONUSAL personnel not been present to mediate, convince Salvadoran authorities on the scene not to resort to violence, and remind participants of the international reputational costs of escalation.[11] Beyond these mechanisms, ONUSAL took critical steps to ensure that the accords were implemented as written, even when the FMLN was willing to bargain away critical provisions such as the integrity of the PNC or lustration of the top ranks of the military. ONUSAL's institution-building efforts were less successful, largely because the government appointed key agency leaders who did not share a vision of a democratically accountable, human rights-promoting state. The main lesson from this is that major institutional changes generate resistance, and the international community needs to be prepared to promote sustained democratising institutional reforms beyond the time frame of a typical peacekeeping mission.

Finally, the Salvadoran peace process demonstrates the importance of providing for public security following cessation of fighting and demobilisation of opposing forces. There are multiple post-war dynamics that may increase violent crime. Although we cannot be certain, it appears that the transition to the new PNC created a security vacuum that allowed a spike in crime a few years after the war ended. The new force was initially too small to meet the country's needs, and the old security forces were demobilised before the PNC was ready to assume full responsibility for policing. This was a genuine dilemma, as the legacy security forces were so corrupted as to be a source of crime themselves, and keeping them deployed in large numbers for a longer period could have undercut confidence in the peace process. It is not obvious how the dilemma could have been avoided, except by deployment of some sort of international interim security force or much more robust international supervision of the old security forces through the transition. What is clear is that the UN underestimated how serious a problem crime and insecurity would become, and that more proactive planning and resource commitments are required anywhere there is a plan to create a new police force while avoiding a post-war crime wave.

The Salvadoran peace process demonstrates what multilateral peacekeeping can accomplish under the right combination of international and domestic circumstances. It also demonstrates some deep-seated weaknesses, including a lack of capacity to provide public security, and a mismatch between the relatively brief time frame of peace missions and the time frame in which major state institutions are built or transformed.

Notes

1 Only rough estimates are possible for the size of the government's military, as the corrupt practice of holding non-existent 'phantom soldiers' on the books was commonplace.
2 Author interview, senior ARENA member, San Salvador, May 1995.
3 Author interview with a former FAN member who opted out of joining ARENA because of the involvement of what he considered criminal elements, San Salvador, October 1989.
4 Author interview with Alvaro Magaña, September 1989.
5 Author interview with ONUSAL official, San Salvador, May 1992.
6 Author interview with UN official who participated in these negotiations, San Salvador, July 1993.
7 Author interviews with Salvadoran and US military officers, San Salvador, September and October 1992.
8 Author interviews with UN and USAID officials, San Salvador, May 1993 and July 1995.
9 Author interview, high ranking ARENA member, San Salvador, May 1995.
10 Author interviews in San Salvador with high ranking Democratic Convergence leader, June 1995; high ranking FMLN leader, June 1995; and former FMLN information officer, May 1995.
11 Multiple author interviews with UN officials in El Salvador, July through December 1992, March through July 1995.

References, further reading, and links to key primary documents

Betancur, Belisario, Reinaldo Figueredo Planchart, and Thomas Buergenthal. 1993. *From Madness to Hope: The 12-Year War in El Salvador: Report of the Commission for Truth in El Salvador.* UN Document S/25500 New York: United Nations Security Council.

Boyce, K. James. (Ed.). 1995. *Adjustment Toward Peace: Economic Policy and Post-War Reconstruction in El Salvador.* San Salvador: United Nations Development Programme.

Byrne, Hugh. 1996. *El Salvador's Civil War: A Study of Revolution.* Boulder and London: Lynne Rienner Publishers.

Call, T. Charles. 2002. "Assessing El Salvador's Transition from Civil War to Peace." In Stephen John Stedman, Donald Rothchild, and Elizabeth M. Cousens (Eds.), *Ending Civil Wars: The Implementation of Peace Agreements*, 383–420. Boulder and London: Lynne Rienner Publishers.

Call, T. Charles. 2007. "The Mugging of a Success Story: Justice and Security Reform in El Salvador." In Charles T. Call (Ed.), *Constructing Justice and Security After War*, 29–68. Washington, DC: United States Institute of Peace Press.

Ching, Erik. 2016. *Stories of Civil War in El Salvador: A Battle Over Memory.* Chapel Hill: University of North Carolina Press.

Costa, Gina. 1999. *La Policía Nacional Civil de El Salvador (1990–1997).* San Salvador: UCA Editores.

Doggett, Martha. 1993. *Death Foretold: The Jesuit Murders in El Salvador.* New York: Lawyers Committee for Human Rights.

Fortna, Virginia Page. 2008. *Does Peacekeeping Work?* Princeton, NJ: Princeton University Press.

Gibb, Tom, and Frank Smyth. 1990. *Is Peace Possible?* Washington, DC: Washington Office on Latin America.

Guerra y Guerra, Rodrigo. 2009. *Un golpe al amanecer: La verdadera historia de la Proclama del 15 de octubre de 1979.* San Salvador: Índole Editores.

Holiday, David, and William Stanley. 1993. "Building the Peace: Preliminary Lessons from El Salvador." *Journal of International Affairs* 46 (2): 415–438.

Human Rights Watch. 1992. *El Salvador: Peace and Human Rights: Successes and Shortcomings of the United Nations Observer Mission in El Salvador (ONUSAL).* New York: Human Rights Watch.

Ladutke, Lawrence Michael. 2004. *Freedom of Expression in El Salvador: The Struggle for Human Rights and Democracy.* Jefferson, NC: McFarland and Company.

Mahoney, James. 2002. *Legacies of Liberalism: Path Dependence and Political Regimes in Central America.* Baltimore: Johns Hopkins University Press.

Mason, T. David, and Dale A. Krane. 1989. "The Political Economy of Death Squads: Towards a Theory of the Impact of State-Sanctioned Terror." *International Studies Quarterly* 33 (1): 175–198.

Miles, Sara, and Bob Ostertag. 1989. "D'Aubuisson's New ARENA." *NACLA Report on the Americas* 23 (1): 14–38.

Paige, Jeffery. 1997. *Coffee and Power: Revolution and the Rise of Democracy in Central America.* Cambridge, MA: Harvard University Press.

Peceny, Mark, and William Stanley. 2001. "Liberal Social Reconstruction and the Resolution of Civil Wars in Central America." *International Organization* 55 (1): 149–182.

Peceny, Mark, and William Stanley. 2010. "Counterinsurgency in El Salvador." *Politics and Society* 38 (10): 67–94.

Popkin, Margaret. 2000. *Peace Without Justice: Building the Rule of Law in El Salvador.* University Park: Pennsylvania State University Press.

Rosa, Herman. 1993. *AID y las transformaciones globales en El Salvador.* Managua: CRIES.

Samayoa, Salvador. 2003. *El Salvador: La Reforma Pactada.* San Salvador: UCA Editores.

Smyth, Frank. 1989. "Caught with Their Pants Down." *Village Voice*, 5 December.

Spence, Jack, David R. Dye, and George Vickers. 1994. *El Salvador: Elections of the Century.* Cambridge, MA: Hemisphere Initiatives.

Stanley, William. 1996a. *The Protection Racket State: Elite Politics, Military Extortion, and Civil War in El Salvador.* Philadelphia: Temple University Press.

Stanley, William. 1996b. *Protectors or Perpetrators: The Institutional Crisis of the Salvadoran Civilian Police.* Washington: Washington Office on Latin America.

Stanley, William. 2007. "Business as Usual? Justice and Policing Reform in Postwar Guatemala." In Charles T. Call (Ed.), *Constructing Justice and Security After War*, 113–158. Washington, DC: United States Institute of Peace Press.

Stanley, William. 2013. *Enabling Peace in Guatemala: The Story of MINUGUA.* Boulder and London: Lynne Rienner Publishers.

Stanley, William, and David Holiday. 1997. "Peace Mission Strategy and Domestic Actors: UN Medication, Verification, and Institution Building in El Salvador." *International Peacekeeping* 4 (2): 22–49.

Stedman, S. John. 1997. "Spoiler Problems in Peace Processes." *International Security* 22 (2): 5–53.

United Nations. 1994. *Report of the Joint Group for the Investigation of Politically Motivated Illegal Armed Groups.* New York: United Nations. 22 October. S/1994/989.

United Nations. 1995. *The United Nations and El Salvador 1990–1995.* The United Nations Blue Book Series, Volume IV. New York: Department of Public Information, United Nations.

Wade, J. Christine. 2016. *Captured Peace: Elites and Peacebuilding in El Salvador.* Athens: Ohio University Press.

Whitfield, Teresa. 1995. *Paying the Price: Ignacio Ellacuría and the Murdered Jesuits of El Salvador.* Philadelphia: Temple University Press.

Williams, Robert. 1986. *Export Agriculture and the Crisis in Central America*, Chapel Hill: University of North Carolina Press.

Williams, Robert. 1994. *States and Social Evolution: Coffee and the Rise of National Governments in Central America.* Chapel Hill: University of North Carolina Press.

Wolf, H. Daniel. 1992. "ARENA in the Arena: Factors in the Accommodation of the Salvadoran Right to Pluralism and the Broadening of the Political System." *LASA Forum* 23 (1): 10–18.

Wood, J. Elisabeth. 2000. *Forging Democracy from Below: Insurgent Transitions in South Africa and El Salvador.* Cambridge: Cambridge University Press.

8

LIBERIA

Sukanya Podder

Introduction

The case of Liberia has been selected in order to study trends in similarities and differences between the two phases of conflict and peacebuilding (1989–1994 and 1999–2003). This helps us to ascertain the underlying causes of conflict relapse amid attempts to negotiate peace settlements outside of established explanations. The case study reveals three important lessons for the study of African civil wars. First, ethnicity in conflicts and their role in peace settlements need to be better analysed in a given context. Ethnicity is often a mobilisation tool at the inception of conflicts but can, however, become less relevant over time as the conflict expands, drawing in more actors and more political and economic interests. Situating the role of ethnic differences vis-à-vis political, structural, and economic factors can offer a more balanced narrative of African civil conflicts.

Second, the role of conflict entrepreneurs and political elites in deciding the fate of power-sharing arrangements is well understood in the literature on spoiler violence. This factor, however, requires more thorough examination with respect to peace negotiations. The Liberian case reveals that elite compacts reinforce structural conflict drivers that mostly benefit the 'guys with the guns' already in positions of privilege and status to subsequently entrench inequalities that will be increasingly difficult to remedy.

Finally, the role of the international community as peace and security guarantors can be particularly important in the context of weak states with low institutional development such as Liberia. Ensuring the neutrality of third-party guarantors of peace agreements can be a key factor in avoiding conflict relapse. In particular, the role of regional players needs in peacemaking, while attractive, must be applied with caution. ECOMOG's role in Liberia offers important lessons in this regard.

Conflict analysis

The Liberian state as was founded in 1847 by a small group of freed slaves who had been resettled in Liberia under the philanthropic enterprise of the American Colonisation Society in 1820. The descendants of this group of 'Americo-Liberians' constituted merely 5 per cent of the population but gradually came to dominate the politics and economics of the country by consolidating a strong oligarchic, exclusionist, and discriminatory set-up. Liberia has 16 different indigenous ethnic groups. The largest are the Kpelle (21 per cent), followed by the Bassa (15 per cent), and the Gio, Kru, Grebo, and Mano (8 or 9 per cent each). The relationship between the Americo-Liberians and the indigenous population was both initiated and grew on an unequal and inimical basis.

Liberia under Americo-Liberian domination

Liberian politics came to be dominated by a single political party, the True Whig Party, between 1870 and 1980. The Americo-Liberian elite played a brokerage role between the indigenous population and external trade and commercial interests. Resembling colonial practices, the growing elite control of Liberia's social and political life perpetuated the evolution of racial lineage driven discrimination (Osaghae 1995: 2). The indigenous people were denied citizenship until 1904 and were demarcated into 16 tribal clusters through a redefinition of administrative boundaries (Ellis 1999: 37). Liberia progressively transitioned from a fluid multi-ethnic and tribal mosaic to a more rigid and territorially disaggregated distribution of specific tribal groups under the Americo-Liberian elite (Moore 1990; Outram 1997: 358). A complex system of pyramidal patron–client relationships was established for administrative and political purposes. Access to the state and an ability to manipulate its administrative, fiscal, legal, and military resources became central to the process of Americo-Liberian domination (Outram 1997: 358; Ellis 1999; Pham 2004; Gberie 2005).

This exclusionist set-up, where revenue was monopolised and controlled by the elite, resulted in indigenous people being employed as unskilled labour and fomented opposition in the form of student and labour groups with greater awareness of power disparities. Opposition became more acute under the Tolbert regime (1971–1980), and regular riots provoked attempts at military suppression. Efforts to extend employment opportunities to the hinterland populace under President Tolbert had implications for the composition of the army. A growing opposition to Tolbert's economic policies, especially an arbitrary increase in the price of rice, provoked a great deal of resentment. This also created an opportunity for a successful coup by Master Samuel Doe in April 1980, thereby marking the demise of the long-standing monopoly of the Americo-Liberian minority (Ellis, 1995).

Samuel Doe and polarisation of ethnic identity politics

Samuel Doe's April 1980 seizure of power needs to be contextualised as essentially a coup within a marginal institution, namely the Army. The military had played second fiddle to the political leadership under President Tubman and later Tolbert. Doe's arrival also marked the rise of the hitherto socially marginal element, the Krahn, into the echelons of state power and patronage networks. Given that Doe was relatively unconnected politically, he forged alliances with the Krahn and Mandingo communities, into a new neo-patrimonial set up. This alliance monopolised access to state power through its control over jobs, commercial opportunities, and related benefits (Outram 1997; Hoffman 2006: 310). Following rigged elections in 1985, a purge of the military followed. The People's Redemption Council (PRC) regime, led by Doe, undertook a bloody beachside execution of leading opposition members during 1985. As a result, ordinary soldiers and non-commissioned officers gained control of the government machine (Outram 1997). Following an unsuccessful coup attempt in 1985 by Thomas Quiwonkpa, a Gio man from Nimba and Doe's former army commander, Doe unleashed a cruel purge against Gio and Mano soldiers in the AFL as well as ethnically targeted civilian killings in Nimba and Monrovia. Ethnic cleavages became far more pronounced from this point onwards. Political instability was worsened by Doe's mismanagement of the economy. Aid support from the US became less forthcoming during the final phase of Cold War politics (Levitt 2005).

The structural factors which contributed to the Liberian Civil War, namely the ethnicisation of political and social life, were therefore complete in the Doe era. However, the proximate trigger that sparked this conflict into life came in the form of the National Patriotic Front of Liberia (NPFL) insurgency in 1989. Charles Taylor and his NPFL cadres readily exploited these grievances to gain support among the Mano and Gio and to advance Taylor's own personal ambitions for resource extraction and later the presidency.

Charles Taylor and the onset of the first civil war

The NPFL incursion on Christmas Eve 1989 should be viewed not only as a result of domestic political instability but also through the prism of regional political alliances (Bøås 2001: 709). The initial response of the populace was support. Young people in Nimba county, especially Gio and Mano tribesmen who had been targeted and persecuted under the Doe regime, willingly joined the ranks of Taylor's forces. As a result, it was not long before the roughly 100 men recruited from among a selection of Ivorian, Sierra Leonean, and Burkinabe fighters who had launched a strike in Nimba from Côte d' Ivoire swelled in number, and within eight months they had control over nearly 90 per cent of the country's territory.

An initial nonchalance on part of the Doe regime resulted in a wholly ineffective effort to quell the rebellion. Given its previous experience of effectively suppressing the 1985 coup attempt, there was neglect on part of the AFL, and in no time the insurgency was knocking on the gates of the presidential palace in Monrovia (Outram 1997). At this juncture, a power struggle developed within the NFPL ranks and resulted in the formation of a splinter faction – the Independent (I) NPFL – under Prince Yeomie Johnson, a Krahn. This split cost the main insurgency in terms of professional soldiers who left the main NPFL fold and supported the Johnson faction. As a result, the NPFL ranks came to be filled by inexperienced civilians who saw in the rebellion an opportunity for economic gain, physical security, and the desire for social change.

Regional players

Taylor's NPFL invasion also introduced important international and regional actors into the civil war. Prominent among them were Côte d' Ivoire, Burkina Faso, and Libya. President Houphouët-Boigny of Côte d' Ivoire supported Taylor as part of his broader strategy to counter Nigerian regional hegemony. He was also keen to overthrow Samuel Doe's undemocratic rule. Through Houphouët-Boigny, Taylor befriended President Blaise Campaoré of Burkina Faso and Muammar Gaddafi of Libya. As a result, Taylor received Burkinabe troops and weapons transfers for his campaign, while through Gaddafi, he secured training and weapons for NPFL troops. Gaddafi's interest was partly fuelled by a desire to overthrow Doe's regime, initially close to the US, and also to extend Libyan influence in sub-Saharan Africa. During the initial phase, President Doe's counterinsurgency campaign was also supported covertly by Nigeria and the United States due to a perceived anti-Nigerian character of the alliance supporting Taylor and due to US opposition to Libya (Bøås 2005; Levitt 2005).

Armed factions during the first civil war

The next phase of the civil war witnessed the emergence of new and competing factions, often organised along ethnic lines but rooted in the personality of a single leader. Gradually Liberia became a battleground for control over natural resource exploitation by the different warring factions (Table 8.1). There was also a marked shift in the rationale for violence. Civilians were increasingly targeted. A progressive fragmentation of political life complicated efforts to negotiate and implement peace agreements.

TABLE 8.1 Profile of armed groups in Liberia 1995–1996

Faction	*Leader*	*Territory*	*Combatants*
AFL	Lieutenant General Hezekiah Bowen	Barracks within ECOMOG zone	8,734
ULIMO-J	Roosevelt Johnson	South-west	7,776
ULIMO-K	Alhaji Kromah	North-west	12,460
LDF	Francois Massaquoiy	Lofa county, North west	750
LPC	George Boley	Eastern counties	4,650
NPFL	Charles Taylor	Nimba, Bong and adjacent areas	25,000
ECOMOG	ECOWAS	Monrovia and surrounding areas from Kakata to Buchanan	7,269

(*Source*: Outram 1997: 356)

Fourteen different accords were signed at different points during six years of conflict, culminating in the Abuja II accords (1995), which finally paved way for elections and a superficial disarmament, demobilization, and reintegration process (DDR).

Eight different factions and splinter groups were active during the first civil war (1989–1995). Apart from the NPFL headed by Charles Taylor and its splinter faction the INPFL formed under the leadership of Prince Johnson, there was also an anti-Krahn faction of the NPFL called the NPFL–Central Revolutionary Council (NPFL-CRC) formed by Tom Woewiyu (Sesay 1996b). Ethnicity played an important role in the configuration of factions. The Krahn–Mandigo alliance forged under the regime of Samuel Doe was reunited in the form of a joint opposition rebel front of the ULIMO, formed from among exiled Krahn and Mandingo soldiers, politicians, and civilian refugees in Sierra Leone in 1991. The ULIMO received patronage and support from the government in Freetown as well from the Nigerian components of the ECOMOG. The Sierra Leonean government also recruited from among these refugees to bolster its weak army and augment its counterinsurgency strategy. It provided logistical support and bases from which ULIMO first undertook a cross-border strike on NPFL troops in August 1991 (Sesay 1996a, 1996b; Ellis 1995: 183; Outram 1997).

In addition to the groups above, there was also the Doe government's own forces, the AFL, composed primarily of ethnic Krahn soldiers. Sesay (1996b) suggests that this force functioned in the nature of a rebel faction and was primarily entrusted with defending and protecting ethnic Krahn people. The Liberian Peace Council (LPC), formed in 1993 by George Boley, a former minister in the Doe government, recruited a cohort of dissatisfied Krahn soldiers formerly with the AFL. The LPC was essentially an anti-Taylor outfit engaged in attacks on the NPFL in select areas, with the support of the ULIMO and the AFL. The LDF was formed in Guinea in 1993 and sponsored by Taylor to fight the ULIMO-K. The latter responded by aiding the creation of another anti-Taylor force called the Bong Defense Force (BDF). Another small faction called the Liberia New Horizons (LNH) was formed by ethnic Krahns in the US; it made a failed bid, under the leadership of former AFL commander General Charles Julu, to overthrow the interim government in 1994 (Adeleke 1995; ICG 2003).

ECOMOG: a non-neutral peacekeeper

The possible spill-over of the conflict and the continuous outflow of refugees prompted neighbouring countries in West Africa (Jaye 2003: 234) to take action, in the face of staunch opposition from Côte d'Ivoire, to place the Liberian issue on the agenda of the United Nations Security Council (UNSC) (Adibe 1997: 471). US preoccupation with the collapse of the Soviet Union and the Iraqi invasion of Kuwait also made a regional resolution and intervention inevitable (Adibe 1997). On 7 August 1990, the ECOWAS Ceasefire Monitoring Group (ECOMOG) was established under the leadership of Nigeria as a regional peacekeeping force (Alao 1998: 62–65; Olonisakin 1999; Aboagye et al. 2004).

The results of the Peace Plan proposed by ECOWAS were as follows: immediate cessation of hostilities by all factions; the formation and immediate deployment of ECOMOG to Liberia; generalised disarmament of the warring parties by ECOMOG; an embargo on the importation and acquisition of arms by the warring parties in Liberia; and the formation of an Interim Government of National Unity pending the conduct of general and presidential elections in Liberia (see ECOWAS, Decision A/DEC.1/8/90 in Adibe 1997: 474).

Regional rivalries in West Africa have traditionally been aligned along colonial competition lines between Francophone and Anglophone legatees of their previous colonisers. The question of troop contribution to the ECOMOG peacekeeping force deepened this dichotomy, with most of the initial troop contribution from Anglophone states, including Nigeria Ghana, Gambia, and Sierra Leone (Grant-Thomas and Taw 1999: 60). Guinea received the largest influx of Liberian refugees and was the only Francophone state to contribute troops to the mission. Given the political nature of its composition, then, the neutrality of the ECOMOG was dubious at best. Nigerian officers of the ECOMOG co-opted and cooperated with various faction leaders, such as Prince Johnson of the INPFL, and this resulted in the gruesome murder of President Doe by Johnson, which was videotaped and circulated in the media in a brutal testimony to rebel triumph (Bøås 2001, 2005).

The conflict resolution process

During the first Liberian civil war, regional intervention under ECOWAS, supported by the Organisation of African Unity (OAU) and the UN, led to 14 short-lived peace accords between 1990 and 1995 (Dupuy and Detzel 2007). Intermittent peacemaking efforts during the initial years led to five sets of peace agreements. These were the four Banjul Agreements of August–December 1990, the Lomé Agreement of February 1991, the four Yamoussoukro Agreements between April and September 1991, the Cotonou Peace Agreement of July 1993, the Akosombo Agreement and Accra Clarification of September 1994, and finally the Abuja Peace Agreement 1995 and Abuja II 1996 (ibid.).

The reason for so many multiple attempts can be understood from the factionalised nature of the first civil war. The first ceasefire was signed in Bamako, Mali in 1990 and was followed by the Banjul peace agreement the same year. Most of the warring factions were not committed to disarm, however, and therefore this ceasefire did not hold. Another attempt at negotiating a more substantive peace agreement was made in Yamoussoukro, Côte d'Ivoire, in 1991. This resulted in the formation of an Interim Government of National Unity. However, following a lethal attack (Operation Octopus) by the Taylor forces on the ECOMOG forces stationed in Monrovia in 1992, the ECOMOG was drawn into a confrontation with the NPFL. The ECOMOG started supporting the remnant AFL cadres in their anti-Taylor campaign to free Monrovia from NPFL siege.

The emergence of ULIMO in 1991 complicated the civil conflict further. As it was not a party to the 1991 Yamoussoukro Agreement and its provisions, it was difficult to honour the ceasefire agreement. The next ceasefire was signed in Geneva, and a peace agreement between active warring factions was concluded in Cotonou, Benin in 1993. These efforts at negotiating peace were also interrupted by the emergence of two new factions in 1993 – the LPC and the LDF (Outram 1997; Bøås 2001; Dupuy and Detzel 2007). This turn of events and failure to reach a substantial ceasefire prompted UN action with the creation of the UN observer mission in Liberia (UNOMIL) in an attempt to control volatility of the situation.

A split in ULIMO ranks in 1994 added more parties to the negotiating table at Akosombo. The NPFL, AFL, and ULIMO-K negotiated an interim agreement. However, an unsuccessful coup attempt against the interim Liberian government, together with new splits in the NPFL ranks due to the formation of the NPFL-Central Revolutionary Council (CRC) faction, delayed implementation.

The Abuja Accord followed in 1995 and installed a new caretaker government. Elections mandated under Abuja I were postponed on account of internecine and factional fighting between the NPFL and ULIMO-K factions, on the one hand, and the ULIMO-J, LPC, and remnant AFL troops, on the other, in April 1996 (Dupuy and Detzel 2007).

A few key developments at the sub-regional and external levels spurred progress in negotiations. First, former NPFL backers Burkina Faso and Côte d'Ivoire, along with Francophone Benin and Niger, contributed troops to ECOMOG. As a result, a genuinely sub-regional peacekeeping force was formed for the first time in the mission's history.

At the external level, the US decided to dissociate its strained bilateral relationship with Nigeria, which constituted ECOMOG's dominant contingent, from its multilateral support for ECOMOG. The US provided all peacekeepers with logistical support they had previously lacked. This problem of inadequate logistics had thwarted three previous efforts at disarmament. The EU also played an important role in providing logistical support to ECOMOG. Nigeria, which had lacked the logistical and financial resources to end the civil war, was finally provided support by external actors. The US, EU, and UN assisted with demobilisation, reintegration programmes for former combatants, and the electoral process.

Peace also needed the cooperation of the warlords, who decided to enter the political process in August 1995, enabling disarmament. The strongest of the Liberian factions, Taylor's NPFL, made peace with Nigeria, which under General Sani Abacha's leadership was no longer obstructive of Taylor's political ambitions. Elections held in July 1997 saw former warlords take on the mantle of politicians and transform their organisations into numerous political parties. Charles Taylor had maximum resources and manpower and won a clear mandate from a war-weary, tortured populace which chose Taylor to avoid prolonging the conflict and their misery.

This negotiated settlement in 1996 and Taylor's ensuing electoral victory did not, however, result in a comprehensive resolution. Among the proximate triggers that led to conflict relapse in 1999 were (1) the insecure nature of peace and (2) the incomplete disarmament of warring factions.

Insecure peace: the incomplete disarmament, demobilisation, and reintegration of 1996–1997

The DDR programme (1996–1997) was the culmination of a longer process that had been continuously hampered by the lack of political will of parties to the conflict to disarm and demobilise, and the changing or inclusion of new actors in the planning process. From the Yamoussoukro IV Accord (30 October 1991) onwards, all accords contained provisions for the encampment, disarmament, and demobilisation of the warring factions, which multiplied over time. The first attempt, in March 1994, collapsed due to inter-factional fighting, following which a task force on DDR was formed. This task force consisted of representatives from the UNOMIL, ECOMOG, UN agencies, USAID, the EU, and the new Liberian transitional government (LNTG).

The LNTG was installed when the Abuja Accord was signed in August 1995, with the National Disarmament and Demobilisation Commission (NDDC) created subsequently (Detzel and Dupuy 2007). At the start of disarmament and demobilisation operations (22 November 1996), seven of the original 13 sites were opened at Voinjama, Camp Naama, Zwedru, Buchanan, Camp Scheifflin, Barclay Training Center, Tubmanburg, Bo Waterside, Kakata, Tappita, and five other sites, comprising a total of 18 which were operational towards the close of the process (Creative Associates International 1997: 16–17).

The legal framework for the first DDR process was outlined in the Cotonou Accord (July 1993). It was subsequently elaborated, amended, and clarified by the Akosombo Agreements of September 1994, Accra (December 1994), and Abuja 1995. But these agreements only broadly described the modality of disarmament and demobilisation, leaving the financing and most of the planning to the designated organisations. ECOWAS, ECOMOG, the UN, and other international groups such as the United Nations Department of Humanitarian Affairs–Humanitarian Assistance Coordination Office in Liberia (UNDHA-HACO) were responsible for demobilisation from late 1995.

Different modalities were used in the disarmament process across the country, and disarmament criteria were variant and fluctuated at various sites. Criteria for the acceptance of weapons also varied from site to site and from time to time. While initially 40 rounds of ammunition (with or without a weapon) were enough to register as a combatant, later increases in the number of proxies meant the qualifying requirement was revised to 100 rounds (ibid.: 16). The actual registration of former combatants at DDR sites was also much less compared to initial estimates.

The international community's support for the Liberian DDR was less enthusiastic than desired. According to Kelly (1998), the annual budget for UNOMIL was equivalent to spending on four days of UN peacekeeping in former Yugoslavia. As a result, the entire demobilisation process for ex-combatants in Liberia lasted a maximum of 12 hours, with no provision for encampment or prolonged trauma counselling either for adult or child soldiers.

Insufficient logistical preparation led to delays and confusion at the demobilisation centres; fighters were not adequately screened, and there was no encampment and no civic education facilities. The demobilised fighters were directed to other activities within 24 hours of registering at demobilisation centres. By 9 February 1997, nearly 24,500 of the estimated 33,000 fighters (74 per cent) had been disarmed and demobilised. These included 4,306 child fighters and 250 adult female fighters. More than 9,570 weapons and 1.2 million rounds of ammunition were also surrendered, and ECOMOG's cordo and search operations yielded another 917 weapons and 122,162 rounds of ammunition later. Yet this was only a miniscule portion of the weapons actually used during the seven-year civil conflict, and in some respects the disarmament was far from complete. According to media reports, some commanders discouraged disarmament and also intimidated their fighters to prevent them from demobilising (Creative Associates International 1997: 21–25).

Many of the weapons collected were in poor condition, and almost 20 per cent were unserviceable. In the name of reintegration, some labour-intensive programmes were introduced to absorb ex-combatants into productive labour, but these discontinued following the 19 July 1997 elections. Importantly, Charles Taylor's new government was uninterested in reintegrating combatants from factions previously opposed to the NPFL into the new AFL (Bruthus 2004: 5–6). The economy was weak and struggled to absorb returning combatants, who found few employment choices. The mistrust and ethnic cleavages exploited in the course of the civil war were also not adequately addressed or reconciled, and moreover, political targeting of opponents under the Taylor regime reinforced fear and prevented establishment of a positive peace.

In addition to a weak DDR process, the nature of the state under Taylor operated much in line with his warlord control over 'Greater Liberia' (Outram 1997). As president, he resorted to targeted elimination of opponents and economic aggrandisement. These developments were accompanied by a complete collapse of public services. Shifting regional alliances and changing international dynamics resulted in the creation of new factions aimed at ousting Taylor. An increasingly cross-border dimension resulted in embroiling the whole West African landscape into rebel group activity. Conditions for conflict recurrence and the historical events that shaped the outbreak of the second civil war in Liberia are examined next.

The second civil war: the LURD and MODEL insurrections (1999–2003)

Several studies have elaborated that successful negotiated settlements must offer a high degree of institutionalised guarantees relating to military, political, economic, and territorial power-sharing. On the issue of commitment to peace accords, Walter (1999) contends that peace settlements are more likely to endure when effective third-party guarantees provide credible commitments to enforce the terms of a negotiated settlement. On both these counts, the Abuja Accord had its own flaws. Unlike Contonou, which had extant provisions for DDR, the Abuja I accord

(1995, August) delineated broad procedures on DDR and did not provide for specific provisions on planning and coordination. Further to this, the implementation of the provisions of the Abuja II accord was incomplete given that the enforcers, ECOMOG, left the country in October 1999, in a period when a new anti-Taylor group, the Liberians United for Reconciliation and Democracy (LURD), had begun making inroads into Lofa county in the north-west. An under-funded, short, inadequate disarmament and demobilisation process, with a non-existent reintegration and rehabilitation phase, prolonged the conflict. Reno (2000) laments that the 1995 Agreement excluded all civil society groups, effectively legitimising warlord control over Liberia's political structure and economic resources.

Conflict recurrence in Liberia

The recurrence of conflict in Liberia can be explained through a number of approaches to civil war relapse. First was the presence of spoilers and dissatisfied pockets (Stedman 1997, 2002). Second, there were ineffective third-party guarantees to disarm and demobilise factions (Jervis 1978; Walter 2002). Third was the presence of warring factions with their organisational structure intact (Wagner 1993: 255; Licklider 1995). Fourth, the weak institutionalisation of the power-sharing agreement (Hartzell 1999). Finally, a previous civil war can increase the risks of future violence in a state, to the extent that it preserves or intensifies earlier grievances and helps create new ones (Collier 2000: 2)

Charles Tilly suggests that a rebel victory is less likely to be followed by a recurrence of civil war than either a government victory or negotiated settlement because rebel victory is more likely to eliminate the condition of dual sovereignty (Tilly 1978). However, in Liberia, a rebel victory resulted in more insurrections and insurgent movements, backed by regional actors (Cousens and Call 2008). Liberia was a state whose antecedent conditions, i.e. collapsed state apparatus, lootable natural resources, and traditional gerontocratic, exclusionist society lent greater susceptibility to conflict onset and recurrence. This, coupled with the frail nature of democracy and the monopoly of power following Taylor's electoral victory in 1997, provided fertile proximate conditions for conflict resumption (Skocpol 1979; Goldstone 1991; Goodwin 2001). Although the elections in 1997 eliminated the problem of dual sovereignty, it did not create a more stable polity. The hasty and incomplete DDR process, together with inadequate implementation of the terms of the Abuja Peace accord following the departure of the 10,500-strong ECOMOG force in October 1999, resulted in a fragile peace. Internally, the Taylor government continued in the form of his earlier personalised warlord economic dealings, and the delivery of public services was minimal. This laxity in governance was accompanied by a policy of brutal elimination of opposition and reprisals against opponents once Taylor assumed the presidency. Most Krahns faced persecution, hostile behaviour, and neglect during Taylor's elected political leadership.

Opposition to Taylor also crystallised at an international level, with US and regional governments, especially Sierra Leone and Guinea, taking lead in financing and providing bases for operations by anti-Taylor elements; this resulted in the formation of two new insurgencies between 2000 and 2002, namely the Liberians United for Reconciliation and Democracy (LURD) and Movement for Democracy in Liberia (MODEL).

The LURD movement emerged essentially from the ashes of the Liberian civil war and the ethnic persecution, particularly against ethnic Mandingos and Krahns, that followed Taylor's electoral victory in 1997. Many of them were ex-fighters of the ULIMO-K faction forced into exile for fear of reprisal under Taylor's new government.

As part of a shifting matrix of regional political alliances, the Guinean government also provided logistical support to LURD in retaliation for Taylor's support of Guinean dissidents who were trying to overthrow Lansana Conté in 2001 (Jaye 2003). Taylor's difficult relations with the regime in Guinea also created roadblocks to a successful diplomatic settlement. The leadership of LURD, including Chairman Sekou Koneh, were based in the Guinean capital Conakry to liaise with Guinean President Lansana Conté. Lofa county, in the north-west, was at the centre of the LURD uprising due to its contiguity with the Guinea border, where a considerable number of anti-Taylor Mandingo tribespeople had taken refuge (Brabazon 2003; Reno 2004).

Other regional shifts included reversal in the trend ofTaylor's relations with Côte d' Ivoire. Following the death of his initial Ivorian patron, President Houphouët-Boigny, Taylor's ties with that country were strengthened under the regime of General Robert Guei, who was in charge of the army during the onset of Taylor's rebellion against the Doe government. However, after Guei's fall from power, a new Ivorian leadership under President Laurent Gbagbo responded to Liberian and Burkinabe support for two new rebel factions on its western corridor, especially the Mouvement Populaire Ivoirien du Grand-Ouest (MPIGO) faction (formed to avenge killing of Guei), by supporting the MODEL insurgency. Pugel (2008) notes that there is little academic writing on the character of rebel groups operative during the second civil war. There are several theories about the origins of MODEL. Some observers suggest that when LURD attack had permeated Lofa, Bong, Gbarpolu, and Bomi counties, a split developed within its leadership between the Krahns and Mandingos, resulting in the separate faction called MODEL (HRW 2004; Alusala 2008).

With fighting intensifying between LURD and government forces in 2003, Monrovia was besieged in three rounds, locally famous as World Wars I, II, and III. Most of the counties in the south-east, like Grand Gedeh, River Gee, Grand Kru, Sinoe, and Maryland, were under MODEL control even as international negotiators met at Akosombo (Ghana) to find a solution (Alusala 2008: 4; Bøås 2005). As fighting escalated, so did the destruction. Cumulatively, the two episodes of civil war in Liberia resulted in large-scale human displacement and immense infrastructural destruction. According to a 2007 estimate, Lofa, Bomi, Bong, and Gbarpolu were the most affected counties in terms of the displaced (CCF 2007: 7). With respect to death toll, roughly between 200,000 and 300,000 were estimated dead due to the war, a high percentage in a population of just over three million (Loden 2007: 297).

The second civil war came to a close with the signing of a truce on 11 June 2003 between the three main factions – Taylor's AFL and allied militias, the LURD, and MODEL. This was followed by a ceasefire declaration on 17 June 2003 in Accra, Ghana, which paved the way for instituting a transitional government excluding Charles Taylor. Although Taylor was keen on continuing in office until the end of his term as president in 2004, external factors as well as internal opposition made it impossible for him to remain in office. UN sanctions were imposed on him in 2000 and 2001 for his support for the Revolutionary United Front in Sierra Leone and the trade in conflict diamonds. Diplomatic pressures from the US at this time were followed by an indictment on war crime charges by the Special Court of Sierra Leone. Charles Taylor accepted the offer of asylum from Nigeria, and this paved the way for his exit.

The Accra Accords were signed in August 2003 and provided for the creation of a robust UN peacekeeping mission in Liberia (UNMIL), which was entrusted with the responsibility for comprehensive security sector reform and a large DDR programme. On 14 October 2003, Charles Gyude Bryant became the chairman of the National Transitional Government of Liberia (NTGL), which included representatives of LURD and MODEL, loyalists of former President Charles Taylor, and the civilian opposition. The UNMIL also oversaw elections in 2005, while the interim government continued in office, culminating in the election of Ellen Johnson Sirleaf to the presidency in January 2006. The election was lauded as remarkably fair and democratic, and marked a return to constitutional government, fulfilling a key objective of the Comprehensive Peace Agreement (CPA) (Pham 2006).

Lessons to be learned from the case study

By way of a conclusion, it is possible to identify three key points about the Liberian peace process that can inform other peace processes in terms of contextual insights. First, the ethnic element is often overemphasised in conflicts. Mobilisation processes in civil wars are complex. While ethnicity can be a key variable for insurgent success, over time other factors, such as security, economic interests, and external actors, can become more prominent. In Liberia, some of the original armed groups did apparently split along ethnic lines. For instance, the ULIMO fractured into ULIMO-K, based on Mandingo and Krahn affiliation respectively. In reality, these splits were informed by power struggles and clash of personalities in the leadership ranks rather than purely ethnic differences (Outram 1997: 361; Johnson et al. 2008). Anti-Doe or anti-Taylor identification, rather than ethnicity, was the key factor in deciding who was attacked.

Second, the role of elites in conflicts needs to better analysed. This is important from a political settlement perspective. Allowing elites to dictate peace processes through a resort to violence can become a guaranteed formula for post-peace instability. In Liberia, the key leaders of the warring factions were elites at different points in the earlier Americo-Liberian regime and later the Doe regime. Charles Taylor, George Boley, and Alhaji Kromah held ministerial positions and important posts in the Doe government (Reno 2004). These elites were allowed to come to power after the first civil war without appropriate vetting of their wartime involvement. The instability that ensued can be partly attributed to this.

Finally, third-party involvement can become a source of conflict intensification. Involving regional actors in peacekeeping in Liberia's case was a reason for conflict prolongation. Regional solutions to civil conflicts, and in the case of Africa, African solutions to African problems, is a noble ideal. However, political and economic interests of regional players can often mar such an objective. The role of ECOMOG in Liberia and that of regional backers such as Guinea and Côte d' Ivoire, who became involved in the conflict, compromised the much-needed neutrality that third-party guarantees to peace settlements demand. This dynamic was also repeated with the UN mission in Sierra Leone. In both cases, ECOMOG became one of the parties to the conflict, and Nigerian military officials engaged in rent seeking behaviour, profiting from the sale of diamonds by colluding with armed groups such as the Revolutionary United Front (RUF) (La Guardia 2000).[1] To transform regional third-party spoilers into constructive peacemakers requires a more thorough understanding of the objectives and motivations of external players, especially their role as patrons for armed groups. Whether external patrons have a commercial relationship with an armed group, or are merely interested in destabilising a neighbouring state must be carefully ascertained. Experiences from the Mano River conflicts present important lessons in this respect.

Note

1 Interview with Maj Gen Vijay Jetley, Force Commander UNAMSIL, New Delhi, 2 April 2018.

References, further reading, and links to key primary documents

Aboagye, Festus B., and Alhaji M.S. Bah. 2004. "Liberia at a Crossroads: A Preliminary Look at the United Nations Mission in Liberia (UNMIL) and the Protection of Civilians." *ISS Paper 95*. https://oldsite.issafrica.org/uploads/PAPER95.PDF.

Adeleke, Ademola. 1995. "The Politics and Diplomacy of Peacekeeping in West Africa: The Ecowas Operation in Liberia." *The Journal of Modern African Studies* 33 (4): 569–593.

Adibe, Clement E. 1997. "The Liberian Conflict and the ECOWAS-UN Partnership." *Third World Quarterly* 18 (3): 471–488.

Alao, Abiodun. 1998. *The Burden of Collective Goodwill: The International Involvement in the Liberian Civil War*. Aldershot: Ashgate.

Alusala, Nelson. 2008. "Disarmament, Demobilisation, Rehabilitation and Reintegration in Liberia." *DDR and Human Security Project Case Study, ISS/CICS*. www.ddr-humansecurity.org.uk.

Bøås, Morten. 2001. "Liberia and Sierra Leone-Dead Ringers? The Logic of Neo-patrimonial Rule." *Third World Quarterly* 22 (5): 697–723.

Bøås, Morten. 2005. "The Liberian Civil War: New War/Old War?" *Global Society* 19 (1): 73–88.

Brabazon, James. 2003. "Liberia: Liberians United for Reconciliation and Democracy (LURD)." Africa Programme Armed Non-State Actors Project Briefing Paper 1. London: The Royal Institute of International Affairs. www.chathamhouse.org.uk/file/3733_brabazon_bp.pdf.

Bruthus, L. 2004. "The Stockholm Initiative on DDR: Liberia at the Crossroads." http://forsvar.regeringen.se/content/1/c6/53/96/34e491ae.pdf.

Call, Charles T., and Elizabeth M. Ending. 2008. "Ending Wars and Building Peace: International Responses to War-Torn Societies." *International Studies Perspectives* 9 (1): 1–21.

CCF. 2007. "Revitalization of War Affected Communities and Reintegration of Women and Children Associated with the Fighting Forces." *RWAC Program Evaluation Report*. http://pdf.usaid.gov/pdf_docs/PDACK459.pdf.

Collier, Paul. 2000. "Policy for Post-Conflict Societies: Reducing the Risks of Renewed Conflict." Paper presented at the Economics of Political Violence Conference, Princeton, 18–19 March.

Creative Associates International. 1997. "Assessment of the demobilization and disarmament process in Liberia." Final Report. Liberia: USAID.

Dupuy, Kendra, and Helga Malmin Binningsbø. 2007. "Power-Sharing and Peace-Building in Sierra Leone. Power-Sharing Agreements, Negotiations and Peace Processes." *PRIO*.

Ellis, Stephen. 1995. "Liberia 1989–1994: A Study of Ethnic and Spiritual Violence." *African Affairs* 94: 165–197.

Ellis, Stephen. 1999. *The Mask of Anarchy: The Destruction of Liberia and the Religious Dimension of an African Civil War*. London: Hurst & Company.

Gberie, Lansana. 2005. "Liberia's War and Peace Process: A Historical Overview." In Festus Aboagye, and Alhaji M.S. Bah (Eds.), *A Tortuous Road to Peace: The Dynamics of Regional*. Pretoria: ISS.

Goldstone, Jack. 1991. *Revolution and Rebellion in the Early Modern World*. Berkeley: University of California Press.

Goodwin, Jeff. 2001. *No Other Way Out: States and Revolutionary Movements: 1945–1991*. Cambridge: Cambridge University Press.

Hartzell, Caroline A. 1999. "Explaining the Stability of Negotiated Settlements to Intrastate Wars." *Journal of Conflict Resolution* 43 (1): 3–22.

Hoffman, Daniel. 2006. "Despot Deposed: Charles Taylor and the Challenge of State Reconstruction in Liberia." In Roger Southall, and Henning Melber (Eds.), *Legacies of Power: Leadership Change and Former Presidents in African Politics*, 308–331. Uppsala: Nordic Africa Institute.

Human Rights Watch. 2004. "Living in Fear: Child Soldiers and the Tamil Tigers in Sri Lanka." http://hrw.org/reports/2004/srilanka1104/srilanka1104.pdf.

International Crisis Group. 2003. "Liberia: Security Challenges. Dakar/Brussels: Africa." Report No. 71, 3 November. www.crisisgroup.org/~/ . . . /liberia/Liberia%20 Security%20Challenges.ashx.

Jaye, Thomas. 2003. "Briefings Liberia: An Analysis of Post-Taylor Politics." *Review of African Political Economy* 30 (98): 643–686.

Jervis, Robert. 1978. "Cooperation Under the Security Dilemma." *World Politics* 30 (2): 167–214.

Johnson, Kirsten, Jana Asher, Stephanie Rosboroug, Amisha Raja, Rajesh Panjabi, Charles Beadling, and Lynn Lawry. 2008. "Association of Combatant Status and Sexual Violence with Health and Mental Health Outcomes in Post-Conflict Liberia." *Journal of the American Medical Association* 300: 676–690.

Kelly, David. 1998. "Assessment of the Demobilisation and Disarmament Process in Liberia." *UNICEF Final Report.* http://repository.forcedmigration.org/showmetadata.jsp?Pid=fmo:3259.

Levitt, Jeremy I. 2005. *The Evolution of Deadly Conflict in Liberia.* Durham: Carolina Academic Press.

La Guardia, Anton. 2000. "Indian Troops to Pull Out of Sierra Leone." *The Telegraph*, 22 September. www.telegraph.co.uk/news/worldnews/asia/india/1356408/Indian-troops-to-pull-out-of-Sierra-Leone.html.

Licklider, Roy. 1995. "The Consequences of Negotiated Settlements in Civil Wars, 1945–1993." *American Political Science Review* 89 (3): 681–690.

Loden, Alexander. 2007. "Civil Society and Security Sector Reform in Post-Conflict Liberia: Painting Moving Train Without Brushes." *The International Journal of Transitional Justice* 1: 297–307.

Moore, Bai T. 1990. "Problems of Vai Identity in Terms of My Own Experience." *Liberian Studies Journal* 15 (2): 10–12.

Olonisakin, Funmi, and Emmanuel Kwesi Aning. 1999. "Humanitarian Intervention and Human Rights: The Contradictions in ECOMOG." *International Journal of Human Rights* 3 (1): 16–39.

Osaghae, Eghosa E. 1995. "Amoral Politics and Democratic Instability in Africa: A Theoretical Explanation." *Nordic Journal of African Studies* 4 (1): 62–78.

Outram, Quentin. 1997. "It's Terminal Either Way: An Analysis of Armed Conflict in Liberia 1989–1996." *Review of African Political Economy* 24 (73): 355–371.

Pham, John-Peter. 2004. *Liberia: Portrait of a Failed State.* New York: Reed Press.

Pham, John-Peter. 2006. "Reinventing Liberia: Civil Society, Governance and a Nation's Post-War Recovery." *The International Journal of Not-for-Profit Law* 8 (2). www. icnl.org/knowledge/ijnl/vol8iss2/art_2.htm.

Pugel, James. 2008. "Disaggregating the Causal Factors Unique to Child Soldiering: The Case of Liberia." In Scott Gates, and Simon Reich (Eds.), *Child Soldiers: Children and Armed Conflict in the Age of Fractured States*, 160–182. Pittsburgh: University of Pittsburgh Press.

Reno, William. 2000. "Liberia and Sierra Leone: The Competition for Patronage in Resource-Rich Economies." In E. Wayne Nafziger, Frances Stewart, and Raimo Väyrynen (Eds.), *War, Hunger, and Displacement: The Origins of Humanitarian Emergencies*, 231–259. Oxford: Oxford University Press.

Reno, William. 2004. "Reconstructing Peace in Liberia." In Taisier Mohamed Ahmed Ali, and Robert O. Matthews (Eds.), *Durable Peace: Challenges for Peacebuilding in Africa*, 115–141. Toronto: University of Toronto Press.

Sesay, Max Ahmadu. 1996a. "Bringing Peace to Liberia." www.c-r.org/our-work/accord/liberia/index.php/.

Sesay, Max Ahmadu. 1996b. "Politics and Society in Post-War Liberia." *The Journal of Modern African Studies* 34 (3): 395–420.

Stedman, Stephen John. 1997. "Spoiler Problems in Peace Processes." *International Security* 22 (2): 5–53.

Skocpol, Theda. 1979. *States and Social Revolutions: A Comparative Analysis of France, Russia and China.* New York: Cambridge University Press.

Stedman, Stephan John. 2002. *Ending Civil Wars: The Implementation of Peace Agreements.* Boulder and London: Lynne Rienner Publishers.

Taw, Jennifer Morrison, and Andrew Grant-Thomas. 1999. "US Support for Regional Complex Contingency Operations: Lessons from ECOMOG." *Studies in Conflict and Terrorism* 22 (1): 53–77.

Tilly, Charles. 1978. *From Mobilisation to Revolution*. Reading, MA: Addison Wesley.
Wagner, Robert H. 1993. "Ten Causes of Peace." In Roy Licklider (Ed.), *Stopping the Killing: How Civil Wars End*, 235–268. New York: New York University Press.
Walter, Barbara F. 1999. "Designing Transitions from Civil War: Demobilisation, Democratisation, and Commitments to Peace." *International Security* 24 (1): 127–155.
Walter, Barbara F. 2002. *Committing to Peace: The Successful Settlement of Civil Wars*. Princeton, NJ: Princeton University Press.

9

MINDANAO

Ayesah Abubakar and Kamarulzaman Askandar

Introduction

The struggle of the Bangsamoro people in Mindanao can be traced to the history of struggle against the conquest of the western world in this part of Southeast Asia. Spain arrived to the Philippine islands in the early 1520s and met with a civilisation of datus and sultans who had already formed a concept of their own 'bangsa', or nation–states. The two Sultanates of Sulu and Maguindanao led the Muslim resistance against Spain for 300 years when the Philippines was made into a Spanish colony. When the Americans came and took over from the Spaniards, the Bangsamoro people remained defiant and refused to take part in the new Philippine nation, expressing their aspirations for freedom and right to self-determination.[1] Eventually, the Philippine Commonwealth government was successfully installed and later succeeded by the Republic of Philippines. Throughout this history of Philippine state making, the Bangsamoro people have been constant in their struggle for freedom through various means, including diplomatic means and an armed revolutionary movement.

This chapter presents the case of a struggle for self-determination between the Bangsamoro revolutionary movements and the Government of the Philippines (GPH). It is one of the longest running armed conflicts in Southeast Asia and is an example of a protracted and intractable conflict that has evolved from a historical past of state formation to a modern-day revolutionary movement for right to self-determination and freedom. The chapter covers the evolution of the conflict and peace processes involving the Moro National Liberation Front (MNLF) and the Moro Islamic Liberation Front (MILF) with the GPH. The fact that the MNLF and the MILF have had strong support from their own people, gained recognition as representatives of the Bangsamoro cause, and proven difficult to defeat on the ground has compelled the Philippine government to engage them in a formal peace process. The peace process can be separated into two tracks, one each with the MNLF and the MILF. While pursued separately and at different times, the two tracks actually complemented each other, with many successes and failures from the MNLF process, which started in the 1970s and continued through to 1996, being used as lessons learned for the MILF process, which started in 1997. Presently, only the MILF process is still active. It has seen some innovations and achievements since it began in 1997, including bringing in Malaysia as a third-party facilitator in 2001, the involvement of an International Monitoring Team (IMT), and the introduction of an International Contact Group (ICG) in 2009 to act as guarantors to the peace process. The process has also seen a combination of top-down and bottom-up approaches, with civil society organisations playing a crucial role to support the process. All these are part of creative measures to overcome obstacles along the way. It is argued that the hybridity and creativity, especially of the MILF–GPH process, is something that we can learn from.

Conflict analysis

In a 1903 census, 76 per cent of the 327,741 people living in Mindanao were identified as Bangsamoro, with 24 per cent identified as non-Bangsamoro population. This distribution was reversed in the 1980 census, with 23 per cent Bangsamoros and 77 per cent non-Bangsamoros.[2] This reversal has been the result of the successful resettlement programme of Filipinos from the Luzon and Visayas islands to Mindanao, which started during the American administration and continued through the succeeding Philippine governments. It is this phenomenon that dispossessed the Bangsamoro from their traditional ancestral domain practice (as part of the Sultanate system) and enforced a new Torrens titling system. The arrival of migrant settlers greatly affected the Bangsamoro and has been irreversible.[3] It has altered the political, social, and economic dynamics in Mindanao. In the Philippine Census of 2000 by the National Statistics Office, out of the Mindanao total population of 18,856,451, the Bangsamoros or Moros numbered 19.59 per cent, the Lumads and other indigenous groups 8.39 per cent, and the migrant settlers 72.02 per cent.[4] This marked shift of population distribution has led to uneven development and weak political participation from the regional to the national levels. It has further compounded the marginalisation among the Bangsamoros and other indigenous peoples in many ways given the unitary state and majority–minority political dynamics within the country.

The dominance of the Filipino-Christian culture and religion has also had an impact on the Bangsamoro and other indigenous peoples. The Catholic Church was constant in its missionary efforts in Mindanao. The church widely operated schools and other social institutions throughout the islands and from time to time have been a source of tension between Muslims and Christians. While this is not a religious conflict, it does not also discount a number of realities, such as (1) Islam unites the various Bangsamoro ethno-linguistic groups; (2) when Spain colonised the Philippines, its mission was to convert the people into Christianity; and (3) Spain had a history of conflict with the *Moors* or Muslims in Africa, and parallels can be seen in the treatment of the Bangsamoro. As a result, deeply rooted bias against the Bangsamoros can be traced from this historical influence.

The Bangsamoro have been in a cycle of armed violence from the time of the Spanish colonisation until the establishment of the Philippine government. Historical records show a number of massacres that were perpetrated by the rulers and state forces. During the American period, there were massacre incidences in Bud Dajo in 1906, Bud Bagsak in 1913, and the Manobo indigenous people in the Alangkit Movement in Cotabato in 1926–1927.[5] Upon the establishment of the Philippine Commonwealth (1935), and later the Republic (1946), there were no major armed encounters between the government and the Bangsamoro people, but there have been smaller insurrections in areas in Sulu, Lanao, and Cotabato, where some leaders became uncooperative with government. For the most part, it appeared that the assimilation and integration processes have somewhat controlled the increasing dissatisfaction in the communities.[6] Nonetheless, the imposition of the new government and system of laws demotivated the Bangsamoro people and made them feel like second-class citizens in their own homeland. Their sultanate system and their own laws were suddenly disregarded. Many of them have become reluctant to send their children to the public school system and express scepticism towards the Western-oriented values that it introduced.

To some extent, the Philippine government succeeded in attracting some Bangsamoro leaders to participate in national politics. However, these were very few, and their voice had no impact on the national discourse in protecting their people's welfare. They have also sponsored the education of thousands of Moro youth to study in universities in Manila and overseas. It is through this new generation that a group of professionals and religious leaders among their ranks emerged. The Filipino leaders in Manila believed that the Bangsamoro only needed to be educated in order for them to be part of mainstream Philippine society.[7] They underestimated the Bangsamoro worldview, which sees itself as a civilisation that has continuously resisted colonisers and whose culture, religion, and social fabric remains intact. This is in contrast to the Filipinos, who have adapted the Spanish and American ways of life.

It is clear that the shared history of struggle and resistance against the Filipino government has effectively led to the consolidation of Bangsamoro identity, despite having 13 ethno-linguistic groups under the Bangsamoro umbrella. This became more apparent after the Jabidah massacre incident, which occurred under President Ferdinand Marcos on 18 March 1968. The execution of a number of Bangsamoro youth (mainly of Tausug and Samal ancestry), who were initially recruited for a military mission to invade the state of Sabah in Malaysia, highlighted the grave sense of impunity and human rights abuses of the Philippine government towards the Bangsamoro people. This unfortunate history strongly affected the Bangsamoro. It reinforced their insecurities and loss of freedoms under the Philippine State.[8] The Jabidah incident was strongly viewed by Malaysia as a threat to their own independence and national security. Beyond Malaysia, this also received attention from Arab and Muslim countries, e.g. Libya, that are members of the Organization of Islamic Conference.[9] As a consequence, the Jabidah incident hastened the formal formation of the Moro National Liberation Front (MNLF) as a uniting force of resistance against the state.

The Bangsamoro revolutionary movement had its beginning in the formation of the Muslim Independence Movement (MIM) (1 May 1968). Soon after the Jabidah massacre, some Moro leaders organised themselves in order to express their grievances to the Philippine government. This group was led by Datu Udtog Matalam, who was a prominent and well-respected traditional leader. The MIM published a manifesto that asserted the independence of the Moros in the Mindanao, Sulu, and Palawan areas, with a desire to establish an Islamic state. The said manifesto was sent to the United Nations Secretary General's Office, to all Muslim international leaders, and to then-President Ferdinand Marcos.[10] While it seemed that the MIM manifesto had no concrete intention, it did elicit some attention. President Marcos took this message seriously and invited Datu Matalam to talk in Malacanang Palace. The manifesto was also perceived as a threat by Christians in Cotabato and paved the way for the establishment of their own militias, which were known as *Ilagas* or rats as defenders.[11] On the other hand, it was the emergence of MIM that further inspired the younger Bangsamoro to take part in military trainings that were reportedly conducted in Malaysia and in some parts of Mindanao.[12] This eventually started the formation of the forces of the Moro National Liberation Front and its leadership.[13]

During the period of 1970 to 1972, several massacres of Moro communities were committed by the *Ilagas*, who were at times perceived to be in collusion with the security forces and other officials of the government. As a response, it was believed that the MIM organised the Blackshirt group to help defend the Moros. The killings and violence further escalated, up until President Marcos declared martial law throughout the country on 21 September 1972.[14] The Organization of Islamic Conference (OIC), through Libya, learned about the atrocities in Mindanao and became concerned about what might be becoming the potential genocide of Muslims in the Philippines. More Muslim leaders were sympathetic and became more vocal in asking President Marcos and his government to explain what was happening in Mindanao. This presented an opportunity for dialogue between the Moro revolutionary movements and the Philippine government.

The conflict resolution process

There are two tracks of the peace process with the Bangsamoro revolutionary movements. The first was started in 1975 between the government and the Moro National Liberation Front (MNLF), while the second commenced in 1997 between the government and the Moro Islamic Liberation Front (MILF).

The MNLF–GRP peace process

Philippine president Ferdinand Marcos declared martial law on 21 September 1972. Mindanao and the whole country became more chaotic, not only because of the civil unrest but also because of the increasing conflict between Marcos' allies and their political opposition. It was in 1973 that the government and the Moro National Liberation Front (MNLF) forces began to engage in armed confrontations. There were immediate calls for peace talks by the international community, but President Marcos did not wish to recognise the MNLF. Marcos was persuaded to talk to the MNLF after some OIC member countries threatened to impose an oil embargo on the Philippines. Through the mediation of the OIC, the MNLF and the Philippine government conducted their first attempt at peace negotiations. The MNLF, led by Chair Nur Misuari, mainly articulated a demand for freedom and autonomy in Muslim-inhabited areas in the Southern Philippines.[15] The Philippine government, on the other hand, recognised this demand but within the framework of the Philippine constitution which upholds undertaking constitutional procedures and the territorial integrity and sovereignty of the country. Thus, the 1976 Tripoli Agreement was signed by both parties. In this agreement, 14 areas were identified to be included in a referendum that shall eventually form part of the autonomous government envisioned.[16] The territories identified are mainly land-based areas.[17] The 1976 Tripoli Agreement did not reach a successful implementation, as the government attempted to implement it unilaterally. The MNLF was mainly opposed to the government's condition that the inclusion of these land-based areas/provinces would be decided through a constitutional process – a plebiscite. A plebiscite would put the Bangsamoro population in a losing position, given that many of these historically Bangsamoro areas had more recently been populated by Christian settlers. Therefore, the negotiations were suspended, and the MNLF continued with its armed struggle. One of the results of this failure was the fractionalisation of members within MNLF and the emergence of another group, the Moro Islamic Liberation Front (MILF), in 1978.[18]

The Bangsamoro revolutionary movement continued to gain local support throughout the change of government leadership from President Marcos to President Corazon Aquino and then to President Fidel Ramos. In 1996, through the mediation of the OIC – represented by the Government of Indonesia – the Final Peace Agreement (FPA) between the MNLF and the Government of the Philippines was signed. The agreement was translated into the Republic Act (RA) 9054 as the basis of governing the Autonomous Region in Muslim Mindanao (ARMM). This also resulted in the MNLF ruling the ARMM until 2005.[19] The present and existing ARMM areas include the Provinces of Sulu, Tawi-Tawi, Basilan, Maguindanao, and Lanao del Sur and the City of Marawi.

During the period of governance by MNLF leaders in the ARMM, there were many lingering questions as to the extent of powers that they are able to exercise under RA 9054. One example of this lack of power is on the issue of bodies of water within the ARMM areas. In the 1996 FPA and RA 9054, the theme of jurisdiction on bodies of water and maritime territory remained mostly under the purview of the national government, except those that are already defined as part of municipal waters covered under Philippine laws. This issue holds importance with the realisation that bodies of water, like the Lake Lanao, are exploited as a power generation resource outside any authority of the autonomous government. Other natural resources within the region have already been foreseen as potential sources for oil and gas (Liguwasan Marsh, Sulu Seas), and rivers and seas covering the ancestral domain of the Bangsamoro (Sulu Seas, Moro Gulf, etc.) have become inaccessible and underdeveloped for the purpose of connectivity in transportation, marine industry, security, and as a hub for trade and commercial relations within the greater BIMP-EAGA region.[20] The latter is part of the historical social and economic life of the Bangsamoro. The MNLF had a litany of complaints regarding what powers were in fact given to the ARMM. These issues continued to be the agenda of formal discussions as the MNLF demanded a review of the peace deal with the government, again through the facilitation of the OIC.

Soon after the 1996 FPA was reached, President Ramos initiated direct negotiation with the Moro Islamic Liberation Front (MILF), in 1997. However, this was short-lived and was caught during the political transition with the election of a new leader, President Joseph Estrada, in 1998. Over the years, the implementation of the 1996 FPA and the ARMM project was largely viewed as a failure in delivering a more peaceful Mindanao. Peace continued to be elusive, and the people remained sceptical towards the political will of the national government in resolving the Bangsamoro conflict. This was happening amid the MILF–GRP peace negotiations, which had a slow beginning and a low profile given the absence of any international third party.

The MILF–GRP peace process was catapulted to national consciousness when President Estrada decided on a military solution with the hope of ending the influence of the MILF in central Mindanao in 1999, better known as the 'all-out-war'. Contrary to the government's view that fighting the MILF and taking back its camps would win points for the government, the revolutionary group instead gained more local support. While the nine months of armed confrontations between the government and MILF forces awakened deep-seated biases and discrimination of Filipinos against the Bangsamoro people in general, it also fuelled the Bangsamoro revolutionary movements and communities to articulate their demands for right to self-determination. Subsequently, President Estrada's 'all-out-war' became one of the main things, among others, that led to his impeachment and forced his departure from office in 2001 following mass protests against his leadership. He was quickly replaced by Vice President Gloria Macapagal-Arroyo. President Gloria Macapagal-Arroyo wasted no time in asking Malaysia to persuade the MILF to return to peace negotiations with her new government as part of bringing stability back to the country. Thus began the MILF–GRP peace process with Malaysia as third-party facilitator.[21]

The MILF–GHP peace process[22]

The peace process between the Moro Islamic Liberation Front (MILF) and the Government of the Philippines (GPH) illustrates a systematic type of peacemaking. At the early stages, the agenda was divided into three core themes: security arrangements, rehabilitation and development, and ancestral domain. This compartmentalisation of negotiating themes was a novel idea, taking the approach of discussing the easy to hard topics in the negotiating process and dissecting the roots of the conflict. In the ancestral domain theme, there were also sub-topics: concept, territory, resources, and governance. It is in this regard that clear discussions were made on identifying not only geographical land territories but also bodies of water and marine territory that have historically been part of the envisioned Bangsamoro region. The MILF pursued this topic as crucial not only to political governance but also, and most importantly, in terms of sustainable development, regional economic connectivity, and social integration covering the Western Mindanao islands to Central Mindanao areas. On the side of the Philippine government, they needed to ensure that the interest of the national and other local governments outside the envisioned Bangsamoro region were fulfilled, especially in the access and exploitation of bodies of water and marine territory. This aspect of power over resources (in the covered regions) is particularly relevant given the involvement of investors and industrialists close to the national government. An example of this is the case of the control of Lake Lanao, which was mainly controlled by a government-owned corporation with foreign direct investment interests. Lake Lanao not only has a resource and economic value to the people in this region but, more importantly, also has historical and social value as well. Thus, the issue of control over resources is crucial to the discussion of ancestral domain for the MILF.

Since 2001, the GPH–MILF peace process has not only provided a peacemaking platform but also evolved a comprehensive structure in peacekeeping and peacebuilding infrastructures. The peacemaking is formally facilitated and hosted by the Government of Malaysia. These negotiations and meetings were held in Kuala Lumpur or Putrajaya in Malaysia. However, despite encouraging progress up to 2008, the formal signing of the Memorandum of Agreement on Ancestral Domain (MOA-AD) was halted due to a restraining order by the Philippine Supreme Court.[23] Eventually, the Court decided that the MOA-AD was unconstitutional, leading the GPH panel to abandon this document and suspended the peace talks. In 2009, efforts were restarted towards the resumption of peace negotiations. One of these initiatives was the holding of a Consolidation for Peace (COP3) for Mindanao: Strategic Planning for Peace Post MOA-AD in Penang, Malaysia.[24] This event became the first meeting for the negotiating panels and Filipino civil society groups (mostly from Mindanao), soon after the MOA-AD debacle. Participants were involved in a dialogue, self-reflection, and brainstorming exercise on how to move the process forward. This kind of informal and non-commitment type of avenue proved to be useful, especially when the formal peace process was confronted with difficulties in renewing trust among the parties and supporters themselves. One important proposal that came out of the COP3 was the proposal of establishing the 'Friends of the Peace Process'. Upon the resumption of the GPH–MILF peace process, this idea was carried out in the formal introduction of a group of international guarantors or actors to serve as official observers.[25] This group was later named the International Contact Group (ICG). The ICG included the Governments of the United Kingdom, Japan, Turkey, Saudi Arabia; and international organisations like the Centre for Humanitarian Dialogue (Switzerland), Conciliation Resources (UK), The Asia Foundation (US), and Muhammadiyah (Indonesia).

The first ceasefire between the MILF and GPH armed forces began in 1997. Since then, peacekeeping and peace monitoring has evolved from the setting up of the local monitoring teams (organised by the main parties) to the eventual acceptance and inclusion of independently organised, civilian-led monitors, more popularly known as *Bantay Ceasefire*. The *Bantay Ceasefire* was organised by a coalition of local non-governmental networks and organisations – the Mindanao People's Caucus (MPC). In January 2003, this group conducted a successful investigative mission that evaluated ceasefire violations, which had become more frequent despite the ongoing peacemaking process. As a result, the *Bantay Ceasefire* network produced a report of this mission and recommended to both MILF and GPH that there was a need to deploy a more independent monitoring and peacekeeping team.[26] This same report was also submitted to the Government of Malaysia as the third-party facilitator of the peace talks.[27] The network also noted that for purpose of management, Malaysia should also take a leadership role in this task. The following year, the International Monitoring Team (IMT) was formed and led by Malaysia, including monitors from Brunei and Libya. The presence of the IMT led to an abrupt decrease of ceasefire violations after its deployment in 2004. From a height of 698 violations in 2002, and 569 in 2003, these violations dropped as low as 16 violations in 2004. From 2012 to 2014, no violations were recorded by the IMT.[28] Another important innovation introduced in 2004 was the Ad Hoc Joint Action Group (AHJAG), which was tasked with ensuring that there would be a working relationship between the MILF and GPH forces in the pursuit of suspected criminals or actors involved in acts of terrorism in MILF-controlled areas.[29] In many incidences, the work of the AHJAG proved to be important in preventing conflicts, with the government forces and the MILF cooperating in times of police or military operations on suspected criminals thought to be hiding in MILF areas.

Security was not the only mandate of the International Monitoring Team. Three other aspects – mainly socio-economic monitoring, civilian protection, and humanitarian and rehabilitation – became more prominent with the addition of other actors to the IMT. In 2006, Japan participated and deployed socio-economic monitors as part of the IMT.[30] This was followed in 2010 by the incorporation of Norway, together with other non-governmental organizations as members under the Civilian Protection Component; and a European Union representative to lead the focus on the Humanitarian, Rehabilitation, and Development Component. The IMT in itself has developed into a complex structure with the involvement of both local and international actors serving specific roles of monitoring.[31] The IMT also expanded to include security forces and civilian members from Indonesia.

The Philippines has had a history of building a robust NGO community since the re-establishment of a more democratic government under President Corazon Aquino in 1989. However, it was during the resumption of peace talks between the MILF and GPH in 2001 that peacebuilding strategies and activities immensely increased. Many of these activities were organised by the NGOs and the academe based in Mindanao. There was wide interest in getting involved in the peace process, given that it was widely hoped to be the final track in the search for peace in Mindanao. The conglomeration of NGOs, like the Mindanao People's Caucus (MPC) and the Mindanao Peace Network, were visible in organising the annual Mindanao Peace Week, mainly in the cities of Zamboanga, Davao, Cotabato, and Marawi. Also during this time, more Bangsamoro NGOs and academics were drawn into working for advocacy and peace. For the first time, at least 60 Bangsamoro NGOs formed their own network, the Consortium of the Bangsamoro Civil Society.[32] Civil society organizations' (CSO) peacebuilding work gained momentum, and a more united voice of representation was finally heard. In times of deadlocks and many challenges in the peacemaking and peacekeeping arena, it was this CSO component that provided another pillar to the whole peace process.

When the process was confronted with the non-signing of the Memorandum of Agreement on Ancestral Domain (MOA-AD) in 2008, this presented an opportunity for the CSOs to lead and initiate a dialogue while filling the vacuum that often comes when the formal peace process is faced with a setback.[33] Interestingly, this point in the history of GPH–MILF engagement made the CSOs reflect on their experiences, and several lessons were learned in this setback. Some of these reflections included the realisation that the CSOs themselves needed to be in constant dialogue with each other in order to develop a united front. Second, they observed that the efforts of many years of peacebuilding should be scaled up and turned into a national project, not only concentrated in Mindanao.[34] This is important as it showed that the dissenters and spoilers emanated not only from some Mindanao traditional politicians but also from the general public outside of the conflict areas (as far away as Manila), for whom the search for peace in the Bangsamoro region was less urgent. Crucially, they realised that the traditional politicians identified as 'spoilers' in the beginning, and assumed to be under the purview of the government, cannot be left behind but instead must be included in their peacebuilding advocacy. The peace process would need all the support it could get from various sectors, including politicians, bureaucrats, business and investors, government security forces, youth, and many other Filipinos, who needed to be convinced that a peaceful Mindanao would benefit the entire country.

In the succeeding years, President Benigno Aquino Jr. took over from President Gloria Arroyo and continued the GPH–MILF peace process. The resumption of this new chapter of the peace process was, again, confronted with a sense of uncertainty. However, in a bold move, President Aquino personally met the MILF Chair Ebrahim Murad in Tokyo, Japan as an initial effort of rebuilding confidence and trust among negotiating parties.[35] In spite of challenges in pursuing his own brand of peacemaking, it is during his term that the 17-year-old MILF–GPH peace process reached the signing of the Framework of Agreement of the Bangsamoro (FAB) on 12 October 2012 and the Comprehensive Agreement on the Bangsamoro (CAB) on 27 March 2014. The CAB presented a collection of agreements and detailed discussion on the Framework of Agreement of the Bangsamoro (FAB),[36] Annex on Transitional Arrangements and Modalities, Annex on Revenue Generation and Wealth Sharing, Annex on Power-Sharing, Annex on Normalisation, and the Addendum on the Bangsamoro Waters and Zones of Joint Cooperation.

From these agreements, several institutions were established, namely, the Independent Commission on Policing, Transitional Justice and Reconciliation Commission, and the Bangsamoro Transition Commission (BTC). It is the BTC that was mainly tasked to draft the Bangsamoro Basic Law as the charter of the new governing institution to be entrenched in the envisioned Bangsamoro political entity.

The Aquino government worked the hardest with the completion and initial implementation of the agreements, like the fulfilment of a socio-economic package to MILF fighters (called *Sajahatra* Program), charting of a Bangsamoro Development Plan and the first step of a symbolic turn-over of decommissioning of weapons from senior MILF fighters, and the successful inclusion and participation of more international actors (governments and donor agencies) as part of the bigger peace support infrastructure. The defining moments of President Aquino's accomplishment were the signing of the two previously mentioned agreements: the FAB on 15 October 2012 and the CAB on 27 March 2014 – both signed in Manila and witnessed by the Malaysian government as facilitator, members of the International Contact Group (ICG), and many other international and local supporters of the peace process.

However, while the Aquino government pushed the peace process to its highest point, it also brought it down to its lowest. This happened when the Mamasapano incident[37] led to the failure of the Bangsamoro Basic Law (BBL) to be passed in the Congress and Senate. The BBL was to be the foundation law that would constitutionally establish the new form of government agreed in the FAB and CAB. On that fateful day of 25 January 2015, armed hostilities broke out between the government and MILF forces. As a result, President Aquino and the MILF as peace partners were both put in the critical public eye as they were held responsible for the violent killing of 44 SAF troopers. It turned out that the biggest casualty was the BBL. President Aquino ended his term in June 2016 without the passing of the BBL in the parliament. Hence, the implementation of the CAB awaited the incoming government of President Rodrigo Duterte.

The Duterte presidency and the Bangsamoro peace process

The Philippines witnessed another turning point in its political life upon the assumption of Rodrigo Duterte as the 16th president of the country. He is widely perceived as a populist leader, in contrast to the general perception that national leadership is reserved for the elite from Luzon or Visayas regions. President Duterte made history by being the first president to come from the Mindanao region. With his origin and personal history, President Duterte appears to be highly familiar with the history of armed conflicts between the Bangsamoro groups, the communists, and the Philippine government. He has personally met all leaders of these non-state actor groups. As such, there are some expectations that he should be keener to broker peace with all of these groups.

The two Bangsamoro revolutionary groups – the MILF and the MNLF (under the leadership of Muslimin Sema, Yusof Jikiri, and Abul Khayr Alonto) – have forged unity in supporting the BBL, as a result of the Bangsamoro Coordination Forum between the two groups, which was established by the Organization of Islamic Conference and the Government of the Philippines. It is thought that the MILF peace track can succeed only if the MNLF and its 1996 Final Peace Agreement is merged with a future MILF agreement implementation. As such the OIC has worked on this unity initiative since 2005.[38] However, on most occasions, Chair Misuri remained ambivalent towards this idea.[39] This dilemma, however, was finally resolved when MNLF Chair Misuari officially stated that he is not opposed to the BBL but will instead take part in President Duterte's campaign for federalism.[40] Henceforth, the BBL continues its journey through the legislative process in the House of Congress, while allies of President Duterte are constant in their work towards a shift to a federal type of government – and with it is a Bangsamoro region as envisioned by Misuari and President Duterte.

The MILF peace agreement implementation continues to be confronted by the same legislative process as in the past government. There are two possible scenarios: Scenario A – the submitted BBL by the duly installed Bangsamoro Transition Commission (BTC) will be unadulterated, pass the scrutiny of both Congress and Senate, and be enacted as the law in reconstructing a new Bangsamoro government; or, Scenario B – a new and revised BBL will result from the deliberations in Congress and Senate and in the process be unable to stay close to the Comprehensive Agreement of the Bangsamoro (CAB). Scenario B is reminiscent of what happened in 2016, during the time of President Benigno Aquino Jr., which ended in the failure of the legislative bodies to pass the BBL. The main difference between the events of 2016 and 2018 is that (1) there is a parallel move by Congress to shift from a unitary to a federal type of government, which appears to be an important vision of President Duterte and his allies; and (2) in 2016, even if the Mamasapano event of 2015 diminished the social capital of then-President Benigno Aquino Jr. as the champion of the BBL, in 2018 the military success of the Marawi crisis[41] has, in fact, made President Duterte appear to be the strong leader needed to champion the BBL. However, in spite of all these and an open communication line between the two groups – the MILF and the MNLF – directly with President Duterte, the future of the Bangsamoro peace process remains unpredictable and highly volatile.[42] Nevertheless, in contrast to the termination of the peace process with the Communist Party of the Philippines, led by its Chair Joma Sison, the Bangsamoro process appears to be more stable.[43]

Lessons to be learned from the case study

The Bangsamoro conflict resolution process presents a number of interesting lessons regarding political will and leadership, the role of civil society, the involvement of third-party mediators, and the potential for creative solutions.

The political will to resolve, especially by the leaderships on both sides, must be there. While inputs by other actors and stakeholders are important to pressure the main actors to start and maintain a peace process, the decision to be involved in a peace process itself is top-down. The same applies to sustaining it over time. On the government side, the relevant presidents made the decision based on personal and national interests, as well as influence and pressure by other actors, including political allies and enemies, international actors, and national and local constituents. The MNLF and MILF were also influenced by their leaderships. Nur Misuari, Salamat Hashim, and Ebrahim Murad have all been influential in determining the direction of their struggles, both for war and peace. The roots of the groups' transformation can be traced to personal transformation on the part of the leaderships. Another plus point has been continuity and consistency, especially of the MILF negotiating panel. Changes to this team were made only when necessary, such as in the case of death or health problems of a panel member.

Any decision and transformation for peace from the top cannot be started and sustained if the base and platform for peace on the ground is not strong. The Bangsamoro case has shown that grassroots activities and civil society peacebuilding go hand in hand and complement the peace process. The roots of peace are local. The emergence of the civil society in peacebuilding came about during the peace process. Constituent building within the community, network-building, peace advocacy, peace monitoring, use of alternative media, reconciliation activities, inter-faith dialogues, peace education, and many others are just some of the activities engaged in in the Bangsamoro areas to promote support for peace on the ground. These activities keep up the pressure on the main armed actors to continue with the peace process.

The Bangsamoro case also shows that even though the solution and support for peace must come from the roots of the conflict on the ground, wider national support is crucial for its success. The decisions and agreements still need to be ratified by national bodies, as well as transformed into national laws for implementation. Without support at the national level, this will not happen.

The involvement of a third party to kick-start the process and guide it towards an agreement is important. The role played by the third party will be determined by the mandate given by the main actors. It was thus that Malaysia and the OIC (represented by Libya and Indonesia) both played the roles of intermediaries or facilitators at different times in the conflict. The role in the formal peace process has mainly been to facilitate the talks and provide guidance for the process to move forward. Indonesia was successful in guiding the GRP–MNLF process towards the 1996 Final Peace Agreement (FPA), while Malaysia was successful in getting the government and the MILF to sign the FAB in 2012 and the CAB in 2014.

Third parties can also come in different forms, either formal or informal, and be involved in different types of activities. Countries (UK, Turkey, Japan, Saudi Arabia) and international non-governmental organisations (CR, CHD, Asia Foundation, Muhammadiyah) have come in as the International Contact Group (ICG) and have played the role of monitors and guarantors in the formal meetings. International actors (Malaysia, Libya, Brunei, Japan, Indonesia) have also come in to monitor the situation on the ground and investigate ceasefire violations by the armed actors; they have also supported socio-economic programmes (Japan, UNDP, WB) within the communities and have with local partners provided support for civilian protection mechanisms (EU). An innovative way of peacebuilding can also be seen in the creation of a second parallel informal track as shown by the Consolidation for Peace (COP) programmes (SEACSN, REP-USM) organised in Malaysia, as a way of providing civil society and other stakeholders access to the main actors and to have a two-way dialogue between them in an informal setting away from the conflict zones.

The GPH–MILF process has shown that a well-structured peace process is necessary to ensure sustainability, commitment, and success. It began by looking at immediate concerns such as security and preventing armed contacts on the ground, before progressing to include other issues, including ancestral domain, socio-economic and political issues, and a long-term political solution to address the generations-long injustices felt by the Bangsamoro people. A look at the agreements signed between the government and the MILF over the years will show that these are detailed documents. Everything is spelled out and made as detailed as possible. This is to ensure that they are not misunderstood and to make sure that the implementation process is well guided. The agreements are also regarded as cumulative, meaning that what has been agreed today stays, and adds on to whatever decisions that have been agreed upon before. It will also be used as a platform or building block for future documents.

The durability of the process has also been influenced by the way challenges and obstacles have been overcome over the years. Each hurdle has in fact made the process stronger and acted as a building block for peace. For example, the collapse of the process in 1999 resulted in Malaysia being appointed as the facilitator; the clashes on the ground and violations of the ceasefire agreement brought in the International Monitoring Team (IMT) in 2004; the collapse of the process in 2008 due to the MOA-AD rejection by the Supreme Court resulted in the creation of the International Contact Group (ICG) to act as guarantors; the rejection of the Bangsamoro Basic Law (BBL) in the legislative bodies due to the Mamasapano incident in 2015 brought in greater commitments by the next president (Duterte) to resolve the issue, through a stronger and more inclusive Bangsamoro Transition Commission (BTC), identifying the BBL as an urgent bill in Congress, and the introduction of federalism as a long-term solution to address the Bangsamoro problem and the whole of the country's governance structure.

Lastly, this durability of the Bangsamoro peace process reflects the creativity of the architects and others involved in the process. Some decisions were made by design, some as responses to emerging issues or incidences. It has the ingredients of a generic peace process, but it has also shown elements of creativity and hybridity by combining local and international contributions and involvement and marrying peacemaking–peacebuilding–peacekeeping/monitoring together. It also combines and uses different lenses when looking at finding a long-term solution to the Bangsamoro conflict – it looks at addressing past injustices; it looks at current realities, both challenges and opportunities; and it looks at the creation of new and innovative institutional reforms that will finally resolve the socio-economic and political issues of the Bangsamoro people. This comprehensive approach will hopefully end the Bangsamoro conflict once and for all.[44]

Notes

1 Under the Treaty of Paris, signed on 10 December 1898, Spain ceded the Philippine Islands to America with a payment of 20,000 Mexican dollars. Earlier, during the declaration of the First Philippine Republic in 1896, then President Emilio Aguinaldo wrote a letter to the Sulu Sultan (dated 18 January 1899) recognising their sovereignty and independence. He asked the Bangsamoro people to be part of the formation of the new state. Eventually, the Sulu Sultan disregarded this offer and instead decided to sign the Bates Treaty with the Americans.
2 See the table of population in Che Man (1990).
3 This settler migration was mainly a problem in mainland Mindanao. By the year 1950, it became apparent that the settlers had gained full control of the political and economic life of many towns. On the other hand, the Bangsamoro-populated towns became underdeveloped, which fuelled more frustration on their part.
4 In the Philippine Census of 2000 by the National Statistics Office (NSO), but the disaggregated populations according to Moro and Lumad groups were adapted from Rodil (2010).
5 The Bud Dajo and Bud Bangsak massacres happened among the Tausugs in Sulu, while the Alangkit Movement was another massacre incident that involved the non-Moro indigenous peoples known as Manobos, in the area of Cotabato. All were perpetrated by the Americans.
6 This Philippine government policy also has its origins in the policy of attraction that the American government employed in the Moro Province. It also has to be noted that American rule in the Philippines was interrupted by the Japanese occupation (1942–1945). During this time, it is interesting that some Moro leaders played crucial roles and defended the country side by side with the Filipino and American militaries. The Bangsamoro leader, Salipada Pendatun from Cotabato, became a Brigadier General and successfully led the defence of Central Mindanao areas against the Japanese soldiers.
7 Cesar Majul writes about this period in time, when Senator Domocao Alonto, from Lanao, led a committee in 1954 to study the Moro Problem. In the end, recommendations were made, but only one was fulfilled – the establishment of the Commission on National Integration. See Majul (1985).
8 The Jabidah Massacre was an alleged secret operation by the government of President Marcos. A group of young Tausug men from Sulu were recruited by the military and trained in the island of Corregidor. On the day of their mission, they were told to invade Sabah, Malaysia. These young men did not wish to follow the orders, and thus, they were killed. A lone survivor lived to tell this story, Jibin Arula. A more recent interview is in Arguillas (2009).
9 Later, in the succeeding section, the involvement of Malaysia and the OIC will be further discussed as part of the internationalisation of the peace process. Majul (1985) tells the story of the experiences of massacres in the Moro areas and the armed hostilities among the Moros and the Christians
10 In Jubair (1999).
11 Ibid. A list of massacres perpetrated by the *Ilagas* in Mindanao can be found in Salah Jubair's book. The killings occurred from March 1970 to January 1972. It is also said that the *Ilagas* were mainly organised by local Christian politicians in central Mindanao.
12 The first group was known as Batch 90 and the second was Batch 300 – these became the core military force of the Moro National Liberation Front.
13 The founding of the MNLF was led by Salleh Loong (Tausug from Sulu), Hashim Salamat (Maguindanao from Cotabato), Nur Misuari (Sama-Bangingi from Tawi-Tawi and Sulu), and Abul Khayr Alonto (Maranaw from Lanao).

14 There were many reasons given why President Marcos declared martial law in the Philippines at that time – because of the communist threat and increasing opposition from the university student movement, including what has been labelled as a Mindanao secessionist movement. However, there were also early indications that President Marcos made use of martial law in order for him to stay in power for a long time.
15 This track with the MNLF has evolved in terms of its party representations. The agreements signed with the MNLF were under the leadership of Chair Nur Misuari (1978 to 1997). However, within the last ten years of implementing and reviewing the peace agreement, the government has been confronted by negotiating and dealing with several leadership factions within the MNLF, apart from Chair Nur Misuari. These factions involve the groups under the leadership of Muslimin Sema, Abulkayr Alonto, Hatimil Hassan, and Alvarez Isnaji, among many others. In spite of this complexity of representation, one thing remains constant – Chair Nur Misuari as a key player of the MNLF and his official relationship with the OIC. Nur Misuari remains a recognised leader–representative of the MNLF during the formal OIC meetings. However, in recent years, the OIC meetings has also invited the MILF Chair Ebrahim Murad, besides Misuari, as part of an effort to encourage both leaderships to have a platform for dialogue and a more consolidated voice in this type of meetings.
16 The Tripoli Agreement was reached on 23 December 1976 with the participation of the Quadripartite Ministerial Commission Members of the Islamic Conference and the Secretary General of the Organization of Islamic Conference (OIC). Its key provisions include the establishment of an autonomous region in the Southern Philippines 'within the realm of the sovereignty and territorial integrity of the Republic of the Philippines'. The region shall comprise the following 13 provinces: Basilan, Sulu, Tawi-Tawi, Zamboanga del Norte, Zamboanga del Sur, North Cotabato, Maguindanao, Sultan Kudarat, Lanao del Norte, Lanao del Sur, Davao del Sur, South Cotabato, and Palawan; and all the cities and villages situated in the above-mentioned areas. The Tripoli Agreement also provided for Shari'a law courts and special regional security forces. MNLF Tripoli Agreements 1976.
17 This aspect of land-based territory identification was further developed in the MILF peace process as they have successfully included the bodies of water and other sea-based territories in the agreements – Addendum on Bangsamoro Waters.
18 There were actually two groups that emerged from the MNLF – the MILF, led by Hashim Salamat, and the Reformist Group by Dimas Pundato.
19 To be noted is the fact that the ARMM was created during the time of President Corazon Aquino. Aquino and Misuari were engaged in direct negotiations but failed to reach an agreement. In the end, she organised the ARMM and supported a new group of local Moro politicians to become the leaders of this new autonomy project. While the Organic Act, or enabling law of the ARMM, was drafted in 1988, with broad-based participation of leaders from the Bangsamoro, Christians and Lumads, or Indigenous Peoples, the end result – the creation of the ARMM – remained highly criticised and was mostly seen as a unilateral act without cooperation and agreement, especially from the Bangsamoro communities.
20 Brunei, Indonesia, Malaysia, Philippines–East Asia Growth Area.
21 A comprehensive analysis of Malaysia's entry into and role in this process can be found in Santos (2003).
22 During the earlier peace process, the Government of the Philippines used GRP in the documents, but sometime in 2010 this was replaced with GPH to follow ISO naming standards. This change of name was officially recorded in the succeeding documents to avoid any miscommunication.
23 The MOA-AD was agreed upon by the parties on 16 July 16 2008 and was to be officially signed on 5 August. However, this agreement was confronted with opposition. Some political leaders went to the Supreme Court to question the legality and constitutionality of the MOA-AD. In the morning of 4 August, while all the GPH–MILF representatives were on their flight from Manila to Kuala Lumpur, the Supreme Court enacted a restraining order in regard to the signing of the agreement.

24 The COP is a joint peacebuilding program between the Southeast Asian Conflict Studies Network, Research and Education for Peace–Universiti Sains Malaysia, and the Japan International Cooperation Agency. A report proceedings of this COP3 can be found in Askandar and Abubakar (2009).

25 The MILF proposed this idea of international guarantors or observers to the newly installed GPH peace panel upon the resumption of the peace talks.

26 See Arguillas (2009).

27 This report was submitted to the Office of the Prime Minister of the Government of Malaysia by a member of the Bantay Ceasefire Mission.

28 In a formal report by the IMT Head of Mission in the Consolidation for Peace (COP6) held 23–25 June 2014, Hiroshima, Japan. This was organised by the SEACSN, REP-USM, and JICA.

29 At that time, many of the ceasefire violations were found to be occurring during the height of kidnap-for-ransom activities and other criminal acts that did not necessarily involve the MILF forces and dragged them into armed confrontation with the GPH forces. This context and operation of AHJAG is often tested on the ground on many occasions and proves how this entity is key to any mis-encounter and escalation of armed conflicts.

30 This is one of the important suggestions that came out during the Consolidation for Peace (COP1) on 23–26 January 2006. This list of suggestions was also formally submitted to then-President Gloria Macapagal-Arroyo through the Office of the Presidential Adviser on the Peace Process (OPAPP).

31 As of 2017, the IMT contingent remains to be led by Malaysia with the participation of members from Brunei, Indonesia, Japan, EU, and Norway. The government of Libya withdrew its four-member delegation in 2009.

32 This development of emergence of Bangsamoro NGOs is important given that during the time of the MNLF–GPH process and implementation, the only NGOs were mostly those that had been organised by the MNLF or government.

33 There were many instances throughout the GPH–MILF process at which the CSO peacebuilding work proved to be crucial in supporting the peace process.

34 As results of discussions during a peacebuilding forum, Consolidation for Peace 3 held in Penang in 2009.

35 This event happened despite the advice that President Aquino should not be meeting with the MILF Chair in person.

36 The FAB is like a road map that gave the details of key sections to be completed in the CAB, including the timeline of the whole process up to the implementation and post-implementation stage.

37 On 24 January 2015, there were almost 400 members of the police special action forces (SAF) that conducted an operation to arrest a suspected terrorist named Marwan, who was allegedly hiding in an MILF-controlled area in a small village in Mamasapano, Maguindanao. This event led to a bloody encounter between the SAF and the MILF fighters and resulted in the killing of 44 SAF troopers, 17 MILF fighters, and three civilians. The whole country woke up on 25 January to this sudden and violent news. The MILF insisted that it was a mis-encounter and no coordination had been made by the government security forces with their group given that there is an existing mechanism within the International Monitoring Team in relation to this type of operation against suspected criminals in MILF areas. See Mordeno (2015). The Houses of Senate and Congress conducted high-profile investigations into this incident that eventually led to a loss of credibility for the BBL as it was about to be deliberated by both branches of the parliament. The government has also lost its credibility due to the fact that this SAF operation was only privy to a small group of leadership and President Aquino himself; not involving the highest officials of the Philippine National Police and the Department of Interior and Local Government and the Armed Forces of the Philippines, as such, it effectively put the lives of the SAF in danger without proper planning and protocols.

38 The Secretary General of the OIC, for the first time, attended the supposed signing of the Memorandum of Ancestral Domain (MoA-AD) in Putrajaya, Malaysia in September 2005 as part of its first steps in bringing together the two peace tracks. In this official document, Secretary-General Ambassador Sayed Elmasry was stated as an endorser of this agreement. Becoming a formal witness to the signing of this document was planned to show recognition of the MILF peace process in parallel to the OIC's official role in the earlier MNLF peace process.
39 See Arguillas (2017).
40 See Cornelio (2017).
41 It is interesting that during the implementation phase of the MILF peace agreement, another armed conflict occurred in Mindanao – the Marawi crisis brought about by the local group called Maute brothers, which evolved into a full-scale terror group. The Marawi armed conflict commenced on 23 May 2017 and lasted for five months. It brought Marawi City to ground zero. While this was not related to either the MILF or the MNLF groups, this event clearly demonstrated the fragile security conditions in Bangsamoro areas like Marawi City and the real and present danger of other groups exploiting Bangsamoro historical grievances. More than ever, the hope of resolving the Bangsamoro conflict has become urgent, and Marawi is becoming a symbol of this desperation to reach a durable peace in Mindanao.
42 President Duterte's latest assurances include that both BBL and federalism are part of his government's commitment and strategy in seeking peace in Mindanao. See Arguillas (2018).
43 The peace process with the CPP/NPA was terminated on 23 November 2017, and the group was declared as a terrorist organisation by President Duterte. See Mallari Jr. (2018).
44 Note: Research for this chapter has benefited from the financial support of the SHAPE-SEA Research Grants Program 2017 under the research project on "Revolutionary Peace: Transformative Roles of Movement Leaders and Insiders in the Self-Determination Conflict in Patani, Thailand and the Bangsamoro areas, Philippines."

References, further reading, and links to key primary documents

Abdulhaqq, Nu'ain. 2005. *We Must Win the Struggle! – Salamat Hashim*. Bangsamoro Darul Jihad: Agency for Youth Affairs-MILF.

Arguillas, O. Carolyn. 2000. *Free the Bangsamoro- A Compendium of Essays on MILF and Interviews with Chairman Sheikh Salamat Hashim*. Bangsamoro Darul Jihad: Agency for Youth Affairs-MILF.

Arguillas, O. Carolyn. 2009. "Q and A with Jibin Arula: 41 Years After the Jabidah Massacre (1)." *Minda News*, 15 March. www.mindanews.com/top-stories/2009/03/q-and-a-with-jibin-arula-41-years-after-the-jabidah-massacre/.

Arguillas, O. Carolyn. 2017. "OIC Convenes Meeting of MNLF, MILF Leaders in Jeddah; Nur a No-Show." *Minda News*, 8 May. www.mindanews.com/peace-process/2017/05/oic-convenes-meeting-of-mnlf-milf-leaders-in-jeddah-nur-a-no-show/.

Arguillas, O. Carolyn. 2018. "BBL Will Be Passed Ahead Shift to Federalism-Duterte." *Minda News*, 15 January. www.mindanews.com/peace-process/2018/01/bbl-will-be-passed-ahead-of-shift-to-federalism-duterte/.

Askandar, Kamarulzaman. 2007. *Building Peace: Reflections from Southeast Asia*. Penang: Southeast Asian Conflict Studies Network.

Askandar, Kamarulzaman, and Ayesah Abubakar. 2009. *Peace for Mindanao*. Penang: SEACSN, REP-USM and JICA.

Baclagon, S. Uldarico 1988. *Christian-Moslem Guerillas of Mindanao*. Manila: Lord Avenue Printing Press.

Che Man, Wan Kadir. 1990. *Muslim Separatism: The Moros of Southern Philippines and the Malays of Southern Thailand*. Singapore: Oxford University Press.

Cornelio, Claire. 2017. "Bangsamoro, Federalism Plans on Table as Duterte, Misuari talk." *ABS-CBN News*, 17 September. http://news.abs-cbn.com/news/09/17/17/bangsamoro-federalism-plans-on-table-as-duterte-misuari-talk.

Diaz, Patricio. 2011. "'GRP' to 'GPH': Why?" *Minda News*, 22 January. www.mindanews.com/mindaviews/comment/2011/01/%E2%80%9Cgrp%E2%80%9D-to-%E2%80%9Cgph%E2%80%9D-why/.

Iribani, Abraham. 2006. *Give Peace a Chance: The Story of the GRP-MNLF Peace Talks*. Mandaluyong City: MKFI/PCID.

Jubair, Salah. 2007. *The Long Road to Peace: Inside the GRP-MILF Peace Process*. Cotabato City: Institute of Bangsamoro Studies.

Majul, C. Adib. 1985. *The Contemporary Muslim Movement in the Philippines*. Berkeley: Mizan Press.

Mallari, Jr. Delfin. 2018. "Joma's Wish: For Duterte to Revive Peace Talks." *Inquirer*, 1 January. http://newsinfo.inquirer.net/956579/jomas-wish-for-duterte-to-revive-peace-talks.

Mindanao Peoples Caucus. "What Is Bantay Ceasefire?" www.eprpinformation.org/files/peaceprocesses/ceasefires/What-is-Bantay-Ceasefire.pdf.

Mordeno, H. Marcos. 2015. "MILF on Mamasapano Clash: SAF Was at Fault for Not Coordinating." *Minda News*, 25 March. www.mindanews.com/top-stories/2015/03/milf-on-mamasapano-clash-saf-was-at-fault-for-not-coordinating/.

REP-USM, SEACSN, and JICA. 2006. *Proceedings Report on the Consolidation for Peace (COP1) Conference held in USM Penang in January 23–26, 2006*. Penang: REP-USM, SEACSN, JICA.

REP-USM, SEACSN, and JICA. 2014. *Proceedings Report on the Consolidation for Peace (COP6) Conference held in Hiroshima, Japan in June 23–24, 2014*. Penang: REP-USM, SEACSN, JICA.

Rodil, B. Rudy. 2000. *Kalinaw Mindanao: The story of the GRP-MNLF Peace Process 197–1996*. AFRIM: Davao City.

Rodil, B. Rudy. 2010. "Achieving Peace and Justice in Mindanao Through the Tri-People Approach." *Mindanao Horizons* 1 (2): 25–46.

Salah, Jubair. 1999. *Bangsamoro, a Nation Under Endless Tyranny*, 3rd edn. Kuala Lumpur: IQ Marin Sdn. Bhd.

Salmi, H. Ralph, Adib Cesar Majul, and George K. Tanham. 1998. *Islam and Conflict Resolution, Theories and Practices*. Lanham, MD, and Oxford: University Press of America.

Santos, Soliman. 2003. "Malaysia's Role in the Peace Negotiations Between the Philippine Government and the Moro Islamic Liberation Front." In *Peace and Conflict Research Report Number 2*. Penang: Southeast Asian Conflict Studies Network.

Tan, Samuel. 1977. *The Filipino Muslim Armed Struggle, 1900–1972*. Manila: Filipinas Foundation Inc.

Primary documents

Memorandum of Agreement on Ancestral Domain (MOA-AD). 2005. http://muslim mindanao.ph/ancestral_domain1.html.

Various Authors. 2014. *Bangsamoro Documents and Materials, Volumes 1 & 2*. Davao City: Mindanews-Ateneo de Davao University.

10
MYANMAR

Stefano Ruzza

Introduction

Myanmar, known as Burma until 1989, gained its independence from the United Kingdom in 1948 and was plagued with civil war immediately thereafter. From then until now, a situation of internal strife has continued uninterruptedly, with different insurgent groups rising up against the government and sometimes clashing among themselves. Beginning in 1989, ceasefires were established between the government and some of the insurgent groups, but these agreements never entailed any real conflict resolution nor any demobilisation.

The ongoing democratic transition that many link to the coming into office of Nobel laureate Aung San Suu Kyi and her cabinet, but that actually dates back at least to 2010, has given momentum to the need to find a more comprehensive and long-lasting peace settlement for the country. In 2011, President Thein Sein, a former general who led Myanmar's first civilian government after almost 50 years of military rule, launched his peace plan. This achieved some significant results, such as the so called Nationwide Ceasefire Agreement (NCA) in October 2015. Notwithstanding the name, the NCA is not really nationwide as it does not include the largest share of the insurgents. The peace process is still in its infancy: some insurgent groups have formal talks with the government in an institutionalised setting, while others are still stuck at the pre-talk phase. Hence, many of the aspects that are usually associated with a peace process (a peace accord, SSR, and DDR) have not yet come about. No further landmarks have been achieved after the signing of the NCA at the time of writing, notwithstanding the coming into office of Aung San Suu Kyi.

Exploring Myanmar's peace process is relevant for four main reasons. First, the long duration of Myanmar's civil war and its legacies. For decades, Myanmar's governments have relied mostly on the use of military might and a 'divide and impera' policy to contain the insurgencies. The ongoing peace process is relatively young, as it formally started only in 2011. It has to deal with long-lasting conflicts, entrenched identities, and a dynamic situation.

Second, the conflict sees different causes mix together and feed on each other. The focus of this chapter is on borderland insurgencies, which mostly have a secessionist/autonomist agenda. However, demands for an end of military and authoritarian rule have been a near constant issue in Myanmar and have heavily influenced both the insurgencies and the peace process. Political demands are also heavily linked to an economic dimension and the need to devise an equitable system of resource-sharing, as the borderlands are rich in natural resources.

The third reason for the relevance of this peace process is the extremely high number of warring parties, as more than 20 insurgent organisations are active in the country. Conflicts tend to be defined more often by a common enemy instead of a shared agenda and consequently are relatively volatile. This applies to both sides, not only the insurgents, as even government actors do not always agree or cooperate among themselves.

The fourth and last reason is the degree of fragmentation characterising the Myanmar peace process, as there are at least five relevant groups to be considered besides the government: ethnic armed organizations that have joined the 2015 ceasefire; those that have not yet but are willing to do so; those that have not yet and are not willing to do so but have a separate ceasefire; those that are in a condition of open conflict; and those who are not deemed by the government as entitled to join the talks table. This last category is made of only one organisation, the Arakan Rohingya Salvation Army, which is not recognised by the government as a legitimate party.

Conflict analysis

There are three main rationales for violent conflict in Myanmar. The first is contestation over the form of government and about who should rule the country (a military or a civilian leadership). After independence in 1948, the country was run by a liberal government until 1962, when it was toppled by a military coup. The Tatmadaw (Myanmar Armed Forces) then uninterruptedly ran the country until 2010, when they yielded to a limited democratic turn. This change was substantiated in a semi-civilian government led by former General Thein Sein (2011–2015) and was preceded by the introduction of a new constitution in 2008 and by the first open general election in 2010. The main opposition party – the Aung San Suu Kyi-led National League for Democracy (NLD) – boycotted the 2010 elections but ran in the following round (2015) and achieved a landslide victory. This led to the Aung San Suu Kyi cabinet, which is in power at the time of writing (2018). The contest over who should rule the country is mostly intra-Bamar, the majority ethnic group in Myanmar, which accounts for about 70 per cent of the population.

The second rationale for violence is about who should rule the periphery of the country and how. Border areas are generally underdeveloped but wealthy in natural resources (high quality timber, precious gems, opium poppy), characterised by difficult terrain and permeable borders. These regions are also mostly inhabited by non-Bamar people. Myanmar's independence was based on the Panglong agreement, a deal between Bamar and other ethnic minority groups. At the core of the agreement was the possibility for some ethnic minorities to negotiate secession after independence was achieved, a tenet that was included in the 1947 constitution. One of the reasons behind the 1962 military coup was fear on the side of the Tatmadaw of seeing the country dissolve under secessionist demands. The demands coming from insurgents were originally about independence but have reoriented over the years toward autonomy or some sort of federalism. Economic issues are also on the table, especially a fair redistribution of the income derived from the exploitation of natural resources and an adequate supply of public goods in border areas.

Insurgent groups are usually labelled as ethnic armed organizations (EAOs), and there are 21 such groups officially recognised in contemporary Myanmar. This high number of insurgent organisations is one of the main causes of complexity in the peace process. Some EAOs are large, with tens of thousands of members, while others are small, able to mobilise only a few hundred individuals. While there is a common resolve among all the EAOs – namely some sort of self-government or federalism – each one is active in a different region of the country, draws its strength from different ethnic groups, and has different sources of financing, its own set of external relations (with foreign governments and diasporas), and a more or less lenient attitude towards the central government. China and Thailand have been supportive of some EAOs in different phases of Myanmar history, but while Thailand ceased this several decades ago, China has not yet entirely done so. Taking into account spinoffs, mergers, and alliances made and broken among different groups is helpful in understanding why there are cyclical phases of conflict reduction, with ceasefires between EAOs and the government holding up, then phases of conflict escalation as ceasefires fall apart. Splits mean that spoiler groups might continue the armed struggle or new insurgent groups emerge. The Tatmadaw is also active in this process, as it is able to change the opportunity cost of armed uprising by providing economic incentives to those accepting peace on the Tatmadaw's terms or by increasing military pressure on unrelenting opponents.

The third kind of violence is communal violence. In the last few years, the media has been filled with images of attacks in Rakhine state (the westernmost region of Myanmar) and with displaced Rohingya seeking shelter in Bangladesh. But not all of this violence has been perpetrated by the Tatmadaw or by government forces, as there have also been riots and lynchings. The most famous are perhaps the Rakhine riots of June 2012, which left about 200 dead and several thousand displaced. The Rohingya are a stateless minority without citizenship rights and are not even counted in the national census. About 90 per cent of Myanmar's population is Buddhist, while the Rohingya are Muslim. Rakhine state is also inhabited by the Rakhine people, a non-Bamar Buddhist ethnic group which hosts anti-Rohingya feelings, but at the same time has grudges against the central government and the

Bamar leadership of the country. It should also be noted that there are Muslims minorities with regular rights living in Myanmar (e.g. the Kaman), and that clashes have occurred between Buddhists and non-Rohingya Muslims outside of Rakhine state in the last few years (March 2013 in Meiktila, August 2013 in Kanbalu, June 2014 in Mandalay), although without reaching the level of violence seen in Rakhine (McCharty and Menager 2017). Last but not least, it should be kept in mind that instances of communal violence are to be found not only between Buddhist and Muslims or between Rohingya and non-Rohingya, but also between different ethnic groups.

These three kinds of violent conflict – contestation over who rules the centre, contestation over who rules the periphery, and communal violence — often overlap with and influence each other. For example, the Karen insurgency centred around the Karen National Union (KNU) has traditionally placed the request for a democratic turn in government at the forefront of its political demands and obstinately refused dialogue with the military junta. While in power, the Tatmadaw had enemies in both the ethnic armed organisations and the democratic opposition, and the military government engaged actively to avoid cooperation between them. Communal violence can be found at the base of several insurgencies, and the most recent example can be found in Rakhine state, where the long-lasting oppression against the Rohingya has led to the creation the ARSA. This chapter will focus on insurgencies, as these are at the centre of the peace process in Myanmar. However, the other sources of violent conflict have to be kept present and will be recalled when they feed back on the peace process.

In order to shed more light on the actors who take centre stage in the peace process, to understand cycles of violence and peace in Myanmar, and to grasp how the relative ripeness that brought to the (limited) ongoing peace process came to be (Zartman 2003; Lederach 1999), it is necessary to briefly recall the history of the ceasefires preceding the democratic transition. Before 1989, the government's policy regarding insurgencies was almost exclusively muscular, but from 1989 onward several ceasefires were agreed with different insurgent groups. This happened for two main reasons. First, in 1988 a democratic opposition to military rule emerged, as the uprising in Yangon and in the rest of the country demonstrated. The junta feared possible cooperation or transfer of skills between opponents of the regime and insurgents. Second, in 1989 the Communist Party of Burma (CPB), the only ideological insurgency active in the country, fell apart, with a number of ethno-nationalist insurgencies rising from its ashes. This created the possibility of alliances between old and new insurgent groups, previously impossible because of different ideological orientations and international allegiances. To keep these risks in check, the military government decided to act first and to strike deals with the CPB spinoffs. The agreements were very basic and entailed just a ceasefire, the recognition of economic self-management on a temporary basis, and pushed the idea of political negotiations in the future. Back then, the constitution was suspended as a consequence of the 1988 pro-democracy uprisings. The junta used this as an argument to state it has no right to make political concessions, and that political talks would be postponed until a new constitution was in place (South 2008; Sherman 2003; Smith 1999).

Ceasefires were not agreed with every insurgent group; only a few were offered the option, and not all of them accepted. A relatively small CPB spinoff, the Myanmar National Democratic Army Alliance (MNDAA), was the first to receive and accept such an offer. A second CPB spinoff, the United Wa State Army (UWSA) followed suit. The importance of the UWSA cannot be overstated, as it is the largest EAO active in Myanmar, at about 20-30,000 strong, with control over a large part of Shan state (Eastern Myanmar) and internationally notorious for drug production and trade. It is also close to China, from which it receives support in many ways (allegedly also in the shape of two Mi-17 'Hip' medium transport helicopters outfitted with air-to-air missiles) (Kramer 2007). Ceasefire offers were later extended to EAOs that were not CPB spinoffs. The Kachin Independence Organization (KIO), operating in Kachin state (Northern Myanmar) agreed to a ceasefire in 1994, although this was a consequence of a mounting Tatmadaw offensive. The KIO is the second largest EAO in Myanmar, at about 10,000 strong. As has already been mentioned, the KNU (South-East Myanmar) was not open to negotiations before the end of the military government and did not agree a ceasefire until 2012. For this reason, it suffered heavily at the hands of the Tatmadaw (Ruzza 2015; Zaw Oo and Win Min 2007).

The system of ceasefires allowed the Tatmadaw to concentrate its forces and single out one or a few enemies at a time, instead of facing many foes at once. Hence, while the ceasefires generated a conflict reduction, they also changed the balance of forces in favour of the government. This shift also had a political impact, as the declaration of ceasefire areas allowed the government to gradually insert its own economic and legal model in border areas under the guise of development assistance (Ruzza 2015; Grundy-Warr and Dean 2011; Woods 2011).

The conflict resolution process

The democratisation process had a central role in making the peace process possible. While Myanmar's limited democratisation cannot be analysed in detail here, it should be mentioned that while pressures from civil society and the international community certainly played a role in favour of regime change, this was ultimately decided on by the military elite, which set up its own plan for the transition and played it at its own pace (Ruzza and Gabusi 2018; Jones 2014). The desire for change in the military junta was founded on the willingness to realign internationally (i.e. to break out from the grasp of China) and to escape economic underdevelopment by opening up to international markets.

In its history, the Tatmadaw has always held onto three guiding principles. These are called the Three National Causes and are: (1) non-disintegration of the Union; (2) non-disintegration of national solidarity; and (3) perpetuation of national sovereignty. Hence, secession is unacceptable from the military standpoint. These guiding principles were included in the 2008 constitution and complemented with three more, of which the last is of particular interest: 'enabling the Defence Services to be able to participate in the National political leadership role of the State'. This is just the first hint at the many safeguards that the Tatmadaw enshrined in the 2008 constitution in order to hold onto power.

Myanmar's constitution assigns three key ministries (Borders, Defence, and Home) to the Tatmadaw, along with 25 per cent of parliamentary seats. Reforming the constitution requires a majority of 75 per cent of seats in parliament plus one, hence it is impossible without military consent. The constitution also sets legal immunities and budgetary independence for the Tatmadaw and includes several clauses defining the armed forces as the supreme authority in case of an emergency. On top of this, the Tatmadaw also has substantial economic power, in both the form of two massive economic holdings (Union of Myanmar Economic Holdings Limited, UMEHL, and Myanmar Economic Corporation, MEC) and informal control of commodities in border areas where counter-insurgency operations are ongoing.

In 2009, after the new constitution came into force but before elections were held, the military government put forward a programme called 'Border guard forces plan' (BGF) to integrate EAOs in the state security forces. The BGF was refused by all but one of the EAOs, as it would have entailed dismantling insurgent organisations before any of their political demands had been met. The fact that the military junta previously used the lack of a constitution to postpone political negotiations, and then after 2008 pushed in favour of a programme that looked like DDR instead of political talks, prompted EAOs to reject the BGF.

The Tatmadaw reacted angrily to the BFG rejection, opening a new round of military offensives. In 2009, it attacked the MNDAA, the first EAOs with which a ceasefire was arranged in 1989, leading to the collapse of the agreement. It also attacked other EAOs active in Shan state (notably the National Democratic Army Alliance, NDAA, and the Shan State Progressive Party, SSPP). It is interesting to note that the largest EAO, the UWSA, was not attacked, and it is reasonable to assume that the Tatmadaw's hope was to send the UWSA a message without having to engage with it directly, as all the attacked EAOs were UWSA neighbours.

Another important ceasefire that collapsed during this phase was that with the KIO. Since its inception in 1994, the Tatmadaw military presence in Kachin state continued to grow, and the local economy was brought increasingly under government control. This did not generate the perception of improved wealth and development among the Kachin people but rather fed the idea of a land stripped of its riches by the government. The BGF added to the discontent, and the refusal by the Union Election Commission to accept the registration of a Kachin party (the Kachin State Progressive Party, KSPP) to run in the 2010 general election was the final straw. In June 2011, hostilities reopened between the Tatmadaw and the KIO (Brenner 2015; Farrelly 2012).

In line with expectation expressed in much of the academic literature, democratisation has been synonymous with an increase in violent conflict in Myanmar as well (Nilsen 2013; Cederman et al. 2013). After the coming into force of the new constitution, the use of military might in Myanmar reached peaks unequalled since the 1980s. Casualties and displaced figures got on an upward trend, and while Myanmar civil war is not among the most lethal (with a few hundred battle-related death per year), there have been hundreds of thousands of displaced persons. Most notably, the conflict in Kachin has generated about 100,000 IDPs since 2011, while there are another 550,000 in the rest of the country at the time of writing. This overall figure (650,000) more or less matches with that of the Rohingya that have been pushed out of Myanmar through the use of force.

In August 2011, a few months after having entered office, the new president, Thein Sein, decided on a change, relinquishing the muscular approach followed since the inception of the new constitution. Two reasons can be found behind this decision. First, the military campaigns were not as decisive as hoped. The MNDAA and the KIO are still belligerent at the time of writing (early 2018), and only one of the EAOs had accepted the BGF. Second, for the democratic transition to be convincing – and hence to achieve the results the military elite wanted to obtain from it – a credible peace process needed to be in place, as it would demonstrate the capability of the new regime to manage ethnic politics democratically and its willingness to include ethnic minorities in the governance of the country. Having a credible peace process in place is also relevant for economic reasons, as it provides the government in Naypyidaw more legitimacy to negotiate investments or manage trade related to border areas with foreign partners attentive (or at least paying lip service) to democratic values and human rights (Woods 2016).

Thein Sein shelved the BGF and launched his own peace plan, calling for negotiations to be held with all the EAOs. His plan was structured in three steps: (1) ceasefires at the regional and state level; (2) confidence-building measures, political dialogue, and plans for economic development conducted at the national (union) level; and (3) stipulation of a nationwide 'agreement for eternal peace' in front of parliament and other authorities. As can be seen, ceasefires were still a precondition for political dialogue. Preparations to launch the plan began in earnest, with 'peacemaking committees' created at the national and regional levels, and credible negotiators were hand-picked. A team conducted by Aung Min (Railway Minister until August 2012, then Minister of the President's Office of Myanmar) was in charge of dealing with the KNU and with other four EAOs. A second team led by Aung Thaung (former Ministry of Industry-1 and then MP) and Thein Zaw (former Minister of Communication and then MP) was tasked with the KIO, UWSA, NDAA, and SSPP.

Thein Sein's plan was able to achieve substantial results quickly: between late 2011 and early 2012, several ceasefires were renewed (UWSA, NDAA, and SSPP), while new ones were agreed. Most notable here was a ceasefire with the KNU, which has been at war since 1949, and with the Restoration Council of Shan State (RCSS). War weariness, credible negotiators, signs of progress toward democracy, and intra-Karen competition for leadership all helped to achieve these results (Brenner 2017).

In November 2012, the Myanmar Peace Centre (MPC), a government-affiliated non-profit organisation, was inaugurated in Yangon. Originally led by Aung Min, the mission of the MPC was stated as 'to contribute to sustainable peace and an overall political settlement to the benefit of all the citizens of Myanmar' (Myanmar Peace Center 2015). The European Union provided a start-up grant of 700,000 EUR and kept funding it until 2016, along with the UN and a few other donors (mostly Western). It should be noted, though, that while the MPC was open to civil society and the international community, it was not a third party in the peace process, but rather a government-affiliated institution.

On the insurgents' side, in February 2011 (hence before the breaking of the KIO ceasefire and the launch of Thein Sein's plan) the United Nationalities Federal Council (UNFC) was founded, with the aim of coordinating EAOs' demands and to push for the creation of an authentic federal union. The major divergences among EAOs were about conditions attached to ceasefires, and if they should be called before or after political concessions. Originally, the UNFC grouped together 14 EAOs, but although it aimed to be an umbrella organisation for EAOs, it never managed to gather all of them.

By invitation of the KIO, EAOs convened a meeting in Laiza (Kachin state) in late 2013 in order to try to overcome differences among them and to define a common ground for the process ahead. Laiza hosts the KIO headquarters, and it is under rebel control. While the Myanmar government has traditionally been very suspicious of any gathering of EAOs, this time it gave its blessing to the encounter. The major outcome of the Laiza meeting was the creation of a Nationwide Ceasefire Coordination Team (NCCT) that partly overcame differences between EAOs (although it still did not group all of them) and that was recognised by the government as its counterpart in the negotiations for a nationwide ceasefire agreement. At this point it should be mentioned the UWSA was not a member of the UNFC nor of the NCCT. As the single largest and most powerful EAOs, the UWSA did not see any advantage coming from negotiating along with the others at the time.

In Myanmar, ceasefires were traditionally bilateral, a condition that allowed the government to apply a 'divide et impera' policy and to concentrate military means against a few opponents at a time. The shift towards a nationwide ceasefire was important as it signalled a distancing of the government from the old policy. Furthermore, in order to advance negotiations, the government generally committed to a federal and democratic system, although a ceasefire was still seen as a precondition to allow for the achievement of such goals. After several rounds of negotiations, in March 2015 a draft Nationwide Ceasefire Agreement (NCA) was agreed at the MPC between the government and representatives of 16 EAOs. However, EAOs representatives claimed they did not have the authority to sign the NCA; hence, they referred it up to their leaders. In turn, these asked for several amendments and, more importantly, for the possibility for all the NCCT members to be present for the official signing. Given the condition of open conflict between the Tatmadaw and several EAOs which were NCCT members, that request could not be met, and the process stalemated.

In October 2015, just before the general election that brought the Aung San Suu Kyi cabinet into office, an NCA agreement was signed nonetheless, although with only eight EAOs. Of these eight, only the RCSS, the KNU, and a third one (DKBA-5) are of a significant size, while the others number a few hundred effectives each. Not surprisingly, the UWSA was not among the NCA signatories. Roughly speaking, about 20 per cent of the combatants active in Myanmar are included in the NCA, while 30 per cent are in open conflict and the remaining 50 per cent are part of organisations that have a bilateral ceasefire. The EAOs that remained at war with the government were the KIO, the MNDAA, the Arakan Army (AA, a Rakhine insurgent organisation but originally active in Kachin and North Shan state), and the Ta'ang National Liberation Army (TNLA, operating in Shan state as well). Armed conflict is concentrated in North-East Myanmar, in the Kachin and Shan states. Even if the NCA signed in October 2015 was just a partial result, it was a historical landmark, as no other agreement of such scope had been signed before in the history of the country.

In the elections held in November 2015, the NLD achieved a landslide victory, but it should be noted that there were two areas in Myanmar where it did not get a majority vote: Rakhine and Shan states (Oh 2016). The NLD won the elections in Kachin state, but that result was due to a KIO demand to vote for NLD instead of for Kachin ethnic parties as the former was the only one deemed able to beat the party of the military (Union Solidarity and Development Party, USDP) in a national election. The NLD cabinet and Aung San Suu Kyi in particular placed the peace process on the top of their agenda. As the daughter of Aung San, a key figure in Myanmar independence and the architect of the Panglong agreement, she decided to rename the peace process the '21st Century Panglong Conference' (21CPC). The MPC was rebranded as well, becoming the National Reconciliation and Peace Center (NPRC), falling entirely under government control, and moving from Yangon to Naypyidaw (the new capital city, founded in 2005). Aung San Suu Kyi herself took on the chairmanship of the NRPC, replacing Aung Min. Rebranding aside, the most significant innovation introduced by the new government was a channel of dialogue with NCA non-signatories. Five parties are officially part of the 21CPC: Tatmadaw, government, parliament, political parties, and EAOs, while previously Tatmadaw and parliament were not explicitly acknowledged. For all practical effects, though, it makes more sense to consider the relevant stakeholders in the peace process as four: Tatmadaw, government, ceasefire EAOs and non-ceasefire EAOs.

While the peace process was being reshaped by Aung San Suu Kyi and her cabinet, there were developments on the ethnic front as well. In March 2016, the UWSA hosted a meeting of EAOs active in Shan state and in Kachin at their headquarters in Pangsang (also known as Pangkham, Shan state). It gathered all the EAOs in open conflict with the government (KIO, MNDAA, TNLA, and AA), as well as the SSPP and the NDAA, which held bilateral ceasefires. Major conclusions from the meeting included a rejection of the NCA process and a request to get back to the authentic Panglong agreement. The first point can be easily understood once it is considered that some of the EAOs involved had very disappointing experiences with ceasefires (namely the KIO), while others were openly ostracised by the Tatmadaw and faced demands to disarm before entering any talks (namely, the three smaller belligerents: the AA, MNDAA, and TNLA). The second request was intrinsically problematic, since it implicitly referred to the option of secession that was part of the original Panglong agreement, and which is unacceptable for the

Tatmadaw and impossible under the current constitution. Since five of the seven EAOs that took part at the Pangsang meeting were also members of the UNCF, and not all of the UNCF members were invited to Pangsang, this created a crack in the ethnic front's unity.

The Pangsang meeting also produced a call to China to act as a mediator and as a provider of local development through the 'One Belt One Road' (OBOR) initiative. This call on China is not surprising, as the UWSA has strong ties with it (including the provision of military hardware) and inside the Wa-administered special region, Chinese language and money are routinely used. Chinese visitors and businesses play a large role in the economic life in the area under NDAA control, and MNDAA insurgents received sanctuary in China after the Tatmadaw offensives of 2009. Relations between China and the KIO (or the Kachin people more in general) are more problematic, but nonetheless Chinese businesses (if not the Chinese authorities) have been necessary partners in sustaining the KIO both before and after the breaking of the ceasefire in 2011 (Woods 2016).

In August 2016, the first session of the 21CPC began, with UN Secretary Ban Ki-moon attending the opening ceremony. The UWSA left the conference on the second day, claiming it was allowed in as an observer only and had not been given permission to address the audience. In March 2017, the UNFC, which still included all of the non-signatories of the NCA and all of the belligerent EAOs, submitted a nine-point proposal to the government. In the talks that followed there was agreement, at least in principle, on the political points (formation of a federal union, constitutional reform) but not on the military and technical points (ceasefire monitoring, troops relocation). Due to the lack of an agreement on its nine points, the UNFC was allowed to join the second session of the 21CPC (which was held in May 2017) only as an observer, which the UNFC refused.

The divide between the UNFC members able and willing to join the NCA and those either not allowed or unwilling to join grew larger, and ultimately brought about the substantial dissolution of the UNFC. After several defections, at the time of the writing it includes only four minor EAOs, or 1,500 personnel (less than 2 per cent of the whole insurgent force). On the other hand, the initiative launched by the UWSA with the Pangsang meetings, which have been repeated several times, gained momentum and led to the creation of the Federal Political and Negotiation Consultative Committee (FPNCC) in April 2017. It gathered together the UWSA and its NDAA satellite, the three small belligerent groups (AA, TNLA, MNDAA), the KIO, and the SSPP. All the EAOs that joined the FPNCC and were members of the UNFC left the latter. The leadership of the FPNCC is in the hands of the UWSA, and it is noteworthy that while the UWSA had an agenda that steered away from any comprehensive peace process since the inception of Thein Sein plan, the same was not true for all the other EAOs that joined the FPNCC. Yet, dissatisfaction with official channels, both before and after Aung San Suu Kyi entered office, led these EAOs to align with the UWSA in the search for alternative paths for the negotiations. The most relevant consequence of this is that UWSA increased its political weight. This, in turn, means a likely bigger role for China in the future of the peace process, both formally and informally.

In May 2017, the second session of the 21CPC convened, while combat operations intensified in North-East Myanmar (Kachin and Shan states). Issues related to the right to secession proved to be the most contentious, and no agreement was found on them between the hard-line EAOs and the government. The FPNCC members attended the session but left before its end. Later on, the FPNCC declared that any further negotiations with the Tatmadaw or the government would have to involve the FPNCC as a bloc, and that separate talks with its members would not be accepted. The third session of the 21CPC was originally planned for early 2018, but has been postponed. The UNFPC, in its diminished form, restated its nine points, and it is possible that now that its membership has reduced an agreement will be found. This could lead some or all of the EAOs still part of the UNFC to join the NCA.

After the inception of the NCA and the change of government, the overall trend on the ethnic front has been of polarisation, with one side constituted by the NCA and all the actors that tend to converge on it, and the other by all the actors that move away from it and hence tend to gravitate around the UWSA and the FPNCC. The reasons for this dynamic can be traced back to the activities of two actors in particular, the Tatmadaw and the UWSA. By ostracising some EAOs, the Tatmadaw forced them to find alternative channels of dispute resolution. On its end, while the UWSA did not actively sabotage the peace process, it exploited its own relative weight and privileged position to give itself more leverage. The UWSA is now the most prominent actor of a block resisting the NCA that has gathered together about 70 per cent of Myanmar insurgents.

As has been mentioned, a major consequence of the rise of the FPNCC is also an increased role for China in the peace process. China was also able to regain influence on Myanmar through the Rohingya crisis, where it acted as the chief facilitator between Bangladesh and Myanmar. This is quite paradoxical, since Myanmar's military elite started the democratisation to contain China's influence on Myanmar, and that influence now is returning with a person in office who has been considered a pro-Western standard-bearer of democracy, Aung San Suu Kyi.

The points of contention that remain on the table and are unlikely to be solved soon are the distribution of power between the centre (Naypidaw and the government) and the periphery of the country (the various ethnic border areas). Although everyone is eager to mention concepts like 'Panglong spirt' or 'federalism', the meaning attached to these words is extremely variable and ranges from limited autonomy to the right to secession. A related problem is about the so called federal army, or the idea of creating an army that could include the EAOs without dismantling them. While the notion sounds fascinating, it is difficult to translate it into a practicable plan. Furthermore, the Tatmadaw rejects the idea entirely and would hardly consider it in any form different from what was entailed in the BGF (Taylor 2017).

Lessons to be learned from the case study

The peace process in Myanmar can hardly be defined as a success, as the largest share of the insurgents are currently either at war with the government or holding on to a bilateral ceasefire as previously. It is also sadly true that there is more war in Myanmar now than there was before the advent of the democratisation. However, it is worth recalling that some relevant deals were successfully closed. Perhaps the best example is provided by the ceasefire with the KNU, which ended more than six decades of conflict. It should also be mentioned that while the NCA is not as 'nationwide' as its name suggests, its scope is unequalled in the history of independent Myanmar. Last but not least, the limited results achieved so far have to be put in perspective, as the Myanmar peace process is still in its early phases and will definitely take more time to mature and bear fruit.

Four points can be drawn from this overview of the Myanmar peace process. The first point is about speed and reversibility. Given the high number of actors involved, it is inevitable for time to stretch on, as parties require time to define and redefine their positions, and as alliances are made and broken. It should be noted, though, that while the pace of the peace progress has progressively slowed, there were no backward steps, and even if the process fragments in the future (with the NCA becoming a multilateral ceasefire without managing to extend to all the EAOs), that does not imply it has to collapse. Paradoxically, the best guarantees of this relative irreversibility are to be found in the Tatmadaw. While the armed forces certainly are not open to many concessions and would like to defeat some EAOs, they also need a peace process to give credibility to the ongoing democratisation, a project in which they have a vested interest.

The second point is about the relative value of polarisation. As the process moved forward, the very complex ethnic front progressively gathered around two positions: those more favourable to the NCA and those against it. While this may mean that the gap between the parties is widening, it also generated clarification of a complex picture that can perhaps open opportunities for future progress, as it makes it easier to identify interests and needs of the involved parties.

The third point is about the return of China, or rather its persistence in Myanmar. While the democratisation process was launched to provide Myanmar with geopolitical alternatives, China has managed to maintain a relevant position in its neighbour through several channels. Leaving aside the crisis in Rakhine, the relationship that China has held, formally and informally, with insurgents and authorities in Myanmar has granted it a role in the peace process that likely cannot be matched by any Western counterpart or any international organisation.

The fourth and last point is about redistribution of revenues from Myanmar's natural richness and how this might be managed through federal arrangements. It is not incidental that among the UNCF's nine points there was a demand for 'big scale development plans to adhere to the Extractive Industries Transparency Initiative (EITI), in cooperation with the concerned public and the EAOs'. This demand is related to the abusive exploitation of natural resources in borderlands. Redistribution of wealth from commodity revenues has a key role in influencing peace and war in Myanmar. In the post-1989 era, ceasefires were agreed as they provided opportunities for EAOs and their related communities to enjoy part of the wealth of their lands. Dissatisfaction with the sharing agreement is one of the factors that led to the collapse of the KIO ceasefire in 2011. Resource management and equitable distribution of revenues will likely influence the peace process in the future, and perhaps talks focusing on this topic could provide a way to de-politicise hotly contentious issues.

As a concluding remark, it is worth mentioning that the peace process, by itself, would not be enough to reach a deep and long-lasting peace in Myanmar. Even if the 21CPC achieved the most outstanding possible results and struck a deal with all of the EAOs (a slim possibility), issues of communal violence in Myanmar are entirely removed from the process, as well as the right to citizenship of part of Myanmar's population. Negative peace would perhaps be reached, but there would be a lot more road to cover before achieving positive peace.

References, further reading, and links to key primary documents

Key primary documents

"The Border Guard Force Scheme." 2009. *Myanmar Peace Monitor*. www.mmpeacemonitor.org/background/border-guard-force.

"Constitution of the Republic of the Union of Myanmar." 2008. *Burma Library*. www.burmalibrary. org/docs5/Myanmar_Constitution-2008-en.pdf.

"The Constitution of the Union of Burma." 1947. *Burma Library*. www.ilo.org/dyn/natlex/docs/ELECTRONIC/79573/85699/F1436085708/MMR79573.pdf.

"The Government's Roadmap for National Reconciliation and Union Peace." 2016. *Myanmar Peace Monitor*. www.mmpeacemonitor.org/images/2016/Statement/mpm_bni_the%20government%20road map%20peace_oct16.pdf.

"The Laiza Agreement, Briefing Paper." 2013. *Burma Centre for Ethnic Studies Peace and Reconciliation*, November. www.burmalibrary.org/docs16/BCES-BP-19-Laiza-en-red.pdf.

Myanmar Peace Center. 2015. Overview. http://www.mmpeacemonitor.org/stakeholders/myanmar-peace-center?format=pdf. accessed 4 January 2019.

"The Nationwide Ceasefire Agreement Between the Government of the Republic of the Union of Myanmar and the Ethnic Armed Organizations." 2015. *Myanmar Peace Monitor*. www.mmpeace monitor.org/images/2015/oct/nca%20contract%20eng.pdf.

"Panglong Agreement." 1947. *United Nations Peacemakers*. https://peacemaker.un.org/sites/peacemaker.un.org/files/MM_470212_Panglong%20Agreement.pdf.

"Thein Sein plan." 2011. *Myanmar Peace Monitor*. www.mmpeacemonitor.org/peace-process/government-peace-plan.

"United Nationalities Federal Council (UNFC) 9 Points Proposal." 2017. *Myanmar Peace Monitor*. www.mmpeacemonitor.org/images/2016/Statement/unfc%209-point%20proposal_bur.pdf.

Monographs, book chapters, and scientific articles

Brenner, David. 2015. "Ashes of Co-Optation: Armed Group Fragmentation and the Rebuilding of Popular Insurgency in Myanmar." *Conflict, Security, and Development* 15 (4): 337–358.

Brenner, David. 2017. "Inside the Karen Insurgency: Explaining Conflict and Conciliation in Myanmar's Changing Borderlands." *Asian Security* 14 (2): 83–99.

Cederman, Lars-Erik, Kristian Skrede Gleditsch, and Simon Hug. 2013. "Elections and Ethnic Civil War." *Comparative Political Studies* 46 (3): 387–417.

Farrelly, Nicholas. 2012. "Ceasing Ceasefires? Kachin Politics Beyond the Stalemates." In Nick Cheesman, Monique Skidmore, and Trevor Wilson (Eds.), *Myanmar's Transitions: Openings, Obstacles and Opportunities*, 52–71. Singapore: ISEAS.

Grundy-Warr, Carl, and Karin Dean. 2011. "Not Peace, Not War: The Myriad Spaces of Sovereignty, Peace and Conflict in Myanmar/Burma." In Scott Kirsch, and Colin Flint (Eds.), *Reconstructing Conflict*, 91–114. Burlington: Ashgate.

Jones, Lee. 2014. "Explaining Myanmar's Regime Transition: The Periphery Is Central." *Democratization* 21 (5): 780–802.

Kramer, Tom. 2007. *The United Wa State Party: Narco-Army or Nationalist Party?* Washington, DC: East West Center.

Lederach, Jean Paul. 1999. *Building Peace: Sustainable Reconciliation in Divided Societies*. Washington, DC: United States Institute of Peace Press.

Marte, Nilsen. 2013. "Will Democracy Bring Peace to Myanmar?" *International Area Studies Review* 116 (2): 115–141.

McCharty, Altmetric, and Jacqueline Menager. 2017. "Gendered Rumours and the Muslim Scapegoat in Myanmar's Transition." *Journal of Contemporary Asia* 47 (3): 396–412.

Oh, Su-Ann. 2016. "Making Sense of the Election Results in Myanmar's Rakhine and Shan States." *Trends in South-East Asia* 1. ISEAS-Yusof Ishak Institute.

Oo, Zaw, and Win Min. 2007. *Assessing Burma's Ceasefire Accords*. Washington, DC: East-West Center.

Ruzza, Stefano. 2015. "There Are Two Sides to Every COIN: Of Economic and Military Means in Myanmar's Comprehensive Approach to Illiberal Peacebuilding." *European Journal of East Asian Studies* 14 (1): 76–97.

Ruzza, Stefano, and Giuseppe Gabusi. 2018. "Myanmar: Democratization in Slow-Motion." In Roger Mac Ginty, and Hans J. Giessmann (Eds.), *Research Handbook on Post-Conflict Transition*. Cheltenham: Edward Elgar Publishing.

Sherman, Jake. 2003. "Burma: Lessons from the Cease-Fires." In Karen Ballentine, and Jake Sherman (Eds.), *The Political Economy of Armed Conflict: Beyond Greed and Grievance*, 225–255. Boulder: Lynne Rienner Publishers.

Smith, Martin. 1999. *Burma: Insurgency and the Politics of Ethnicity*. London and New York: Zed Books.

South, Ashley. 2008. *Ethnic Politics in Burma: States of Conflict*. Abingdon and New York: Routledge.

Steinberg, David I. 2010. *Burma/Myanmar: What Everyone Needs to Know*? Oxford and New York: Oxford University Press.

Taylor, Robert. 2017. "Myanmar's Military and the Dilemma of Federalism." *ISEAS Perspective* 7. ISEAS Yusof Ishak Institute.

Woods, Kevin. 2011. "Ceasefire Capitalism: Military – Private Partnerships, Resource Concessions and Military-State Building in the Burma-China Borderlands." *Journal of Peasant Studies* 38 (4): 747–770.

Woods, Kevin. 2016. "The Commercialisation of Counterinsurgency: Battlefield Enemies, Business Bedfellows in Kachin State, Burma." In Mandy Sadan (Ed.), *War and Peace in the Borderlands of Myanmar: The Kachin Ceasefires, 1994–2011*, 114–145. Copenhagen: Nordic Institute of Asian Studies.

Zartman, I. William. 2003. "The Timing of Peace Initiatives: Hurting Stalemates and Ripe Moments." In John Darby, and Roger Mac Ginty (Eds.), *Contemporary Peace Making: Conflict, Violence and Peace Processes*. Basingstoke: Palgrave Macmillan.

Online resources

Euro-Burma Office. www.euro-burma.eu/.
The Irrawaddy. www.irrawaddy.com/.
Mizzima News. www.mizzima.com/.
Myanmar Peace Monitor. www.mmpeacemonitor.org.

11

NEPAL

Elly Harrowell and Varsha Gyawali

Introduction

By the time the peace agreement was signed that would bring Nepal's civil war to an end in 2006, the country had endured a decade of violent conflict between Maoist insurgents and government forces, bringing misery and destruction to the country's poorest, rural communities. Given that the conflict was driven by deep-rooted grievances around inequality, caste, ethnic and gender-based discrimination, poverty, and citizenship rights, any effective attempt to resolve it would have to address these thorny issues. As this chapter will demonstrate, Nepal's peace process certainly took steps to address these questions through a number of provisions included in the Comprehensive Peace Agreement, and the prospect of a return to open conflict with the Maoists now seems inconceivable, as they have been fully integrated into the mainstream political process. However, more than a decade on from the signing of this agreement, many of the same grievances that fuelled the conflict remain significant, and these continue to contribute to social conflict in the country, including the violent protests in the Tarai region which left more than 50 people dead in 2015. As such, we argue below that Nepal's peace process should be considered a work in process and serves as an important reminder that work to restore peace does not end with the signing of a peace accord – in fact, this is just the beginning.

Nepal is one of the poorest countries in South Asia, largely dependent on agriculture and remittances through labour migration from abroad. Nestled between the emerging Asian powers India and China, the country's location has played an important role in its political and economic development. With a population of approximately 29 million people, Nepal has an incredibly diverse society comprising 125 groups defined along caste, ethnicity, linguistic, and religious lines. It is also geographically diverse, home to both the towering peaks of the Himalayas and the fertile Tarai plains along the country's southern border, which plays a key role in its economic and agricultural production. Although the country remains predominantly rural, it is urbanising at one of the fastest rates in the region, creating both problems and opportunities in a country which still finds itself firmly on the list of Least Developed Countries (LDCs). Since the end of the war, the country has been undergoing a political transition characterised by political instability, endemic corruption, and slow economic growth. It is against this backdrop that the country has wrestled with the challenge of moving from war to peace.

Conflict analysis

The Nepali Civil War lasted a decade from its inception on 13 February 1996, when the conflict exploded into life through a series of attacks against police posts, to the signing of a Comprehensive Peace Agreement on 21 November 2006. The conflict caused around 13,000 deaths, thousands more disappearances, and resulted in the internal displacement of up to 200,000 people, claiming a particularly heavy toll on impoverished rural communities. It pitted the Nepali government against a Maoist insurgency, the then-Communist Party of Nepal–Maoist (CPN-Maoist, hereafter referred to as 'the Maoists'). The Maoists sought to address pernicious inequalities in the country through a programme of land reform, state restructuring (including abolishing Nepal's powerful monarchy and installing a 'People's Republic' in its place), the development of a secular state, and a comprehensive programme of social reform, including the end to discrimination on the basis of caste, gender, or ethnicity.

At first glance, the main actors in the Nepali civil war seem quite clear cut, with the insurgent Maoists taking on the established government for control of the country and its polity. However, as is so often the case, behind these two groupings lay a more complex balance of interest groups, whose relative power and prominence would wax and wane throughout the conflict and the peace process that followed. The CPN-Maoist's immediate predecessor, the CPN-Unity Centre, had united three smaller communist parties, participating in the pro-democracy protests known as *Jana Andolan I* that had swept the country in the 1990, bringing the return of multi-party democratic elections for the first time since these were suspended by King Mahendra in 1960. The CPN-UC would participate in elections in 1991, winning nine seats, although by the end of the year they had already adopted a motion stating their intention to usher in a revolution via a 'people's war'. In 1994, the CPN-UC split with the more radical faction led by Pushpa Kamal Dahal (more commonly known by his *nom de guerre* Prachanda) renaming itself the CPN-Maoist and eventually initiating hostilities in 1996. Crucially, however, during the 10 years of conflict the Maoists would come to represent the grievances of a range of actors, overwhelmingly drawn from the country's impoverished countryside, that felt disenfranchised by the elites based in Kathmandu and regional centres. Women, *Dalits* (lower caste communities), ethnic minorities and indigenous groups known as *Adivasi Janajatis*, and Madhesi communities from the southern Tarai plains had all been excluded from power, and saw in the Maoists demands an opportunity to redress this situation. Of course, it would be these groups that suffered the most from the conflict and the actions of both the state and Maoist forces.

On the side of the government, it is important to distinguish between the political parties and leadership that made up successive governments throughout the duration of the conflict (largely represented by the dominant Nepal Congress Party (NC) and the Communist Party of Nepal–United Marxist Leninist (UML)) and the monarchy, whose influence decreased following the reintroduction of democracy in 1990, after which King Birendra took on a more symbolic role as the head of state. As we shall see, the rise to power of King Gyanendra following the royal massacre in 2001, which claimed the life of King Birendra, would have a significant impact. The entry of the army into the conflict, which drastically increased casualty numbers, and King Gyanendra's decision to dismiss the government and take executive control of the country in 2005 provided the Maoists and mainstream parties with a common enemy, creating the 'ripe moment' for negotiations to begin.

Mapping the phases of the conflict

The conflict in Nepal can be broken down into three main phases: a low-level insurgency that lasted from the outbreak of violence in 1996 to 2001; the rapid intensification of violence from both parties following the murder of King Birendra and nine other members of the royal family by Crown Prince Dipendra (including himself) in June 2001; and the restoration of absolute monarchy by King Gyanendra in February 2005, which gave the Maoists and mainstream political parties common cause to work together towards the restoration of representative democracy.

On 4 February 1996, Baburam Bhattarai, representing the political wing of the CPN-Maoist, the United People's Front Nepal (UPFN), presented a list of 40 demands to the prime minister at the time, Sher Bahadur Deuba. This list covered a range of demands, including social and economic reforms, an end to Indian interference in national politics, extensive state restructuring including the abolition of the monarchy, and an end to discrimination on the basis of gender, caste, or nationality (HRW 2004; Whitfield 2008). Many of the issues raised in the CPN-Maoist's list echoed the grievances of marginalised rural and indigenous communities, increasing the Maoist's traction in these areas (Lawoti 2015). These demands were rejected by the government, prompting the beginning of armed hostilities by the Maoist People's Liberation Army, a force which, according to the United Nations, would number almost 20,000 fighters by the conflict's end. To an extent this can be understood as a response to a government crackdown on the Maoists from 1995 onwards, including the brutal Operation Romeo, which resulted in severe human rights violations against suspected dissidents and villagers in the Maoist stronghold of Rolpa (HRW 2004). Over the next few years, the Maoists were able to quickly extend their reach through the territory of Nepal, aided by an ineffective government response which framed the conflict as a law and order issue, to be dealt with by a police force that was ill-equipped to counter such an insurgency, rather than the Royal Nepali

Army (RNA) (Do and Iyer 2010). While the police response was clearly inadequate and fuelled brutal human rights abuses against local populations, as Whitfield (2008: 4) notes, 'whether to mobilize the Royal Nepal Army (RNA) against the Maoists was a controversial issue, principally because the army – as its name implied – was not under the control of the civilian government, but the king'. By 2001, the Maoists had extended their control to 22 of Nepal's 75 districts, and the government seemed no closer to finding an effective response to the conflict.

The events of 2001 would shock the nation and the wider world, setting the civil conflict on an entirely new course and remaining a source of speculation in the country to this day. On 1 June 2001, in circumstances that remain shrouded in mystery to this day, Crown Prince Dipendra gunned down King Birendra, Queen Aishwarya, and eight other members of the royal family, gathered for a dinner, before turning the gun on himself. The massacre brought King Birendra's brother Gyanendra, who had been away from Kathmandu at the time and tended to support a more aggressive approach to the conflict, to the throne. Gyanendra was not a widely popular figure and would be dogged by rumours about the manner of his accession to the throne throughout his reign. In the aftermath of the massacre and the ascendancy of King Gyanendra to the throne, the Maoists and government declared a ceasefire on 23 July; however, on 21 November the Maoists withdrew from this ceasefire and resumed hostilities. A state of emergency was declared by the government in response, with King Gyanendra authorising the entrance of the RNA into the conflict for the first time. From this point, the intensity of the conflict increased markedly, with deaths caused by both government and Maoist forces rocketing (Figure 11.1).

The increased ferocity of the Nepali government's response to the insurgency found resonance with the US-led global War on Terror from 2001, and in 2002 the Maoists were declared a terrorist organisation, subject to sweeping new legislation

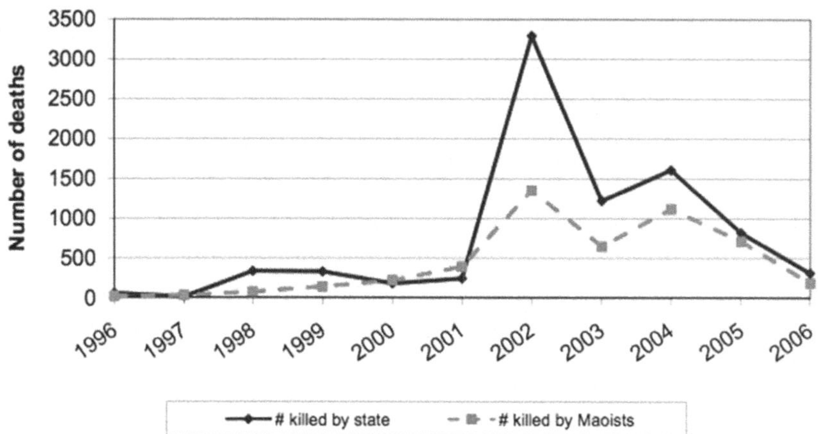

FIGURE 11.1 Conflict deaths in the Nepal Civil War

Source: (Do and Iyer 2010)

that, as human rights organisations have noted, fostered a culture of impunity in the security forces and encouraged further rights abuses in a conflict already marked by brutality (HRW 2004). A second ceasefire from January 2003 to August 2003 fell apart after it became clear the government was not willing to countenance key Maoist demands regarding the restructuring of the state (Thapa and Sharma 2009), and after the murder of 21 civilians by RNA soldiers in Doramba. In this period, the Maoists started to succeed in urbanising the conflict, calling a number of general strikes and gradually increasing violence in urban areas (Do and Iyer 2010). This was important, since the capital until that time had largely avoided the impact of the insurgency, with the rural and mountainous regions bearing the brunt of the violence. As the violence began to encroach on Kathmandu, however, it became more difficult for the urban elites to ignore.

In this febrile mix, King Gyanendra made what was to prove a devastating strategic blunder. Faced with a conflict that had not been resolved despite four years of military engagement, and in the context of increasing pro-democracy demonstrations, Gyanendra moved to restore absolute monarchy in February 2005, dismissing the government, imprisoning political leaders, targeting human rights defenders, curtailing press freedom, and declaring another state of emergency. In one stroke, Gyanendra's actions achieved what years of stalled talks and brutal conflict had not – his decisions united the Maoists and the Seven Party Alliance (SPA) of mainstream political parties, simultaneously alienating the country's main foreign allies (the UK, India, and the United States, all of whom had overwhelmingly supported the government against the insurgency). The united front presented by Nepali political parties across the spectrum, alongside widespread civil society-led public protests in Kathmandu, would force King Gyanendra to renounce control by April 2006. At the same time, this turbulent period provided the impetus for the parties to the conflict to proceed with a series of peace talks, culminating in the Comprehensive Peace Agreement signed on 21 November 2006.

Understanding the root causes of conflict

So, what root causes lay behind Nepal's conflict? As Sharma (2006) points out, the conflict could not be traced to questions of ethnicity or religion, nor could it be attributed to a lack of political freedom, breaking out as it did at a time when the reinstatement of multi-party democracy in 1990 meant that civil liberties and political freedoms seemed to be improving. Instead, the war was widely understood to be linked to the widespread and pernicious inequality that had defined Nepali society for decades (if not centuries). This inequality was embodied in the country's highly stratified social structure, its economy, and the gaping urban–rural divide, all of which provided fertile ground for dissatisfaction to develop into open conflict. The country was plagued by deep-seated structural grievances related to spatial inequality and elite domination, caste, ethnic, and gender-based discrimination, poverty, and landlessness, among others.

One of the defining features of Nepali society has long been its strict social stratification, along both caste and ethnic lines, which has seen political power concentrated in the hands of a small group. From the eighteenth century to the fall of the monarchy (with a few short interludes of attempted parliamentary democracy), the country was ruled either by a monarch from the Shah family or by a hereditary prime minister from the Rana clan (Lunn 2013). Discrimination on the basis of caste or ethnicity is a feature that permeates every part of society. Hill Brahmins and Chhetris have dominated society, monopolising political and economic power despite the fact they constitute less than 30 per cent of the population. At the other end of the scale, Dalits (commonly known as 'untouchables'), indigenous or *Janajati* groups, women, Madhesis (a large minority group from the southern Tarai region), and the unlanded (such as bonded labourers) have traditionally made up the most marginalised groups in the state, despite together comprising the overwhelming majority (Lawoti 2015). This extreme discrimination had serious consequences for the ability of many to gain citizenship, particularly for the Madhesis. Neither the monarchy nor the nascent parliamentary democracy in place at the outbreak of the conflict presented a credible opportunity, nor even a convincing interest, in addressing the pervasive inequality that excluded so many people from full and free participation in the state.

Analysis of the civil war has overwhelmingly identified economic inequality and poverty as another of its root causes (Do and Iyer 2010; Tiwari 2009; Sharma 2006). The country's rural areas, where the insurgency was to take hold and eventually dominate, were devastatingly poor. Sharma notes that by 1996 the GDP per capita of people living in rural areas was less than half than that of their urban counterparts, a gap which had widened significantly over the preceding ten years. This inequality, he notes,

> was also reflected by the limited access to public goods and services in the rural areas. For example, in urban areas a health post was accessible within a few minutes as opposed to over an hour in the rural areas. Access to market, banking services and reliable road networks was even worse in the rural areas.
> *(Sharma 2006: 1244)*

Once again, a large majority of the country's population was excluded from development gains and basic services. Crucially, there was a significant overlap between most economically marginalised and the most socially and politically marginalised groups, such as women, Dalits, Madhesis, and *Adivasi Janajatis*.

An important impact of this social, political, and economic marginalisation that was to prove another key driver of conflict was the question of land. The hugely unequal, and often exploitative, patterns of land ownership in the country both reflected wider problems of social stratification and marginalisation and served as a trap which kept the most vulnerable sections of society mired in poverty. Land reform would emerge as a key demand tabled by the Maoists throughout the insurgency, as would calls for the dissolution of the monarchy, the nationalisation of private property, the curbing of foreign influence (particularly by India), an end to discrimination based on gender, caste, or ethnicity, and a comprehensive programme of state restructuring. These demands allowed the Maoists to draw on support from marginalised groups keen to have their grievances addressed, although these groups would also be the ones that suffered the most violence during the conflict, at the hands of both the police and army and the Maoists.

The conflict resolution process

In many ways, the extent to which Nepal's conflict resolution process can be deemed to be successful depends on where you draw the boundaries of assessment. If, like some, one considers the period from the fall of King Gyanendra in 2006 until the democratic election of the Maoist leader Prachanda to the position of Prime Minister in 2008, then the peace process can be understood as a significant success. As Whitfield (2008: 2) notes, 'the distance travelled from war to peace, as Nepalis elected a constituent assembly in which the Maoists represented the largest single party, abolished the monarchy and declared the country a federal republic, was enormous'. However, widening the scope of enquiry to include the nearly ten years since Prachanda's symbolically crucial election – a decade in which the architecture of peacebuilding envisaged in the CPA was introduced and supported by the international community – would lead to a more cautious appraisal of the process' success. To be sure, there has been no return to the levels of violence of the civil war, but neither have the underlying inequalities that drove that violence been effectively addressed, and the post-2006 period has been marked by waves of protest by identity-based groups, often resulting in violence. Perhaps the most marked of these was the violence that broke out in response to the 'fast-tracked' constitution that followed the devastating earthquakes in 2015, demonstrating clearly the tensions and conflicts the country had yet to successfully address.

Moving from war to peace

Although the conclusion of the civil war, when it came, seemed to move quite quickly, in actual fact the groundwork for this had been laid by continuing contacts between the Maoists and representatives of the mainstream political parties for some time. Formal talks, such as those that followed a ceasefire in 2003, were supplemented by ongoing contact between Maoist representatives and senior establishment figures, even after the breakdown of the ceasefire (Whitfield 2008). Although prospects for further formal peace talks foundered as King Gyanendra seized the reins of power in early 2005, this also provided the parties to the conflict with common cause to rally against – presenting perhaps the 'ripe moment' for conflict resolution envisaged by Zartman (2000). Informal negotiations restarted between the main political parties – now organised into the Seven Party Alliance (SPA) – and the Maoists, with talks taking place in New Delhi, Kathmandu, and in the India–Nepal border regions in 2005. These talks would result in the adoption of a 12 Point Understanding between the SPA and Maoists. This document affirmed both parties' commitment to a peaceful resolution of the conflict, the restoration of democracy, and end to the King's autocratic rule and support for the people's movement that had emerged in protest at the King's coup. The international community, and particularly the Indian government, played a supportive role in these negotiations and in mediation between the SPA, the Maoists, and the King.

The role of the people's movement, which would come to be known as *Jana Andolan II*, in reference to the previous popular movement for democracy that had emerged in the 1990s, was crucial in bringing an end to the conflict in Nepal and providing the impetus for peace. Not only did it mobilise huge numbers of citizens to go on strike and demonstrate against the King's actions, but it also threw the weight of the people behind calls for an end to the conflict and for action on questions of social inclusion and state restructuring that were at the heart of the Maoists' demands for change. The 19 days of strikes and demonstrations that took place in April 2006 were at times met with violence but were eventually successful at forcing the King to reinstate parliament on 24 April, paving the way for a resumption of formal peace talks between the SPA and Maoists the following month. Civil society actors would continue to play a vital role in peace talks, for example through the 'track 1.5' diplomacy mechanism the Nepal Transition to Peace Initiative, led by two prominent civil society actors (Sapkota 2017). From the resumption of talks in May, progress was made to approve a series of intermediate agreements (for example, requesting UN assistance and setting the terms for a ceasefire), leading to the signing of a Comprehensive Peace Agreement (CPA) in November 2006. This progress was by no means smooth – a number of contentious issues related to the disposal of Maoist arms, the form of interim institutions, and the status of the monarchy threatened to derail the nascent peace process, and the two parties disagreed about the speed they wished talks to progress, with the Maoists keen to capitalise on the social awareness generated by the April protests (International Crisis Group 2006). However, in spite of the pattern of brinkmanship and recriminations being played out on the public stage, in private positions were often subtler, and progress was sustained by face to face meetings between key high-level figures from either side (ibid.).

The CPA itself has at once been lauded as 'fairly exhaustive' (Thapa 2017: 54) in terms of the breadth of issues it sought to address, and problematically vague on the details of how these issues could be resolved (Suhrke 2011). Building on the principles set out in the 12 Point Understanding of 2005 and a further 8 Point Understanding of June 2006, the CPA envisaged a range of measures. It provided for the cantonment of both Maoist fighters and the Nepali Army, while also delineating terms for a ceasefire. It set out political next steps, including elections to a Constituent Assembly, and identified timeframes by which these should occur. The CPA took steps to set up an architecture of peacebuilding and transitional justice (explored in greater detail below), envisaging the establishment of bodies such as the Truth and Reconciliation Commission and a High-level State Restructuring Recommendation Commission, and invited the United Nations to play a role in monitoring key elements of the CPA's implementation. Perhaps most significantly, the document incorporates large sections dedicated to human rights as well as political, social, and economic transformations. Accordingly, Clause 3.5 affirms that

> In order to end discriminations based on class, ethnicity, language, gender, culture, religion and region and to address the problems of women, Dalits, indigenous ethnic minorities (*Adivasi Janjatis*), Tarai communities (Madhesis), oppressed, neglected and minority communities and the backward areas by deconstructing the current centralised and unitary structure, the state shall be restructured in an inclusive, democratic and forward looking manner
>
> *(Comprehensive Peace Agreement 2006)*

This serves to further underline the importance placed on effectively addressing questions of inclusion and federalism – identified as key drivers of the conflict – if a lasting peace is to be achieved.

The year that followed the adoption of the CPA proved to be something of a mixed bag. While initial deadlines for the installation of the interim government and interim legislature were missed, by January 2007 the legislature had met, including 83 Maoist delegates, and the UN-monitored process of registering and securing of weapons had begun. The UN's political mission (UNMIN) was also established in January 2007 to support the peace process, and by April 2007 the Maoists had also joined the interim government, taking responsibility for five cabinet ministries. At the same time, though, tensions were brewing, both within the Maoist ranks and in the large Madhesi minority community, who felt their needs were not adequately reflected in the CPA and interim institutions that had followed it (Lunn 2013). Protests by Madhesi groups would become a recurring theme throughout 2007 and 2008, as well as the Maoists' own protests in the autumn of 2007, and although a series of talks with both parties enabled elections to the Constituent Assembly envisaged in the CPA to take place on 10 April 2008, Madhesi claims remain a thorny and unresolved issue even to this day. These elections produced a result that perhaps no one expected, as the Maoists won 220 of the 601 seats, becoming the largest party in the body (which would also serve as a parliament).

A local or internationally driven process?

Throughout this period, a number of external actors would play a role in the peace process, though this was always secondary to the Nepali stakeholders driving the process. Most significant among these were the parts played by India, Nepal's large and influential southern neighbour, and the United Nations. India has long played a key role in Nepal's politics, with their tacit support being widely viewed as 'indispensable' to any political party seeking to take power in Kathmandu (Jha 2012: 332). The Indian government's approach to the Nepali conflict shifted significantly through the early 2000s. At first, they resisted interventions by international actors in Nepal, preferring to pursue a 'two pillars' approach which supported constitutional monarchy and multi-party democracy through bilateral engagement with the King and mainstream political parties (Upreti 2010; Muni 2012). There was considerable mistrust between India and the Maoists, with the former wary of its own Naxalite Maoist insurgencies, and the latter making the lessening of Indian influence in Nepal a key feature of the 40 demands they had presented in 1996. India's stance on the Maoists hardened further in light of the US-led War on Terror in 2001, which saw the Maoists characterised as a terrorist group. However, following King Gyanendra's power grab in 2005, the Indian government increasingly perceived that the two pillars that had been the bedrock of their policy towards the Nepali civil war had become incompatible – the monarchy was now a direct threat to multi-party democracy. In this new context, India increasingly supported peace talks, the involvement of international actors such as the UN, and direct engagement with the Maoists. They provided a supportive atmosphere for the talks leading to the 12 Point Understanding between the SPA and Maoists, and were widely seen as the 'guarantor of the agreement' (Jha 2012: 332), even though they did not directly participate in or mediate the talks. The Indian government also dispatched an intermediary to put pressure on King Gyanendra to reinstate the Prime Minister and legislature, hoping that this would be enough to save the monarchy. Despite these positive steps, tensions remained between the Maoists and the Indian government, and India would continue to play an influential role in Nepal's domestic affairs, including in the collapse of the Prachanda-led government in 2009 and again in their response – much criticised in Nepal – to the violent Tarai protests and fuel blockade of 2015.

The United Nations did not play a particularly active role in the peace negotiations; although they had been offering their good offices in the pursuit of peace for some time (something the Maoists had been particularly open to), their engagement had previously been discouraged by India. Following the announcement of the 12 Point Understanding, however, the UN stepped up its involvement, receiving a request from Prime Minister Koirala and Maoist leader Prachanda to contribute to the peace process in a number of important, albeit limited, ways. The UN Mission in Nepal (UNMIN) worked from 2007 to 2011 to support the peace process in three main ways: military monitoring of the ceasefire, surrender of arms, and cantonment of combatants; elections monitoring; and civil affairs. These functions complemented the ongoing presence of the Office for the High Commissioner for Human Rights (OHCHR), which had begun work in Nepal in response to the upsurge in rights abuses in the 2005 royal coup. UNMIN has been characterised as narrow in focus and particularly 'light touch' with regards to its military component, which was composed of former and active military officers acting in a civilian capacity (as a noted contributor of peacekeeping troops, Nepal was highly reluctant to be a recipient of a full peacekeeping mission) (Martin 2012). While this limited scope allowed UNMIN to focus on achieving their goals, it also set the mission up for criticism due to the inherent 'tensions [. . .] between a limited mandate and high expectations' (Martin 2012: 201). As time wore on, UNMIN was variously criticised by members of the SPA for favouring the Maoists, for over-registering

PLA fighters, for under-registering PLA weapons, and for involving itself too much in the Madhesi question. Ultimately, UNMIN played an important and eminently practical role in the Nepali peace process from 2006 to 2008 but shared the fate that Prashant Jha (2012: 358) has eloquently identified of most international actors who sought to intervene in Nepal;

> As long as the key principal domestic actors see an incentive in working together to maintain a consensus, the involvement of international actors can be channelled constructively. When that consensus unravels and politics begin to fragment, those international actors with major interests in the country end up contributing to instability deliberately or inadvertently.

In contrast, the Nepali peace process has been lauded by many, especially by actors within the country, as an essentially 'home grown' achievement (Whitfield 2008; Upreti 2012). That is to say, the impetus for the peace process, negotiations, drafting, and implementation of the CPA were all principally led by Nepali stakeholders. Although key external players such as India and the UN would play influential roles, the UN Special Representative of the Secretary General in Nepal during the peace process, Ian Martin, characterised the Nepali case as 'exceptional in the extent to which it was truly a national achievement and not one mediated by any international actor' (Martin 2012: 201). At a time when the wider academic discourse has turned towards the notion of hybridity in peacebuilding and increasingly notes the value of integrating local approaches to peace rather than relying on externally imposed models (Richmond 2009), Nepal's experience provides an interesting possible example of hybridity within a peace process.

A significant feature of the 'home grown' nature of Nepal's peace process was the prominent role of civil society. Post the 1990 *Jana Andolan I*, along with the ushering in of democratic politics and freedom of speech in the country, Nepal also witnessed a period of exponential rise in various civil society groups, particularly NGOs, who became very active in the development sector and in supplementing the government's service delivery. The insurgency period saw an emergence of human rights NGOs, who challenged the state and Maoists for the atrocities they committed on civilians during the conflict and sought accountability for the human rights violations that were committed. Many of these prominent civil society groups, however, were viewed as part of an elite (higher-caste, educated) Kathmandu-based network with close affiliations with different political parties.

During Nepal's second democracy movement, i.e. *Jana Andolan II* in 2006, the civil society movement took a prominent role in mobilising the general civilians into the political process for overthrowing the monarch while mediating between the SPA and the Maoists and their political agendas. The Citizens' Movement for Democracy and Peace was a civil society initiative that became instrumental in laying the ground for the 2006 movement and encouraging a greater participation of the common people in the struggle to bring in democracy for the second time. While the role of civil society cannot be overstated in Nepal's *Jana Andolan II*, they were almost immediately side-lined during the peace negotiations (only five civil society representatives were invited as observers to the peace talks), and their work was limited to providing ad-hoc support in breaking deadlocks during the negotiations (Farasat and Hayner 2009). Post-2006, the role of civil society as a guarantor of the peace process has diminished, and successive governments have closed down the space for civil society groups to meaningfully engage in the political process. Although civil society groups remain active in some areas – particularly post-disaster work following the devastating earthquakes in 2015 – they have never regained the heights of *Jana Andolan II* in terms of their ability to bring about political change. Besides the lack of support for such activism by the state, there have been stringent policies implemented against the civil society groups, particularly NGOs, to access funding from the government and foreign sources in recent times.

Taking into account the period from the initial talks in New Delhi in 2005 to the democratic election of a Maoist-led government in 2008, then, the Nepali peace process should be considered a success, at the very least in terms of installing a negative peace. Perhaps crucially, since the early days of the process it never seemed likely that the Maoists would take up arms again. The fragile peace has held, and a return to the organised and widespread violence of 1996–2006 seems unthinkable, especially as the Maoists have been fully integrated into the political system since their 2008 electoral victory. Another success of the peace process by 2008 was the mainstreaming of language and discussion around questions such as inclusion, women's rights, and federalism. The Maoists were successful in ensuring that these grievances – at the heart of their demands in 1996 – were at the heart of the CPA and further advanced through mechanisms such as the progressive quota system in the 2008 elections to the Constituent Assembly, which saw more women and Dalits elected than ever before. That the success in ensuring these key questions was placed firmly on the public agenda in the years following the CPA and not brushed under the carpet as the threat of violence receded was significant and should not be underestimated. All the same, some researchers (Suhrke 2011) have noted that although the vague nature of many references to such issues in the CPA may have enabled their quick adoption and mainstreaming into political discourse, this also stored up problems for later, since there was little detail about how these lofty aims would actually be achieved.

From quick wins to long-term problems

Taking a longer view of the peace process in Nepal, however, leads to a more critical appraisal of its success. More than a decade on from the signing of the CPA, many of its core provisions have been only partially implemented, and some not at all. The key conflict drivers identified in that document – such as inequality, discrimination, citizenship, and access to land and resources – remain highly problematic today. Emblematic of this situation have been the explosive protests by Madhesi and Tharu communities in the wake of the adoption of a 'fast-tracked' and, to many, regressive constitution in 2015. These protests, and the often brutal police response to them, clearly demonstrate the continued potential for conflict stemming from issues that the CPA and peace process were meant to address. In particular, it is important to highlight three key elements of the CPA which continue to pose very real problems to the success of the peace process in Nepal today – land reform, transitional justice, and identity-based movements.

Land reform

One area of the peace process in which very little has been achieved since 2006 is land reform. The question of access to and ownership of land cuts to the heart of the questions of gender, caste, and ethnicity-based discrimination and pernicious poverty that drive conflict in Nepal. The country's land tenure system has long been characterised as 'feudal' and directly linked to practices such as bonded labour, leaving many marginalised rural communities as landless or land-poor. Although the CPA included a provision to 'end feudal land ownership and formulate the policies for scientific land reform' (CPA Clause 3.7), as well as to return lands and property seized in the conflict, in reality very little has been done in this respect. Although the question of land reform and restitution periodically rises to the top of the political agenda, this is rarely matched by clear structures and legislative commitments to seriously address the issue (Carter Center 2012), and land ownership in Nepal remains deeply unequal. This was thrown into stark relief by the devastating earthquakes of 2015, after which reconstruction has been severely hampered by poor land records, gender inequality in land tenure, and the challenge of rebuilding for the landless, in many cases resulting in a rise in social conflict at the local level.

Transitional justice

Among the several key commitments in the CPA, one was to establish a Truth and Reconciliation Commission (TRC) 'to probe into those involved in serious violation of human rights and crimes against humanity in the course of the armed conflict for creating an atmosphere for reconciliation in the society' (Article 5.2.5, Comprehensive Peace Agreement 2006). The Maoist-led government that emerged after the first constituent assembly elections in 2008 and the subsequent governments showed little interest in setting up the transitional justice mechanisms agreed upon within the CPA. After widespread calls by Nepali civil society – particularly human rights agencies and the international community on accountability for the mass atrocities committed during the armed conflict – the government enacted the Enforced Disappearances Enquiry, Truth and Reconciliation Commission Act (TRC Act) in 2014. In accordance with the Act, two Commissions were established in February 2015 – the Truth and Reconciliation Commission (TRC) and the Commission of Investigation on Enforced Disappeared Persons (CIEDP). Although the setting up of the two Commissions was seen as a positive step forward, several provisions under the TRC Act 2014 have provoked wide criticisms and are considered to fall below the international legal standards. A big contention has been the discretionary powers offered to the Commissions to grant amnesties for serious human rights violations for disclosures, along with provisions that allow forced reconciliation without victims' informed consent and lack of criminalisation of war crimes like torture and enforced disappearances under the country's domestic law, among other things (TRC Act 2014).

In its fourth year, the two commissions have reportedly received over 65,000 complaints, although it continues to struggle with restricted scope, outreach, and resources (Selim 2017). The directives by the Nepali Supreme Court to amend the act (e.g. on issues around amnesties, forced reconciliation) is yet to be implemented by the state. Sharma argues that the government's act of defying court orders, refusing vetting processes against senior government and army personnel, and withdrawing criminal charges against alleged perpetrators dilutes efforts for a meaningful transitional justice process in the country (Sharma 2017: 34). Another important component of the Nepali transitional justice process is the government's Interim Relief Program (IRP), which it has equated to reparation since it was rolled out to the victims and their families in 2007. With a focus on financial compensation, the IRP has also been marred by inconsistencies along with discriminatory practices, as the victims of sexual violence and torture are not recognised as a qualifying category under the scheme, and an official acknowledgement of human rights violations during the insurgency is absent from the state discourse (Sajjad 2015; Selim 2017).

Madhesi and other identity-based movements

The post-insurgency period in Nepal saw the emergence of various identity-based movements, particularly from the Madhesis and *Adivasi Janjatis*, who were historically marginalised from political power and representation. One of the first and most prominent of these movements took place in the Tarai, led by the then-*Madhesi* People's Rights Forum, Nepal in 2007, which led to an agreement within the Interim Constitution to recognise Nepal as a federal state and incorporate 'right to social justice' (Jha 2017). In the 2008 Constituent Assembly election, a progressive quota or proportional representation system was introduced to ensure participation from marginalised communities, resulting in the most diverse elected body in the history of Nepali politics. However, serious disagreements continued around key issues of reservations (quotas), electoral system, citizenship rights, and federal structure. The political leaders were unable to reach an acceptable compromise, leading to the dissolution of the Constituent Assembly in 2012 among heightened identity-group tensions and widespread protests (often violent) across the country and particularly in the Tarai region. The 'fast-track' promulgation of the 2015 constitution created further rifts where Madhesis and *Tharus* blamed the government for backtracking from its constitutional commitments on guarantees of inclusion, participation, and representation of the historically marginalised communities and expressed strong reservations against the delineation of new federal state boundaries. Among fears that these commitments would be further diluted, political protests spread across the Tarai region, resulting in border blockade and violent demonstrations killing over 50 people in late 2015. There still remain deep divisions between the marginalised communities and the government on these issues, and the Tarai belt continues to reel from political instability.

Lessons to be learned from the case study

Taking stock of the peace process in Nepal a decade after the CPA was signed, then, it becomes clear that this has produced mixed results. On the one hand, there have been notable successes. The warring parties have not taken up arms again, and the Maoists have become fully integrated into the democratic process. Local actors, particularly drawn from civil society, played a central role in bringing an end to armed violence, meaning that the 'home-grown' peace process that followed was locally grounded and owned by the Nepali people. In addition, ambitious responses to pernicious problems such as inequality were included in the CPA, suggesting that it would henceforth be impossible to brush these issues under the carpet. However, when it comes to long-term implementation, the picture is not so rosy. Despite these promising beginnings, many of the most challenging elements of the CPA – such as land reform, transitional justice, and the Madhesi question – have not been satisfactorily addressed. As a result, the same old grievances caused by inequality, discrimination, and poverty continue to fuel conflict in Nepal today, albeit at a lower level than in the decade from 1996 to 2006.

So what lessons can be learned from this? As in many of the cases in this volume, Nepal's experience once again underlines the significance of Zartman's 'ripe moment' for conflict resolution. In Nepal, King Gyanendra's increasingly authoritarian rule, encapsulated in his restoration of absolute monarchy in 2005, provided the Maoists and Seven Party Alliance with common cause, kickstarting peace talks between them. The Nepali peace process also highlights the complicated and at times contradictory role played by international actors. As noted earlier in the chapter, Indian interventions have at sometimes supported peace talks, while at other times they have undermined this process. Similarly, the UN made some important contributions to the peace process, particularly between 2006 and 2008, but as time went on their role became more contested.

Perhaps one of the most important lessons to emerge from the Nepali experience is the importance of local ownership of the peace process. From the events of *Jana Andolan II*, and the role of local civil society organisations in supporting these, to the initial negotiations that led to the CPA and the elections to the Constituent Assembly, the peace process was largely driven by Nepali actors. While international actors did play a role (as mentioned above), the fact that local ownership was retained over Nepal's peace process is significant and goes some way to explaining why this process has not experienced the same kind of crisis in legitimacy witnessed in other cases. This has been something of a double-edged sword in later years, however, as the peace process has increasingly become hostage to national politics.

The failure of all parties to effectively address the fundamental issues that drove the conflict in Nepal – inequality, discrimination on the basis of caste, ethnicity, and gender, the rural–urban divide, and crippling poverty – has undermined the peace process. Ironically, success in swiftly integrating the Maoist insurgents into formal institutions of government has been a mixed blessing, preventing a return to large-scale violence but leaving much of the progressive agenda advocated in the Maoist's original 40 demands and the eventual CPA bogged down in the drawn out processes of politics-as-usual in Nepal. The devastating earthquakes that hit the country in 2015 once again highlighted pernicious inequalities in Nepali society, throwing into relief these faultlines as the poorest and most vulnerable were once again hit hardest by the effects of this tragedy (and the painfully slow recovery that has followed). The emergence of identity-based movements drawn from communities such as the Madhesis and *Adivasi Janajatis*, whose actions have been violently countered by the state in recent years, suggest that until these core grievances are properly addressed, marginalised communities will continue to seek means of pursuing this aim. In spite of ten years of conflict and 12 years of CPA implementation and peacebuilding programmes, the concerns raised in the recent Tarai protests are fundamentally the same as those that were raised in the civil war. As long as this is the case, then the Nepali peace process cannot be considered to be complete.

References, further reading, and links to key primary documents

Carter Center, The. 2012. "Land Commitments in Nepal's Peace Process: An Update on Implementation." https://www.cartercenter.org/resources/pdfs/peace/democracy/nepal-land-062012-eng.pdf

Comprehensive Peace Agreement between the Government of Nepal and the Communist Party of Nepal (Maoist). 2006. https://peacemaker.un.org/nepal-comprehensive agreement2006

Do, Quy Toan, and Lakshmi Iyer. 2010. "Geography, Poverty and Conflict in Nepal." *Journal of Peace Research* 47 (6): 735–748.

Farasat, Warisha, and Priscilla Hayner. 2009. "Negotiating Peace in Nepal: Implications for Justice." *IFP Mediation Cluster Country Case Study: Nepal*. Institute for Peacebuilding/ International Centre for Transitional Justice

Human Rights Watch. 2004. "Between a Rock and a Hard Place: Civilians Struggle to Survive in Nepal's Civil War." www.hrw.org/sites/default/files/reports/nepal1004.pdf.

International Crisis Group. 2006. "Nepal's Peace Agreement: Making It Work." *Asia Report* 126. www.refworld.org/pdfid/45a4b4b82.pdf.

Jha, Dipendra. 2017. "Comparing the 2007 and 2015 Constitutions." In Deepak Thapa, and Alexander Ramsbotham (Eds.), *Two Steps Forward, One Step Back: The Nepal Peace Process*, 64–67. London: Conciliation Resources.

Jha, Prashant. 2012. "A Nepali Perspective on International Involvement in Nepal." In Sebastian von Einsiedel, David M. Malone, and Suman Pradhan (Eds.), *Nepal in Transition: From People's War to Fragile Peace*. Cambridge: Cambridge University Press.

Lawoti, Mahendra. 2015. "Prolonged Transition and Setback in Reforms: Timing, Sequencing, and Contestations Over Reforms in Post-Conflict Nepal." CRPD Working Paper No. 43,

KU Leuven. https://soc.kuleuven.be/crpd/files/working-papers/working-paper-lawoti-2.pdf.

Lunn, Jon. 2013. "Nepal's Endless Peace Process, 2006–12." *International Affairs and Defence Section, House of Commons*, October 2011. Accessed 31 July 2014. http://researchbriefings. files.parliament.uk/documents/SN04229/SN04229.pdf.

Martin, Ian. 2012. "The United Nations and Support to Nepal's Peace Process: The Role of the UN Mission in Nepal." In Sebastian von Einsiedel, and David M. Malone (Eds.), *Nepal in Transition: From People War to Fragile Peace*. Cambridge: Cambridge University Press.

Muni, S.D. 2012. "Bringing the Maoists Down from the Hills: India's Role." In Sebastian von Einsiedel, David M. Malone, and Suman Pradhan (Eds.), *Nepal in Transition: From People's War to Fragile Peace*. Cambridge: Cambridge University Press.

Richmond, Oliver P. 2009. "Becoming Liberal, Unbecoming Liberalism: Liberal-Local Hybridity Via the Everyday as a Response to the Paradoxes of Liberal Peacebuilding." *Journal of Intervention and Statebuilding* 3 (3): 324–344.

Sajjad, Tazreena. 2015. "Heavy Hands, Helping Hands, Holding Hands: The Politics of Exclusion in Victims' Networks in Nepal." *International Journal of Transitional Justice* 10 (1): 25–45.

Sapkota, Bishue. 2017. "Architecture of Peace in Nepal." In Deepak Thapa, and Alexander Ramsbotham (Eds.), *Two Steps Forward, One Step Back: The Nepal Peace Process*, 64–67. London: Conciliation Resources.

Selim, Yvette. 2017. "Examining Victims and Perpetrators in Post-Conflict Nepal." *International Review of Victimology* 23 (3): 275–301.

Sharma, Kishor. 2006. "The Political Economy of Civil War in Nepal." *World Development* 34 (7): 1237–1253.

Sharma, Mandira. 2017. "Transitional Justice in Nepal: Low Priority, Partial Peace." In Deepak Thapa, and Alexander Ramsbotham (Eds.), *Two Steps Forward, One Step Back: The Nepal Peace Process*, 64–67. London: Conciliation Resources.

Suhrke, Astri. 2011. "Virtues of a Narrow Mission: The UN Peace Operation in Nepal." *Global Governance: A Review of Multilateralism and International Organizations* 17 (1): 37–55.

Thapa, Deepak. 2017. "Looking Back at the CPA: An Inventory of Implementation." In Deepak Thapa, and Alexander Ramsbotham (Eds.), *Two Steps Forward, One Step Back: The Nepal Peace Process*, 54–57. London: Conciliation Resources.

Thapa, Ganga B., and Jan Sharma. 2009. "From Insurgency to Democracy: The Challenges of Peace and Democracy-Building in Nepal." *International Political Science Review* 30 (2): 205–219.

Tiwari, Bishwa Nath. 2009. "12 an Assessment of the Causes of Conflict in Nepal." In Mahendra Lawoti, and Anup K. Pahari (Eds.), *The Maoist Insurgency in Nepal: Revolution in the Twenty-First Century*, 241–257. London: Routledge.

Upreti, Bishnu Raj. 2012. "Nepal from war to Peace." *Peace Review* 24: 1.

Whitfield, Teresa. 2008. "Masala Peacemaking: Nepal's Peace Process and the Contribution of Outsiders." Conflict Prevention and Peace Forum, October.

Zartman, I. William. 2000. "Ripeness: The Hurting Stalemate and Beyond." *International Conflict Resolution After the Cold War* 2: 225–250.

12

NORTHERN IRELAND

Roger Mac Ginty

Introduction

Consider the Northern Ireland conflict in March 1988. The conflict had been going on for almost 20 years, and the prospects for a negotiated settlement looked bleak. March 1988 saw undercover British soldiers shoot dead three members of the Irish Republican Army (IRA) in Gibraltar. The funeral of the three IRA members, held in Belfast, was attacked by a loyalist (pro-United Kingdom) militant who killed three mourners. When the funeral was held again, three days later, two undercover British soldiers were abducted by the crowd and later found murdered. Elsewhere in Northern Ireland that month, an IRA member was killed in a gun battle with the British Army, a policeman was shot dead by the IRA, and a Protestant civilian was murdered by the IRA (http://cain.ulst.ac.uk/othelem/chron.htm). Northern Ireland seemed trapped in a cycle of violence. The political process was moribund, and there was little sign of initiatives that could lessen violence and tension. Militant groups were well-established. They were unable to achieve their objectives by force, but, at the same time, the British state was unable (or unwilling) to fully suppress them. While citizens and business had become somewhat inured to persistent violence and had developed elaborate coping mechanisms, Northern Ireland was a sick society. Many areas were heavily militarised with frequent vehicle checkpoints and military patrols. The schooling system was a virtual apartheid with Catholics and Protestants educated separately. Unemployment for Catholic males was almost three times the rate for their Protestant counterparts (Bryson et al. 2005: 3). Most Catholics and Protestants lived apart, in areas in which their group was the majority (Harland 2011: 414).

Yet, if we fast-forward ten years to April 1998, the situation was significantly different. The main militant groups had called ceasefires and the British state had begun a process of demilitarising many parts of Northern Ireland. This had a major impact on the ground in terms of the everyday ability of people to move around securely and contributed to business confidence and popular optimism. A major peace accord (the Belfast Agreement or the Good Friday Agreement) had been reached following a lengthy period of talks between the main political parties in Northern Ireland. The British and Irish governments, along with support from the United States and the European Union, had engineered a peace process that meant that a number of parties could claim an 'honourable peace', at least to their own supporters. The Agreement was comprehensive and dealt with a wide range of constitutional, identity, security, and social issues. It also legislated for the establishment of a power-sharing Assembly in Northern Ireland. The Belfast Agreement did not, however, usher in an immediate and comprehensive peace; a significant proportion of Northern Ireland's population remained suspicious of the intentions of 'the other side', and many issues remained to be dealt with, particularly the sectarianism that was deeply rooted in Northern Ireland's society. Despite these outstanding issues, Northern Ireland in 1998 was a very different place to Northern Ireland in 1988. What allowed the changes in a seemingly intractable conflict?

This chapter seeks to explain the evolution of the Northern Ireland peace process and identify the main actors, processes, and incidents that facilitated the transition to a lower level of violence. The peace process confronted all actors (politicians and security officials, militants and their supporters, and the general citizenry) with a series of difficult choices. Many of these choices were highly contentious, even offensive. For example, as part of the Belfast Agreement, militant prisoners – many of whom had been convicted of serious offences – were released from jail. Often these choices put political parties, militant groups, and others under huge pressure, and threatened the unity of these groups and therefore threatened the peace process with splits and spoilers. When the peace process was underway, political and militant actors were forced to spend considerable energy keeping their own colleagues 'on board'. So not only was the peace process about reaching an accommodation with political adversaries; it was also about maintaining working relationships with allies.

The peace process was as much about perception as it was about actual changes and political agreements. The dominant perceptions were of winning and losing. Political parties exploited this perception and developed narratives of loss and gain in order to mobilise their supporters. When compromises had to be made, political parties worked hard to shepherd their supporters, always aware that others within their group were waiting to make accusations of 'weakness' and 'treachery'.

Perhaps the most important perception, and one that took root very gradually, was that there *was* a viable peace process. At times, political movement seemed very slow and was threatened by security incidents or political intransigence. Given Northern Ireland's history of violence and of failed political initiatives to deal with the conflict, it took a long time to convince some actors that there was a peace process. The episodic and 'stop–start' nature of the peace process meant that the process was 'running on empty' and relied on hope and faith rather than observed evidence. Showcase events, like major speeches by political leaders or a visit by a US President, often gave the impression of momentum while there was little substantive movement.

The peace process did not see the political parties, or the British and Irish governments, disavow their fundamental aims. It was not an occasion in which political actors 'came to their senses', realised that their strategies had been mistaken, and that their opponents had been correct. Unionists continued to want to remain in the United Kingdom, and Irish nationalists continued to want unification of the island of Ireland. The scourge of sectarianism remained largely intact. All sides tried to maximise the advantages for their own group. Yet, as the peace process emerged, it became a complex series of interlocking compromises and agreements. Gradually the environment changed, especially in terms of who would talk to who. Some unionist politicians moved from a position of declaring that they would never talk to terrorists, to sharing government with them. This was a remarkable transition and involved complex negotiations within and between groups.

The chapter will begin with a conflict analysis that sets out the 'who, where, how, and why' of the conflict. It will then describe the armed actors, their motivations, methods, and role in the peace process, before giving an account and analysis of the peace process that began in the early 1990s. The chapter ends by reflecting on whether there are any lessons that can be learned from the Northern Ireland experience (Darby 2008). As is usual in thinking about comparisons between peace processes, it is useful to be cautious. Many factors in the Northern Ireland conflict were specific to Northern Ireland and the peculiarities of its conflict, geography, and demographics. Perhaps the greatest lesson that Northern Ireland can offer other cases does not lie in specific mechanisms, laws, or initiatives that formed part of the peace process. Instead, the greatest lesson is that a peace process was possible despite the apparently intractable nature of the conflict. There was a very understandable fatalism among political leaders and the general population in the late 1980s and early 1990s. The conflict seemed to be stuck in a repetitive cycle of low level but persistent violence, political impasse, and sectarian conflict. Yet the cycle was broken. The rest of this chapter tells the story of how that happened.

The concentration in this chapter is on the negotiation of the Good Friday Agreement and the immediate implementation period. The 20+ years since reaching the Good Friday Agreement have been turbulent, with a number of long-lasting collapses of the power-sharing Assembly. These relate to the fundamental lack of trust between the two sides and the continuing popular relevance of the them versus us narrative. Yet, importantly, Northern Ireland has not reverted back to pre-peace process levels of violence, and it seems very unlikely to do so. As a result, Northern Ireland's peace process can be judged as reasonably successful: lives have been saved and improved as a result of it.

Conflict analysis

By the standards of many civil wars, the Northern Ireland conflict was a low-level affair. Between 1969 and 2010, a total of 3,568 people were killed, the majority of them civilian (1,879). Over a thousand members of the security forces (British Army and Police) were killed, along with almost four hundred republican (pro-united Ireland) militants and over 150 loyalist (pro-United Kingdom) militants (Sutton 1994). Yet the small size of Northern Ireland meant that the conflict had an intimate feel: it was highly local, with virtually everyone affected by knowing a relative or friend killed, injured, imprisoned, or displaced.

This conflict analysis section is comprised of two parts. The first part is a very brief history of the conflict that sets out the context from which the peace process developed from the mid-1990s onwards. It sets out the history of the colonisation of Ireland, the formation of the state of Northern Ireland (1921), and the course of the violent conflict (1969–1994). The second part follows a traditional conflict analysis model that outlines the 'who, where, how, and why' of the modern conflict.

A very brief history

The most recent violent phase of the Northern Ireland conflict began in 1969, but the conflict has much longer roots. The islands of Britain and Ireland are proximate, a mere 12 miles or 19.3 kilometres at the closest point. It is not surprising that there has been a long history of political, military, cultural, and economic exchange between the islands over many thousands of years (well illustrated in O'Toole 2013). Between the twelfth and sixteenth centuries, British rule gradually extended across Ireland, often in league with indigenous Irish chiefs and warlords. But in the late sixteenth century, a new system of British colonisation began, one that would sow the seeds for enduring conflict in Ireland. The new system was a form of plantation. Small farmers from Scotland and England were sponsored to settle and farm in Ireland. This form of colonisation especially took root in the northern part of Ireland. These farmer–settlers were Protestant, while the native Irish were Catholic. Given that the farmer–settlers were small farmers, and were given relatively small parcels of land, their form of settlement spread across the territory. With further waves of settlement, and as time progressed, these settlers became entrenched and developed their own communities and practices. In many places they lived in close proximity to Irish Catholics, thus giving the conflict its intimate nature. Protestants tended to own the better land or enjoy positions of privilege, and so many Catholics held grievances against their Protestant neighbours. But Protestants were in the minority (except in the north-east of the island) and so often felt isolated and insecure.

There were regular bouts of conflict and tension between the native Irish and the Protestant settlers. Many of these conflicts involved differences over religion and identity, but they were also linked with land and resources. Over time, the British state strengthened its administrative and security control over Ireland. By the nineteenth century, Ireland was largely pacified, and the 1801 Acts of Union formally brought Ireland into the United Kingdom. Ireland was ruled from London, and many Irish people served as soldiers and administrators in the expanding British Empire. While many people retained an Irish identity or part Irish identity, they also were part of a British-dominated economy and were culturally influenced by Britain.

By the end of the nineteenth century, however, a movement in favour of Irish independence, and of a stronger cultural expression of Irishness, began to develop among Catholics. This led to calls for 'Home Rule' or increased autonomy for Ireland under overall British rule. These calls were mainly peaceful, although many Protestants, mainly settled in the north-east of the island, found them unsettling and organised to defend the link with Britain. In the early twentieth century, an increased radicalism impacted on both those who wanted to maintain the link with the United Kingdom (unionists, loyalists, and mainly Protestant) and those who wanted increased independence or complete separation (nationalists, republican, and mainly Catholic). During the First World War, a small group of Irish nationalists in Dublin declared independence from British rule (McGarry 2010). Their uprising was quickly put down, but the British response to the rising inflamed tensions and led to a growth of pro-independence sentiment among many Irish Catholics.

By 1919, a guerrilla war had developed between the Irish Republican Army, a community-based insurgent movement that wanted Irish independence, and the British state. Irish nationalists were pushing at an open door (Hart 2003). The British state was exhausted following WWI and realised that it could not maintain order in most of Ireland without severe repression. The result was the partition of Ireland in late 1921. Most of Ireland, including Dublin, its principal city, was granted independence from Britain. The Irish Free State, later the Republic of Ireland, had a massive Catholic majority and claimed that the whole island should be freed from British rule. The six north-east counties remained under British rule. This territory had a Protestant, pro-British majority, and became Northern Ireland.

The state of Northern Ireland

While Protestant-unionists were the majority in Northern Ireland (60/40), they were the minority on the island of Ireland (80/20). The new state of Northern Ireland had its own parliament, although constitutionally it was firmly within the United Kingdom and relied on London for its budget. The Northern Ireland administration was overwhelmingly Protestant, and active steps were taken to exclude Catholics from civic and political life. Protestants, generally, had better employment prospects, protection from the state, and access to public goods such as education and housing. By the middle and late 1960s, and inspired by civil rights movements in France and the United States, a civil rights movement developed in Northern Ireland with (mainly) Catholic protesters calling for greater equality. The Protestant-unionist administration, and the Protestant-unionist majority population, tended to see the civil rights movement as a threat to their security and privilege. Attempts to suppress and intimidate the civil rights movement led to a hardening of attitudes on both sides (ÓDochartaigh 1997). The civil rights issue lessened in prominence, and the emerging conflict adopted a more sectarian and nationalist tone. Thus, the outlines of the modern Northern Ireland conflict took shape: Protestant–loyalist–unionist and pro-United Kingdom versus Catholic–republican–nationalist and pro-united Ireland.

The 'Troubles', 1969–1994

By the late 1960s, Northern Ireland was increasingly unstable. Marches by one side were met by counter-marches by the other. Some politicians used inflammatory language and mobilised their populations. The police force made few attempts to be even-handed and was clearly on the side of the Protestant majority. In August 1969, the British State intervened by sending troops onto the streets of Northern Ireland to maintain order. At first many Catholic-nationalists welcomed this; the British troops offered protection from a largely sectarian police force. But with time, many Catholics came to resent the British Army, regarding them as occupiers and defending a political system in which Catholics were second-class citizens. The early 1970s saw the period of greatest violence. There were no viable political initiatives that could satisfy both the Protestant majority (who wanted security and order, within the United Kingdom) and the Catholic minority (who wanted equality and a recognition of their Irishness). In 1972, the British government put the Northern Ireland Parliament on hold and powers were transferred to London. Northern Ireland would be under 'direct rule' from London until after the Good Friday Agreement 25 years later.

Amid political stalemate, a three-cornered low-level conflict developed. In one corner were the Irish Republican Army (IRA) and a number of smaller pro-united Ireland militant groups. They aimed to oust the British from Northern Ireland through force. These groups tended to be small in numbers of personnel, perhaps with no more than a few hundred active members. In the second corner was the British state, with its regular army, a militarised police force and police reserve, and a locally recruited pro-state militia. At times there were in excess of 30,000 security personnel serving, and parts of Northern Ireland became militarised with checkpoints, fortifications, and surveillance systems. Many Protestants found employment with the security forces and drew much comfort from their presence. Many Catholics, on the other hand, found the security forces to be intrusive and intimidating. The security forces did engage in multiple excesses and human rights abuses, but they did not engage in total war against militants. In the third corner were a number of militant pro-United Kingdom loyalist groups. These groups targeted Catholic militants, though more often than not their targets were Catholic civilians who were unconnected with violence. Officially and unofficially, the security forces assisted the loyalist militants through the supply of weapons, lists of targets, and protection from prosecution.

The conflict that developed through the 1970s, 1980s, and early 1990s was both sectarian (Catholic versus Protestant) and nationalist (pro-Irish versus pro-British). The vast majority of the population in Northern Ireland sought to get on with their lives. While they overwhelmingly fell into one of the two camps (Catholic–nationalist–republican or Protestant–unionist–loyalist), they did not directly engage in militant activity. People were outraged at particular events, but life settled into a low-level civil war of bombings, shootings, rioting, and intimidation. The state did not collapse; public services such as schooling and healthcare were maintained. Political initiatives to forge some sort of agreement between moderate Catholic-nationalist and Protestant-unionist politicians failed, but since the British State was still providing a safety net of social services, life – for most people – was bearable. By the early 1990s, the situation was in a stalemate. No side could win militarily, but all sides were aware of the cost of continuing the violence. Northern Ireland was in a mutually hurting stalemate (Zartman 2008).

A brief conflict analysis

Who?

Given that the conflict was ongoing for many decades (at different levels of intensity), it is worth noting that the 'who?' question is complicated. Certainly, many issues in the conflict remained constant, especially the wider issue of the constitutional status of Northern Ireland. But each generation approached the conflict in slightly different ways. There were new controversies and new methods of politics, violence, and coping. So, the conflict evolved over time as each new generation took custody of it. As the conflict was multi-generational and spanned many decades, it involved successive British governments (Labour and Conservative), each of which took a slightly different tack. New political parties and militant groups emerged in Northern Ireland, and some older ones faded. The key point is that although the broad outlines of the conflict remained largely constant, there was dynamism among the actors. To use a theatrical analogy, the plot stayed the same but there were some changes to the script and the cast.

Northern Ireland's population was little over 1.8 million in 2011, having risen from 1.5 million in 1971 (2012). The 2011 census revealed that 48 per cent of the population was of a Protestant background, and 45 per cent of Catholic background (Nisra 2011; Moriarty 2012). The Catholic population has been growing, albeit slowly, over the past few decades. Generally, the east of Northern Ireland is Protestant dominated, and the west is Catholic dominated (although Belfast is roughly 50:50). Although the labels 'Catholic' and 'Protestant' are widely used, the conflict is not about religion. Instead, it is about competing nationalisms (one pro-united Ireland and the other pro-United Kingdom).

Politics is organised according to the constitutional issue, namely whether Northern Ireland should remain part of the United Kingdom. The Protestant-unionist and Catholic-nationalist camps have long-standing political parties that have sought to serve both the moderate and less moderate parts of their constituencies. One of the main dynamics in Northern Ireland, and one that shaped much of the peace process, is the in-group nature of politics, with Catholic-nationalist and Protestant-unionist parties claiming to be the true defenders of their group and accusing their in-group rivals of being weak or treacherous. A small cross-communal party, the Alliance Party, was founded in 1970 but has struggled to attract large support. Virtually no Catholics vote for pro-United Kingdom parties and virtually no Protestants vote for pro-united Ireland parties. The story of the peace process has been of the groups and political parties on the extremes moderating their stances, and of the moderate parties accepting that deals must be done with less moderate parties.

One of the key relationships in the peace process has been between the British and Irish governments. They have moved from a relationship of tension in the 1970s and 1980s to an enduring relationship in which they co-shepherded the peace process in the 1990s and early 2000s. As part of this, and because of long-term historical and cultural ties, the British government acted as a proxy for the pro-United Kingdom parties and the Irish government acted as a proxy for the pro-united Ireland parties. While the British and Irish governments often disagreed on the direction and speed of the peace process, they realised that they had a shared interest in the peace process continuing and bearing fruit.

Where?

Northern Ireland is situated in the north-east of the island of Ireland. It is small; it takes 90 minutes to drive from one side to the other. It shares a lengthy border with the Republic of Ireland (360km). Note also Northern Ireland's proximity to Britain. It was, until 2019, part of the European Union (with Great Britain). The territory is largely comprised of low hills, and most land is given over to agriculture. While few areas were completely 'safe' during the violent conflict, some areas (for example, north Belfast) experienced much more violence than others. Militant groups did not hold any territory during the conflict. Instead, they took the form of underground groups who lived among their support community. The security forces had access to all areas during the conflict, although extra security precautions had to be taken in some areas.

Importantly, apart from relatively isolated incidents, mass violence between Catholics and Protestants was rare. This was for a number of reasons. First, residential segregation meant that Catholics and Protestant often lived and socialised in separate areas, and so violence was restricted to interface areas. Second, when mass inter-communal violence did break out, the security forces usually intervened to separate the crowds. Third, each community had its own 'violent specialists' in the form of militant groups. As a result, most direct violence was the preserve of relatively small groups.

The British strategy during much of the 'Troubles' was to contain the conflict within Northern Ireland. The local police force was militarised and strengthened, and a militia was recruited, in order to ease the burden on the regular British Army. Northern Ireland had its own terrorist legislation, courts system, and prisons.

The main impact of the conflict was contained in Northern Ireland itself, but there was a spill-over effect into the Republic of Ireland and the United Kingdom. Pro-united Ireland militants sometimes prepared and staged attacks from the Republic of Ireland, and the issue of Northern Ireland often caused controversy in the politics of the Republic. It was not a dominant issue, however. While the Republic of Ireland maintained a constitutional claim over Northern Ireland (until the 1998 Good Friday Agreement), the issue was effectively 'parked' in its public discourse, and most of the population and political parties were preoccupied with economic and other issues.

Pro-united Ireland militants repeatedly staged attacks on the island of Britain, believing that such attacks gained much more media attention ('more bang for the buck') and circumvented British attempts to contain the conflict within Northern Ireland. These attacks usually took the form of shootings and bombings on military targets, although civilians were often the victims. In the early 1990s, the IRA exploded a number of very large bombs in London's financial district. These bombs caused huge damage, and some commentators believe that they were influential in encouraging some within the British government to seek a negotiated outcome. Indeed, there is speculation that the decision to locate the European Central Bank in Frankfurt rather than London was the result of the IRA revealing the vulnerability of the City of London to attack (Coaffee 2003: 106).

Beyond the islands of Britain and Ireland, all sides sought to gain moral and material support for their cause (Guelke 1988). Pro-united Ireland militants sought weapons, money, and support from the large Irish diaspora in the United States and also secured arms from Libya and illegal sources. They also had limited links with the Palestinian Liberation Organisation and a number of other 'liberation' movements. Pro-United Kingdom loyalists obtained arms from the apartheid South African regime. All sides, including the British and Irish governments, worked hard on the 'propaganda war'. The British government sought to portray the conflict as an internal or domestic matter. United Nations interest was strongly rebuffed, although British governments were regularly embarrassed during Cold War negotiations when Soviet officials would raise the issue of human rights abuses in Northern Ireland. Irish governments sought international diplomatic support to help nudge British governments towards a negotiated settlement. Irish governments also worked hard to prevent the Irish-American diaspora from arming the IRA. As the peace process took root in the 1990s, international actors played a very important role in encouraging the Northern Ireland political parties to investigate negotiations, and the European Union in particular was important in giving large-scale financial assistance for peace and reconciliation projects.

When?

The Northern Ireland 'Troubles' are usually dated from 1969 (the onset of serious violence) to 1994 (when the militant groups called ceasefires) or 1998 (when the Good Friday Agreement was reached). But, as the history section above shows, the conflict had a very long heritage. Over the centuries there were long periods of tense calm, interspersed with upsurges in violence. The tense calm was maintained by a complex set of power relations and legal frameworks. The violence that began in 1969 was of a different order than previous upsurges during the previous decades:

- The violence was of such a magnitude that the Northern Ireland Parliament was suspended by London
- The regular British Army was deployed to maintain order, a deployment that would last 36 years
- Militant groups (both pro-united Ireland and pro-United Kingdom) were able to sustain their campaigns over long periods

The conflict that began in 1969 stabilised into a regular pattern by 1972. The overall trend was towards a lessening of violence after the initial very bloody years of the early 1970s. Four hundred and eighty people were killed in 1972, but no more than one hundred people were killed annually after 1989.

There were a number of reasons for the long-term decline in casualty figures.

- The security forces became very defensive-focused (body armour, surveillance from the air, electronic jamming devices to thwart bombs) with the result that it became increasingly difficult for militants to kill soldiers
- The use of informers by the security forces to jail large numbers of militants and disrupt their activities
- All sides conformed to unwritten 'rules' of engagement and targeting
- Both communities quickly learned survival mechanisms, such as keeping within their own districts at night and being guarded in what they said in mixed company

Although the conflict had stabilised into a semi-regular pattern by the mid-1970s, there was no obvious conflict ending in sight. No side was able to defeat the other. Each was able to inflict damage on the other, but not deliver a knock-out blow. Along the way there were upsurges in violence, or spectacular incidents (such as the 1984 bombing of Margaret Thatcher's Conservative Party conference). There were a number of political initiatives to attempt to 'solve' the conflict. All of these initiatives failed. They usually took the same format: an attempt to get the political moderates (the pro-United Kingdom Ulster Unionist Party and pro-united Ireland Social Democratic and Labour Party (SDLP), and the cross-community Alliance Party) to agree to some sort of interim political deal. Such activity excluded militants and those on the political extremes, but these actors had the power to derail any attempts to reach agreement. The peace process that developed in the 1990s was very different in that it sought to be inclusive, specifically including the very actors that had the power to hold a veto.

Why?

The conflict principally revolved around two incompatible nationalisms. One nationalism believed that Northern Ireland should have a British identity and remain part of the United Kingdom. The other nationalism believed that Northern Ireland should be subsumed within the Republic of Ireland to reflect an overall Irish identity. Although the conflict is often described in terms of religion (Catholic versus Protestant) the conflict is *not* about interpretations of the Bible or any matter of religious faith. The terms 'Catholic' and 'Protestant' are simply used as labels to differentiate between the two identity groups.

The Irish nationalist versus British nationalist dimension of the conflict was added to by at least two other dimensions. First, as the conflict intensified, an element of revenge set in. Many of those who joined militant groups did so because they were outraged by attacks on their own community. Some were motivated because they lost relatives and friends. Second, the political economy of the conflict is important. Catholic-nationalists felt grievances towards Protestant-unionists and the British state because they suffered from higher unemployment and generally poorer socio-economic conditions.

'Non-state armed groups': targets, methods, and sources

The armed actors in the conflict were the British state (its military, intelligence services, a militarised police force, and a local militia), pro-united Ireland militants, and pro-United Kingdom militants. This section will only examine the non-state armed actors.

Pro-united Ireland militants

The largest group was the Irish Republican Army (IRA) (English 2004; Maloney 2003). There were other minor pro-united Ireland groups, such as the Irish National Liberation Organisation, but these were strategically and politically unimportant. It claimed to be the successor organisation of the IRA that had waged the war of independence against the British in 1918–1921. Its aim was to secure a united Ireland through military means and to defend the Catholic-nationalist population. The organisation was quite small, with a cadre of militants in the hundreds, and a larger network of people who supplied safe-houses, alibis, and logistical assistance. As membership of the IRA was illegal, it was an underground movement. Most of its militants lived at home, and many kept regular jobs, operating as militants in their spare time.

The IRA regarded itself as a legitimate army fighting a 'liberation struggle' against the British in Ireland. Its main targets were British soldiers, the militarised police force in Northern Ireland, the locally recruited militia, and economic and symbolic targets of Britain in Ireland. In its own propaganda, it saw itself as only attacking 'legitimate targets'. Yet, its opponents saw it as conducting a terrorist and sectarian campaign. Given that most members of the police and the militia were Protestant, many in the Protestant community saw attacks on the security forces as attacks on their own community. The IRA also killed many civilians in cases of 'mistaken identity' or botched attacks. In general, it attempted to avoid civilian mass casualty attacks, but it spectacularly failed in this aim on a number of occasions. It also 'policed' the Catholic-nationalist community, issuing summary justice to those suspected of anti-social behaviour, and murdering those suspected of collaborating with the security forces.

The IRA's main methods were shooting and bombing. In the main, its attacks were small-scale 'hit and run' attacks. With time, it gained increased technological sophistication, for example acquiring surface to air missiles and Semtex explosives. Although the IRA campaign had the ability to shock, particularly through 'spectacular' incidents in Britain, its campaign was contained. Large numbers of its militants were imprisoned (often through dubious legal processes). While enough members of the Catholic-nationalist population supported the organisation in order to sustain it, not all Catholics supported the IRA. Indeed, many – perhaps a majority – were opposed to it, believing that its armed campaign was actually a hindrance to the aim of Irish unification rather than a help to that cause.

The organisation funded itself through community support, donations from the Irish-American diaspora, bank robberies, and (voluntary and involuntary) 'contributions' from businesses. By the late 1980s, it had invested significant amounts of money in the legitimate economy. For example, it was reported to own several petrol stations and bars. It secured arms from supporters in the United States, from Colonel Gaddafi in Libya, and the illegal market. It sought to legitimise itself by making common cause with anti-colonialist or anti-authoritarian struggles by Palestinians, Basques, black South Africans, and various groups in Latin and Central America. Most of these links were symbolic and rhetorical rather than practical. While some of its supporters constructed an ideological case for a united Ireland (often drawing on socialism), the vast majority of members and supporters were motivated by Irish nationalism and anti-Britishness. Many were provoked by excesses by the security forces, and by what they regarded as an anti-Irish and Catholic bias from successive British governments.

For much of the 1970s, the IRA had an underdeveloped political wing. Its main concentration was on its militant campaign and the belief that this would be enough to oust Britain from Ireland. By the late 1970s, there was an increasing recognition of the need to develop a political wing. The IRA's political cousins, Sinn Féin, was populated by many former (and perhaps some serving) IRA members. The Party would have a number of aims. First, it could help justify the IRA's campaign among the Catholic population. The Catholic Church, the moderate nationalist Social Democratic and Labour Party, and the Irish government were strong opponents of IRA violence, so a political wing was useful to deflect this criticism. Second, it could justify the IRA's campaign and the Catholic-nationalist cause internationally. Third, and crucially for the onset of the peace process, it could provide a semi-legitimate conduit for any negotiations that could develop.

During the 1970s, Sinn Féin boycotted elections in Northern Ireland, believing that participation in such elections would admit that Northern Ireland was a legitimate political entity. This strategy changed over time, as Sinn Féin developed what it called the 'armalite and ballot box' strategy, or a combination of physical force nationalism and political opportunism. The potential of electoral politics was realised in 1981 when Bobby Sands, an IRA prisoner on hunger strike, was elected to the British Parliament in London. Thereafter Sinn Féin engaged in electoral politics, though maintained an abstentionist position in relation to Westminster (i.e. Sinn Féin Members of Parliament (MPs) do not take their seats in Westminster). During the 1980s and early 1990s, Sinn Féin's support was smaller than that of the Social Democratic and Labour Party (SDLP), a rival pro-united Ireland political party that did not advocate violence. This position reversed as the peace process took root in the 1990s and Sinn Féin's support grew. By this stage, the IRA was on ceasefire, suggesting that a majority of Catholic-nationalists favoured a non-violent approach to politics.

The electoral rise of Sinn Féin during the 1980s and 1990s was significant in the course of the conflict and subsequent peace process. It meant that there was a public interface available should negotiations become a reality. During the 1980s and early 1990s, Sinn Féin was excluded from most political processes as unionist political parties and the British government refused to meet with it. They saw it as merely a mouthpiece for terrorism, and Sinn Féin spent much of its time attempting to justify IRA violence. But the electoral rise of Sinn Féin revealed that support for the IRA was not restricted to a tiny minority who could be ignored. Instead, it showed that substantial numbers of Catholic-nationalists supported the IRA campaign. The electoral rise of Sinn Féin in the 1980s, and the continued IRA campaign, prompted the British government to take action. There was a more robust security response, and Sinn Féin spokespersons were banned from television and radio. There was also a very significant political initiative. In 1985 the British and Irish governments signed an international treaty on the management of the Northern Ireland conflict. In the Anglo-Irish Agreement, the British and Irish governments recognised that Northern Ireland was part of the United Kingdom, but that situation could change if a majority of people wanted it. They also agreed to enhanced cooperation on security matters. Crucially, they established an Intergovernmental Conference, or ongoing Irish government involvement in the running of Northern Ireland. While this role was largely consultative, it began a permanent relationship between the British and Irish governments on the Northern Ireland issue. This was particularly important at the level of senior bureaucrats, as this tier of government played an important role in the development of the peace process in the 1990s.

The Anglo-Irish Agreement was very unpopular with unionists, who resented a role for the Irish government in the affairs of Northern Ireland. The Agreement was also designed to blunt the electoral rise of Sinn Féin by bolstering the constitutional nationalist party, the SDLP. There was partial success in this agenda, in that the Sinn Féin vote fell in the late 1980s, but this setback was temporary. By the early 1990s, Northern Ireland seemed stuck in *Groundhog Day* politics: there was no sign of a political accommodation between the Northern Ireland political parties; sectarian divisions between the two communities were still strong; and there seemed to be no end to the long-running violence.

Pro-United Kingdom militants

Northern Ireland was home to a number of pro-United Kingdom militant groups: the Ulster Defence Association, the Ulster Volunteer Force, and Ulster Freedom Fighters (Taylor 1999; Smithey 2011). These groups saw themselves as defenders of Northern Ireland's position within the United Kingdom. The pro-United Kingdom militants justified their campaigns by saying that they targeted IRA members. In reality, the majority of their victims were Catholic civilians, again reinforcing the sectarian element to the conflict. Like the IRA, they were small organisations, with a relatively small cohort of members involved in direct violence. Protestant-unionists who wanted to defend the Union with Great Britain could also join the police force and the state-sponsored militia, the Ulster Defence Regiment. As a result, many of those with an urge to 'fight back' or protect their own community could do so through legal means rather than joining illegal militant groups.

Perhaps the most controversial aspect of the pro-United Kingdom militant campaigns was the extent to which they were assisted by the British State. In recent years, evidence of collusion between the security forces and pro-United Kingdom militants has surfaced. What is not clear is the extent to which this practice was sanctioned by the British government and senior security officials. Certainly, members of the security forces used the pro-United Kingdom militants as proxies to attack the IRA. These groups were very heavily infiltrated by the security forces and were provided with intelligence and legal protection by their security force 'handlers'.

Again, mirroring militant groups on the Catholic-nationalist side, pro-United Kingdom militants did not hold territory. They lived among their community support base, and many engaged in violence on a part-time basis. These groups were mainly restricted to the east of Northern Ireland, especially in the Belfast area, and funded themselves through extortion and drug dealing. They also were involved in neighbourhood 'policing', or delivering 'rough justice' to youths believed to be responsible for anti-social behaviour. The groups also engaged in regular bouts of feuding, often connected with who had the right to claim particular districts of Belfast as their own.

Unlike the IRA, pro-United Kingdom militant groups did not develop viable political parties. The support base for the pro-United Kingdom militants was geographically restricted, and so they found it difficult to achieve success in electoral politics. Moreover, mainstream Protestant-unionist political parties (the Democratic Unionist Party (DUP) and the Ulster Unionist Party (UUP)) shared a pro-United Kingdom agenda with the militants. Indeed, these political parties, although not directly involved in violence, were equivocal about some forms of violence, especially that against (alleged) IRA members. When elections were held to allow for the entry of political parties into the multi-party talks, an elaborate 'top up' mechanism was introduced to 'help' parties associated with pro-United Kingdom militants get into the talks.

Although Northern Ireland had a three-cornered conflict (British State, pro-united Ireland militants, and pro-United Kingdom militants), the most important conflict was between the British State and the IRA. The British State wielded coercive and legal power. The IRA, while unable to force the British out of Northern Ireland, was able to cause significant headaches for the British state. The principal focus of the British government in the peace process was to stop IRA violence and disarm the IRA. The principal focus of Sinn Féin was to wrestle concessions from the British government.

The conflict resolution process

A very brief account of the peace process

Northern Ireland's peace process began at the intra-party level with a dialogue between Catholic-nationalist political actors. Moderate nationalists in the Social

Democratic and Labour Party, the Catholic Church, and the Irish government had repeatedly told Sinn Féin and the IRA that their violent campaign was the chief obstacle to movement towards Irish unity. Sinn Féin eventually took this view on board, and the IRA declared a ceasefire in 1994. Protestant-unionists were deeply suspicious of the ceasefire and believed that the peace process could only result in concessions to nationalists. They urged the British government to ignore Sinn Féin calls for talks. Despite their reservations, pro-United Kingdom militants also called a matching ceasefire in 1994. The British government moved very cautiously and avoided direct talks with Sinn Féin and the IRA. In part this was due to British Prime Minister John Major's government relying on unionist votes in the British Parliament. The British government demanded that the IRA disarm before talks would begin. The IRA refused, saying that a ceasefire was enough. In a sign of their dissatisfaction with the slow pace of events, the IRA called off their ceasefire in February 1996, although their violent campaign was restrained. A new ceasefire was called after Tony Blair was elected Prime Minister in May 1997. He had given assurances that multi-party talks would begin if the IRA called another ceasefire.

Multi-party talks, sponsored by the British and Irish governments and chaired by US Senate leader George Mitchell, began in autumn 1997. These talks were boycotted by the Democratic Unionist Party, but the Ulster Unionist Party did attend them. The Good Friday Agreement was reached in April 1998. It established a new power-sharing Assembly in Northern Ireland, recognised the right of people in Northern Ireland to have a dual identity (British and Irish), and ushered in significant security reforms.

The establishment of the power-sharing Assembly was delayed. Unionists insisted that the IRA disarm its weapons before they would share power. Although political movement seemed slow, the ceasefires held (apart from limited spoiler violence), and there were significant quality of life improvements for the majority of people in Northern Ireland. With time, the Northern Ireland Assembly has taken root. The most significant change came in 2006 when the Democratic Unionists became the largest unionist political party and shared the top positions (First Minister and Deputy First Minister) with Sinn Féin. This was a quite remarkable change, as the DUP had been the most trenchant critics of Sinn Féin and had boycotted the 1996–1998 talks.

Pre-negotiations

In November 1993, British Prime Minister John Major told the British Parliament that the idea of sitting down and talking with the IRA 'would turn my stomach'. His statement came after a particularly violent few weeks in which significant numbers of civilians – including children – had been killed both in England and in Northern Ireland.

Despite the Prime Minister's protestations, secret talks had been going on for three years between the IRA and the British government. These talks were held at a deniable level. They involved a retired British spy and a former Catholic priest who acted as message carriers. The systems of information exchange were regular.

Martin McGuinness, the deputy leader of Sinn Féin and reputedly a senior figure in the IRA, claimed that he could have a message on the Prime Minister's desk within 30 minutes, faster than many cabinet ministers (Personal communication with McGuinness). These secret talks involved the British government and the IRA seeking to find out each other's 'bottom line', and the extent to which the other side was serious about negotiations that would facilitate an end to violence. Both sides wanted to end the violence, but it was politically difficult for them to do so. The British government was committed to securing its citizens and its armed forces. The IRA had pledged to free Ireland through force. In addition to these secret IRA–British government talks, there were also secret talks between the Catholic-nationalist political parties, Sinn Féin and the SDLP. These involved the SDLP (increasingly acting in concert with the Irish government) encouraging Sinn Féin to explore political options rather than rely on IRA violence.

While secret 'talks about talks' were underway in the early 1990s, the British and Irish governments attempted to begin formal public talks among the constitutional political parties: the Ulster Unionists (UUP), the Democratic Unionists, the Social Democratic and Labour Party, and the Alliance Party of Northern Ireland. Sinn Féin were excluded from these talks because of the IRA's continued campaign. The British and Irish governments hoped that these talks could allow for the devolution of power back to Northern Ireland and a recalibration of the relationship between Northern Ireland and the Republic of Ireland. The different parties wanted different things from the talks. The British and Irish governments wanted the security situation to be stabilised. Many within the British government (and the wider British population) wanted the Northern Ireland problem to go away. It was a constant source of bad news and a drain on resources. The Irish government, increasingly acting as a proxy for Catholic-nationalists within Northern Ireland, also wanted an end to violence, and a warming of relations with Northern Ireland's unionists. Many Protestant-unionists were suspicious any political initiatives that involved the Irish government. For them, a peace process risked being a concession process. They were alarmed that the Irish government (in their eyes a foreign state) was automatically included in talks. But the British government responded by saying that the only way to lessen the role of the Irish government would be for unionists to make a deal with Northern Ireland's nationalists. These formal public talks between the constitutional parties made very slow progress. They were marred by walkouts and the parties setting preconditions before they would talk with their opponents.

During the 1991–1993 period, British government ministers made a number of speeches in which they noted that Britain was 'neutral' in relation to Northern Ireland, and had 'no pre-selected constitutional outcome' in mind on Northern Ireland's status. We now know that these phrases were deliberately placed in speeches as confidence-building measures. They had been suggested by the IRA in its secret talks with the British government. So the British government, which officially said it would never talk to terrorists, was actually using in its speeches phrases suggested to it by the IRA. In return, the IRA held unofficial ceasefires of up to several weeks. All of this was only known to a tiny handful of people.

For most people, it seemed to be 'business as usual'; armed campaigns and security responses continued, and political talks failed to make headway. Frustrated at the lack of progress by Northern Ireland's political parties, the British and Irish governments announced the Downing Street Declaration in December 1993 (http://cain.ulst.ac.uk/events/peace/docs/dsd151293.htm). The Declaration was a statement of intent by the British and Irish governments that they intended to press ahead with efforts to reach a political solution. It caused much public debate, and Sinn Féin made calls for clarification. Although there was no direct public contact between Sinn Féin and the British government, they did engage in some form of dialogue through the media. The dialogue revolved around a British demand that the IRA get rid of its weapons before any direct talks could begin. In January 1993, Gerry Adams, the leader of Sinn Féin, was granted a visa to visit the United States. This was a signal from the US administration that it was encouraging Sinn Féin and the IRA to investigate all possible opportunities for a negotiated settlement. It seemed as though the components for a peace process were falling into place.

In May 1994, amid continuing violence, the British government replied to a list of 20 questions submitted by Sinn Féin. The questions had been seeking clarification on the Downing Street Declaration, or the basis of negotiations. In August 1994, the IRA declared a 'cessation of military operations' in order to facilitate political negotiations. Many unionists were suspicious that the ceasefire had come about as a result of a secret deal with the IRA. In October 1994 pro-United Kingdom militants called a matching ceasefire.

Ceasefires and collapse

The ceasefires brought about significant changes for everyday life. The security forces relaxed many of their patrols and economic confidence developed. The European Commission, British government, and the United States all announced aid packages in support of the peace process. Political progress was slow, though. The British government was very cautious about making major concessions while the IRA still retained its weapons. The IRA would not give up its weapons before a peace agreement was reached. Northern Ireland's unionists were suspicious of the peace process, believing that it would threaten their position within the United Kingdom. Another factor was at play: the British government under John Major had a very small parliamentary majority and relied on support from Northern Ireland's unionist MPs. Much of 1995 was taken up with circular debates on the decommissioning issue. The British government met with Sinn Féin for 'exploratory talks' but would not engage on substantive issues, nor would they begin multi-party talks. There were no direct negotiations between Sinn Féin and Northern Ireland's unionists. In February 1995, the British and Irish governments launched the 'Framework for Agreement' document. This set out, in rough form, the agenda for multi-party talks. They would cover two principal areas. The first area would be to manage relations within Northern Ireland. This would involve a power-sharing representative body. The second area would involve relations between Northern Ireland and the Republic of Ireland. This would involve establishing some sort of North–South body. Unionists feared that it would have executive power and amount to joint sovereignty. Nationalists wanted to enhance the North–South element of any agreement.

While a tentative agenda for talks was in place, there was still political stalemate. Unionists refused to talk to Sinn Féin, believing them to be 'terrorists'. The British government refused to admit Sinn Féin to formal substantive talks because the IRA retained its arms. The IRA refused to disarm because it would then lose its principal bargaining card. The governments had established an International Body on Decommissioning Arms to investigate how militant weapons could be destroyed. In January 1996 this Body, headed by former US Senate majority leader George Mitchell, published a report that recommended that arms should be decommissioned during talks. The report also set down a number of conditions relating to the importance of non-violence during talks. The ceasefires by the militant groups had largely held, although as they held onto their weapons, the threat of a resumption of violence was ever present. The militant groups also engaged in training, and some punishment attacks on their own communities. The 'Mitchell Principles' were essentially confidence-building measures and were applied when multi-party negotiations eventually began.

The stalemate was broken in February 1996 when the IRA declared an end to its ceasefire, blaming the British government for squandering the opportunity for negotiations. The ending of the ceasefire met with widespread condemnation. The renewed IRA campaign was not of the same intensity of its 1969–1994 violence. Care seemed to be taken in targeting to avoid provoking pro-United Kingdom militants into violence. Many of the IRA attacks were in Britain. The British government announced that elections would take place in Northern Ireland in June to decide which political parties could be represented at multi-party negotiations. Talks then began in Belfast shortly after the elections. The British and Irish governments chaired the talks, although Sinn Féin was excluded from these talks because of continuing IRA violence. These talks made little progress.

Negotiations

Little of significance occurred until May 1997, when a Labour government was elected under Tony Blair. He had a large majority and thus freedom to act on Northern Ireland. A new government was also elected in the Republic of Ireland in June 1997, with a prime minister determined that the peace process should succeed. Blair's government announced that Sinn Féin could be admitted to multi-party talks if the IRA renewed its ceasefire (thus dropping the demand of prior decommissioning). The IRA renewed its ceasefire in July 1997, paving the way for talks. The Democratic Unionist Party refused to take part in the talks because of the presence of Sinn Féin, while the Ulster Unionist Party believed that the best option was to confront Sinn Féin. The UUP, however, refused to talk directly with Sinn Féin, and contact was through intermediaries

Multi-party negotiations (without the DUP) began in September 1997. The decommissioning issue was side-stepped with the establishment of an Independent International Commissioning of Decommissioning led by international experts. The negotiations had three strands. Strand one would deal with relations within Northern Ireland, especially the establishment of a representative body. Strand two would deal with North–South relations. Strand three would deal with East–West relations, between Britain and Ireland. This third strand was in the context of a devolution process in the United Kingdom in which Scotland and Wales were granted more powers and their own Parliament and Assembly respectively. While the formal talks were underway in Belfast, a large number of bilateral talks (especially between Tony Blair and the Northern Ireland political parties) took place. Blair invested significant time on the Northern Ireland issue, and even hosted visits by Sinn Féin to Downing Street – a situation unimaginable only a few years previously.

The backdrop to the talks was continuing violence, though at a lower level than before the ceasefires. Some of the violence was from splinter groups from the pro-united Ireland camp who exploded a series of large bombs in town centres across Northern Ireland. Their aim was to goad pro-United Kingdom militants into an over-reaction, which would then collapse the peace process. Pro-United Kingdom militants also staged an assassination campaign, mainly against Catholic civilians. Both Sinn Féin and a political party linked to pro-United Kingdom militants were suspended from the negotiations for short periods.

The formal negotiations took a very long time. Often the parties recounted historical grievances rather than dealing with pressing issues. In order to speed progress, the Chair of the talks, George Mitchell, reduced the size of each party's nominated negotiated team from five to two. The British and Irish governments also introduced a 'Heads of Agreement' document that attempted to solidify the broad outlines of an agreement. The talks were mainly held in Belfast, but occasionally moved to London and Dublin. The Chair of the talks set a series of deadlines to try to concentrate the minds of the negotiators, and intensive talks sessions were held with the British and Irish Prime Ministers. A comprehensive peace accord, the Good Friday Agreement or Belfast Agreement, was reached on 10 April 1998. Both governments and all political parties, except the Democratic Unionist Party, signed up to the Agreement, which would be put to the people of Northern Ireland and the Republic of Ireland in a referendum (Table 12.1).

TABLE 12.1 Techniques used to help progress in the multi-party negotiations

- Militant prisoners allowed out of prison to consult with political representatives
- Negotiating teams cut in size
- Break-out sessions to lower tension in talks
- Deadlines
- Ground rules on non-violence, and suspensions for those breaking the rules
- Setting up commissions outside of the talks to deal with particularly tricky issues
- Nothing is agreed until everything is agreed (to prevent premature collapse of talks)
- Moving the talks venue and 'hot-housing' some issues through intensive discussions
- Bilateral talks between political parties and the British and/or Irish governments
- The provision of framework documents and heads of agreement notes by the governments
- Shuttle diplomacy and good offices mediation provided by a minor party that declared itself neutral: Northern Ireland Women's Coalition

The Good Friday Agreement

At 10,000 words long, the Good Friday Agreement was a complex document.[1] It involved an international treaty between the United Kingdom and Northern Ireland, and an agreement between the Northern Ireland political parties on the formation of a series of institutions to manage relationships. It also introduced a large number of reforms that would mean changes in policing and the expression of identity.

The Agreement followed three strands. Strand one involved the establishment of a power-sharing Assembly in Northern Ireland. A complicated electoral formula meant that both Catholic-nationalists and Protestant-unionists would jointly form a government. Strand two involved North–South relations and established a North–South Ministerial Council whereby the Northern Ireland Assembly and the Parliament of the Republic of Ireland would have regular meeting to discuss issues of common concern, such as waterways or sharing energy or healthcare provision. Strand three involved the East–West dimension and established a Council of the Isles in which representatives from London and Dublin, as well as from the devolved institutions in Scotland, Wales, and Northern Ireland could come together to discuss common concerns.

The Agreement reaffirmed Northern Ireland's constitutional position within the United Kingdom, and that any change to that position would have to be through consent. It pledged to hold a constitutional referendum if there was a mood for change. The Irish government withdrew the clauses in its constitution that staked a claim over the territory of Northern Ireland. The Agreement recognised that people in Northern Ireland could have Irish citizenship, British citizenship, *or both*. There was provision for the 'normalisation' of security, such as the removal of security installations, for major reforms to the policing and justice sectors, and for the introduction of human rights and equality legislation. Militant prisoners were to be released from prison (a proposal that many of the families of victims of violence disagreed with). The Agreement made several platitudes about the victims of violence and the need for reconciliation but did not have any concrete proposals.

What was not in the agreement?

A number of issues were not covered in the Agreement or were covered in a vague way:

1 Arms decommissioning

This became the key sticking point in the implementation of the Good Friday Agreement. Unionists wanted the IRA to decommission its weapons before they would share power with Sinn Féin and make the Assembly work. While the Agreement called on those with weapons to disarm in association with the Independent International Commission on Decommissioning, there was no mechanism to force decommissioning. The issue would become toxic, and the prolonged IRA refusal to disarm (and a matching refusal by pro-United Kingdom militants) meant that there were low levels of political and inter-community trust. The IRA finally disarmed in 2005.

2 Trust

There was little trust between the main political parties. Once the Good Friday Agreement was reached, they did not suddenly begin to like each other. They still wanted to gain as many votes as possible and represent *their* community. With time, however, some level of grudging unspoken respect did develop between some nationalists and some unionists as they realised that they could work together. Perhaps the most remarkable example of working trust was between the Reverend Ian Paisley, the leader of the Democratic Unionist Party, and Martin McGuinness, deputy leader of Sinn Féin and reputed one-time commander of the IRA. They served as First and Deputy First Minister and built up a strong personal rapport to the extent that they were known as 'the chuckle brothers' after being repeatedly photographed laughing together. This inter-personal trust did not extend to their political parties.

3 Inter-communal relations

While the Belfast Agreement set up new political institutions and established reviews of policing and security, it could not legislate for how Catholics and Protestant interacted with one another on a day-to-day basis. Trust levels between many Catholic-nationalists and Protestant-unionists remained poor. There were regular bouts of inter-communal rioting and tensions. Levels of residential segregation remained high; most Catholics and Protestants continued to live, socialise, and be educated apart. A shared 'Northern Irish' identity took root only very slowly and did not spread to all sections of the community. Only in 2013, 15 years after the Good Friday Agreement was reached, did the Northern Ireland government publish proposals to tackle sectarianism. These efforts largely failed.

Post-Agreement fall-out

The Agreement was put to the people of Northern Ireland and the Republic of Ireland in referendums. It was passed with a 70 per cent majority in Northern Ireland and a massive majority in the Republic of Ireland. But the 70 per cent majority in Northern only consisted of 50 per cent of Protestant-unionists. With time, that support leached away and a majority of Protestant-unionists came to be against the Agreement.

This had a significant impact on the Ulster Unionist Party, which suffered splits and dissensions. The Democratic Unionist Party, which advocated a 'No' vote in the referendum, attracted greater support and had a trenchant narrative that the peace process was a bad deal for unionists.

The power-sharing Assembly was established after elections, with the Ulster Unionist Party and the Social Democratic and Labour Party taking the positions of First and Deputy First Minister. These early days of the Assembly were rocky, with many walkouts and strong evidence of a lack of trust between nationalists and unionists. The British and Irish governments were repeatedly called upon to mediate between the squabbling parties. The electoral balance was also changing, with the DUP overtaking the UUP on the Protestant-unionist side, and Sinn Féin overtaking the SDLP on the Catholic-nationalist side. Significant sticking points remained, principally over the refusal of the IRA to disarm and the refusal of Sinn Fein to recognise the newly reformed police service. The Assembly collapsed a number of times, and power was transferred back to London.

A breakthrough came with the St Andrews Agreement in 2006.[2] This paved the way for Sinn Féin and the DUP to share power in the Assembly, as the two leading parties. They eventually led the power-sharing government from May 2007. This was quite a remarkable change. The First Minister, Ian Paisley, had been present at the start of the Troubles as a Protestant firebrand preacher who had an uncompromising attitude to Catholic-nationalists. The Deputy First Minister, Martin McGuinness, had been a leading member of the IRA for three decades. Yet, the two men had agreed to work together. By early 2016 the power-sharing Assembly began what would turn out to be a long-term collapse. There was no sign of its reinstatement by mid-2019.

Away from the Assembly, progress was made in many other areas of the Good Friday Agreement. The police force underwent huge reform, including a stipulation that recruitment must be 50/50 Catholic/Protestant in order to redress the significant shortfall of Catholic members. A human rights body was also established, and militant prisoners were released. A number of commissions looked into the issue of victims and reconciliation, but little progress was made in this area. While there was spoiler violence, mainly from pro-united Ireland militants, these groups attracted little public support.

Lessons to be learned from the case study

10 lessons from the Northern Ireland peace process

We must be very careful in recommending lessons from one context to another. What works in one context may have little relevance in another. Nevertheless, the following ten points can be taken from the Northern Ireland experience.

1 *Change can happen*

The Northern Ireland conflict, and especially the campaigns of violence, seemed never-ending. Virtually no one could have predicted that a sustained peace process, ending in a major peace accord, could have happened. It took perseverance and risks, but it did happen.

2 *Peace processes occur at the intra-group level as well as at the inter-group level*

Much of the focus during the Northern Ireland peace process was on negotiations between opponents (for example, between the British government and Sinn Féin). Yet, serious negotiations also took place within governments, political parties, militant groups, and communities. These negotiations and disagreements often took place in secret, yet they had a significant impact on the course of the peace process. Political and militant leaderships had to invest significant energy into keeping their comrades 'on board'.

3 *The elite and non-elite peace processes were not linked*

Northern Ireland's formal peace talks were restricted to the British and Irish governments, the political parties, and the militant groups. Yet, outside of the building where the talks were held, there was a vibrant civil society, much of it very supportive of a peace deal, but it had no access to the negotiations. The formal political talks often did not reflect the 'mood on the street'. There was little sense of popular ownership of the peace process. This had serious consequences in that 50 per cent of Protestant-unionists voted against the 1998 peace deal.

4 *Movement and momentum matter*

For long periods, little was happening in the Northern Ireland peace process. Political parties and governments engaged in delaying tactics and deliberately thwarted the demands of their opponents. Yet, it was possible to inject a sense of momentum into the peace process through events that were more symbolic rather than substantive. Thus, for example, visits to Northern Ireland by US President Bill Clinton or announcements of additional funding for economic development, had little actual impact on the peace process but kept alive the idea that the peace process was ongoing.

5 *Money helps*

For most of its duration, the Northern Ireland peace process took place during a time of economic growth. House prices and salaries were growing, so there was a 'feel good factor' among the general population. The British and Irish governments were able to invest in the peace process. This involved giving money to civil society and peace projects. It also involved 'buying off' groups linked with militant groups. The European Union in particular was generous with peace support funding.

6 *Ground rules can be useful*

The peace process had a number of ground rules, the main one being a ceasefire before admission to talks. These were formalised and extended in the form of the 'Mitchell Principles', or rules of non-violence that all political parties had to sign up to in order to gain admittance to the multi-party talks. Parties were suspended from the multi-party talks if they broke them.

7 *Reaching a peace agreement is only Part I. Part II is implementation*

Although reaching a peace deal was difficult, that did not introduce immediate and comprehensive peace. The Belfast Agreement had to be implemented (a long process), and certain elements had to be renegotiated. Moreover, some of the parties to the deal had to confront internal divisions. If the Belfast Agreement was a wedding, then what followed was a marriage, and marriages require work.

8 *Nothing is agreed until everything is agreed*

In order to prevent parties from simply leaving the talks when they got the concessions they wanted, the rule 'nothing is agreed until everything is agreed' was introduced.

9 *Inclusive talks are difficult, but they worked*

Multiple attempts were made in the 1970s, 1980s, and early 1990s to reach a political deal in Northern Ireland. They were all based on the principle of exclusion: those who engaged in violence were excluded and only the moderate parties were admitted. The problem with this model was that the parties on the extremes had the power to wreck any agreement that the moderate parties made. The Northern Ireland peace process was inclusive in that political parties linked to militant groups were admitted. But the militant groups had to call ceasefires, and the political parties had to sign up to the Mitchell Principles of non-violence. The strategy of inclusive was, of course, highly offensive to many people who believed that all non-state armed actors were terrorists and should never be negotiated with.

10 *No one wants to be blamed for the collapse of the peace process*

None of the parties involved in the peace wanted to be seen to wreck the process. They may have wanted delays or to renegotiate certain elements of the process, but they were careful not to be seen to derail or force the collapse of the process. This was unlike the spoiler groups, who actively wanted to bring about a collapse of the peace process.

It is worth restating that all conflicts and peace processes are unique. Yet they do face many common dilemmas and problems:

- Negotiations before or after a ceasefire?
- What to do with arms: decommission them or let them rust?
- What to do with militants: have a formal DDR process, or let them drift away?
- What to do with militant prisoners?
- Sequencing: what issues are dealt with in what order?
- Negotiations: in public or in private?
- How are spoilers to be dealt with: concessions or security?

While many of the questions above demand either/or answers, the Northern Ireland experience highlights the importance of 'constructive ambiguity' and a lack of transparency in places to smooth the passage of the peace process. This meant that the British and Irish governments often 'looked the other way' with regard to illegality. The peace process required what John Darby called 'the hard swallow, and the weak smile'. The parties in the peace process were not always consistent or truthful. Yet the peace process would not have been possible if all parties adhered to a strict ideological script. It required very human (and indeed humane) qualities such as deal-making, dissembling (saying one thing and meaning another), delaying, grand gestures, and private grumbling. This meant that the peace process was rarely a palatable sight. Yet it has proved itself to be robust enough to withstand significant pressures, and it has delivered a form of peace that is vastly superior to the situation in the 1970s and 1980s.

Notes

1 The text of the Good Friday Agreement can be found here: http://cain.ulst.ac.uk/events/peace/docs/agreement.htm.

2 The text of the St Andrews Agreement can be found here: www.legislation.gov.uk/ukpga/2006/53/contents.

References

Bryson, Jonathan, Eric H Hanvey, Richard Marsh, Irene Mosca, and Fabian Zuleeg. 2005. *Report on Labour Market Dynamics. Phase Two: Exploring Northern Ireland Labour Market Outcomes*. Edinburgh: DTZ Pieda Consulting and Belfast: Office of the First and Deputy First Minister. Accessed 8 May 2013. www.ofmdfmni.gov.uk/phase2.pdf.

Coaffee, Jon. 2003. *Terrorism, Risk and Global City: Towards Urban Resilience*. London: Ashgate.
Darby, John. 2008. "Borrowing and Lending in Peace Processes." In John Darby, and Roger Mac Ginty (Eds.), *Contemporary Peacemaking: Conflict, Peace Processes and Post-War Reconstruction*, 2nd edn., 339–351. Basingstoke: Palgrave Macmillan.
English, Richard. 2004. *Armed Struggle: A History of the IRA*. Oxford: Oxford University Press.
Guelke, Adrian. 1988. *Northern Ireland: The International Perspective*. Dublin: Gill and Palgrave Macmillan.
Harland, Ken. 2011. "Violent Youth Culture in Northern Ireland: Young Men, Violence and the Challenges of Peacebuilding." *Youth and Society* 43 (2): 414–432.
Hart, Peter. 2003. *The IRA at War, 1916–23*. Oxford: Oxford University Press.
Maloney, Ed. 2003. *A Secret History of the IRA*. New York: WW Norton.
McGarry, Fearghal. 2010. *The Rising: Easter 1916*. Oxford: Oxford University Press.
Moriarty, Gerry. 2012. "Figures Reveal Just 54,000 More Protestants Than Catholics in NI." *Irish Times*, 12 December. www.irishtimes.com/news/figures-reveal-just-54-000-more-protestants-than-catholics-in-ni-1.2386.
Nisra. 2011. "The Population of Northern Ireland." www.nisra.gov.uk/publications/default.asp10.htm.
ÓDochartaigh, Niall. 1997. *From Civil Rights to Armalites: Derry and the Birth of the Irish Troubles*. Cork: Cork University Press.
O'Toole, Fintan. 2013. *A History of Ireland in 100 Objects*. Dublin: Royal Irish Academy.
Smithey, Lee, A. 2011. *Unionists, Loyalists and Conflict Transformation in Northern Ireland*. Oxford: Oxford University Press.
Sutton, Malcolm. 1994. *An Index of the Deaths from the Conflict in Ireland 1969–1993*. Belfast: Beyond the Pale Publications.
Taylor, Peter. 1999. *Loyalists: War and Peace in Northern Ireland*. London: TV Books.
Zartman, I. William. 2008. "The Timing of Peace Initiatives: Hurting Stalemates and Ripe Moments." In John Darby, and Roger Mac Ginty (Eds.), *Contemporary Peacemaking: Conflict, Peace Processes and Post-War Reconstruction*, 2nd edn, 22–35. Basingstoke: Palgrave Macmillan.

13

ISRAEL AND THE PALESTINIANS

Mandy Turner

Introduction

It is now a standard cliché, frequently uttered by critics, that the Israel–Palestinian peace process (IPPP) has been all process and no peace.[1] However, this does not do justice to what has been one of the most extreme examples of a travesty created under the rubric of modern 'peacemaking': the 1993 'Declaration of Principles on Interim Self-Government Arrangements' (hereafter the DOP, otherwise known as the Oslo Accords) between Israel and the Palestine Liberation Organisation (PLO). Initially the DOP was hailed as a success story, because it seemed to signal a historic compromise, i.e. it enshrined the principle of partition and thus the end to disagreements over who had the right to the land (Shlaim 2005a). It was hugely feted and regarded as a model of what conflict resolution could achieve – because it appeared to bring to a peaceful conclusion one of the world's most intractable conflicts. In recognition of this, the DOP earned its protagonists, Yitzhak Rabin (Israel's prime minister) Shimon Peres (Israel's foreign minister), and Yasser Arafat (PLO chairman), the Nobel Peace Prize in 1994. In actuality, however, the DOP and the resulting 'Oslo framework' provided the stronger party (Israel) with multiple benefits while trapping the weaker party (the Palestinians) in a state of limbo that is neither peace nor conflict, but something in-between. In order to understand how and why the situation got to this point, this chapter will analyse the conflict causes and dynamics, the conflict resolution processes, and the main lessons we should learn from the IPPP. Despite initially being lauded as a 'success' and now hailed a 'failure', this chapter will argue that the measure of 'failure' or 'success' is not straightforward because one party has succeeded in gaining most of its demands, while the other has not – and so failure and success depend on the eye of the beholder. Indeed, as argued by Mouin Rabbani, 'failed agreements normally do not last several decades' (Rabbani 2013: 31). What the DOP was about therefore needs to be unpacked carefully and critically.

In order to do this, the chapter is split into three parts. The first section focuses on the structural and proximate causes of the Israel–Palestine conflict; it briefly reviews the different ways in which the conflict is understood by the two actors themselves, and ends by explaining the context that led to the signing of the DOP. The second section critically assesses the DOP and subsequent agreements; the economic, political, and geographical framework implemented as a result; and the negotiations themselves. The third section concludes the chapter with a short discussion of the most important lessons learned from the IPPP. While different perspectives, particularly those of the two sides, are presented so that the reader gets a sense of the contrasting (and often clashing) understandings, the core argument presented here is that the IPPP has served to facilitate, solidify, and give international legitimacy and cover for a victor's peace. This is the result of the huge power asymmetry between the two actors involved, which both facilitates (and in turn is facilitated by) a fundamental misrepresentation of the causes of the Israel–Palestine conflict, its dynamics, and how to solve it. The chapter will conclude by introducing possible future scenarios in the absence of the creation of a sovereign Palestinian state.

Conflict analysis

The roots of the Israel–Palestine conflict lie, as with many conflicts in the global south, in the experience of western colonialism and perfidious imperial decisions. However, this is a highly contentious conflict; thus, who you read dictates what explanation you are given. This section therefore briefly provides the official narratives given by both Israel and the PLO, while critically assessing the historical record.[2] As with other conflicts, understanding the causes is essential for conceiving of possible solutions, as well as the way that conflict resolution should be undertaken.

The official Israeli state narrative is that it has re-established a Jewish state back in the ancestral homeland of 2,000 years ago (MFA 2003a). This view is expressed in the Declaration of the Establishment of the State of Israel of 14 May 1948 issued by the Jewish People's Council, led by David Ben Gurion, leader of the Jewish community in Palestine during the Mandate period and first prime minister of Israel (MFA 1948). This perspective is underpinned by the belief that God promised the land of Israel to the Jewish people as enshrined in the Bible (MFA 2003a; *The Guardian* May 22, 2003). Israel thereafter presents the establishment of the modern state as the outcome of the Zionist strategy of migration to Ottoman and then British Mandate Palestine in the late nineteenth and early twentieth centuries that built the New Yishuv,[3] followed by an anti-colonial struggle against British rule (MFA 2013a, 2013b). Israel portrays itself as being thereafter forced to fight with an 'iron wall strategy' to defend its existence as the Jewish state in a hostile environment surrounded by Arab countries that seek to destroy it (Shlaim 2010). Furthermore, the history of Jewish persecution, particularly in Europe (that climaxed in the Nazi Holocaust), is regarded to be the driving force of Zionism, which originated as a secular movement for a Jewish state and is now the official state ideology of Israel. Zionists (which include a large portion of evangelical Christians as well as the majority of Jews worldwide) regard the existence of a Jewish state to be an essential bulwark in a world presented as being fundamentally hostile to Jews (Shlaim 2000). Those who are critical of Zionism – Jewish and non-Jewish alike – are labelled and dismissed as being anti-Semites (Gordon 2018). Palestinians (which Israel refers to as 'Arabs') are regarded as having been temporary residents, who should now give the land back to its rightful owners and move to Jordan or other neighbouring Arab states (MFA 2013b; Op-Ed 2016). A common Zionist claim is that they 'made the desert bloom', thus implying they are more deserving owners and have an intimate bond with the land (George 1979). The official Israeli interpretation of its history has not changed much over the past 70 years; indeed, these perspectives pepper the speeches of all Israeli leaders and state documents.

The Palestinian perspective (as represented by the official position of the PLO), on the other hand, regards the origins of the Israel–Palestine conflict as residing in the nature of Zionism (and thus Israel as the Zionist state) as a European settler colonial movement.[4] With the support of powerful imperial allies – initially Britain, then the USA – Zionist forces displaced Palestinians, the native population, from their homeland and established a state with inbuilt privileges for Jews (PLO Negotiations Affairs Department 2017; Sayegh 2012). Palestinian opposition to the 'Jewish national homeland' was consistent throughout the mandate period and underpinned the 'first wave' nationalist movement that led the 1936 revolt and opposition to the partition plan (Khalid 2006: 131–139). Mass Zionist settlement, which created the New Yishuv, threatened Palestinian land rights and land use (Segev 2001: 273–276). However, the real turning point was the Nakba of 1948, which displaced three-quarters of the Palestinian-Arab population, turning them into refugees in neighbouring Arab lands, including in the West Bank and Gaza Strip, which were controlled by Jordan and Egypt, respectively, when the first Arab–Israeli war ended. Palestinians regard themselves to be the indigenous inhabitants of historic Palestine .who have been displaced, occupied, and repressed by a state that has racial discrimination at its core – as expressed by (codified and uncodified) privileges for Jews and protected by segregation practices (Beinin and Stein 2006: 166–171). This perspective underpins the 1964 Palestinian National Charter that established the PLO (Palestine Ministry of Information 1999).

British colonial rule over Palestine was crucial for its subsequent history and the current situation. Britain supported 'the establishment in Palestine of a national home for the Jewish people', which it announced via a letter from Arthur Balfour (then British foreign secretary) to Lord Rothschild (a leader of the British Jewish community) on 2 November 1917, thus creating an alliance of British imperialism with Zionist settler ambitions (Shlaim 2005b). The Balfour Declaration had enormous repercussions, as Britain occupied Jerusalem one month later and subsequently became the administering power for the League of Nations Mandate over Palestine, the text of which was based on Zionist proposals that obliged Britain to implement its support for a 'Jewish national home' (Renton 2010). Due to the genocidal Nazi Holocaust that wiped out two-thirds of European Jewry, international support for the creation of a Jewish state in Palestine was high at the end of the Second World War, including at the newly created United Nations, as reflected in the 1947 UN Partition Plan. This plan granted the proposed future Jewish state

62 per cent of the territory of the land of Mandate Palestine (Aderet 2017), even though demographically the Arab population was double that of the Jews and Jewish land ownership was spread out, thus not constituting the basis for a state (Abu-Sitta 2010). Unsurprisingly, the Palestinian leadership rejected the plan, but the Jewish leadership accepted it and announced the State of Israel; the first Arab–Israeli War broke out; and the expulsions of the Nakba took place. After the UN-brokered ceasefire, Palestine disappeared from the map: Israel had possession of 78 per cent of historic Palestine (whereas the New Yishuv had only controlled/owned 6–8 per cent of the land), while Jordan and Egypt shared the other 22 per cent (thus controlling the West Bank and Gaza respectively) (Beinin and Hajjar 2014). These 1949 armistice lines (more commonly known as the 'green line') remained in place until 1967, when the West Bank and Gaza Strip were thereafter captured and occupied by Israel during the 1967 Arab–Israeli War.

The methods of dispossession and control developed by Israel inside the 'green line' to contain Palestinians that remained after the Nakba were extended when Israel occupied the West Bank and Gaza Strip (and annexed East Jerusalem) after the 1967 War (PLO Negotiations Affairs Department 2012). However, Israel regards the West Bank and Gaza Strip to be 'disputed territories', not 'occupied' (MFA 2003b), and insists that Jerusalem is its eternal undivided capital (Newman 2015). Israel regards (and has labelled) the occupied West Bank as 'Judea and Samaria' (thus referencing the ancient kingdoms which were part of the biblical Land of Israel), and it is designated as an Israeli administrative region (but that only represents Jewish communities). The settlement strategy, which was designed to integrate the conquests of 1967 with those of 1948, began immediately after the occupation, and has been pursued since by *every* Israeli government (irrespective of political affiliation) (Sela 2009: 125). In 2017, it was estimated that there are 600,000 Jewish settlers living in the West Bank and East Jerusalem (The Office of the European Union Representative 2017), who are subject to Israeli law and enjoy military protection from the Israeli army. Israel regards these settlements as fulfilling its historic right and mission to gain control and (re)populate the ancient biblical Land of Israel. Palestinians regard these actions as constituting a continuation of more than 100 years of Zionist settler colonialism. International law regards the settlements to be illegal and a war crime under the Fourth Geneva Convention, as confirmed by the UN Security Council as recently as December 2016 (UN Security Council Resolution 2334, UN Press Office 2016). The UN and most member states have continually condemned Israel for creating new settlements and expanding existing ones.

Further complicating the issue has been the regional character of the Israel–Palestine conflict. Full-blown wars between Israel and Arab states have erupted on six occasions (1948, 1956, 1967, 1973, 1982, 2006), and Israel has been involved in frequent battles with PLO guerrilla forces resident initially in Jordan and then in Lebanon, as well as with various Palestinian political factions in the OPT after 1967 (Shlaim 2000). The PLO emerged as a national liberation movement with the expressed goal of liberating the whole of historic Palestine through armed resistance, with its basis of operations in neighbouring Arab states. Acting as an umbrella movement for the majority (but not all) political factions, the PLO was a government in exile, with a variety of bodies and a constitution (Sayigh 2000: 217–221). The Palestinian national movement has employed a variety of tactics – including high-profile plane hijacks, kidnappings, and suicide bombings; popular resistance strategies such as consumer/workers' strikes, demonstrations, and international boycotts; as well as seeking international support and recognition (through the UN and from states) – to achieve Palestinian liberation and self-determination.

Israel has continually sought to control and suppress Palestinian political activity and resistance to its colonisation practices, which are designed to expand its state. Towards this end, Israel employs a variety of counterinsurgency strategies involving the use of 'kinetic' techniques that cover direct military intervention; extensive repression through mass incarceration, detention without trial, torture, and house demolitions; and targeted assassinations and collective punishment. Israel has also developed bureaucratic pacification techniques that involve methods of population control such as 'stratified citizenship' and restrictions on movement, marriage, and residency; a closure regime of checkpoints, barriers, and the Separation Wall; and the use of local proxies and collaborators.[5]

Like Israel, the PLO's understanding of the causes of the Israel–Palestine conflict has not changed much. However, the PLO has had to radically alter its goals to be given a place at the negotiations table. This has meant accepting the existence of the state of Israel, and accepting the principle of a Palestinian state only on the land of the territory occupied since 1967 – which amounts to only 22 per cent of historic Palestine and vastly less than that envisaged by the UN Partition Plan.[6] These altered goals were confirmed in changes made to the Palestinian National Charter in 1996 that made it compliant with what the PLO had agreed to during the peace process as codified in the DOP. However, these had been acknowledged earlier, in 1988, when the PLO accepted the three requirements imposed on it by the US: to accept UN Security Council Resolutions 242 and 338; to acknowledge the borders of 1967 and the right of Israel to exist in peace; and to renounce and condemn terrorism (Shaath 2013: 23).

While the PLO enjoyed the overwhelming support of the developing world and the Soviet Union, and had been recognised by the UN as the 'legitimate representative of the Palestinian people' (and awarded Observer Status at the General Assembly in 1974), Israel had the support of the USA – which has constantly offered diplomatic and political support and has guaranteed Israel's regional military supremacy (through extensive aid and a special alliance) (Khalidi 2014). This created a situation of stasis. However, this changed in the early 1990s due to events that transformed the international and regional environment and weakened the PLO – thus pushing it towards accepting conditionalities and peace plans it had previously rejected. These events were: the collapse of the PLO's superpower ally, the Soviet Union; and the defeat of Iraq in the 1991 Gulf War. The USSR had been the PLO's main source of weapons and political support, and had acted as a balancing force against US support for Israel. And so, its departure from the international scene made the PLO vulnerable to US pressure. The PLO's isolation was further compounded by the defeat of its regional ally, Iraq, in 1991. Up until this point, the PLO had enjoyed the support of two major regional allies – Iraq and Kuwait. By choosing to support Iraq's invasion of Kuwait in 1990, which was defeated by a US-led coalition (that included some Arab states), the PLO incurred the wrath of Kuwait and other Gulf states. Kuwait responded by expelling around 400,000 Palestinians, and the Gulf Cooperation Council countries ended their financial and political support for the PLO (Khatib 2010: 50–58). These two factors formed the backdrop to the PLO signing the DOP.

Some commentators propose that there were a number of factors that also pushed Israel towards the negotiation table and recognition of the PLO. The First Intifada – a popular uprising in the OPT against Israel's occupation, which erupted in 1987 and ran until 1993 – had a huge impact on Israel. It ended the illusion that Palestinians in the OPT would continue to be compliant under Israeli control; it negatively affected the Israeli economy; and it damaged Israel's reputation abroad (Neff 1997). Furthermore, in 1988, Jordan surrendered its claims on the West Bank, which ended the illusion of a 'Jordanian option' and meant that Israel had to negotiate directly with the Palestinians. However, the biggest push appears to have come from the US, who, according to Nabil Shaath (who has played a leading role in the PLO and the peace negotiations), 'dragged' Israeli Prime Minister, Yitzhak Shamir, to Madrid (Shaath 2013: 24). A further push factor was the changes that had taken place in Israel's economy throughout the 1980s – it had exchanged its state-led economic policies for a neoliberal marketisation strategy, i.e. privatisation, trade liberalisation, and opening up its economy to overseas investment (Hanieh 2003: 14–15). The emergence and development of a new capitalist class with its head turned towards further globalisation of the Israeli economy thus created a constituency interested in ending the Arab economic boycott, which had successfully isolated Israel from large parts of the world market (Bouillon 2006: 51–53). This is because, while the boycott was enforced by the Arab League, most of the leverage came from other states who did not want to go against the Arab position. The Arab League's position was that the economic boycott would only be ended through a peace deal with the PLO. This remains the Arab League's official position, although some of its member states have subsequently signed peace deals with Israel that ended the boycott, and some publicly support it but privately have trade links with Israel (Weiss 2017).

This changing context and the potential 'push' and 'pull' factors would appear to confirm the utility of Zartman's concept of 'ripeness' (Zartman 2000). The situation that led to the DOP was certainly 'ripe' in one sense: that the PLO was weakened, the US spotted an opportunity for a deal, and Israel saw it as a way to implement its original idea for the OPT as codified in the 1967 Allon Plan, discussed below (Haddad 2016: 36–54). However, we should ask the question: 'ripe' for what or whom?[7] While the signing of the DOP indicates that there was a willingness to move from hostility to cooperation by both sides, negotiations and relations between them quickly deteriorated – leading to the situation that currently exists. The following section therefore offers an overview of the negotiations and details of the DOP, as well as an analysis of its implementation.

The conflict resolution process

There is a vast literature on the DOP and the IPPP.[8] Akin to analyses of the Israel–Palestine conflict itself, there are fundamental disagreements between the two parties on: the minimum (yet necessary) requirements for peace, who is to blame for important aspects of the DOP (and subsequent agreements) *not* being implemented, why there has not been a move towards final status negotiations, and what is the future of the space between the Jordan River and the Mediterranean Sea (as well as the future of Palestinian refugees). While an objective assessment can be made (based on weighing up the evidence), this will not be neutral – an often unreasonable demand made when discussing the Israel–Palestine conflict.

The US has been the dominant third-party actor in attempting to broker peace in the Middle East, not only between Israel and the Palestinians, but also between Israel and its Arab neighbours; indeed, it facilitated the signing of the 1979 Israel–Egypt Peace Treaty, the 1994 Israel–Jordan Peace Treaty, and a few rounds of (failed) peace talks between Israel and Syria. It has used aid, trade agreements, and the sale of military hardware (or the promise thereof) to facilitate these talks and treaties and ensure their continuation (Baxter and Akbarzadeh 2008: 46–69). However, as regards peace with the Palestinian people, the US initially accepted Israel's stipulations of refusing to negotiate with the PLO and refusing to discuss Palestinian self-determination. The proposal advanced during the 1988 Shultz Initiative, for instance, was that parts of the OPT be autonomous but under the jurisdiction of Jordan, an option that mirrored aspects of the Allon Plan proposed by Israel, which would ensure that it remained in control of key parts of the West Bank (Khatib 2010: 53). The PLO refused to negotiate on this basis, and so talks never took place. Fast forward to the early 1990s and the radically transformed international context which weakened the PLO (as outlined in the previous section) compelled it to consider the previously unthinkable.

The DOP was signed after two and a half years of laborious negotiations that took place along two different yet parallel tracks: the official US-led process and the Oslo back channel. The official negotiations were launched at the October 1991 Madrid Conference and continued in Washington DC at the invitation of the US and the USSR. And yet even at these talks, Israel refused to directly negotiate with the PLO, and so the Palestinian team, which consisted of political leaders from inside the OPT and not explicitly the PLO (although they were negotiating under the direction of the PLO), had to be part of a joint Jordanian–Palestinian delegation (Khatib 2010: 51–61). These talks were based on UN Security Council Resolutions 242 and 338, and thus on the principle of land for peace, i.e. that Israel would withdraw from land it occupied in 1967 in exchange for peace with its Arab neighbours. The ideas proposed for implementing withdrawal from the OPT bore a remarkable similarity to what eventually was agreed through the Oslo channel: a two-phase process – negotiations for interim arrangements for a period of five years, and then negotiations on permanent status. However, the official Palestinian delegation in Washington expressed huge reservations about this approach and thus rejected it, because it fell far short of self-determination and statehood, it was too ambiguous, and it was feared that Israel would not agree to ending settlement expansion (Kassis 2013). And yet the PLO delegation to the Oslo back channel negotiations accepted this two-phase process – a move that surprised the official delegation.[9] Indeed, chief negotiator of the official delegation, Haidar Abdel-Shafi, regarded it as a disastrous agreement, and prominent Palestinian academic Edward Said called it 'an instrument of Palestinian surrender, a Palestinian Versailles' (Said 1993).

The Oslo negotiations were conducted via a secret channel that brought together a PLO delegation and a succession of Israeli delegations whose membership changed and increased in importance as the talks were recognised by the Israeli leadership as being fruitful (Qurei 2006). Beginning in December 1992 in London and then lasting for eight months from January 1993 at various locations in Norway (under the auspices of the Norwegian government), the outcome was the Declaration of Principles on Interim Self-Government Arrangements (DOP), which was signed in a public ceremony at the White House on 13 September 1993. There are a variety of explanations for why the PLO accepted principles that the official delegation did not – that it was already in a weakened position and was afraid of being further side-lined both internationally and within the OPT (Hilal 1995); that the two delegations were ultimately controlled by the PLO, which used the official channel to push a 'strong' position while using the secret channel to be more flexible; that the official delegation was subject to Palestinian public opinion while the secret one was not (Khatib 2010: 84–91); and that the secret delegation was more focused on PLO recognition while the official delegation was more focused on the end goal (Ashrawi 1996). The most important thing, however, is that the DOP was not radically different from the proposals put forward in the 1980s or indeed those proposed during the official Washington talks, but it did give the PLO the recognition it so sorely desired. This historic recognition, however, came at the cost of accepting the autonomy scenario.

A number of agreements were thereafter signed between Israel and the PLO: the 1993 Israel–PLO Letters of Recognition; the 1993 DOP; the 1994 Paris Protocol on Economic Relations; the 1994 Gaza–Jericho Agreement; the 1994 Agreement on the Preparatory Transfer of Power and Responsibilities; the 1995 Interim Agreement (otherwise known as Oslo II); the 1997 Protocol Concerning the Redeployment in Hebron; the 1998 Wye River Memorandum; and the 1999 Sharm el-Sheikh Memorandum. The Letters of Recognition established mutual recognition between Israel and the PLO, which was crucial in creating the basis for further negotiations, and were the preamble to the DOP. The 1993 DOP outlined the permanent status issues to be negotiated (Jerusalem, borders, settlements, water, security, and refugees); a 'transitional period' to last no more than five years that would lead to the implementation of UN Security Council Resolutions 242 and 338; Palestinian elections; and an outline of the first Israeli military redeployment (The Oslo Declaration of Principles 1993). The 1994 Paris Protocol on Economic Relations created the framework for economic cooperation between the Palestinian Authority and the government of Israel (Bamya 2013: 61). The 1994 Gaza–Jericho Agreement (Oslo II) signalled the beginning of the five-year transitional period and the transfer of limited powers and responsibilities to the Palestinian Authority; it also specified the redeployment of the Israeli army from parts of Gaza and Jericho city. The 1994 Agreement on the Preparatory Transfer of Power and Responsibilities transferred powers to the Palestinian Authority in five specified areas: education and culture, health, social welfare, direct taxation, and tourism. The 1995 Interim Agreement (Oslo II) set out the bulk of the Oslo Agreements, established the powers and remit of the Palestinian Authority, and delineated Areas A, B, and C which instituted different modes of control and governance across the West Bank (and, until 2005, in Gaza); Oslo II superseded all previous agreements apart from the DOP. The 1997 Protocol Concerning the Redeployment in Hebron divided the city into two spheres: H1 controlled by the Palestinian Authority and H2 (where Israeli settlers live) controlled by Israel (Khatib 2010: 83). The 1998 Wye River Memorandum was designed to restart the implementation of Oslo II and set out a timetable for Israel's redeployment, as did the 1999 Sharm el-Sheikh Memorandum following Israel's failure to abide by the provisions of Oslo II (Buttu 2019)

These thousands of pages of agreements had, at their core, four main principles: (1) PLO recognition of Israel and Israel's recognition of the PLO; (2) Israel's military redeployment from parts of the West Bank and Gaza Strip; (3) the creation of an 'interim administration' to govern Palestinians in Areas A and B, and a security force capable of ensuring that Palestinians would not carry out armed attacks against Israeli civilians, settlers, and soldiers; and (4) entrenchment of the 'two state' framework, with track-one bilateral negotiations as the only means of ending Israel's military rule over the OPT (Buttu 2019). The international legality of these agreements, however, are questionable: not only are they an anomaly in that they are not treaties concluded between states, but they have never been registered with the UN Secretariat. Furthermore, the final status negotiations should have taken place by 4 May 1999 – and so an interim agreement with transitional measures that have long lapsed, which codified such a huge imbalance of power but never had a termination clause, could well be deemed inconsistent with the basic principles of law and violate the internationally recognised principle of self-determination (Kattan 2013: 40). However, as with international law *per se*, their legality (or otherwise) is subject to conflicting interpretations.[10]

But whether they are deemed to be legal or illegal documents, the DOP and all the other agreements did not end the Israel–Palestine conflict. In fact, what we have witnessed instead is 20 years of 'summits' and 'initiatives'. These include: the 2000 Camp David Summit and the Clinton Parameters, the 2001 Taba Summit, the 2002 Road Map for Peace, the 2003 Geneva Initiative, the 2007 Annapolis Conference, the 2010 Direct Negotiations, the 2012 Amman Talks, and the 2013–2014 Kerry Initiative.[11] So, why did all these initiatives fail? While this cannot be answered seriously without going into the details of each context, some conclusions can be drawn from the hundreds of confidential documents compiled during the peace talks that spanned the period 1999 to 2010 (including minutes of high-level meetings between US, European, Israeli, and Palestinian Authority officials), which were obtained and released by the news network Al Jazeera in January 2011. *The Palestine Papers*, as they were thereafter called, exposed how much Palestinian negotiators were willing to concede, and how little Israel was willing to concede. The fundamental issues of Jerusalem, borders, settlements, water, security, and refugees were – and remain – the sticking points. However, while the PLO shifted towards the principle of 'land for peace' and thus a two-state solution even before the signing of the DOP, successive Israeli governments have refused a solution to the conflict based on international law and sovereign Palestinian statehood (Sela 2009: 115–125). Israel has continually expanded Jewish settlements in the OPT and refuses to negotiate an acceptable solution for both parties on the status of Jerusalem, instead asserting its claim of sovereignty over it all. While Palestinian statehood and the two-state solution (with Jerusalem as a shared capital) were *not* mentioned in the DOP, they constituted the basis for the 'Roadmap' (which attempted to save the IPPP after the outbreak of the Second Intifada) – and thereafter these have been regarded as the foundation for the solution to the conflict.

The Palestine Papers also document how the US and its European allies continually pressured the Palestinian negotiators to lower their demands, but did not use the same pressure on Israel; it also reveals their persistent attempts to manipulate internal Palestinian politics (Swisher 2011). After the failure of the Kerry Initiative, there have been no further talks, or indeed initiatives to restart talks. Although at the time of writing (March 2018), there is much talk of a 'Trump peace plan'.

And yet, despite the failure of these peace talks and initiatives, the Oslo framework (which was the result of the agreements signed in the 1990s) remains in place and governs the Palestinian people – politically, geographically, and economically. Politically, a limited form of self-rule was created, embodied in the institution of the Palestinian Authority (PA). The PA was given limited autonomy over the civil affairs of the majority of Palestinians living in the West Bank and Gaza (but not over the land) as Israel's military forces formally withdrew from high-density population areas while continuing to control access to and from them (and making frequent military incursions and arrest raids into them). Geographically, the OPT was divided into administrative parcels: in the West Bank (excluding East Jerusalem) into Area A (under PA civilian and security control), Area B (under PA civilian control and Israeli military control) and Area C (under full Israeli control); in Hebron into H1 (akin to Area A) and H2 (akin to Area C); and in Gaza into Yellow and White areas (until Israel's unilateral withdrawal in 2005). In the West Bank, 18 per cent of the territory was designated as Area A (which held 55 per cent of the Palestinian population), 20 per cent of the territory was designated as Area B (which held 41 per cent of the Palestinian population), and 62 per cent of the territory was designated as Area C (which held 5.8 per cent of the Palestinian population) (EU Heads of Mission 2011). Israel's military withdrawal and plans to transfer more areas to the control of the PA was frozen in 2000, and there has been no significant redeployment since, apart from Gaza in 2005 (which was thereafter put under siege). Areas A and B are surrounded by Area C, meaning there is no geographical contiguity for areas under PA administration, thus allowing Israel to control the movement of people and goods. This geographical framework has had hugely negative economic effects that have been compounded by the Paris Economic Protocol (PEP), which established a quasi-customs union between the PA and Israel. The PEP gave the PA extremely limited economic powers, thus putting the OPT at the mercy of being tied to a tariff structure appropriate to an advanced industrialised globalised economy, not that of an underdeveloped economy emerging out of decades of military occupation and neglect. It also put a large proportion of PA finances under the direct control of Israel because it collects (and transfers) Palestinian tax and custom duties, which have often been withheld by Israel (Husseini and Khalidi 2013: 57).

PEP enshrined, however, the principles of free movement of Palestinian labour and goods to the Israeli market. These were regarded by the Palestinian negotiators to be beneficial for economic development in the OPT, but Israel has repeatedly violated these principles (Bamya 2013). The Oslo framework necessitated huge and continuing amounts of aid to mitigate and manage the economic and social problems created by it, which Arab and western donors have provided to keep the situation stable, purportedly in order to provide space and support for the negotiations to take place. While attempts to deal with final status issues have repeatedly failed, the framework instituted by the DOP has continued – and so have the problems created by it.

If a cost–benefit analysis were to be undertaken of the IPPP, there is little doubt that Israel has benefited the most. While the exiled PLO elite were able to return to the OPT and establish the symbols of statehood, which was initially a source of optimism and national pride, this long ago dissipated in the harsh reality of the continuation of Israel's control and colonisation regime. In general, the PLO has been forced to change its position and goals and accept things it had previously rejected; but still it has not managed to achieve self-determination or sovereignty – no doubt this is not what its leadership envisaged or sought. For the general Palestinian population, who experience the negative impacts more acutely, by 2018 the situation was highly differentiated across the OPT. In the West Bank, the population is under authoritarian rule; a political and economic elite has consolidated its control through monopolistic practices and its links with Israel and the donors; and security coordination between the PA and Israel (under US supervision) is tighter than it has ever been. Gaza (institutionally divided from the PA in the West Bank since 2007) is also under authoritarian rule, its economy is on the verge of collapse due to a crippling blockade (but sustained as an international charity case), and its population is largely imprisoned within its 'borders' which are policed by Israel and Egypt. East Jerusalem is leaderless, marginalised, and ignored; and struggles over the status of the religious sites (particularly over the Haram al-Sharif, which Jews claim as the site of the biblical Jewish Temple) are frequent and constitute a potential tinderbox. Meanwhile, Palestinian refugee communities continue to suffer from varying degrees of statelessness, which means that they often have difficulty accessing basic rights. In light of all this, Palestinians have few avenues to pursue their cause for rights and self-determination.

Israel, on the other hand, has gained huge benefits from the IPPP – particularly that it ended its international isolation and allowed it to continue its colonial expansion and counterinsurgency repression under the veneer of respectability. In the negotiations leading to the 1991 Madrid peace conference, Israel made revocation of UN Resolution 3379 (which determined that Zionism was a form of racism and racial discrimination) a condition of its participation – a demand that was implemented. Provoked by the peace talks, further international acceptance brought Israel in from the cold: between 1992 and 1999, 45 countries established diplomatic ties with Israel – more than in the four preceding decades combined. Moreover, Israel signed a peace treaty with Jordan in 1994, which probably would not have happened without the DOP. In addition to these diplomatic ties, the DOP also brought economic opportunities for Israel through the opening of trade offices in Morocco, Tunisia, Oman, Qatar, and Mauritania – all members of the Arab League (which had previously adhered to the boycott) (Buttu 2019). Other global south states followed suit after the Arab stamp of approval. Israel was thereafter able to discard the coloniser reputation it had earned after 1967. Furthermore, after the creation of the Palestinian Authority, Israel was no longer obliged to provide services for Palestinians in the OPT, which has saved it some money; although, of course, it has continued to heavily invest in methods of control (both military and bureaucratic). No doubt the assassination of Yitzhak Rabin (the Israeli prime minister that signed the DOP) by a right-wing religious Jew, Palestinian suicide attacks in the mid-1990s, and the Second Intifada bolstered the Zionist right in Israel (Mendel and Dimi 2019). However, Israel's position has not actually changed that much – Rabin did not agree to Palestinian statehood nor an end to the occupation, and neither has any subsequent Israeli leader (Sela 2009: 119). The DOP, therefore, has been a failure for one side, but a success for the other.

Lessons learned from the case study

In 2016, a play entitled *Oslo* premiered in New York City, won critical acclaim and awards, and subsequently toured to London. Written by J.T. Rogers, a playwright known for tackling difficult political issues, it brought together on one stage all of the *dramatis personae* involved in the negotiations and signing of the DOP. Describing his play as seeking 'to capture the spirit of these real events' but having 'taken dramatic liberties', Rogers seemed unable to decide whether the play should be a tragedy or a farce – and so it appears to be both (Rogers 2017). The PLO delegation is portrayed as being split between two characters – one is contemplative but eager to please, the other makes radical proclamations – representing a PLO desperate to sign a deal. The Israeli delegation is depicted as initially being made up of bumbling academics, but then taken over by tough and ruthless negotiators focused on details – representing an Israeli state desperate, to the last minute, to undermine the PLO. The Norwegian hosts are characterised as being reluctant to intervene (unless it was to prevent the talks disintegrating), and the main protagonist, Terje Rød-Larsen, is represented as a dilettante trying out his academic theory of 'gradualism' in conflict resolution. And the Americans are painted as being rather mysterious but as having the power to force both parties to do what they want. While this is perhaps a gross oversimplification of the historical record, nevertheless in some ways it captures an essence of the situation. First, that the PLO was desperate to reach an agreement and so signed a peace deal that was ambiguous and fell far short of self-determination. Second, that Israel was happy to discuss the finer details of the duties and responsibilities of the Palestinian Authority, but less happy to discuss the larger, and more important issues, of self-determination and statehood. And third, that the role of third-party actors has been crucial, especially that of the US. Unfortunately, however, the curtains have not closed on the DOP; indeed, the encores to the mythical peace process and two-state solution appear to be never-ending.

There are two main lessons, therefore, that should be learned from the DOP and the IPPP. First, that an occupation and process of colonisation cannot be resolved via bilateral dispute settlement mechanisms but rather requires the application of international law and a process of decolonisation. Second, that power discrepancies between parties must be balanced by a third party willing to use pressure to stop the powerful party dictating the process – otherwise a victor's peace is the likely outcome. The power discrepancy embedded in the IPPP allowed Israel to postpone agreed-upon target dates and unilaterally dictate a 'performance-based' approach, which it used to violate the terms and spirit of the agreements. By accepting that questions of land and sovereignty be postponed until final status negotiations, the West Bank and Gaza thereafter became 'disputed territories' with Israel granted an equal claim to them (Said 1993: 18). While the DOP stated that none of the parties should do anything that could prejudice the outcome of the permanent settlement, no third-party actors were willing to use sufficient pressure or leverage against Israel. This is in stark contrast to 1992 when the US used its role as an aid provider as leverage to stop Israel building settlements (Goshko 1992). Indeed, if a two-state solution was really what Israel wanted, then settlement expansion would not have continued and accelerated since the signing of the DOP. And if the US had really wanted to force Israel to stick to the principles of the DOP, particularly as regards settlement expansion, then it could have – including rejecting the Israeli argument that expansion is largely propelled by 'natural growth' (Eldar 2009). There is little doubt that settlement expansion is *the* main obstacle to the creation of a sovereign Palestinian state and thus the two-state solution, despite claims to the contrary from Israel and its supporters. There is much to say about the strategy of the Palestinian leadership, and criticisms abound; however, *The Palestine Papers* reveal a lot about their weakness, and the fact that no one stood by them to uphold international law despite a major historical compromise on their part to accept Israel and a truncated Palestinian state.

Some narratives define the Israel–Palestine conflict as one predominantly over religion – and, of course, this has come to play a role (Pfeffer 2014). However, fundamentally the conflict is one over land and resources; Israel controls access to both of these and has gained ownership over more and more through an aggressive colonisation strategy of settling its own people in the OPT, land-grabbing, and using a variety of tactics to push Palestinians off their land and into more confined urban spaces, or even to emigrate. The DOP did not change this – on the contrary, it provided a veneer of international legitimacy and respectability for these processes to continue under the guise of a peace process. Why did the IPPP turn out this way? The short answer is that it has suited Israel, the PLO has been unable or unwilling to muster a viable resistance to it, and the key third-party actors appear unwilling to use pressure against Israel but are willing to support a situation that ensures some level of stability through the use of vast amounts of aid to the Palestinian Authority and for the UN Relief and Works Agency for Palestinian Refugees in the Near East (UNRWA). The fact that this 'stability' is experienced as a violent colonial one by Palestinians is unlikely to lead to a policy change. In a situation of such profound power imbalances, proposing 'confidence-building' measures and mediation strategies is not only inappropriate but also ineffective.

In the absence of the two-state solution as represented by the creation of a sovereign Palestinian state existing side-by-side with Israel, there are only two avenues left. The first is the full implementation of the Allon Plan – usually referred to as the 'Jordan option' – where the current PA-governed areas in the West Bank federate with Jordan, and Israel annexes its settlement blocs and strategic areas; Gaza is dealt with separately; East Jerusalem remains part of Israel; and the refugees continue to be ignored (Op-Ed 2016). The second avenue is to decolonise the space from the Jordan River to the Mediterranean Sea to create one state that represents all religions and nationalities; this would require a separation of religion and state, massive investment in Palestinian areas long neglected under the current system, and a total rethink of how political representation and participation could operate. The first avenue would swing the pendulum back to Israel's original plan, allowing it to expand *Eretz Israel*; the second avenue would swing the pendulum back to the PLO's original plan of one democratic state in the whole of historic Palestine. In a situation where there is no clear journey towards one of these options, the colonial peace that was initiated and legitimised by the DOP and implemented through the Oslo framework will continue.

Notes

1 I prefer to use the formulation 'Israel–Palestinian peace process' because it underlines the asymmetrical character of the situation where a sovereign state (Israel) enjoys all the benefits of international recognition and legality (and which is the stronger party) but is portrayed as an equal 'combatant'/conflict actor to a stateless people (the Palestinians), who do not enjoy sovereignty and its benefits (and which is the weaker party).

2 Of course, the PLO does not represent *all* Palestinians, as there are other groups, such as Hamas and Islamic Jihad, that remain outside of its membership. However, I am trying to capture the *mainstream* dominant positions of the conflict narratives as represented by the political leadership of each community. Indeed, it would also be true to say that 'the state of Israel' does not necessarily represent the view of *all* Israelis. Furthermore, Hamas and Islamic Jihad accept the settler colonial explanation for the conflict.

3 Literally meaning 'settlement' in Hebrew, the Yishuv was the term used to describe Jewish communities in Ottoman Palestine and Mandate Palestine. A distinction is made

between the 'old' Yishuv (pre-Zionist community of Palestinian Jews) and the 'new' Yishuv (post-1880s Zionist Jewish immigrants), which transformed the community into an organised political body (Reinharz 1993/4).

4 President Mahmoud Abbas' speech to a PLO meeting on 14 January 2018 is a good example of this perspective. Levy (2018).

5 For a full list of sources and further elaboration of Israel's counterinsurgency practices and techniques, see Turner (2016).

6 See Arafat's letter to the Camp David Summit in July 2000, in Qurie (2008: 163–164).

7 I am thankful to Toufic Haddad for this point.

8 My top five are: Khatib (2010), Kurtzer (2008), LeVine (2008), Said (2001), Enderlin (2003).

9 Nabil Kassis, Hanan Ashrawi, Raja Shehadeh, and Haidar Abdel-Shafi (all part of the official Washington delegation) all expressed surprise at what was signed (see Khatib 2010: 84–92). Indeed, Abdel-Shafi, the head of the delegation, broke with the delegation and did not attend the signing of the DOP because 'he feared its outcome' (Kassis 2013: 53).

10 For an assessment of this, see Watson (2000).

11 There have also been a number of initiatives undertaken by Arab states and the Arab League – e.g. the 2002 Beirut Summit (which launched the Arab Peace Initiative), and the 2005 Sharm el-Sheikh Summit (which sought an end to the second intifada).

References, further reading, and links to key primary documents

Abu-Sitta, Salman. 2010. *Atlas of Palestine, 1917–1966.* London: Palestine Land Society.

Aderet, Ofer. 2017. "Why the Mysterious Swede Who Drew Up Israel's Map Favored the Jews." *Ha'aretz*, 25 November. www.haaretz.com/israel-news/.premium-1.824757.

Ashrawi, Hanan. 1996. *This Side of Peace: A Personal Account.* New York: Touchstone Publishers.

Associated Press. 2015. "Israel's New Deputy Foreign Minister: This Land Is Ours, All of It Is Ours." *The Guardian*, 22 May. www.theguardian.com/world/2015/may/22/israels-new-deputy-foreign-minister-this-land-is-ours-all-of-it-is-ours.

Avalon Project. "Palestinian National Charter." 1964. http://avalon.law.yale.edu/20th_century/plocov.asp.

Bamya, Saeb. 2013. "The Economics of the Oslo Accord." In *20 Years Since Oslo: Palestinian Perspectives*, published by the Heinrich Böll Stiftung, 61–67. Ramallah: Heinrich Boll Stiftung.

Baxter, Kylie, and Shahram Akbarzadeh. 2008. *US Foreign Policy in the Middle East: The Roots of Anti-Americanism.* Abingdon: Routledge.

Beinin, Joel, and Rebecca L. Stein. 2006. *The Struggle for Sovereignty: Palestine and Israel, 1993–2005.* Stanford: Stanford University Press.

Bouillon, Markus E. 2006. *The Peace Business: Money and Power in the Israeli-Palestinian Peace Process.* London: IB Tauris.

Buttu, Diana. 2019. "The Oslo Agreements – What Happened?" In Mandy Turner (Ed.), *From the River to the Sea: Domination, Disintegration and Reintegration in Israel and Palestine in the Shadow of 'Peace'.* Lanham, MD: Rowman and Littlefield.

Beinin, Joel, and Lisa Hajjar. 2014. "Palestine, Israel and the Arab-Israeli Conflict, Middle East Research and Information Project." www.merip.org/sites/default/files/Primer_on_PalestineIsrael (MERIP_February2014)final.pdf.

"Declaration of the Establishment of the State of Israel." 1948. Published in the Official Gazette 14 May. www.mfa.gov.il/mfa/foreignpolicy/peace/guide/pages/declaration%20of%20establishment%20of%20state%20of%20israel.aspx.

Eldar, Akiva. 2009. "Peace Now: 'Natural Growth', Israel's Trick for West Bank Expansion." *Haaretz*, 17 May. www.haaretz.com/1.5053357.

Enderlin, Charles. 2003. *Shattered Dreams: The Failure of the Peace Process in the Middle East, 1995–2002*. New York: Other Press.

EU Heads of Mission. 2011. "Area C and Palestinian Statebuilding." July. www.ipk-bonn.de/downloads/EU-Report-Area-C.pdf.

George, Alan. 1979. "'Making the Desert Bloom', a Myth Examined." *Journal of Palestine Studies* 8 (2): 88–100.

Gordon, Neve. 2018. "The New Anti-Semitism." *London Review of Books* 30 (1). www.lrb.co.uk/v40/n01/neve-gordon/the-new-anti-semitism.

Goshko, John M. 1992. "Baker Bans Israeli Loan Aid Unless Settlements Are Halted." *Washington Post*, 25 February. www.washingtonpost.com/archive/politics/1992/02/25/baker-bars-israeli-loan-aid-unless-settlements-are-halted/e7311eea-e6d3-493b-8880-a3b98e0830a1/?utm_term=.e8992973bbf8.

Haddad, Toufic. 2016. *Palestine Ltd: Neoliberalism and Nationalism in the Occupied Territory*. London: IB Tauris.

Hanieh, Adam. 2003. "From State-Led Growth to Globalization: The Evolution of Israeli Capitalism." *Journal of Palestine Studies* 32 (4): 5–21.

Hilal, Jamil. 1995. "The PLO: Crisis of Legitimacy." *Race & Class* 37 (2): 1–18.

Israeli Ministry of foreign Affairs. 1948. "Declaration of Establishment of State of Israel." 14 May. https://mfa.gov.il/mfa/foreignpolicy/peace/guide/pages/declaration%20of%20establishment%20of%20state%20of%20israel.aspx

Israeli Ministry of Foreign Affairs. 2003a. "The Land of Promise: The State of Israel." 27 March. http://mfa.gov.il/MFA/MFAArchive/2003/Pages/The%20Land%20of%20Promise.aspx.

Israeli Ministry of Foreign Affairs. 2003b. "Disputed Territories: Forgotten Facts About the West Bank & Gaza Strip." 1 February. http://mfa.gov.il/MFA/MFA-Archive/2003/Pages/DISPUTED%20TERRITORIES-%20Forgotten%20Facts%20About%20the%20We.aspx.

Israeli Ministry of Foreign Affairs. 2013a. "History: Foreign Domination." http://mfa.gov.il/MFA/AboutIsrael/History/Pages/HISTORY-%20Foreign%20Domination.aspx.

Israeli Ministry of Foreign Affairs. 2013b. "Israel's War of Independence." http://mfa.gov.il/MFA/AboutIsrael/History/Pages/Israels%20War%20of%20Independence%20-%201947%20-%201949.aspx.

Husseini, Hiba I., and Raja Khalidi. 2013. "Fixing the Paris Protocols Twenty Years Later: Some Lessons for Diehard Reformers." In *20 Years Since Oslo: Palestinian Perspectives*, published by the Heinrich Böll Stiftung, 56–61. Ramallah: Heinrich Boll Stiftung.

Kattan, Victor. 2013. "Are the Oslo Accords Still Legally Binding: Ten Points to Consider." In *20 Years Since Oslo: Palestinian Perspectives*, published by the Heinrich Böll Stiftung, 38–42. Ramallah: Heinrich Boll Stiftung.

Kassis, Nabeel. 2013. "Interview: We Had Too Much Trust in Our Ability to Turn the Situation to Our Favour." In *20 Years Since Oslo: Palestinian Perspectives*, published by the Heinrich Böll Stiftung, 49–53. Ramallah: Heinrich Boll Stiftung.

Khalidi, Rashid. 2006. *The Iron Cage: The Story of the Palestinian Struggle for Statehood*. New York: Beacon Press.

Khalidi, Rashid. 2014. *Brokers of Deceit: How the US Has Undermined Peace in the Middle East*. Boston: Beacon Press.

Khatib, Ghassan. 2010. *Palestinian Politics and the Middle East Peace Process: Consensus and Competition in the Palestinian Negotiating Team*. Abingdon: Routledge.

Kurtzer, Danile C., and Scott B. Lasensky. 2008. *Negotiating Arab-Israeli Peace: American Leadership in the Middle East*. Washington, DC: United States Institute of Peace.

LeVine, Mark. 2008. *Impossible Peace: Israel/Palestine Since 1989*. London: Zed Books.
Levy, Elio. 2018. "PA President Abbas: 'Israel a colonial project, has nothing to do with Jews.'" *YNet News*, 14 January. www.ynetnews.com/articles/0,7340,L-5070977,00.html.
Mendel, Yonatan, and Dimi Reider. 2019. "A New Nationalistic Political Grammar: Jewish-Israeli Society 25 Years After Oslo." In Mandy Turner (Ed.), *From the River to the Sea*.
Neff, Donald. 1997. "The First Intifada Erupts, Forcing Israel to Recognize Palestinians." *Washington Report on Middle East Affairs*, December.
Newman, Marissa. 2015. "Netanyahu: Israel Will Not Be Divided Again." *Times of Israel*, 18 May. www.timesofisrael.com/netanyahu-jerusalem-construction-our-natural-right/.
The Office of the European Union Representative (West Bank and Gaza Strip). 2017. "Six Month Report on Israeli Settlements in the West Bank, Including East Jerusalem (January–June 2017)." 15 December. https://eeas.europa.eu/delegations/palestine-occupied-palestinian-territory-west-bank-and-gaza-st rip_id/37466/Six-Month%20Report%20on%20Israeli%20settlements%20in%20the%20occupied%20West%20Bank,%20including%20East%20Jerusalem%20(%20January%20-%20June%202017.
Op-Ed. 2016. "Is This Netanyahu's Palestinian State?" *Miami Herald*, 9 June. www.miamiherald.com/opinion/op-ed/article82891167.html.
"The Oslo Declaration of Principles." 1993. http://avalon.law.yale.edu/20th_century/isrplo.asp.
"The Palestinian Charter." 1999. *Palestinian American Council*, Amended in 1968. www.pac-usa.org/the_palestinian_charter.htm.
Pfeffer, Anshel. 2014. "The Israel-Palestine Conflict Is Not Just About Land. It's a Bitter Religious War." *The Guardian*, 20 November. www.theguardian.com/commentisfree/2014/nov/20/israel-palestine-conflict-religious-war.
PLO Negotiations Affairs Department. 2012. "Nakba: The Untold Story of a National Disaster." www.nad.ps/sites/default/files/the_untold_story_of_a_cultural_catastrophe_al_nakba.pdf.
PLO Negotiations Affairs Department. 2017. "Israel's Settler Colonialism Exposed." www.nad.ps/en/videos/israels-settler-colonialism-exposed.
Qurei, Ahmed. 2006. *From Oslo to Jerusalem: The Palestinian Story of the Secret Negotiations*. London: IB Tauris.
Qurie, Ahmed. 2008. *Beyond Oslo: The Struggle for Palestine*. London: IB Tauris.
Rabbani, Mouin. 2013. "Twenty Years of Oslo and the Future of the Two-State Paradigm." In *20 Years Since Oslo: Palestinian Perspectives*, published by the Heinrich Böll Stiftung, 29–33. Ramallah: Heinrich Boll Stiftung.
Reider, Dimi. 2019. "Israeli Society 25 Years After Oslo: Entrenchment and Annexation." In Mandy Turner (Ed.), *From the River to the Sea: Domination, Disintegration and Reintegration in Israel and Palestine*. Lanham, MD: Rowman and Littlefield.
Reinharz, Jehuda. 1993/1994. "Old and New Yishuv: The Jewish Community in Palestine at the Turn of the Twentieth Century." *Jewish Studies Quarterly* 1 (1): 54–71.
Renton, James. 2010. "Flawed Foundations: The Balfour Declaration and the Palestine Mandate." In Rory Miller (Ed.), *Britain, Palestine and Empire: The Mandate Years*, 15–37. Farnham: Ashgate.
Rogers, J.T. 2017. *Oslo: A Play*. London: Nick Hern Books.
Said, Edward. 1993. "The Morning After." *London Review of Books* 15 (20): 3–5.
Said, Edward. 2001. *The End of the Peace Process: Oslo and After*. London: Vintage.
Sayegh, Fayez. 2012. "Zionist Colonialism in Palestine (1965)." *Settler Colonial Studies* 2 (1): 206–225.
Sayigh, Yezid. 2000. *Armed Struggle and the Search for State: The Palestinian National Movement, 1949–1993*. Oxford: Oxford University Press.

Segev, Tom. 2001. *One Palestine, Complete: Jews and Arabs Under the British Mandate*, translated by Haim Watzman. New York: Henry Holt and Company.

Sela, Avraham. 2009. "Difficult Dialogue: The Oslo Process in Israeli Perspective." *Macalester International* 23. http://digitalcommons.macalester.edu/macintl/vol23/iss1/11.

Shaath, Nabil. 2013. "Today the Peace Process Has Died." In *20 Years Since Oslo: Palestinian Perspectives*, published by the Heinrich Böll Stiftung, 23–29. Ramallah: Heinrich Boll Stiftung.

Shlaim, Avi. 2000. *The Iron Wall: Israel and the Arab World*. London: Penguin.

Shlaim, Avi. 2005a. "The Rise and Fall of the Oslo Process." In Louise Fawcett (Ed.), *International Relations of the Middle East*, 241–261. Oxford: Oxford University Press.

Shlaim, Avi. 2005b. "The Balfour Declaration and Its Consequences." In Wm. Roger Louis (Ed.), *Yet More Adventures with Britannia: Personalities, Politics and Culture in Britain*, 251–270. London: IB Tauris.

Swisher, Clayton E. 2011. *The Palestine Papers: The End of the Road?* London: Hesperus Press.

Turner, Mandy. 2016. "Peacebuilding as Counterinsurgency in the Occupied Palestinian Territory." *Review of International Studies* 41 (1): 73–98.

UN Security Council Resolution 2334, UN Press Office. 2016. "Israel's Settlements Have No Legal Validity, Constitute Flagrant Violation of International Law, Security Council Reaffirms." 23 December. www.un.org/press/en/2016/sc12657.doc.htm.

Watson, Geoffrey R. 2000. *The Oslo Accords: International Law and the Israeli-Palestinian Peace Agreements*. New York: Oxford University Press.

Weiss, Martin A. 2017. "Arab League Boycott of Israel." *Congressional Research Service*, 25 August, Washington, DC. https://fas.org/sgp/crs/mideast/RL33961.pdf.

Zartman, William. 2000. "Ripeness: The Hurting Stalemate and Beyond." In Paul Stern and Daniel Druckman (Eds.), *International Conflict Resolution after the Cold War*, 225–249. Washington: National Academy Press.

Links to key primary documents

Essential Primary Documents and Descriptions of Key Events Have Been Collated and Annotated by the European Institute for Research on Mediterranean and Euro-Arab Cooperation. www.medea.be/en/themes/arab-israeli-conflict/.

14

SOMALILAND

Louise Wiuff Moe

Introduction

In a conversation about how Somaliland managed – in a context of very low external support – to bring about a remarkably stable peace in the absence of a strong state, the former Somaliland foreign minister explained me, 'we knew you cannot build a house starting from the roof'.[1]

This chapter discusses the process of peacebuilding and reconstruction that took place in Somaliland, in the aftermath of the collapse of the state in Somalia in 1991. The case of Somaliland is significant in illustrating that the Somali context does not merely feature fragility, insecurity, and armed conflict but also holds important lessons on peace processes.

The above quotation speaks to one such lesson; namely, that sometimes reconciliatory achievements can be enabled by the *absence* of a centralised state or internationally led coordination and management. The chapter explores in greater detail how the decentralised peace and reconciliation processes unfolded. It also highlights the role of historical contingencies that allowed for both preserving and mobilising certain 'socio-cultural capital'[2] – specifically, customary institutions – that subsequently came to serve as key resources for peacemaking. Hence, differing from highly formalised peace processes – i.e. processes facilitated by third parties, and involving a clearly defined framework with sequenced steps – the Somaliland peace process evolved more organically and drew on customary practices and skills rather than externally pre-defined negotiation schemes. The related approach of building upon reconciliatory outcomes of localised peace processes as the basis for wider political reconstruction offers insights of broader significance for issues of legitimacy and political authority. Specifically – and in contrast to a framework of 'building states to build peace' (Call 2008) – the Somaliland approach allowed for a process whereby political arrangements were born out of, and as such validated through, the negotiations and settlements reached among local communities. Against this backdrop, Somaliland emerged as the most stable polity within the Somali territories.

Somaliland has by now received significant attention, and rightly so, for its self-reliant path to peace. Yet, external intervention has not been absent altogether and merits further attention. This is especially since the internationally un-recognised status of Somaliland has encouraged more flexible and 'low-key' models of intervention than is usually the case in post-conflict states. Following on from this, the chapter explores examples of, first, low-key facilitative support to reconciliation processes in the 1990s and early 2000s and, second, more recent examples (based on the author's field research from 2014; see Moe 2015) of interventions allegedly seeking to 'secure the peace' through counterterrorism initiatives. The two types of examples allow for drawing out the ambiguous effects of flexible 'low key' intervention on local peace: from facilitative support of already ongoing peace processes, to subtle securitisation of local peace.

The chapter is structured as follows. The first section offers a brief historical contextualisation, discussing the different colonial experiences of Somaliland and Somalia, post-colonial competitions over state resources, and the eruption of civil war under the dictatorship of Siad Barre (1969–1991). The section traces the dynamics and nature of northern (Somaliland) resistance and armed struggle against Barre, up until the eventual defeat of the latter in 1991. The second section turns to an analysis of the nature of, and key agency behind, the peace processes in Somaliland, following its declaration of independence and the defeat of Barre. The latter half of the section provides a discussion of different instances of intervention and ensuing effects on local peace and order.

Conflict analysis

With colonisation in late nineteenth century, Somalis were for the first time subordinated to a central state, ruled by the Italians in the south and the British in the north, which led to a shift of the locus of power and politics. While in pre-colonial Somali society politics took place on the community level, during colonialism, politics and power were transferred by the colonial rulers to the urban administrative centres.

The colonial experience of the north and the south, becoming a British protectorate and an Italian colony, respectively, differed in important respects (Spears 2003; Reno 2003; Jhazbhay 2007). Since the main interests of the British forces in Somaliland were to secure food supply – Somali mutton – for their military garrison in Aden and to prevent other colonial powers from taking control, economic and political interference was kept to a minimum (WSP 2005; Reno 2003; Spears 2003). To the extent that the British colonisers did exercise authority over the rural population (the vast majority of the population), they did so through the customary authorities (Bradbury 2008; Reno 2003). This method of indirect rule created some degree of 'decentralized despotism' (Mamdani 1996) but also left the traditional structures – which later became the basis for peacebuilding and state formation – largely intact (Spears 2003). The Italians, in contrast, pursued a strategy of direct rule and thus imported a whole new political system to southern Somalia, with centralised economic planning, state appropriation, and substantial support for big enterprises. In this 'modernization process', Somali custom was perceived as something to be 'overcome' (Jhazbhay 2007; Reno 2003).

The nationalist movements and parties emerging in the 1950s, across the north and south, increasingly pushed for independence, which finally was granted by the British on 26 June 1960, and a few days later, on 1 July, by the Italians. On the latter day, the two territories united into the new 'Somali Republic'. However, the Republic was only a few months old when northern dissatisfaction with the unification started to rise (Bryden 2003; WSP 2005; Ahmed 1999). There was a perception in the north that it was being politically under-represented, and the hasty merger of the two different systems of administration left little room for articulation of northern interests and furthermore did little to address the British legacy of severe economic underdevelopment in the north (Ahmed 1999).

Elite competition over state resources and related processes of the degeneration of the political party system eventually paved the way for a bloodless military coup in 1969. The coup initiated more than 20 years' dictatorship under General Mohamed Siyad Barre, which worsened the situation for Somalis in general and for the populations in the north in particular.

Geographically located far away from the economic hub of Mogadishu, and therefore politically, militarily, and economically marginalised, the clans from the north had little chance of effectively tapping into state resources and were largely excluded from the patron–client networks of Barre (Reno 2003). Simultaneously, the marginalisation of the northern clans (in particular the Isaaq and Dir) markedly worsened and became increasingly violent in its expression, especially from the late 1970s onwards.

On this basis, the northern political elite adopted a strategy of resisting rather than adapting to the Somali national state (Doornbos and Markakis 1994; Simons 1998) – a development which created a significant measure of social cohesion in terms of alliances and networks developing outside Barre's political reach (Reno 2003). Specifically, in the late 1980s, northern resistance against Siad Barre produced close cooperation between the northern customary leadership of the largest clan family in Somaliland, the Isaaq, and the regionally based resistance movement the Somali National Movement (SNM). The SNM did not operate as a distinct guerrilla front, but rather as 'an armed expression of the Isaaq people' (Prunier 1994: 62). This embeddedness of the SNM within the Isaaq communities and the lack of any substantial external funding led SNM to rely upon customary authorities. The customary authorities, which are the key clan representatives, became the driving forces behind the mobilisation of resistance among the Isaaq communities and organised a council – known as a Guurti[3] – specifically for coordinating purposes.

The SNM was one of several movements in a wider mobilisation of armed opposition, in response to Barre's increasing loss of political and economic power, and corresponding increasing reliance on violent repression. The SNM expanded rapidly as the struggle against Barre intensified during the late 1980s, and in 1988 in a 'surprise offensive' managed to capture Burco and Hargeisa. Barre reacted with an indiscriminate bombing of Hargeisa, which laid the city to ruin but also triggered an unprecedented large-scale mobilisation of support for SNM (Bradbury 2001). In 1991, Barre's support bases – internally as well as externally – had disintegrated to the extent that he was forced to flee Somalia.

This marked a critical juncture in the Somali civil war, and in the north–south conflict. Yet, peace was far from assured in Somaliland. While the northern resistance against Barre had mainly been mobilised among the Isaaq clan, segments of other clans, such as the Gardabursi and Harti, had been armed by Barre to combat the SNM. Deep divisions and fear of revenge therefore shaped the post-Barre Somaliland environment. Moreover, as the common enemy was defeated, internal divisions among the Isaaq sub-clans resurfaced. The destabilising potentials of such tensions were heightened by the post-war conditions of displacement; lack of infrastructure, social services, and governmental structures; instances of looting and livestock raiding (ongoing since the civil war); and a high number of weapons among the population. As Bradbury notes, while the mobilisation of resistance fighters along clan lines had worked as a strategy of the SNM during the war against Barre, after the war, 'the difficulties of managing multiple clan militia with no central command became readily apparent' (Bradbury 2008: 88).

The next section turns to an analysis of the shift from resistance politics to the challenges of post-conflict reconciliation in Somaliland.

The conflict resolution process

Since the end of the war against Barre, Somaliland has gone through several phases of peacebuilding and reconstruction, allowing it to gradually emerge as the most stable political entity within the Somali territories. This section first outlines key aspects and outcomes of the early local peace and reconstruction processes and discusses some of the central factors that explain these outcomes. It then moves on to explore different ways in which external actors have engaged with this 'home-grown' peace.

Reconciliation and the emergence of the Somaliland state

Within a month of the defeat of Barre in January 1991, the SNM convened the first of many clan-conferences, aimed at peace and reconstruction. It was held in Berbera and provided a platform for signalling a commitment to reconciliation politics by the liberation elite – i.e. SNM and leading Isaaq clan members – while also serving as a forum for pre-negotiations laying the foundation for a larger 'national' (i.e. Somaliland-wide) clan-conference held in Burco. The latter resulted in the declaration of Somaliland's independence from Somalia on 18 May 1991. The declaration was made by the liberation elite but was pushed forward by wider public pressure. Subsequently, the SNM central committee, headed by Cabdiraxmaan Axmad Cali – known as Tuur – formed the first Somaliland administration and was faced with the task of constructing security and a government from scratch. This was particularly challenging for an organisation that, after all, had been established as a liberation movement – not a government.[4]

While the Burco clan-conference was critical in terms of creating peace between the Isaaq and other clans in Somaliland, especially the Dir in the north and the Harti in the east, it had not addressed the grievances between Isaaq sub-clans. Therefore, internal conflicts between different factions of SNM – which had been suppressed out of necessity during the fight against Barre – soon broke out. After a little less than two years with the Tuur administration, sporadic fighting between Isaaq sub-clans was ongoing, and new irregular militias had taken up weapons and engaged in predatory activities. It was clear that the rising tensions, if left unaddressed, could have spill-over effects strong enough to undermine the longer-term project of re-establishing peace and political order in Somaliland.

Security and reconciliation thus emerged as the main objectives, and the application of customary conflict resolution mechanisms became the means to reach this objective. Against this backdrop, the customary authorities and their councils remained highly influential. They went from being mobilising forces behind the resistance against Siad Barre to developing as the driving actors behind the peace, reconciliation, and reconstruction processes. As such, the administration under Tuur increasingly relied on the Guurti's (i.e. the council of customary authorities established during the resistance against Siad Barre; see above) capacities rather than the SNM charter (Renders 2006). However, the charter in any case envisioned a political programme grounded in Somali traditions, also reflecting the historical alignments of SNM and customary authorities.

During a peace conference in Sheik in 1992 the Guurti mediated a large intra-Isaaq clan conflict that had erupted over tax revenues in the Berbera port. The leading mediating roles were taken by elders from the Gardabursi clan, so as to ensure third-party (non-Isaaq) neutrality. This formed the basis for expanding the Guurti beyond only Isaaq membership, and it was this more inclusive council that became part of a new Somaliland government the year after.

One of the key dynamics characterising peacebuilding and reconstruction in Somaliland during this 1990s period was a synergy between localised context-specific reconciliation processes and Somaliland-wide clan conferences. Thus, numerous local and regional negotiations between customary authorities from different clans dealt with civil, security, and justice issues, such as restoring collaborative relations and agreements to facilitate trade and remove roadblocks, negotiating access to grazing for livestock and reducing livestock raids, returning looted property, and reaching agreements on mutual reconciliation politics (i.e. making oaths to abstain from attacks). These negotiations were critical for containing violence on the local level and paving the way for large-scale peace conferences, bringing all the northern clans together to negotiate the pillars and institutional framework for a new political order (see Bradbury 2008:107). As explained by a Somaliland political analyst, who had been active participant in the peace processes:

> Every clan had to accept the rebirth of Somaliland, and to accept Somaliland they had to deal with the 'next door' clan, to address all the grievances and

> to exchange xeer.[5] Only then could we start to agree on how to build a state. The local and regional conferences were handling conflicts of certain areas, and these conflicts would otherwise have destabilised the whole situation.[6]

A huge clan-conference in the city of Boroma in 1993 was particularly significant in regard to providing institutional substance to Somaliland's political order. It was largely financed by the communities of Somaliland and lasted for about four months. An estimated 2,000 people attended, including 150 voting delegates from customary authorities (Bradbury 2008).

The most important results were:

- The adoption of a national charter defining a hybrid system of governance which institutionalised the Guurti council of 82 clan elders in the upper house of parliament
- The nomination of a lower house of parliament, selected on the basis of clan-representation
- The formulation and adoption of a peace charter, which 'elaborated a code of conduct for the people of Somaliland, in accordance with their traditions and Islamic values' (Bradbury 2008: 98). The charter outlined the responsibilities of the customary authorities for mediating conflicts and leading the demobilisation process. Furthermore, it demanded that all communities make an oath to refrain from attacking any other clans. In brief, the charter spelled out a 'national xeer',[7] aimed at restoring the relationships among the northern clans and also providing the foundation for political order (Menkhaus 2000; Bradbury 2008)
- The nomination of a new president, Mohamed Haji Ibrahim Egal, and vice president Daahir Rayaale Kahiin (Menkhaus 2000; WSP 2005; Bradbury 2008)

As Menkhaus rightly notes: 'By any standard, this was an impressive accomplishment for a traditional peacemaking mechanism facing entirely new types of political challenges' (Menkhaus 2000: 189).

After a more stable peace was established towards the end of the 1990s, a new constitution was drafted, which outlined the steps for a transition from a clan-based to a multi-party political system (Renders 2006). The final constitutional draft, which proposed this multi-party system as well as an independent Somaliland, was sent out to public referendum in 2001 and was endorsed. On this basis, the clan-system was reconfigured into a system whereby the Head of State and the House of Representatives are elected. The Upper House of Elders – the Guurti – remained in place, however, so as to continue to allow a balancing of party politics with clan-representation.

Somaliland has gone through significant political changes, developments, and also crises since the early years of reconciliation. During this period, the *de facto* state institutions have continuously consolidated, and Somaliland has completed three rounds of direct presidential elections and six direct elections overall, including parliamentary and local council elections. Tensions, in particular with Puntland (at times supported by Somalia), concerning territorial control cause ebbs and flows of armed conflict, yet Somaliland has remained by far the most stable and secure territory in the Somali context.

Three factors, in particular, stand out in explaining these outcomes. First, historical contingencies appear to have played a significant role. During colonial times, Somaliland mainly suffered what Prunier terms 'benign neglect' as a British protectorate (Prunier in Spears 2003: 93); and such 'neglect' in fact allowed for preserving the socio-cultural capital – i.e. customary institutions – which in turn became a key resource in later reconciliation and reconstruction processes. Moreover, during the struggle against Siad Barre in the 1970s and 1980s, the mobilisation against a 'common enemy' created a significant measure of social cohesion in terms of alliances and networks developing outside of the reach of the state. In particular, the alignment of the SNM and the customary authorities during this struggle translated into post-war collaboration, combining the efforts of reconciliation and political reconstruction. While not all segments of the Somaliland population had supported the resistance against Barre, it was clear that with the defeat of the Somali army, SNM had emerged as the winner and evidently most powerful force in the region. Consequently, the movement had no need to enforce its rule over competitors and could choose a path of reconciliation politics (Bradbury 2008: 79).

Second, the sequence of first prioritising local processes of reconciliation and letting achievements from such context-specific processes feed into wider processes of 'national' peacemaking and political reconstruction was particularly suitable in a context where centralised power and decision-making had been de-legitimised through historical experiences of abusive state practices. In brief, the absence of a state was not – as is often assumed in mainstream peacebuilding literature – an impediment to peace. Similarly, state-building was also not the precondition for peace, but rather vice versa. As Bradbury accurately observes, 'by removing the state as a primary object of conflict, social relations could be addressed through customary institutions' (Bradbury 2008: 107).

Third, and similarly challenging mainstream views, the very low level of intervention – from benign neglect during the colonial period, to very limited external interference in the reconciliation process – necessitated and facilitated heterogeneous processes of bargaining, accommodation, and cooperation between a range of different local actors (Bradbury 2008; Renders and Terlinden 2010; Moe 2011). In this regard, Somaliland illustrates that sometimes reconciliatory achievements are made possible because of the *absence* of international attempts to manage the process.

International engagement has, however, not been absent altogether, and in recent years interventions have in fact increased. The following discussion will tease out the ambiguous effects of past and recent interventions on peace in Somaliland.

International support to conflict resolution

Against the backdrop of non-recognition of the Somaliland state, donors did not as a point of departure have a strong interest in dominating peace and reconstruction agendas to the extent seen in many other post-conflict societies, including in Somalia. This has in turn made possible more flexible and low-key models of engagement. For example, the large-scale 1993 Boroma clan-conference which provided institutional substance to Somaliland's claim to independence was in fact enabled by a combination of clan-based regional facilitation and funds as well as small-scale targeted external support. The latter included air transportation made available by the United Nations Development Programme (UNDP) for delegates travelling from the eastern regions to Boroma and funds supplied by a range of foreign governments, the Norwegian, French, and US embassies, and several international non-governmental organizations (INGO) (Walls et al. 2008: 50), which helped in making the organisation of the four-month conference possible. As Walls and Elmi (2012: 13) note, 'by channeling this support through existing channels and in a manner that avoided its "politicisation", the engagement was constructive and non-disruptive, but still vital', and as such enabled autonomous peace and state making (beyond the parameters of internationally led state-*building*).

Another noteworthy example of low-key facilitative support of already ongoing local initiative is the engagement of an INGO, namely the Danish Refugee Council (DRC). In 2003 the DRC was approached by a group of Somaliland customary authorities who asked for support to begin dialogues and experience-sharing among prominent clan leaders, and to facilitate better cooperation and coordination between customary and religious leaders as well as state actors on matters of peace and security.[8] There had been an increase in revenge killings during the early 2000s, particularly in the Toghdeer region of Somaliland. Revenge killings typically happen when a clan or sub-clan involved in a conflict is unable or unwilling to pay compensation as per the Somali customary law, the Xeer, and the aggrieved clan responds by killing the perpetrator or other members of his clan. This may set off a spiral of revenge killings.

The customary authorities which approached the DRC considered that stronger joint efforts among representatives from different clans and sub-clans in Somaliland, and between them and other security providers, would be necessary to deal with this growing insecurity. Recognising the importance of the customary system as the primary source of conflict resolution, DRC decided to support the initiative. DRC was one of the first INGOs to systematically engage with this type of authority in Somaliland (despite the fact that customary authorities take care of about 80–85 per cent of everyday disputes and crime; Gundel 2006).

The first dialogue took place in the Toghdeer region in Somaliland and brought together policing actors, religious leaders, and over 100 customary authorities from five clans in this region. Interest in the initiative spread, and the Toghdeer dialogue was followed by a series of regional dialogue meetings in Sahel, Awdal, Maroodi Jeex, Sool, and Sanag regions. Later, in the mid-2000s, the initiative spread to Puntland. The role of the DRC was mainly one of facilitating the consultations by providing support and funding for logistics, such as transportation, food, and planning (lack of such basic logistics, and resources for hosting dialogues, can oftentimes be *the* barrier to local peace meetings).

During focus group discussions in Ceel Afweyn and Hargeisa districts, customary authorities that had been involved in the initiative expressed that relationships and networks between the leaders of different clans and sub-clans had been strengthened through the dialogues. Some noted that this was the first time they had an opportunity to come together, take the time to share insights and concerns over peace and security issues, and attend to long-standing unresolved clan conflicts. Following the dialogues, a number of both local and regional conflicts (in particular, cases of revenge killing and conflicts over water, grazing, and land) had been addressed in both Somaliland and Puntland (Moe and Simojoki 2013).

Also, with regard to the aim of strengthening the cooperation between the customary authorities and the Somaliland state providers, field studies have reported indications of positive developments, with a decrease in cases of revenge killings and clan protection being provided for perpetrators, coupled with a corresponding increase in the number of murder cases being handed over to, and processed by, the courts after the dialogues took place (Simojoki 2010).

Yet another example, illustrating more recent external engagement in the arena of government politics, is the role played by international actors in the deep political crisis in 2009 related to the upcoming presidential elections. Clashes occurred over the extension of the Guurti's and the president's term, the establishment of the election committee, and the annulment of voter registration. Stakes were high in terms of consolidating and demonstrating Somaliland's continued democratic progress (APD and Interpeace Regional Office for Eastern and Central Africa 2010). Here the external donors were involved in brokering a six-point agreement providing the basis for a consensus, and in enabling the formation of a new Electoral Commission. Ultimately, this 'proved critical to the process and provided the turning point in the electoral process' (APD and Interpeace Regional Office for Eastern and Central Africa 2010: 18). Again, given the condition of international non-recognition, external donors could not dictate the terms, but engaged in both assertive and supportive diplomacy, including the drafting of a 'non-paper' which subsequently was taken up as a suitable draft for the six-point memorandum that eventually was signed by the key Somaliland stakeholders (Walls and Elmi 2012; Kibble and Walls 2009; Walls 2009).

Resonating with the above examples, Somaliland analysts who have more widely reviewed international support in the Somaliland context suggest that the common features of the 'successful cases' of external intervention are: that 'external funding did not disproportionally dominate', that 'outsiders did not establish frameworks and deadlines beyond the immediate release of funds', and that the form of engagement was 'smaller in scale and (built) actively on local initiatives' (Walls and Elmi 2012: 83).

In recent years, however, a number of international actors have developed a more vested interest in Somaliland, as the stability of the polity is seen to offer a bulwark against the spread of the al-Shabaab insurgency (which is understood to pose not only a local but also an international threat). Against this backdrop, recent internationally driven counterterrorism initiatives, which have produced new securitised institutions, are cast as efforts to secure the peace in Somaliland. As will be discussed in the following, however, the effects of such initiatives on local order are in fact often far from peaceful.

New international security trends: securing the Somaliland peace – or jeopardising it?

While the need for more contextual and culturally adapted intervention approaches has long been emphasised in scholarship on peacebuilding (Mac Ginty 2008; Richmond 2009), and specifically with reference to Somaliland (Boege et al. 2009), less attention has been paid to how 'bottom-up discourse' and the vocabulary of 'peace' have been taken up by international security actors seeking to make counterterrorism and counter-insurgency approaches more flexible and capable of engaging 'local' agency and institutions (Moe 2016). When I visited Somaliland in 2014, a British security contractor explained to me that for him, Somaliland's condition of relative peace makes it an ideal entry point for interventions aimed at containing 'extremism', following an approach that focuses on 'investing in and helping indigenous communities and institutions build up the [. . .] security infrastructure. And help them combat al-Shabaab'.[9] Indeed, the influx of international security contractors, and related efforts of building up the defence sector, are on the rise in Somaliland, and are commonly framed as support for maintaining the polity's 'impressive strides towards democratic governance and stability' against 'violent crime, arms trafficking and terrorism' (Adam Smith International 2016: 13). Somaliland indeed deserves support in maintaining its stability, and beyond doubt al-Shabaab constitutes a genuine concern. Yet, the kind of institutions and practices produced by interventions that securitise capacity-building and reform efforts in the pursuing of counterterrorism are unlikely to support foundations for a sustainable inclusive peace.

One example of the far from peaceful effects is the 2012 establishment of the Rapid Response Unit (RRU), tasked with targeting al-Shabaab. This example is also more widely illustrative as it mirrors US support in the south of Somalia, and Puntland. Trained and supported by British contractors, the Somaliland RRU is far better equipped than the Somaliland forces; yet, officially it is described as 'Somaliland police', and the establishment of the RRU was thereby 'sold' as a security sector reform programming, designed to 'help Somalilanders keep their hard-won peace'.[10] This stands in stark contrast to widespread local complaints noting that the force has been used not only against al-Shabaab suspects but also as a political tool against people and institutions critical of the Somaliland political elite. Examples mentioned in my personal communication with people in Somaliland and in a report by the Human Rights Center Somaliland (2014) include a number of night-time arrests by the RRU of Somaliland citizens, including an opposition party member, a regional deputy governor, and a former Vice-Minister of the Interior. The RRU has moreover been behind several violent crackdowns on peaceful public demonstrations.[11]

Many saw the RRU as but one example of a broader trend towards a significant increase of internationally established and supported security and defence institutions, which are cast of means of securing the peace, but in fact hold risks of rather jeopardising it.

Risks highlighted include: first, the security actors created by counterterrorism support are understood as not locally embedded, and also not locally restrained or accountable. Whereas the established Somaliland security structures have evolved through domestic processes (as illustrated above), the internationally created units – such as the RRU – are new appointees, who have received substantially more training and funding than the former.[12] Moreover, people I spoke to expressed the concern that access to positions within new, internationally supported forces could become a bone of contention among clans and among other providers (this has been the case for example with regard to Oil Protection Units set up in the contested eastern regions of Somaliland).[13]

Second, while at times international support to Somaliland is framed as 'decentred support' – i.e. targeting institutions and actors beyond the level of the Mogadishu-based recognised government – counterterrorism agendas in fact tend to feed into profoundly centralising logics within Somaliland. The manner in which the RRU has been deployed as a political tool is seen as a sign of centralised and authoritarian security command, which risks having de-legitimising effects for both Somaliland government institutions and international actors. Framed as part of the Somaliland police, yet lacking a public mandate, clear command structures, or procedures for reporting arrests,[14] the RRU pointedly illustrates a wider double-sided development born out of contemporary forms of 'light footprint' counterterrorism approaches; namely, 'the centralization of coercion by externally supported yet fragmented government elites and, simultaneously, a de-bureaucratization that enables the evasion of transparency and legality' (Moe 2018: 338).

Third, Somaliland does not have a legal framework in place to define 'terrorism' or spell out the scope and procedures for counterterrorism. This, in conjunction with the un-recognised environment, put few legal constraints on international actors. In fact, the Somaliland government became the entry point for international attempts of 'updating' the legal environment, to provide the legal foundation for initiatives along the lines of the RRU. Thereby, the government has been approached by donors, with the UK taking the lead, for the endorsement of a ready-drafted 'anti-terror bill', presented as legal support to enable Somaliland to protect 'its development, rule of law, democracy and the right of its citizens to live in peace, freedom and security'.[15] The bill has been strongly criticised by local human rights activists for containing an open-ended definition of terrorism that would permit secret court hearings with no defendants and, as a result, dubious prosecutions. Furthermore, it would invest the government with powers to intercept communications and the police with powers to make arrests without warrants. As I have argued elsewhere, this exposes both the contradiction of permitting violations of civil and human rights while

> constructing such violations as peaceful and democratic measures to counter terrorism and insurgency, through the lawful enforcement of legal provisions,

> and the contradiction of seeking to install such new 'state law' through a state which is not granted *de jure* recognition in the first place.
>
> (Moe 2018: 340)[16]

Overall, these developments are apt to significantly affect how peace and order-making are understood and can be pursued. This is particularly apparent when comparing historical and contemporary dynamics in Somaliland. While the war between Somalia and Somaliland in the 1980s, and the intra-Somaliland conflicts in the 1990s, generated incentives for bargaining and consultative processes with various local constituencies, elites, and civilians, the current global geo-politics of counterterrorism, which today significantly shapes most local Somali orders, is a context in which the need for local bargaining is decreasing as selected sections of the elite instead can strike deals with external actors in order to expand security rents and coercive capacities.

Lessons learned from the case study

This chapter has shown how the Somali context is not only a showcase for failure and insecurity but also features impressive examples of decentred peace and reconstruction processes, which showcase the significance of customary reconciliation skills. It was discussed how these processes in the context of Somaliland were shaped by historical contingencies and characterised by synergies between localised reconciliation processes and wider inclusive political reconstruction. It followed that the political arrangements that emerged generally reflected, and were born out of, the settlements and accommodations achieved through the reconciliation processes.

Somaliland thereby challenges approaches that have prioritised top-down state and peacebuilding as a means of achieving lasting peace, and also serves as a reminder that it is sometimes better to limit external intervention to facilitation and allow internal processes of reconciliation, political negotiations, and institutional reform to evolve on their own. Along these lines, the chapter discussed a number of concrete examples where international engagement in Somaliland positively contributed to peace. These examples were characterised by 'low-key' engagement where external actors took facilitative and logistical roles (rather than agenda setting powers), maintained transparency, and avoided external funding or frameworks dominated processes. Such 'low key' approaches were partly prompted by the condition of official non-recognition of the state (and related avoidance of directly pursuing internationally led state-*building*).

In turn, the chapter also discussed more recent interventions that propose to 'secure' Somaliland's peace by building up counterterrorism capacities. Such interventions are rapidly on the rise, and consequently, the boundary between war and peace is becoming increasingly blurred, also well beyond Somaliland.[17] Moreover, counterterrorism and counterinsurgency approaches have acquired significant flexibility in terms of more widely engaging with actors and structures beyond formally recognised state institutions (also as these pose less legal and accountability constraints). According to Menkhaus (2014: 7), practically every polity within

Somalia has 'benefited' from internationally promoted post-9/11 security-driven institution-building to beef up counterterrorism capacities, often at the expense of human rights and development. This unavoidably has a profound impact on processes of order-making and on what forms of local 'peace' are produced.

The above analysis highlighted the counterproductive potentials of the reconceptualisation of 'peace' as counterterrorism containment by demonstrating through examples from Somaliland how such interventions have produced practices and institutions that run counter to the political negotiation and the gradual democratisation processes that have historically been key for Somaliland's peace. More widely, the current reframing of 'peace' as counterterrorism tends to sidestep policies and efforts seeking to address political and social causes behind armed conflict.[18] Of course, the tensions between counterterrorism, on the one hand, and consultation, reconciliation, and human rights, on the other, currently mark politics on a global scale. Yet, in contexts where efforts of securing a lasting peace and crafting sustainable and representative institutions are ongoing and under significant pressures from wider internal and external violent conflict dynamics and limited resources to ensure accountability (including the accountability of interveners), the stakes are particularly high.

Acknowledgements

I would like to thank the research team at the Social Research and Development Institute (SORADI) in Hargeisa for invaluable discussions and assistance in relation to conducting parts of the research that forms the basis for this chapter. Thanks also to Roger Mac Ginty and Stephanie Jänsch for reading through earlier drafts.

Notes

1 Interview with former foreign minister of Somaliland, Abdilahi Mohamed Dualeh, Addis Ababa, 16.03.08.
2 Here the term 'socio-cultural' (used for lack of a better term) also refers to profoundly *political* repertoires.
3 The concept of Guurti traditionally refers to the highest political council of titled as well as non-titled elders in pastoral Somali society (Jhazbhay 2007).
4 Interview with former general of the SNM, Hargeisa, 02.05.08.
5 Somali customary law.
6 Interview, Hargeisa, 17 April 2008.
7 Xeer is Somali customary law and is also referred to as a social contract, negotiated and agreed upon between clan linage entities (diya-paying groups).
8 Everyday 'rule of law' matters in Somaliland are shaped by legal pluralism, where religious law (shari'a), customary law (xeer), and secular law systems co-exist and interlink.
9 Author's field notes, personal communication with British security contractor, Hargeisa, Sept. 2014. See also Moe (2018: 23).
10 Author's field notes, personal communication with the British office (part of the British Embassy Mogadishu), Hargeisa, Sept. 2014.
11 Author's personal communications with local analysts and human rights activist, Hargeisa, Sept. 2014. See also Human Rights Center Somaliland (2014).
12 This is not to say that the established providers like the Somaliland police are accountable. There are concerns regarding abuse and unaccountability regarding the police as

well. This speaks to the importance of not further complicating accountability by introducing specialised forces with no clear mandate and command.

13 See Moe (2018: 338).

14 See Human Rights Center Somaliland (2014).

15 (In the name of) Republic of Somaliland, *Law on Prevention and Combatting Terrorism* (unofficial translation), Law No: xx/2012. See also Moe (2018, 340).

16 To the knowledge of the author, the law remains under consideration but has not yet been endorsed at the time of writing.

17 See, for example, Bell (2011), Charbonneau (2017).

18 See also Charbonneau (2017).

References, further reading, and links to key primary documents

Academy for Peace and Development and Interpeace Regional Office for Eastern and Central Africa. 2012. "Vote for Peace II. A Report on the 2010 Somaliland Presidential Election Process." Accessed 21 June 2018. https://apd-somaliland.org/wp-content/uploads/2014/12/vote-for-peace-II.pdf.

Adam Smith International. 2016. "Justice Security & Peacebuilding brochure." Accessed 21 June 2018. https://issuu.com/adamsmithinternational/docs/justice_security___peacebuilding_br.

Ahmed, Ishmail. 1999. "Understanding Conflict in Somalia and Somaliland." In Adebayo Adedeji (Ed.), *Comprehending and Mastering African Conflicts*, 236–257. London: Zed Books.

Bell, Colleen. 2011. "Civilianising Warfare: Ways of War and Peace in Modern Counterinsurgency." *Journal of International Relations and Development* 12 (3): 309–332.

Boege, Volker, Anne Brown, Kevin Clements, and Anna Nolan. 2009. "Building Peace and Political Community in Hybrid Political Orders." *International Peacekeeping* 16 (5): 599–615.

Bradbury, Mark. 2001. *Somaliland*. CIIR Country Report. London: The Catholic Institute for International Relations (CIIR).

Bradbury, Mark. 2008. *Becoming Somaliland*. London: Progression.

Bryden, Matt. 2003. "The Banana Test: Is Somaliland Ready for Recognition?" *Les Annales d'Ethiopie* 19: 1–24.

Call, Charles T. 2008. "Building States to Build Peace? A Critical Analysis." *Journal of Peacebuilding and Development* 4 (2): 60–74.

Charbonneau, Bruno. 2017. "Intervention in Mali: Building Peace Between Peacekeeping and Counterterrorism." *Journal of Contemporary African Studies* 35 (4): 415–431.

Doornbos, Martin, and John Markakis. 1994. "Society and State in Crisis: What Went Wrong in Somalia?" In Mohamed Abdel Rahim Mohamed Salih, and Lennart Wohlgemuth (Eds.), *Crisis Management and the Politics of Reconciliation in Somalia*. Uppsala: Nordiska Afrikainstitutet.

Gundel, Joakim. 2006. "The Predicament of 'Oday'." In *Report for Danish Refugee Council and Novib/Oxfam*. Nairobi: Oxfam.

Human Rights Center Somaliland. 2014. "Somaliland Government: Accountable to No One." Annual Report on Human Rights Situation in Somaliland.

Jhazbhay, Iqbal. 2007. "Somaliland: Post-War Nation-Building and International Relations, 1991–2006." PhD diss., University of the Witwatersrand, Johannesburg, South Africa.

Kibble, Steve, and Michael Walls. 2009. "Tradition and Modernity in Somaliland – Beyond Polarity: Negotiating a Hybrid State." Paper presented at Democratisation in Africa conference, Leeds University Centre for African Studies (LUCAS), Leeds, December.

Mac Ginty, Roger. 2008. "Indigenous Peace-Making Versus the Liberal Peace." *Cooperation and Conflict* 43 (2): 139–163.

Mamdani, Mahmood. 1996. *Citizen and Subject. Contemporary Africa and the Legacy of the Late Colonialism*. Princeton: Princeton University Press.

Menkhaus, Ken. 2000. "Traditional Conflict Management in Contemporary Somalia." In William Zartman (Ed.), *Traditional Cures for Modern Conflict: African Conflict 'Medicine'*. Boulder: Lynne Rienner Publishers.

Menkhaus, Ken. 2014. *Aid and Institution-Building in Fragile States: The Case of Somali-Inhabited Eastern Horn of Africa.* Working paper 2014/002, 1–13. Helsinki: World Institute for Development Economics Research.

Menkhaus, Ken, and Henri-Michel Yéré. 2008. "Arrangements sécuritaires locaux dans les régions somalies de la Corne de l'Afrique [Local Security Arrangements in Somali-Inhabited Areas of the Horn of Africa]." *Politique Africaine* 3: 22–43.

Moe, Louise Wiuff. 2011. "Hybrid and 'Everyday' Political Ordering: Constructing and Contesting Legitimacy in Somaliland," *Journal of Legal Pluralism* 63: 143–178.

Moe, Louise Wiuff. 2016. "The Strange Wars of Liberal Peace; Hybridity, Complexity and the Governing Rationalities of Counterinsurgency in Somalia." *Peacebuilding* 4 (1): 99–117.

Moe, Louise Wiuff. 2018. "Counter-Insurgency in the Somali Territories: The 'grey zone' Between Peace and Pacification." *International Affairs* 94 (2): 319–341.

Moe, Louise Wiuff, and Maria Vargas Simojoki. 2013. "Custom, Contestation and Co-Operation: Peace and Justice Promotion in Somaliland." *Conflict, Security & Development* 13 (4): 393–416.

Moe, Louise Wiuff. 2015. "Security in Somaliland: Between Decentred Stabilisation and External Intervention," in Hoffmann, Kasper and Louise Moe (eds.), *Protection and (In)Security beyond the State*, DIIS Report 2015 (01)

Prunier, Gerard. 1994. "Somaliland: The Birth of a New Country?" In Charles Gurdon (Ed.), *The Horn of Africa*, 61–76. London: UCL Press.

Renders, Marleen. 2006. "Traditional Leaders and Institutions in the Building of the Muslim Republic of Somaliland." PhD diss., University of Ghent, Belgium.

Renders, Marleen and Ulf Terlinden. 2010. "Negotiating statehood in a hybrid political order: The case of Somaliland." *Development and Change* 41 (4): 723–746.

Reno, William. 2003. *Somalia and Survival in the Shadow of the Global Economy*. Queen Elizabeth House Working Paper No.100. Chicago: Northwestern University.

Richmond, Oliver P. 2009. "Becoming Liberal, Unbecoming Liberalism: Liberal-Local Hybridity Via the Everyday as a Response to the Paradoxes of Liberal Peacebuilding." *Journal of Intervention and Statebuilding* 3 (3): 324–344.

Simojoki, M. Vargas. 2010. "Unlike Allies: Working with Traditional Leaders to Reform Customary Law in Somaliland." In Erica Harper (Ed.), *Working with Customary Systems: Post-Conflict and Fragile States*, 33–51. Rome: IDLO.

Simons, Anna. 1998. "Somalia: The Structure of Dissolution." In Leonardo Alfonso Villalón, and Phillip A. Huxtable (Eds.), *The African State at a Critical Juncture, Between Disintegration and Reconfiguration*, 57–75. London: Lynne Rienner Publishers.

Spears, Ian. 2003. "Reflections on Somaliland and Africa's Territorial Order." *Review of African Political Economy* 30 (95): 89–98.

Walls, Michael. 2009. "The Election: Obstacles in the Path of Somaliland's Democracy." *Journal of the Anglo-Somali Society* 46: 27–28.

Walls, Michael, and Hodan Elmi. 2012. "Indigenous Forms and Èxternal Interventions in a Somali Context." In *Reflections and Lessons of Somaliland's Two Decades of Sustained Peace, Statebuilding and Democratization*, 70–87. Hargeisa, Somaliland: SORADI & HBF Publishers.

Walls, Michael, Mohamud Omar Ali, and Koss Mohammed. 2008. "Peace in Somaliland: An Indigenous Approach to State Building." In *The Search for Peace Series*. Geneva and Hargeysa: Interpeace/Academy for Peace and Development.

WSP International Somali Programme. 2005. *Rebuilding Somaliland, Issues and Possibilities*. Eritrea: The Red Sea Press Inc.

15

SOUTH AFRICA

Adrian Guelke

Introduction

Throughout the period from the end of the Second World War, to the fall of the Berlin Wall in 1989, South Africa was a byword for racism, and the policies of its government attracted widespread international opprobrium that increased in intensity with the passage of time. The open practice of racial discrimination had by no means been confined to South Africa. However, what ensured conflict with the international community was that the *direction* of South African policies ran counter to the global rejection of racism after 1945. In the decades following the war, there was an intensification of racial discrimination in South Africa, underpinned by the racial classification of the entire population of the country and an elaborate ideology that justified the differential treatment of racially defined population groups from the cradle to the grave. In 1948, the country's overwhelmingly white electorate voted the National Party into power on its platform of apartheid. The principal aim of the new policy was to reverse the erosion of racial segregation that had taken place in South Africa during the Second World War. But apartheid amounted to more than just a revival of segregation. It contained novel elements, including seeking to control the operation of the market economy so as to prevent it from becoming an agent of integration.

The roots of white domination could be traced back to the late nineteenth century, before the creation of South Africa as a unified political entity. Decisive in establishing white control was the mineral revolution that resulted from the discoveries of diamonds and gold. It transformed the power relationship between the country's European settlers and its African natives in favour of the former. During the early years of the Union of South Africa, politics tended to revolve around divisions within the white community. However, with the triumph of Afrikaner nationalists in the 1948 elections, the conflict more clearly became one between Afrikaner and African nationalists. This conflict took a violent turn after 1960 when the two main African nationalist movements, the African National Congress (ANC) and the Pan Africanist Congress (PAC), were outlawed in the wake of the Sharpeville massacre. South Africa became a Republic in 1961, fulfilling a long-term ambition of Afrikaner nationalists. In the 1980s, the National Party government sought to broaden support for the system of white domination through the establishment of a power-sharing facade that involved the co-option of representatives of the Coloured and Indian minorities under a tri-cameral constitution.

By the end of the 1980s, it was apparent that the reforms that had been made by the government after the 1976 Soweto uprising had failed to end the country's crisis of governability. Negotiations with authentic representatives of the African majority became unavoidable. The removal of the ban on the ANC, PAC, and the South African Communist Party (SACP) followed, along with the release of Nelson Mandela from jail in February 1990. This paved the way to South Africa's far from smooth transition to democracy. The four years of the transition from February 1990 to Mandela's inauguration as the president of a fully democratic country in May 1994, were the bloodiest in South Africa's history. Yet, remarkably, there was legal continuity between the institutions that enacted apartheid and those of the democratic dispensation that came into existence in 1994.

Conflict analysis

A case might be made that conflict at the southern tip of Africa should be dated back to 1652, the year of the first permanent European settlement at the Cape, since relations between the settlers and the indigenous population were marked by friction from the outset. The settler–native divide provides one obvious way of viewing the conflict, and it remains the interpretation favoured by Africanists and the PAC. But a more serviceable set of dates for the framing of the conflict in its modern form remains those given in the remit of the Truth and Reconciliation Commission (TRC), 1 March 1960 and 10 May 1994. The starting date was chosen to ensure that the Sharpeville massacre of 21 March 1960 fell within the terms of reference of the report. The closing date coincided with Mandela's inauguration as president of a democratic South Africa.

The Sharpeville massacre, in which 69 people were shot dead outside a police station in a township in the Transvaal, was a turning point in the country's history.[1] The victims of the massacre had been participating in a PAC protest against the pass laws that controlled the influx of Africans into the urban areas. The massacre had a profound impact on external opinion. While Western governments continued to have close relations with South Africa for strategic and economic reasons, increasingly, these governments were forced to take cognisance of public hostility towards apartheid.

But the regime's loss of international legitimacy was not matched by loss of control internally. Suppression of the African nationalist movements followed the Sharpeville massacre, while the crisis led to an increase in support for the government among whites. The government responded to the challenge of an African nationalist turn towards violence by introducing harsh new security measures. Legislation was passed to permit detention without trial for lengthy periods. Torture of suspects in police custody became commonplace. The government was able to marginalise most of the opposition to its rule through the course of the decade. A study carried out for the Nixon Administration in 1969 concluded that there was no likelihood in the foreseeable future that the African nationalist movements could pose a serious threat to white rule (Kissinger 1975).

However, the apartheid regime's position of predominant power started to be eroded in the course of the 1970s. The change was a product of fundamental social and economic trends and of events, both inside South Africa and in the region. The number of whites as a proportion of the total population was continuing to decline (from 19.3 per cent in 1960 to 17.1 per cent in 1970 and 14.8 per cent in 1985). Urbanisation of the African population was also expanding, despite the operation of influx control and economic stagnation. A military coup d'état in Portugal in April 1974, which paved the way to the rapid dismantlement of the Portuguese empire in Africa, gave fresh hope to the apartheid's opponents. The failure of the government's military intervention in Angola demonstrated the limitations of South African power, as well as emboldening a new generation of internal opponents of the regime.

How this generation was able to arise in an era of repression is a significant part of the story. While the government's security measures had crushed both the ANC and the PAC inside the country, the government's own quest for legitimacy ended up by creating space for others to take their place. The government put forward its view of South Africa as a multinational state to counterpoise the liberal vision of South Africa as a common society and, in this context, the authorities mistakenly saw advocates of black power as potential allies in furthering the government's separatist ideology. The consequence was the growth of the black consciousness movement and a revival of political activism in South Africa's subordinate communities. This formed the backdrop to the outbreak of violence in Soweto outside Johannesburg.

The trigger for the revolt was the imposition of Afrikaans as a medium of instruction in African secondary schools. During a mass demonstration against the policy on 16 June 1976, police shot dead two pupils. This prompted widespread unrest across the country in which hundreds died. The Soweto uprising created an even more profound crisis for white rule than the Sharpeville massacre had done, as the initial loss of confidence in the country was not followed by a restoration of the government's authority, let alone by an economic boom. A prolonged crisis of governability followed the Soweto uprising.

Repression was not the government's sole response to the crisis. The country entered an era of what two analysts dubbed 'reform apartheid'.[2] While the government pressed ahead with its plans for granting independence to four of the ten Bantustans it had established to be the repository of African political rights, there were efforts to address some of the grievances of urban Africans through reform of the labour laws. The government also sought to broaden the base of the regime through the co-option of representatives of the Coloured and Indian minorities. To this end a new, tri-cameral constitution was put into place in the 1980s. However, this also meant that the government could not repress all political activity among blacks if it was to ensure a minimal level of credibility for the new institutions. That provided the opening for the creation in 1983 of a mass movement, the United Democratic Front (UDF), that sought the same political aim as the ANC of one-person-one-vote in a unitary state.

South Africa's aggressive policies towards its neighbours, though intended to demonstrate the country's worth in countering Soviet influence on the continent, also further alienated Western opinion. The extent of the regime's international isolation was underlined in 1986 when Congress imposed far-reaching economic sanctions on South Africa, overriding President Reagan's veto. Influencing opinion was an uprising in townships in South Africa in September 1984 in response to rent increases. By this point, it was apparent that the government's quest for legitimacy had failed both internally and internationally. That forced the government to contemplate entering into negotiations with the ANC so a new dispensation might be forged. However, its shape was by no means pre-determined and would only emerge after a prolonged power struggle.

Formed in 1912, the ANC was one of the longest standing political organisations in Africa. But it did not become a mass movement until after the Second World War. The impetus for the organisation's transformation came from the ANC Youth League, formed in 1944. The Youth League was endowed with a remarkably talented set of leaders, including Nelson Mandela, Walter Sisulu, and Oliver Tambo. The Youth League persuaded the ANC to adopt a Programme of Action in December 1949 that envisaged civil disobedience. This was put into effect in the 1952 Defiance Campaign, which the government suppressed. By this time, the National Party was in government and had begun implementing its policy of apartheid. In 1955, the ANC and a number of other organisations, which together formed the multiracial Congress Alliance, took another initiative. They adopted the Freedom Charter as a statement of their political aspirations. The government's response to this development was to charge the signatories of the Freedom Charter with treason.

Following the Sharpeville massacre, the government banned the two main African nationalist movements, the ANC and the PAC. After its prohibition the ANC went underground, attempting to sustain mass passive resistance along with its commitment to the use of exclusively non-violent methods. However, the brutal suppression by the authorities of the stay-away from work the ANC called to coincide with the proclamation of the Republic of South Africa in May 1961 prompted consideration of a resort to violence. The decision to form Umkhonto we Sizwe was made in June 1961 as a joint initiative of the SACP and a number of leading figures in the ANC. The name, Umkhonto we Sizwe (meaning Spear of the Nation in Zulu), was commonly abbreviated as MK. Initially, the MK campaign was limited to one of sabotage.[3]

While MK had little impact militarily over the next three decades and never posed a significant threat to the regime's survival, it nonetheless enhanced the reputation of the ANC politically, particularly through such spectacular attacks as the one on 1 June 1980 which damaged a plant at Sasolburg that produced oil from coal, an important symbol of the country's self-sufficiency and capacity to overcome an oil embargo. However, MK and the ANC played little part in the township uprisings in 1976 and in 1984 that did most to underline the failure of apartheid and to force the government to negotiate on the terms for a new political dispensation representative of the whole of the society.

The ANC and the SACP were not the only organisations to turn to violence after Sharpeville. In its response to Sharpeville and the suppression of peaceful political activity, the PAC made preparations for an insurrection inside the country under the name, Poqo, Xhosa for 'pure' or 'alone'. However, the government gained prior knowledge of the PAC's plans, and the insurrection was a complete failure. At the end of the 1960s, the PAC established the Azanian People's Liberation Army (APLA), which was recognised by the Organization of African Unity as a liberation movement. APLA carried out a few attacks in South Africa in the 1980s and 1990s. However, it was less effective than MK, and the indiscriminate nature of its attacks on whites alienated potential supporters.

The conflict resolution process

By the mid-1980s, the government had arrived at an impasse in its quest for legitimacy, and this provided the incentive for it to explore more radical options. The conflict resolution process in South Africa went through a number of phases. They can most conveniently be listed under the eight headings set out in Table 15.1.

Secret talks

The context in which the government began to explore the possibility of negotiations with the ANC on a new political dispensation was the boycott of the elections to the Coloured and Indian Houses in the country's tri-cameral parliament, the outbreak of serious unrest in African townships throughout the country, and the

TABLE 15.1 Phases of the South African conflict resolution process

1 – Secret talks
2 – Talks about talks
3 – CODESA
4 – The NP-ANC Pact
5 – Negotiating to a deadline
6 – Bringing in the others
7 – The final constitution
8 – Dealing with the past

external response to this crisis in the form of backing for the anti-apartheid movement across the Western world and the imposition of economic sanctions. Secret talks took place with leaders of the ANC along two parallel tracks.

One track involved Nelson Mandela, who was in prison. A meeting took place between the Minister of Justice, Kobie Coetzee, and Mandela in November 1985. Talks between Mandela and government ministers continued up to his release in February 1990. When Mandela was finally released from prison on 11 February 1990, he recognised that in his exploration of the possibility of negotiations he had gone beyond simply stating the official position of the ANC and also that he needed to allay fears of a secret deal with the government. In his first speech as a free man, he stressed that he was 'a loyal and disciplined member of the African National Congress'[4] and that the purpose of his talks with the government had solely been directed towards paving the way to negotiations between the government and the ANC. The official position of the ANC on conditions for negotiations at this time was set out in the Harare Declaration, endorsed by the Organisation of African Unity in a meeting in Zimbabwe in August 1989.

A second track of negotiations had been taking place. This comprised talks between members of the Afrikaner elite in communication with but independent of the government, and leaders of the ANC in exile, headed by Thabo Mbeki. Throughout the 1980s the ANC in exile had engaged in a diplomatic offensive to engage with different components of civil society in South Africa, including business leaders, academics, lawyers, writers, and the heads of sports organisations. Despite condemnation by government of such contacts with the ANC, members of the Afrikaner community were at the forefront of a number of these initiatives. It underscored the extent to which elite opinion in the country had moved towards acceptance of the need for an entirely new political dispensation.

Talks about talks

On 2 February 1990, President F.W. de Klerk, who had succeeded P.W. Botha in August 1989, dramatically announced in a speech to open a new session of parliament that the ban on the ANC, PAC, SACP, and a number of other organisations was being lifted and that Nelson Mandela would shortly be released from prison. A number of factors influenced President de Klerk to adopt such a radical approach. First, he calculated correctly that very dramatic changes were needed to bring about the lifting of sanctions. Second, he was influenced by the set of circumstances in which he had become president. Through the course of several months of 1989, De Klerk had been caught up in a conflict with his predecessor, as Botha declined to resign the presidency when De Klerk was elected leader of the party following Botha's resignation for health reasons. In the ensuing power struggle between the two men, Botha had been supported by the security apparatus. De Klerk would necessarily have had to rely on these personnel if he had opted instead for a new effort to suppress the African nationalist opposition. Third, De Klerk calculated (wrongly) that with the fall of the Berlin Wall, the ANC would be politically weakened by its links with the SACP and its reliance for aid on the Soviet bloc.

It was expected that the legalisation of the ANC and the release of Mandela from prison would be immediately followed by full negotiations between the government and the ANC. However, an episode in which the police opened fire on demonstrators, killing 11, in April 1990 delayed a meeting between the two sides until early May 1990. Out of the meeting, which took place over three days, came the Groote Schuur Minute, under which the two sides agreed to a peaceful process of negotiations and the government agreed to lift the state of emergency, while both sides agreed to establish a joint working group to deal with such matters as the release of political prisoners and the return of exiles. The report of the joint working group established the definition of a political offence and dealt with the question of the release of prisoners, thereby providing the basis for the Pretoria Minute, under which the ANC suspended all armed actions on 6 August 1990.

MK's ceasefire fulfilled one of the government's requirements for the setting of a formal negotiating forum. However, it did not end political violence.[5] Indeed, not only did the suspension of the armed struggle not lead to any lessening of violence, but in fact the opposite was the case. The explanation for this paradox was that agreement between the government and the ANC coincided with Buthelezi's decision to mount a direct challenge to the ANC, through the formation of the Inkatha Freedom Party (IFP). The civil war that was already raging in Natal intensified and spread to the townships of the Witwatersrand centred on the country's commercial capital of Johannesburg.

The government was subsequently embarrassed by revelations in July 1991 that it had financed and provided military training for members of the IFP. They lent weight to demands made by the ANC over the continuing violence, the outcome of which was the National Peace Accord of September 1991. This was a multilateral agreement that included the IFP. It provided for the creation of a nationwide network of volunteers to monitor the violence and assist in the resolution of local disputes that gave rise to violence. While the impact of the Accord on the level of violence was limited, it did help to clear the way to the establishment of a forum for all-party negotiations.

CODESA

Formal, multilateral negotiations are a necessary phase in practically any peace process. In South Africa's case, the name given to the forum for this process was the Convention for a Democratic South Africa (CODESA). Invitations were extended to political parties represented in the different Houses in the country's parliament and to representatives of homeland administrations, as well as to the main anti-apartheid political groupings. The PAC and parties of the extreme right boycotted CODESA. There was an initial public plenary of CODESA on 20 December 1991. Thereafter, the business of CODESA was conducted through working groups that focused on particular aspects of the transition. A wide gulf still existed between the National Party and the ANC. The National Party wanted the negotiations to provide the basis for the entrenchment of minority rights, through provisions for power-sharing and the like, while the ANC's main objective was that there should be democratic elections and that representatives of the people should draw up the country's new constitution. The National Party remained wedded to group rights as an important element in any new dispensation, while the ANC insisted on majoritarianism. The government also faced a challenge from the extreme right to the existence of CODESA. It met this challenge by holding a referendum on 17 March 1992 in which the National Party asked for a mandate to continue the negotiations. It was a controversial step to hold a vote confined to the white electorate. However, the positive outcome (with 69 per cent voting yes) did not make agreement in CODESA any easier, as, during the campaign for a yes vote, the government's position on the entrenchment of group rights had hardened.

As a consequence, agreement could not be reached, and in May the CODESA process collapsed. It was followed by the ANC's organisation of a campaign of rolling mass action. Tensions increased and there were a number of serious episodes of violence, including the Boipatong massacre in which IFP-supporting hostel-dwellers attacked and killed 38 people in an informal settlement in the township on 17 June 1992. The violence in South Africa prompted consideration of the situation by the United Nations Security Council and warnings by Western governments to the South African authorities, who were blamed for orchestrating the violence as a response to the ANC's mass action campaign. Another serious episode of violence occurred on 7 September 1992 when 29 ANC supporters were shot dead by soldiers in the Ciskei Defence Force.

The NP-ANC Pact

The crisis that gripped the process in the middle of 1992 was resolved by an agreement between President de Klerk and Nelson Mandela on 26 September 1992. The content of the agreement was less important than the signal it gave that the government and the ANC were determined to find a way of reconciling their differences. The pact was a consequence of talks that had been going on behind the scenes between the main negotiators for the government and the ANC. The Record of Understanding was followed by further bilateral agreements between the two. In this context, Slovo put forward the notion of sunset clauses as a way of bridging the divide over power-sharing. Under Slovo's proposal, there would be a transitional period in which all political parties above an agreed threshold of support would be represented in government. The ANC also gave assurances over the job security of civil servants, a major concern of government supporters. For some months, there was no attempt to revive a multi-party negotiating forum, given the headway that bilateral talks were making, but both sides recognised that a formal process would be needed to give legitimacy to what they had agreed, while they also saw it as an opportunity to secure the participation of parties that had boycotted CODESA. On 1 April 1993, the first session of the Multi-Party Negotiating Forum (MPNF) took place. In total, 26 parties took part in its deliberations.

Negotiating to a deadline

On 10 April 1993, a popular figure in the SACP, Chris Hani, was murdered by a supporter of the extreme right. The reaction in the townships to the murder threatened once again to raise the spectre that the country would become ungovernable. Mandela stepped in to appeal for calm, and it became clear at that moment that the country was dependent on his leadership to maintain any semblance of political stability. This enhanced the ANC's bargaining power in the negotiations. It was reflected in an agreement in the MPNF to give urgency to the process through providing that democratic elections would be held in the country by the end of April 1994.

The effect of the deadline was to force the parties to reach agreement as best they could on contentious issues. Considerable reliance was placed on technical committees, involving academic experts to devise solutions in line with international norms on governance and the protection of human rights. Where agreement could not be reached in terms of the rule of sufficient consensus under which the MPNF operated, the issue had to be left to be dealt with by the incoming government. However, there was agreement on an interim constitution to provide a bridge to a new era and on principles for the final constitution, but not including any commitment to power-sharing. Among the last issues on which a deal was reached was that of the integration of military forces. The agreement was that the existing South African Defence Force (SADF) would be transformed into the South African National Defence Force (SANDF) with the addition of units from the homelands and from both MK and APLA, and that the SANDF would come into being as the interim constitution took effect on 27 April 1994.[6]

Bringing in the others

Once the ANC and the National Party had reached agreement on the modalities of the transition, including the formation of the Transitional Executive Council to oversee the holding of one-person-one-vote elections under independent supervision and the detailed provisions of an interim constitution, the efforts of both became directed at securing the inclusion and participation in the elections of potential spoilers. This included the extreme right, the IFP, and homelands still holding out against being part of the new polity. Resistance to incorporation in South Africa by the leader of the independent homeland of Bophuthatswana, Lucas Mangope, had prompted strikes by civil servants fearful of the economic consequences of their exclusion from the new South Africa. A mutiny by his army followed that paved the way to the rapid reincorporation of the territory into South Africa. What happened to Mangope's bid to stay out of the process also persuaded Constand Viljoen, a leading figure on the extreme right, to register a party for the elections so as to provide a vehicle for extreme right voters. Even the IFP agreed to take part at the last possible moment, on 19 April, a week before polling was due to begin. Stickers for the IFP had to be added to the ballot papers to reflect Buthelezi's change of mind.

The efforts to ensure inclusion of the entire spectrum of opinion in the country were vindicated when voting took place at the end of April against the backdrop of an unprecedented racial truce in which people of all races patiently queued for hours on end to cast their ballots. The outcome (as shown in Table 15.2) was a triumph for both the ANC and the National Party. The ANC fell short of the two-thirds majority that would have enabled the party to draw up the final constitution without considering any input from other parties, but it suited the ANC that fears about the party's intentions were thereby allayed. The surprises included the strong showing of the IFP and the poor showing of the PAC, which had been seen as a major rival of the ANC prior to the prohibition of both parties after the Sharpeville massacre. There were some widely observed electoral irregularities, but careful handling by the Independent Electoral Commission helped to ensure the acceptability of the outcome to the main parties and hence the legitimacy of the whole process.

The last phase of any successful conflict resolution process is the consolidation of the new dispensation that the process has led to. This can only happen once a settlement has been reached and implemented and the whole process legitimised through some form of electoral process. This is also the terminal point at which a political settlement can unravel. In South Africa's case, the point of consolidation was the coming into force of the final constitution in February 1997. Even though the final constitution did not provide for power-sharing or other political guarantees for minorities that the National Party had sought when it embarked on the transition, there was wide acceptance of the constitution, not least because of the complex constitutional process that it had gone through.

The drawing up of the final constitution was one of the primary functions that had been entrusted to the institutions elected under the terms of the country's interim constitution in April 1994. The parliament established under the interim constitution was a bicameral one, with a National Assembly of 400 members, elected by proportional representation across the country, and a Senate composed of ten representatives from each of the nine provinces the country had been divided into. The Constituent Assembly tasked with drawing up the final constitution was composed of the National Assembly and Senate sitting together. The ANC did not have on its own the two-thirds majority required for the adoption of the final constitution. However, the provision for a referendum in the event of deadlock

TABLE 15.2 General election results, 1994*

Party	*Seats*	*Percentage of votes*
African National Congress	252	62.6
National Party	82	20.4
Inkatha Freedom Party	43	10.5
Freedom Front	9	2.2
Democratic Party	7	1.7
Pan Africanist Congress	5	1.2
African Christian Democratic Party	2	0.5

* Only listing parties winning seats in the National Assembly.

provided a powerful incentive for the parties to reach agreement. The requirement that the Constitutional Court should certify that the constitution was compliant with the principles set out in the interim constitution provided further protection for the opposition parties. In fact, the court declined to certify the constitution as originally drafted and insisted on a number of amendments to secure full compliance with the 34 principles. These were duly made before the constitution came into force.

Dealing with the past

The most internationally eye-catching aspect of post-apartheid South Africa was not the drawing up of the final constitution, which received very little attention outside the country, but the manner in which the new government sought to address the issue of dealing with the past through the establishment of the Truth and Reconciliation Commission (TRC). The TRC had its origins in a short epilogue to the interim constitution. It was headed 'National Unity and Reconciliation' and its key sentence stated: 'In order to advance such reconciliation and reconstruction, amnesty shall be granted in respect of acts, omissions and offences associated with political objectives and committed in the course of the conflict in the past'.[7] The whole of this portion of the interim constitution was composed by two assistants to the ANC and National Party chief negotiators in the final days before the adoption of the interim constitution in November 1993. It was more a statement of aspirations than a legally enforceable commitment.

The epilogue did not put forward a mechanism for the implementation of amnesty. The choice of the mechanism of the TRC was a decision made by the ANC. It was put into effect under the Promotion of National Unity and Reconciliation Act of 1995. Both the National Party and the IFP opposed the setting up of the TRC and afforded it minimal cooperation in practice. However, because of the TRC's connection to the interim constitution, a very common misconception is that the TRC was the product of agreement among the parties. The National Party's hostility towards the setting up of the TRC was encapsulated in a comment by F.W. de Klerk, now one of two Deputy Presidents, that it risked tearing the stitches from the wounds of the past that were beginning to heal.

The TRC began its work in December 1995. Three committees were established to carry out its mandate. The Committee on Human Rights Violations was to gather information and hold hearings with a view to producing a comprehensive report on the nature, cause, and extent of human rights violations between 1960 and 1994. The Committee on Amnesty had responsibility for adjudicating on applications for amnesty in respect of actions carried out between 1 March 1960 and 10 May 1994. The Committee on Reparation and Rehabilitation was asked to make recommendations for compensation for victims and for suitable symbolic reparation in the form of memorials or monuments. From its first public hearing on 15 April 1996 to the presentation of its final report on 29 October 1998, the TRC attracted huge coverage.[8]

Lessons to be learned from the case study

There are a number of ways in which the South African transition might be seen as providing lessons applicable to other cases of violent conflict and their resolution. Some elements, such as the balance of power, the normative dimension, and leadership, play a role in most peace processes. More specific to the South African case was the confounding of expectations. However, it would be a mistake to regard any of these elements as establishing a model that could be used as a template, particularly as there were aspects of South Africa's successful peace process that by their nature cannot be replicated. For example, the power struggle that occurred between Botha and De Klerk in 1989 arose in unusual circumstances due to the former's recovery from illness that could not possibly have been predicted or factored into any model for conflict resolution. Its contribution to South Africa's liberalisation was simply serendipitous. De Klerk's miscalculation of the impact of the end of the Cold War on the ANC's standing can be seen in a similar light (Sparks 1994).

The commonest term used to describe South Africa's transition, both at the time of Mandela's inauguration and since, has been miracle.[9] It reflected how unexpected the transition to majority rule through a process of negotiations had been. It had long been considered a truism of South African politics that the white minority would never voluntarily surrender power, and a long-established assumption had existed that apartheid would come to an end in a racial bloodbath. This nightmarish scenario helped to influence the conduct of the principal political actors during crises in the country's transition, when the need for the parties to step back from the brink of the abyss was very widely acknowledged. The impact on the conduct of the political leaders was reflected in their determination to maintain open lines of communication with their adversaries, notwithstanding public hostilities. An example was the role that the relationship between Cyril Ramaphosa (for the ANC) and Roelf Meyer (for the National Party) played in the aftermath of the breakdown of CODESA and then of the Boipatong massacre.

The balance of forces in any conflict cannot be ignored and tends to set the parameters within which talks on a settlement take place. If one side or the other holds out the hope of prevailing by coercive force, then the prospects for negotiations are likely to be poor. The converse of that is encapsulated in Zartman's influential concept of a hurting stalemate.[10] However, the fit with the South African case is not perfect. The more future-oriented notion of mutually enticing opportunities was arguably of greater relevance. A common observation made by analysts of the South African transition was that in the 1990s the government had possessed the power to resist majority rule for many more years (Adam et al. 1997). Reasons for the government to embark on negotiations stemmed from its recognition that demographic trends would continue to weaken its position and that both apartheid and reform apartheid had failed, while the stagnation of the economy and the prospect of continuing sanctions provided additional incentives. And, significantly, when President de Klerk embarked on the transition, he clearly did not envisage that it would result in majority rule. Further, the government considered the end of the Cold War as presenting the opportunity for avoiding such an outcome.

Settlements that simply reflect the existing balance of forces in a society and have no independent normative foundation are unlikely to prove durable. The obvious reason is that over time the balance of forces in a society is likely to change, and if the force of circumstances is the sole incentive for parties to maintain their adherence to a settlement, their defection from the settlement and its breakdown are likely to follow any change in the distribution of power. An advantage enjoyed by the ANC during South Africa's transition was that its demand for one-person-one-vote in an undivided country was in line with prevailing international norms. At the same time, the impact of globalisation and the consensus behind the pursuit of a neoliberal macro-economic strategy provided the white minority with guarantees that were as valuable to protecting white economic interests as a political veto would have been.

Peace processes require a change in relations between formerly strongly antagonistic parties. That means that leaders who are capable of persuading their supporters to adopt a different attitude towards former enemies are necessary in any successful process of conflict resolution. South Africa was fortunate that both Mandela and De Klerk were exceptionally adept and forward-looking in their leadership. Finally, while South Africa is justifiably seen as one of the most successful cases of conflict resolution in the post-Cold War world, it is also important to acknowledge what the transition did not achieve. The country has not ceased to be highly polarised along racial lines, and South Africa remains both a very violent and highly unequal society. Under President Jacob Zuma, who came to office in 2009, corruption has loomed even larger as an issue than crime or inequality. However, the election of Cyril Ramaphosa as President of the ANC in December 2017 and the party's choice as Zuma's successor as President of South Africa holds out the prospect that corruption at the highest level, encapsulated in the illuminating concept of state capture, will be addressed.

Notes

1 For an excellent account of the massacre and its repercussions, see Lodge (2011).
2 See Giliomee and Schlemmer (1989).
3 Mandela was convicted with others of engaging in a campaign of sabotage directed at the violent overthrow of the government and sentenced to life imprisonment.
4 ANC: www.anc.org.za/show.php?id=4520
5 For monthly totals of political fatalities in South Africa between 1985 and 1996, see Sidiropoulos et al. (1997).
6 MK contributed 22,000 personnel out of a total in the SANDF of 130,000.
7 See quoted in full in Spitz and Chaskalson (2000).
8 See the account of Krog (1998).
9 See, for example, Waldmeir (1997).
10 See, for example, Zartman (2008).

References, further reading, and links to key primary documents

Adam, Heribert, Frederik van Zyl Slabbert, and Kogila Moodley. 1997. *Comrades in Business: Post-Liberation Politics in South Africa*. Cape Town: Tafelberg.

ANC. "Nelson Mandela's Address to Rally in Cape Town on His Release from Prison, 11 February 1990." www.anc.org.za/show.php?id=4520.

Giliomee, Hermann, and Lawrence Schlemmer. 1989. *From Apartheid to Nation-Building.* Cape Town: Oxford University Press.

Kissinger, A. Henry. 1975. "National Security Study Memorandum 39." In Barry Cohen, and Mohammed A. El-Khawas (Eds.), *The Kissinger Study of Southern Africa.* Nottingham: Spokesman Books. The book reproduced the NSC study in full.

Krog, Antjie. 1998. *Country of My Skull.* London: Jonathan Cape.

Lodge, Tom. 2011. *Sharpeville an Apartheid Massacre and Its Consequences.* Oxford: Oxford University Press.

Sidiropoulos, Elizabeth, Anthea Jeffery, Shaun Mackay, Rory Gallocher, Herma Forgey, and Cheryl Chipps. 1997. *South Africa Survey 1996/97.* Johannesburg: South African Institute of Race Relations.

Sparks, Allister. 1994. *Tomorrow is Another Country: The Inside Story of South Africa's Negotiated Revolution.* Sandton: Struik Book Distributors.

Spitz, Richard, and Michael Chaskalson. 2000. *The Politics of Transition: A Hidden History of South Africa's Negotiated Settlement.* Oxford: Hart Publishing.

Waldmeir, Patti. 1997. *Anatomy of a Miracle: The End of Apartheid and the Birth of the New South Africa.* London: Viking.

Zartman, I. William. 2008. "The Timing of Peace Initiatives: Hurting Stalemates and Ripe Moments." In John Darby, and Roger Mac Ginty (Eds.), *Contemporary Peacemaking: Conflict, Peace Processes and Post-War Reconstruction*, 2nd edn, 22–35. Basingstoke: Palgrave Macmillan.

Further reading

Abel, L. Richard. 1995. *Politics by Other Means: Law in the Struggle against Apartheid, 1980–1994.* New York: Routledge.

Adam, Heribert, and Kogila Moodley. 1993. *The Negotiated Revolution: Society and Politics in Post-Apartheid South Africa.* Johannesburg: Jonathan Ball.

Barber, James. 1999. *South Africa in the Twentieth Century: A Political History – In Search of a Nation State.* Oxford: Blackwell.

Barber, James, and John Barratt. 1990. *South Africa's Foreign Policy: The Search for Status and Security 1945–1988.* Cambridge: Cambridge University Press.

Beinart, William. 1994. *Twentieth-Century South Africa.* Cape Town: Oxford University Press.

Butler, Anthony. 2009. *Contemporary South Africa*, 2nd edn. Basingstoke: Palgrave Macmillan.

Davenport, Thomas, and Christopher Saunders. 2000. *South Africa: A Modern History*, 5th edn. Basingstoke: Palgrave Macmillan.

Dubow, Saul. 2014. *Apartheid, 1948–94.* Oxford: Oxford University Press.

Friedman, Steven, and Doreen Atkinson. (Eds.). 1994. *The Small Miracle: South Africa's Negotiated Settlement.* Johannesburg: Ravan Press.

Giliomee, Hermann. 2003. *The Afrikaners: Biography of a People.* Cape Town: Tafelberg.

Guelke, Adrian. 1999. *South Africa in Transition: The Misunderstood Miracle.* London: IBTauris.

Guelke, Adrian. 2005. *Rethinking the Rise and Fall of Apartheid: South Africa and World Politics.* Basingstoke: Palgrave Macmillan.

Harvey, Robert. 2001. *The Fall of Apartheid: The Inside Story from Smuts to Mbeki.* Basingstoke: Palgrave Macmillan.

Jeffery, Anthea. 1997. *The Natal Conflict: 16 Years of Conflict.* Johannesburg: South African Institute of Race Relations.

Keegan, Timothy. 1996. *Colonial South Africa and the Origins of the Racial Order.* Cape Town and Johannesburg: David Philip.

Lipton, Merle. 1986. *Capitalism and Apartheid: South Africa, 1910–86.* Aldershot: Wildwood House.

Lodge, Tom. 2002. *Politics in South Africa: From Mandela to Mbeki*. Cape Town: David Philip.

Mandela, Nelson. 1994. *Long Walk to Freedom*. London: Little Brown and Company.

Matisonn, John. 2015. *Gods, Spies and Lies: Finding South Africa's Future Through Its Past*. Vlaeberg: Missing Ink.

Minter, William. 1994. *Apartheid's Contras: An Inquiry into the Roots of War in Angola and Mozambique*. Johannesburg: Witwatersrand University Press.

Nolutshungu, C. Sam. 1982. *Changing South Africa: Political Considerations*. Manchester: Manchester University Press.

O'Meara, Dan. 1996. *Forty Lost Years: The Apartheid State and the Politics of the National Party 1948–1994*. Randburg: Ravan Press.

Posel, Deborah. 1991. *The Making of Apartheid 1948–1961: Conflict and Compromise*. Oxford: Clarendon Press.

Potter, Elaine. 1975. *The Press as Opposition: The Political Role of South African Newspapers*. London: Chatto and Windus.

Rich, Paul. 1996. *State Power and Black Politics in South Africa, 1912–51*. Basingstoke: Palgrave Macmillan.

Seekings, Jeremy. 2000. *The UDF: A History of the United Democratic Front in South Africa, 1983–1991*. Claremont: David Philip.

Sisk, D. Timothy. 1995. *Democratization in South Africa: The Elusive Social Contract*, Princeton, NJ: Princeton University Press.

Sparks, Allister. 2003. *Beyond the Miracle: Inside the New South Africa*. Johannesburg and Cape Town: Jonathan Ball Publishers.

Steinberg, Jonny. 2008. *Thin Blue: The Unwritten Rules of Policing South Africa*. Johannesburg and Cape Town: Jonathan Ball Publishers.

Terreblanche, Sampie. 2002. *A History of Inequality in South Africa, 1652–2002*. Pietermaritzburg: University of Natal Press.

Welsh, Frank. 2000. *A History of South Africa*. London: Harper Collins.

Links to key documents of transition

African National Congress. Accessed October 2016. www.anc.org.za/. This website provides access to the party documents in the lead up to and during the transition.

O'Malley Archive. Accessed October 2016. www.nelsonmandela.org/omalley/index.php/site/q/03lv00000.htm. This website provides a vast array of material on the transition, including interviews and a detailed chronology.

South African Constitution. Accessed October 2016. www.gov.za/documents/constitution/constitution-republic-south-africa-1996-1. This provides the text of the constitution that came into force in 1997, as well as of previous constitutions, including the interim constitution of the transition.

Truth and Reconciliation Commission. Accessed October 2016. www.justice.gov.za/trc/. This official website provides access to the TRC's huge archive of material, as well as the TRC multi-volume final report.

16
SRI LANKA

David G. Lewis

Introduction

On 22 February 2002, after more than 25 years of armed conflict, the Liberation Tigers of Tamil Eelam (LTTE) and the Sri Lankan government signed a ceasefire agreement (CFA). The two sides began talks, and there were genuine hopes that the peace process might resolve the long-standing separatist conflict through peaceful negotiations. However, peace talks soon stalled over fundamental political disagreements, and by late 2005 the peace process had effectively broken down. After the election of President Mahinda Rajapaksa in 2006, the government began a full-scale counterinsurgency campaign, and on 3 January 2008 the government unilaterally abrogated the CFA, formally ending the peace process. In May 2009, government forces finally defeated the LTTE in a violent military assault on LTTE positions, accompanied by mass killings of civilians and allegations of war crimes. The result was an 'authoritarian peace', in which mass armed violence was ended and the political situation stabilised, but the authorities largely failed to address continuing grievances among minority Tamils.

The Sri Lankan peace process has become a key case study in a growing debate about the nature of post-liberal peace, particularly the apparent shift in approaches to peacebuilding from liberal to illiberal forms of conflict management (Goodhand 2010; Goodhand et al. 2010; Lewis 2010; Lewis et al. 2018; Sørbø et al. 2011; Piccolino 2015). The basic tenets of the Sri Lankan peace process – third-party mediation by Norway, a strong role for civil society and track II negotiations, a commitment to conflict resolution through peaceful negotiation in neutral venues with parity among parties to the peace talks – were classic components of a liberal peace process. The reasons behind the collapse of the peace process into renewed war, the nature of the subsequent counterinsurgency, and the sustainability of the post-conflict political order are all highly contested. While there is broad agreement that domestic politics, particularly the rise in influence of Sinhalese nationalist sentiments, played a primary role in the demise of the peace process (Goodhand 2010), the reasons why they were able to gain popular support and the extent to which international factors played a role are all disputed.

One area of critique has focused primarily on the role of the international community. Perhaps the most radical critique of the peace process argues that the location of the peace process within a broadly Westphalian philosophy of international relations ensured that it would always be hostile to the legitimate aspirations of Tamils for self-determination (Fernando 2014; Rampton and Nadarajah 2017). In this view, the underlying tenet of international negotiations – that Sri Lanka's territorial integrity was essentially non-negotiable – made a relapse into war inevitable. A very different view, but also focused on the international system, points to a geopolitical shift of power away from Western, liberal powers towards China and other 'rising powers' that made it easier for the Sri Lankan government to resort to war and to defend its position in the UN and other bodies (Lewis 2010). A third area of discussion focused on the international examines the role of external meditation in peace processes and has led to some soul-searching among peace negotiators, particularly for the key negotiator, Norway, about their future engagement in complex peace processes (Sørbø et al. 2011).

A second area of critique focuses on the design and implementation of the peace process in the national context (Sørbø et al. 2011). One area of discussion addresses inclusivity. The Sri Lankan peace process was exclusive and narrowly defined, imposing a bipolar framework on a myriad of complex conflicts and tensions in the post-colonial state. Parties excluded from the talks – particularly Sinhala nationalist forces – used criticism of the peace process to mobilise and gain popular support (ICG 2006). Another area of debate involves attention to human rights abuses and questions of internal politics on both sides. Negotiators and parties to the process overlooked human rights abuses by both parties, but there was particular reluctance to confront the LTTE, for fear of upsetting the peace process (Keenan 2007). This debate also has more and less radical positions. For some, with hindsight, there were problems in implementation, sequencing, and design that might have been addressed differently, but the overall effort was still worthwhile. A more critical position, however, argues that the poor design and implementation of the process contributed to the subsequent turn to full-scale military counterinsurgency (Lewis 2010).

Conflict analysis

The analysis of the conflict is highly contested, both among scholars and within the different traditions largely represented by Sinhala and Tamil political movements. A simple bipolar description of the conflict is based on an historic ethnic divide on the island between the majority Sinhala community, who are traditionally Buddhist in faith and inhabit largely the central and southern regions of the country, and an ethnic Tamil community, predominantly settled in the north and east, who primarily practice Hinduism; both groups have sizeable Christian minorities. Even the demographics are disputed. The last full census was conducted in 1981, and internal and external displacement of populations has caused significant shifts in population. In 1981, Sri Lankan Tamils constituted about 12.7 per cent of the population, with a majority living in the north and east of the island. The Sinhalese made up 74 per cent, while 'Upcountry' Tamils – communities brought into Sri Lanka as indentured labour by the British in the late nineteenth century – formed 5.5 per cent and Tamil-speaking Muslims formed some 7.3 per cent (ICG 2006).

At its most simplistic, the four 'Eelam Wars' between 1983 and 2009 that together are considered to constitute the Sri Lankan civil war were a struggle over territory between an armed separatist movement, the LTTE, which aimed to establish an independent Tamil homeland, and successive Sri Lankan governments, dominated by Sinhalese political leaders, who sought to maintain the country as a unitary state. Ethnicity had already become a salient political divide following the introduction of universal suffrage in 1931 (Spencer 2008). Following independence from Britain in 1948, ethnicity became the most salient cleavage at elections, with Sinhalese political parties engaged in 'ethnic outbidding' against each other, each advocating nationalist policies, including the disenfranchisement of upcountry Tamils in 1949, the Sinhala-only language law of 1956, and increasing constraints on employment of Tamils in the new state apparatus and restrictions on their entry to university (DeVotta 2004). This increasing marginalisation of Tamils provided the impetus for a powerful nationalist movement, which eventually developed into armed militancy against the Sri Lankan state.

However, this binary view of ethnic and political divisions is a highly simplistic framework through which to understand Sri Lanka's multiple conflicts. Both the civil war of 1983–2009 and the peace process of 2002–2006 can also be understood as representing the suppression of a whole set of other conflicts within each ethnic community by the reification of one bipolar conflict regarding the territorial division of the state. As Uyangoda (2011) has argued, the civil war is best understood as a crisis of state-building, or even of two-state-building projects, that of the Sinhalese polity in the south and a parallel process among Tamils in the north. The crisis of the legitimacy and identity of the post-colonial state emerged in a wide range of conflicts informed by multiple cleavages, not only that of ethnicity. In the 1960s and 1970s, class and revolutionary movements, inspired by issues of distributive justice, were nevertheless intertwined with issues of ethnicity and failed to overcome the ethnic divide (Spencer 2008). A mass rebellion by the Sinhalese Maoist movement, the Janatha Vimukthi Peramuna (JVP), in 1971 was brutally suppressed by the military, representing a significant shift towards the normalisation of violence and militarisation of Sri Lankan society.

The JVP uprising demonstrated the deep divisions with Sinhalese society. Political divisions ran deep, particularly between the leftist Sri Lankan Freedom Party (SLFP), which represented rural voters in the south and claimed to be more representative of authentic Sinhalese communities, and its main political rival, the United National Party (UNP), the party of the urban English-speaking Colombo elite and of business. Although it was the UNP that launched the 2001 peace process and an

SLFP administration that presided over the 2006–2009 war, previous UNP administrations had also been deeply implicated in episodes of anti-Tamil violence. The ability of both parties to appeal to nationalist constituencies ensured that support for extreme nationalist parties, such as the JVP – and a later party, shaped by militant Buddhism, the Jathika Hela Urumaya (JHU) – was always relatively limited; such parties were capable of mobilising vocal opposition to conciliatory policies and setting the political agenda, particularly during elections. The JVP and the JHU became the most powerful opponents of the peace process and played significant roles in its collapse (DeVotta and Stone 2008; ICG 2007b). Moreover, the project of a unitary Sinhala-Buddhist state promoted by the JHU became part of the political mainstream, particularly under the SLFP government of President Rajapaksa.

The rise of the JVP in the south illustrated the extent to which the conflicts in Sri Lanka were intertwined crises of ethnic politics, post-colonial identities, and socio-economic questions. During the 1960s and 1970s, the SLFP led a socialist economic policy, which restricted private sector business and vastly expanded the state bureaucracy. This both closed off the private sector as an area for ethnic Tamils to fulfil aspirations and led to a rapid Sinhalisation of the state, as patronage networks and ethnicity-based recruitment became widespread. However, more pro-market policies under the UNP after 1977 did little to undermine ethnic cleavages: indeed, some argue that the pursuit of market reforms also increased the Sinhalisation of the state. Moreover, many Tamils viewed state development programmes, such as the huge Mahaweli dam programme, as vehicles for more Sinhalese settlement in traditional Tamil homelands. Certainly, such projects increased the competition over land and water that lay behind many local ethnic tensions (Bandarage 2008).

In the north, Tamil activists claimed that the possibility of campaigning for change by peaceful means had been largely exhausted by the early 1970s, after successive government crackdowns. The new Constitution of 1972 consolidated the 'Sinhala-only' language policy and imposed a duty on the state to protect and foster Buddhism (Coomaraswamy 2013: 126–129). It contributed to a new radicalism, evident in the adoption by Tamil leaders of the 1976 Vaddukoddai resolution, which advocated an independent Tamil state. The commitment to a separate state (Tamil Eelam) remained the primary aim of the LTTE throughout the war and the peace process, although discussions were beginning about potential confederal or federal solutions to the conflict. The LTTE refused to permit debate with Tamil political leaders calling for different models of devolution. In 1999, the LTTE assassinated the moderate Tamil leader Neelan Tiruchelvam, who had authored a more moderate proposal for Tamil autonomy within the Sri Lankan state.

Some of the underlying grievances of Tamils over language and university admissions were addressed in a series of concessions won by Tamil parliamentary parties in 1977–1978. The changes were too late and too limited to calm growing militancy among Tamil youth, particularly in the Jaffna peninsula, which had already entered a cycle of violence between state and rebel forces. The LTTE, led by the charismatic Velupillai Prabhakaran, was just one of many militant groups active on the Jaffna peninsula in the 1970s. They first came to prominence through the assassination of Alfred Duraiappah, the mayor of Jaffna, in 1975, and soon gained a reputation as the best organised and most ruthless of the new militants. Rebel attacks sparked government counter-actions and mass pogroms and riots, including the deliberate burning of Jaffna library in 1981. After LTTE militants killed 13 Sri Lankan policemen in Jaffna in July 1983, there were mass communal pogroms in Colombo and other southern districts against ethnic Tamils. Estimates of those killed in the riots varied from 400 to 3,000. Many Tamils fled the country after the 'Black July' events, creating a highly politicised diaspora in the UK, Canada, and other Western countries, which proved to be a significant source of funding for militant activities in Sri Lanka.

After 1983, sporadic militant attacks developed into a full-scale guerrilla war, punctuated by attacks on civilians, such as the 1984 Kent and Dollar Farm massacre, when militants hacked to death hundreds of civilians at night, and the 1985 killing of over 100 civilians at the Jaya Sri Maha Bodhi shrine at Anuradhapura. The massacres prompted brutal government responses, in what became a self-sustaining cycle of violence and revenge. Militants effectively took control of large parts of the Jaffna peninsula, the heart of Tamil life in the north of the country. A major military offensive by the government in 1987 might have succeeded in retaking control of Jaffna from militant groups but for the intervention of the Indian government, which put pressure on the Sri Lankan government to halt military activities. India, which had covertly armed and trained many Tamil militant groups, pressured the government into signing the Indo–Sri Lanka Peace Accord of 29 July 1987, which provided important concessions to the Tamils, including territorial autonomy in the north-east of the island, through the 13th amendment to the Constitution. Militant groups were to disarm and an Indian peacekeeping force (IPKF) was introduced into conflict-affected areas. However, the Indian intervention quickly turned into a disaster, after the LTTE refused to disarm and became involved in a conflict with Indian troops; the government, meanwhile, faced another JVP-led uprising in the south.

The consequences of the IPKF's intervention in Sri Lanka were far-reaching. In 1991, an LTTE suicide bomber assassinated former Prime Minister Rajiv Gandhi, in Tamil Nadu. Thereafter, although India never intervened militarily, the sympathy of official India and particularly of the Gandhi dynasty for the Tamil political struggle and for the LTTE dissipated considerably. More significantly, in the short term, the rapid withdrawal of the IPKF allowed the LTTE to seize control of large swaths of territory in the north and east and to begin to establish a *de facto* state (Stokke 2006). From 1990 to 2001, government forces faced the LTTE in two long periods of military confrontation, sometimes termed 'Eelam War II' and 'Eelam War III'. The wars were marked by enormous brutality, frequent massacres, and ethnic cleansing. The LTTE dominated Tamil politics and asserted its claim to be the sole representative of Sri Lankan Tamils through a campaign of violence and killing of other Tamil political figures (Hoole et al. 1988). The LTTE attacked not only Sinhalese civilians (assassinations included Sri Lankan President Premadasa in 1993) but also Muslims, who also traditionally inhabited the east and north of the island. In 1990, in an act of ethnic cleansing, the LTTE forced over 70,000 Muslims to leave Jaffna. The Muslim community had little political consciousness until the

1980s, when the Sri Lankan Muslim Congress (SLMC) was formed to advocate for better representation of Muslim interest, and as a defence against the LTTE (Vellaithamby 2006). Relations between Muslims and the LTTE were fatally damaged by the ethnic cleansing in Jaffna and several massacres, particularly in Eastern Province (ICG 2007a; McGilvray 2011). The failure to represent Muslim interests in the peace process became a growing source of tension in the negotiations after 2003.

There were hopes of a breakthrough in the conflict following the election of SLFP leader Chandrika Kumaratunga in 1994. Initial talks with the LTTE broke down in 1995 amid mutual recriminations, and were followed by a new government military offensive, dubbed the 'War for Peace'. The Sri Lankan military's campaign had early successes but soon ground to a halt against the LTTE's effective guerrilla campaign. The LTTE launched a new campaign of terrorist bombings, including numerous suicide bombings, killing hundreds of civilians in attacks on the Central Bank in Colombo in 1996, the World Trade Centre in 1997, and the Temple of the Holy Tooth in Kandy in 1998. The LTTE also held the advantage in conventional warfare, despite the makeshift nature of its armed forces. The extreme nature of the violence gave the conflict a momentum of its own, with each violent attack by the rebels prompting counter-attacks by government forces. By the late 1990s, the military advantage began to swing towards the LTTE. The LTTE enjoyed several spectacular military successes, winning the battle of Elephant Pass in 2000 against superior conventional forces, and culminating in a daring raid on Katanayake international airport near Colombo in 2001, which destroyed almost half of the country's aircraft. Despite the failure of the 'War for Peace' policy, President Kumaratunga was narrowly re-elected in 1999, perhaps boosted by popular sympathy after she was wounded in an LTTE assassination attempt earlier that year. But the SLFP lost parliamentary elections in December 2001, with UNP leader Ranil Wickremasinghe becoming prime minister in 2001 after running a pro-peace campaign.

By 2001, the conflict appeared to many observers have reached a moment of 'ripeness' for resolution. On the government side, there was a widespread view that the war was militarily unwinnable and that a political solution was required. The attack on Colombo airport badly damaged the tourist industry, and the economy went into recession. Although the war had developed a political economy of its own, the damage caused by LTTE attacks to the economy outweighed any influence of the war economy (Sørbø et al. 2011: 24). For the LTTE, the peace process offered a possibility of turning military success into political recognition, including international legitimacy. Having lost India's support, the LTTE faced a hostile international environment, compounded by the US announcement that it was launching a War on Terror in the aftermath of the terrorist attack by Al-Qaeda on New York in September 2001. The LTTE undoubtedly believed that they had an opportunity to consolidate their existing territorial gains and achieve a new political status quo. In retrospect, it is clear that neither side was as ready for genuine negotiations as some external actors believed. Whatever their many political differences, Sinhalese politicians of all parties were still united in their opposition to Tamil secession. The LTTE, meanwhile, remained committed to an independent Tamil state.

The conflict resolution process

Using an external mediator was widely seen as an important first step in bridging this divide. In 1999 the Kumaratunga government had secretly asked Norway to engage in talks with the LTTE. Norwegian diplomats began a process of shuttling between LTTE representatives in exile and political leaders in Colombo, attempting to broker a ceasefire (Sørbø et al. 2011). However, it was only with the election of Prime Minister Wickremasinghe in 2001 that there was a real shift in policy. The LTTE surprised everybody with a unilateral ceasefire in December 2001, and a Ceasefire Agreement was concluded by the two sides in February 2002. The CFA was a major breakthrough after decades of war. The two sides agreed 'the total cessation of all military action', to be monitored by a Sri Lanka Monitoring Mission (SLMM), staffed by around 70 personnel from Nordic states (CFA 2002). It had offices across the north and east of the country and was permitted to travel freely to report on any CFA violations. In this aspect, the CFA was relatively successful, with direct attacks by the LTTE and government forces largely ceasing until late 2005. The CFA also agreed the opening of long-closed transport corridors, including the main Jaffna–Kandy road, and allowed both civilians and unarmed combatants to move freely across lines once more. The CFA had several immediate positive impacts, not least an end to the everyday violence and military activity on fronts in the north and east of the country, and increased freedom of trade across the country. The government set up a Secretariat for Coordination of the Peace Process, SCOPP, to support the process from the government side.

The most controversial aspects of the CFA were the benefits it granted to the LTTE. The agreement recognised existing frontlines, effectively entrenching the LTTE as the sole governing body in areas under its control. Although the CFA ordered parties to 'abstain from hostile acts against the civilian population, including such acts as torture, intimidation, abduction, extortion and harassment', the LTTE continued its long-standing practice of recruiting child soldiers, extorting Tamil and Muslim businesses, and mounting political assassinations of its rivals. The vast majority of recorded violations of the CFA were by the LTTE. Of 1,996 complaints to the SLMM in 2003, 670 concerned the recruitment of children by the LTTE as soldiers (Höglund 2005: 161). Operating in conditions of constant warfare, the LTTE had developed a highly authoritarian regime, which controlled all media production, permitted no dissent, and punished any political deviation severely. Using the protection of the CFA, the LTTE further solidified its claim to *de facto* statehood, developing a police force, a judiciary, and other rudimentary government structures, but rejecting any calls for more pluralist politics (Stokke 2006). The Sri Lankan government continued to fund state agencies based in what it termed 'uncleared areas', territories outside government control, but in practice these state bodies and officials were under the control of the LTTE. In Eastern Province, where the government and LTTE shared control in a complex patchwork of jurisdiction, LTTE political and intelligence officers were permitted to travel in government-controlled areas. In practice, this often meant a further extension of LTTE indirect control over Tamil businesses and communities in those areas. According to human rights activists:

> The LTTE moved into towns to freeload from Muslim shops and to extort from Tamils and Muslim civilians alike. In areas along the main road from Valaichenai to Kallar where the LTTE's movements were hitherto inhibited, the LTTE came in and started demanding children and money to set up offices. Where the children were extremely young, the LTTE often demanded a written declaration from the parents that they would give the first child that [came] of age – reportedly 12 years.
>
> *(UTHR 2002)*

LTTE violations of the CFA posed a major challenge for the negotiators. For the most part, the SLMM and international negotiators preferred to downplay evidence of violations, for fear of upsetting the delicate peace negotiations. In effect, the LTTE was permitted to further its vertical control over the north and east in exchange for its agreement to horizontal negotiation with the government. The LTTE, as with all parties to the agreement, wished to transform a complex, multi-layered conflict with multiple participants into a simple, binary peace process with two main actors who could represent their respective communities. The LTTE viewed itself as the sole representative of Tamil-speaking people in Sri Lanka, but this position was rejected by many dissident Tamil groups and by Muslim communities, who asserted their own separate identity, despite their use of the Tamil language.

Peace talks

There were various contacts between different parties during 2002, but formal peace talks began on 16 September 2002 in Sattahip in Thailand between a government delegation headed by G.L. Peiris, a lawyer, and Anton Balasingham, a London-based negotiator, who had long-standing, close connections with LTTE leader, Prabhakaran. Although the talks were reported to be cordial, the focus was on CFA implementation and humanitarian issues rather than any substantive political questions. During a further round (31 October–3 November 2002) of talks, also held in Thailand, the two sides agreed to establish three sub-committees: a Sub-committee on Political Affairs (SPA), a Sub-committee on De-escalation and Normalization (SDN), and a Sub-committee on Immediate Humanitarian Rehabilitation Needs (SIHRN). Despite the establishment of the SPA, it never met, and political issues were often side-lined in favour of humanitarian and development issues (ICG 2006).

Talks in Oslo in December 2002 were initially seen as a breakthrough, when both sides agreed to

> explore a solution founded on the principle of internal self-determination in areas of historical habitation of the Tamil speaking peoples, based on a federal structure within a united Sri Lanka.
>
> *(Waldman 2002)*

The assertion that the LTTE had agreed to work within a federal Sri Lanka was seen as a positive step forward by the mediators, but it apparently caused severe strains among LTTE negotiators (Sørbø et al. 2011: 42). Balasingham (2004: 464) complained that the statement had been 'blown up as a paradigm shift', when in reality it merely expanded on an existing LTTE position, outlined by Prabhakaran during a speech on Martyrs' Day in November 2002. The Oslo Communiqué exposed the difficulties faced by the LTTE in maintaining an unwavering commitment to an independent state, in the light of almost universal international opposition. After Oslo, Balasingham and other LTTE moderates appear to have been side-lined, and LTTE suspicion of the peace process intensified. Certainly, any short-lived optimism engendered by progress in Oslo began to fade during talks held in Nakorn Pathom, Thailand (6–9 January 2003), where the two sides struggled to agree on the working of the sub-committees and clashed over the issue of so-called High Security Zones (HSZ), areas in which many Tamils had been forced out of their homes to make way for military bases. These humanitarian concerns were particularly acute in Jaffna, but efforts to find a way to link dismantling HSZs to demobilisation of LTTE offensive weapons led nowhere (Sørbø et al. 2011: 41).

The fifth round of talks, held in Berlin (7–8 February 2003), continued the contentious discussion on the HSZs and appeared to reach an agreement between the LTTE and UNICEF to resolve the problem of child soldiers, although its implementation was deeply flawed (ICG 2006). Although the LTTE did release some child soldiers, it also continued to recruit underage soldiers. A series of violations of the CFA during February/March 2003 by the LTTE also began to fuel criticism of the government and of the Norwegian mediators. SLMM monitors intercepted LTTE arms shipments, and there was concern over the activities of the LTTE's small navy, the 'Sea Tigers'. Meanwhile, Muslim anger at increased LTTE violence in Eastern Province sparked a new political activism and sense of identity among Muslims (ICG 2007a: 10). In January 2003, as many as 20,000 Muslims gathered to acclaim the 'Oluvil declaration', which laid out Muslims' claim for rights and status. The exclusion of the Muslim community from the peace talks continued to rankle and caused continual problems for the Norwegian negotiators over the next two years (Mohideen 2006).

A sixth round of talks was held in Hakone, Japan (18–21 March). At this meeting, in response to mounting concerns over the human rights abuses obscured by the CFA, Ian Martin, the former head of Amnesty International, encouraged both sides to adopt a human rights agenda. Both sides – and international mediators – had reasons to resist such an imposition, and the idea was never implemented. After Hakone, in April 2003, the LTTE pulled out of further talks. The ostensible reason was the LTTE's exclusion from a donors' conference, to be held in Washington DC. (The LTTE was not invited because it was proscribed as a terrorist group in the US.) However, as Balasingham admitted, the real problem for the LTTE was its fear of being caught in a so-called peace trap, whereby an institutionalised, internationalised peace process gradually reduced the LTTE's space for manoeuvre (Goodhand and Walton 2009: 309). The nature of the LTTE, a mobilisational, authoritarian movement, made it particularly vulnerable to a relaxation of military and political pressures. It was more difficult to justify the LTTE's forced recruitment of child soldiers, its maximalist political demands, and its repressions against dissidents in an environment of relative peace. On 21 April, the LTTE unilaterally suspended negotiations with the government, although it reiterated its commitment to the CFA. The LTTE was invited to a donors' conference in Tokyo in June 2003, where donors pledged some $4.5 billion in aid, but the LTTE boycotted the conference.

The Tokyo conference appointed the US, Japan, and the EU as three co-chairs of the peace process, alongside Norway's established mediation role. However, the increasing internationalisation of the peace process coincided with a decline in the influence of international actors. From late 2003, the fate of the peace process was effectively determined by increasingly divisive domestic political factors. On 31 October 2003, the LTTE presented a proposal for an Interim Self-Governing Administration (ISGA). The ISGA proposal guaranteed LTTE control over the whole of the north-east of the island, which would be vacated by the Sri Lankan military, and granted them effective autonomy over all domestic governance within the ISGA region. The ISGA sharpened a growing divide between the stance of the mediators and non-LTTE political elites inside Sri Lanka. While Norway viewed the ISGA as a starting point for negotiations and welcomed the fact that the LTTE had put forward a formal proposal for a structure short of immediate independence, government critics viewed the ISGA as little more than a proto-state, which would guarantee LTTE de facto statehood in the north-east and offer a viable road map to secession via a proposed referendum after five years.

The ISGA proposal was never viable in the context of a negotiated settlement, but it served to crystallise existing divisions in the government. President Kumaratunga had long been unhappy with the conduct of the peace process and had been effectively side-lined. But in the wake of the ISGA proposal, she intervened against Prime Minister Ranil Wickremasinghe and declared a state of emergency. The move reflected increasing popular disapproval of the UNP government and its international allies, largely fuelled by its refusal to condemn LTTE ceasefire violations or to dismiss the ISGA proposal (Sørbø et al. 2011: 48). These machinations at the top took place in the context of a broader shift in nationalist politics, with growing public support for the JVP and for militant Buddhist organisations, such as the Sinhala Urumaya (Sinhala Heritage) movement, which set up the Jathika Hela Urumaya (JHU) as a political party in 2004. The JHU unexpectedly won nine seats at parliamentary elections in April 2004 and attracted support from many influential middle-class Sinhalese, including government officials. Both the JVP and the JHU opposed the peace process, instead advocating a full-scale military campaign to defeat the LTTE, a position that was marginal in mainstream political thought at the time. The SLFP – running as the United People's Freedom Alliance coalition – won a convincing victory at April 2004 elections, and Mahinda Rajapaksa was appointed prime minister. In retrospect, it was probably impossible to have rescued the peace process after the April 2004 elections: both the new prime minister and President Kumaratunga were opposed to fundamental aspects of the peace process, albeit for different reasons.

The other critical turning point in 2004 emerged from growing dissension within the Tamil community. Despite LTTE efforts to stamp out any dissent against its monopoly of power, the peace process made it more difficult for Prabhakaran to assert total control over the movement. In March 2004, the commander of LTTE forces in Eastern Province, Vinayagamoorthy Muralitharan (more commonly known as 'Colonel' Karuna Amman), announced a breakaway from the LTTE leadership of Prabhakaran. This was a huge blow to the LTTE, from which it never completely recovered. Karuna led some of the most effective military units in the LTTE, and his defection gave the government access to invaluable intelligence on the LTTE's armed forces and operations. Although the LTTE defeated Karuna's forces and recovered most territory in the east in the aftermath of the defection, some of Karuna's forces began working with the Sri Lankan military as paramilitaries, who knew the terrain well and could effectively challenge the LTTE on the ground. Karuna claimed that it had been his engagement with the wider world that persuaded him to move against what he saw as Prabhakaran's inflexible position, although long-standing disagreements between Eastern and Northern Tamil communities probably also played a role (ICG 2006). Whatever the real reasons, the split with Karuna was exactly the outcome that some LTTE hardliners had feared from the 'peace trap'; the continued existence of the Karuna faction soured further peace talks and became a constant source of tension between the two sides.

The Karuna split probably ended the LTTE's genuine interest in further negotiations, although they reaffirmed their commitment to the CFA. A period of phony peace began. In reality, both sides appeared to be preparing for war, but conflict was forestalled by the Indian Ocean tsunami on 26 December 2004. Amid the devastation (much of it on the eastern and north-eastern shores, populated predominantly by Tamil and Muslim communities), there was hope that responding to the tsunami would bring the two sides together. There was cooperation between the different communities in the north and east, but this period of relative pluralism was short-lived. For the LTTE, this 'very open and flexible space of opportunity posed a threat and needed to be filled as soon as possible' (Walker 2013: 75). With the Norwegians mediating once more, both sides supported a Post-Tsunami Operational Management Structure (P-TOMS) as a new, joint mechanism for distributing aid, which appeared to offer more influence for Muslim communities (which were badly affected by the tsunami) and a balance between the government and LTTE over how aid would be spent. P-TOMS was the last initiative that reflected a long-standing belief among negotiators that foreign aid and economic development offered a way to bring the two sides together, without addressing underlying political issues (Sriskandarajah 2003). However, the political implications of the P-TOMS mechanisms were clear and immediately fuelled political opposition. Eventually the P-TOMS structure was ruled unconstitutional by the Supreme Court, but in any case it had become irrelevant as the momentum for war resumed in the summer of 2005.

Against this backdrop of renewed controversy, Prime Minister Mahinda Rajapaksa, a southern politician from the more nationalist wing of the SLFP, won presidential elections in 2005, narrowly defeating the UNP's Ranil Wickremasinghe. With hindsight, the election of Rajapaksa was the key event in shifting the Sri Lankan state towards a full-scale military campaign, although at the time of the election Rajapaksa advocated a more moderate stance and was viewed as a pragmatist by international mediators. One important factor in Rajapaksa's victory was the LTTE's decision to enforce a boycott of the election among Tamil voters, rather than supporting their partner in the peace process, Ranil Wickremasinghe. The absence of Tamil votes in the north provided Rajapaksa with the necessary 2 per cent margin for victory. The LTTE decision was perhaps the clearest strategic mistake of the entire peace process, based on a false belief that a new war with the Sri Lankan state would leave them in a much stronger position both domestically and internationally. The decision reinforced the view that the LTTE lacked a well-informed political strategy. Prabhakaran had a strong reputation as a military tactician but lacked good political advice or a well-developed political vision.

Although Rajapaksa won on a clearly nationalist platform, he initially advocated a continuation of the peace process, at least publicly. However, in reality the war had already resumed, with killings and assassination by both sides, including the murder of Tamil MP Joseph Pararajasingham while celebrating Christmas Mass in Batticaloa. Although the mediators and the SCOPP remained active, by April 2006 Defence Minister Gotabaya Rajapaksa was telling negotiators he could envisage a military solution to the conflict (Sørbø et al. 2011: 54). This conviction was matched by a new military build-up, with Sri Lanka on a buying spree for new equipment, including fighter planes and new offensive weapons; and a diplomatic offensive, stressing the fight against terror and building up relations with sympathetic non-Western states, such as Pakistan and China (Lewis 2010). A shift in international opinion against the LTTE was particularly marked after the assassination of Sri Lankan Foreign Minister Lakshman Kadirgamar in August, almost certainly by the LTTE. The EU proscribed the LTTE in May 2006, and many countries began to investigate LTTE activities among Tamil diasporas and block fundraising. The JVP and the JHU intensified a campaign of demonstrations and protests against Norway and the CFA.

By June 2006, full-scale military confrontations had resumed, particularly in Eastern Province, where fighting was accompanied by reports of massacres by government troops or paramilitaries, including the killing in August 2006 of 17 aid workers from the French NGO *Action Contre la Faim*. Although peace talks did continue in 28–29 October 2006 in Geneva between the two sides, in practice the government was beginning to believe that it could win a military confrontation outright. This was not the view among diplomats. Norwegian diplomats agreed that 'all observers think that this is a conflict that cannot be won by military means and most believe that the government cannot beat the LTTE militarily' (Sørbø et al. 2011: 63). This belief was pervasive in the international and diplomatic community, and partly explains the continued willingness of Norway and other EU states to maintain the peace process mechanism, with the hope that the government would be forced to resume talks once its military offensive began to falter. This was a fundamental error in analysis but was widely shared.

In reality, the LTTE turned out to be much weaker militarily than expected. Although it managed a symbolic air attack on Colombo in April 2007, it proved no match for the better-equipped Sri Lankan military. Indeed, the discovery that the LTTE had developed an air force prompted India to offer radar and other support to the Sri Lankan government (Sørbø et al. 2011: 54). By July 2007, the government had driven the LTTE out of Eastern Province. On 2 January 2008, the government withdrew from the CFA and the SLMM was terminated. Government forces launched a military campaign against LTTE strongholds in the north and quickly overran LTTE positions. International efforts to organise a ceasefire were rejected by both sides. The government campaign culminated in the military defeat of the LTTE in May 2009, amid accusations of war crimes and mass killings of civilians in the final few days of battle (Lewis 2011). According to the International Crisis Group, civilian deaths in the final few weeks of battle may have exceeded 30,000 (ICG 2010).

Lessons to be learned from the case study

There are multiple lessons to be learned from the Sri Lanka peace process, and many have been explored in detail elsewhere (ICG 2006; Goodhand et al. 2005, 2011; Sørbø et al. 2011; Orjuela 2010). Three key issues that have wider application are (1) the over-reliance on foreign aid and a development agenda to have positive impacts on the conflict; (2) a poor understanding of the fundamental political dynamics at stake in the conflict, including – above all – the internal politics of the LTTE; and (3) the misreading of a shifting international environment, in which Western leverage became increasingly irrelevant as the peace process developed.

Aid and development

A key point through the process was the 'inflated assessment of the leverage of aid' (Goodhand and Walton 2009: 310), and the undue influence on the peace process of development professionals, aid workers, and humanitarian NGOs. Donors believed that foreign aid would offer a 'peace dividend' that would boost support for the peace process and improve cooperation between the two sides (Sriskandarajah 2003; Goodhand et al. 2005; Bastian 2007; Goodhand and Walton 2009). This was a profound misreading of the nature of the conflict. An emphasis on humanitarian and development issues during the peace process did not act as a process of confidence-building to lay the ground for later political discussions. Instead, efforts to create joint development initiatives merely reproduced the fundamental divisions in the peace process, but in different form.

Institutions designed to deliver aid, such as the North–East Reconstruction Fund (NERF), funded by international donors, or the SIHRN and P-TOMS, were often viewed by international negotiators as 'soft' mechanisms to achieve cooperation and confidence-building. In reality, both sides viewed the control of aid and development funds as primarily a political question and refused to acknowledge demands for recognition of the neutrality of humanitarian space. The LTTE viewed the control and channelling of foreign aid as an important way for them to achieve greater local legitimacy and to further develop their nascent state structures (Sørbø et al. 2011: 107). Engagement with international donors was seen as a form of partial international recognition (Burke and Mulakala 2011). NGOs were constantly subject to LTTE controls or were persuaded to channel their aid through the LTTE's development wing, the Tamil Rehabilitation Organisation (TRO). The post-tsunami influx of aid organisations into Sri Lanka, far from supporting the peace process, often created local conflicts among different communities and local leaders (Sørbø et al. 2011: 109), and sometimes fuelled nationalist, anti-Western sentiments in the south. This manipulation of aid and the failure to achieve humanitarian space during the peace process was followed by even more cynical politicisation of aid during 2006–2009, when 'information control and the manipulation of aid – granting partial humanitarian access in return for silence – [became] a key part of the SL government's strategy' (ODI 2010: 3).

Politics

The partial attempt to de-politicise the peace process through a development track was compounded by insufficient attention to the politics of peace, both the everyday domestic politics that ultimately undermined the whole process and the underlying political questions that divided the two sides. Although it was unrealistic to expect a peace process to address the full range of complex historical cleavages of a post-colonial state, the insistence on a bipolar framework made it extremely difficult to address the challenges of intra-community divisions, among both Tamils and Sinhalese, and also to address the inclusion of other communities, such as the Muslims. The non-viability of the LTTE's plans for independence, given universal international opposition, should have been part of the guiding framework for the talks. Instead, this principle was often fudged through academic discussions of federal alternatives, which were unlikely to be accepted by the LTTE leadership. Moreover, the highly authoritarian nature of LTTE rule, which made many Tamils and Muslims nervous about granting substantial autonomy to the LTTE, was hardly addressed. The failure to respond adequately to serious human rights abuses by the LTTE in the first year of the CFA discredited the process for many democratic Tamil voices and provided ammunition to potential spoilers among Sri Lankan nationalists (Höglund 2005; ICG 2006; Keenan 2007). In neither of the state-building projects – that of the LTTE or of the Sinhala state – was there any attempt at political reform during this period, yet reform of the state was a precondition for sustainable peace (Uyangoda 2010). During 2004–2005, it was advocates of extremist state-building projects – the LTTE on the one hand and the proponents of the Sinhala-Buddhist hegemonic state on the other – that accrued most influence, with liberal and moderate voices becoming discredited by their association with the peace process. In this sense, the conduct of the peace process made its eventual failure much more dangerous than it might otherwise have been by fuelling Sinhalese nationalist sentiment, which came to insist on a maximalist military solution to the conflict (Lewis 2010).

Shifting international environment

The third major lesson of the Sri Lankan peace process regards the role of external mediators and the international community in general. There have been numerous specific criticisms of the modalities of Norway's involvement in the peace process, prompting a broader discussion of the role of external mediators in peace processes (Sørbø et al. 2011). Certainly, the assumption that Norway would be viewed as an honest broker and perceived as neutral by all sides, was naive. Instead, Norwegian negotiators became the focus of nationalist anger, protests, and demonstrations. The international community was complacent about public opinion, possibly misled by opinion polls suggesting strong support for the peace process in 2003–2004. Once military conflict resumed in 2006, however, the public swung quickly behind the government and backed the military counterinsurgency (Lewis 2010). International actors struggled to engage with the public more widely, or with a broad spectrum of political forces outside a narrow Colombo elite of UNP politicians and civil society actors. While external actors had some influence over the policies of the UNP government of 2001–2004, they struggled to find ways to influence the LTTE. Moreover, EU states rapidly lost influence with the government after the election of Rajapaksa in 2005.

The decline of Western influence was more than matched by President Rajapaksa's new diplomatic ties. He found China ready to offer financial support and military hardware and discovered diplomatic allies among non-Western powers, including Russia, India and China. Indeed, the Sri Lankan case demonstrated that all peace processes now have to operate within a new geopolitical constellation, in which the leverage of Western powers is sharply reduced and the concept of small, liberal powers such as Norway acting as 'neutral brokers' is increasingly difficult to maintain. Instead, major powers such as China and Russia play a decisive role, both directly by backing governments facing internal conflicts and diplomatically in the UN Security Council. These shifts in power are accompanied by changes in norms. The liberal norms that have informed peace processes since the late 1980s are now contested and challenged at every level. The failure of the Sri Lankan peace process marked the beginning of a new era in which illiberal and authoritarian responses to internal conflicts have become increasingly normalised.

References, further reading, and links to key primary documents

Balasingham, Anton. 2004. *War and Peace: Armed Struggle and Peace Efforts of Liberation.* Vienna: Fairfax Publishing.

Bandarage, Asoka. 2008. *The Separatist Conflict in Sri Lanka: Terrorism, Ethnicity, Political Economy.* London: Routledge.

Bastian, Sunial. 2007. *The Politics of Foreign Aid in Sri Lanka: Promoting and Supporting Peace.* Colombo: ICES.

Bastian, Sunial. 2011. "Politics of Market Reforms and the UNF-Led Negotiations." In Jonathan Goodhand, Benedikt Korf, and Jonathan Spencer (Eds.), *Conflict and Peacebuilding in Sri Lanka: Caught in the Peace Tramp?* 132–149. London and New York: Routledge.

Burke, Adam, and Anthea Mulakala. 2011. "Aiding Peace? An Insider's View of Donor Support for the Sri Lankan Peace Process, 2000–2005." In Jonathan Goodhand, Benedikt Korf, and Jonathan Spencer (Eds.), *Conflict and Peacebuilding in Sri Lanka: Caught in the Peace Tramp?* London and New York: Routledge.

CFA. 2002. "Agreement on a Ceasefire Between the Government of the Democratic Socialist Republic of Sri Lanka and the Liberation Tigers of Tamil Eelam." www.regjeringen.no/no/dokumenter/agreement_on_a_ceasefire_between/id260701/.

Coomaraswamy, Radhika. 2013. "The 1972 Republican Constitution of Sri Lanka in the Postcolonial Constitutional Evolution of Sri Lanka." In Asanga Welikala (Eds.), *The Sri Lankan Republic at 40: Reflections on Constitutional History, Theory and Practice.* Sri Lanka: Centre for Policy Alternatives.

DeVotta, Neil, and Jason Stone. 2008. "Jathika Heia Urumaya and Ethno-Religious Politics in Sri Lanka." *Pacific Affairs* 81 (1): 31–51.

DeVotta, Neil. 2004. *Blowback: Linguistic Nationalism, Institutional Decay, and Ethnic Conflict in Sri Lanka.* Stanford: Stanford University Press.

DeVotta, Neil. 2009. "The Liberation Tigers of Tamil Eelam and the Lost Quest for Separatism in Sri Lanka." *Asian Survey* 49 (6): 1021–1051.

De Silva, Kingsley M. 1998. *Reaping the Whirlwind: Ethnic Conflict, Ethnic Politics in Sri Lanka.* London: Penguin Books.

Fernando, Jude Lal. 2014. "Negotiated Peace Versus Victor's Peace: The Geopolitics of Peace and Conflict in Sri Lanka." *Cambridge Review of International Affairs* 27 (2): 206–225.

Goodhand, Jonathan. 2010. "Stabilising a Victor's Peace? Humanitarian Action and Reconstruction in Eastern Sri Lanka." *Disasters* 34: S342–S367.

Goodhand, Jonathan, and Oliver Walton. 2009. "The Limits of Liberal Peacebuilding? International Engagement in the Sri Lankan Peace Process." *Journal of Intervention and Statebuilding* 3 (3): 303–323.

Goodhand, Jonathan, Bart Klem, Dilrukshi Fonseka, S.I. Keethaponcalan, and Shonali Sardesai. 2005. *Sri Lanka: Strategic Conflict Assessment.* Sri Lanka: The Asia Foundation.

Goodhand, Jonathan, Benedikt Korf, and Jonathan Spencer. (Eds.). 2010. *Conflict and Peacebuilding in Sri Lanka: Caught in the Peace Trap?* London: Routledge.

Höglund, Kristine. 2005. "Violence and the Peace Process in Sri Lanka." *Civil Wars* 7 (2): 156–170.

Hoole, Rajan, Daya Somasundaram, K. Sritharan, and Rajani Thiranagama. 1988. *The Broken Palmyra: The Tamil Crisis in Sri Lanka – An Inside Account.* Sri Lanka: Sri Lanka Studies Inst.

ICG. 2006. "Sri Lanka: The Failure of the Peace Process." International Crisis Group, *Asia Report* 124, 28 November.

ICG. 2007a. "Sri Lanka's Muslims: Caught in the Crossfire." International Crisis Group, *Asia Report* 134, 29 November.

ICG. 2007b. "Sri Lanka: Sinhala Nationalism and the Elusive Southern Consensus." International Crisis Group, *Asia Report* 141, 7 November.

ICG. 2010. "War Crimes in Sri Lanka." International Crisis Group, *Asia Report* 191, 17 May.

ICG. 2011. "India and Sri Lanka After the LTTE." International Crisis Group, *Asia Report* 206, 23 June.

ICG. 2012. "Sri Lanka: Tamil Politics and the Quest for a Political Solution." International Crisis Group, *Asia Report* 239, 20 November.

Keenan, Alan. 2007. "The Temptations of Evenhandedness: On the Politics of Human Rights and Advocacy in Sri Lanka." In Michel Feher (Ed.), *Non-Governmental Politics*. New York: Zone Books.

Lewis, David. 2010. "The Failure of a Liberal Peace: Sri Lanka's Counterinsurgency in Global Perspective." *Conflict, Security and Development* 10 (5): 647–671.

Lewis, David. 2011. "A 'successful' Model of Counterinsurgency? The Sri Lankan Government's War Against the LTTE." In Paul B. Rich, and Isabelle Duyvesteyn (Eds.), *The Routledge Companion to the Study of Insurgency and Counter Insurgency*. London: Routledge.

Lewis, David. 2015. "Illiberal Peace? Authoritarian Approaches to Conflict Management." Presented at Seminar Emerging Powers and Conflict Management: Lessons from Central Asia, New York, 21 April.

Lewis, David, John Heathershaw, and Nick Megoran. 2018. "Illiberal Peace? Authoritarian Modes of Conflict Management." *Cooperation and Conflict*.

McGilvray, Dennis B. 2011. "Sri Lankan Muslims: Between Ethno-Nationalism and the Global Ummah." *Nations and Nationalism* 17: 45–64.

Mohideen, M.I.M. 2006. "Sri Lanka Peace Process and the Muslim Question." In Kumar Rupesinghe (Ed.), *Negotiating Peace in Sri Lanka: Efforts, Failures and Lessons*, 313–337. Colombo: Foundation for Co-Existence.

ODI. 2010. "Humanitarian Space in Sri Lanka: What Lessons Can be Learned?" Overseas Development Institute, Humanitarian Policy Group, London, 18–19 November, Meeting Summary.

Orjuela, Camilla (Ed.). 2010. *Power and Politics in the Shadow of Sri Lanka's Armed Conflict*. Stockholm: Sida.

Piccolino, Giulia. 2015. "Winning Wars, Building (illiberal) Peace? The Rise (and possible fall) of a Victor's Peace in Rwanda and Sri Lanka." *Third World Quarterly* 36 (9): 1770–1785.

Rampton, David, and Suthaharan Nadarajah. 2017. "A Long View of Liberal Peace and Its Crisis." *European Journal of International Relations* 23 (2): 441–465.

Rupesinghe, Kumar. (Ed.). 2006. *Negotiating peace in Sri Lanka: Efforts, Failures, and Lessons* (Vol. 2). Colombo: Research & Documentation Centre, Foundation for Co-Existence.

Sørbø, Gunnar, Jonathan Goodhand, Bart Klem, Ada Elisabeth Nissen, and Hilde Selbervik. 2011. *Pawns of Peace Evaluation of Norwegian Peace Efforts in Sri Lanka, 1997–2009*. Oslo: Norwegian Agency for Development Cooperation.

Spencer, Jonathan. 2008. "A Nationalism without Politics? The Illiberal Consequences of Liberal Institutions in Sri Lanka." *Third World Quarterly* 29 (3): 611–629.

Sriskandarajah, Dhananjayan. 2003. "The Returns of Peace in Sri Lanka: The Development Cart Before the Conflict Resolution Horse?" *Journal of Peacebuilding & Development* 1 (2): 21–35.

Stokke, Kristian. 2006. "Building the Tamil Eelam State: Emerging State Institutions and Forms of Governance in LTTE-Controlled Areas in Sri Lanka." *Third World Quarterly* 27 (6): 1021–1040.

Subramanian, Nirupamam. 2005. *Sri Lanka, Voices from a War Zone*. New Delhi: Vijitha Yapa Publications.

Swamy, Narayan. 2002. *Tigers of Lanka: From Boys to Guerrillas*. Columbia: South Asia Books.

UTHR. 2002. "In the Name of 'Peace': Terror stalks the North-East." *University Teachers for Human Rights Jaffna* 28, 1 February. www.uthr.org.

Uyangoda, Jayadeva. 2010. "Politics of Political Reform: A Key theme in the Contemporary Conflict." In Camilla Orjuela (Eds.), *Power and Politics in the Shadow of Sri Lanka's Armed Conflict*, 29–78. Stockholm: Sida.

Uyangoda, Jayadeva. 2011. "Travails of State Reform in the Context of Protracted Civil War in Sri Lanka." In Kristian Stokke and Jayadeva Uyangoda (Eds.), *Liberal Peace in Question*. London: Anthem Press.

Vellaithamby, Ameerdeen. 2006. *Ethnic Politics of Muslims in Sri Lanka*. Michigan: Centre for Minority Studies.

Waldman, Amy. 2002. "Sri Lanka to Explore a New Government", *New York Times*, 6 December, https://www.nytimes.com/2002/12/06/world/sri-lanka-to-explore-a-new-government.html

Walker, Rebecca. 2013. "Taking a Back Seat: The Uses and Misuses of Space in a Context of War and Natural Disaster." *Journal of Human Rights* 12: 69–86, 75.

Wilson, A. Jeyaratnam. 2000. *Sri Lankan Tamil Nationalism*. London: Hurst & Company.

17
SUDAN

Alex de Waal

Introduction

Signed in January 2005 following more than 20 years of civil war, Sudan's Comprehensive Peace Agreement (CPA) was hailed as that country's 'second independence' and the last, best chance for a united, democratic, and peaceful Sudan. A few years later, the story was written differently: as the stepping stone to an independent South Sudan which collapsed into a bloody internal war and as a temporary truce between north and south (Johnson 2012).

Observers of Sudan must be careful, because whichever way they choose to read the country, it will appear like this. The dominant narrative is of hope, derailed by errors and misfortune, culminating in calamity (Copnall 2014; Johnson 2016). There is also a version that blames the international mediators for imposing a 'liberal peace' (Young 2012) or for simplistically advocating secession (Mamdani 2016). The story in this chapter is more complicated. In some respects, it is more forgiving: it sees the Sudanese conflict as a 'wicked problem' that is inherently difficult to resolve because of its combination of apparently chaotic reconfiguration, multiple dimensions, and indeterminacies (De Waal 2007). In other respects, it is more pessimistic: the flaws in the process were evident at the time. The mediators were not in charge of the process at any point. Sometimes they were able to leverage the alignment of factors to help the Sudanese make a step forward, but more often they were reacting to events outside their control or unaware of the driving forces determining Sudan's politics. The most skilful Sudanese politicians are able to hold different and contradictory analyses and scenarios in their heads at the same time, plan on the basis of multiple contingencies, and keep their political ships afloat in the rough seas of national and regional affairs. Rarely can they steer those ships to a destination.

The mediators, drawn from the neighbouring countries and the 'troika' of the United States, United Kingdom, and Norway, made heroic simplifications in order to develop a formula based on a single text, with space for just two signatories. The main effort was distilling the complexities of Sudan's wars down to what they supposed was its essence: a conflict between the north (represented by the Government of Sudan and the ruling National Congress Party (NCP)) and the south (represented by the Sudan People's Liberation Movement and Army (SPLM/A)). The hope was that by resolving this primary conflict and stopping the fighting that the other issues, such as democratic inclusiveness, could be addressed in due course.

Even the text of the CPA, however, is an ironic paradigm of indeterminacy, as the title 'Comprehensive Peace Agreement' means different things in the two definitive languages, English and Arabic. The 260 pages of the Agreement include six protocols and two implementation matrices signed over the previous three years. This was one reason for calling it 'comprehensive'. Another reason was that it was intended as the central pillar of a political settlement that would be buttressed by several other agreements – to resolve the wars in Darfur and Eastern Sudan, recommence the stalled 'south–south dialogue' of internal reconciliation among southern armed groups and political parties, along with national elections that would bring in all the civilian opposition parties that had constituencies under-represented in the CPA's power-sharing formula.

The Arabic translation of 'Comprehensive Peace Agreement' is *al itifag al salam al shamil*. The first two words – 'peace agreement' – are unproblematic. But the third – *al shamil* – implies a sealed completeness. It shares a root with *shumuliya*, 'totalitarianism', and *al da'awa al shamla*, 'the all-encompassing religious call to God', an Islamist project of societal transformation pursued a few years earlier. Unsurprisingly and perceptively, many Sudanese saw the CPA differently: as an exclusive carve-up by the NCP and SPLM.

The immediate goal of the CPA was to stop the war between the Government of Sudan and the SPLM/A that had raged since 1983. Beyond that, it had two ambitious goals: prepare for the exercise of southern Sudanese self-determination and democratise the country. Each of these on its own would have been ambitious. Attempting both together was exceptionally so. There were tensions within each one. The agreement called on both parties to support unity, well aware that the majority of the southern electorate had an undeclared sympathy for separation (Deng 2005). The agreement provided for elections after three years, a process that could potentially sweep the signatories from power.

In due course, the CPA became a checklist of actions preparatory for the southern referendum and its pre-ordained outcome. The elections were held in year five (2010), far too late to allow for a democratically elected government to demonstrate the virtues of a unified country, and the NCP and SPLM swept the vote and consolidated their power in north and south respectively. International observers certified the election as 'free and fair', explicitly conceding that they were doing so in order not to endanger the referendum scheduled for just nine months later. The international community was astonishingly ill-prepared for the process of separation and its ramifications. Although the referendum was conducted in an orderly and peaceable manner in January 2011 and South Sudan duly celebrated its independence six months later, there was a brief but disastrous war between Sudan and South Sudan in 2012, and a calamitous civil war in South Sudan broke out in 2013.

In analysing Sudan's peace process, we face a huge difficulty of source material. The main writers on the negotiations are the mediators themselves, who are inevitably subjective and selective (Waihenya 2006; Johnson 2011). Documentation of peace processes remains a scarce scholarly resource, which means that much of the contemporary history of Sudan and South Sudan, and much of the analysis of peace processes, is based on surmise rather than evidence. To date there is only one account of peace talks between Khartoum and the southern Sudanese based on texts and first-hand accounts from the process itself (Wöndu and Lesch 2000), though more resources are gradually becoming available for scholars (World Peace Foundation 2013).

Conflict analysis

Sudan's independence, achieved on 1 January 1956, was ambiguous. For the parliamentary leader, Ismail al-Azhari, the vote to expedite independence was a tactical ploy to hold on to a parliamentary majority for a few more months, and the creation of the republic was a modernising project. For many in his Unionist Party, it was a stepping stone to unification with Egypt. For his parliamentary rivals, the Umma Party, it was the country's second independence – reviving the Mahdist state that had existed at the end of the nineteenth century. The southern Sudanese members of parliament supported the independence vote because they had been promised that there would be a federal system in which the southern region, severely underdeveloped and culturally distinct, would be able to run its own affairs.

A few months before independence, southern Sudanese soldiers had already mutinied against the prospect of being transferred north and placed under a northern command. The promise of a federal system was not honoured, and the parliamentary government collapsed in crisis, handing power to the military in 1958. From 1963 to 1972, separatist guerrillas known as the Anyanya waged a bush war. This was resolved with the Addis Ababa peace agreement of 1972, which granted southern Sudan regional autonomy. President Jaafar Nimeiri, the architect of the agreement, began to unpick it before the decade was out, as he embraced Islamist parties and played divide-and-rule across the country. In 1983, southern troops mutinied and, under the leadership of Colonel John Garang, founded the SPLA. They were welcomed and hosted by the Ethiopian government of the time, headed by President Mengistu Haile Mariam, who was fighting his own civil wars and was fiercely opposed to secessionism. Garang wrote a manifesto calling for a united, secular, socialist Sudan. His aim was that the SPLA should win support not just from the marginalised non-Arab constituencies in northern Sudan (notably the 'two areas') but also from northern radicals opposed to Nimeiri.

Sudan's long civil war lasted for more than 20 years. It was complicated in several ways.

First: the parties' positions and constituencies shifted over time

Nimeiri was overthrown in 1985 by a non-violent popular uprising, whose leaders (perhaps naively) expected that Garang would welcome their exemplary democratic credentials and join the government. He refused – in part because there was no functional 'M' (Movement) at the time, and he was unprepared for governing as part of a coalition. Garang thereby condemned Sudan's democratic spring to failure. A year later, the Umma Party leader Sadiq al Mahdi was elected prime minister but, faced with an escalating civil war and financial bankruptcy, lurched from one crisis to the next until he was deposed in a coup in 1989. The new president, Brigadier Omar al Bashir, ruled in tandem with the sheikh of the Muslim Brothers, Hassan al-Turabi, seeking to create an Islamic state – and in doing so, more deeply antagonising the southerners. In 1999, the government's prospects were transformed by oil, increasing its budget tenfold in just six years. Meanwhile, the Islamists fell out among themselves. Bashir removed al-Turabi and consolidated a more conventional security state, in doing so sparking Islamist opposition that contributed to the 2003 war in Darfur. Having hosted Usama bin Laden from 1992–1996, along with other radical Islamists, Sudan was on the US list of state sponsors of terrorism, and was a target of military action by its neighbours (Egypt, Eritrea, Ethiopia, and Uganda) and a cruise missile strike by the US. Fearing that it might be in line for a regime change intervention after 11 September 2001, the Sudanese government cooperated with the US on counterterrorism and peace negotiations. Now in opposition, al-Turabi relentlessly criticised Bashir, going so far as to sign a Memorandum of Understanding with the SPLM/A and openly expressing his sympathies for Darfurian Islamists in rebellion.

In parallel, the SPLM changed, too. Following the collapse of its Ethiopian sponsor in 1991, it abandoned socialism and instead espoused a 'secular, democratic, united Sudan'. It escalated the war to the north, recruiting in the 'two areas' (the Nuba Mountains of Southern Kordofan and Blue Nile, which are north of the internal north–south boundary) and sending forces to Eastern Sudan and Darfur. But in the south itself, the SPLA split – rival commanders accused Garang of dictatorial ways, including failing to build civil institutions. Garang's rivals put self-determination on the agenda, gaining popular support among southerners, most of whom had wanted separation all along. Ironically, Khartoum was ready to back anti-SPLA southern militia that espoused separation, even while Garang stuck with his agenda of unity. In parallel to the government-sponsored Islamisation of the north, the southerners – many of them believers in theistic spirituality – embraced Christianity *en masse*, and the SPLM/A (now with an identifiable political wing) in turn welcomed Christian solidarity groups, notably in America.

The bloodshed and turmoil of the internecine fighting was such that junior commanders, local leaders (notably church people), and foreign well-wishers combined to press the SPLA to reform and reunify, and Garang complied. In 1994, the north-east African regional organisation, the Inter-Governmental Authority for Development (IGAD), drafted a Declaration of Principles (DoP) for resolving the

Sudanese conflict, which included self-determination. African intergovernmental organisations have been consistently opposed to separatism, and had IGAD not included self-determination in this text, it is very hard to see how secession could ever have become an option for southern Sudanese. The 'frontline states' of Eritrea, Ethiopia, and Uganda also began backing the SPLA with their own troops, in retaliation for Sudanese destabilisation of their countries, notably including terrorist attacks such as the attempt to assassinate Egyptian President Husni Mubarak in Addis Ababa in 1995. The IGAD member states were therefore both mediators and belligerents, and in both roles they were supported by the US (El-Affendi 2001).

The key lesson from this is that turmoil is the norm, stability the exception. For a political–military leader, it is a rational strategy to hang on in reasonable expectation that things might change in one's favour. There's even a vernacular term for it: the politics of delay. In this context, any mutually hurting stalemate (Zartman 2001) will soon be reconfigured.

Second: the conflict was expressed in different registers

The journalists' shorthand was that Sudan's civil war was between an 'Arab Islamic north and a Christian, animist South'. This contains grating simplifications but an element of truth, in that many Sudanese describe the conflict in such a language of everyday primordialism (Fearon and Laitin 2000). But in the next breath, Sudanese will freely admit that their ethnic and racial labels are historically constructed and that everyone is mixed. The word 'Arab' is used colloquially with several meanings; the term 'Sudanese' has shifted over the decades, from referring to de-tribalised black Sudanese (principally southerners and Nuba) to referring to the social and cultural elite. After centuries in which there has been mixing from north, south, east, and west, the great majority of Sudanese have mixed ancestry. Elaborate efforts are needed to translate the terms 'African' and 'Arab' into meaningful social and political terms.

Sudanese identity politics is better seen as competing political–ideological projects: Arabisation, Islamisation, Africanisation, and secularisation (F. Deng 1995; Jok 2007). All gesture towards seeking unity in diversity, but it is a gesture only. The Arabisation has both a forcible manifestation and a more subtle process of adopting normatively 'Sudanese' cultural practices (Doornbos 1988). Sudanese Islamism experimented with taking a distinctively African character (El Affendi 1990), but the subsequent failure of 'African' Islamists, especially Darfurians, contributed to the rancorous split within the Islamist movement in 1999 and the war in Darfur. In popular discourse, however, these agendas were expressed as invocations of primordial identities and conflicts. The 1990s Islamist programme 'return to the roots' was intended to make Islamic traditions more salient in social life but had the unanticipated consequence of legitimising non-Arab communities' use of their own languages and customs. The SPLM/A never fully resolved its identity politics, postponing them for later decision. Among its many currents were authoritarian secularism, celebrating traditional cultures (notably in the Nuba Mountains and

Blue Nile (Mekki 2001)), stressing the 'African' character of Sudan as a whole, and – most consistently – opposing Arabisation and Islamisation. Primordialist identity politics was amplified in the echo chamber of partisan advocacy and media, whether Arab-Islamist or Christian solidarity and the absolutist language of the Save Darfur campaign. The foci of high-profile international campaigns – slavery and genocide – presupposed a clash of identities.

A second means of framing the conflict, favoured by Sudanese intellectuals, was inequality. An elite at the centre, controlling Khartoum and its environs, was systematically marginalising the rest of the country – the south, the Nuba Mountains and Blue Nile, Darfur, and Eastern Sudan. This critique was articulated by Garang in the SPLM Manifesto (Garang 1987, 1992), by the Nuba and Blue Nile people who joined the SPLM/A, by the Beja Congress in Eastern Sudan, and by the Darfurians who rose in rebellion in 2003 – notably including the Darfurian Islamists whose Black Book detailed the unequal distribution of power and wealth (Flint and De Waal 2008). Some figures in the government unabashedly defended inequality, such as the Minister of Finance in the mid-1990s, Abdel Rahim Hamdi, who proposed concentrating economic investment in an area limited by a day's drive from Khartoum. Known as 'Hamdi's Triangle', this zone indeed received the vast majority of spending on services and infrastructure (World Bank 2007).

Linked to this was a narrative of the war as a struggle for resources and an exercise in predation. This was a long-standing issue in Sudanese politics: the flag of the Beja Congress, designed in 1953, has an image of the inland delta of the River Gash, once the dry-season grazing grounds for the Beja camel herds but turned into a cotton plantation in the final years of colonial rule. By the 1980s and 1990s, these processes had advanced much further. Land expropriation by well-connected merchants, civil servants, and army officers was probably the single greatest source of resentment and recruits to the SPLA in the Nuba Mountains and Blue Nile (African Rights 1995). In southern Sudan, the resources included water (the construction of a canal through the marshes to increase the flow of the Nile downstream), oil, and (when the war was underway) cattle, cheap or unpaid labour, and timber. In Darfur, the contestation over land had a different pattern, but the issue was equally central (Tubiana 2007).

Another register was competing agendas for political transformation. Both the Islamists and the SPLM/A had slogans of a 'New Sudan', though they meant completely different things. Each had a mixture of transforming Sudan's socio-cultural identity and its political economy. Al-Turabi was famous for his political creativity, from championing democracy to strategic accommodation with military dictatorship, and back to democracy. During his long career he coined an entire lexicon of political vocabulary. Perhaps most revealing was his concept of 'the jurisprudence of necessity', whereby the ends could justify the means (De Waal and Abdel Salam 2004). Other new terms included *al-mashru' al-hadhari* (the 'civilization project' – a fusion of Arabisation and Islamisation, of which the 'comprehensive call to God' was a part) and *al-tawali* ('the way ahead' – the civilianisation of the military regime).

Another leading Islamist, Ali Osman Mohamed Taha, led Khartoum's delegation to the peace talks. He had far-sighted and bold ideas, including a new political party in which he and Garang would lead the country to a transformed future. This plan died when Garang was killed in a helicopter crash in 2005. Meanwhile, President Bashir's support for the CPA was equivocal: he opposed military withdrawal from southern Sudan and made it clear that he believed that too much had been surrendered for too little gain.

Garang was also a creative thinker (Deng 2013). Having begun with a slightly diluted Marxist analysis of Sudan's political economy, his signature political programme became 'the New Sudan' (Johnson 2013). This meant several things: a democratic governance system in which all citizens were equitably represented; the chance for the marginalised 'African' majorities of all the peripheries combined to rule the country for the first time; and the territories and communities under the military control and political authority of the SPLM/A. Each of these formulations had a political strategy attached. Therefore, during the peace talks, Garang was pursuing several strategies in parallel. One was seeking a negotiated peace with the government. A second was a military victory, in the reasonable anticipation that the talks would fail. This involved not only continuing the war in the south (until that became politically impossible) but also supporting the Darfurian insurgents, to the extent of jointly writing their manifesto and pushing them to change their name from 'Darfur Liberation Front' to 'Sudan Liberation Movement'. Third was support for a popular uprising in alliance with the northern civilian parties, a strategy that evolved into holding out the option of an electoral alliance with those parties to remove the NCP through the ballot box. During the CPA negotiations, this option faded in favour of a partnership between Garang and Ali Osman jointly to transform the country. Meanwhile, Garang's lieutenants – notably his deputy and successor Salva Kiir – simply wanted separation.

The lesson from this dimension of complexity is that we must problematise the idea of a 'political settlement' to end an internal conflict as a means of establishing 'the rules of the game' (Leftwich 2010; Khan 2017). There were *several* games being played at once, each with different rules, and the key players were themselves playing different games at the same time – and were also contemplating using executive power to break those rules and set new ones following the agreement. How to formulate a settlement and commonly understood rules in such circumstances? How to specify this in a single text that organises power, wealth, and security arrangements?

Third: the war was conducted at different levels

North versus south was just one level of conflict. There was an array of conflicts within the north and within the south, and myriad local conflicts, often associated with local rivalries over administrative positions and boundaries, and resources such as grazing land and water.

There were contests for leadership within each of the major parties. Throughout the war, the rule of thumb for explaining any decision by the leader on either side was to look to the threat of his closest internal rivals. Thus, many of Bashir's key decisions were taken because of the challenges posed by al-Turabi, while Garang's were taken to pre-empt threats from his distrusted lieutenants. Even in November 2004, just a few weeks before the CPA was signed, senior SPLA commanders summoned Garang to a meeting to confront him with charges of making secret deals with the NCP that would leave them behind when he joined the collective presidency. For Salva Kiir, the southern armed groups excluded from the CPA – especially the Khartoum-backed South Sudan Defence Forces – were the key actor in the bargains that made viable the independence project.

From the outset, the war was internationalised: the SPLA was set up in Ethiopia, where it obtained training, political orientation, and weaponry. This was in retaliation for Sudanese facilitation of the Eritrean, Tigrayan, and Oromo liberation fronts, fighting against the Ethiopian government. One military operation encapsulates this complexity. In November 1989, the SPLA (with Ethiopian military support) occupied Kurmuk and Geissan, two small border towns, which lie in Blue Nile within northern Sudan. President Mengistu, who was facing defeat in Eritrea, informed President Bashir that unless Sudanese support for the Eritrean People's Liberation Front (EPLF) was cut off, he would ensure that the Blue Nile dam was captured, cutting Khartoum's electricity supply and the water for the Gezira irrigated scheme, thus probably causing the downfall of the Sudanese government. The counterattack was led by the EPLF, which defeated the SPLA on Sudanese soil, defeated Ethiopian troops in the rearguard, and then inserted Oromo Liberation Front fighters inside Ethiopia, before returning (De Waal 2004). This phase of regional war ended with Mengistu's defeat in 1991, but from 1994 onwards, there was another phase of cross-border military action. In 1997–1998, the main SPLA offensives were conducted with Ugandan and Ethiopian officers and heavy armour, while Eritrean troops fought in Eastern Sudan and tried to open a front in Darfur.

Libya and Egypt were also involved, militarily and politically. Cairo and Tripoli tried to put together a peace initiative to rival IGAD's, with the twin aims of bringing a broader-based government to Khartoum and eliminating self-determination from the agenda. However, the distrust between President Mubarak and Colonel Muammar Gaddafi meant that the Libyan–Egyptian Initiative never became a serious contender.

The war was globalised. After al-Turabi declared support for Saddam Hussein's invasion of Kuwait, anticipating Islamist revolutions across the Arab world, Sudan was ostracised. It became the hub for jihadists of all kinds, including al-Qaeda. In turn, this brought US political pressure and, in retaliation for al-Qaeda's 1998 attacks on the US embassies in Nairobi and Dar es Salaam, a cruise missile strike on Khartoum. However, while President Bill Clinton's administration had sought regime change by proxy, using the SPLA and the 'frontline states', the George W. Bush administration pursued a peace deal. It did so for several reasons: it hoped that US oil companies could gain a stake in Sudan's oilfields; it had no confidence that the SPLA could win militarily because of its past shortcomings and because the Sudanese army was re-equipping with its new oil funds; and the 'frontline states' had gone to war with one another in 1998 (Ethiopia *versus* Eritrea and Rwanda *versus* Uganda), and so were no longer willing to fight Sudan. Having just invaded Afghanistan, the Pentagon had no appetite to take on the job itself.

The idea of peace negotiations as a two-level game is familiar (Putnam 1988). This refers to the negotiations between the principals, and between each principal and his followers. This is relevant to the CPA insofar as the peace negotiations consolidated the authority of each of the principals. But the negotiations were in fact a *five*-level game: international, regional, national, internal within each party, and between the parties and other national political actors. It is akin to five linked pendulums, which will swing in chaotic motion until each pendulum is stabilised in turn.

For a peace process to be workable, the top three levels needed to be aligned. In late 2001, this occurred: the US and the regional players, the Government of Sudan and the SPLM/A, were all ready to talk peace. With the Egyptians and Libyans absent, dynamics within northern Sudan were relegated to secondary status. The fourth level – the relations between the principal and his party – was stabilised by the negotiations themselves. The fifth level – wider conflicts in north and south – was postponed for later, or ignored. This allowed the two principals to focus on the middle, third level – the deal between the government and the SPLM/A. It worked, but only for a moment.

The conflict resolution process

The CPA is an elaborate text. It was the foundational text for the Interim National Constitution and the subsequent subnational peace agreements in southern Sudan (The Juba Declaration of January 2006), Darfur (May 2006), and Eastern Sudan (October 2006) as well as the secession and independence of the Republic of South Sudan (July 2011). Its chapters cover power-sharing, wealth sharing, security arrangements, Abyei Area, and the 'two areas' in addition to the foundational agreement (The July 2002 Machakos Protocol) and implementation schedules. Its core is a 'one country two systems' interim period, with separate administrations and armies in the north and south, leading to a referendum in southern Sudan after six years, and democratic elections throughout the country at the mid-point of the interim period.

The reason for the detail lies in the process whereby it was crafted. The SPLM delegation entered the talks deeply suspicious of the north. There was, in the words of one of southern Sudan's elder statesmen, a history of 'too many agreements dishonoured' (Alier 1992). The southerners expected that the northerners would make concessions at the negotiating table and then claw them back in the implementation, and so wanted as much specified on paper as possible. This strategy had a flaw, which was that the SPLM had too few qualified and experienced bureaucrats and lawyers to fill all the positions necessary – alongside the parallel challenges of economic reconstruction, delivering services to their people, turning the SPLA into a professional army, and setting up a working government more or less from scratch. Meanwhile, the mediators, backed by their team of specialist lawyers, worked on the basis of texts and the operating procedure that every problem should have a solution formulated in writing.

In several places, the text was indeterminate in ways that subsequently proved damaging. A notable case is the provisions for the disputed area of Abyei, on the north–south boundary. This had been a thorny issue since the first civil war, and even including Abyei within the negotiations was a contentious issue. After a protracted stalemate, the negotiators agreed to accept an American-drafted text without amendment. The American draft contained a confusing mix of different kinds of terms, including ethnic labels such as 'Ngok Dinka' and 'Misseriya', along with 'nomadic peoples' and 'residents'. The intent of the drafters was to distinguish between autochtonous Dinka residents and seasonally transient Arab Misseriya cattle herders, and to identify the boundaries of Abyei Area based on reading these identities back in time to 1905, the date when the administration of the area was transferred from south to north. It was a sociologically naïve framing of identities, livelihoods, and territories that soon became unstuck, confronted with the complexities of history and ethnicity, and the legal manoeuvres of the Government of Sudan, which had no intention of letting the Ngok Dinka transfer Abyei into southern Sudan.

Another indeterminacy was the provision for 'popular consultations' in the 'two areas'. This was another track of negotiation reluctantly conceded by the Government of Sudan, which initially did not want to enter into talks on any issue outside southern Sudan, but had no option but to do so because of the strength of the SPLM/A in these areas. Garang faced down the demands of his commanders in the two areas, who wanted the same rights as the southerners. What they got instead was limited autonomy in the interim period, during which time there would be a 'popular consultation' in which the members of the local state assemblies would decide whether these arrangements were satisfactory, or not. This provision was well short of what the SPLM/A members in these areas demanded and had no provisions for what would happen should southern Sudan become independent, leaving them stranded as a diminished minority within a pared-down and embittered northern Sudan. The security arrangements provisions for the two areas were even weaker. During the interim period, the two SPLA divisions, drawn entirely from the people of the areas, who had fought there for 15 years, were to be withdrawn to the south. In the event of the secession of the south, the Nuba and Blue Nile soldiers within the SPLA were to be demobilised entirely, which would amount to abandoning the people on whose behalf they had fought to the mercies of the northern army. The SPLM tried *not* to explain these provisions to its constituents. Unsurprisingly, the provisions counted for nothing when the southerners voted to secede, and a new war promptly broke out.

These examples point to the fundamental tension in the CPA. For the principals – Ali Osman and Garang – it was the launchpad for their private agreement to lead jointly the transformation of a united Sudan. Some indications of this agenda can be seen in the dynamism of the two men in the collective presidency in July 2005 (Deng 2013). It is likely that their plan not only aimed to maintain a united Sudan but also to change the national political conversation in a way that would reduce the CPA text as such into a curiosity, a stack of paper that served its purpose for the political moment and then became another national foundational document, to which people referred without actually reading what they contained. This would have made the deficiencies of the Abyei and 'two areas' protocols into no more than a historical footnote. The biggest challenge for such a project was how to deal with self-determination, and the likely solution would have been a deal under which the two formed a new national political party, Garang became president of a united Sudan, and the referendum on self-determination was indefinitely postponed.

For the internationals, and for the second-order politicians who had no such mastery of the political arena, the CPA was a text that should be interpreted detail-by-detail. This was the default option when Garang died and Ali Osman thereby lost his political partner.

The CPA made scant mention of two of the biggest international policy questions that followed: the UN peacekeeping mission and international development assistance. Neither transpired as anticipated.

During the negotiations, the Sudanese had come to expect that the UN peacekeeping presence would be small and with a limited mandate. The US Special Envoy John Danforth said the Sudanese should work out their own agreement, and they could not expect UN peacekeepers. Additionally, the peace support operation that was actually functional during this period – the Joint Military Commission to oversee the ceasefire in the Nuba Mountains – was extremely modest and very effective. At its height, it consisted of 39 unarmed international monitors with a budget of $18 million per year.

The CPA provided for the UN Security Council to mandate a peacekeeping force with the principal task of providing 'good offices and political support for the peace process, security aspects, governance, and humanitarian assistance and development'. Following the standard arithmetic for force protection for ceasefire monitors, the size of the UN Mission in Sudan (UNMIS) was specified as 10,000 troops and 700 civilian police. While UNMIS operated primarily under a Chapter VI mandate, it also had limited Chapter VII responsibilities to use force in protection of itself, its mission, and civilians in imminent danger of harm. It also included political and civil affairs and human rights. Troops were stationed not only in the war-affected areas but also in Khartoum itself. The Sudanese government saw this as a highly visible transgression on its sovereignty, and moreover one that had been undertaken by stealth.

No sooner had UNMIS begun deployment then the Save Darfur campaign began advocating for a military intervention in Darfur for forcible civilian protection. The US Administration did not want to send its own troops and instead made its policy that UN peacekeepers should be deployed, and in 2006 the UN Security Council authorised an additional 20,000 UNMIS troops for Darfur, under a Chapter VII mandate. The Sudanese government not only rejected this (later compromising on a hybrid African Union–UN force) but developed a near-paranoid attitude towards international peacekeepers in general. The southern Sudanese meanwhile saw the UN as an ally, to the extent that in 2011, the South Sudanese asked for a Chapter VII UN Mission in South Sudan, initially expecting that its forces would be deployed on the border with the north to deter northern aggression.

The second big post-CPA international policy issue was aid and economic normalisation. For the Sudanese government, one of the main incentives of the CPA was America's promise of lifting sanctions, removing it from the list of state sponsors of terror, and American corporations' investment in the oil industry. Because of the Darfur war, none of these happened. This penalised both north and south: southern Sudanese oil remained subject to sanctions, and thus sold at a discount, even after South Sudan became independent, because it was pumped to market using a pipeline through northern Sudan. For the southern Sudanese, there was a promise of massive international assistance for reconstruction. Shortly after the CPA, the World Bank organised a Joint Assessment Mission (JAM) to draw up plans for infrastructure, services, and investment in agriculture and industry. The JAM appeal was seriously under-funded, principally because donor interest and funds were consumed by the humanitarian crisis in Darfur. Nonetheless, southern Sudan was relatively generously assisted, and Western donors and international financial institutions arrived in Juba enthused with a spirit of solidarity with the newly emancipated people and government of southern Sudan.

This was all that the southern Sudanese expected, and they came to see uncritical support as an entitlement. At every stage of the CPA negotiations, the international community – the members of the American, British, and Norwegian delegations, the observers and experts from the UN, staff from the World Bank and other development agencies – openly or implicitly encouraged the SPLM with an assurance that they would assist with resources, expertise, and guarantees. When the Garang–Ali Osman dynamo was removed, the southern Sudanese fell back upon the presumption that their Western friends would ensure that the technocratic template was implemented.

A representation of this paradigm of state-building-by-numbers that would be comedic were it not uttered without an iota of irony, was provided by the Deputy Special Representative of the UN Secretary General for South Sudan, speaking to a television reporter in 2012. She said, entirely in earnest:

> About two years ago when it became clear that the South was going to vote for secession, at that point there became a real worry and preoccupation with the possibility of state failure. What we could see was a new state being born but one that was going to fail very early on because essential functions weren't yet in place. What happened was a team of international experts, they were funded by the U.S. Government, came and spent four months in the south and analyzed the functions that needed to be in place to make sure that the state survived. At that stage what we did was sit down with the government leadership and say, 'here's what the analysis shows, you need these 144 functions.' And in an extraordinary process of prioritization the government

> got that list down to nineteen essential functions, what we often just in shorthand call 'survival functions.
>
> *(Lise Grande speaking in Martin-Kessler and Poiret 2012)*

The southern Sudanese leadership was also earnest in welcoming the international technocracy. But it was playing a parallel game, which was the real politics of Sudan. The goal of Salva Kiir, President of the autonomous southern government (2005–2011), was the independence of the Republic of South Sudan by means of simple power alone: money and guns. Lacking the organisational means to mobilise a conventional army, this meant dominating the military–political marketplace in southern Sudan by buying military loyalty at a scale never before seen in the country. The enormous inflow of oil money provided the means to do this.

In 2004, the SPLA had perhaps 30,000 men under arms. By 2011, the payroll was about ten times higher, although the number of actual soldiers who could turn out to fight was considerably fewer. This massive expansion began when President Salva reconciled with his principal military rival, General Paulino Matiep, in the Juba Agreement of January 2006, bringing at least 30,000 troops formerly paid by Khartoum into the SPLA. More militia followed, according to the same formula. Officers kept their ranks, which Khartoum had inflated, and the SPLA had to promote its own commanders en masse to keep parity, so that within a few years the SPLA had over 700 generals. Two months after the Juba Agreement, the southern Sudanese legislature doubled the army's salaries compared to those of their counterparts in northern Sudan, and then doubled them again as independence approached. The reason was less to establish a large conventional army and more to make it too expensive for the Sudanese intelligence services to pursue their well-honed strategy of renting allegiances for cash and guns. In pursuing this strategy, the SPLA received assistance from foreign donors for security sector reform programmes, but ensured that all effort was directed to their main goal of a vast army with a single allegiance, at least until independence had been won.

During the CPA interim period (2005–2011), both north and south massively increased their military spending, in what was partly an arms race but more correctly a patronage race, the winner being the side that outspent the other in terms of buying loyalties in the political marketplace. Southern Sudan won. The cost was high: an entrenched system of militarised kleptocracy that bankrupted itself and plunged the new country into civil war (De Waal 2015).

Looking back on the CPA and the six years of relative stability that it brought, a period that coincided with unprecedented prosperity on account of oil exports, we see many missed opportunities. The oil-and-peace dividend was squandered. Instead of development and welfare programmes that could have reduced the country's gross inequalities and alleviated the extreme poverty of the south and other marginalised areas, the prior political–economic pathologies were exacerbated. Instead of an open national discussion about an inclusive political settlement, the political arena was occupied by men almost entirely preoccupied with narrow short-term interests.

Lessons learned from the case study

The promise of the CPA was peace, democracy, unity, and normalised relations between Sudan and the international community. None were achieved.

The independence of South Sudan was the default option for the CPA: a mechanical reading of the text and its political logic led automatically to that conclusion. The 'one country two systems' model was inherently centrifugal, and the six years of the interim period were far too short for the agenda of 'making unity attractive', even if the parties had been fully committed to that goal. Salva Kiir was intent on leading southern Sudan to independence, but maintained the public front that he was committed to unity for as long as possible. The NCP leadership appeared to be in denial about the imminence of separation until it was almost upon them: they did little to modify their programme to make it acceptable to the southerners. Both spent the peace dividend mainly on their militaries and the precious six years of the interim period preparing for a new war. Most strikingly, the internationals were almost entirely unprepared for the process of dividing Sudan and the implications that would follow.

The internal divisions within each of the main parties were frozen rather than resolved by the CPA and the interim period. Within the SPLM, these differences resurfaced at the party's 2008 Convention, at which point the US Special Envoy headed off an acrimonious leadership dispute by proposing that all leadership positions be kept as they were. In the months before independence, some SPLM leaders argued that a new war with the north was inevitable and should be initiated now, while the two SPLA divisions in the Nuba Mountains and Blue Nile were still part of the integrated command. Others argued for postponing the war until South Sudan could fight as an independent country. The option of a peaceful and cooperative separation was a minority position. Within the Sudanese government, paranoia was driven by the international response to the war and massacres in Darfur, culminating in the International Criminal Court arrest warrant issued for President Bashir in 2009. In these circumstances, it is perhaps remarkable that the CPA did not collapse into a renewed war before the 2011 referendum: that at least was achieved.

This evaluation of the CPA is pessimistic. It implies that the epistemological starting point for envisaging a peace agreement, a political settlement, or an institutional arrangement of the 'rules of the game' is insufficient for a conflict that has multiple dimensions and levels, and in which the political principals are skilled at the practical political management of turmoil and unpredictability. The potential salvation of the CPA lay not in the specifications of its text, but the opportunity it provided for Sudan's leaders to transcend the mechanical details and instead reinvent the political rules of the country. Under any circumstances that would have been a difficult challenge, but with one of the principals dead and the other side-lined, it became impossible. The implementation of the CPA was reduced to two parallel processes: an arms-and-patronage race to determine whether southern Sudan could become independent, and a technocratic exercise in constructing a plausible imitation of a bureaucratic state in southern Sudan.

References, further reading, and links to key primary documents

African Rights. 1995. *Facing Genocide: The Nuba of Sudan*. London: African Rights.

Alier, Abel. 1992. *Southern Sudan: Too Many Agreements Dishonoured*. London: Paul & Co.

Copnall, James. 2014. *A Poisonous Thorn in Our Hearts: Sudan and South Sudan's Bitter and Incomplete Divorce*. London: Hurst & Company.

Deng, Francis Mading. 1995. *War of Visions: Conflict of Identities in the Sudan*. Washington, DC: Brookings Institution Press.

Deng, Francis Mading. 2005. "African Renaissance: Towards a New Sudan." *Forced Migration Review* 24: 6–8.

Deng, Lual A. 2013. *The Power of Creative Reasoning: The Ideas and Vision of John Garang*. Bloomington, IN: Iuniverse.

De Waal, Alex. 2004. "The Politics of Destabilization in the Horn, 1989–2001." In Alex de Waal (Ed.), *Islamism and Its Enemies in the Horn of Africa*. London: Hurst & Company.

De Waal, Alex. 2007. "Sudan: The Turbulent State." In Alex de Waal (Ed.), *War in Darfur and the Search for Peace*. Cambridge, MA: Harvard University Press.

De Waal, Alex. 2015. *The Real Politics of the Horn of Africa: Money, War, and the Business of Power*. Cambridge: Polity Press.

De Waal, Alex, and A.H. Abdel Salam. 2004. "Islamism, State Power and *Jihad* in Sudan." In Alex de Waal (Ed.), *Islamism and Its Enemies in the Horn of Africa*. London: Hurst & Company.

Doornbos, Paul. 1988. "On Becoming Sudanese." In Tony Barnett, and Abbas Abdelkarim (Eds.), *Sudan: State, Capital and Transformation*. London: Croom Helm.

El-Affendi, Abdelwahab. 1990. "Discovering the South: Sudanese Dilemmas for Islam in Africa." *African Affairs* 89: 371–389.

El-Affendi, Abdelwahab. 2001. "The Impasse in the IGAD Peace Process for Sudan: The Limits of Regional Peacemaking." *African Affairs* 100: 581–599.

Fearon, D. James, and David D. Laitin. 2000. "Violence and the Social Construction of Ethnic Identity." *International Organization* 54 (4): 845–877.

Flint, Julie, and Alex de Waal. 2008. *Darfur: A New History of a Long War*. London: Zed Books.

Garang, John. 1987. *John Garang Speaks*. London: Kegan Paul.

Garang, John. 1992. *The Call for Democracy in Sudan*. London: Kegan Paul.

Johnson, H. Douglas. 2012. *The Root Causes of Sudan's Civil Wars: Peace or Truce?* Oxford: James Currey.

Johnson, H. Douglas. 2013. "New Sudan or South Sudan? The Multiple Meanings of Self-Determination in Sudan's Comprehensive Peace Agreement." *Civil Wars* 15 (2): 141–156.

Johnson, F. Hilde. 2011. *Waging Peace in Sudan: The Inside Story of the Negotiations That Ended Africa's Longest Civil War*. Brighton: Sussex Academic Press.

Johnson, F. Hilde. 2016. *South Sudan: The Untold Story*. London: IB Tauris.

Jok, Jok Madut. 2007. *Sudan: Race, Religion and Violence*. London: OneWorld.

Khan, H. Mushtaq. 2017. "Introduction: Political Settlements and the Analysis of Institution." *African Affairs* 1–20. https://academic.oup.com/afraf/advance-article/doi/10.1093/afraf/ad x044/4690667.

Leftwich, Adrian. 2010. "Beyond Institutions: Rethinking the Role of Leaders, Elites and Coalitions in the Institutional Formation of Developmental States and Strategies." *Forum for Development Studies* 37 (1): 93–111.

Mamdani, Mahmoud. 2016. "Who's to Blame in South Sudan?" *Boston Review*, 28 June. http://bostonreview.net/world/mahmood-mamdani-south-sudan-failed-transition.

Martin-Kessler, Florence, and Anne Poiret. 2012. *State Builders: The First Year of South Sudan's Independence*. Link TV. www.linktv.org/shows/state-builders/episodes/state-builders.

Mekki, Yousif Kuwa. 2001. "Things Would No Longer Be the Same." In Suleiman Rahhal (Ed.), *The Right to Be Nuba: The Story of a Sudanese People's Struggle for Survival*. Trenton, NJ: Red Sea Press.

Putnam, D. Robert. 1988. "Diplomacy and Domestic Politics: The Logic of Two-Level Games." *International Organization* 42 (3): 427–460.

Tubiana, Jérôme. 2007. "Darfur: A War for Land?" In Alex de Waal (Ed.), *War in Darfur and the Search for Peace*. Cambridge, MA: Harvard University Press.

Waihenya, Waithaka. 2006. *The Mediator: Gen. Lazaro Sumbeiywo and the Southern Sudan Peace Process*. Nairobi: Kenway Publications.

Wöndu, Steven, and Ann Lesch. 2000. *Battle for Peace in Sudan: An Analysis of the Abuja Conferences 1992–1993*. Lanham, MD: University Press of America.

World Bank. 2007. *Sudan: Public Expenditure Review, Synthesis Report*. Washington, DC: World Bank, Poverty Reduction and Economic Management Unit. Report No. 41840-SD, December.

World Peace Foundation. 2013. *Sudan Peace Archive*. Somerville MA: World Peace Foundation. https://sites.tufts.edu/wpf/sudan-peace-archive.

Young, John. 2012. *The Fate of Sudan: The Origins and Consequences of a Flawed Peace Process*. London: Zed Books.

Zartman, William. 2001. "The Timing of Peace Initiatives: Hurting Stalemates and Ripe Moments." *Global Review of Ethnopolitics* 1 (1): 8–18.

18

TURKEY

Bahar Başer and Alpaslan Özerdem

Introduction

The roots of the Turkish–Kurdish conflict can be traced back to well before the fall of the Ottoman Empire and the foundation of the Turkish Republic in 1923. As a result of nation-building efforts in the early republican era, a number of harsh measures were implemented to suppress any kind of dissent against the newly emerging and fragile authority of the state, with the aim of creating a unified nation under one flag from an ethnically, religiously, and linguistically divided country.

The Kurdish conflict, often coined as the 'Kurdish Question' in Turkey, can be understood as a constant resistance against the Turkish state's assimilation policies. These policies have resulted in the systematic suppression of Kurdish identity and subsequently a demand for the recognition and restitution of this group's basic political, cultural, and linguistic rights. As a typical asymmetric conflict, the two sides of the conflict have employed different warfare strategies and repertoires of action which have shifted according to the changes in political leadership, needs of time, and demands from their constituencies, among other factors.

The Kurdish resistance against the Turkish state's oppression and assimilation policies has not always been violent. There have been Kurdish movements in the form of student organisations, leftist sections of various political parties, and elite initiatives. However, over the last few decades the conflict turned violent, making it the country's primary political challenge, not to mention a high priority security problem that threatens the country's territorial integrity, to say the very least.

There has been an armed conflict between the Turkish state and the Kurdish armed group PKK (Kurdistan Workers' Party) since the early 1980s. For a long time, the Turkish state had a 'no negotiation with terrorists'[1] approach and opted for a military solution, as many other countries do while they are dealing with asymmetric conflicts. Simultaneously, starting from the mid-1980s, the state formulated a policy of recruiting Kurds who are not supporters of the PKK and arming them as a paramilitary structure called Village Guards. The idea was to curb potential support for the PKK by offering benefits such as salaries and status to certain tribes. Overall, nearly 50,000 people were killed in this armed conflict, and it is estimated that up to two million Kurds were displaced, lost their properties, and suffered from the consequences of this low-intensity civil war (see Çelik 2005; Ayata and Yükseker 2005). The conflict also increased societal polarisation among different Kurdish groups as well as between Turkish and Kurdish communities in Turkey.

In the political realm, on the other hand, various leaders from different political backgrounds, such as Turgut Özal or Erdal İnönü, tried to establish a soft recognition approach towards the plight of the Kurds; however, no concrete steps were taken until the AKP (Justice and Development Party) came to power in 2002. In the light of the demands from the European Union (EU) as preconditions for a potential membership, the newly elected government showed significant efforts in demonstrating their will to democratise the country. For instance, the 'Kurdish Opening' launched by the AKP in 2009 paved the way for public discussions of several issues previously considered taboo in Turkey. However, it fell short of corresponding to the demands of the Kurdish movement in Turkey.

After a secret negotiation process in Oslo from 2009 onwards and various democratisation packages in the country, Turkey finally experienced a resolution period. The Turkish–Kurdish peace process is said to have started in 2013, and it did not take long for it to be stalled, mostly due to unfolding domestic and regional developments. The hopes for a peaceful resolution were high considering the fact that both sides had public legitimacy and the leaders on both sides were able to consolidate their charismatic leadership due to their strong appeal over the crowds. However, the peace talks collapsed in the summer of 2015 and armed clashes resumed with even higher intensity than before. As the conflict continues, it destabilises Turkey and not only affects the national and international politics of the country but also has a major impact on many neighbouring countries with Kurdish populations, such as Iran, Iraq, and Syria.

Conflict analysis

As the founder of the Republic, Mustafa Kemal Atatürk oversaw the revolutionary remaking of Turkey from the ashes of the Ottoman Empire, while also introducing certain measures to keep the newly founded state intact. Considering the multicultural/multi-ethnic structure of the Empire and the territory that remained as its legacy, it was a hard task to establish a homogenous nation–state under one flag. A nationalist project was established which included a significant Turkification mechanism in order to create 'Turks' as the citizens of the new Republic.

There had been resistance to the reforms, mainly in the Kurdish areas, which engendered a significant amount of rebellion by various segments of society, including the Sunnis and the Alevites.[2] These rebellions were crushed by the Turkish military, and the leaders of the rebellions were severely punished in order to discourage any future unrest in the region. Under the martial law in the Kurdish populated areas, the Kurdish language was banned, Kurdish schools were closed down, and the Kurdish identity was left to disappear, with an expectation that Kurds, who constituted almost one-fourth of the population of Turkey, would eventually assimilate and become Turks.

The Turkish History Thesis and the Sun Language Theory were fabricated 'scientifically' by Turkish 'academics' who made it possible to deny the Kurdish existence in the political atmosphere of that period (Zeydanlıoğlu 2008). First, in 1938 Turkish was declared as the only official language of the Turkish Republic. Education was reformed and made compulsory, and the sole language of education was to be Turkish. The existence of a distinct Kurdish identity was denied; the Kurds were referred to as 'Mountain Turks' in order to define them in a Turkish context. Gradually, the use of Kurdish names was banned, causing the names of places and people to be changed. Even terms such as 'Kurd', 'Kurdish', 'Kurdistan', and 'the Kurdish language' were banned. It was a clear sign that the 'overlapping projects of functioning citizenship and democratisation have managed to bypass the Kurds, as Kurds, in modern Turkey' (White 2000: viii), and there was persistence in creating a homogenous Turkish nation derived from its geography's own multi-ethnic structure.

However, it was only after the 1960s that Kurdish student movements and other organisations with leftist tendencies started to emerge, campaigning about 'Kurdish rights' and taking a critical point of view vis-à-vis the Turkish state. In the mid-1970s, armed resistance was increasingly discussed by certain Kurdish groups; however, it was only with the foundation of the PKK in 1978 that these ideas were solidified. In the meantime, Turkey experienced three military coups in 1960, 1971, and 1980. The 1980 coup became a turning point especially for the Kurdish movement, as it aimed at erasing mostly the leftist ideology from the Turkish political scene, and the Kurdish movements at that time suffered the most from its iron fist. Many Kurds were put in prison, tortured, or compelled to leave the country, which created a significant diaspora population outside Turkish borders (Başer 2015). As a result of the military coup, the PKK gained a recruitment base due to the brutal policies of the Turkish state. Many Kurds released in the mid-1980s joined the PKK or started to become more sympathetic to it. In the meantime, the PKK extended its hegemony over the other Kurdish movements by actively fighting with or silencing them, as well as absorbing their constituencies. The PKK has waged an armed conflict against the Turkish state since 1984, which has been labelled as 'terrorism' by the state. Their initial aim was to establish a separate Kurdish state based on Marxist–Leninist principles, which the organisation gradually played down according to the changing political atmosphere in the world.

According to Mesut Yeğen (2015: 3), a prominent scholar of Kurdish studies, the Turkish state's engagement with the Kurdish question from 1923 to the 1990s stood on three pillars: assimilation, repression, and containment. These policies worked up until the 1990s but then started failing for two main reasons: (1) Kurdish resistance reached uncontainable proportions and the PKK turned into an insurgent group that had the capacity to conduct a low-level war with the Turkish state and its army for many decades without having recruitment problems. On top of that, the resistance movement influenced other establishments, such as Kurdish media, TV channels, political parties, and civil society organisations; and (2) after the 1991 Gulf War, some dynamics changed in the Middle East, which shifted the balance of power especially in favour of the Kurds in Iraq. This could explain why the Turkish state then opted for a harsher security policy in the region.

The 1990s have a significant place in Kurdish memory. Those years became the time when the Kurdish armed movement was turning into a social movement while receiving significant support from the Kurdish population. The state answered these uprisings with constant states of emergency in the region, which also included forced displacement of many Kurds from their villages due to allegations that they were providing material help and recruitment to the PKK. There have also been a significant number of disappearances, kidnappings, torture, and extra-judicial killings, which Ensaroğlu calls 'terror from above' by the state as a response to 'terror from below' by the PKK (Ensaroğlu 2013: 8). These surely became issues during the peace talks with regards to reconciliation and transitional justice. When the conflict reached a peak at the end of the 1990s, the PKK leader, Abdullah Öcalan, was captured in Kenya (Van Bruinessen 2000).

After the imprisonment of the PKK leader in 1999, the Kurdish movement rapidly transformed itself into a political power in Kurdish regions. The movement also dropped the idea of a separate Kurdish state and instead adopted a strategy that foresees a semi-federal solution demanding the decentralisation of the Turkish state. Altering their strategies according to the unfolding developments in the region, the Kurdish resistance then started to embed itself in civil society organisations and diaspora movements. The Kurdish diaspora managed to lobby European parliaments as well as the European Union itself towards a resolution. This has been an important strategy, considering the fact that Turkey was declared as an eligible country for EU membership candidacy in 1999. Several political parties mushroomed, which were defined as pro-Kurdish; however, they were banned one after another by the Turkish Constitutional Court for terrorist propaganda or for supporting separatism (Watts 2014). Up until the 2000s, Kurds struggled to open a political space for representation in Turkish politics; however, their attempts were pushed back by the Turkish establishment.

The AKP came to power in 2002, and its rise to power was a turning point in Turkey for many reasons. It started implementing a conservative agenda and, at the same time, 'taboo' topics such as Kurdish identity and peace negotiations were opened to discussion. The AKP gradually began implementing reforms to accommodate Kurdish identity in order to align itself with the membership ideals of the European Union. This tactic brought electoral success to the AKP in the 2007 elections due to the Kurdish votes that it poached from other parties. This enabled them to further consolidate their power (Gürbüz 2016) but at the same time gave them enough confidence to proceed with a reform process.

Regional developments also compelled the government to act this way. First, it was clear that the Kurdish autonomous region in Iraq was there to stay, and its willingness to collaborate with Turkey made Turkey understand that the Kurdish region was an ally rather than an eternal security threat. Turkey was also aiming to establish a new foreign policy which would make it a rising power in the Middle East and enable it to play a bigger role in determining the politics of the region in the future. Therefore, it would be of interest to Turkey to end its domestic problems as soon as possible. Moreover, there was a positive atmosphere towards peace despite the uproar from opposition parties such as the MHP (Nationalist Movement Party) and CHP (Republican Peoples' Party). The conflict had been going on for a long time, and it was obvious that Turkey could not win the war by conventional military methods, since the PKK had no problems with recruitment or arms supply. Moreover, its societal support base had been growing daily. Although this situation cannot be defined as a mutually hurting stalemate in Zartman's terms, it seemed like a ripe moment for establishing covert or secret communication channels. Considering the conflict had had a huge human toll and the Turkish state has set aside an annual 15 billion US dollars over the past 20 years to tackle this problem, negotiations were obviously considered as a rational step (Ensaroğlu 2013: 9).

The conflict resolution process

The PKK ended its ceasefire in 2004 and launched attacks against the Turkish military two years after the AKP came to power. Understanding the necessity of containing the problem, Yeğen suggests in his 2005 Diyarbakir speech that 'Erdoğan used the most liberal discourse a prime minister had ever employed in Turkey' (Yeğen 2015: 5) by saying 'the Kurdish problem is my problem'. He admitted that the state had made mistakes with regards to its treatment of the Kurdish population in Turkey and that he would make sure that local cultures flourished under the umbrella of the Turkish Republic.

Starting with the 2007 election, the AKP showed clear intentions with regard to serious reforms in terms of resolving the Kurdish Question. By doing so, the AKP increased its popularity among the religious Kurds, enhancing its voter base while also gaining the approval of the international community. A timeline of significant events, considered to be crucial parts of the pre-negotiation and negotiation process, can be seen in Figure 18.1. Concurrently, we discuss the outcome of negotiations and explain the reasons for failure. However, before that, it is important to remember that such conflict resolution terms as 'negotiations' should be used loosely in the Turkey peace process context because of the overall opaqueness of what took place and whether they were negotiations in conventional sense. This is one of the most interesting and unique characteristics of the Turkey peace process; while it seemed to employ a wide range of typical conflict resolution tools, their implementation, as will be seen below, was rather unorthodox.

FIGURE 18.1 Phases of the Turkish–Kurdish conflict resolution process

Source: Authors

Oslo Talks: After the 2007 elections, the AKP decided to implement a new policy of negotiation with the PKK.

> Between September 2008 and 2011, these reform efforts were accompanied by several meetings, apparently in Oslo, between high-level representatives from the National Intelligence Agency (MİT) and top PKK leaders [in exile] like Zübeyir Aydar, Sabri Ok, Remzi Kartal and Adem Uzun, with the presence of an international mediator.
>
> *(ICG Report 2014)*

There is no credible source which states the exact start date of the secret negotiations, and it is clear that the initial talks were conducted with extreme caution (Yeğen 2015: 5; Ensaroğlu 2013: 13). It is said that several meetings occurred in Europe; however, these talks are usually referred to as the Oslo Talks.[3] The exact number of people, their statuses and roles were not shared with the public. The transcription of meetings was later leaked to the public in 2011 and brought no concrete results. However, it was a sign that the Turkish state was now addressing the primary actor of the Kurdish movement, the PKK. 'The Oslo Process collapsed in 2011 and many important issues such as conditional amnesties; returns, transitional justice and disarmament remained unsolved' (ICG Report 2014).

The Kurdish Opening:[4] In parallel with the Oslo Talks, the AKP government declared the beginning of a process of reforms with the potential to lead to a resolution of the Turkish–Kurdish conflict in 2009, called the 'Kurdish Opening'. A state TV channel (TRT 6) broadcasting in Kurdish was opened, several departments at universities started offering curricula in Kurdish, and the existence of a Kurdish Question was acknowledged by politicians, including the then-Prime Minister Erdoğan. The AKP also ended the state of emergency as a gesture of good will to show that they were determined to find a peaceful solution to this problem. They also prepared an amnesty law aimed at PKK fighters.

Despite these 'gestures', the PKK and Kurdish activists also still questioned the sincerity of the government on the route to a potential resolution and were sceptical of its actions. During the rapprochement period, it was still possible to observe the oppression of Kurdish identity and freedom of speech. Many Kurdish politicians and journalists were arrested; pro-Kurdish parties were outlawed or criminalised; Turkish opposition politicians constantly referred to the Kurdish movement as 'terrorist'; and ceasefires were violated, though on a fairly small scale. At the same time, the 'peace project' was alive and kicking, and the media was paying a great deal of attention to the whole process. Despite uproar from the opposition, who did not have enough teeth to spoil the process, the AKP and PKK showed determination in continuing with the process, which resulted in the return of 34 PKK fighters from the Qandil Mountains, where the PKK is based, and from Maxmur refugee camp, both of which are in the neighbouring Iraq. Turkish media picked up on the fact that these fighters returned with guerrilla clothes and were welcomed by huge crowds. This unusual scene, shown on every TV station, backfired and rekindled Turkish nationalist 'sensitivities', which then compelled the government to take a step back from the process. The process deadlocked, and violence resumed (Yeğen 2015: 6–7).

Between 2010 and 2013, many people lost their lives. Some significant events also occurred during this period, such as the closure of the pro-Kurdish political party DTP (Democratic Society Party) (2009), which created aftershocks among Kurdish society; the Roboski incident[5] (2011); the KCK (Kurdistan Communities Union) trials;[6] and the assassination of three Kurdish activist women in Paris (2013),[7] among others, which widened the gap between the two sides.[8] One other significant event to mention is the hunger strikes in Turkish prisons initiated by Kurdish political prisoners in 2012. The strikes lasted for so long that it became a political debate in the parliament. The prisoners demanded that Öcalan should be allowed to see his lawyers and convey messages to the PKK. It is said that at that time the minister of justice, Sadullah Ergin, had individual meetings with prisoners to end the strike, which were not shared with the public at that time (Çelik et al. 2015: 36, Ensaroğlu 2013: 14). As a result of the hunger strikes, among other developments, the communication channels with Öcalan were opened again to refresh the process.

Another critical impact on the resolution process, on the other hand, came from the 2013 Gezi protests. At the end of May in 2013, a protest in Gezi Park sparked a massive wave of protests all around Turkey, starting from Istanbul. Although initially the protests were against the demolition of the Gezi Park, they turned into demonstrations of extreme disapproval with the AKP government's policies with regard to freedom of speech and assembly, freedom of press, and the secular values on which the Turkish Republic was founded. During the Gezi protests, leftists, Kemalists, and nationalists formed an unconventional alliance, which was short term and consequential. Many individual Kurds also participated in the protests in metropoles of Turkey, but the protests did not create a visible echo in the Kurdish region. The Kurdish political party was also cautious and hesitant to make declarations as the protestors were a heterogeneous group, and some involved, such as the nationalists and Kemalists, were against the peace process altogether. Moreover, the Kurdish movement did not fully support the protests for fear that this would stall the peace process (Gourlay 2013). The protests caused uproar among the ranks of the government, which then started implementing more and more authoritarian politics in order to curb the opposition. As Turkey became less and less democratic under an elected government, the space in which the peace process could flourish also started disappearing.

Öcalan's road map and the İmralı meetings: Öcalan had previously prepared a road map for the resolution process, but it was not accessible to public until early 2011 (Yeğen 2015: 7). However, the real impact of Öcalan's communications came to the fore when regular visits to his prison cell began. A committee established by the deputies of the pro-Kurdish Party, BDP (and then consecutively HDP), has visited the PKK leader Öcalan at the İmralı Island prison in the Marmara Sea on a number of occasions and acted as mediator/messenger between the different segments of the Kurdish resistance movement. The negotiation process was complicated due to the existence of a number of proxy actors. Yeğen defines this mechanism as the following: 'the state and Öcalan would keep talking, Öcalan would inform the PKK headquarters in Kandil and be informed by them through the BDP deputies visiting İmralı' (Yeğen 2015: 8). It meant that the state was not directly negotiating with a group which it has called 'terrorist' for the last four decades.

First, on 3 January 2013, two Kurdish MPs went to İmralı Island to visit Öcalan. In the same year, other visits were paid by Kurdish MPs in February and April. Following the meetings, the BDP officials then visited the PKK and KCK leaders. Thus, 2013 became the year in which the negotiations became known to the public. It was also a significant moment of taboo-breaking when the government let the Kurdish MPs convey Öcalan's messages to the symbolically important Newroz celebrations in March that year. Öcalan's letter was read out loud in Diyarbakır to the public; he called for peace, stating that armed struggle should be a thing of the past and the Kurdish movement should opt for a democratic struggle. He suggested that PKK fighters should retreat from Turkey, democratic reforms should be put into place by the government, and the PKK should be integrated in civil and political circles in Turkey (Çelik et al. 2015: 37). The PKK then declared a ceasefire on 23 March.

Öcalan's Newroz call significantly decreased the violence between the Turkish military and the PKK. Authors such as Çicek and Coşkun (2015: 7) claim that the peace process actually symbolically started with Öcalan's Newroz declaration. Similar to the South African example, these events showed that an imprisoned leader could still have an influence on both the PKK and its constituency; he therefore proved himself to be the right person to talk to for a potential resolution of the conflict.

In late 2013, the PKK stated that they had done their share by withdrawing from Turkey, and that it was time for the Turkish state to realise its promises. What was expected from the government were legal reforms to guarantee Kurdish rights in the constitution, making these rights irreversible, rather than a democratisation rhetoric which has not yet been solidified into laws or regulations. Obviously, there was significant mistrust between the two parties which the Newroz declaration could not erase. The Turkish state kept building military posts and dams[9] in south-east Turkey, as well as increasing the number of village guards during the peace process; this was a clear sign that the state was actually considering going back to fighting and was taking security measures by increasing its presence in the region (Gunter 2014).

Wise People Commissions: In April 2013, then-Prime Minister Erdoğan appointed 63 people as 'wise men'[10] in order to formulate fact-finding commissions that would be responsible for the seven different regions of Turkey. Within two months of observations and trips to various locations, they were expected to report back to the prime minister about their findings. This exercise was a kind of 'testing the waters' strategy, but it was tailored for testing Turkish sensitivities towards the process rather than Kurdish ones. Members of the 'wise people' committees included journalists, authors, actors, academics, and public intellectuals who were thought to have the capacity to understand the people's expectations of the peace process. Each commission wrote a report on their expectations. These above all else emphasised the confusion experienced by people during the peace process (Oran 2014). These reports have not been shared with the public, and there is significant doubt about their impact. Nevertheless, it was quite a revolutionary attempt by the Turkish state to engage the general public on an issue which would traditionally remain in the domain of top-down policy making. It was never clear whether there was genuine interest from the government in making the peace process participatory by incorporating the public's views on peace and peacebuilding, but at least the formation of such commissions showed a new departure point and approach to conflict resolution in Turkey.

Resolution Commission: The Turkish Parliament also founded a 'Resolution Commission' that included ten MPs from the ruling AKP and one member from the pro-Kurdish party, which at the time was called the BDP (Peace and Democracy Party).[11] A significant number of civil society organisations, political parties, academics, and intellectuals were invited to share their thoughts on the resolution process. Two contributors to this volume – Professor Jenny Pearce and Professor Alpaslan Özerdem – were among those academics who took part in this Commission's proceedings. At the end of the commission meetings, the AKP and the BDP[12] published their own interpretations of the meetings. The opposition parties refused to provide members for this committee.

Promises and disappointments: Since the beginning, PKK's demands were clear: release of political prisoners, improvement of Öcalan's prison conditions, elimination of the 10 per cent threshold for parliamentary elections (which would enable the movement to have political representation), introduction of mother-tongue education in Kurdish populated areas, legalisation of the PKK, and an acknowledgement of its role in the peace process. The reform package offered by the government, however, hardly met these conditions except for offering a few cosmetic changes on cultural and linguistic issues, such as allowing the use of the letters X, Q, and W as well as freedom to campaign in Kurdish (Gunter 2014: 22). The Turkish state also repetitively underlined that they expected PKK's withdrawal and disarmament as a precondition for a peaceful resolution. The Kurdish side constantly demanded that a third party be involved in the peace negotiations. This would bring not only a neutral party to monitor the process but would also a mediator to reconcile potential conflicts between the two sides on the way to a peace agreement. The government rejected the idea until the Dolmabahçe Accord in 2015, which suggested an independent monitoring commission. In 2014, the AKP formulated two legal frameworks that could constitute the basis of a legal settlement to the conflict. The first amendment of the law on the National Intelligence Service (NIS) gave the NIS the authority to 'negotiate with the terrorists', and then a law which was entitled 'Law to End Terror and Strengthen Social Integration' was prepared (Yeğen 2015: 10; Çelik et al. 2015: 47–50).

Rapidly changing dynamics in the Middle East also affected the psyche of the peace process. The Kurdish movement in Syria, which is very sympathetic to the PKK, started fighting with the so-called Islamic State (IS) in Northern Syria around the Turkish border. The Turkish state never wanted to acknowledge the agency of this group, PYD (Democratic Union Party), and their armed wing, YPG (The People's Protection Units) as a separate actor in Syria; instead, they kept referring to them as a part of the PKK. Their successes against IS were perceived as a possible security threat for Turkish territorial integrity, as it meant that an autonomous Kurdish region in Syria might also mean that same thing could happen in Turkey. Moreover, they did not want to see a PKK-friendly structure just next to the border. Therefore, when IS attacked Kobane and formed a siege in September 2014,[13] Turkish attitude towards the Kurds in Kobane became a determining factor for the success of the peace process in Turkey.

For some Kurds, Turkey has been supporting IS or other Islamic movements in Syria with the aim of preventing the formulation of an autonomous Kurdish region, and therefore the siege was a cause for satisfaction rather than dismay among Turkish nationalist political circles, including the government (Yanmış 2016: 15). In October 2014, there were mass protests by the Kurds all around Turkey which turned violent. The protestors were demonstrating their anger against both IS and Turkey at the same time. Dozens of civilians lost their lives, as did some military personnel. Some argue that Kobane protests actually mark the end of the resolution process, although both sides declared that they would keep negotiating. These events clearly showed that the government had gradually eliminated its 'winning hearts and minds of the Kurdish population' strategy while at the same time making it clear that the PKK cannot opt for disarmament when their sister organisation is waging a fight for survival against the IS. The cards of the game were being reshuffled due to the swiftly sprouting events in the Middle East.

Dolmabahçe Accord

After nearly two years of a dialogue process following Öcalan's Newroz declaration, the Dolmabahçe Meeting took place on 28 February 2015. This meeting was highly significant since it was the first time that representatives from both sides were present at a press declaration on the peace process. The HDP MP, Sırrı Süreyya Önder, read the report of the İmralı Committee and stated that the negotiations were at a breaking point. He stated that Öcalan had called the PKK to have an extraordinary meeting in spring 2015 to end the armed struggle in order to arrive a democratic solution for the Turkish–Kurdish conflict. AKP representatives also made statements underlining that the resolution was near and that there had been a serious progress (Çiçek and Coşkun 2015: 10). What ended this 'dialogue' process were the developments that occurred after the Dolmabahçe Accord. Less than a month after the Dolmabahçe press declaration, Öcalan's Newroz declaration of 2015 brought a precondition for the gathering of the extraordinary PKK Congress: a Truth and Reconciliation Commission whose members would be selected from the members of parliament and the monitoring commission. On the other hand, President Erdoğan declared that he did not agree with the declarations and was strongly opposed to a monitoring commission for the negotiations.

By late March, campaigns for the forthcoming national elections on 6 June were taking place all around Turkey, which were particularly important for Turkey's political future. On the one hand, the AKP desired a supermajority in the parliament to be able to have enough number of deputies to change the regime of Turkey from a parliamentarian to an ambiguous presidential one. At the same time, the HDP, a pro-Kurdish leftist leaning party, decided to participate in the elections, despite the 10 per cent threshold, rather than putting forward independent candidates. If the HDP passed the threshold, it would prevent the AKP gaining the desired percentage of the votes. A fierce campaign took place between the AKP and the HDP where both sides targeted each other in election speeches. The AKP was aware that due to the peace process it had been losing nationalist votes, and it seemed like the process was favouring the HDP rather than the AKP when it came to Kurdish voters. The AKP and the President then adopted a nationalist rhetoric that criminalised the PKK and continued to call the Kurdish movement and their representatives in the parliament 'terrorists'. In the meantime, HDP's election slogan was directly against Erdoğan, stating 'We will not make you the President!' The HDP passed the threshold and received more than 13 per cent of the votes in the elections, becoming the biggest barrier facing the AKP's desires to change the regime. Moreover, the new Parliament failed to produce a coalition government, thanks to President Erdoğan's direct and indirect interventions, which led the country to hold follow-up national elections on 1 November 2015.

Before and after the elections, the government lobbied the international community to put the PYD in Syria on the terrorist lists of the EU, NATO, and the USA. This caused displeasure among the Kurdish population. As the process was becoming extremely vulnerable towards the conflict taking place in Syria, a bomb attack targeted Kurdish activists and leftist students in Suruç on 20 July while they were planning on bringing some aid materials to Kobane. The Kurdish viewpoint was that the attack was orchestrated by ISIS, but enabled by the Turkish state. The PKK, as a retaliation, killed two policemen on 22 July, and the Turkish military started bombing PKK camps in northern Iraq. This date is accepted as marking the official collapse of the peace process.

Unfolding events after the collapse of the peace process

After the collapse of the peace process, clashes between the PKK and the Turkish armed forces resumed, with the government simultaneously starting to put more pressure on opposition groups. While observers suggested that Turkey was becoming more and more authoritarian and experiencing a democratic backslide,[14] the clashes reached a peak point when the urban wing of the PKK declared self-rule in certain districts of south-eastern Turkey, digging trenches and building barricades against the security forces. The response to these developments by the authorities were 24-hour curfews in many cities, which prevented people from leaving their homes and reaching supplies such as food and medicine. It was reported that many civilians lost their lives during the security operations.[15]

Both sides went back to a mood of 'total war' starting from 2017, and the traces of the peace process gradually disappeared as peace journalism turned into mainstream media spreading hatred, and politicians using a polarising discourse increased tensions among the different segments of Turkish society. Meanwhile, on 15 July 2016, Turkey witnessed one of its most critical political junctures when a coup was attempted by a small segment of the Turkish army. The Gülen Movement, a religious brotherhood that was in a close relationship with the AKP until only a few years ago, was identified as the plotter of the failed coup attempt, which was followed by a declaration of a state of emergency for three months. This three-month state of emergency was extended twice. The government used this as an opportunity and implemented a massive purge in the name of cleansing the infiltration of the Gülenists from all public institutions, including the judiciary, bureaucracy, police, army, and academia.

Since the end of the peace process, Turkey has also experienced 33 bomb attacks carried out by ISIS and TAK (a PKK splinter group), killing 446 people, 363 of whom were civilians. During the purge orchestrated under the states of emergency, many journalists, academics, and opposition party members were arrested. Elected politicians from the HDP, including the co-leaders of the party, have been put in prison. Under these circumstances, resuming the peace process seems highly unlikely, but lessons learned from other cases reveal that confluence of various factors can actually push both sides to negotiate with one another in the near future.

The reasons for failure

According to a quantitative study conducted by Mehmet Yanmış in Kurdish-populated areas such as Hakkari, Silopi, and Cizre, among others, 57.8 per cent of the interviewees think that what ended the peace process was the attitude of the state and government.

This is followed by 28.6 per cent who state it was the failure and insincerity of the parties, 17.6 percent that it was the PKK's distrust of process and politics, 13.9 per cent that it was the inability of the PKK and HDP to manage the post-June 7 election period, 12.5 per cent that it was the government's attitude towards Kobane, and 7.3 per cent blaming foreign powers (Yanmış 2016: 11). With these survey results in mind, the reasons for failure in achieving a full political settlement of the Kurdish Question in Turkey could be grouped under two main headings: political shifts and changing priorities for both parties, and ineffective management of the process.

Political shifts and changing priorities

The 7 June 2015 elections became a litmus test for the peace process. Since President Erdoğan rejected the Dolmabahçe meeting resolutions and put an end to further negotiations, there was no room for further discussion before the elections. In the meantime, significant events such as the Suruç Massacre and Kobane made it clear that both sides would take up arms again and keep blaming each other for the failure of the process.

The Erdoğan factor and his expectations from a peaceful settlement of the Kurdish Question has changed over time. Once he realised he could no longer win elections on the basis of making peace with the Kurds, the only realistic option left to him was to go war instead. Similarly, the entire process was also an internal power struggle between the three segments of PKK – Qandil, Diaspora, and HDP – as well as Öcalan, and when it became clear to Qandil that peace might be a total loss of power for them, then the continuation of violence was the way forward. With the Syrian war particularly, they had fewer reasons for a peaceful settlement and hoped that an alliance with PYD could, in fact, bring them what they always wanted – independence from Turkey.

Ineffective management of the process

Throughout the process, the parties – but particularly the state actors – behaved in a rather reactive and inexperienced way. They gave an impression of making up strategies as the process progressed rather than setting up a coherent plan of actions. Not engaging Parliament fully in this process is a good example. Insisting on a full disarmament of PKK without providing the necessary political guarantees also showed a significant level of immaturity and lack of understanding of realistic demands of such environments. It can also be argued that the power asymmetries have been kept throughout the process, and the government never accepted the PKK as an equal partner in negotiations. Also, the connections between Öcalan and the PKK or other civil society organisations were stalled by the Turkish government, which hindered healthy channels of communication (Gunter 2014). This prevented a constant dialogue being sustained throughout the whole process. Permissions to visit Öcalan were granted in an arbitrary fashion that upset the Kurdish side.

The Kurdish side also constantly demanded that a third party be involved in the peace negotiations. This would have brought not only a neutral party to monitor the process but also a mediator to reconcile the potential conflicts between the two sides on the way to a peace agreement. The government persistently rejected the idea. Furthermore, the public's concerns were ignored, and it was hoped that the Wise People Commission alone could deal with them. It is also important to remember that the Kurdish conflict in Turkey has never been a solely domestic matter. In fact, it always had very strong regional and international dimensions. Therefore, such dynamics should have also been tackled more effectively to enable a successful conclusion to the talks.

Last but not least, the EU could not use its leverage on Turkey throughout the whole process. Although in the early 2000s, the EU pushed Turkey for further reforms and democratisation due to membership negotiations, the Syrian refugee crises changed the balance of power between the two actors. The refugee deal between the EU and the Turkish state to keep the flow of Syrian refugees crossing to Europe through the Aegean Sea between Turkey and Greece gave Turkey a strong hand. Subsequently, the EU started to be less and less critical towards Turkey and, in time, became an invisible actor, even though some serious human rights violations took place beginning with the collapse of the negotiations.

Lessons to be learned from the case study

The peace process seemed to be beneficial for both sides for a variety of reasons while it lasted: the AKP enhanced its voter base while at the same time increasing its prestige globally and managing to create a positive image of itself, especially in the USA and in Europe. The PKK also used the negotiations as a potential platform to legitimise itself and gain prestige by showing their peaceful demands. Also, the peace process enabled the PKK to shift its attention to Syria. There has always been mistrust between these two actors, but the PKK was aware that they could only sit at the negotiation table with this political party, as opposition parties such as the MHP or CHP never once employed a peace rhetoric during the resolution process.

However, the process showed that the so-called ripe moment can be fluid and is vulnerable to domestic and external factors. The peace process took place at a time when regional dynamics were constantly shifting. Both sides had interests in alternative outcomes of the war in Syria, and what was happening next door had an immense impact on the process. Moreover, domestically, the AKP and President Erdoğan's desire to cling to power exceeded the desire for a peaceful resolution. The government backed the peace process as long as it served its own interests. As soon as it started losing votes, there was a U-turn towards nationalist rhetoric to attract more votes from nationalist voters who were disturbed by the peace process in general. Before this point, when both sides were committed, they did not let spoilers derail the process – so much so that the negotiations went on despite the murders of three Kurdish activists in Paris, leakage of the secret talks, etc. Negative and positive developments went hand in hand throughout the whole process.

Both sides learned from each other during this process. They developed skills in terms of dealing with opponents on the negotiation table. Examples from other cases such as South Africa and Northern Ireland show us that resuming peace processes are possible when conditions become ripe again. When the time is right, the Turkish establishment must come up with a better road map for negotiations by understanding the complexities of the situation and, rather than making impossible demands, should be more assertive in terms of coming up with a more realistic plan. The PKK should also open up more space for pro-Kurdish political parties to play the role of mediators in the process and should not undermine their efforts. A peaceful resolution would only come to Turkey through the 'peace by democratization' method. Considering the current developments in the region, such as continuation of war in Syria, Turkey's rapprochement with Russia, and abandoning the ideal of becoming a member of the EU, at least in rhetoric, one can see that a ripe moment is not on the horizon. However, it should be noted that moments can also be ripened by a desire for peace from the political leaders of both sides. The rapidly changing internal and external dynamics currently blur the potential road map for a peaceful settlement in Turkey.

Notes

1 Turkey is not the only country which considers the PKK a terrorist organisation. The European Union, NATO, and the USA also define it as such.
2 The most well-known rebellions are Seyh Said (1925), Agrı (1926–1930), and Dersim (1937).
3 President Erdoğan officially confirmed in 2012 that these talks took place and that some international organisations were involved as third parties; however, the details have not been shared with the public.
4 The name of this initiative was later revised as the 'Democratic Opening', then 'the National Unity and Fraternity Project' led by then-Interior Minister Beşir Atalay.
5 On 28 December 2011, Turkish F-16 fighter jets bombed and killed 19 people who were crossing the Turkish–Iraqi border. Most of the victims were children. They were smuggling petrol and cigarettes from Iraq to Turkey and were crossing the border with donkeys. The Turkish state declared that they were mistaken as PKK fighters. The lack of an official apology caused uproar and had a negative impact on the peace process.
6 Starting from April 2009, thousands of people were detained on charges of being members of the KCK, allegedly the urban wing of the PKK. The detainees included politicians, journalists, academics, and human rights activists, among others. The trials and pre-trial detentions lasted until 2012.
7 Three Kurdish women were assassinated in Paris on 9 January 2013: Sakine Cansız (one of the co-founders of the PKK), Fidan Doğan, and Leyla Söylemez, who were active in Kurdish politics. The murderer was a Turkish man who infiltrated a Kurdish organisation and disguised himself as Kurdish until the murders. He then died in prison without the trial ending in France.
8 However, it should be noted that these events, despite creating trust issues, did not visibly affect the commitment of either side towards the peace process.
9 The so-called security dams were a crucial issue during the peace process. Construction of dams in Kurdish-populated areas in south-eastern Turkey causes eradication of Kurdish cultural heritage in these areas as well as displacement of many Kurds. The Kurdish activists usually refuse dam construction as they perceive it a 'cultural genocide'. Environmentalists also warned that the dams affect the climate and vegetation in the area in a negative way. The dams also separate the Kurdistan region of Iraq from Kurdish-populated areas in Turkey.

10 The term 'wise men' was changed to 'wise people' as a reaction to its sexist connotations through an intervention by Professor Özerdem on a TV programme – 5N1K – which was then widely accepted by the public.
11 The BDP was active on the political scene between 2008 and 2014. It was succeeded by People's Democratic Party (HDP).
12 'BDP Kürt Sorunu Komisyon Raporu' [*BDP Kurdish Question Report*], available online [https://serdargunes.files.wordpress.com/2015/08/bdp-kurt-sorunu_komisyonu_raporu.pdf]
13 The siege and attacks created around 20,000 Kurdish refugees at the Turkish border.
14 The Turkish establishment mobilised all its state apparatuses for suppressing opposition in Turkey, starting with the November 2015 elections. For example, see Öztürk (2016).
15 For more information, see www.hrw.org/news/2015/12/22/turkey-mounting-security-operation-deaths.

References, further reading, and links to key primary documents

Ayata, B., and D. Yükseker. 2005. "A Belated Awakening: National and International Responses to the Internal Displacement of Kurds in Turkey." *New Perspectives on Turkey* 32: 5–42.

Başer, B. 2015. *Diasporas and Homeland Conflicts: A Comparative Perspective*. Farnham: Ashgate.

Bozarslan, H. 2001. "Human Rights and the Kurdish Issue in Turkey." *Human Rights Review* 3 (1): 45–54.

Casier, M., J. Jongerden, and N. Walker. 2013. "Turkey's Kurdish Movement and the AKP's Kurdish Opening: A Kurdish Spring or Fall?" In M. Ahmed, and G. Michael (Eds.), *The Kurdish Spring: Geopolitical Changes and the Kurds*. Costa Mesa, CA: Mazda Publishers.

Çelik, B.A. 2005. "I Miss My Village!" Forced Kurdish migrants In İstanbul and their representation in Associations, New Perspective on Turkey.

Çelik, B.A., E. Balta, L. Korkut, M. Çelikkan, and Nil Mutluer. 2015. "Barış Sürecine Giden Yol." In A. Necmiye, and T. Hakan (Eds.), *Barış Açısını Savunmak: Çözüm Sürecinde Ne Oldu?* Istanbul: Metis.

Çiçek, C. 2015. "Çözüm Sürecinde Kırılmalar: Çatışmalar, Müzakereler ve Sınırlar." In A. Necmiye, and T. Hakan (Eds.), *Barış Açısını Savunmak: Çözüm Süreci'ne Ne Oldu?* İstanbul: Metis: Siyah Beyaz.

Çiçek, C., and V. Coşkun. 2015. "Dolmabahçe'den Günümüze Çözüm süreci: Başarısızlığı Anlamak ve Yeni Bir Yol Bulmak." In *Barış Vakfı*. Ankara: Politika Raporu 1.

Ensaroğlu, Yılmaz. 2013. "Turkey's Kurdish Question and the Peace Process." *Insight Turkey* 15 (2): 7–17.

Gourlay, W. 2013. "After Gezi: Turkish-Kurdish Fault Lines." *Open Democracy*, 27 September 2013. www.opendemocracy.net/william-gourlay/after-gezi-turkish-kurdish-fault-lines.

Gunter, Micheal. 2014. "The Turkish-Kurdish Peace Process Stalled in Neutral." *Insight Turkey* 16 (1): 19–26.

Gürbüz, M. 2016. *Rival Kurdish Movements in Turkey: Transforming Ethnic Conflict*. Amsterdam: Amsterdam University Press.

International Crisis Group Report. 2014. "Turkey and the PKK: Saving the Peace Process." International Crisis Group Report, No. 234, 6 November 2014. https://www.crisisgroup.org/europe-central-asia/western-europemediterranean/turkey/turkey-and-pkk-saving-peace-process.

Jongerden, J., and A.H. Akkaya. 2011. "Born from the Left: The Making of the PKK." In C. Marlies, and J. Jongerden (Eds.), *Nationalisms and Politics in Turkey: Political Islam, Kemalism and the Kurdish Issue*. New York: Routledge.

Oran, B. 2014. *Ben Ege'de Akilken . . . .* İstanbul: İletişim Yayınları.

Öztürk, A.E. 2016. "Turkey's Diyanet Under AKP Rule: From Protector to Imposer of State Ideology?" *Southeast European and Black Sea Studies* 16 (4): 619–635.

Sarıgil, Z., and O. Fazlıoğlu. 2014. "Exploring the Roots and Dynamics of Kurdish Ethno-Nationalism in Turkey." *Nations and Nationalism* 20 (3): 436–458.

Van Bruinessen, M. 2000. *Turkey, Europe and the Kurds After the Capture of Öcalan*. Kurdish ethno-nationalism versus nation-building states. Istanbul: ISIS Press.

Watts, Nicole. 2014. *Sandıkla Meydan Okumak: Türkiye'de Kürtlerin Siyasi Yolculuğu*. Ankara: İletişim Yayınları.

White, Paul. 2000. *Primitive Rebels or Revolutionary Modernizers? The Kurdish National Movement in Turkey*. London/New York: Zedbooks.

Yanmış, M. 2016. *Resurgence of the Kurdish Conflict in Turkey: How Kurds View It*. Rethink Institute. Washington, DC: Rethink Paper 25.

Yeğen, Mesut. 2015. *The Kurdish Peace Process in Turkey: Genesis, Evolution and Prospects*. IAI Working paper 11. www.iai.it/sites/default/files/gte_wp_11.pdf.

Zeydanlıoğlu, W. 2008. *The White Turkish Man's Burden: Orientalism, Kemalism and the Kurds in Turkey*. In G. Rings, and A. Ife (Eds.), *Neo-Colonial Mentalities in Contemporary Europe? Language and Discourse in the Construction of Identities*. Newcastle Upon Tyne: Cambridge Scholars Publishing.

Further reading

Bilgin, Fevzi, and Sarihan Ali. (Eds.). 2013. *Understanding Turkey's Kurdish Question*. Lanham, MD: Lexington Books.

Jacoby, T., and A. Özerdem. 2012. *Peace in Turkey 2023: The Question of Human Security and Conflict Transformation*. Lanham, MD: Lexington Books.

Kuzu, D. 2016. "The Politics of Identity, Recognition and Multiculturalism: The Kurds in Turkey." *Nations and Nationalism* 22: 123–142.

Tekdemir, Ö. 2016. "Conflict and Reconciliation Between Turks and Kurds: The HDP as an Agonistic Actor." *Southeast European and Black Sea Studies* 16 (4): 651–669.

Tezcur, G.M. 2010. "When Democratization Radicalizes: The Kurdish Nationalist Movement in Turkey." *Journal of Peace Research* 47 (6): 775–789.

Weiss, Matthew. "From Constructive Engagement to Renewed Estrangement? Securitization and Turkey's Deteriorating Relations with Its Kurdish Minority." *Turkish Studies* 17 (4): 567–598.

Zeydanlıoğlu, W. 2009. "Torture and Turkification in Diyarbakır Military Prison." In W. Zeydanlıoğlu, and J.T. Parry (Eds.), *Rights, Citizenship and Torture: Perspectives on Evil, Law and the State*, 73–92. Oxford: Inter-disciplinary Press.

Key documents

Akil İnsanlar Heyeti [Wisemen Commission]. 2013. "Akil İnsanlar Güneydoğu Raporu." [Wisemen Commission South East Report]. https://barisicinakademisyenler.net/sites/default/files/raporlar/akil-insanlar-guneydogu-raporu.pdf.

"BDP Kürt Sorunu Komisyon Raporu." [BDP Kurdish Question Report]. https://serdargunes.files.wordpress.com/2015/08/bdp-kurt-sorunu_komisyonu_raporu.pdf.

19

CONCLUSION

What have we learned?

Alpaslan Özerdem and Roger Mac Ginty

Introduction

Armed conflict is experienced differently according to context and circumstances, and similarly, once it is achieved, the experience of peace is likely to be different for different communities and individuals. A wide range of factors from demographics to the socio-political and economic characteristics of population mean that peace not only is a context-based phenomenon but also very much depends on how it is lived, enacted, and embodied in everyday lives. With this in mind, the question of assessing the success or failure of peace processes becomes a difficult task. A peace process might be judged – overall – as a success, but for some communities and individuals it might mean a loss of power or a reduction in life opportunities. As we pointed out in the Introduction, it is prudent to use a wide range of indicators to gain an overall sense of what a peace process has achieved.

This volume selected 18 'peace processes' as case studies, some of which were completed quite a while ago, such as South Africa and Northern Ireland, while others have recently started, i.e. Colombia; some are still in their infancy, such as Afghanistan. Our cases also differ in terms of whether or not they have reached a clear conclusion of signing a comprehensive peace accord, such as Cambodia and El Salvador, or completely failed, such as Turkey. There are also significant differences in the way the peace processes took place, such as in Basque, where there was very little engagement of the Spanish state; Somaliland, which has been more about building peace between different clans in community-based approaches; and Bosnia-Herzegovina, in which the international community led the state-building/peacebuilding exercise. Most of our case studies focused on peace processes in which the parties were mainly a state and a secessionist armed group, such as Aceh, Nepal, and Mindanao. Other cases, such as Myanmar, involved more than 20 parties to the conflict. It is also worth noting the geographical spread and diversity of the cases, and how they involve both the global north and south. Needless to say, our case studies also differ from each other in terms of different geographies across the world, with which we wanted to underline the fact that armed conflict is a challenge for not only the global south but also very much the global north. Importantly, the cases considered in this volume are international and transnational, meaning that they are of global significance and often involve regional and global powers as well as international organisations.

As explained in the Introduction, we identified 11 variables to apply to our 18 case studies. This approach comes with a number of explanations and caveats, especially as we have decided to use a numerical approach to map out the 'successes and failures' for each of those variables. The approach is designed to maximise comparability across the cases. The first caveat concerns the enormous difficulty of comparing peace processes which are not only heavily informed by their own socio-economic, political, and geographic realities but are also very much the product of their own time periods. In other words, the case studies of Colombia, Nepal, Sri Lanka, and Turkey may have a number of similarities in terms of the political economy of the conflict but also significant differences such as the resources, capacities, and capabilities of each party to the process in each context, and the way things were carried out because of the wider international environment. Therefore, it is important we acknowledge the fact that what we compare here, to a large extent, are not the successes and failures of peace processes, but more the challenge of making and building peace in those very different environments. Where a peace process and a context that informs that peace process begin and end are very difficult to identify. The second caveat is to acknowledge the variety in peace processes, especially the nature of the parties to the conflict. While social scientific robustness might emphasise the requirement for a clear-cut comparative framework, the case studies are marked by variety and exceptions. A third caveat, and one discussed too rarely by the scholarly community, is that in order to arrive at a numeric assessment of a peace process, we have to make a judgement call. This call is guided by the evidence available to us from the case study chapters and the 'tightness' of definitions of the variables. Yet, at the end of the day, a judgement is made that might be prone to a series of subjective factors. Moreover, many factors pertaining to the case studies are open to debate and defy definitive judgement.

Having pointed out the three main caveats for our comparative analysis, we can now turn to the definitions that guide our assessment of peace processes. Table 19.1 provides a brief summary of the 18 case studies and through it a mapping exercise. Here it is possible to see the wide scope of the peace processes considered in this volume. However, even the apparently simple exercise of mapping was not free from the pitfalls of taxonomy development. For example, creating clear-cut boundaries for when peace processes start and come to an end is often open to debate. Therefore, as Editors, we have made a number of executive decisions! First of all, to define the starting context for peace processes, we have not used a single categorisation, but instead, based on the Uppsala Conflict Data Programme (UCDP) definitions and others, we opted for keywords that best define each case context or type of conflict. The conflict type in most of our case studies can be defined as 'internal armed conflict' that 'occurs between the government of a state and one or more internal opposition group(s) without intervention from other states' (i.e. Colombia, El Salvador, Nepal). Meanwhile, some of the cases are described as internationalised internal armed conflict that 'occurs between the government of a state and one or more internal opposition group(s) with intervention from other states (secondary parties) on one or both sides' (i.e. Afghanistan, Cambodia,

TABLE 19.1 A summary of peace process case studies

Peace process cases		*Peace process starting context*		*Passage of time*		*Current state of peace process*	*Main outcomes of peace process*
Aceh Indonesian State vs GAM	1	Subnational armed conflict	2	1999–2005	3	Completed	Autonomy for Aceh within Indonesia Integration of GAM in mainstream politics Post-disaster/post-conflict reconstruction in the aftermath of the 2004 tsunami
Afghanistan Afghan State vs. the Taliban	4	Internationalised internal armed conflict	5	2015–present	6	Efforts to start peace talks with continuing internal armed conflict	In February 2018 President Ashraf Ghani issued a call for peace talks with the Taliban 'without preconditions', including promises of amnesty and government posts for the Taliban
Basque Spanish State vs. ETA	7	Subnational armed conflict	8	1975–2017	9	Completed	Widening levels of autonomy for the Basque region Self-dissolution of ETA
Bosnia-Herzegovina Bosniaks vs. Croats vs. Serbs	10	Internationalised internal armed conflict	11	1992–1995	12	Completed	Bosnia-Herzegovina preserved its internationally recognised borders but was internally divided in a threefold way: administratively, ethnically, and territorially
Cambodia PRK vs. CGDK	13	Internationalised internal armed conflict	14	1989–1993	15	Completed	Ended the armed conflict in the country Established Supreme National Council Paved the way for a comprehensive framework for peacebuilding Organisation of democratic elections
Colombia Colombian State vs. FARC	16	Internal armed conflict	17	2011–2016	18	Peace Accord signed but its implementation is ongoing	Ended the armed conflict with FARC Paved the way for a comprehensive framework for peacebuilding

El Salvador El Salvadoran State vs. FMLN	19	Internal armed conflict	20	1990–1992	21	Completed	A stable and complete ceasefire, demobilisation of the rebel forces, and halving of the government's military, as well as extensive political reforms that substantially addressed the repression and political exclusion that had contributed to outbreak of war
Liberia NPFL vs. AFL vs. ULIMO-K vs. AFL vs. LURD vs. MODEL	22	Internationalised internal armed conflict	23 24 25 26 27 28	 1990–1996 2002–2003	29	Completed	Ended the armed conflict between various armed groups Paved the way for the establishment of a democratic government Implementation of peacebuilding
Mindanao Philippines State vs. MNLF MILF	30	Subnational armed conflict	31 32 33 34	 1976–1996 1997–2014	35	Implementation of different aspects of the peace process is ongoing	Independent Commission on Policing, Transitional Justice, and Reconciliation Commission, and the Bangsamoro Transition Commission (BTC), which has mainly been tasked to draft the Bangsamoro Basic Law as the charter of the new governing institution to be entrenched in the envisioned Bangsamoro political entity
Myanmar Myanmar State vs. high number of warring parties (over 20)	36	Borderland insurgencies	37	2011–present	38	Ongoing insurgencies and humanitarian crises	Roughly speaking, about 20 per cent of the combatants active in Myanmar have been included in the peace agreement, while 30 per cent are in open conflict and the remaining 50 per cent are part of organisations that have a bilateral ceasefire

(*Continued*)

TABLE 19.1 (Continued)

Peace process cases	*Peace process starting context*	*Passage of time*	*Current state of peace process*	*Main outcomes of peace process*
Nepal Nepali State vs. the Maoists	39 Internal armed conflict	40 2003–2006	41 Completed	The Maoists have become fully integrated into the democratic process. A wide range of socio-economic, justice, security, and governance measures have been undertaken, though some of them have been more successful than others
Northern Ireland British State vs. IRA	42 Subnational armed conflict	43 1968–1998	44 Completed	A complete end of armed conflict Power-sharing arrangements for governance Disarmament of armed groups and demilitarisation
Israel and the Palestinians Israel vs. the Palestinians	45 'Interstate' armed conflict – Occupation – Colonialism	46 1990–1999 47 1999–2010	48 Ongoing occupation	More failed peace talks Continuing occupation Intensification of colonisation
Somaliland Various clans	49 Inter-clan armed conflict	50 1990–present	51 Ongoing	The most stable and secure territory within the Somali context
South Africa The apartheid regime vs. ANC	52 Apartheid	53 1985–1998	54 Completed	End of the apartheid regime A new Constitution and democratic governance Truth and Reconciliation Commission
Sudan South Sudan	55 Subnational armed conflict	56 2005–2011	57 Ongoing internal armed conflict in South Sudan	South Sudan gained independence
Sri Lanka Sri Lankan State vs. LTTE	58 Subnational armed conflict	59 1999–2009	60 Failed	The government campaign culminated in the military defeat of the LTTE in May 2009, amid accusations of war crimes and mass killings of civilians in the final stages of the battle
Turkey Turkish State vs. PKK	61 Subnational armed conflict	62 2013–2015	63 Failed	Both sides went back to 'total war' starting from 2017, and the traces of the peace process gradually disappeared

Liberia) (UCDP 2018). We also opted for the term 'subnational armed conflict' that 'can be defined as armed conflict over control of a subnational territory, within a sovereign state, where an opposition movement uses violence to contest for greater self-rule for the local population' (i.e. Aceh, Mindanao, Turkey) (The Asia Foundation 2018). In our perspective, the main difference between (internationalised) internal and subnational conflict is around the latter being for more secessionist goals while the former aims to take over full control of the sovereign state. For a more nuanced understanding of internal conflict, we also defined the context in Myanmar as 'Borderland insurgencies', Somaliland as 'Inter-clan armed conflict', and South Africa as 'Apartheid'. While we made a decision to highlight the distinctiveness of these case studies, they could all in fact be included within the category of 'internal armed conflict'. The case study of Israel–Palestine did not quite fit in any of the above-mentioned categories. It could be considered as 'interstate armed conflict', if the Palestinian Authority (PA) is assumed to represent as a separate state. Yet the PA lacks meaningful autonomy, many of the Palestinian territories are occupied by Israel, and there is also a strong characteristic of colonialism – something that we noted in our mapping.

For the 'Passage of time', we faced similar difficulties in deciding what to take as the beginning and end of peace processes. The earliest initiatives in peace processes often informed our decision as the starting point, and for the end, if there was a fully-fledged peace accord framework, we included the period of its implementation in the passage of time. However, as Editors we recognise that such decisions were subjective at best and could be considered differently from different point of views. The answer to the question 'When does a post-conflict society cease being a post-conflict society?' may be 'Never' given the long legacy of violent conflict in terms of demographics and economic and social dislocation. For the 'Current state of peace process', the main distinctions we made were around whether it was completed, ongoing, or failed before it reached the stage of signing an accord. However, it is important to note that with 'completed', we do not mean a successful implementation of the peace accord. Rather, it indicates that the context concerned is already beyond the political framework of the peace accord programmes.

The 11 variables we identified to assess 'success and failure' in the case studies can be grouped into four categories: *Context*, *Procedural*, *Responsiveness*, and *Participation and inclusion*. These categories, and indeed the variables, can be thought of as interdependent rather than discrete. The variables 'Level of symmetry between the parties' and 'Level of engagement and supportiveness by the international community' fit within the *Context* category. The *Procedural* category is populated by two variables: 'Existence and effectiveness of confidence-building measures' and 'Level and supportiveness of third-party engagement'. The *Responsiveness* category concerns the ability of the process and accord to respond to four issues: 'Security', 'Effective governance', 'Justice and legacy', and the 'Political economy of peace and conflict'. The final category, *Participation and inclusion*, is concerned with the 'Level of public participation', 'Level of gender inclusion', and 'Level of youth inclusion' (in the process and accord). On the basis of the case studies in this volume we have made numeric assessment of the peace processes in relation to each of the variables (Table 19.2). The numeric scores range from 1 (low attainment) to 5

TABLE 19.2 Variables contributing to successes and failures of case study peace processes

	Variables contributing to failures and successes of peace processes (1: Low – 5: High)										
Peace process cases	*Level of symmetry between the parties*	*Level of engagement and supportiveness by the international community*	*Existence and effectiveness of confidence-building measures*	*Level and supportiveness of third-party engagement*	*Ability of the process and accord to deal with security issues*	*Ability of the process and accord to deal to produce effective governance*	*Ability of the process and accord to deal with justice and legacy issues*	*Ability of the process and accord to deal with the political economy of peace and conflict*	*Level of public participation in the process and accord*	*Level of gender inclusion in the process and accord*	*Level of youth inclusion in the process and accord*
Aceh	3	5	4	5	5	4	3	4	2	1	1
Afghanistan	3	1	1	1	N/A	N/A	N/A	N/A	1	1	1
Basque	2	4	4	5	5	5	1	2	5	3	2
Bosnia–Herzegovina	4	2	3	3	4	3	4	2	3	2	2
Cambodia	4	3	5	4	4	4	3	3	2	2	2
Colombia	3	4	5	5	4	4	3	3	4	4	3
El Salvador	3	4	5	5	3	4	3	2	3	2	2
Liberia	5	2	2	2	4	3	4	3	2	4	2
Mindanao	3	4	4	5	3	4	4	3	4	4	2
Myanmar	2	3	4	3	2	3	1	2	2	1	1
Nepal	3	4	4	2	4	4	3	2	4	3	3
Northern Ireland	3	5	4	5	5	4	4	4	4	3	2
Israel–the Palestinians	1	2	2	2	2	2	1	1	2	2	2
Somaliland	5	2	5	2	4	4	1	2	5	3	2
South Africa	2	4	2	3	3	5	4	2	4	3	3
Sudan	3	3	2	3	3	4	1	2	2	2	2
Sri Lanka	2	3	4	3	3	3	3	2	3	2	2
Turkey	2	2	2	2	2	N/A	1	N/A	2	2	2

(high attainment). The main benefit of this approach is in terms of highlighting the most obvious 'successes' and 'failures' for each variable among the 18 case studies. It should be noted that in the cases of Afghanistan and Turkey, we opted for not making a judgement on certain variables, as the former is a potential peace process in its infancy and the latter is failed in its relatively early stages. The case studies of Israel–Palestine, Liberia, and Mindanao include a number of conflict and peace process periods, and in such cases, our grading reflects the entire period rather than just a single peace process. Finally, it is worth reiterating the subjectivity of the grading exercise, but the exercise was useful in encouraging us to make specific and overall judgements about peace processes, and in encouraging us to judge peace processes across a range of issues and not just on security and constitutional matters. In the remaining part of this chapter, the discussions will be structured around the 11 variables and will highlight the most obvious examples of success and failure.

Comparative analysis

Level of symmetry between the parties

In all 18 case studies, the level of symmetry between the parties played a significant role in the way that the peace process was shaped or failed to take off with the conclusion of a political settlement. The asymmetry factor seems to have been a less significant issue in Bosnia-Herzegovina, Cambodia, Liberia, and Somaliland (those rated as 4/5) than the others, where the parties' resources, control of territories, and international sponsors in relative terms played a significant role in influencing peace processes and their subsequent outcomes. With Bosnia-Herzegovina, it might be argued that the Bosniak population and, to some extent, Croats, were much weaker in comparison to Serbs, but the former communities, especially in later stages of the conflict, received strong backing from the international community. In three other case studies of this group, the asymmetries between the parties do not seem to be particularly significant for the peace process. For a large group of case studies (Aceh, Afghanistan, Colombia, El Salvador, Mindanao, Nepal, Northern Ireland, and Sudan) – all rated 3 – the asymmetry between the parties has been a contributing factor. Yet, in these cases, there was some form of balancing between the non-state armed groups and the state in relation to factors such as territory, population bases, or economic resources.

To make a distinction between this group of case studies with the next one (those rated 2) was not easy, but we considered that the asymmetries between the parties to the conflict in the Basque Country, Myanmar, South Africa, Sri Lanka, and Turkey were particularly significant. However, due to other contributing factors, the peace process outcomes in each of those case studies were quite different from each other. For example, in the case of the Basque Country, the non-state actor dissolved itself as part of considerable autonomy gains for the Basque region, while in South Africa the outcome was the end of the apartheid regime. In the case of Sri Lanka, the conflict came to an end with a military victory of the state over the non-state armed group after the failure of the peace process. In Myanmar, despite asymmetries, the peace accords were set up with more than 20 insurgency groups. In the case of Turkey, a significant asymmetry has always existed, as the Turkish state considered a military victory as a viable option based on its overall resources and capacities and was not prepared to go for a win–win solution with the non-state actor. Among our 18 case studies, the Israel–Palestine case represented the most severe asymmetry, and this played a highly decisive role in the long history of a failed peace process. Israel's upper hand in both conflict and peacemaking dictated the outcome of every conflict resolution effort. The heavy US sponsorship of Israel, particularly in recent years, has accentuated these power imbalances, making the prospects of a future peace accord slim.

Level of engagement and supportiveness by the international community

The level of engagement and supportiveness by the international community was a significant factor in many peace processes because of neighbourhood effects, and the possibility of proxy war and peace waged by powerful regional or international actors. There are some interesting exceptions. We rated a number of case studies as 4 or 5 for this variable, such as Aceh, Basque, Colombia, El Salvador, Mindanao, Nepal, Northern Ireland, and South Africa, because the influence of 'bad' neighbourhood was not really a critical issue, and the engagement of the international community was overall constructive and, to a large extent, free from proxy agendas. The case of El Salvador may seem to be an odd one in this group, considering that the US waged a proxy war in the country for a long time, but in the peace process, the US acted in a much more constructive way. Considering that all of these case studies also represent a peace accord and some degree of political transformation afterwards, we conclude that this variable is highly significant for peace processes. For Cambodia, Myanmar, Sri Lanka, and Sudan, which were rated as 3, this variable requires a more nuanced understanding. The influence of neighbourhood was much more significant in Cambodia and Myanmar than the other two case studies in this group, but they received constructive engagement from the international community. In the case of Sri Lanka, this variable was overall quite positive, as there was not any significant negative influence from the region and the engagement of Norway as a mediator was constructive, but the process nevertheless failed. The constructive engagement of the international community was one of the primary reasons in the way that the Sudan peace process concluded with a political settlement and secession of South Sudan.

The contexts which were rated as 2 in our assessment were Bosnia-Herzegovina, Israel–Palestine, Liberia, Somaliland, and Turkey – all cases in which peace prospects have been heavily affected by regional and international factors. In the case of Liberia and Turkey, prevailing factors were the civil wars in neighbouring countries and the way that the non-state armed groups concerned were supported by neighbours; in the case of Israel and the Palestinians, the Middle East provides a very unstable environment in which all major powers have a strong interest; the civil war in Bosnia-Herzegovina must be contextualised in the overall disintegration of

Yugoslavia; and Somaliland can be seen as part of a wider failed state context; these were all factored in for such an assessment. Afghanistan is awarded the overall lowest rating of 1 given the extraordinary levels of international engagement/interference. For a peace accord to be achieved and have successful implementation, one of the key priorities for Afghanistan needs to be around the management of regional and international engagement in proxy conflict and potentially proxy peace dynamics.

Existence and effectiveness of confidence-building measures

The review of our 18 case studies shows that confidence-building measures are very much part and parcel of conflict resolution processes and, in most cases, play a highly significant role in the development and successful signing of a peace accord. In terms of success, the case studies of Aceh, Basque, Cambodia, Colombia, El Salvador, Mindanao, Nepal, Northern Ireland, Somaliland, and Sri Lanka all benefited from such measures, but they were particularly critical in the contexts of Cambodia, Colombia, El Salvador, and Somaliland (those rated as 5). Apart from Sri Lanka, all the other cases achieved a peace accord or context of peaceful relations between the parties to the conflict (for example, a reduction in inter-clan fighting in Somaliland). Even in Sri Lanka, there seemed to be a real chance of reaching a comprehensive political settlement, especially in the context of the post-2004 Tsunami disaster aid context. The Cambodia case study is particularly important given the wide range of confidence-building measures undertaken by the international community and the relatively high success of their implementation. While some cases involved a high degree of international engagement (as was the case with the UN in Nepal), other cases had little third-party engagement. The cases of Bosnia-Herzegovina, Myanmar, South Africa, and Sudan had their fair share of confidence-building measures initiated by the international community, although their record of success was more mixed. In Bosnia-Herzegovina, it would not be an exaggeration to claim that some confidence-building measures did more harm than good. In the case of Myanmar, confidence-building measures by China seemed to have worked particularly well, pointing out the importance of the relative power of the mediator over the parties to the conflict.

The next group of contexts, rated as 2, included Liberia, Israel–Palestine, and Turkey. Each has its own story to tell, but in general confidence-building measures were not a significant catalyst for a more substantive peace. The case of Israel–Palestine witnessed many confidence-building measures introduced by the US, EU, and UN. It was not, therefore, the lack of them but rather their effectiveness that was our main consideration for such a low assessment result. Here, too, it is important to raise the significance of asymmetry between the parties, as discussed above. For confidence-building measures to lead to trustworthiness between the parties, the overall asymmetry is a significant contextual challenge to bear in mind. This was also the case with the peace process in Turkey and the way it failed. Both sides to the conflict were unwilling to develop confidence-building measures, though it should be acknowledged that the Turkish state was more active in its attempts. In the case of Liberia, the majority of confidence-building measures were initiated by the regional actors, and because of their direct and indirect engagement in the conflict itself, they did not prove to be effective. Finally, Afghanistan scores the lowest rating of 1. In the case of the potential peace talks between the Afghan government and the Taliban, there is a real need for such measures, but in the current political and security framework, both parties face a real dilemma in terms of how such confidence-building measures might be used as tactical advantage by the other party. The overall regional and international context that surrounds this potential peace process is hostile. A confidence-building measure by one party is likely to be viewed with extreme suspicion by other parties.

Level and supportiveness of third-party engagement

With the variable of how third-party engagement played a successful role in peace processes, our assessment shows that the cases of Aceh, Basque, Colombia, El Salvador, and Northern Ireland (those rated as 5) were particularly fortunate. It is important to point out that such a high rating does not mean that third parties were always effective in their approach; this is a tall order given the political fluidity of peace process environments, but it could be argued that the third-party engagement in all of these cases was not only significant in relation to the scope of activities, but also to a very large extent, effective. In the cases of Cambodia, Mindanao, and Myanmar (those rated as 4), there was significant third-party engagement, and it was overall quite supportive in reaching a peaceful resolution. Mindanao is a particularly good example of this, and the pivotal role played by Malaysia and other countries deserves specific mention. Similarly, in the case of Cambodia and Myanmar, it was the UN and China respectively that played critical and supportive roles. We rated the third-party engagement as 3 in the contexts of Bosnia-Herzegovina, Sudan, and Sri Lanka. Third-party engagement was active in these contexts and often involved multiple actors, although internal actors were – at different times – able to resist the ministrations and exhortations of third parties. Norway was an active facilitator of the Sri Lankan peace process until the Sri Lankan government effectively locked it out and ignored it, instead pursuing a military outcome.

The next group of cases – Liberia, Nepal, Israel–Palestine, South Africa, Somaliland, and Turkey – is probably the most interesting sub-unit for this variable. In the case of Nepal, South Africa, and Turkey, the third-party engagement was relatively low, but while the former two contexts achieved a successful resolution, Turkey failed. In the case of Israel–Palestine, there has been extensive third-party engagement, but over the longer term this can be seen to reinforce the asymmetry between the two sides. US bias towards Israel has, arguably, emboldened Israel to hold out against a meaningful peace process. As the Oslo Process withered, US influence over Israel waned to the extent that much of the US political establishment seems scared to criticise Israel. The case of Somaliland is interesting in that there was relatively little third-party engagement, but what little there has been has been quite effective in supporting conflict resolution. In the case of Afghanistan, there has been significant third-party meddling, but little of this can be regarded as supportive of a nascent peace process. Indeed, many actions by third parties are deliberately designed to thwart the development of a peace process. Overall, we conclude that third-party engagement is significant for successful conflict resolution, as indicated by a high number of case studies in this volume, but it is not necessarily a must as there are also other cases that have had effective peace processes without significant third-party engagement.

Ability of the process and accord to deal with security issues

Apart from Afghanistan, which is still in early stages of peace talks, all other peace processes took security issues as a primary area of concern, with some achieving more success than others. In the cases of Aceh, the Basque Country, and Northern Ireland (those rated as 5), the transformation of the non-state armed groups has been such that a return to armed conflict has become an unlikely possibility. The process and accord in those three cases and for those rated as 4 (Bosnia-Herzegovina, Cambodia, Colombia, and Somaliland) all made specific provisions on security issues and undertook them successfully to a large extent. However, it should be noted that even with those cases, there is still a certain level of fragility, such as the dependence on an international presence in Bosnia-Herzegovina, and the threats posed by other non-state armed groups which were not part of the peace accord in Colombia. The successes, so far, in dealing with security issues in Somaliland remain vulnerable to insecurity challenges in other Somalia territories.

The next category of contexts (those rated as 3) – El Salvador, Liberia, Mindanao, South Africa, Sri Lanka, and Sudan – are probably the most interesting ones for this variable as, although they all attempted to address security issues, their current contexts show a mix of success and failure. In the cases of El Salvador and South Africa, the political violence has turned into a high level of criminal violence, and therefore it is difficult to consider them as success stories. The security situations in Liberia and Mindanao have been reasonably calm, but processes of demilitarisation and the disarmament, demobilisation, and reintegration of ex-combatants have not been without problems. In the case of the Sudanese peace process, which resulted in South Sudan becoming an independent country, Sudan still faces secessionist and rebellious pressures in Darfur and elsewhere, while South Sudan has suffered an extremely destructive civil war. The peace process in Sri Lanka failed to reach an accord, and the continuation of internal conflict afterwards resulted in a victor's peace for the state. In the current security context, there is no more internal conflict, but any settlement imposed through mass state violence is likely to cause resentment and grievance among subordinated populations. Finally, in the cases of Israel–Palestine, Myanmar, and Turkey (those rated as 2), the conflict continues. The Myanmar peace process has involved over 20 conflict parties, but it seems legitimate to question the extent to which the Myanmar regime simply wants ceasefire agreements from armed non-state actors or wants something more akin to a meaningful peace process. The 2017–2018 humanitarian crisis experienced by the Rohingya minority provided a stark reminder that the country is far from a secure place for all of its population groups. Although it has never reached to a peace accord stage, the peace talks in Turkey made some reference to the future of the non-state armed group, but the political sensitivities surrounding this issue prevented the parties from taking significant steps towards demilitarisation.

Ability of the process and accord to deal to produce effective governance

As well as security issues, almost all of the peace processes concerned in this volume attempted to produce effective governance. The case of Somaliland provides the only exception to this, as the process there has focused on building peace between different clans first rather than the common practice of state-building found in other contexts. In our ratings, we did not include Afghanistan as the process is in its infancy, but it is important to point out that if a peace process does take off, a key focus is likely to be on who will govern Afghanistan and how. Also, we did not rate the peace process in Turkey, as the talks failed before considering any issues of power-sharing for the Kurdish dominated provinces. For the case study of Israel–the Palestinians, which is rated as 2, the governance issue in relation to the control of different territories and whether or not a two-state solution would be viable form the backbone of disagreements. Those contexts that are rated as 3 have different stories to tell in terms of how governance issues were addressed. In the case of Bosnia-Herzegovina, the peace accord made detailed references to governances and created highly complex structures. It is questionable, however, whether these complex governing structures have facilitated or obstructed effective governance. The peace process in Liberia was relatively less specific about governance issues apart from setting up frameworks for a return to a democratic governance. Thus far, however, there has been considerable success, especially given the starting point. The victor's peace in Sri Lanka is a far cry from what the peace process discussed in this volume aimed to achieve in terms of power-sharing. Moreover, the current trend of the delivery of governance is still very much focused on the capital Colombo.

For the remaining case studies in this volume (those rated as 4 and 5), governance issues were both included and addressed in the peace processes, with the notable exception of Somaliland, in which progress was made on governance issues following the establishment of peaceful relations between different clans. In the case of Colombia, it is still early days, but the accord itself makes detailed reference to governance issues. Northern Ireland was considered as one of the most successful peace process examples in the way that it has created effective power-sharing arrangements, but there have been significant challenges in recent years, and the post-Brexit context is likely to be challenging. One of the overall lessons from a consideration of the governance issue is that those cases that managed to mainstream the issue into their peace process negotiations tended to have success. Those processes that take seriously issues of governance indicate that political elites realise that ongoing service delivery and legitimacy will have a bearing on how peace is cemented.

Ability of the process and accord to deal with justice and legacy issues

On this variable, it is more difficult to be specific, and therefore our ratings in Table 19.2 should be considered with extra caution. The main reason for this is that although most comprehensive peace accords include matters of justice and legacy, they tend to have much less priority during the implementation process of any peace process. The rise of transitional justice matters in peacebuilding across the world is a positive indicator, but the 18 case studies in this volume show that the parties to conflicts are often much less interested in the complexities of justice reform, amnesty, and reconciliation than in other issues such as security and constitutional matters. Some of the most prominent – and ostensibly successful – examples for this variable include Bosnia-Herzegovina, Liberia, Northern Ireland, and South Africa given their provisions for Special Courts for the trial of war crimes, judicial and police reforms, and Truth and Reconciliation Commissions. But even here, questions can be asked. Structure reform of the judicial system is relatively easy when compared to the thorny issue of legacy and the extent to which people 'feel' (always a subjective matter) that their concerns and hurt have been dealt with.

For those cases rated as 3 – Aceh, Cambodia, Colombia, El Salvador, Mindanao, and Nepal – judicial and legacy issues were considered and made part of the peace accord. Cambodia and El Salvador were relatively more successful in this than others. Nepal is yet to fully implement many aspects of its 2006 peace accord. The peace processes in Aceh and Mindanao made detailed references to such matters as land reform and judicial reform, but again, they are yet to be fully implemented. In the case of Colombia, there was considerable innovation in the peace process with the involvement of victims' delegations in the Havana negotiations. Victims' and legacy issues received considerable attention in the peace accord, but only time will show how they have been addressed in the implementation. For the remaining case studies in this volume – the Basque Country, Israel–The Palestinians, Myanmar, Somaliland, Sri Lanka, Sudan, and Turkey – we opted for a rating of 1. In contexts like the Basque Country, Myanmar, and Somaliland, the issue did not arise because of the nature of the peace process. In the case of Sri Lanka, the peace process – when in existence – did give the impression that justice and legacy issues would be covered but did not make any substantive advances on the issue. With Israel–The Palestinians, it is worth noting that much of the Palestinian cause is focused squarely on justice and legacy issues (whether grievances based on ongoing human rights abuses and the historical issue of the right of return for displaced Palestinians), but it is fair to say that Israel ignored these issues and was able to do so because of the oft-mentioned power asymmetry. During the peace talks, if not directly but at least in various political platforms, the need for a Truth and Reconciliation Commission was tabled in the context of Turkey. Given the termination of the peace process, this discussion never bore fruit.

Ability of the process and accord to deal with the political economy of peace and conflict

Among the four variables that we identified for *Responsiveness*, this is the one that presents the most pessimistic picture. For a significant majority of the peace process contexts in this volume, it was not a significant issue considered in the peace process. Even in cases where the issue appeared in a peace accord, it rarely moved beyond declaratory statements. Fundamentally, capitalist global and national economies can be unforgiving for economies and societies emerging from violent conflict. Bosnia-Herzegovina, El Salvador, Nepal, and South Africa, which were rated as 2, are the prime examples of how the political economy of the conflict has not changed significantly following the conflict/collapse of the previous regime, with the result that war-affected communities still face similar or worse economic challenges in terms of employment and livelihood opportunities. In the cases of Myanmar and Somaliland, such issues have yet to be considered in a comprehensive manner, and although the Sri Lankan peace process failed, since 2009 the government has been implementing its own victor's political economy of peace. South Sudanese independence wasn't envisaged in the CPA peace process, and the wealth sharing was supposedly designed to maximise the attractiveness of national unity. The other case studies in this group – Cambodia, Liberia, and Mindanao – have, in relative terms, made progress in the implementation of this variable. In the case of Colombia, it is too early to reach a verdict, although it is important point out that the peace accord includes significant provisions for the transformation of the war economy into a peace economy, especially around threats posed by narcotics.

The cases of Aceh and Northern Ireland (those rated as 4) are the best examples for this variable, as in both cases there was a concerted effort in changing the political economy of war. In the case of Northern Ireland, the peace process and post-accord dispensation benefited from a generally growing UK economy and very generous sums from the UK and Irish governments, and the European Union and United States, that directly targeted peacebuilding needs. In the case of Aceh, wide-scale reconstruction work undertaken by the international community in the aftermath of the 2004 Tsunami disaster gave the economy a boost. Finally, Afghanistan and Turkey have not been included in the rating exercise as their peace processes did not/have not taken off. Both economies are the site of substantial illicit activity. In the case of Afghanistan in particular, the economy has been skewed by the conflict, with the state security apparatus constituting a massive job creation scheme. For peace to be sustainable, and to avoid a lot of disgruntled and militarily trained young men who experience a peace deficit, the economy would need to be recalibrated away from a conflict footing.

Level of public, gender, and youth participation in the process and accord

For the level of public, gender, and youth participation the peace process and implementation of the accord, the overall picture that emerged from our 18 case studies is not encouraging, underlining the fact that conflict resolution processes are often restricted to the elite level. In terms of public participation, the best case study examples were the Basque Country and Somaliland (those rated as 5), where without civil society the outcomes achieved could not be realised. In the case of the Basque Country, civil society was heavily involved. Indeed, in what might be called the unilateral peace process, it was the engagement of Basque civil society with Basque nationalists that bore results in the sense of the disbandment of the militant organisation. In Somaliland, traditional conflict resolution structures and actors took the lead in both the formation and implementation of the peace process. Questions can be asked about the inclusive nature of these informal actors, but they did act in accordance with customary understandings and there were attempts at consensus decision-making. In the cases of Colombia, Mindanao, Nepal, Northern Ireland, and South Africa (those rated as 4), there was a significant engagement by civil society both in the peace process and implementation phases. While referendums present people with a yes/no decision on a *fait accompli*, they do – in theory at least – create space for a public discussion of the pros and cons of a peace process and accord.

It is also possible to consider the cases of Bosnia-Herzegovina, El Salvador, and Sri Lanka (those rated as 3) as having considerable public engagement; in the former two contexts, this was more in the implementation phase. Meanwhile, in terms of gender participation, good examples are, unfortunately, fewer. In Colombia, Liberia, and Mindanao (those rated as 4), there was a visible engagement by women's organisations in the peace process, while the case studies of Basque, Myanmar, Nepal, Northern Ireland, Somaliland, and South Africa (all rated 3) had also some input from women's organisations. On the other hand, when it comes to youth participation, the overall picture does not indicate any emerging trends, apart from very limited means for young people to get their voices heard in peace processes. There does seem to be international peacebuilding policy and practitioner pressure for greater women's participation in peace processes, but this does not seem to be replicated in relation to youth inclusion.

Concluding remarks

Failures in peace processes are discouraging, but they should no means be a reason to claim that diplomacy does not work. On the contrary, as the majority of case studies in this volume indicate, conflict resolution through negotiation is the most effective way of achieving sustainable peace. This is particularly important to remember in the current international context for conflict response, which is often dictated by military interventionism and a default securitisation rather than an investigation of negotiated outcomes. The alternative of not engaging militarily should not be a non-engagement type of response, either. As the 18 case studies in this volume indicate, there is now a wealth of experience showing that political engagements undertaken in a constructive way can achieve peace accords and the implementation of those accords. Indeed, this exemplar effect – the notion that a peace process is possible – is perhaps the most important lesson that one peace process can give to another. This volume does not underestimate the real difficulties faced by peace processes, but it is aware of the 'prizes' to be gained in terms of life opportunities, livelihoods, and the addressing of grievances.

The contextual variables of asymmetry between the parties to the conflict and the international contexts that surround those conflicts have a critical bearing on the success or failure of peace processes. However, even the most intractable conflicts might have a chance to reach a peaceful settlement, if such factors are effectively considered in the initiation and development of peace processes. The asymmetry might be a reality, but it is not insurmountable if mediators recognise such realities and act upon them accordingly. The problem arises when mediating actors make the assumption that such asymmetries do not exist or ignore them deliberately because of their own proxy peace interests. For a win–win type of conflict resolution, the asymmetry between the parties is a factor that acts as a litmus test for potential successes and failures. Similarly, the regional and international contexts, in the way that they sustain the conflict or enable a peace process to realise its full potential, emerged strongly as a critical variable in the case studies of this volume. Those conflicts among our case studies that had a constructive external context had a significant advantage to developing an effective peace process than those others suffering in the quagmire regional and international politics.

The procedural variables of confidence-building measures and third-party engagement are also critical, but the case studies indicated the need for a more nuanced understanding of them. The ripeness to intervene for such confidence-building measures is highly significant, as they can do more harm than good if their timing is ill judged. Hasty responses by external actors due to their own political agendas could easily deepen the environment of untrustworthiness further. It should also be noted that for confidence-building measures, although it is helpful in their facilitation, an external third party might not always be necessary. Such measures could be undertaken by internal actors or could be made as part of political processes in that context. Almost all of the 18 case studies included in this volume had some engagement of a third party, but in terms of the level, type, and intensity of such an engagement, there is also evidence that a third party is not always a must for peace processes. In some cases, such a third party might be an individual, organisation, or country, but in others, the context might require a wide range of such third parties to engage in different periods and aspects of the peace process.

The investigation of 18 case studies in this volume also indicates that contemporary peace processes are largely about governance and security matters, while those issues around justice and political economy of the conflict get much less interest in the development of peace accords. This might be considered as a natural outcome of what political settlements are all about, and governance and security being the main tools of politics, this is perhaps unsurprising. However, without the issues of economics, justice, and legacy addressed effectively, the transformation from negative to positive peace is not likely to take place, posing serious threats to the sustainability of peace in the long term. This phenomenon has been a particularly stark reminder with the peace process environments where violence transformed into a high level of personal insecurity due to criminality even though the political violence has come to an end. More worryingly, even as such considerations are made and incorporated in comprehensive peace accords, their implementation tends to get much less attention, and they are often postponed as issues to be responded in due course. Even in our successful peace processes case studies, the political economy of conflict in many contexts showed little change, and in some cases, they have been showing worsening trajectories.

Finally, in terms of the engagement of the public and specific groups such as women and the youth in peacebuilding, the discussions in this volume present a highly concerning reality. In many environments, peace processes are designed by the international and national elites, leaving little room for meaningful participation of the public. Local participation is often an afterthought, and in many contexts, it does not go beyond lip service. Meanwhile, some of the case studies in this volume show that civil society could be a resourceful and effective actor that not only contributes to such processes but also actually leads them. Traditional conflict resolution responses could be, if not more so, at least as effective as Western-centric modalities in certain environments. The current practice of conflict resolution needs to stop perceiving conflict-affected publics as a mere recipients and come up with the modalities of involving them in both the development of peace accords and their implementation. To make such processes more effective and sustainable, the engagement of women and young people is a must and there is now a big body of evidence to claim why this is necessary. However, it seems that the peace process practice still has a long way to go to catch up with this knowledge, as neither women nor young people are an integral part of decision-making in such environments.

References

The Asia Foundation. 2018. "The Contested Corners of Asia: Subnational Conflict and International Development Assistance." https://asiafoundation.org/resources/pdfs/ContestedCornersofAsiaExecutiveSummary.pdf.

UCDP. 2018. "Definitions." www.pcr.uu.se/research/UCDP/.

INDEX

Note: Page numbers in *italics* indicate a figure and page numbers in **bold** indicate a table on the corresponding page.